YOUR COMPLETE AFTERSALES SERVICE

DEDICATED TO ALL MAKES OF BUS AND COACH

- **Specialist service centres in London, Rotherham and Scotland**
- **Nationwide all makes parts supply**
- **All makes accident damage and mechanical repairs**
- **Mobile technicians**
- **Technical services and training**
- **Speedline dedicated warranty response: 08000 285626**

At Unitec our priority is getting and keeping your vehicles on the road... whatever make, whatever model we're here to help you.

Whether it's servicing, repairs, parts or training, call us today.

London — **01708 892440**
london.service@optare.com

Rotherham — **01709 535101**
rotherham.service@optare.com

Scotland — **01236 726738**
scotland.service@optare.com

Parts — **01709 792000**
www.unitecparts.co.uk

Unitec, Denby Way, Rotherham S66 8HR, a division of Optare Group Ltd

CW01281449

The UK's biggest selling PSV magazine

Subscribe today and SAVE 10% on the normal price

Delivering prompt and informed coverage every month, **BUSES** magazine has provided an essential overview of the UK's PSV industry for over fifty-five years.

Supported by quality editorial features and the latest news, **BUSES** magazine is essential reading for decision-makers within the bus industry.

The magazine is notable for its most unique feature, 'Fleet News', now an 18-page section detailing the latest additions to and departures from major and less major bus and coach fleets in the UK and Ireland.

Every month BUSES editorial features cover key areas of interest, including vehicle operation, technical developments, ticketing and publicity.

Subscribe today to receive **BUSES** on your desk every month, and keep abreast of the latest news and developments in the bus industry.

12 ISSUES	NORMAL RATE	DISCOUNT RATE	YOU SAVE
UK	£44.40	£39.96	£4.44
EUROPE	£53.20	£47.88	£5.32
ROW	£58.20	£52.38	£5.82

Great subscriber benefits!

A subscription to BUSES comes with FREE MEMBERSHIP to the **Ian Allan Publishing Subs Club.**

As a member of the **Ian Allan Publishing Subs Club**, you will receive a personalised Subscription Loyalty Card, plus a quarterly newsletter with great subscriber benefits, discounts, offers and competitions!

Offer valid until 30/09/08

BUSES PRIORITY SUBSCRIPTION FORM

LRB08

I would like to subscribe to *BUSES*, starting with the........................ issue

- 12 issues UK   DISCOUNT RATE £39.96
- 12 issues Europe   DISCOUNT RATE £47.88
- 12 issues ROW   DISCOUNT RATE £52.38

Mr/Mrs/Miss/Ms: .... Forename: ....
Surname: ....
Address: ....
....
....
Post Code: ....
Tel No: ....
Email: ....

1. Debit / Credit Card
Please debit my card for the amount £...............

☐ Mastercard   ☐ Visa   ☐ Switch / Maestro Card

Exp date: .... Start date: .... Issue No: ....
Cardholders signature: .... Date: ....

2. Cheque
I enclose a cheque to the value of ....
(Please make cheque payable to Ian Allan Publishing Ltd. Eurocheques are not accepted.)

3. Invoice
☐ Please invoice me

Please complete and send to: Buses Subscriptions Department, Ian Allan Publishing Ltd, Riverdene Business Park, Molesey Road, Hersham, Surrey, KT12 4RG
Tel: +44 (0)1932 266622   Fax: +44 (0)1932 266633   Email: subs@ianallanpublishing.co.uk

THE LITTLE RED BOOK
2008

THE PASSENGER TRANSPORT DIRECTORY FOR THE BRITISH ISLES

Editor: Tony Pattison

Ian Allan
PUBLISHING

Riverdene Business Park, Molesey Road, Hersham, Surrey KT12 4RG
Tel: 01932 266600 Fax: 01932 266601

PSV GLASS - WE'VE GOT IT COVERED!

It would be nice to think that there really was one place to go for all your public service vehicle glass solutions. There is - PSV Glass can help you with all aspects of replacement glazing:

IMMEDIATE PARTS IDENTIFICATION > FULL STOCK RANGE > NATIONWIDE DELIVERY SERVICE
ON-SITE TECHNICAL SUPPORT > CUSTOMISED GLASS STORAGE SYSTEMS
MANAGED IMPREST STOCK > GLASS INSTALLATION TRAINING > GLASS ASSOCIATED PRODUCTS
GLASS FILMING PROTECTION MANAGEMENT

Just call PSV Glass on 01494 533131 or visit www.psvglass.com

contents

List of Abbreviations	4
Index to Advertisers	4
Foreword	5

Section 1:
Trade Directory	7

Section 2:
Tendering & Regulatory Authorities	59
Traffic Commissioners,	64
Department for Transport	64

Section 3:
Organisations and Societies	67

Section 4:
British Isles Operators	80

Section 5:
Index (Trade)	226
Index (British Isles Operators)	232

Index to Advertisers

Airconco	18
Bus & Coach Preservation magazine	66
Buses magazine	iv
Camira	46
Crewe Engines	29
Cummins-Allison	23
Eminox	5
Grasshopper Inn	129
Ian Allan Bookshops	16
Midland Counties Publications	216
Prestolite	26
PSV Glass	Front cover, 2
Scan Coin	21
Transport Benevolent Fund	Bookmark
Unitec	Front endpaper
Voith	Front endpaper
Walsh's Engineering	30
ZF Great Britain	45

First published 2007

ISBN (10) 0 7110 3270 X
ISBN (13) 978 0 7110 3705

All rights reserved. No part of this book may be reproduced or transmitted in any form or by any means, electronic or mechanical, including photocopying, recording or by any information storage and retrieval system, without permission from the Publisher in writing.

© Ian Allan Publishing Ltd 2007

Published by Ian Allan Publishing; an imprint of Ian Allan Publishing Ltd, Riverdene Business Park, Hersham, Surrey KT12 4RG; and printed by Ian Allan Printing Ltd, Riverdene Business Park, Hersham, Surrey KT12 4RG.

Code: 0709/A1

Visit the Ian Allan Publishing web site:
www.ianallanpublishing.com

List of Abbreviations

Acct = Accountant
Admin = Administrative
Asst = Assistant
Ch = Chief
Chmn = Chairman
Co = Company
Comm Man = Commercial Manager
Cont = Controller
Dep = Deputy
Dir = Director
Eng = Engineer
Exec = Executive
Fin = Financial
Gen Man = General Manager
Insp = Inspector
Jnt = Joint
Man = Manager
Man Dir = Managing Director
Mktg = Marketing
Off = Officer
Op = Operating
Ops = Operations
Plan = Planning
Pres = President
Prin = Principal
Prop = Proprietor(s)
Ptnrs = Partner(s)
Reg Off = Registered Office
sd = single-deck bus
Sec = Secretary
Supt = Superintendent
Svce = service
Traf Man = Traffic Manager
Traf Supt = Traffic Superintendent
Tran Man = Transport Manager

Foreword

This is a special year for the directory as 2008 marks its 70th anniversary.

New for LRB this year in the A-Z section is Mirrors/Mirror Arms.

We have also re-named the Trade Directory from A-Z Listing of Bus, Coach & Tram Suppliers to A-Z Listing of Bus, Coach & Rapid Transit Suppliers and the Tramway & Light Transit Equipment sub-section in the Trade Directory to Rapid Transit/Priority Equipment and also re-naming of Exhibition Organisers to Exhibition/Event Organisers. Also re-named is Coach Hire Broker to Coach Hire Broker/Vehicle Rental to acknowledge that important part of coach operation.

The Refreshment Facilities section has been re-named to Tourist Venues/Refreshment Facilities.

More than 30 entries have been added to the address list in 2007.

We are very grateful to all who returned their entries - we know it is not easy to find the time to do chores like this. This year we were able to update many more entries than last year through replies received and further research carried out - thank you to all who replied and helped with the research.

If there is no change to your entry there is no need to re-write it all - just say something like "as for last year" but please say who you are. We have had forms returned complete but with no indication as to who they are from.

For the next edition we hope to include a category for operators offering wedding transport. We also hope to expand the coach parking listings in the A-Z section.

There will be the continuing challenge of sorting out the problem of entries for which there has been no reply for a number of years and for which it has been impracticable to gain information from other sources. We have increased the input from other experts in the bus industry so that more accuracy can be attained. Some pruning has been carried out in this edition and will be taken forward for the next.

I would like to welcome industry expert, Ian Barlex, who will be the Editor from the next issue onwards.

Tony Pattison, Editor
August 2007

Clean up for the London LEZ ...with Eminox particulate filter systems

- Exhaust system upgrades to meet London Low Emission Zone standards
- RPC approved CRT® and FBC systems virtually eliminate particulate matter
- Fitting, electronic service indicators and filter exchange available
- Proven technology, almost 50,000 systems in London, Paris and across Europe

Eminox

Eminox Ltd, North Warren Road, Gainsborough, DN21 2TU. Tel: +44 (0)1427 810088 Fax: +44 (0)1427 810061 Email: lez@eminox.com Web: www.eminox.com

Acknowledgements

I am very grateful to Alan Butcher for all his help and advice with layout, production and support for both the entries and the mailing list.

I would like to thank Ian Barlex and Chris Bushell for their major help in updating and correcting many entries throughout the whole book.

I would also like to thank Norman Kemp, Nu-Venture, Coaches Ltd for all his help with compiling the Kent entries.

I would also like to thank Mary Webb and Colin Oggelsby for their substantial input to the current edition and Ann Pattison for compiling the index.

Thanks, too, must go to Irena Cornwell, our Advertising Manager, who has not only worked so hard liaising with our advertisers but has been an important source of new entries.

Finally, thanks to our many advertisers who support the Little Red Book. Please use them and say you saw the advert in the LRB.

How *LRB* entries are compiled

As usual, every operator, manufacturer, supplier and other organisation featured in *LRB 2008* received an invitation to correct their entry for this edition free of charge.

Not all operators responded, which means that some existing unchanged entries are repeated. This is done reluctantly, and we are aware that there must be some entries for companies that are no longer in business; unless we are told of these, perhaps by neighbouring operators, it is impossible to follow up every non-response, although we do try to correct as much information as possible from whatever sources we can obtain. We have used an asterisk to signify those companies that have responded this time.

By the same token, new entrants to the bus and coach market should not wait for *LRB* to make contact. If you are in the bus or coach business, and would like to appear (free of charge) in the next *LRB*, please write to the Editor of *LRB* at Ian Allan Publishing Ltd, Riverdene Business Park, Molesey Road, Hersham, Surrey KT12 4RG, requesting to receive a form for the next edition.

LRB is used by a substantial number of bus and coach operators, as well as by national and local government, trade organisations, tendering authorities, group travel organisers, hotels and leisure attractions.

Advertising in *LRB*

For information regarding advertising contact:
David Lane, Little Red Book Advertising, Foundry Road, Stamford, Lincolnshire PE9 2PP
Tel: 01780 484632   Fax: 01780 763388.

Do you want to keep your LITTLE RED BOOK up-to-date?
Buses magazine is now carrying updates every month.
See opposite title page for Subscription details

section 1

Trade Directory

Vehicle suppliers and dealers	**8**
A-Z listing of suppliers and manufacturers	**17**
Bus & Coach industry service providers	**48**

VEHICLE SUPPLIERS & DEALERS
Full-size bus and coach chassis and integrals

Trade Directory

*ALEXANDER DENNIS LTD
Dennis Way, Guildford GU1 1AF
Tel: 01483 571271
Fax: 01483 306836
Web sites: www.alexander-dennis.com
Range: hybrid single-deck bus, rear-engined low-floor single-deck bus, chassis for rear-engined low-floor midibus, rear-engined low-floor single-deck bus, mid-engined coach, rear-engined coach, rear-engined low-floor double-deck bus, two- or three-axle, low-floor schoolbus.

AUTOSAN UK
UK Supplier: **Autoholdings**
Bedworth Road, Coventry CV6 6BP
Tel: 024 7636 0011
Web site: www.autosanuk.com
Range: High-floor school bus, single-deck bus, coach

AYATS
UK Supplier: **AYATS (GB) LTD**
Meadow Drive, Earith, Cambridge PE28 3SA
Tel: 01487 843333
Fax: 01487 843285
E-mail: david@sunfunholidays.co.uk
Web site: www.carroceriasayats.es
  Ireland supplier: **BARTONS TRANSPORT**
  Straffan Road, Maynooth, Co Kildare
  Tel: 00 353 1 628 6026
  Fax: 00 353 1 628 6722
  E-mail: info@bartons-transport.ie
Models: Rear-engined integral coach range - up to 15m

BMC UK LTD
UK Supplier: **Autoholdings**
Bedworth Road, Coventry CV6 6BP
Tel: 024 7636 3003
Website: www.bmcukltd.com
Models: integral front-engined schoolbus, integral front-engined midicoach, integral rear-engined 11m low-floor single-deck bus

IRISBUS (UK) LTD
Iveco House, Station Road, Watford WD17 1SR
Tel: 01923 259660
Fax: 01923 259623
E-mail: info@irisbus.co.uk
Web site: www.irisbus.co.uk
  UK Supplier: **UK COACH & BUS**
  Carlton House, Euroway Estate, Hellaby, Rotherham S66 8QL
  Tel: 01709 705570
  Fax: 01709 705569
Web site: www.uk-cb.com
Models: midibus, low-floor midibus, minibuses, guided bus system, low-floor rear-engined single-deck bus, rear-engined single-deck coach.

KING LONG PLC
UK Supplier: **Autoholdings**
Bedworth Road, Coventry CV6 6BP
Tel: 024 7636 3004
Models: single-deck coach

MAN
UK Supplier: **Neoman Bus UK**
Frankland Road, Blagrove, Swindon SN5 8YU
Web site: www.man.co.uk
UK Dealer: **Mentor Coach & Bus Ltd**
Carlton House, Euroway Industrial Estate, Hellaby, Rotherham S66 8QL
Tel: 01709 700600
Web site: www.mentorplc.com
  Ireland supplier: **BRIAN NOONE**
  Straffan Road, Maynooth, Co Kildare
  Tel: 00 353 1 628 6311

Fax: 00 353 1 628 5404
Web site: www.briannooneltd.ie
Models: single-deck low-floor bus, rear-engined coach

MERCEDES-BENZ
UK Supplier:
EVOBUS (UK) LTD
Cross Point Business Park, Ashcroft Way, Coventry CV2 2TU
Tel: 024 7662 6000
Website: www.evobus.com
Models: rear-engine coach, rear-engine integral low-floor single-deck bus, rear-engine integral low-floor single-deck articulated bus

NEOPLAN
UK Supplier: **Neoman UK**
UK Dealer: **Mentor Coach & Bus Ltd**
Carlton House, Euroway Industrial Estate, Hellaby, Rotherham S66 8QL
Tel: 01709 705570
Fax: 01709 705569
E-mail: sales@mentorplc.com
Web site: www.mentorplc.com
Models: single-deck and double-deck rear-engine integral coaches

OPTARE GROUP LTD
Manston Lane, Leeds LS15 8SU
Tel: 0113 264 5182
Fax: 0113 260 6635
E-mail: info@optare.com
Web site: www.optare.com
Models: low-floor minibus, rear-engined integral low-floor single-deck midibus, rear-engined integral low-floor single-deck bus
  UK supplier: **OPTARE COACH SALES**
  Denby Way, Hellaby Industrial Estate, Hellaby, Rotherham S66 8HR
  Tel: 01709 535120
  Fax: 01709 535102
  E-mail: coachsales@optare.com
  Web site: www.optare.com

PLAXTON
Plaxton Park, Cayton Low Road, Eastfield, Scarborough YO11 3BY
Tel: 01723 581500
Fax: 01723 5813238
E-mail: sales@plaxtonlimited.co.uk
Web site: www.plaxtonlimited.co.uk
Range: coaches, buses, midicoach and midibus bodies
(Part of Alexander Dennis)

*SCANIA (GB) LTD
Tongwell, Milton Keynes MK15 8HB
Tel: 01908 210210
Fax: 01908 215040
Web site: www.scania.com
Range: rear-engined low-floor single-deck and double-deck bus chassis, integral low-floor single-deck bus, integral low-floor double-deck bus, rear-engined coach.

SETRA
UK Supplier:
EVOBUS (UK) LTD
Cross Point Business Park, Ashcroft Way, Coventry CV2 2TU
Tel: 024 7662 6000
Website: www.evobus.com, www.setra.de
Models: rear-engined integral coaches

VAN HOOL
Bernard Van Hoolstraat 58, B-2500 Lier-Koningshooikt, Belgium
Tel: 00 32 3 420 20 20
Fax: 00 32 3 482 33 68
Website: www.vanhool.be
Models: integral coaches

Trade Directory

VDL BOVA
Web site: www.vdlbova.nl
UK Suppliers: **MOSELEY (PCV) LTD**
Elmsall Way, Dale Lane, South Elmsall, Pontefract WF9 2XS
Tel: 01977 609000
Fax: 01977 609900
Web site: www.moseleycoachsales.co.uk
  MOSELEY IN THE SOUTH LTD
  Summerfield Avenue, Chelston Business Park, Wellington TA21 9JF
  Tel: 01823 653000
  Fax: 01823 663502
  E-mail: enquiries@moseleysouth.co.uk
Models: Lexio, Magiq, Futura single-deck luxury coach; *Synergy* double-deck coach

VDL BUS INTERNATIONAL
UK Supplier: **ARRIVA BUS AND COACH**
Lodge Garage, Whitehall Road West, Gomersal, Cleckheaton BD19 4BJ
Tel: 01274 681144
Web site: www.arriva.co.uk
Models: rear-engined low-floor single-deck bus, rear-engined low-floor double-deck bus, rear-engined coach, rear-engined three-axle single- or double-deck coach.

VOLVO BUS LTD
Wedgnock Lane, Warwick CV34 5YA
Tel: 01926 401777
Fax: 01926 407407
Website: www.volvobuses.volvo.co.uk, www.volvo.com
Models: rear-engined low-floor single-deck bus, rear-engined low-floor articulated single-deck bus, mid-engined coach, rear-engined integral coach, rear-engined low-floor double-deck bus.

Bus Rapid Transit Vehicles

IRISBUS (UK) LTD
Iveco House, Station Road, Watford WD17 1SR
Tel: 01923 259660
Fax: 01923 259623
E-mail: info@irisbus.co.uk
Web site: www.irisbus.co.uk
Models: guided bus system

MINITRAM SYSTEMS LTD
12 Waterloo Park Estate, Bidford on Avon B50 4JH
Tel: 01789 490707
Fax: 01789 490592
E-mail: enquiries@tdi.uk.com
Website: www.minitram.com
Models: Rubber tyre-guided/unguided/rail 7.8m vehicle

VOLVO BUS LTD
Wedgnock Lane, Warwick CV34 5YA
Tel: 01926 401777
Fax: 01926 407407
Website: www.volvobuses.volvo.co.uk, www.volvo.com
Models: rear-engined low-floor single-deck bus, rear-engined low-floor articulated single-deck bus, rear-engined low-floor double-deck bus *(chassis can be equipped with guidewheels for operation on guideways)*.

*WRIGHT GROUP
Galgorm, Ballymena, Northern Ireland BT42 1PY
Tel: 028 2564 1212
Fax: 028 2564 9703
E-mail: info@wright-bus.com
Web site: www.wright-bus.com
Models: StreetCar rapid transit vehicle *(further models - see bodybuilders section).*

Light Rail Vehicles

ALSTOM TRANSPORT
Worldwide headquarters: 48 rue Albert Dhalenne, F-93482 Saint-Ouen Cedex, France
Tel: 00 33 1 41 66 90 00
Fax: 00 33 1 41 66 96 66
Web site: www.transport.alstom.com
Models: rail vehicles including light rail vehicles, traction equipment, infrastructure and maintenance services.

BOMBARDIER TRANSPORTATION
Management Office: 1101 Parent Street, Saint-Bruno, Quebec J3V 6E6, Canada
Tel: 00 1 450 441 20 20
Fax: 00 1 450 441 15 15
Web site: www.transportation.bombardier.com
BOMBARDIER TRANSPORTATION METROS
Litchurch Lane, Derby DE24 8AD
Tel: 01332 344666
Fax: 01332 266271
Models: light rail vehicles, trams, guided or unguided bi-mode rubber tyred electric vehicle.

MINITRAM SYSTEMS LTD
12 Waterloo Park Estate, Bidford on Avon B50 4JH
Tel: 01789 490707
Fax: 01789 490592
E-mail: enquiries@tdi.uk.com
Website: www.minitram.com
Models: Rubber tyre-guided/unguided/rail 7.8m vehicle

*PARRY PEOPLE MOVERS LTD
Overend Road, Cradley Heath, Dudley B64 7DD
Tel: 01384 569171
Fax: 01384 637753
E-mail: jpmparry@aol.com
Website: www.parrytech.com
Models: Ultra light rail vehicles and trams

TRAM POWER LTD
Unit 4, Carraway Road, Gillmoss Industrial Estate, Liverpool L11 0EE
Tel: 0151 547 1425
Fax: 0151 546 6066
Website: www.trampower.co.uk/CityClass.html
Models: Articulated lightweight low-cost tram

Bodybuilders (large vehicles)

SALVADOR CAETANO (UK) LTD
Mill Lane, Heather, Coalville LE67 2QA
Web site: www.caetano.co.uk
Tel: 01530 263333
Fax: 01530 263379
E-mail: enquiries@caetano.co.uk

SC COACHBUILDERS LTD
Hambledon Road, Waterlooville PO7 7UA
Tel: 023 9225 8211
Fax: 023 9225 5611
E-mail: sccaetano.co.uk
Web site: www.caetano.co.uk
Models: single-deck coach, single-deck low-floor midibus.

*EAST LANCASHIRE COACHBUILDERS LTD
Lower Philips Road, Whitebirk Industrial Estate, Blackburn BB1 5UD
Tel: 01254 504150
Fax: 01254 504197
E-mail: john.horn@elcb.co.uk
Web site: www.elcb.co.uk
Models: double-deck low-floor bus, single-deck low floor bus, single-deck low-floor midibus

Trade Directory

ESKER BUS & COACH SALES LTD
Comagh Business Park, Kilbeggan, Co Westmeath, Ireland
Tel: 00 353 506 33070
Fax: 00 353 506 33070
E-mail: info@eskerbusandcoach.com
Web site: www.eskerbusandcoach.com
Models: single-deck coach, single-deck low-floor midibus.

IRIZAR
UK spares supplier: **TRAMONTANA**
Chapelknowe Road, Carfin, Motherwell ML1 5LE
Tel: 01698 861790
Fax: 01698 860778
E-mail: wdt90@tiscali.co.uk
Web site: tramontanacoach.co.uk

JONCKHEERE
Importer: *VOLVO BUS AND COACH CENTRE
Belton Road West, Loughborough LE11 5HP
Tel: 01509 217777
Fax: 01509 239362
Web site: www.volvo.com
Models: single-deck coach
  UK service: **TRAMONTANA**
  Chapelknowe Road, Carfin, Motherwell ML1 5LE
  Tel: 01698 861790
  Fax: 01698 860778
  E-mail: wdt90@tiscali.co.uk
  Web site: tramontanacoach.co.uk

LEICESTER CARRIAGE BUILDERS
Marlow Road, Leicester LE3 2BQ
Tel: 0116 282 4270
Fax: 0116 263 0554
E-mail: rick.johnson@midlandsco-op.com
Web site: www.leicestercarriagebuilders.co.uk

***MCV BUS AND COACH LTD**
Sterling Place, Elean Business Park, Sutton, Ely CB6 2QE
Tel: 01353 773000
Fax: 01353 773001
E-mail: info@mcv-uk.com

***MOSELEY DISTRIBUTORS LTD**
Elmsall Way, Dale Lane, South Elmsall, Pontefract WF9 2XS
Tel: 01977 609000
Fax: 01977 609900
Web site: www.moseleycoachsales.co.uk

NEOPLAN
UK Supplier: *MENTOR
Mentor Coach & Bus Ltd, Carlton House, Euroway Industrial Estate, Hellaby, Rotherham S66 8QL
Tel: 01709 700600
Fax: 01709 700007
E-mail: sales@mentorplc.com
Web site: www.mentorplc.com
Models: single-deck coach, also integral coach.

NOGE
UK Supplier: *MENTOR
Mentor Coach & Bus Ltd, Carlton House, Euroway Industrial Estate, Hellaby, Rotherham S66 8QL
Tel: 01709 700600
Fax: 01709 700007
E-mail: sales@mentorplc.com
Web site: www.mentorplc.com
  Ireland supplier: **BRIAN NOONE**
  Straffan Road, Maynooth, Co Kildare
  Tel: 00 353 1 628 6311
  Fax: 00 353 1 628 5404
  Models: two-axle and three-axle integral coach bodies.

OPTARE LTD
Manston Lane, Leeds LS15 8SU
Tel: 0113 264 5182
Fax: 0113 260 6235
E-mail: info@optare.com
Web site: www.optare.com
Models: double-deck and single-deck buses, also integral
  UK supplier: **OPTARE COACH SALES**
  Denby Way, Hellaby Industrial Estate, Hellaby, Rotherham S66 8HR

Tel: 01709 535120
Fax: 01709 535102
E-mail: coachsales@optare.com
Web site: www.optare.com

PLAXTON
Plaxton Park, Cayton Low Road, Eastfield, Scarborough YO11 3BY
Tel: 01723 581500
Fax: 01723 5813238
E-mail: sales@plaxtonlimited.co.uk
Web site: www.plaxtonlimited.co.uk
Range: coaches, buses, midicoach and midibus bodies
(Part of Alexander Dennis)

VAN HOOL
Bernard Van Hoolstraat 58, B-2500 Lier-Koningshooikt, Belgium
Tel: 00 32 3 420 20 20
Fax: 00 32 3 482 33 60
E-mail: info@vanhool.be
Web site: www.vanhool.be
Models: coach bodies

VDL BERKHOF
UK Supplier: *ARRIVA BUS AND COACH
Lodge Garage, Whitehall Road West, Gomersal, Cleckheaton BD19 4BJ
Tel: 01274 681144
Models: rear-engined three-axle or two-axle single-deck coach.

***WRIGHT GROUP**
Galgorm, Ballymena, Northern Ireland BT42 1PY
Tel: 028 2564 1212
Fax: 028 2564 9703
E-mail: info@wright-bus.com
Web site: www.wright-bus.com
Models: double-deck low-floor bus body, single-deck low-floor articulated bus body, FTR advanced bus rapid transit vehicle, single-deck low-floor bus, single-deck low-entry coach, single-deck low-floor midibus.

Chassis and integral vehicles (small vehicles - under 9m)

***ALEXANDER DENNIS**
Dennis Way, Guildford GU1 1AF
Tel: 01483 571271
Fax: 01483 306836
Web site: www.alexander-dennis.com
Range: rear-engined low-floor midibus

FORD MOTOR COMPANY
Ford Motor Co Ltd, Eagle Way, Brentwood CM13 3BW
Tel: 0845 7111 888
Web site: www.fordvans.co.uk/peoplemovers
Models: Transit, complete minibus or chassis-cowl.

IRISBUS (UK) LTD
Iveco House, Station Road, Watford WD17 1SR
Tel: 01923 259660
Fax: 01923 259623
E-mail: info@irisbus.co.uk
Web site: www.irisbus.co.uk

JOHN BRADSHAW LTD
New Lane, Stibbington, Peterborough PE8 6LW
Tel: 01780 781801
Web site: www.john-bradshaw.co.uk
Models: Electric minibus/taxi

KVC MANUFACTURING LTD
Comagh Business Park, Kilbeggan, Co Westmeath, Ireland
Tel: 00 353 506 32699
Fax: 00 353 506 32691
E-mail: info@kvc.ie
Web site: www.kvc.ie

LDV LTD
Bromford House, Drews Lane, Birmingham B8 2QG
Tel: 0121 322 2000
Fax: 0121 327 4487
Web site: www.ldv.co.uk
Models: Complete minibus or chassis-cowl

MERCEDES-BENZ
UK Supplier:
EVOBUS (UK) LTD
Cross Point Business Park, Ashcroft Way, Coventry CV2 2TU
Tel: 024 7662 6000
Website: www.evobus.com
Models: Complete low-floor minibus or chassis cowl

MINITRAM SYSTEMS LTD
12 Waterloo Park Estate, Bidford on Avon B50 4JH
Tel: 01789 490707
Fax: 01789 490592
E-mail: enquiries@tdi.uk.com
Web site: www.minitram.com
Models: Rubber tyre-guided/unguided/rail 7.8m vehicle

NU-TRACK LTD
Steeple Industrial Estate, Antrim BT41 1AB
Tel: 028 94 469 550
Fax: 028 94 465 430
E-mail: enquiries@nu-track.co.uk

OPTARE LTD
Manston Lane, Leeds LS15 8SU
Tel: 0113 264 5182
Fax: 0113 260 6635
Web site: www.optare.com
Models: front-engined integral low-floor minibus, rear-engined integral low-floor midibus.
UK supplier: **OPTARE COACH SALES**
Denby Way, Hellaby Industrial Estate, Hellaby, Rotherham S66 8HR
Tel: 01709 535120
Fax: 01709 535102
E-mail: coachsales@optare.com
Web site: www.optare.com

RENAULT UK LTD
Rivers Office Park, Denham Way, Maple Cross, Rickmansworth WD3 9YS
Tel: 01923 855500
Web site: www.renault.co.uk
Models: Complete minibus or chassis-cowl; electric vehicle.

TOYOTA (GB) PLC
Great Burgh, Burgh Heath, Epsom KT18 5UX
Tel: 01737 363633
Mobile: 07785 238798
E-mail: steve.prime@tgb.toyota.co.uk
Web site: www.toyota.com
UK suppliers:
A&D Coach Sales
Tel: 01884 860767
Holloway Commercials
Tel: 01902 636661
Salvador Caetano
Tel: 01530 26333
Models: Optimo midicoach, chassis cowl

VAUXHALL MOTORS LTD
Luton LU1 3YT
Tel: 020 7439 0303
Vauxhall Mobility: 0800 731 5267
Web site: www.vauxhall.co.uk
Models: Complete minibus or chassis-cowl.

VOLKSWAGEN COMMERCIAL VEHICLES
Yeomans Drive, Blakelands, Milton Keynes MK14 5AN
Web site: www.volkswagen-vans.co.uk
Models: Complete minibus or chassis-cowl.

Bodybuilders (small vehicles)
Minibus conversions

ADVANCED VEHICLE BUILDERS
Upper Mantle Close, Clay Cross S45 9NU
Tel: 01246 250022
Fax: 01246 250016
E-mail: info@minibus.co.uk

BLUE BIRD VEHICLES LTD
Unit 7, Plaxton Park, Cayton Low Road, Eastfield, Scarborough YO11 3BY
Tel: 01723 860800
Fax: 01723 585235
E-mail: info@bluebirdvehicles.com
Web site: www.bluebirdvehicles.com

BURNT TREE VEHICLE SOLUTIONS
Burnt Tree House, Knights Way, Battlefield Enterprise Park, Harlescott Lane, Shrewsbury SY1 3JE
Tel: 01743 457650
Web site: www.burnt-tree.co.uk

CHASSIS DEVELOPMENTS
Grovebury Road, Leighton Buzzard LU7 8SL
Tel: 01525 374151
Web site: www.chassisdevelopments.co.uk

*CONCEPT COACHCRAFT
Far Cromwell Road, Bredbury, Stockport SK6 2SE
Tel: 0161 406 9322
Fax: 0161 406 9588
E-mail: sales@conceptcoachcraft.com
Web site: www.conceptcoachcraft.com

COURTSIDE CONVERSIONS LTD
1 Woodward Road, Howden Industrial Estate, Tiverton EX16 5HS
Tel: 01884 256048
Fax: 01884 256087
E-mail: courtsidesales@aol.com

CROWN COACHBUILDERS LTD
32 Flemington Industrial Park, Flemington, Motherwell ML1 1SN
Tel: 01698 276087
Fax: 01698 276144
E-mail: davidgreer@hotmail.com
Web site: www.crowncoachbuilders.co.uk

CVI (COMMERCIAL VEHICLE INNOVATION)
Moorfoot View, Bilston, Edinburgh EH25 9SL
Tel: 0131 473 9300
Web site: www.c-v-i.co.uk

ESKER BUS & COACH SALES LTD
Comagh Business Park, Kilbeggan, Co Westmeath, Ireland
Tel: 00 353 506 33070
Fax: 00 353 506 33070
E-mail: info@eskerbusandcoach.com
Web site: www.eskerbusandcoach.com

ESKER BUS & COACH (UK) LTD
Unit 3, Haigh Moor Drive, Brooklands Park, Church Lane, Dinnington, Sheffield S25 2JY
Tel: 01909 552244
Fax: 01909 569242
E-mail: info@eskerbusandcoach.co.uk
Web site: www.eskerbusandcoach.co.uk

EURO COACH BUILDERS LTD
Deerybeg Industrial Estate, Gweedore, Co Donegal, Ireland
Tel: 00 353 75 31528
Fax: 00 353 75 31930
Web site: www.eurocoachbuilders.ie

EXCEL CONVERSIONS LTD
Excel House, Durham Lane, Armthorpe, Doncaster DN3 3FE
Tel: 01302 835388
Fax: 01302 835389
E-mail: admin@excelconversions.co.uk
Web site: www.excelconversions.co.uk

Trade Directory

Trade Directory

GM COACHWORK LTD
Trusham, Newton Abbot TQ13 0NX
Tel: 01626 853050
Fax: 01626 853083
Web site: www.gmcoachwork.co.uk

INDCAR SA
Poligono Industrial Torres Pujals, E-17401 Arbucies (Girona), Spain
Web site: www.indar.com

JDC - JOHN DENNIS COACHBUILDERS
25 Westfield Road, Guildford GU1 1RR
Tel: 01483 501457
Web site: www.jdcbus.co.uk

JUBILEE AUTOMOTIVE GROUP
Woden Road South, Wednesbury WS10 0NQ
Tel: 0121 502 2252
Fax: 0121 502 2258
E-mail: sales@jubileeauto.co.uk

LEICESTER CARRIAGE BUILDERS
Marlow Road, Leicester LE3 2BQ
Tel: 0116 282 4270
Fax: 0116 263 0554
E-mail: rick.johnson@midlandsco-op.com
Web site: www.leicestercarriagebuilders.co.uk

*MCV BUS AND COACH LTD
Sterling Place, Elean Business Park, Sutton, Ely CB6 2QE
Tel: 01353 773000
Fax: 01353 773001
E-mail: info@mcv-uk.com

MELLOR COACHCRAFT
Miall Street, Rochdale OL11 1HY
Tel: 01706 860610
Fax: 01706 860042
E-mail: mcsales@woodhall-nicholson.co.uk
Web site: www.woodhall-nicholson.co.uk

MINIBUS OPTIONS LTD
Bingswood Industrial Estate, Whaley Bridge, High Peak SK23 7LY
Tel: 01663 735255
Fax: 01663 735352
E-mail: info@minibusoptions.co.uk
Web site: www.minibusoptions.co.uk

NU-TRACK LTD
Steeple Industrial Estate, Antrim BT41 1AB
Tel: 028 9446 9550
Fax: 028 9446 5430
E-mail: enquiries@nu-track.co.uk

OLYMPUS COACHCRAFT LTD
7 Temperance Street, Manchester M12 6DX
Tel/Fax: 0161 273 4259
E-mail: geoffolympus@aol.com
Web site: www.olympuscoaches.co.uk

OPTARE LTD
Manston Lane, Leeds, LS15 8SU
Tel: 0113 264 5182
Fax: 0113 260 6235
Web site: www.optare.com

PLAXTON LIMITED
Plaxton Park, Cayton Low Road, Eastfield, Scarborough YO11 3BY
Tel: 01723 581500
Fax: 01723 5813238
Web site: www.plaxtonlimited.co.uk
Range: coaches; midicoach and midibus bodies.

PVS MANUFACTURING LTD
8 Ardboe Business Park, Kilmascally Road, Ardboe, Dungannon BT71 5BP
Tel: 028 8673 6969
Fax: 028 8673 7178
E-mail: mail@pvsltd.com
Web site: www.conversionspecialists.com

STANFORD COACH WORKS
Mobility House, Stanhope Industrial Park, Wharf Road, Stanford-le-Hope SS17 0EH
Tel: 01375 676088
Fax: 01375 677999
E-mail: sales@stanfordcoachworks.co.uk
Web site: www.stanfordcoachworks.co.uk
Range: mini- and midibuses, mini- and midicoaches

JOHN STEWART & CO (WISHAW) LTD
Smith Avenue, Garrion Business Park, Wishaw ML2 0RY
Tel: 01698 373483
Fax: 01698 357185

TAWE COACHBUILDERS LTD
Tawe House, Alloy Industrial Estate, Pontardawe SA8 4EN
Tel: 01792 832040
Fax: 01792 832041
Web site: www.tawecoachbuildersltd.co.uk

TVAC (THE VEHICLE APPLICATION CENTRE)
Centurion Way, Leyland PR26 6TZ
Tel: 01772 457116
Web site: www.tvac.com
Range: low-floor mini- and midibuses, mini- and midicoaches

UVMODULAR
Locksley Road, Armytage Road Industrial Estate, Brighouse HD6 1QF
Tel: 01484 400200
Fax: 01484 401125
E-mail: sales@uvmodular.co.uk

WILKER GROUP
Frederick Street, Clara, Co Offaly, Ireland
Tel: 00 353 506 31010
E-mail: info@wilkergroup.com
UK subsidiary
Sandy lane, Ettiley Heath, Sandbach CW11 3NG
Tel: 01270 705999
E-mail: info.uk@wilkergroup.com
Range: low-floor mini- and midibuses, mini- and midicoaches

Dealers

AD COACH SALES
Newbridge Coach Depot, Witheridge EX16 8PY
Tel: 01884 860767
E-mail: ggoodwin@adcoachsales.co.uk
Web site: www.adcoachsales.co.uk

AJP COMMERCIALS
305-317 Wednesbury Road, Walsall WS2 9QJ
Tel: 01922 639652
Fax: 01922 611700

ALLIED VEHICLES LTD
230 Balmore Road, Glasgow G22 6LJ
Tel: 0800 916 3046
Web site: www.alliedvechicles.co.uk/bus
E-mail: info@alliedvechicles.co.uk

*ARRIVA BUS AND COACH
Lodge Garage, Whitehall Road West, Gomersal, Cleckheaton BD19 4BJ
Tel: 01274 681144

AVONDALE INTERNATIONAL LTD
451 Clifton Drive North, Lytham St Annes FY8 2PS
Tel: 01253 727211
Fax: 01253 714210

B.A.S.E. LTD
129 Clydesdale Place, Moss Side Industrial Estate, Leyland PR26 7QS
Tel: 01772 425355
Web site: www.basecoachsales.co.uk

Trade Directory

BLYTHSWOOD MOTORS LTD
1175 Argyle Street, Glasgow G3 8TQ
Tel: 0141 221 3165
Fax: 0141 221 3172
E-mail: blythswoodmotors@aol.com
Web site: www.blythswoodmotors.co.uk

BOB VALE COACH SALES
Kingshill House, Spurlands End Road, Great Kingshill,
High Wycombe HP15 6PE
Tel: 01494 716996
Fax: 01494 716331
E-mail: bobvalecoachsale@btconnect.com
Web site: www.bobvalecoachsale.com

BRIAN NOONE
Straffan Road, Maynooth, Co Kildare, Ireland
Tel: 00 353 1 628 6311
Fax: 00 353 1 628 5404
Web site: www.briannooneltd.ie

*BRISTOL BUS & COACH SALES
6/7 Freestone Road, St Philips, Bristol BS2 0QN
Tel: 0117 971 0251
Fax: 0117 972 3121
E-mail: simon.munden@bristolbusandcoach.co.uk
Web site: www.bristolbusandcoach.co.uk

*BRITISH BUS SALES
Mike Nash, PO Box 534, Dorking RH5 5XB
Tel: 07836 656692
E-mail: nashionalbus1@btconnect.com
Web site: www.britishbussales.co.uk

SALVADOR CAETANO (UK) LTD
Mill Lane, Heather, Coalville LE67 2QA
Tel: 01530 263333
Fax: 01530 263379
E-mail: enquiries@caetano.co.uk
Web site: www.caetano.co.uk
Models: single-deck coach, single-deck low-floor midibus.

DAWSONRENTALS BUS AND COACH LTD
Delaware Drive, Tongwell, Milton Keynes MK15 8JH
Tel: 01908 218111
Fax: 01908 610156
E-mail: info@dawsongroup.co.uk
Web site: www.dawsongroup.co.uk

EAST LANCASHIRE COACHBUILDERS LTD
Lower Philips Road, Whitebirk Industrial Estate, Blackburn BB1 5UD
Tel: 01254 504150
Fax: 01254 504197
E-mail: john.horn@elcb.co.uk
Web site: www.elcb.co.uk

ENSIGN BUS CO LTD
Juliette Close, Purfleet Industrial Estate, Purfleet RM15 4YF
Tel: 01708 865656
Fax: 01708 864340
E-mail: sales@ensignbus.com
Web site: www.ensignbus.com

ERRINGTONS OF EVINGTON LTD
Glenrise Garage, London Road (A6), Oadby LE2 4RG
Tel: 0116 259 2131
Fax: 0116 259 2313

EVOBUS (UK) LTD
Cross Point Business Park, Ashcroft Way, Coventry CV2 2TU
Tel: 024 7662 6000
Website: www.evobus.com

DAVID FISHWICK VEHICLE SALES
North Valley, Colne BB8 0RF
Tel: 01282 615138/867772

FLEET AUCTION GROUP
Brindley Road, Stephenson Industrial park, Coalville LE67 3HG
Tel: 01530 833535
E-mail: fleet.master@btinternet.com
Web site: www.fleetauctiongroup.com

FLEETMASTER BUS & COACH LTD
Regent House, Silverwood, Snow Hill, Copthorne RH10 3ED
Tel: 01342 859058
Fax: 01342 859059
E-mail: fleet.master@btinternet.com
Web site: www.fleetmaster.co.uk

FURROWS COMMERCIAL VEHICLES
Kemberton Road, Halesfield, Telford TF7 4QS
Tel: 01952 684433

GM COACHWORK LTD
Teign Valley, Trusham, Newton Abbot TQ13 0NX
Tel: 01626 853050
Fax: 01626 853083
Web site: www.gmcoachwork.co.uk
E-mail: david.vadght@gmcoachwork.co.uk

THOMAS HARDIE - WIGAN
Lockett Road, Ashton-in-Makerfield WN4 8DE
Tel: 01942 505124
Fax: 01942 505119

IAN GORDON COMMERCIALS
Schawkark Garage, Stair KA5 5JA
Tel: 01292 591764

HOLLOWAY COMMERCIALS
60 Walsall Road, Willenhall WV13 2EF
Tel: 01902 636661
Fax: 01902 609652
E-mail: sales@hollowaycommercials.co.uk
Web site: www.hollowaycommercials.co.uk

B & D HOLT LTD
Cuthbert Street, Bolton BL3 3SD
Tel: 01204 650999
Fax: 01204 665300
E-mail: bevholt@bdholt.co.uk
Web site: www.bdholt.co.uk

IRISH COMMERCIALS (SALES)
Naas, Co Kildare, Ireland

LVD
Leinster Vehicle Distributors Ltd, Urlingford, Co Kilkenny, Ireland
Tel: 00 353 56 31189/88 3 1899
Web site: www.lvd.ie

LONDON BUS EXPORT
PO Box 12, Chepstow NP6 7NQ
Tel: 01291 689741
Fax: 01291 681361
E-mail: lonbusco@globalnet.co.uk
Web site: www.london.bus.co.uk

LOUGHSHORE AUTOS LTD
26 Killycanavan Road, Ardboe, Dungannon BT71 5BP
Tel: 028 8673 7325
Fax: 028 8673 5882
E-mail: michael@loughshoreautosltd.com
Web site: www.loughshoreautosltd.com

MAJORLINE ENGINEERING LTD
Baybridge Industrial Units, Baybridge Lane, Owslebury, Winchester SO21 1JN
Tel: 01962 777077
Fax: 01962 777661, 777667
E-mail: majorline@compuserve.com

MASS SPECIAL ENGINEERING LTD
Anston, Sheffield S25 4SD
Tel: 01909 550480
Fax: 01909 550486

*MENTOR COACH & BUS LTD
Carlton House, Euroway Industrial Estate, Hellaby, Rotherham S66 8QL
Tel: 01709 700600
Fax: 01709 700007
E-mail: sales@mentorplc.com
Web site: www.mentorplc.com

Trade Directory

MID WEST CHELTENHAM LTD
The Coach Centre, Golden Valley, Staverton, Cheltenham GL51 0TE
Tel: 01452 859111
Fax: 01452 859222
Web site: www.bussales.co.uk

MISTRAL GROUP (UK) PLC
PO Box 130, Knutsford WA16 6AG
Tel: 0870 241 5786
Fax: 0870 241 5784
E-mail: sales@mistral-group.com
Web site: www.mistral-group.com

MOSELEY (PCV) LTD
Elmsall Way, Dale Lane, South Elmsall, Pontefract WF9 2XS
Tel: 01977 609000
Fax: 01977 609900
Web site: www.moseleycoachsales.co.uk

MOSELEY IN THE SOUTH LTD
Summerfield Avenue, Chelston Business Park, Wellington TA21 9JF
Tel: 01823 653000
Fax: 01823 663502
E-mail: enquiries@moseleysouth.co.uk

*MOSELEY DISTRIBUTORS
Rydenmains, Condoratt Road, Glenmavis, Airdrie ML6 0PP
Tel: 01236 750501
Fax: 01236 750503
E-mail: enquiries@moseleydistributors.co.uk
Web site: www.moseleydistributors.co.uk

NEXT BUS LTD
Vincients Road, Bumpers Farm Industrial Estate, Chippenham SN14 6QA
Tel: 01249 462462
Fax: 01249 448844
E-mail: sales@next-bus.co.uk
Web site: www.next-bus.co.uk

W. NORTHS (PV) LTD
Moor Lane Trading Estate, Sherburn in Elmet LS25 6ET
Tel: 01977 682415
Fax: 01977 681119

OPTARE COACH SALES
Denby Way, Hellaby Industrial Estate, Hellaby, Rotherham S66 8HR
Tel: 01709 535120
Fax: 01709 535102
E-mail: coachsales@optare.com
Web site: www.optare.com

OWENS OF OSWESTRY BMC
Unit 3, Foxen Monor Industrial Park, Four Crosses, Llanymynech SY22 6ST
Tel: 01691 652126
Fax: 01691 831142
E-mail: sales@owens-bmc.co.uk
Web site: www.owens-bmc.co.uk

H W PICKRELL
Gardiners Lane North, Crays Hill, Billericay CM11 2XE
Tel: 01268 521033
Fax: 01268 284951
Web site: www.hwpickrell.co.uk

PLAXTON COACH SALES CENTRE
Ryton Road, Anston, Sheffield S25 4DL
Tel: 01909 551155
Fax: 01909 567994
E-mail: coaches@plaxtonlimited.co.uk
Web site: www.plaxtonlimited.co.uk

*SCANIA (GB) LTD
Tongwell, Milton Keynes MK15 8HB
Tel: 01908 210210
Fax: 01908 215040
Web site: www.scania.com

SOMERBUS
Paulton, Bristol BS39 7YR
Tel/Fax: 01761 415456
Web site: www.somerbus.co.uk
E-mail: somerbus@tinyworld.co.uk

SOUTHDOWN PSV LTD
Silverwood, Snow Hill, Copthorne RH10 3EN
Tel: 01342 715222
Fax: 01342 719619
E-mail: bussales@southdownpsv.co.uk
Web site: www.southdownpsv.co.uk

*STAFFORD BUS CENTRE
Unit 27, Moorfields Industrial Estate, Cotes Heath ST21 6QY
Tel: 01782 791774
Fax: 01782 791721
E-mail: martin@staffordbuscentre.com

STEPHENSONS OF ESSEX
Riverside Industrial Estate, South Street, Rochford SS4 1BS
Tel: 01702 541511

STOKE TRUCK & BUS CENTRE
Bute Street, Fenton, Stoke-on-Trent ST4 3PS
Tel: 01782 598310
Fax: 01782 598674
Web site: www.bmcstoke.co.uk

TAYLOR COACH SALES
102 Beck Road, Isleham, Ely CB7 5QP
Tel (mobile): 07850 241848
Tel: 01638 780010

TOYOTA (GB) PLC
Great Burgh, Burgh Heath, Epsom KT18 5UX
Tel: 01737 363633
Fax: 01737 367713
E-mail: steve.prime@tgb.toyota.co.uk
Web site: www.toyota.com
UK suppliers:
A&D Coach Sales
Tel: 01884 860767
Holloway Commercials
Tel: 01902 636661
Salvador Caetano
Tel: 01530 263333

TRAMONTANA COACH DISTRIBUTORS
Chapelknowe Road, Carfin, Motherwell ML1 5LE
Tel: 01698 861790
Fax: 01698 860778
E-mail: wdt90@tiscali.co.uk

UK COACH & BUS
Carlton House, Euroway Estate, Hellaby, Rotherham S66 8QL
Tel: 01709 705570
Fax: 01709 705569
Web site: www.uk-cb.com

USED COACH SALES
PO Box 166, Warrington WA4 5FG
Tel: 0870 062 0616
Fax: 0870 062 4499
Web site: www.usedcoachsales.co.uk

VENTURA BUS + COACH SALES
Unit 39, Hobbs Industrial Estate, Newchapel, Lingfield RH7 6HN
Tel: 01342 835206
Fax: 01342 835813
E-mail:info@venturasales.co.uk

*VOLVO BUS AND COACH CENTRE
Belton Road West, Loughborough LE11 5HP
Tel: 01509 217777
Fax: 01509 239362
Web site: www.volvo.com

WACTON COACH SALES & SERVICES
Linton Trading Estate, Bromyard HR7 4QL
Tel: 01885 482782
Fax: 01885 482127

*WEALDEN PSV LTD
The Bus Garage, 64 Whetsted Road, Five Oak Green, Tonbridge
TN12 6RT
Tel: 01892 833830
Fax: 01892 836977
E-mail: sales@wealdenpsv.co.uk
Web site: www.wealdenpsv.co.uk

ALAN WHITE COACH SALES
135 Nutwell Lane, Doncaster DN3 3JR
Tel: 01302 833203
Fax: 01302 831756
E-mail: sales@alanwhitecoachsales.com
Web site: www.alanwhitecoachsales.com

TREVOR WIGLEY & SONS BUS LTD
Baulder Bridge Road, Carlton, Barnsley S71 3HJ
Tel: 01226 713636/716479
E-mail: wigleys@btconnect.com
Web site: www.twigley.com

*YORKSHIRE BUS & COACH SALES
254A West Ella Road, West Ella, Hull HU10 7SF
Tel: 01482 653302
Fax: 01482 653302
E-mail: craig.porteous@virgin.net

**Do you want to keep your
LITTLE RED BOOK
up-to-date?
Buses magazine is now carrying updates every month.
See opposite title page for Subscription details**

Whatever your interests, historic or modern, we have possibly the most extensive range for the bus enthusiast.

Birmingham
47 Stephenson Street
Birmingham | B2 4DH
Tel: 0121 643 2496 | Fax: 0121 643 6855
Email: bcc@ianallanpublishing.co.uk

Cardiff
31 Royal Arcade
Cardiff | CF10 1AE
Tel: 029 2039 0615 | Fax: 029 2039 0621
Email: cardiff@ianallanpublishing.co.uk

London
45/46 Lower Marsh | Waterloo
London | SE1 7RG
Tel: 020 7401 2100 | Fax: 020 7401 2887
Email: waterloo@ianallanpublishing.co.uk

Manchester
5 Piccadilly Station Approach
Manchester | M1 2GH
Tel: 0161 237 9840 | Fax: 0161 237 9921
Email: manchester@ianallanpublishing.co.uk

Ian Allan PUBLISHING

IAN ALLAN BOOKSHOPS

- Books
- Magazines
- Diecast Models
- DVDs
- CD-ROMs

& much more...

Visit our website:
www.ianallanpublishing.co.uk

A-Z Listing of Bus, Coach & Tram Suppliers

Trade Directory

LIST OF CATEGORIES

Air Conditioning/Ventilation
Audio/Video Systems
Badges - Drivers/Conductors
Batteries
Bicycle Carriers
Body/Electrical Repairs & Refurbishing
Brakes & Brake Linings
Bus Stops/Shelters - see Shelters/Street Furniture
Cash Handling Equipment
Chassis Lubricating Systems
Clutches
Cooling Systems
Destination Indicator Equipment
Door Operating Gear
Drinks Dispensing Equipment
Driving Axles and Gears
Electrical Equipment
Electronic Control
Emission Control Devices
Engineering
Engines
Engine Oil Drain Valves
Exhaust Systems
Fans & Drive Belts
Fare Boxes
Fire Extinguishers
First Aid Equipment
Floor Covering
Fuel, Fuel Management & Lubricants
Garage Equipment
Gearboxes
Hand Driers (Coach Mounted)
Handrails
Headrest Covers/Curtains
Heating & Ventilation Systems
Hub Odometers
In-Coach Catering Equipment
Information Displays - *see* Passenger Information Systems
Labels, Nameplates & Decals
Lifting Equipment
Lifts/Ramps (Passenger)
Lighting/Lighting Systems
Mirrors/Mirror Arms
Model Buses
Oil Management Systems
Painting/Signwriting
Parts Suppliers
Passenger Information Systems
Pneumatic Valves/Cylinders
Rapid Transit/Priority Equipment
Repairs/refurbishment - *see* Body/Electrical Repairs
Retarders & Speed Control Systems
Reversing Safety Systems
Roller Blinds - Passenger/Driver
Roof Lining Fabrics
Seat Belts
Seats, Seat Cushions & Seat Frames
Shelters/Street Furniture
Shock Absorbers/Suspension
Steering
Surveillance Systems
Tachograph Calibrators
Tachograph Chart Analysis Service
Tachographs
Tickets, Ticket machines and Ticket Systems
Timetable Display Frames
Toilet Equipment
Transmission Overhaul
Tree Guards
Tyres
Uniforms
Upholstery
Vacuum Systems
Vehicle Washing and Washers
Wheels, wheeltrims & Covers
Windows & Windscreens

INDUSTRY SERVICE PROVIDERS

Accident Investigation
Accountancy & Audit
Advertising Contractors
Advisory Services
Artwork
Auctioneers & Valuators
Breakdown & Recovery Services
Cleaning Services
Coach Driver Agency
Coach Hire Broker/Rental
Coach Interchange & Parking Facilities
Computer Systems/Software
Consultants
Driver Supply
Driver Training
Exhibition/Event Organisers
Ferry Operators
Finance & Leasing
Graphic Design
Hotels & Hotel Agents
Insurance
Legal & Operations Advisors
Life Insurance & Pensions
Livery Design
Maps for the Bus industry
Marketing Services
Mechanical Investigation
On-Bus Advertising
Printing
Promotional Material
Publications - Magazines & Books
Quality Management Systems
Recruitment
Refreshment Facilities - *see* Tourist Venues/Refreshment Facilities
Timetable Production
Tour Wholesalers
Tourist Venues/Refreshment Facilities
Training & Marketing Services
Vehicle Certification
Vehicle Rental - *see:* Coach Hire Broker/Rental

Coach Climate Control Systems

Airconco Limited

Carrier Sutrak Northern

Airconco Limited is a Carrier Sutrak Network Partner for the North of England and North Wales

- Servicing
- Repairs
- Parts

Tel: 0845 402 401 4   www.airconco.ltd.uk
Unit 10, Middleton Trade Park, Oldham Rd, Middleton, Manchester, M24 1QZ

Air Conditioning/Ventilation

AIRCONCO
Unit 10, Middleton Trade Park, Oldham Road, Middleton, Manchester M24 1QZ
Tel: 0845 402 4014
Fax: 0845 402 4041
E-mail: mail@airconco.uk
Web site: www.airconco.ltd.uk

AMA LTD
Unit 17, Springmill Industrial Estate, Avening Road, Nailsworth GL6 0BH
Tel: 01453 832884
Fax: 01453 832040
E-mail: ama@ftech.co.uk

CARRIER SUTRAK
Unit 6, I O Centre, Barn Way, Lodge Farm Industrial Estate, Northampton NN5 7UW
Tel: 01604 581468
Fax: 01604 758132
E-mail: kim.neale@carrier.utc.com

*CLAYTON HEATERS LTD
Hunter Terrace, Fletchworth Gate, Burnsall Road, Coventry CV5 6SP
Tel: 02476 691916
Fax: 02476 691969
E-mail: sales@claytoncc.co.uk
Web site: www.claytoncc.co.uk

CONSERVE (UK) LTD
Suite 7, Logistics House, Kingsthorpe Road, Northampton NN2 6LJ
Tel: 01604 710055
Fax: 01604 710065
E-mail: information@conserveuk.co.uk
Web site: www.conserveuk.co.uk

*DIRECT PARTS LTD
Unit 1, Churnet Court, Churnetside Business Park, Harrison Way, Cheddleton ST13 7EF
Tel: 01538 361777
Fax: 01538 369100
E-mail: sales@direct-group.co.uk
Web site: www.direct-group.co.uk

EBERSPACHER (UK) LTD
Headlands Business Park, Salisbury Road, Ringwood BH24 3PB
Tel: 01425 480151
Fax: 01425 480152
E-mail: enquiries@eberspacher.com
Web site: www.eberspacher.com

HISPACOLD
See: Clayton Heaters above
Web Site: www.hispacold.es

JAYCAS MINIBUS SALES
11 John Street, Bamber Bridge, Preston PR5 6TJ
Tel/Fax: 01772 321491
E-mail: john@minibusjaycas.co.uk

*THE LAWTON MOTOR BODY BUILDING CO LTD
Knutsford Road, Church Lawton, Stoke-on-Trent ST7 3DN
Tel: 01270 882056
Fax: 01270 883014
E-mail: sales@lawtonmotorbody.co.uk
Web site: www.lawtonmotorbody.co.uk

M A C LTD
Unit 8, Oldends Lane Industrial Estate, Oldends Lane, Stonehouse GL10 3RQ
Tel: 01453 828781
Fax: 01453 828167
E-mail: sales@macai.uk.com
Web site: www.macair.uk.com

*MENTOR
Mentor Coach & Bus Ltd, Carlton House, Euroway Industrial Estate, Hellaby, Rotherham S66 8QL
Tel: 01709 700600
Fax: 01709 700007
E-mail: sales@mentorplc.com
Web site: www.mentorplc.com

NEALINE WINDSCREEN WIPER PRODUCTS
Unit 1, The Sidings Industrial Estate, Birdingbury Road, Marton CV23 9RX
Tel: 01926 633256
Fax: 01926 632600

PLAXTON COACH SALES CENTRE
Ryton Road, Anston, Sheffield S25 4DC
Tel: 01909 551155
Fax: 01909 567994
E-mail: coaches@plaxtonlimited.co.uk
Web site: www.plaxtonlimited.co.uk

SCANIA
Scania Bus & Coach (UK) Ltd, Claylands Avenue, Worksop S81 7DJ.
Tel: 01909 500822.
Fax: 01909 500165

*UNITEC
Parts Division, Denby Way, Hellaby, Rotherham S66 8HR
Tel: 01709 792000
Fax: 01709 792009
E-mail: parts@optare.com

*UNITEC LONDON
Unit 5, Gateway 25, Weston Avenue, West Thurrock RM20 3ZD
Tel: 01708 892440
Fax: 01708 862125
E-mail: london.service@optare.com

*UNITEC ROTHERHAM
Denby Way, Hellaby, Rotherham S66 8HR
Tel: 01709 535101
Fax: 01709 535103
E-mail: rotherham.service@optare.com

*UNITEC SCOTLAND
Unit 7, Cumbernauld Business Park, Ward Park Road, Cumbernauld G67 3JZ
Tel: 01236 726738
Fax: 01236 795651
E-mail: scotland.service@optare.com

WEBASTO PRODUCT UK LTD
Webasto House, White Rose Way, Doncaster Carr DN4 5JH
Tel: 01302 322232
Fax: 01302 322231
E-mail: info@webastouk.com
Web site: www.webasto.co.uk

Audio/Video Systems

*AFTERMARKET COACH SUPPLIES
Unit A, Shipmans Yard, Station Road, Rushton NN14 1RL
Tel: 01536 711310
Web site: www.acsuk.freeuk.com

AUTOSOUND LTD
4 Lister Street, Dudley Hill, Bradford BD4 9PQ
Tel: 01274 688990
Fax: 01274 651318
Web site: www.autosound.co.uk
E-mail: sales@autosound.co.uk

AVT SYSTEMS LTD
Unit 3, Tything Road, Arden Forest Trading Estate, Alcester B49 6ES
Tel: 01789 400357
Fax: 01789 400359
E-mail: enquiries@avtsystems.co.uk
Web site: www.avtsystems.co.uk

EXPRESS COACH REPAIRS LTD
Outgang Lane, Pickering YO18 7EL
Tel: 01751 475215.

FCAV & CO
Brooklyn House, Coleford Road, Bream GL15 6EU
Tel: 01594 564552
Fax: 01594 564556
E-mail: sales@coachaudiovisual.co.uk
Web site: www.coachaudiovisual.co.uk

INOVAS LTD
1 Glenbervie Business Park, Larbert, Falkirk FK5 4RB
Tel: 01324 682268
Fax: 01324 682269
Web site: www.inovas.co.uk
E-mail: info@inovas.co.uk

Trade Directory

JAYCAS MINIBUS SALES
11 John Street, Bamber Bridge, Preston
PR5 6TJ
Tel/Fax: 01772 321491
E-mail: john@minibusjaycas.co.uk

*MENTOR
Mentor Coach & Bus Ltd, Carlton House,
Euroway Industrial Estate, Hellaby,
Rotherham S66 8QL
Tel: 01709 700600
Fax: 01709 700007
E-mail: sales@mentorplc.com
Web site: www.mentorplc.com

PSV PRODUCTS
PO Box 166, Warrington WA4 5FG
Tel: 0870 062 4488
Fax: 0870 062 4499
E-mail: mike@psvproducts.com
Web site: www.psvproducts.com

*UNITEC
Parts Division, Denby Way, Hellaby,
Rotherham S66 8HR
Tel: 01709 792000
Fax: 01709 792009
E-mail: parts@optare.com

Badges - Drivers/Conductors

ABBOT BROWN
Barnfleet Works, Fleet Street, Beaminster
DT8 3EJ
Tel: 01308 862404
Fax: 01308 863402
E-mail: sales@abbotbrown.co.uk

MARK TERRILL PSV BADGES
5 De Grey Close, Lewes BN7 2JR
Tel: 01273 474816
Fax: 01273 474816
Mobile: 07770 666159

TRANSPORTATION MANAGEMENT SOLUTIONS
PO Box 15174, Glasgow G3 6WB
Tel: 0141 332 4733
Fax: 0141 354 0076
E-mail: tramsol@aol.com

Batteries

BETA RESEARCH & DEVELOPMENT/ZEBRA BATTERIES
50 Goodsmoor Road, Sinfin, Derby
DE24 9GN
Tel: 01332 770500
Web site: www.betard.co.uk

CUMMINS UK
Rutherford Drive, Park Farm South,
Wellingborough NN8 6AN
Tel: 01933 334200
Fax: 01933 334198
E-mail: cduksales@cummins.com
Web site: www.cummins-uk.com

ENECO LTD
Unit 6, Spring Copse Business Park, Slinfold
RH13 0SZ
Tel: 01403 790114
Web site: www.eneco.co.uk

THOMAS HARDIE – WIGAN
Lockett Road, Ashton-in-Makerfield
WN4 8DE.
Tel: 01942 505124
Fax: 01942 505119

LEXCEL POWER SYSTEMS PLC
35 Manor Road, Henley on Thames
RG9 1LU.
Tel: 01491 874414
E-mail: sales@lexcelpower.com
Web site: www.lexcelpower.com

MASS SPECIAL ENGINEERING LTD
Anston, Sheffield S25 4SD
Tel: 01909 550480
Fax: 01909 550486

*MENTOR
Mentor Coach & Bus Ltd, Carlton House,
Euroway Industrial Estate, Hellaby,
Rotherham S66 8QL
Tel: 01709 700600
Fax: 01709 700007
E-mail: sales@mentorplc.com
Web site: www.mentorplc.com

MULTIPART PSV
Pilling Lane, Chorley PR7 3EL.
Tel: 01257 225577
Fax: 01257 225575
E-mail: info@multipart.com
Web site: www.multipart.com

PLAXTON COACH SALES CENTRE
Ryton Road, Anston, Sheffield S25 4DC
Tel: 01909 551155
Fax: 01909 567994
E-mail: coaches@plaxtonlimited.co.uk
Web site: www.plaxtonlimited.co.uk

POWER BATTERIES (GB) LTD
Units 5-8, Canal View Business Park,
Wheelhouse Road, Rugeley WS15 1UY
Tel: 01889 571100
Web site: www.bannerbatteriescom

*UNITEC
Parts Division, Denby Way, Hellaby,
Rotherham S66 8HR
Tel: 01709 792000
Fax: 01709 792009
E-mail: parts@optare.com

*UNITEC LONDON
Unit 5, Gateway 25, Weston Avenue,
West Thurrock RM20 3ZD
Tel: 01708 892440
Fax: 01708 862125
E-mail: london.service@optare.com

*UNITEC ROTHERHAM
Denby Way, Hellaby, Rotherham
S66 8HR
Tel: 01709 535101
Fax: 01709 535103
E-mail: rotherham.service@optare.com

*UNITEC SCOTLAND
Unit 7, Cumbernauld Business Park,
Ward Park Road, Cumbernauld G67 3JZ
Tel: 01236 726738
Fax: 01236 795651
E-mail: scotland.service@optare.com

VARTA AUTOMOTIVE BATTERIES LTD
Broadwater Park, North Orbital Road,
Denham UB9 5AG
Tel: 01895 838999
Fax: 01895 838981
Web site: www.varta.co.uk

Body/Electrical Repairs & Refurbishing

AD COACH SALES
Newbridge Coach Depot, Witheridge
EX16 8PY
Tel: 01884 860787
Fax: 01884 860711
E-mail: ggoodwin@adcoachsales.co.uk
Web site: www.adcoachsales.co.uk

AVS STEPS LTD
Alders Farmhouse, Alders Lane, Whixall
SY13 2BR
Tel: 01948 880010
Fax: 01948 880020
Web site: www.avssteps.co.uk

BLACKPOOL COACH SERVICES
Moss Hey Garage, Chapel Road, Blackpool
FY4 5HU.
Tel/Fax: 01253 698686

BRISTOL BUS & COACH SALES
6/7 Freestone Road, St Philips, Bristol
BS2 0QN
Tel: 0117 971 0251
Fax: 0117 972 3121
E-mail: andrew.munden@bristolbusandcoach.co.uk
Web site: www.bristolbusandcoach.co.uk

BULWARK BUS & COACH ENGINEERING LTD
Gate 3, Bulwark Industrial Estate, Chepstow
NP16 5QZ
Tel: 01291 622326
Fax: 01291 622726.

CARLYLE BUS & COACH LTD
Carlyle Business Park, Great Bridge treet,
Swan Village, West Bromwich B70 0X4
Tel: 0121 524 1200
Fax: 0121 524 1201
E-mail: admin@carlyleplc.co.uk

COBUS UK
Carnaby Industrial Estate, Bridlington
YO15 3QY
Tel: 01262 603 829
Fax: 01262 606 738
E-mail: cobus@btconnect.com

CREST COACH CONVERSIONS
Unit 5, Holmeroyd Road, Bentley Moor
Lane, Carcroft, Doncaster DN6 7BH
Tel: 01302 723723
Fax: 01302 724724

CROWN COACHBUILDERS LTD
32 Flemington Industrial Park, Flemington,
Motherwell ML1 1SN
Tel: 01698 276087
Fax: 01698 276144
E-mail: davidgreer@hotmail.com
Web site: www.crowncoachbuilders.co.uk

DRURY & DRURY
Unit 6, Cobbs Wood Industrial Estate,
Brunswick Road, Ashford TN23 1EH
Tel: 01303 610555.
Fax: 01303 610666.
E-mail: martinstrange@channelcommercials.co.uk

Trade Directory

*EAST LANCASHIRE COACHBUILDERS LTD (ELC)
Lower Philips Road, Whitebirk Industrial Estate, Blackburn BB1 5UD
Tel: 01254 504150
Fax: 01254 504197
E-mail: john.horn@elcb.co.uk
Web site: www.elcb.co.uk

EASTGATE COACH TRIMMERS
3 Thornton Road Industrial Estate, Pickering YO18 7HZ
Tel/Fax: 01751 472229
E-mail: info@eastgate-coachtrimmers.co.uk

EXPRESS COACH REPAIRS LTD
Outgang Lane, Pickering YO18 7EL.
Tel: 01751 475215.

GHE
Unit 30, Fort Industrial Park, Fort Parkway, Castle Bromwich B35 7AR.
Tel: 0121 747 4400.
Fax: 0121 747 4977.

HANTS & DORSET TRIM LTD
Canada Road, West Wellow SO51 6DE.
Tel: 023 8033 4235

THOMAS HARDIE – WIGAN
Lockett Road, Ashton-in-Makerfield, Wigan WN4 8DE.
Tel: 01942 505124.
Fax: 01942 505119

HATTS COACHWORKS & SERVICES
Foxham, Chippenham SN15 4NB
Tel: 01249 740444
Fax: 01249 740447
E-mail: adrian@hattstravel.co.uk
Web site: www.hattstravel.co.uk

INVERTEC LTD
Whelford Road, Fairford GL7 4DT
Tel: 01285 713550
Fax: 01285 713548
Mobile: 07802 793828
E-mail: ian@invertec.co.uk
Web site: www.invertec.co.uk

*THE LAWTON MOTOR BODY BUILDING CO LTD
Knutsford Road, Church Lawton, Stoke-on-Trent ST7 3DN
Tel: 01270 882056
Fax: 01270 883014
E-mail: sales@lawtonmotorbody.co.uk
Web site: www.lawtonmotorbody.co.uk

LEICESTER CARRIAGE BUILDERS
Marlow Road, Leicester LE3 2BQ
Tel: 0116 282 4270
Fax: 0116 263 0554
E-mail: rick.johnson@midlandsco-op.com
Web site: www.leicestercarriagebuilders.co.uk

MARTYN INDUSTRIALS LTD
5 Brunel Way, Durranhill Industrial Esate, Carlisle CA1 3NQ
Tel: 01228 544000
Fax: 01228 544001
E-mail: enquiries@martyn-industrials.co.uk
Web site: www.martyn-industrials.com

MASS SPECIAL ENGINEERING LTD
Anston, Sheffield S25 4SD.
Tel: 01909 550480.
Fax: 01909 550486.

MCV BUS & COACH LTD
Sterling Place, Elean Business Park, Sutton CB6 2QE
Tel: 01353 773000
Fax: 01353 773001
E-mail: vernon.edwards@mcv-uk.com

MELLOR COACHCRAFT
Miall Street, Rochdale OL11 1HY
Tel: 01706 860610
Fax: 01706 860042
E-mail: mcsales@woodhall-nicholson.co.uk
Web site: www.woodhall-nicholson.co.uk

MOSELEY (PCV) LTD
Elmsall Way, Dale Lane, South Elmsall WF9 2XS
Tel: 01977 609000
Fax: 01977 609900

*MENTOR
Mentor Coach & Bus Ltd, Carlton House, Euroway Industrial Estate, Hellaby, Rotherham S66 8QL
Tel: 01709 700600
Fax: 01709 700007
E-mail: sales@mentorplc.com
Web site: www.mentorplc.com

MULTIPART PSV
Pilling Lane, Chorley PR7 3EL
Tel: 01257 225577
Fax: 01257 225575
E-mail: info@multipart.com
Web site: www.multipart.com

*NEXT BUS LTD
The Coach Yard, Vincients Road, Bumpers Farm Industrial Estate, Chippenham SN14 6QA
Tel: 01249 462462
E-mail: sales@next-bus.co.uk
Web site: www.next-bus.co.uk

OLYMPUS COACHCRAFT LTD
7 Temperance Street, Manchester M12 6HR
Tel/Fax: 0161 273 4259
E-mail: geoffolympus@aol.com
Web site: www.olympuscoaches.co.uk

PLAXTON
Plaxton Park, Cayton Low Road, Eastfield, Scarborough YO11 3BY
Tel: 01723 581500
Fax: 01723 5813238
E-mail: sales@plaxtonlimited.co.uk
Web site: www.plaxtonlimited.co.uk

PLAXTON COACH SALES CENTRE
Ryton Road, Anston, Sheffield S25 4DC
Tel: 01909 551155
Fax: 01909 567994
E-mail: coaches@plaxtonlimited.co.uk
Web site: www.plaxtonlimited.co.uk

*RH BODYWORKS
A140 Ipswich Road, Brome, Eye IP23 8AW
Tel: 01379 870666
Fax: 01379 872138
E-mail: mike.ball@rhbodyworks.co.uk
Web site: www.rhbodyworks.co.uk

*TRAMONTANA COACH DISTRIBUTORS
Chapelknowe Road, Carfin, Motherwell ML1 5LE
Tel: 01698 861790
Fax: 01698 860778
E-mail: wdt90@tiscali.co.uk

TRUCKALIGN CO LTD
VIP Trading Estate, Anchor & Hope Lane, London SE7 7RY
Tel: 020 8858 3781
Fax: 020 8858 3781

*UNITEC
Parts Division, Denby Way, Hellaby, Rotherham S66 8HR
Tel: 01709 792000
Fax: 01709 792009
E-mail: parts@optare.com

*UNITEC LONDON
Unit 5, Gateway 25, Weston Avenue, West Thurrock RM20 3ZD
Tel: 01708 892440
Fax: 01708 862125
E-mail: london.service@optare.com

*UNITEC ROTHERHAM
Denby Way, Hellaby, Rotherham S66 8HR
Tel: 01709 535101
Fax: 01709 535103
E-mail: rotherham.service@optare.com

*UNITEC SCOTLAND
Unit 7, Cumbernauld Business Park, Ward Park Road, Cumbernauld G67 3JZ
Tel: 01236 726738
Fax: 01236 795651
E-mail: scotland.service@optare.com

*VOLVO BUS AND COACH CENTRE
Belton Road West, Loughborough LE11 5HP
Tel: 01509 217777
Fax: 01509 239362
Web site: www.volvo.com

Bicycle Carriers

JES BUSCYCLE
27-33 High Street, Totton SO40 9HL
Tel: 023 8066 3535

Brakes and Brake Linings

ARVIN MERITOR
Unit 21, Suttons Park Avenue, Reading RG6 1LA.
Tel: 0118 935 9126
Web site: www.arvinmeritor.com

AUTOMOTIVE PRODUCTS GROUP LTD – AP BORG & BECK / AP LOCKHEED
Tachbrook Road, Leamington Spa CV31 3ER.
Tel: 01926 470000.
Fax: 01926 472000.

BBA FRICTION LTD
PO Box 18, Hunsworth Lane BD19 3UJ.
Tel: 01274 854000.
Fax: 01274 854001.

*DIRECT PARTS LTD
Unit 1, Churnet Court, Churnetside Business Park, Harrison Way, Cheddleton ST13 7EF
Tel: 01538 361777
Fax: 01538 369100
E-mail: sales@direct-group.co.uk
Web site: www.direct-group.co.uk

⟫ SCAN COIN

AUTOMATED CASH DEPOSITING SYSTEM

Fast and accurate processing of bank notes, coins and transport tokens plus dropsafe for depositing of non-cash items.

Safe, secure and easy to use.

Network capability   *Fast coin deposit*   *High capacity printer*   *Envelope dropsafe*   *Note acceptance*

- Easy to install, through-the-wall or free-standing
- Front or rear access for changing vaults and for servicing
- Fully customisable user interface
- All totals displayed on-screen
- Multiple coin acceptance and value counting
- Bank notes accepted in any direction
- Vehicle defect reporting
- Exchange rates can be programmed into the system
- Wide range of additional software available

SCAN COIN Ltd
Dutch House, 110 Broadway Salford Quays
Salford M50 2UW

CALL 0161 873 0505
VISIT www.scancoin.co.uk
EMAIL sales@scancoin.co.uk

Trade Directory

ERENTEK LTD
Malt Kiln Lane, Waddington, Lincoln
LN5 9RT
Tel: 01522 720065
Fax: 01522 729155
E-mail: sale@erentek.co.uk
Web site: www.erentek.co.uk

*HART BROTHERS (ENGINEERING) LTD
Soho Works, Soho Street, Oldham OL4 2AD
Tel: 0161 737 6791

IMEXPART LTD
Links 31, Willowbridge Way, Whitwood,
Castleford WF10 5NP
Tel: 01977 553936
Fax: 01977 604684
E-mail: parts@imexpart.com
Web site: www.imexpart.com

IMPERIAL ENGINEERING
Delamare Road, Cheshunt EN8 9UD
Tel: 01992 6342555
Fax: 01992 630506
E-mail: sales@imperialengineering.co.uk
Web site: www.imperialengineering.co.uk

KELLETT (UK) LTD
8 Stevenson Way, Sheffield S9 3WZ.
Tel: 0114 261 1122
Fax: 0114 261 1199
E-mail: sales@kellett.co.uk

KNORR-BREMSE SYSTEMS FOR COMMERCIAL VEHICLES LTD
Douglas Road, Kingswood, Bristol
BS15 8NL.
Tel: 0117 984 6100
Fax: 0117 984 6101
Web site: www.knorr-bremse.com

MAJORLINE ENGINEERING LTD
Baybridge Industrial Units, Baybridge Lane,
Owslebury, Winchester SO21 1JN.
Tel: 01962 777077
Fax: 01962 777661, 777667
E-mail: majorline@compuserve.com

*MENTOR
Mentor Coach & Bus Ltd, Carlton House,
Euroway Industrial Estate, Hellaby,
Rotherham S66 8QL
Tel: 01709 700600
Fax: 01709 700007
E-mail: sales@mentorplc.com
Web site: www.mentorplc.com

MULTIPART PSV
Pilling Lane, Chorley PR7 3EL.
Tel: 01257 225577
Fax: 01257 225575
E-mail: info@multipart.com
Web site: www.multipart.com

*PARTLINE LTD
Dockfield Road, Shipley BD17 7AZ
Tel: 01274 531531
Fax: 01274 531088
E-mail: sales@partline.co.uk
Web site: www.partline.co.uk

ROADLINK INTERNATIONAL LTD
Strawberry Lane, Willenhall WV13 3RL
Tel: 01902 636210
Fax: 01902 606604
E-mail: sales@roadlink-international.co.uk
Web site: www.roadlink-international.co.uk

*P & P SERGEANT (B&A) LTD
PO Box 11, New Hall Lane, Hoylake
CH47 4DH
Tel: 0151 632 5903
Fax: 0151 632 5908
E-mail: enq@sergeant.co.uk
Web site: www.sergeant.co.uk

*UNITEC
Parts Division, Denby Way, Hellaby,
Rotherham S66 8HR
Tel: 01709 792000
Fax: 01709 792009
E-mail: parts@optare.com

*UNITEC LONDON
Unit 5, Gateway 25, Weston Avenue,
West Thurrock RM20 3ZD
Tel: 01708 892440
Fax: 01708 862125
E-mail: london.service@optare.com

*UNITEC ROTHERHAM
Denby Way, Hellaby, Rotherham
S66 8HR
Tel: 01709 535101
Fax: 01709 535103
E-mail: rotherham.service@optare.com

*UNITEC SCOTLAND
Unit 7, Cumbernauld Business Park,
Ward Park Road, Cumbernauld G67 3JZ
Tel: 01236 726738
Fax: 01236 795651
E-mail: scotland.service@optare.com

WABCO AUTOMOTIVE UK
Texas Street, Leeds LS27 0HQ
Tel: 0113 251 2510
Fax: 0113 251 2844

Cash Handling Equipment

CUMMINS-ALLISON LTD
William H Klotz House, Colonnade
Point, Central Boulevard, Progolis Park,
Coventry CV6 4BU
Tel: 024 7633 9810
Fax: 024 7633 9811
E-mail: sales@cummins-allison.co.uk
Web site: www.cumminsallison.co.uk

CASH PROCESSING SOLUTIONS LTD
Unit 26-27, Portland Court, Kingsway, Luton
LU4 8HA
Tel: 01582 402318
Fax: 01582 402318
E-mail: info@cashprocessing.co.uk
Web site: www.cashprocessing.co.uk

*ELECTRONIC TICKET MACHINE SOFTWARE SERVICES (UK)
9 Dorset Avenue, Ferndown BH22 8HJ
Tel: 0844 800 9299
E-mail: info@etmss.com
Web site: www.etmss.com

JOHN GROVES TICKET SYSTEMS
Unit 5, Rennie Business Units, Factory
Place, Saltcoats KA21 5LZ
Tel: 01294 471133
Fax: 01294 471166
Web site: www.cambist.se

MARK TERRILL TICKET MACHINERY
5 De Grey Close, Lewes BN7 2JR.
Tel: 01273 474816
Fax: 01273 474816
E-mail: mark.terrill@ukonline.co.uk

SCAN COIN LTD
110 Broadway, Salford Quays M50 2UW
Tel: 0161 873 0500
Fax: 0161 873 0501
E-mail: sales@scancoin.co.uk
Web site: www.scancoin.co.uk

*THOMAS AUTOMATICS CO LTD
Bishop Meadow Road, Loughborough
LE11 5RE
Tel: 01509 267611
Fax: 01509 266836
E-mail: sales@thomasa.co.uk
Web site: www.thomasa.co.uk

*TRAN SPORT TICKET SERVICES LTD
Yew Tree Cottage, Newcastle, Monmouth
NP25 5NT
Tel/Fax: 01600 750650
E-mail: ttsservices@tiscali.com
Web site: www.ticket-machines.co.uk

Chassis Lubricating Systems

MULTIPART PSV
Pilling Lane, Chorley PR7 3EL
Tel: 01257 225577
Fax: 01257 225575
E-mail: info@multipart.com
Web site: www.multipart.com

Clutches

AUTOMOTIVE PRODUCTS GROUP LTD – AP BORG & BECK / AP LOCKHEED
Tachbrook Road, Leamington Spa
CV31 3ER.
Tel: 01926 470000
Fax: 01926 472000.

ASHLEY BANKS LTD
5 King Street Estate, Langtoft, Peterborough
PE6 9NF
Tel: 01778 560651
Fax: 01778 560721
E-mail: user@ashleybanks.fsnet.co.uk

BBA FRICTION LTD
PO Box 18, Hunsworth Lane, Cleckheaton
BD19 3UJ.
Tel: 01274 854000
Fax: 01274 854001

BUSS BIZZ
Goughs Transport Depot, Morestead,
Winchester SO21 1JD
Tel: 01962 715555/66
Fax: 01962 714868.

*COACH-AID
Unit 2, Brindley Close, Tollgate Industrial
Estate, Stafford ST16 3SU
Tel: 01785 222666
E-mail: workshop@coach-aid.com
Web site: www.coach-aid.com

Trade Directory

EATON LTD
Truck Components Marketing, PO Box 11,
Worsley Road North,
Worsley M28 5GJ.
Tel: 01204 797219.
Fax: 01204 797204.

IMEXPART LTD
Links 31, Willowbridge Way, Whitwood,
Castleford WF10 5NP
Tel: 01977 553936
Fax: 01977 604684
E-mail: parts@imexpart.com
Web site: www.imexpart.com

KELLETT (UK) LTD
8 Stevenson Way, Sheffield S9 3WZ.
Tel: 0114 261 1122.
Fax: 0114 261 1199.
E-mail: sales@kellett.co.uk

MAJORLINE ENGINEERING LTD
Baybridge Industrial Units, Baybridge Lane,
Owslebury, Winchester SO21 1JN.
Tel: 01962 777077.
Fax: 01962 777661, 777667
E-mail: majorline@compuserve.com

*MENTOR
Mentor Coach & Bus Ltd, Carlton House,
Euroway Industrial Estate, Hellaby,
Rotherham S66 8QL
Tel: 01709 700600
Fax: 01709 700007
E-mail: sales@mentorplc.com
Web site: www.mentorplc.com

MULTIPART PSV
Pilling Lane, Chorley PR7 3EL.
Tel: 01257 225577.
Fax: 01257 225575.
E-mail: info@multipart.com
Web site: www.multipart.com

*PACET MANUFACTURING LTD
Wyebridge House, Cores End Road,
Bourne End SL8 5HH
Tel: 01628 526754
Fax: 01628 810080
E-mail: sales@pacet.co.uk
Web site: www.pacet.co.uk

*PARTLINE LTD
Dockfield Road, Shipley BD17 7AZ
Tel: 01274 531531
Fax: 01274 531088
E-mail: sales@partline.co.uk
Web site: www.partline.co.uk

*P & P SERGEANT (B&A) LTD
PO Box 11, New Hall Lane, Hoylake
CH47 4DH
Tel: 0151 632 5903
Fax: 0151 632 5908
E-mail: enq@sergeant.co.uk
Web site: www.sergeant.co.uk

SHAWSON SUPPLY LTD
12 Station Road, Saintfield BT24 7DU
Tel: 028 9751 0994
Fax: 028 9751 0816
E-mail: shawsondiesel@btopenworld.com
Web site: www.shawsonsupply.com

*UNITEC
Parts Division, Denby Way, Hellaby,
Rotherham S66 8HR
Tel: 01709 792000
Fax: 01709 792009
E-mail: parts@optare.com

*UNITEC LONDON
Unit 5, Gateway 25, Weston Avenue,
West Thurrock RM20 3ZD
Tel: 01708 892440
Fax: 01708 862125
E-mail: london.service@optare.com

*UNITEC ROTHERHAM
Denby Way, Hellaby, Rotherham
S66 8HR
Tel: 01709 535101
Fax: 01709 535103
E-mail: rotherham.service@optare.com

*UNITEC SCOTLAND
Unit 7, Cumbernauld Business Park,
Ward Park Road, Cumbernauld G67 3JZ
Tel: 01236 726738
Fax: 01236 795651
E-mail: scotland.service@optare.com

Cooling Systems

*DIRECT PARTS LTD
Unit 1, Churnet Court, Churnetside Business
Park, Harrison Way, Cheddleton ST13 7EF
Tel: 01538 361777
Fax: 01538 369100
E-mail: sales@direct-group.co.uk
Web site: www.direct-group.co.uk

---

transport **counts on it**

The Jetsort range of coin counter/sorters are Euro ready

High speed, high volume coin processing

Counts & sorts up to 9 denominations at 6000 mixed coins a minute

Optional dual bag and coin discrimination Integrates with industry standard software

We also provide a range of note counters and mixed note scanners

CUMMINS COUNTS EURO

CA CUMMINS
CUMMINS-ALLISON LTD.

0800 0186484
www.cumminsallison.co.uk

IMEXPART LTD
Links 31, Willowbridge Way, Whitwood,
Castleford WF10 5NP
Tel: 01977 553936
Fax: 01977 604684
E-mail: parts@imexpart.com
Web site: www.imexpart.com

MAJORLINE ENGINEERING LTD
Baybridge Industrial Units, Baybridge Lane,
Owslebury, Winchester SO21 1JN
Tel: 01962 777077.
Fax: 01962 777661, 777667
E-mail: majorline@compuserve.com

*MENTOR
Mentor Coach & Bus Ltd, Carlton House,
Euroway Industrial Estate, Hellaby,
Rotherham S66 8QL
Tel: 01709 700600
Fax: 01709 700007
E-mail: sales@mentorplc.com
Web site: www.mentorplc.com

MULTIPART PSV
Pilling Lane, Chorley PR7 3EL.
Tel: 01257 225577
Fax: 01257 225575
E-mail: info@multipart.com
Web site: www.multipart.com

*PARTLINE LTD
Dockfield Road, Shipley BD17 7AZ
Tel: 01274 531531
Fax: 01274 531088
E-mail: sales@partline.co.uk
Web site: www.partline.co.uk

SILFLEX LTD
Coed Cae Lane Industrial Estate, Pontyclun
CF72 9HJ
Tel: 01443 238464
Fax: 01443 237781
E-mail: silflex@silflex.com
Web site: www.silflex.com

*UNITEC LONDON
Unit 5, Gateway 25, Weston Avenue,
West Thurrock RM20 3ZD
Tel: 01708 892440
Fax: 01708 862125
E-mail: london.service@optare.com

*UNITEC ROTHERHAM
Denby Way, Hellaby, Rotherham
S66 8HR
Tel: 01709 535101
Fax: 01709 535103
E-mail: rotherham.service@optare.com

*UNITEC SCOTLAND
Unit 7, Cumbernauld Business Park,
Ward Park Road, Cumbernauld G67 3JZ
Tel: 01236 726738
Fax: 01236 795651
E-mail: scotland.service@optare.com

Destination Indicator Equipment

BRIGHT-TECH DEVELOPMENTS LTD
Fleets Point House, Willis Way, Poole
BH15 3SS
Tel: 01202 679627
E-mail: sales@bright-tech.co.uk
Web site: www.bright-tech.co.uk

HANOVER DISPLAYS LTD
Unit 24, Cliffe Industrial Estate, Lewes
BN8 6JL
Tel: 01273 477528
Fax: 01273 407766
E-mail: nrobertson@hanoverdisplays.com
Web site: www.hanoverdisplays.com

INDICATORS INTERNATIONAL LTD
41 Aughrim Road, Magherafelt BT45 6JX.
Tel: 028 7963 2591.
Fax: 028 7963 3927.
E-mail: sales@indicators-int.com
Web site: www.indicators-int.com

INVERTEC LTD
Whelford Road, Fairford GL7 4DT
Tel: 01285 713550
Fax: 01285 713548
Mobile: 07802 793828
E-mail: ian@invertec.co.uk
Web site: www.invertec.co.uk

McKENNA BROTHERS LTD
McKenna House, Jubilee Road, Middleton,
Manchester M24 2LX
Tel: 0161 655 3244
Fax: 0161 655 3059
E-mail: info@mckennabrothers.co.uk
Web site: www.mckennabrothers.co.uk

MULTIPART PSV
Pilling Lane, Chorley PR7 3EL.
Tel: 01257 225577.
Fax: 01257 225575.
E-mail: info@multipart.com
Web site: www.multipart.com

*NORBURY BLINDS LTD
41-45 Hanley Street, Newtown, Birmingham
B19 3SP
Tel: 0121 359 4311
Fax: 0121 359 6388
E-mail: info@norbury-blinds.com
Web site: www.norbury-blinds.com

*PERCY LANE PRODUCTS LTD
Lichfield Road, Tamworth B79 7TL
Tel: 01827 63821
Fax: 01827 310159
E-mail: sales@percy-lane.co.uk
Web site: www.percy-lane.co.uk

PLAXTON COACH SALES CENTRE
Ryton Road, Anston, Sheffield S25 4DL
Tel: 01909 551155
Fax: 01909 567994
E-mail: coaches@plaxtonlimited.co.uk
Web site: www.plaxtonlimited.co.uk

TOP GEARS DESTINATIONS
46 Fulwood Hall Lane, Fulwood, Preston
PR2 8DD
Tel/Fax: 01772 700536
E-mail: steve@pitlane-2000.com
Web site: www.pitlane-2000.com

WEBASTO PRODUCT UK LTD
Webasto House, White Rose Way,
Doncaster Carr DN4 5JH
Tel: 01302 322232
Fax: 01302 322231
E-mail: info@webastouk.com
Web site: www.webasto.co.uk

Door Operating Gear

AIR DOOR SERVICES
The Pavilions, Holly Lane Industrial Estate,
Atherstone CV9 2QZ
Tel: 01827 11660
Fax: 01827 713577
E-mail: airdoorservices@aol.com

CARLYLE BUS & COACH LTD
Carlyle Business Park, Great Bridge Street,
Swan Village, West Bromwich B70 0X4
Tel: 0121 524 1200
Fax: 0121 524 1201
E-mail: admin@carlyleplc.co.uk

*CRESCENT FACILITIES LTD
72 Willow Crescent, Chapeltown, Sheffield
S35 1QS
Tel/fax: 0114 2451050
E-mail: cfl.chris@btinternet.com
Web site: www.cflparts.com

*DEANS SYSTEMS (UK) LTD
PO Box 8, Borwick Drive, Grovehill,
Beverley HU17 0HQ
Tel: 01482 868111
Fax: 01482 881890
E-mail: customerservice@deanssystems.com
Web Site: www.deanssystems.com

ERENTEK LTD
Malt Kiln Lane, Waddington, Lincoln
LN5 9RT
Tel: 01522 720065
Fax: 01522 729155
E-mail: sale@erentek.co.uk
Web site: www.erentek.co.uk

KELLETT (UK) LTD
8 Stevenson Way, Sheffield S9 3WZ.
Tel: 0114 261 1122.
Fax: 0114 261 1199.
E-mail: sales@kellett.co.uk

*KARIVE LIMITED
PO Box 205, Southam CV47 0ZL
Tel: 01926 813938
Fax: 01926 814898
E-mail: karive.ltd@btinternet.com
Web site: www.karive.co.uk

KNORR-BREMSE SYSTEMS FOR COMMERCIAL VEHICLES LTD
Douglas Road, Kingswood, Bristol
BS15 8NL.
Tel: 0117 984 6100.
Fax: 0117 984 6101.
Web site: www.knorr-bremse.com

*THE LAWTON MOTOR BODY BUILDING CO LTD
Knutsford Road, Church Lawton, Stoke-on-
Trent ST7 3DN
Tel: 01270 882056
Fax: 01270 883014
E-mail: sales@lawtonmotorbody.co.uk
Web site: www.lawtonmotorbody.co.uk

MULTIPART PSV
Pilling Lane, Chorley PR7 3EL.
Tel: 01257 225577.
Fax: 01257 225575.
E-mail: info@multipart.com
Web site: www.multipart.com

*NEXT BUS LTD
The Coach Yard, Vincients Road, Bumpers Farm Industrial Estate, Chippenham SN14 6QA
Tel: 01249 462462
E-mail: sales@next-bus.co.uk
Web site: www.next-bus.co.uk

PETERS DOOR SYSTEMS (UK) LTD
Bradbury Drive, Springwood Industrial Estate, Braintree CM7 2ET
Tel: 01376 555255
Fax: 01376 555292
E-mail: sales@petersdoors.co.uk

PLAXTON
Plaxton Park, Cayton Low Road, Eastfield, Scarborough YO11 3BY
Tel: 01723 581500
Fax: 01723 5813238
E-mail: sales@plaxtonlimited.co.uk
Web site: www.plaxtonlimited.co.uk

PLAXTON COACH SALES CENTRE
Ryton Road, Anston, Sheffield S25 4DL
Tel: 01909 551155
Fax: 01909 567994
E-mail: coaches@plaxtonlimited.co.uk
Web site: www.plaxtonlimited.co.uk

PNEUMAX LTD
Unit 8, Venture Industrial Park, Fareham Road, Gosport PO13 0BA
Tel: 01329 823999
Fax: 01329 822345
E-mail: sales@pneumax.co.uk
Web site: www.pneumax.co.uk

*UNITEC
Parts Division, Denby Way, Hellaby, Rotherham S66 8HR
Tel: 01709 792000
Fax: 01709 792009
E-mail: parts@optare.com

*UNITEC LONDON
Unit 5, Gateway 25, Weston Avenue, West Thurrock RM20 3ZD
Tel: 01708 892440
Fax: 01708 862125
E-mail: london.service@optare.com

*UNITEC ROTHERHAM
Denby Way, Hellaby, Rotherham S66 8HR
Tel: 01709 535101
Fax: 01709 535103
E-mail: rotherham.service@optare.com

*UNITEC SCOTLAND
Unit 7, Cumbernauld Business Park, Ward Park Road, Cumbernauld G67 3JZ
Tel: 01236 726738
Fax: 01236 795651
E-mail: scotland.service@optare.com

VAPOR-STONE UK LTD
2nd Avenue, Centrum 100, Burton-on-Trent DE14 3WF
Tel: 01283 743300
Fax: 01283 743333
Web site: www.wabtec.com

WABCO AUTOMOTIVE UK LTD
Texas Street, Morley LS27 0HQ.
Tel: 0113 251 2510
Fax: 0113 251 2844

Drinks Dispensing Equipment

*BRADTECH LTD
Unit 3, Ladford Covert, Seighford, Stafford ST18 9QL
Tel: 01785 282800
Fax: 01785 282558
E-mail: sales@bradtech.ltd.uk
Web site: www.bradtech.ltd.uk

*DRINKMASTER LTD
Drinkpac House, Plymouth Road, Liskeard PL14 3PG
Tel: 01579 342082
Fax: 01579 342591
Web site: www.drinkmaster.co.uk

*ELSAN LTD
Bellbrook Park, Uckfield BN3 7RA
Tel: 01825 748200
Fax: 01825 761212
E-mail: sales@elsan.co.uk
Web site: www.elsan.co.uk

*THE LAWTON MOTOR BODY BUILDING CO LTD
Knutsford Road, Church Lawton, Stoke-on-Trent ST7 3DN
Tel: 01270 882056
Fax: 01270 883014
E-mail: sales@lawtonmotorbody.co.uk
Web site: www.lawtonmotorbody.co.uk

PLAXTON
Plaxton Park, Cayton Low Road, Eastfield, Scarborough YO11 3BY
Tel: 01723 581500
Fax: 01723 5813238
E-mail: sales@plaxtonlimited.co.uk
Web site: www.plaxtonlimited.co.uk

PSV PRODUCTS
PO Box 166, Warrington WA4 5FG
Tel: 0870 062 4488
Fax: 0870 062 4499
E-mail: mike@psvproducts.com
Web site: www.psvproducts.com

SHADES TECHNICS
Marshgate Drive, Hertford SG13 7AJ
Tel: 01992 501683
Fax: 01992 501669
E-mail: sales@shades-technics.com
Web site: www.shades-technics.com

Driving Axles & Gears

ALBION AUTOMOTIVE LTD
South Street, Scotstoun, Glasgow G14 0DT.
Tel: 0141 434 2400
Fax: 0141 959 6362
E-mail: sales@albion_auto.co.uk
Web site: www.albion_auto.co.uk

ARVIN MERITOR
Unit 21, Suttons Park Avenue, Reading RG6 1LA.
Tel: 0118 935 9126
Fax: 0118 935 9138
E-mail: james.randall@arvinmeritor.com
Web site: www.arvinmeritor.com

BUSS BIZZ
Goughs Transport Depot, Morestead, Winchester SO21 1JD.
Tel: 01962 715555/66.
Fax: 01962 714868.

*CRESCENT FACILITIES LTD
72 Willow Crescent, Chapeltown, Sheffield S35 1QS
Tel/fax: 0114 2451050
E-mail: cfl.chris@btinternet.com
Web site: www.cflparts.com

*DIRECT PARTS LTD
Unit 1, Churnet Court, Churnetside Business Park, Harrison Way, Cheddleton ST13 7EF
Tel: 01538 361777
Fax: 01538 369100
E-mail: sales@direct-group.co.uk
Web site: www.direct-group.co.uk

EATON LTD
Truck Components Marketing, PO Box 11, Worsley Road North, Worsley M28 5GJ
Tel: 01204 797219.
Fax: 01204 797204.

*HART BROTHERS (ENGINEERING) LTD
Soho Works, Soho Street, Oldham OL4 2AD
Tel: 0161 737 6791

HL SMITH TRANSMISSIONS LTD
Enterprise Business Park, Cross Road, Albrighton, Wolverhampton WV7 3BJ
Tel: 01902 373011
Fax: 01902 373608

IMPERIAL ENGINEERING
Delamare Road, Cheshunt EN8 9UD
Tel: 01992 6342555
Fax: 01992 630506
E-mail: sales@imperialengineering.co.uk
Web site: www.imperialengineering.co.uk

*LH GROUP SERVICES LTD
Graycar Business Park, Barton Under Needwood, Burton-on-Trent DE13 8EN
Tel: 01283 722600
Fax: 01283 722622
E-mail: lh@lh-group.co.uk
Web site: www.lh-group.co.uk

MAJORLINE ENGINEERING LTD
Baybridge Industrial Units, Baybridge Lane, Owslebury, Winchester SO21 1JN.
Tel: 01962 777077.
Fax: 01962 777661, 777667
E-mail: majorline@compuserve.com

*MENTOR
Mentor Coach & Bus Ltd, Carlton House, Euroway Industrial Estate, Hellaby, Rotherham S66 8QL
Tel: 01709 700600
Fax: 01709 700007
E-mail: sales@mentorplc.com
Web site: www.mentorplc.com

MULTIPART PSV
Pilling Lane, Chorley PR7 3EL.
Tel: 01257 225577.
Fax: 01257 225575.
E-mail: info@multipart.com
Web site: www.multipart.com

*NEXT BUS LTD
The Coach Yard, Vincients Road, Bumpers Farm Industrial Estate, Chippenham SN14 6QA
Tel: 01249 462462
E-mail: sales@next-bus.co.uk
Web site: www.next-bus.co.uk

Trade Directory

Trade Directory

*PARTLINE LTD
Dockfield Road, Shipley BD17 7AZ
Tel: 01274 531531
Fax: 01274 531088
E-mail: sales@partline.co.uk
Web site: www.partline.co.uk

*UNITEC
Parts Division, Denby Way, Hellaby,
Rotherham S66 8HR
Tel: 01709 792000
Fax: 01709 792009
E-mail: parts@optare.com

ZF POWERTRAIN
Stringes Close, Willenhall WV13 1LE
Tel: 01902 366000
Fax: 01902 366504
E-mail: sales@powertrain.org.uk
Web site: www.powertrain.org.uk

Electrical Equipment

*BRADTECH LTD
Unit 3, Ladford Covert, Seighford, Stafford
ST18 9QL
Tel: 01785 282800
Fax: 01785 282558
E-mail: sales@bradtech.ltd.uk
Web site: www.bradtech.ltd.uk

BRITAX PMG LTD
Bressingby Industrial Estate, Bridlington
YO16 4SJ
Tel: 01262 670161
Fax: 01262 605666
E-mail: info@britax-pmg.com
Web site: www.britax-pmg.com

CARLYLE BUS & COACH LTD
Carlyle Business Park, Great Bridge Street,
Swan Village, West Bromwich B70 0X4
Tel: 0121 524 1200
Fax: 0121 524 1201
E-mail: admin@carlyleplc.co.uk

*CRESCENT FACILITIES LTD
72 Willow Crescent, Chapeltown, Sheffield
S35 1QS
Tel/fax: 0114 2451050
E-mail: cfl.chris@btinternet.com
Web site: www.cflparts.com

DIRECT PARTS LTD
Unit 1, Churnet Court, Churnetside Business
Park, Harrison Way, Cheddleton ST13 7EF
Tel: 01538 361777
Fax: 01538 369100
E-mail: sales@direct-group.co.uk
Web site: www.direct-group.co.uk

IMEXPART LTD
Links 31, Willowbridge Way, Whitwood,
Castleford WF10 5NP
Tel: 01977 553936
Fax: 01977 604684
E-mail: parts@imexpart.com
Web site: www.imexpart.com

.INTELLITEC LTD
VIP Trading Estate, Anchor & Hope Lane,
London SE7 7RY
Tel/Fax: 020 8858 3781

INVERTEC LTD
Whelford Road, Fairford GL7 4DT
Tel: 01285 713550
Fax: 01285 713548
Mobile: 07802 793828
E-mail: ian@invertec.co.uk
Web site: www.invertec.co.uk

*KARIVE LIMITED
PO Box 205, Southam CV47 0ZL
Tel: 01926 813938
Fax: 01926 814898
E-mail: karive.ltd@btinternet.com
Web site: www.karive.co.uk

LEXCEL POWER SYSTEMS PLC
35 Manor Road, Henley on Thames
RG9 1LU.
Tel: 01491 874414.
E-mail: sales@lexcelpower.com
Web site: lexcelpower.com

MAJORLINE ENGINEERING LTD
Baybridge Industrial Units, Baybridge Lane,
Owslebury, Winchester SO21 1JN.
Tel: 01962 777077.
Fax: 01962 777661, 777667
E-mail: majorline@compuserve.com

Prestolite electric

Leece·Neville

Suppliers of rotating electrics to the Bus & Coach Industry

THE POWER OF EXCELLENCE

www.prestolite.com   Sales Tel: + 44 20 8231 1137   Email: eu_info@prestolite.com

Trade Directory

*MENTOR
Mentor Coach & Bus Ltd, Carlton House, Euroway Industrial Estate, Hellaby, Rotherham S66 8QL
Tel: 01709 700600
Fax: 01709 700007
E-mail: sales@mentorplc.com
Web site: www.mentorplc.com

MULTIPART PSV
Pilling Lane, Chorley PR7 3EL.
Tel: 01257 225577
Fax: 01257 225575
E-mail: info@multipart.com
Web site: www.multipart.com

NEALINE WINDSCREEN WIPER PRODUCTS
Unit 1, The Sidings Industrial Estate, Birdingbury Road, Marton CV23 9RX
Tel: 01926 633256
Fax: 01926 632600

PACEL ELECTRONICS
Fleets Point House, Willis Way, Poole BH15 3SS
Tel: 01202 676616
Fax: 01202 681357
E-mail: sales@pacel.co.uk
Web site: www.pacel.co.uk

*PARTLINE LTD
Dockfield Road, Shipley BD17 7AZ
Tel: 01274 531531
Fax: 01274 531088
E-mail: sales@partline.co.uk
Web site: www.partline.co.uk

PLAXTON
Plaxton Park, Cayton Low Road, Eastfield, Scarborough YO11 3BY
Tel: 01723 581500
Fax: 01723 5813238
E-mail: sales@plaxtonlimited.co.uk
Web site: www.plaxtonlimited.co.uk

PLAXTON COACH SALES CENTRE
Ryton Road, Anston, Sheffield S25 4DL
Tel: 01909 551155
Fax: 01909 567994
E-mail: coaches@plaxtonlimited.co.uk
Web site: www.plaxtonlimited.co.uk

PNEUMAX LTD
Unit 8, Venture Industrial Park, Fareham Road, Gosport PO13 0BA
Tel: 01329 823999
Fax: 01329 822345
E-mail: sales@pneumax.co.uk
Web site: www.pneumax.co.uk

PRESTOLITE ELECTRIC
Unit 48, The Metropolitan Park, 12-16 Bristol Road, Greenford UB6 8UP
Tel: 020 8231 1137
E-mail: eu_info@prestolite.com
Web site: www.prestolite.com

*UNITEC
Parts Division, Denby Way, Hellaby, Rotherham S66 8HR
Tel: 01709 792000
Fax: 01709 792009
E-mail: parts@optare.com

Electronic Control

ACTIA UK LTD
Unit 81, Mochdre Industrial Estate, Newtown SY16 4LE
Tel: 01686 621067
Fax: 01686 621068
E-mail: mail@actia.co.uk
Web site: www.actia.co.uk

AVT SYSTEMS LTD
Unit 3, Tything Road, Arden Forest Trading Estate, Alcester B49 6ES
Tel: 01789 400357
Fax: 01789 400359
E-mail: enquiries@avtsystems.co.uk
Web site: www.avtsystems.co.uk

*CRESCENT FACILITIES LTD
72 Willow Crescent, Chapeltown, Sheffield S35 1QS
Tel/fax: 0114 2451050
E-mail: cfl.chris@btinternet.com
Web site: www.cflparts.com

INTELLITEC LTD
VIP Trading Estate, Anchor & Hope Lane, London SE7 7RY
Tel/Fax: 020 8858 3781

KNORR-BREMSE SYSTEMS FOR COMMERCIAL VEHICLES LTD
Douglas Road, Kingswood, Bristol BS15 8NL.
Tel: 0117 984 6100.
Fax: 0117 984 6101.
Web site: www.knorr-bremse.com

*MENTOR
Mentor Coach & Bus Ltd, Carlton House, Euroway Industrial Estate, Hellaby, Rotherham S66 8QL
Tel: 01709 700600
Fax: 01709 700007
E-mail: sales@mentorplc.com
Web site: www.mentorplc.com

*PARTLINE LTD
Dockfield Road, Shipley BD17 7AZ
Tel: 01274 531531
Fax: 01274 531088
E-mail: sales@partline.co.uk
Web site: www.partline.co.uk

*UNITEC
Parts Division, Denby Way, Hellaby, Rotherham S66 8HR
Tel: 01709 792000
Fax: 01709 792009
E-mail: parts@optare.com

VDO KIENZLE UK LTD
36 Gravelly Industrial Park, Birmingham B24 8TA.
Tel: 0121 326 1234.
Fax: 0121 326 1299

WABCO AUTOMOTIVE UK
Texas Street, Morley LS27 0HQ.
Tel: 0113 251 2510.
Fax: 0113 251 2844.

Emission Control Devices

CUMMINS UK
Rutherford Drive, Park Farm South, Wellingborough NN8 6AN
Tel: 01933 334200
Fax: 01933 334198
E-mail: cduksales@cummins.com
Web site: www.cummins-uk.com

*DINEX EXHAUSTS LTD
14 Chesford Garage, Woolston, Warrington WA1 4RE
Tel: 01925 849849
Fax: 01925 849850
E-mail: enquiries@dinex.co.uk
Web site: www.dinex.dk

*MENTOR
Mentor Coach & Bus Ltd, Carlton House, Euroway Industrial Estate, Hellaby, Rotherham S66 8QL
Tel: 01709 700600
Fax: 01709 700007
E-mail: sales@mentorplc.com
Web site: www.mentorplc.com

MULTIPART PSV
Pilling Lane, Chorley PR7 3EL.
Tel: 01257 225577.
Fax: 01257 225575.
E-mail: info@multipart.com
Web site: www.multipart.com

PLAXTON
Plaxton Park, Cayton Low Road, Eastfield, Scarborough YO11 3BY
Tel: 01723 581500
Fax: 01723 5813238
E-mail: sales@plaxtonlimited.co.uk
Web site: www.plaxtonlimited.co.uk

*UNITEC
Parts Division, Denby Way, Hellaby, Rotherham S66 8HR
Tel: 01709 792000
Fax: 01709 792009
E-mail: parts@optare.com

Engineering

ARRIVA BUS AND COACH LTD
Lodge Garage, Whitehall Road West, Gomersal BD19 4BJ.
Tel: 01274 681144
Fax: 01274 651198
Web site: www.arriva.co.uk
E-mail: busandcoachsales@arriva.co.uk

BUSS BIZZ
Goughs Transport Depot, Morestead, Winchester SO21 1JD.
Tel: 01962 715555/66.
Fax: 01962 714868.

*COACH-AID
Unit 2, Brindley Close, Tollgate Industrial Estate, Stafford ST16 3SU
Tel: 01785 222666
E-mail: workshop@coach-aid.com
Web site: www.coach-aid.com

Trade Directory

CUMMINS UK
Rutherford Drive, Park Farm South,
Wellingborough NN8 6AN
Tel: 01933 334200
Fax: 01933 334198
E-mail: cduksales@cummins.com
Web site: www.cummins-uk.com

*DIRECT PARTS LTD
Unit 1, Churnet Court, Churnetside Business
Park, Harrison Way, Cheddleton ST13 7EF
Tel: 01538 361777
Fax: 01538 369100
E-mail: sales@direct-group.co.uk
Web site: www.direct-group.co.uk

ERENTEK LTD
Malt Kiln Lane, Waddington, Lincoln
LN5 9RT
Tel: 01522 720065
Fax: 01522 729155
E-mail: sale@erentek.co.uk
Web site: www.erentek.co.uk

FTA VEHICLE INSPECTION SERVICE
Hermes House, St John's Road, Tunbridge
Wells TN4 9UZ.
Tel: 01892 526171
Fax: 01892 534989
E-mail: enquiries@fta.co.uk
Web site: www.fta.co.uk

THOMAS HARDIE – WIGAN
Lockett Road, Ashton-in-Makerfield, Wigan
WN4 8DE.
Tel: 01942 505124.
Fax: 01942 505119.

*HART BROTHERS (ENGINEERING) LTD
Soho Works, Soho Street, Oldham OL4 2AD
Tel: 0161 737 6791

*HILTECH DEVELOPMENTS
22 Larbre Crescent, Whickham, Newcastle
upon Tyne NE16 5YG
Tel: 0191 488 6258
Fax: 0191 488 9158
E-mail:
executive@hiltechdevelopments.com
Web site: www.hiltechdevelopments.com

IMEXPART LTD
Links 31, Willowbridge Way, Whitwood,
Castleford WF10 5NP
Tel: 01977 553936
Fax: 01977 604684
E-mail: parts@imexpart.com
Web site: www.imexpart.com

IMPERIAL ENGINEERING
Delamare Road, Cheshunt EN8 9UD
Tel: 01992 6342555
Fax: 01992 630506
E-mail: sales@imperialengineering.co.uk
Web site: www.imperialengineering.co.uk

JBF SERVICES LTD
Southedge Works, Hipperholme, Halifax
HX3 8EF
Tel: 01422 202840
Fax: 01422 206070
E-mail: jbfservices@aol.com

*LEYLAND PRODUCT DEVELOPMENTS LTD
Aston Way, Leyland, Preston PR26 7TZ
Tel: 01772 435834
E-mail: sales@lpdl.co.uk
Web site: www.lpdl.co.uk

*LH GROUP SERVICES LTD
Graycar Business Park, Barton Under
Needwood, Burton-on-Trent DE13 8EN
Tel: 01283 722600
Fax: 01283 722622
E-mail: lh@lh-group.co.uk
Web site: www.lh-group.co.uk

*MENTOR
Mentor Coach & Bus Ltd, Carlton House,
Euroway Industrial Estate, Hellaby,
Rotherham S66 8QL
Tel: 01709 700600
Fax: 01709 700007
E-mail: sales@mentorplc.com
Web site: www.mentorplc.com

MAJORLINE ENGINEERING LTD
Baybridge Industrial Units, Baybridge Lane,
Owslebury, Winchester SO21 1JN.
Tel: 01962 777077.
Fax: 01962 777661, 777667
E-mail: majorline@compuserve.com

*MARSHALLS COMMERCIAL ENGINEERING LTD
Firbank Way, Leighton Buzzard LU7 4YP
Tel: 01525 375301
Fax: 01525 850967
Web site: www.mce-ltd.com

MASS SPECIAL ENGINEERING LTD
Anston, Sheffield S25 4SD
Tel: 01909 550480.
Fax: 01909 550486.

PLAXTON
Plaxton Park, Cayton Low Road, Eastfield,
Scarborough YO11 3BY
Tel: 01723 581500
Fax: 01723 5813238
E-mail: sales@plaxtonlimited.co.uk
Web site: www.plaxtonlimited.co.uk

PNEUMAX LTD
Unit 8, Venture Industrial Park, Fareham
Road, Gosport PO13 0BA
Tel: 01329 823999
Fax: 01329 822345
E-mail: sales@pneumax.co.uk
Web site: www.pneumax.co.uk

*QUEENSBRIDGE (PSV) LTD
Milner Way, Longlands Industrial Estate,
Ossett WF5 9JE
Tel: 01924 281871
Fax: 01924 281807
E-mail: enquiries@queensbridgeltd.co.uk
Web site: www.queensbridgeltd.co.uk

TRANSPORT DESIGN INTERNATIONAL
12 Waterloo Road Estate, Bidford on Avon
B50 4JH
Tel: 01789 490370
Fax: 01789 490592
E-mail:enquiries@tdi.uk.com
Web site: www.tdi.uk.com

*UNITEC
Parts Division, Denby Way, Hellaby,
Rotherham S66 8HR
Tel: 01709 792000
Fax: 01709 792009
E-mail: parts@optare.com

*UNITEC LONDON
Unit 5, Gateway 25, Weston Avenue,
West Thurrock RM20 3ZD
Tel: 01708 892440
Fax: 01708 862125
E-mail: london.service@optare.com

*UNITEC ROTHERHAM
Denby Way, Hellaby, Rotherham
S66 8HR
Tel: 01709 535101
Fax: 01709 535103
E-mail: rotherham.service@optare.com

*UNITEC SCOTLAND
Unit 7, Cumbernauld Business Park,
Ward Park Road, Cumbernauld G67 3JZ
Tel: 01236 726738
Fax: 01236 795651
E-mail: scotland.service@optare.com

Engines

BUSS BIZZ
Goughs Transport Depot, Morestead,
Winchester SO21 1JD.
Tel: 01962 715555/66.
Fax: 01962 714868.

CRAIG TILSEY & SON LTD
Unit 7, Moorfield Industrial Estate, Cotes
Heath, Stoke-on-Trent ST21 6QY
Tel: 01782 791524
Fax: 01782 791316
E-mail:
maureen@eyremaureen.wanadoo.co.uk

CREWE ENGINES
Warmingham Road, Crewe CW1 4PQ
Tel: 01270 526333
Fax: 01270 526433
E-mail: sales@creweengines.co.uk
Web site: www.creweengines.co.uk

CUMMINS UK
Rutherford Drive, Park Farm South,
Wellingborough NN8 6AN
Tel: 01933 334200
Fax: 01933 334198
E-mail: cduksales@cummins.com
Web site: www.cummins-uk.com

DAF COMPONENTS LTD
Eastern Bypass, Thame OX9 3FB
Tel: 01844 261111
Fax: 01844 217111
Web site: www.daftrucks.com.

DAYCO – TRANSPORT & TRADE DISTRIBUTION LTD
Davis House, Lodge Causeway Trading
Estate, Fishponds, Bristol BS16 3JB.
Tel: 0117 965 9999.
Fax: 0117 965 4724.

DIESEL POWER ENGINEERING
Goughs Transport Depot, Morestead,
Winchester SO21 1JD.
Tel/Fax: 01962 711314

Mercedes engines

**Highest quality, Lowest price.
Direct from the Uk's No.1 for 25 years.**

also... MAN, Cummins, IVECO, VOLVO, DAF

Join the UK's major bus & coach groups and choose Crewe Engines for Mercedes-Benz engines. From fast delivery of an exchange engine to collection of your vehicle and fitting of the engine, we have the expertise and resources to provide great service at very competitive prices.

ENGINES
- UK's No.1 for remanufactured Mercedes engines
- Also MAN, Cummins, Iveco, Volvo, DAF, etc
- Petrol & diesel, 1950's to present day, 4 cyl to V12
- Fast, friendly & efficient - excellent reputation

ENGINE PARTS
- Full range of highest quality original equipment parts
- Pistons, crankshaft bearings, gasket sets, etc
- Cylinder heads, camshafts, crankshafts, etc

Call now for a quote or free info-pack
☎ **01270 526333**

www.creweengines.co.uk
e-mail: sales@creweengines.co.uk

Crewe Engines Ltd

Trade Directory

---

*HART BROTHERS (ENGINEERING) LTD
Soho Works, Soho Street, Oldham OL4 2AD
Tel: 0161 737 6791

IVECO
Iveco Ford Truck Ltd, Iveco Ford House, Station Road, Watford WD1 1SR.
Tel: 01923 246400.
Fax: 01923 240574.

*LH GROUP SERVICES LTD
Graycar Business Park, Barton Under Needwood, Burton-on-Trent DE13 8EN
Tel: 01283 722600
Fax: 01283 722622
E-mail: lh@lh-group.co.uk
Web site: www.lh-group.co.uk

MAJORLINE ENGINEERING LTD
Baybridge Industrial Units, Baybridge Lane, Owslebury, Winchester SO21 1JN.
Tel: 01962 777077.
Fax: 01962 777661, 777667
E-mail: majorline@compuserve.com

MAN TRUCK & BUS UK LTD
Frankland Road, Blagrove, Swindon SN5 8YU.
Tel: 01793 448000.
Fax: 01793 448262.

*MENTOR
Mentor Coach & Bus Ltd, Carlton House, Euroway Industrial Estate, Hellaby, Rotherham S66 8QL
Tel: 01709 700600
Fax: 01709 700007
E-mail: sales@mentorplc.com
Web site: www.mentorplc.com

MULTIPART PSV
Pilling Lane, Chorley PR7 3EL.
Tel: 01257 225577.
Fax: 01257 225575.
E-mail: info@multipart.com
Web site: www.multipart.com

*NEXT BUS LTD
The Coach Yard, Vincients Road, Bumpers Farm Industrial Estate, Chippenham SN14 6QA
Tel: 01249 462462
E-mail: sales@next-bus.co.uk
Web site: www.next-bus.co.uk

PERKINS GROUP LTD
Peterborough PE1 5NA.
Tel: 01733 567474.
Fax: 01733 582240.
Web site: www.perkins.com

QUEENSBRIDGE (PSV) LTD
Longlands Industrial Estate, Milner Way, Ossett WF5 9JE
Tel: 01924 281871
Fax: 01924 281807
E-mail: craig@queensbridgeltd.co.uk
Web site: www.queensbridgeltd.co.uk

SHAWSON SUPPLY LTD
12 Station Road, Saintfield BT24 7DU
Tel: 028 9751 0994
Fax: 028 9751 0816
E-mail: shawsondiesel@btopenworld.com
Web site: www.shawsonsupply.com

*UNITEC
Parts Division, Denby Way, Hellaby, Rotherham S66 8HR
Tel: 01709 792000
Fax: 01709 792009
E-mail: parts@optare.com

*UNITEC LONDON
Unit 5, Gateway 25, Weston Avenue, West Thurrock RM20 3ZD
Tel: 01708 892440
Fax: 01708 862125
E-mail: london.service@optare.com

*UNITEC ROTHERHAM
Denby Way, Hellaby, Rotherham S66 8HR
Tel: 01709 535101
Fax: 01709 535103
E-mail: rotherham.service@optare.com

*UNITEC SCOTLAND
Unit 7, Cumbernauld Business Park, Ward Park Road, Cumbernauld G67 3JZ
Tel: 01236 726738
Fax: 01236 795651
E-mail: scotland.service@optare.com

WALSH'S ENGINEERING
Barton Moss Road, Eccles, Manchester M30 7RL
Tel: 0161 787 7017
Fax: 0161 787 7038
E-mail: walshs@gardnerdiesel.co.uk
Website: www.gardnerdiesel.co.uk

Trade Directory

WALSH'S ENGINEERING LTD

COMMERCIAL DIESEL ENGINE SPECIALISTS
Barton Moss Road. Eccles. Manchester. M30 7RL

SUPPLIERS OF ALL TYPES OF RECONDITIONED ENGINE UNITS, PARTS AND SERVICE TO THE TRANSPORT INDUSTRY

FOR DETAILS CONTACT
CHARLIE HUGHES
OR
STEVE BRADLEY

TEL:- 0161 787 7017   FAX:- 0161 787 7038
E-MAIL:- walshs@gardnerdiesel.co.uk

WEALDSTONE ENGINEERING
Sanders Lodge Industrial Estate, Rushden NN10 6AZ.
Tel: 01933 316622.
Fax: 01933 358742.
Web site: www.wealdstone.co.uk

Engine Oil Drain Valves

FUMOTO ENGINEERING OF EUROPE
Normandy House, 35 Glategny Esplanade, St Peter Port, Guernsey GY1 2BP
Tel: 01481 716987
Fax: 01481 700374
E-mail: info@fumoto-valve.com

MARTYN INDUSTRIALS LTD
5 Brunel Way, Durranhill Industrial Esate, Carlisle CA1 3NQ
Tel: 01228 544000
Fax: 01228 544001
E-mail: enquiries@martyn-industrials.co.uk
Web site: www.martyn-industrials.com

*MENTOR
Mentor Coach & Bus Ltd, Carlton House, Euroway Industrial Estate, Hellaby, Rotherham S66 8QL
Tel: 01709 700600
Fax: 01709 700007
E-mail: sales@mentorplc.com
Web site: www.mentorplc.com

MULTIPART PSV
Pilling Lane, Chorley PR7 3EL.
Tel: 01257 225577.
Fax: 01257 225575.
E-mail: info@multipart.com
Web site: www.multipart.com

*PARTLINE LTD
Dockfield Road, Shipley BD17 7AZ
Tel: 01274 531531
Fax: 01274 531088
E-mail: sales@partline.co.uk
Web site: www.partline.co.uk

WALLMINSTER LTD
Unit 22, Chelsea Wharf, 15 Lots Road, London SW10 0QJ
Tel: 020 7352 2727
Fax: 020 7352 3990
E-mail: info@tankcontainers.co.uk

Exhaust Systems

ARVIN MERITOR
Unit 21, Suttons Park Avenue, Reading RG6 1LA.
Tel: 0118 935 9126
Fax: 0118 935 9138
E-mail: james.randall@arvinmeritor.com
Web site: www.arvinmeritor.com

ASHLEY BANKS LTD
5 King Street Estate, Langtoft, Peterborough PE6 9NF
Tel: 01778 560651
Fax: 01778 560721
E-mail: user@ashleybanks.fsnet.co.uk

BUSS BIZZ
Goughs Transport Depot, Morestead, Winchester SO21 1JD.
Tel: 01962 715555/66.
Fax: 01962 714868.

CARLYLE BUS & COACH LTD
Carlyle Business Park, Great Bridge Street, Swan Village, West Bromwich B70 0X4
Tel: 0121 524 1200
Fax: 0121 524 1201
E-mail: admin@carlyleplc.co.uk

*CRESCENT FACILITIES LTD
72 Willow Crescent, Chapeltown, Sheffield S35 1QS
Tel/fax: 0114 2451050
E-mail: cfl.chris@btinternet.com
Web site: www.cflparts.com

*DINEX EXHAUSTS LTD
14 Chesford Garage, Woolston, Warrington WA1 4RE
Tel: 01925 849849
Fax: 01925 849850
E-mail: enquiries@dinex.co.uk
Web site: www.dinex.dk

EMINOX LTD
North Warren Road, Gainsborough DN21 2TU
Tel: 01427 810088
Fax: 01427 810061
E-mail: marketing@eminox.com
Web site: www.eminox.com

IMEXPART LTD
Links 31, Willowbridge Way, Whitwood,
Castleford WF10 5NP
Tel: 01977 553936
Fax: 01977 604684
E-mail: parts@imexpart.com
Web site: www.imexpart.com

MAJORLINE ENGINEERING LTD
Baybridge Industrial Units, Baybridge Lane,
Owsleybury, Winchester SO21 1JN.
Tel: 01962 777077.
Fax: 01962 777661, 777667
E-mail: majorline@compuserve.com

*MENTOR
Mentor Coach & Bus Ltd, Carlton House,
Euroway Industrial Estate, Hellaby,
Rotherham S66 8QL
Tel: 01709 700600
Fax: 01709 700007
E-mail: sales@mentorplc.com
Web site: www.mentorplc.com

*PARTLINE LTD
Dockfield Road, Shipley BD17 7AZ
Tel: 01274 531531
Fax: 01274 531088
E-mail: sales@partline.co.uk
Web site: www.partline.co.uk

*UNITEC
Parts Division, Denby Way, Hellaby,
Rotherham S66 8HR
Tel: 01709 792000
Fax: 01709 792009
E-mail: parts@optare.com

*UNITEC LONDON
Unit 5, Gateway 25, Weston Avenue,
West Thurrock RM20 3ZD
Tel: 01708 892440
Fax: 01708 862125
E-mail: london.service@optare.com

*UNITEC ROTHERHAM
Denby Way, Hellaby, Rotherham
S66 8HR
Tel: 01709 535101
Fax: 01709 535103
E-mail: rotherham.service@optare.com

*UNITEC SCOTLAND
Unit 7, Cumbernauld Business Park,
Ward Park Road, Cumbernauld G67 3JZ
Tel: 01236 726738
Fax: 01236 795651
E-mail: scotland.service@optare.com

Fans & Drive Belts

CARLYLE BUS & COACH LTD
Carlyle Business Park, Great Bridge Street,
Swan Village, West Bromwich B70 0X4
Tel: 0121 524 1200
Fax: 0121 524 1201
E-mail: admin@carlyleplc.co.uk

CUMMINS UK
Rutherford Drive, Park Farm South,
Wellingborough NN8 6AN
Tel: 01933 334200
Fax: 01933 334198
E-mail: cduksales@cummins.com
Web site: www.cummins-uk.com

DIRECT PARTS LTD
Unit 1, Churnet Court, Churnetside Business
Park, Harrison Way, Cheddleton ST13 7EF
Tel: 01538 361777
Fax: 01538 369100
E-mail: sales@direct-group.co.uk
Web site: www.direct-group.co.uk

IMEXPART LTD
Links 31, Willowbridge Way, Whitwood,
Castleford WF10 5NP
Tel: 01977 553936
Fax: 01977 604684
E-mail: parts@imexpart.com
Web site: www.imexpart.com

MAJORLINE ENGINEERING LTD
Baybridge Industrial Units, Baybridge Lane,
Owsleybury, Winchester SO21 1JN.
Tel: 01962 777077.
Fax: 01962 777661, 777667
E-mail: majorline@compuserve.com

*MENTOR
Mentor Coach & Bus Ltd, Carlton House,
Euroway Industrial Estate, Hellaby,
Rotherham S66 8QL
Tel: 01709 700600
Fax: 01709 700007
E-mail: sales@mentorplc.com
Web site: www.mentorplc.com

MULTIPART PSV
Pilling Lane, Chorley PR7 3EL.
Tel: 01257 225577.
Fax: 01257 225575.
E-mail: info@multipart.com
Web site: www.multipart.com

*PACET MANUFACTURING LTD
Wyebridge House, Cores End Road,
Bourne End SL8 5HH
Tel: 01628 526754
Fax: 01628 810080
E-mail: sales@pacet.co.uk
Web site: www.pacet.co.uk

*PARTLINE LTD
Dockfield Road, Shipley BD17 7AZ
Tel: 01274 531531
Fax: 01274 531088
E-mail: sales@partline.co.uk
Web site: www.partline.co.uk

PIONEER WESTON
Smithfold Lane, Worsley, Manchester
M28 0GP.
Tel: 0161 703 2000
Fax: 0161 703 2025
E-mail: pioneer.weston@wyko.co.uk

QUEENSBRIDGE (PSV) LTD
Longlands Industrial Estate, Milner Way,
Ossett WF5 9JE
Tel: 01924 281871
Fax: 01924 281807
E-mail: craig@queensbridgeltd.co.uk
Web site: www.queensbridgeltd.co.uk

*UNITEC
Parts Division, Denby Way, Hellaby,
Rotherham S66 8HR
Tel: 01709 792000
Fax: 01709 792009
E-mail: parts@optare.com

Fare Boxes

*M BISSELL DISPLAY LTD
Unit 15, Beechwood Business Park,
Burdock Close, Cannock WS11 7GB
Tel: 01543 502115
Fax: 01543 502118
E-mail: sales@bisselldisplay.com
Web site: www.bisselldisplay.com

CUBIC TRANSPORTATION SYSTEMS LTD
AFC House, Honeycrock Lane, Salfords
RH1 5LA
Tel: 01737 782200
Fax: 01737 789759
Web site: www.cubic.com

*ELECTRONIC TICKET MACHINE SOFTWARE SERVICES (UK)
9 Dorset Avenue, Ferndown BH22 8HJ
Tel: 0844 800 9299
E-mail: info@etmss.com
Web site: www.etmss.com

JOHN GROVES TICKET SYSTEMS
Unit 5, Rennie Business Units, Factory
Place, Saltcoats KA21 5LZ
Tel: 01294 471133
Fax: 01294 471166
Web site: www.cambist.se

MARK TERRILL TICKET MACHINERY
5 De Grey Close, Lewes BN7 2JR.
Tel: 01273 474816
Fax: 01273 474816
E-mail: mark.terrill@ukonline.co.uk

Fire Extinguishers

ASHLEY BANKS LTD
5 King Street Estate, Langtoft, Peterborough
PE6 9NF
Tel: 01778 560651
Fax: 01778 560721
E-mail: user@ashleybanks.fsnet.co.uk

CARLYLE BUS & COACH LTD
Carlyle Business Park, Great Bridge Street,
Swan Village, West Bromwich B70 0X4
Tel: 0121 524 1200
Fax: 0121 524 1201
E-mail: admin@carlyleplc.co.uk

FIREMASTER EXTINGUISHER LTD
Firex House, 174-176 Hither Green Lane,
London SE13 6QB
Tel: 020 8852 8585
Fax: 020 8297 8020
E-mail: info@firemaster.co.uk
Web site: www.firemaster.co.uk

HAPPICH V & I COMPONENTS LTD
Unit 30/31, Fort Industrial Park, Fort
Parkway, Castle Bromwich B35 7AR.
Tel: 0121 747 4400
Fax: 0121 747 4977
E-mail: sales@happich.co.uk
Web site: www.happich.co.uk

KELLETT (UK) LTD
8 Stevenson Way, Sheffield S9 3WZ.
Tel: 0114 261 1122.
Fax: 0114 261 1199.
E-mail: sales@kellett.co.uk

Trade Directory

*THE LAWTON MOTOR BODY BUILDING CO LTD
Knutsford Road, Church Lawton,
Stoke-on-Trent ST7 3DN
Tel: 01270 882056
Fax: 01270 883014
E-mail: sales@lawtonmotorbody.co.uk
Web site: www.lawtonmotorbody.co.uk

MULTIPART PSV
Pilling Lane, Chorley PR7 3EL.
Tel: 01257 225577.
Fax: 01257 225575.
E-mail: info@multipart.com
Web site: www.multipart.com

*PARTLINE LTD
Dockfield Road, Shipley BD17 7AZ
Tel: 01274 531531
Fax: 01274 531088
E-mail: sales@partline.co.uk
Web site: www.partline.co.uk

PLAXTON
Plaxton Park, Cayton Low Road, Eastfield, Scarborough YO11 3BY
Tel: 01723 581500
Fax: 01723 5813238
E-mail: sales@plaxtonlimited.co.uk
Web site: www.plaxtonlimited.co.uk

PLAXTON COACH SALES CENTRE
Ryton Road, Anston, Sheffield S25 4DL
Tel: 01909 551155
Fax: 01909 567994
E-mail: coaches@plaxtonlimited.co.uk
Web site: www.plaxtonlimited.co.uk

PSV PRODUCTS
PO Box 166, Warrington WA4 5FG
Tel: 0870 062 4488
Fax: 0870 062 4499
E-mail: mike@psvproducts.com
Web site: www.psvproducts.com

SAFEGUARD
Kiln Lane, Swindon SN2 2NP
Tel: 01793 512999
Fax: 01793 511345

First Aid Equipment

ASHLEY BANKS LTD
5 King Street Estate, Langtoft, Peterborough PE6 9NF
Tel: 01778 560651
Fax: 01778 560721
E-mail: user@ashleybanks.fsnet.co.uk

*BRADTECH LTD
Unit 3, Ladford Covert, Seighford, Stafford ST18 9QL
Tel: 01785 282800
Fax: 01785 282558
E-mail: sales@bradtech.ltd.uk
Web site: www.bradtech.ltd.uk

CARLYLE BUS & COACH LTD
Carlyle Business Park, Great Bridge Street, Swan Village, West Bromwich B70 0X4
Tel: 0121 524 1200
Fax: 0121 524 1201
E-mail: admin@carlyleplc.co.uk

FIREMASTER EXTINGUISHER LTD
Firex House, 174-176 Hither Green Lane, London SE13 6QB
Tel: 020 8852 8585
Fax: 020 8297 8020
E-mail: info@firemaster.co.uk
Web site: www.firemaster.co.uk

HAPPICH V & I COMPONENTS LTD
Unit 30/31, Fort Industrial Park, Fort Parkway, Castle Bromwich B35 7AR
Tel: 0121 747 4400
Fax: 0121 747 4977
E-mail: sales@happich.co.uk
Web site: www.happich.co.uk

MULTIPART PSV
Pilling Lane, Chorley PR7 3EL.
Tel: 01257 225577
Fax: 01257 225575
E-mail: info@multipart.com
Web site: www.multipart.com

*PARTLINE LTD
Dockfield Road, Shipley BD17 7AZ
Tel: 01274 531531
Fax: 01274 531088
E-mail: sales@partline.co.uk
Web site: www.partline.co.uk

PLAXTON
Plaxton Park, Cayton Low Road, Eastfield, Scarborough YO11 3BY
Tel: 01723 581500
Fax: 01723 5813238
E-mail: sales@plaxtonlimited.co.uk
Web site: www.plaxtonlimited.co.uk

PLAXTON COACH SALES CENTRE
Ryton Road, Anston, Sheffield S25 4DL
Tel: 01909 551155
Fax: 01909 567994
E-mail: coaches@plaxtonlimited.co.uk
Web site: www.plaxtonlimited.co.uk

PSV PRODUCTS
PO Box 166, Warrington WA4 5FG
Tel: 0870 062 4488
Fax: 0870 062 4499
E-mail: mike@psvproducts.com
Web site: www.psvproducts.com

SAFEGUARD
Kiln Lane, Swindon SN2 2NP
Tel: 01793 512999
Fax: 01793 511345

TRAMONTANA
Chapelknowe Road, Carfin, Motherwell ML1 5LE
Tel: 01698 861790
Fax: 01698 860778
E-mail: wdt90@tiscali.co.uk
Web site: tramontanacoach.co.uk

Floor Coverings

ALTRO
Works Road, Letchworth SG6 1NW
Tel: 01462 480480
Fax: 01462 480010
E-mail: lkni@altro.co.uk
Web site: www.altrotransfloor.com

AUTOMATE WHEEL COVERS LTD
California Mills, Oxford Road, Gomersal, Cleckheaton BD19 4HQ
Tel: 01274 862700
Fax: 01274 851989
E-mail: sales@wheelcovers.co.uk
Web site: www.euroliners.com

AUTOMOTIVE TEXTILE INDUSTRIES
Unit 15 & 16, Priest Court, Springfield Business Park, Grantham NG31 7BG
Tel: 01476 593050
Fax: 01476 593607
E-mail: sales@autotex.com
Web site: www.autotex.com

CARLYLE BUS & COACH LTD
Carlyle Business Park, Great Bridge Street, Swan Village, West Bromwich B70 0X4
Tel: 0121 524 1200
Fax: 0121 524 1201
E-mail: admin@carlyleplc.co.uk

COACH CARPETS
Unit 12, Hamilton Street, Blackburn BB2 4AJ.
Tel: 01254 53549.
Fax: 01254 261873.

FIRTH FURNISHINGS LTD
PO Box 22, Flush Mills, Heckmondwike WF16 0EP.
Tel: 01924 406141.
Fax: 01924 401128.

*THE LAWTON MOTOR BODY BUILDING CO LTD
Knutsford Road, Church Lawton, Stoke-on-Trent ST7 3DN
Tel: 01270 882056
Fax: 01270 883014
E-mail: sales@lawtonmotorbody.co.uk
Web site: www.lawtonmotorbody.co.uk

MARTYN INDUSTRIALS LTD
5 Brunel Way, Durranhill Industrial Esate, Carlisle CA1 3NQ
Tel: 01228 544000
Fax: 01228 544001
E-mail: enquiries@martyn-industrials.co.uk
Web site: www.martyn-industrials.com

MULTIPART PSV
Pilling Lane, Chorley PR7 3EL.
Tel: 01257 225577.
Fax: 01257 225575.
E-mail: info@multipart.com
Web site: www.multipart.com

TIFLEX LTD
Tiflex House, Liskeard PL14 4NB
Tel: 01579 320808
Fax: 01579 320802
E-mail: marketing@tiflex.co.uk
Web site: www.tiflex.co.uk

*TRIMPLEX SAFETY TREAD LTD
Trident Works, Mulberry Way, Belvedere DA17 6AN
Tel: 020 8311 2101
Fax: 020 8312 1400
E-mail: safetytread@btconnect.com
Web site: www.safetytread.co.uk

Fuel, Fuel Management & Lubricants

CUMMINS UK
Rutherford Drive, Park Farm South, Wellingborough NN8 6AN
Tel: 01933 334200
Fax: 01933 334198
E-mail: cduksales@cummins.com
Web site: www.cummins-uk.com

Trade Directory

INTERLUBE SYSTEMS LTD
St Modwen Road, Plymouth PL6 8LH
Tel: 01752 676000
Fax: 01752 676001
E-mail: info@interlubesystems.com
Web site: www.interlubesystems.com

JMW
Systems House, Pentland Industrial Estate, Loanhead EH20 9QH
Tel: 0131 440 3633
Fax: 0131 440 3637
E-mail: enquiries@jmw-group.co.uk
Web site: www.jmw-group.co.uk

MULTIPART PSV
Pilling Lane, Chorley PR7 3EL.
Tel: 01257 225577.
Fax: 01257 225575.
E-mail: info@multipart.com
Web site: www.multipart.com

*VBI TRISCAN
Harwood Street, Blackburn BB1 3BD
Tel: 0870 445 2952
Fax: 01254 680 381
E-mail: info@vbilimited.com
Web site: www.vbilimited.com

Garage Equipment

BUTTS OF BAWTRY GARAGE EQUIPMENT
Station Yard, Station Road, Bawtry, Doncaster DN10 6QD
Tel: 01302 710868
Fax: 01302 719481
E-mail: info@jhmbuttco.com
Web site www.jhmbuttco.com

TERENCE BARKER TANKS
Tel: 01376 330661
E-mail: terencebarkertanks.co.uk
Web site: www.terencebarkertanks.co.uk

*DIRECT PARTS LTD
Unit 1, Churnet Court, Churnetside Business Park, Harrison Way, Cheddleton ST13 7EF
Tel: 01538 361777
Fax: 01538 369100
E-mail: sales@direct-group.co.uk
Web site: www.direct-group.co.uk

GEMCO EQUUIPMENT LTD
153-156 Bridge Street, Northampton NN1 1QG
Tel: 01604 828600
Fax: 01604 633159
E-mail: sales@gemco.co.uk
Web site: www.gemco.co.uk

PHIL STOCKFORD GARAGE EQUIPMENT
7 Badger Way, North Cheshire Trading Estate, Prenton CH43 3HQ
Tel: 0151 609 1007
Fax: 0151 609 1008

VARLEY & GULLIVER LTD
Alfred Street, Sparkbrook, Birmingham B12 8JR.
Tel: 0121 773 2441.
Fax: 0121 766 6875.

MAJORLIFT HYDRAULIC EQUIPMENT LTD
Arnold's Field Industrial Estate, Wickwar, Wotton-under-Edge GL12 8JD
Tel: 01454 299299
Fax: 01454294003
Web site: www.majorlift.com
E-mail: info@majorlift.com

SOMERS TOTALKARE LTD
15 Forge Trading Estate, Mucklow Hill, Halesowen B62 8TR
Tel: 0121 585 2700
Fax: 0121 585 2725
E-mail: sales@somerstotalkare.co.uk
Web site: www.somerstotalkare.co.uk

STERTIL UK LTD
Unit A, Brackmills Business Park, Caswell Road, Northampton NN4 7PW
Tel: 01604 677384
Fax: 01604 765181
E-mail: info@stertil.com
Web site: www.stertil.com

V L TEST SYSTEMS LTD
3-4 Middle Slade, Buckingham Industrial Park, Buckingham MK18 1WA
Tel: 01280 822488
Fax: 01280 822489
E-mail: sales@vltestuk.com
Web site: www.vltest.com

Gearboxes

ALLISON TRANSMISSION
Allison House, 36 Duncan Close, Moulton Park, Northampton NN3 6WL

DAVID BROWN VEHICLE TRANSMISSIONS LTD
Park Gear Works, Lockwood, Huddersfield HD4 5DD.
Tel: 01484 422180
Fax: 01484 435292

BUSS BIZZ
Goughs Transport Depot, Morestead, Winchester SO21 1JD.
Tel: 01962 715555/66.
Fax: 01962 714868.

EATON LTD
Truck Components Marketing, PO Box 11, Worsley Road North, Worsley M28 5GJ
Tel: 01204 797219.
Fax: 01204 797204.

GARDNER PARTS LTD
Barton Hall, Hardy Street, Eccles M30 7WA.
Tel: 0161 278 9200
Fax: 0161 787 7549.

*HART BROTHERS (ENGINEERING) LTD
Soho Works, Soho Street, Oldham OL4 2AD
Tel: 0161 737 6791

HL SMITH TRANSMISSIONS LTD
Enterprise Business Park, Cross Road, Albrighton, Wolverhampton WV7 3BJ
Tel: 01902 373011
Fax: 01902 373608

*LH GROUP SERVICES LTD
Graycar Business Park, Barton Under Needwood, Burton-on-Trent DE13 8EN
Tel: 01283 722600
Fax: 01283 722622
E-mail: lh@lh-group.co.uk
Web site: www.lh-group.co.uk

MAJORLINE ENGINEERING LTD
Baybridge Industrial Units, Baybridge Lane, Owslebury, Winchester SO21 1JN.
Tel: 01962 777077
Fax: 01962 777661, 777667
E-mail: majorline@compuserve.com

*MENTOR
Mentor Coach & Bus Ltd, Carlton House, Euroway Industrial Estate, Hellaby, Rotherham S66 8QL
Tel: 01709 700600
Fax: 01709 700007
E-mail: sales@mentorplc.com
Web site: www.mentorplc.com

MULTIPART PSV
Pilling Lane, Chorley PR7 3EL.
Tel: 01257 225577.
Fax: 01257 225575.
E-mail: info@multipart.com
Web site: www.multipart.com

*NEXT BUS LTD
The Coach Yard, Vincients Road, Bumpers Farm Industrial Estate, Chippenham SN14 6QA
Tel: 01249 462462
E-mail: sales@next-bus.co.uk
Web site: www.next-bus.co.uk

QUEENSBRIDGE (PSV) LTD
Longlands Industrial Estate, Milner Way, Ossett WF5 9JE
Tel: 01924 281871
Fax: 01924 281807
E-mail: craig@queensbridgeltd.co.uk
Web site: www.queensbridgeltd.co.uk

SHAWSON SUPPLY LTD
12 Station Road, Saintfield BT24 7DU
Tel: 028 9751 0994
Fax: 028 9751 0816
E-mail: shawsondiesel@btopenworld.com
Web site: www.shawsonsupply.com

*UNITEC
Parts Division, Denby Way, Hellaby, Rotherham S66 8HR
Tel: 01709 792000
Fax: 01709 792009
E-mail: parts@optare.com

*UNITEC LONDON
Unit 5, Gateway 25, Weston Avenue, West Thurrock RM20 3ZD
Tel: 01708 892440
Fax: 01708 862125
E-mail: london.service@optare.com

*UNITEC ROTHERHAM
Denby Way, Hellaby, Rotherham S66 8HR
Tel: 01709 535101
Fax: 01709 535103
E-mail: rotherham.service@optare.com

*UNITEC SCOTLAND
Unit 7, Cumbernauld Business Park, Ward Park Road, Cumbernauld G67 3JZ
Tel: 01236 726738
Fax: 01236 795651
E-mail: scotland.service@optare.com

*VOITH TURBO LTD
6 Beddington Farm Road, Croydon CR0 4XB
Tel: 020 8667 0333
Fax: 020 8667 0403
E-mail: john.domigan@voith.com
Web site: www.voith.co.uk

Trade Directory

*VOR TRANSMISSIONS LTD
Little London House, St Anne's Road, Willenhall WV13 1DT
Tel: 01902 604141
Fax: 01902 603868
E-mail: vor@globalnet.co.uk
Web site: www.vor.co.uk

TREVOR WIGLEY & SONS BUS LTD
Baulder Bridge Road, Carlton, Barnsley S71 3HJ
Tel: 01226 713636/716479
E-mail: wigleys@btconnect.com
Web site: www.twigley.com

ZF POWERTRAIN
Stringes Close, Willenhall WV13 1LE
Tel: 01902 366000
Fax: 01902 366504
E-mail: sales@powertrain.org.uk
Web site: www.powertrain.org.uk

Hand Driers (in coaches)

*BRADTECH LTD
Unit 3, Ladford Covert, Seighford, Stafford ST18 9QL
Tel: 01785 282800
Fax: 01785 282558
E-mail: sales@bradtech.ltd.uk
Web site: www.bradtech.ltd.uk

SHADES TECHNICS
Marshgate Drive, Hertford SG13 7AJ
Tel: 01992 501683
Fax: 01992 501669
E-mail: sales@shades-technics.com
Web site: www.shades-technics.com

Handrails

*ABACUS TUBULAR PRODUCTS LTD
Abacus House, Highlode Industrial Estate, Ramsey PE26 2RB
Tel: 01487 710700
Fax: 01487 710626
E-mail: info@abacus-tp.com

CARLYLE BUS & COACH LTD
Carlyle Business Park, Great Bridge Street, Swan Village, West Bromwich B70 0X4
Tel: 0121 524 1200
Fax: 0121 524 1201
E-mail: admin@carlyleplc.co.uk

CROWN COACHBUILDERS LTD
32 Flemington Industrial Park, Flemington, Motherwell ML1 1SN.
Tel: 01698 276087.
Fax: 01698 276144.
E-mail: davidgreer@hotmail.com
Web site: www.crowncoachbuilders.co.uk

DEANS POWERED DOORS
PO Box 8, Borwick Drive, Grovehill, Beverley HU17 0HQ
Tel: 01482 868111
Fax: 01482 881890
E-mail: info@deans-doors.com

*GABRIEL & CO LTD
Abro Works, 10 Hay Hall Road, Tyseley, Birmingham B11 2AU
Tel: 0121 248 3333
Fax: 0121 248 3330
E-mail: contact@gabrielco.com
Web site: www.gabrielco.com

HAPPICH V & I COMPONENTS LTD
Unit 30/31, Fort Industrial Park, Fort Parkway, Castle Bromwich B35 7AR.
Tel: 0121 747 4400
Fax: 0121 747 4977
E-mail: sales@happich.co.uk
Web site: www.happich.co.uk

JBF SERVICES LTD
Southedge Works, Hipperholme, Halifax HX3 8EF
Tel: 01422 202840
Fax: 01422 206070
E-mail: jbfservices@aol.com

PLAXTON
Plaxton Park, Cayton Low Road, Eastfield, Scarborough YO11 3BY
Tel: 01723 581500
Fax: 01723 5813238
E-mail: sales@plaxtonlimited.co.uk
Web site: www.plaxtonlimited.co.uk

PLAXTON COACH SALES CENTRE
Ryton Road, Anston, Sheffield S25 4DL
Tel: 01909 551155
Fax: 01909 567994
E-mail: coaches@plaxtonlimited.co.uk
Web site: www.plaxtonlimited.co.uk

*UNWIN SAFETY SYSTEMS
Unwin House, The Horseshoe, Coat Road, Martock TA12 6EY
Tel: 01935 827740
Fax: 01935 827760
E-mail: sales@unwin-safety.co.uk
Web site: wwwunwin-safety.com

Headrest Covers & Curtains

DUOFLEX LTD
Trimmingham House, 2 Shires Road, Buckingham Road Industrial Estate, Brackley NN13 7EZ
Tel: 01280 701366
Fax: 01280 704799
E-mail: sales@duoflex.co.uk
Web site: www.duoflex.co.uk

ORVEC INTERNATIONAL LTD
Malmo Road, Hull HU7 0YF.
Tel: 01482 879146
Fax: 01482 878989.
E-mail: service@orvec.co.uk
Web site: www.orvec.co.uk

Heating & Ventilation Systems

AMA LTD
Unit 17, Springmill Industrial Estate, Avening Road, Nailsworth GL6 0BH.
Tel: 01453 832884.
Fax: 01453 832040.
E-mail: ama@ftech.co.uk

CARLYLE BUS & COACH LTD
Carlyle Business Park, Great Bridge Street, Swan Village, West Bromwich B70 0X4
Tel: 0121 524 1200
Fax: 0121 524 1201
E-mail: admin@carlyleplc.co.uk

CARRIER SUTRAK
Unit 6, I O Centre, Barn Way, Lodge Farm Industrial Estate, Northampton NN5 7UW
Tel: 01604 581468
Fax: 01604 758132
E-mail: kim.neale@carrier.utc.com

*CLAYTON HEATERS LTD
Hunter Terrace, Fletchworth Gate, Burnsall Road, Coventry CV5 6SP
Tel: 02476 691916
Fax: 02476 691969
E-mail: sales@claytoncc.co.uk
Web site: www.claytoncc.co.uk

CONSERVE (UK) LTD
Suite 7, Logistics House, Kingsthorpe Road, Northampton NN2 6LJ
Tel: 01604 710055
Fax: 01604 710065
E-mail: information@conserveuk.co.uk
Web site: www.conserveuk.co.uk

EBERSPACHER (UK) LTD
Headlands Business Park, Salisbury Road, Ringwood BH24 3PB
Tel: 01425 480151
Fax: 01425 480152
E-mail: enquiries@eberspacher.com
Web site: www.eberspacher.com

HAPPICH V & I COMPONENTS LTD
Unit 30/31, Fort Industrial Park, Fort Parkway, Castle Bromwich B35 7AR.
Tel: 0121 747 4400
Fax: 0121 747 4977
E-mail: sales@happich.co.uk
Web site: www.happich.co.uk

*KARIVE LIMITED
PO Box 205, Southam CV47 0ZL
Tel: 01926 813938
Fax: 01926 814898
E-mail: karive.ltd@btinternet.com
Web site: www.karive.co.uk

NEALINE WINDSCREEN WIPER PRODUCTS
Unit 1, The Sidings Industrial Estate, Birdingbury Road, Marton CV23 9RX
Tel: 01926 633256
Fax: 01926 632600

PLAXTON COACH SALES CENTRE
Ryton Road, Anston, Sheffield S25 4DL
Tel: 01909 551155
Fax: 01909 567994
E-mail: coaches@plaxtonlimited.co.uk
Web site: www.plaxtonlimited.co.uk

*UNITEC
Parts Division, Denby Way, Hellaby, Rotherham S66 8HR
Tel: 01709 792000
Fax: 01709 792009
E-mail: parts@optare.com

WEBASTO PRODUCT UK LTD
Webasto House, White Rose Way, Doncaster Carr DN4 5JH
Tel: 01302 322232
Fax: 01302 322231
E-mail: info@webastouk.com
Web site: www.webasto.co.uk

Hub Odometers

KELLETT (UK) LTD
8 Stevenson Way, Sheffield S9 3WZ.
Tel: 0114 261 1122
Fax: 0114 261 1199
E-mail: sales@kellett.co.uk

MULTIPART PSV
Pilling Lane, Chorley PR7 3EL.
Tel: 01257 225577.
Fax: 01257 225575.
E-mail: info@multipart.com
Web site: www.multipart.com

*PARTLINE LTD
Dockfield Road, Shipley BD17 7AZ
Tel: 01274 531531
Fax: 01274 531088
E-mail: sales@partline.co.uk
Web site: www.partline.co.uk

PIONEER WESTON
Smithfold Lane, Worsley, Manchester M28 0GP.
Tel: 0161 703 2000
Fax: 0161 703 2025
E-mail: pioneer.weston@wyko.co.uk

ROADLINK INTERNATIONAL LTD
Strawberry Lane, Willenhall WV13 3RL
Tel: 01902 636210
Fax: 01902 606604
E-mail: sales@roadlink-international.co.uk
Web site: www.roadlink-international.co.uk

In-coach Entertainment

AVT SYSTEMS LTD
Unit 3, Tything Road, Arden Forest Trading Estate, Alcester B49 6ES
Tel: 01789 400357
Fax: 01789 400359
E-mail: enquiries@avtsystems.co.uk
Web site: www.avtsystems.co.uk

*BRADTECH LTD
Unit 3, Ladford Covert, Seighford, Stafford ST18 9QL
Tel: 01785 282800
Fax: 01785 282558
E-mail: sales@bradtech.ltd.uk
Web site: www.bradtech.ltd.uk

*ELSAN LTD
Bellbrook Park, Uckfield BN3 7RA
Tel: 01825 748200
Fax: 01825 761212
E-mail: sales@elsan.co.uk
Web site: www.elsan.co.uk

EXPRESS COACH REPAIRS LTD
Outgang Lane, Pickering YO18 7EL.
Tel: 01751 475215.

PLAXTON COACH SALES CENTRE
Ryton Road, Anston, Sheffield S25 4DL
Tel: 01909 551155
Fax: 01909 567994
E-mail: coaches@plaxtonlimited.co.uk
Web site: www.plaxtonlimited.co.uk

PSV PRODUCTS
PO Box 166, Warrington WA4 5FG
Tel: 0870 062 4488
Fax: 0870 062 4499
E-mail: mike@psvproducts.com
Web site: www.psvproducts.com

SHADES TECHNICS
Marshgate Drive, Hertford SG13 7AJ
Tel: 01992 501683
Fax: 01992 501669
E-mail: sales@shades-technics.com
Web site: www.shades-technics.com

Labels, Nameplates & Decals

*FIRST CHOICE NAMEPLATES, LABELS & SIGNS
Lynden 2c, Russell Avenue, Balderton, Newark NG24 3BT
Tel: 01636 678035
Fax: 01636 707066

*THE LAWTON MOTOR BODY BUILDING CO LTD
Knutsford Road, Church Lawton, Stoke-on-Trent ST7 3DN
Tel: 01270 882056
Fax: 01270 883014
E-mail: sales@lawtonmotorbody.co.uk
Web site: www.lawtonmotorbody.co.uk

McKENNA BROTHERS LTD
McKenna House, Jubilee Road, Middleton, Manchester M24 2LX
Tel: 0161 655 3244
Fax: 0161 655 3059
E-mail: info@mckennabrothers.co.uk
Web site: www.mckennabrothers.co.uk

Lifting Equipment

AUTOLIFT LTD
Forge House, Norwell Woodhouse, Newark NG23 6NG
Tel: 01636 636586
Fax: 01636 636101
E-mail: info@autolift.freeserve.co.uk

PLAXTON
Plaxton Park, Cayton Low Road, Eastfield, Scarborough YO11 3BY
Tel: 01723 581500
Fax: 01723 5813238
E-mail: sales@plaxtonlimited.co.uk
Web site: www.plaxtonlimited.co.uk

Lifts/Ramps (Passenger)

COMPAK RAMPS LTD
VIP Trading Estate, Anchor & Hope Lane, London SE7 7RY
Tel/Fax: 020 8858 3781

CROWN COACHBUILDERS LTD
32 Flemington Industrial Park, Flemington, Motherwell ML1 1SN.
Tel: 01698 276087
Fax: 01698 276144
E-mail: davidgreer@hotmail.com
Web site: www.crowncoachbuilders.co.uk

HATTS COACHWORKS & SERVICES
Foxham, Chippenham SN15 4NB
Tel: 01249 740444
Fax: 01249 740447
E-mail: adrian@hattstravel.co.uk
Web site: www.hattstravel.co.uk

MARTYN INDUSTRIALS LTD
5 Brunel Way, Durranhill Industrial Estate, Carlisle CA1 3NQ
Tel: 01228 544000
Fax: 01228 544001
E-mail: enquiries@martyn-industrials.co.uk
Web site: www.martyn-industrials.com

PASSENGER LIFT SERVICES LTD
Unit 10, Crystal Drive, Sandwell Business Park, Smethwick B66 1QG.
Tel: 0121 552 0600.
Fax: 0121 552 0200.
Web site: www.pls-access.co.uk

PNEUMAX LTD
Unit 8, Venture Industrial Park, Fareham Road, Gosport PO13 0BA
Tel: 01329 823999
Fax: 01329 822345
E-mail: sales@pneumax.co.uk
Web site: www.pneumax.co.uk

RATCLIFF TAIL LIFTS LTD
Bessemer Road, Welwyn Garden City AL7 1ET
Tel: 01707 325571
Fax: 01707 327752
Web site: www.ratcliff.co.uk

RICON UK LIMITED
Littlemoss Business Park, Littlemoss Road, Droylsden, Manchester M43 7EF
Tel: 0800 435677
Fax: 0161 301 6050
E-mail: info@riconuk.com
Web site: www.riconuk.com

TRUCKALIGN CO LTD
VIP Trading Estate, Anchor & Hope Lane, London SE7 7RY
Tel: 020 8858 3781
Fax: 020 8858 3781

Lighting & Lighting Design

ATLAS LIGHTING COMPONENTS
3 King George Close, Eastern Avenue, West Romford RM7 7PP.
Tel: 01708 776375
Fax: 01708 776376

BRITAX PMG LTD
Bressingby Industrial Estate, Bridlington YO16 4SJ
Tel: 01262 670161
Fax: 01262 605666
E-mail: info@britax-pmg.com
Web site: www.britax-pmg.com

CARLYLE BUS & COACH LTD
Carlyle Business Park, Great Bridge Street, Swan Village, West Bromwich B70 0XA
Tel: 0121 524 1200
Fax: 0121 524 1201
E-mail: admin@carlyleplc.co.uk

Trade Directory

Trade Directory

*CRESCENT FACILITIES LTD
72 Willow Crescent, Chapeltown, Sheffield
S35 1QS
Tel/fax: 0114 2451050
E-mail: cfl.chris@btinternet.com
Web site: www.cflparts.com

CSM LIGHTING
Suite 1b, Cobb House, Oyster Lane, Byfleet
KT14 7DU
Tel: 01932 349661
Fax: 01932 349991
Web site: www.csmauto.com

HAPPICH V & I COMPONENTS LTD
Unit 30/31, Fort Industrial Park, Fort
Parkway, Castle Bromwich B35 7AR.
Tel: 0121 747 4400
Fax: 0121 747 4977
E-mail: sales@happich.co.uk
Web site: www.happich.co.uk

IMEXPART LTD
Links 31, Willowbridge Way, Whitwood,
Castleford WF10 5NP
Tel: 01977 553936
Fax: 01977 604684
E-mail: parts@imexpart.com
Web site: www.imexpart.com

INVERTEC LTD
Whelford Road, Fairford GL7 4DT
Tel: 01285 713550
Fax: 01285 713548
Mobile: 07802 793828
E-mail: ian@invertec.co.uk
Web site: www.invertec.co.uk

KELLETT (UK) LTD
8 Stevenson Way, Sheffield S9 3WZ.
Tel: 0114 261 1122.
Fax: 0114 261 1199.
E-mail: sales@kellett.co.uk

MULTIPART PSV
Pilling Lane, Chorley PR7 3EL.
Tel: 01257 225577.
Fax: 01257 225575.
E-mail: info@multipart.com
Web site: www.multipart.com

*PARTLINE LTD
Dockfield Road, Shipley BD17 7AZ
Tel: 01274 531531
Fax: 01274 531088
E-mail: sales@partline.co.uk
Web site: www.partline.co.uk

*UNITEC
Parts Division, Denby Way, Hellaby,
Rotherham S66 8HR
Tel: 01709 792000
Fax: 01709 792009
E-mail: parts@optare.com

Mirrors/Mirror Arms

*ASHTREE GLASS LTD
Brownroyd Street, Bradford BD8 9AF
Tel: 01274 546732
Fax: 01274 548525
E-mail: sales@ashtreeglass.co.uk
Web site: www.ashtreeglass.co.uk

Model Buses

MIRROR IMAGE MODELS
A's Models of Bolton, (Dept. LRB/MIM),
PO Box 514, Bolton BL1 5YD
Tel: 01204 467 961.
Web site: www.mirror-image-models.org.uk

Oil Management Systems

IMEXPART LTD
Links 31, Willowbridge Way, Whitwood,
Castleford WF10 5NP
Tel: 01977 553936
Fax: 01977 604684
E-mail: parts@imexpart.com
Web site: www.imexpart.com

INTERLUBE SYSTEMS LTD
St Modwen Road, Plymouth PL6 8LH
Tel: 01752 676000
Fax: 01752 676001
E-mail: info@interlubesystems.com
Web site: www.interlubesystems.com

STERTIL UK LTD
Unit A, Brackmills Business Park, Caswell
Road, Northampton NN4 7PW
Tel: 01604 677384
Fax: 01604 765181
E-mail: info@stertil.com
Web site: www.stertil.com

Painting & Signwriting

BLACKPOOL COACH SERVICES
Moss Hey Garage, Chapel Road, Blackpool
FY4 5HU.
Tel/Fax: 01253 698686

BULWARK BUS & COACH ENGINEERING LTD
Gate 3, Bulwark Industrial Estate, Chepstow
NP16 5QZ
Tel: 01291 622326.
Fax: 01291 622726.

DRURY & DRURY
Unit 6, Cobbs Wood Industrial Estate,
Brunswick Road, Ashford TN23 1EH.
Tel: 01303 610555.
Fax: 01303 610666.
E-mail: martinstrange@channelcommercials.co.uk

EXPRESS COACH REPAIRS LTD
Outgang Lane, Pickering YO18 7EL.
Tel: 01751 475215.

HANTS & DORSET TRIM LTD
Canada Road, West Wellow SO51 6DE.
Tel: 023 8033 4335

HATTS COACHWORKS & SERVICES
Foxham, Chippenham SN15 4NB
Tel: 01249 740444
Fax: 01249 740447
E-mail: adrian@hattstravel.co.uk
Web site: www.hattstravel.co.uk

*LANCES MOBILE PAINTING
20 Hillman Crescent, Boost Town,
Worsley, Manchester M28 1FY
Tel: 07974 862022
Fax: 01249 740447

*THE LAWTON MOTOR BODY BUILDING CO LTD
Knutsford Road, Church Lawton,
Stoke-on-Trent ST7 3DN
Tel: 01270 882056
Fax: 01270 883014
E-mail: sales@lawtonmotorbody.co.uk
Web site: www.lawtonmotorbody.co.uk

McKENNA BROTHERS LTD
McKenna House, Jubilee Road, Middleton,
Manchester M24 2LX
Tel: 0161 655 3244
Fax: 0161 655 3059
E-mail: info@mckennabrothers.co.uk
Web site: www.mckennabrothers.co.uk

*MENTOR
Mentor Coach & Bus Ltd, Carlton House,
Euroway Industrial Estate, Hellaby,
Rotherham S66 8QL
Tel: 01709 700600
Fax: 01709 700007
E-mail: sales@mentorplc.com
Web site: www.mentorplc.com

*NORBURY BLINDS LTD
41-45 Hanley Street, Newtown, Birmingham
B19 3SP
Tel: 0121 359 4311
Fax: 0121 359 6388
E-mail: info@norbury-blinds.com
Web site: www.norbury-blinds.com

PLAXTON
Plaxton Park, Cayton Low Road, Eastfield,
Scarborough YO11 3BY
Tel: 01723 581500
Fax: 01723 5813238
E-mail: sales@plaxtonlimited.co.uk
Web site: www.plaxtonlimited.co.uk

PLAXTON COACH SALES CENTRE
Ryton Road, Anston, Sheffield S25 4DL
Tel: 01909 551155
Fax: 01909 567994
E-mail: coaches@plaxtonlimited.co.uk
Web site: www.plaxtonlimited.co.uk

*RH BODYWORKS
A140 Ipswich Road, Brome, Eye IP23 8AW
Tel: 01379 870666
Fax: 01379 872138
E-mail: mike.ball@rhbodyworks.co.uk
Web site: www.rhbodyworks.co.uk

*UNITEC LONDON
Unit 5, Gateway 25, Weston Avenue,
West Thurrock RM20 3ZD
Tel: 01708 892440
Fax: 01708 862125
E-mail: london.service@optare.com

*UNITEC ROTHERHAM
Denby Way, Hellaby, Rotherham
S66 8HR
Tel: 01709 535101
Fax: 01709 535103
E-mail: rotherham.service@optare.com

*UNITEC SCOTLAND
Unit 7, Cumbernauld Business Park,
Ward Park Road, Cumbernauld G67 3JZ
Tel: 01236 726738
Fax: 01236 795651
E-mail: scotland.service@optare.com

Trade Directory

*VOLVO BUS AND COACH CENTRE
Belton Road West, Loughborough LE11 5HP
Tel: 01509 217777
Fax: 01509 239362
Web site: www.volvo.com

Parts Suppliers

AIR DOOR SERVICES
Unit D, The Pavillions, Holly Lane Industrial Estate, Atherstone CV9 2QZ.
Tel: 01827 711660
Fax: 01827 713577
Web site: www.airdoorservices.co.uk

ARRIVA BUS AND COACH LTD
Lodge Garage, Whitehall Road West, Gomersal BD19 4BJ.
Tel: 01274 681144
Fax: 01274 651198
Web site: www.arriva.co.uk
E-mail: busandcoachsales@arriva.co.uk

ASHLEY BANKS LTD
5 King Street Estate, Langtoft, Peterborough PE6 9NF
Tel: 01778 560651
Fax: 01778 560721
E-mail: user@ashleybanks.fsnet.co.uk

M BARNWELL SERVICES LTD
Reginald Road, Smethwick B67 5AS
Tel: 0121 420 0700
Fax: 0121 420 3080
E-mail: sales@barnwell.co.uk

*BRADTECH LTD
Unit 3, Ladford Covert, Seighford, Stafford ST18 9QL
Tel: 01785 282800
Fax: 01785 282558
E-mail: sales@bradtech.ltd.uk
Web site: www.bradtech.ltd.uk

BRT BEARINGS LTD
Algores Way, Wisbech PE13 2TQ
Tel: 01945 464097
Fax: 01945 464523
Web site: www.brt-bearings.com
Email: brt.sales@brt-bearings.com

BUSS BIZZ
Goughs Transport Depot, Morestead, Winchester SO21 1JD.
Tel: 01962 715555/66.
Fax: 01962 714868.

CARLYLE BUS & COACH LTD
Carlyle Business Park, Great Bridge Street, Swan Village, West Bromwich B70 0X4
Tel: 0121 524 1200
Fax: 0121 524 1201
E-mail: admin@carlyleplc.co.uk

CONSERVE (UK) LTD
Suite 7, Logistics House, 1 Horsley Road, Kingsthorpe Road, Northampton NN2 6LJ
Tel: 01604 710055
Fax: 01604 710065
E-mail: information@conserveuk.co.uk
Web site: www.conserveuk.co.uk

*CRESCENT FACILITIES LTD
72 Willow Crescent, Chapeltown, Sheffield S35 1QS
Tel/fax: 0114 2451050
E-mail: cfl.chris@btinternet.com
Web site: www.cflparts.com

CREST COACH CONVERSIONS
Unit 5, Holmeroyd Road, Bentley Moor Lane, Carcroft, Doncaster DN6 7BH
Tel: 01302 723723
Fax: 01302 724724

CREWE ENGINES
Warmingham Road, Crewe CW1 4PQ
Tel: 01270 526333
Fax: 01270 526433
E-mail: sales@creweengines.co.uk
Web site: www.creweengines.co.uk

CUMMINS UK
Rutherford Drive, Park Farm South, Wellingborough NN8 6AN
Tel: 01933 334200
Fax: 01933 334198
E-mail: cduksales@cummins.com
Web site: www.cummins-uk.com

*DIRECT PARTS LTD
Unit 1, Churnet Court, Churnetside Business Park, Harrison Way, Cheddleton ST13 7EF
Tel: 01538 361777
Fax: 01538 369100
E-mail: sales@direct-group.co.uk
Web site: www.direct-group.co.uk

*EAST LANCASHIRE COACHBUILDERS LTD (ELC)
Lower Philips Road, Whitebirk Industrial Estate, Blackburn BB1 5UD
Tel: 01254 504150
Fax: 01254 504197
E-mail: john.horn@elcb.co.uk
Web site: www.elcb.co.uk

FLIGHTS COACH TRAVEL LTD
Beacon House, Long Acre, Birmingham B7 5JJ
Tel: 0121 322 2222.
Fax: 0121 322 2224.
E-mail: sales@motorcoach.co.uk

GARDNER PARTS LTD
Barton Hall, Hardy Street, Eccles, Manchester M30 7WA.
Tel: 0161 278 9200
Fax: 0161 787 7549.

HAPPICH V & I COMPONENTS LTD
Unit 30/31, Fort Industrial Park, Fort Parkway, Castle Bromwich B35 7AR.
Tel: 0121 747 4400
Fax: 0121 747 4977
E-mail: sales@happich.co.uk
Web site: www.happich.co.uk

THOMAS HARDIE – WIGAN
Lockett Road, Ashton-in-Makerfield WN4 8DE
Tel: 01942 505124.
Fax: 01942 505119.

*HART BROTHERS (ENGINEERING) LTD
Soho Works, Soho Street, Oldham OL4 2AD
Tel: 0161 737 6791

IMEXPART LTD
Links 31, Willowbridge Way, Whitwood, Castleford WF10 5NP
Tel: 01977 553936
Fax: 01977 604684
E-mail: parts@imexpart.com
Web site: www.imexpart.com

IMPERIAL ENGINEERING
Delamare Road, Cheshunt EN8 9UD
Tel: 01992 6342555
Fax: 01992 630506
E-mail: sales@imperialengineering.co.uk
Web site: www.imperialengineering.co.uk

*KARIVE LIMITED
PO Box 205, Southam CV47 0ZL
Tel: 01926 813938
Fax: 01926 814898
E-mail: karive.ltd@btinternet.com
Web site: www.karive.co.uk

KELLETT (UK) LTD
8 Stevenson Way, Sheffield S9 3WZ
Tel: 0114 261 1122.
Fax: 0114 261 1199.
E-mail: sales@kellett.co.uk

KNORR-BREMSE SYSTEMS FOR COMMERCIAL VEHICLES LTD
Douglas Road, Kingswood, Bristol BS15 8NL.
Tel: 0117 984 6100
Fax: 0117 984 6101.
Web site: www.knorr-bremse.com

*THE LAWTON MOTOR BODY BUILDING CO LTD
Knutsford Road, Church Lawton, Stoke-on-Trent ST7 3DN
Tel: 01270 882056
Fax: 01270 883014
E-mail: sales@lawtonmotorbody.co.uk
Web site: www.lawtonmotorbody.co.uk

*LH GROUP SERVICES LTD
Graycar Business Park, Barton Under Needwood, Burton-on-Trent DE13 8EN
Tel: 01283 722600
Fax: 01283 722622
E-mail: lh@lh-group.co.uk
Web site: www.lh-group.co.uk

MAJORLINE ENGINEERING LTD
Baybridge Industrial Units, Baybridge Lane, Owslebury, Winchester SO21 1JN.
Tel: 01962 777077.
Fax: 01962 777661, 777667
E-mail: majorline@compuserve.com

*MENTOR
Mentor Coach & Bus Ltd, Carlton House, Euroway Industrial Estate, Hellaby, Rotherham S66 8QL
Tel: 01709 700600
Fax: 01709 700007
E-mail: sales@mentorplc.com
Web site: www.mentorplc.com

MOCAP LIMITED
Hortonwood 35, Telford TF1 7YW
Tel: 01952 670247
Fax: 01952 670241
Web site: www.mocap.co.uk
E-mail: sales@mocap.co.uk

MULTIPART PSV
Pilling Lane, Chorley PR7 3EL.
Tel: 01257 225577.
Fax: 01257 225575.
E-mail: info@multipart.com
Web site: www.multipart.com

*NEXT BUS LTD
The Coach Yard, Vincients Road, Bumpers Farm Industrial Estate, Chippenham SN14 6QA
Tel: 01249 462462
E-mail: sales@next-bus.co.uk
Web site: www.next-bus.co.uk

*PARTLINE LTD
Dockfield Road, Shipley BD17 7AZ
Tel: 01274 531531
Fax: 01274 531088
E-mail: sales@partline.co.uk
Web site: www.partline.co.uk

PIONEER WESTON
Smithfold Lane, Worsley, Manchester
M28 0GP.
Tel: 0161 703 2000.
Fax: 0161 703 2025
E-mail: pioneer.weston@wyko.co.uk

PLAXTON
Plaxton Park, Cayton Low Road, Eastfield,
Scarborough YO11 3BY
Tel: 01723 581500
Fax: 01723 5813238
E-mail: sales@plaxtonlimited.co.uk
Web site: www.plaxtonlimited.co.uk

PLAXTON COACH SALES CENTRE
Ryton Road, Anston, Sheffield S25 4DL
Tel: 01909 551155
Fax: 01909 567994
E-mail: coaches@plaxtonlimited.co.uk
Web site: www.plaxtonlimited.co.uk

PNEUMAX LTD
Unit 8, Venture Industrial Park, Fareham
Road, Gosport PO13 0BA
Tel: 01329 823999
Fax: 01329 822345
E-mail: sales@pneumax.co.uk
Web site: www.pneumax.co.uk

***PSV GLASS**
Hillbottom Road, High Wycombe
HP12 4HJ
Tel: 01494 533131
Fax: 01494 462675
E-mail: sales@psvglass.co.uk
Web site: www.psvglass.co.uk

QUEENSBRIDGE (PSV) LTD
Longlands Industrial Estate, Milner Way,
Ossett WF5 9JE
Tel: 01924 281871
Fax: 01924 281807
E-mail: craig@queensbridgeltd.co.uk
Web site: www.queensbridgeltd.co.uk

ROADLINK INTERNATIONAL LTD
Strawberry Lane, Willenhall WV13 3RL
Tel: 01902 636210
Fax: 01902 606604
E-mail: sales@roadlink-international.co.uk
Web site: www.roadlink-international.co.uk

SHAWSON SUPPLY LTD
12 Station Road, Saintfield BT24 7DU
Tel: 028 9751 0994
Fax: 028 9751 0816
E-mail: shawsondiesel@btopenworld.com
Web site: www.shawsonsupply.com

***TRAMONTANA COACH DISTRIBUTORS**
Chapelknowe Road, Carfin, Motherwell ML1 5LE
Tel: 01698 861790
Fax: 01698 860778
E-mail: wdt90@tiscali.co.uk

TREVOR WIGLEY & SON BUS LTD
Passenger Vehicle Dismantling/Spares
Works: Boulder Bridge Lane, off Shaw Lane,
Barnsley S71 3HJ
Correspondence: 148 Royston Road,
Cudworth, Barnsley S72 8BN
Tel: 01226 723147
Fax: 01226 700199

***UNITEC**
Parts Division, Denby Way, Hellaby,
Rotherham S66 8HR
Tel: 01709 792000
Fax: 01709 792009
E-mail: parts@optare.com

***VOLVO BUS AND COACH CENTRE**
Belton Road West, Loughborough LE11 5HP
Tel: 01509 217777
Fax: 01509 239362
Web site: www.volvo.com

WABCO AUTOMOTIVE UK LTD
Texas Street, Morley LS27 0HQ.
Tel: 0113 251 2510.
Fax: 0113 251 2844.

WACTON COACH SALES & SERVICES
Linton Trading Estate, Bromyard HR7 4QL.
Tel: 01885 482782.
Fax: 01885 482127

WALSH'S ENGINEERING
Barton Moss Road, Eccles, Manchester
M30 7RL
Tel: 0161 787 7017
Fax: 0161 787 7038
E-mail: walshs@gardnerdiesel.co.uk
Website: www.gardnerdiesel.co.uk

ZF POWERTRAIN
Stringes Close, Willenhall WV13 1LE
Tel: 01902 366000
Fax: 01902 366504
E-mail: sales@powertrain.org.uk
Web site: www.powertrain.org.uk

Passenger Information Systems

***M BISSELL DISPLAY LTD**
Unit 15, Beechwood Business Park,
Burdock Close, Cannock WS11 7GB
Tel: 01543 502115
Fax: 01543 502118
E-mail: sales@bisselldisplay.com
Web site: www.bisselldisplay.com

HANOVER DISPLAYS LTD
Unit 24, Cliffe Industrial Estate, Lewes
BN8 6JL
Tel: 01273 477528
Fax: 01273 407766
E-mail: hanover@hanoverdisplays.com
Web site: www.hanoverdisplays.com

JOURNEY PLAN LTD
12 Abbey Park Place, Dunfermline
KY12 7PD
Tel: 01383 731048
Web site: www.journeyplan.co.uk

McKENNA BROTHERS LTD
McKenna House, Jubilee Road, Middleton,
Manchester M24 2LX
Tel: 0161 655 3244
Fax: 0161 655 3059
E-mail: info@mckennabrothers.co.uk
Web site: www.mckennabrothers.co.uk

***MOTIONAL MEDIA LTD**
Unit 4, Waltham Court, Hare Hatch,
Milley Lane, Reading RG10 9AA
Tel: 01189 406353
Fax: 01189 406352
E-mail: matthew@motionalmedia.tv
Web site: www.motionalmedia.tv

SSL SIMULATION SYSTEMS LTD
Unit 12, Market Industrial Estate, Yatton
BS49 4RF
Tel: 01934 838803
Fax: 01934 876202
E-mail: ssl@simulation-systems.co.uk
Web site: www.simulation-systems.co.uk

VULTRON INTERNATIONAL LTD
Unit 2, Stadium Way, Elland Road, Leeds
LS11 0EW
Tel: 0113 387 7310
Fax: 0113 387 7317
E-mail: jmoorhouse@vultron.co.uk

Pneumatic Valves/Cylinders

PNEUMAX LTD
Unit 8, Venture Industrial Park, Fareham
Road, Gosport PO13 0BA
Tel: 01329 823999
Fax: 01329 822345
E-mail: sales@pneumax.co.uk
Web site: www.pneumax.co.uk

***UNITEC**
Parts Division, Denby Way, Hellaby,
Rotherham S66 8HR
Tel: 01709 792000
Fax: 01709 792009
E-mail: parts@optare.com

Rapid Transit/ Priority Equipment

ALSTOM TRANSPORT SA
48 rue Albert Dhalenne, F-93482 Saint-
Ouen Cedex, France
Tel: 00 33 1 41 66 90 00
Fax: 00 33 1 41 66 96 66
Web site: www.transport.alstom.com

BALFOUR BEATTY RAIL PLANT LTD
PO Box 5065, Raynesway, Derby
DE21 7QZ
Tel: 01332 661491
Fax: 01332 288222
Web site: www.bbrail.com

BRECKNELL WILLIS & CO LTD
PO Box 10, Chard TA20 2DE
Tel: 01460 64941
Fax: 01460 66122
Web site: www.brecknell-willis.co.uk

BRISTOL ELECTRIC RAILBUS LTD
Heron House, Chiswick Mall, London
W4 2PR
Tel: 020 8995 3000
Fax: 020 8994 6060
E-mail: james@skinner.demon.co.uk

JMW
Systems House, Pentland Industrial Estate,
Loanhead EH20 9QH
Tel: 0131 440 3633
Fax: 0131 440 3637
E-mail: enquiries@jmw-group.co.uk
Web site: www.jmw-group.co.uk

***PARRY PEOPLE MOVERS LTD**
Overend Road, Cradley Heath, Dudley
B64 7DD
Tel: 01384 569171
Fax: 01384 637753
E-mail: jpmparry@aol.com
Website: www.parrytech.com

Trade Directory

PRE METRO OPERATION LTD
21 Woodglade Croft, Kings Norton,
Birmingham B38 8TD
Tel: 0121 243 9906
Fax: 0121 243 9906
E-mail: premetro@aol.com
Web site: www.parrytech.com

SIEMENS TRAFFIC CONTROLS LTD
Sopers Lane, Poole BH17 7ER
Tel: 01202 782000
Web site: www.siemenstraffic.com

SUSTRACO LTD
Heron House, Chiswick Mall, London
W4 2PR
Tel: 020 8995 3000
Fax: 020 8994 6060
Web site: www.ultralightrail.com

Repairs/Refurbishment
- see body repairs above

Retarders & Speed Control Systems

BUSS BIZZ
Goughs Transport Depot, Morestead,
Winchester SO21 1JD.
Tel: 01962 715555/66.
Fax: 01962 714868.

CHASSIS DEVELOPMENTS LTD
Grovebury Road, Leighton Buzzard
LU7 8SL.
Tel: 01525 374151.
Fax: 01525 370127
Web site: www.chassisdevelopments.co.uk

MULTIPART PSV
Pilling Lane, Chorley PR7 3EL.
Tel: 01257 225577.
Fax: 01257 225575.
E-mail: info@multipart.com
Web site: www.multipart.com

*P & P SERGEANT (B&A) LTD
PO Box 11, New Hall Lane, Hoylake
CH47 4DH
Tel: 0151 632 5903
Fax: 0151 632 5908
E-mail: enq@sergeant.co.uk
Web site: www.sergeant.co.uk

TELMA RETARDER LTD
25 Clarke Road, Mount Farm, Milton Keynes
MK1 1LG
Tel: 01908 642822
Fax: 01908 641348
E-mail: telma@telma.co.uk
Web site: www.telma.co.uk

*VOITH TURBO LTD
6 Beddington Farm Road, Croydon
CR0 4XB
Tel: 020 8667 0333
Fax: 020 8667 0403
E-mail: john.domigan@voith.com
Web site: www.voith.co.uk

WABCO AUTOMOTIVE UK LTD
Texas Street, Morley LS27 0HQ.
Tel: 0113 251 2510.
Fax: 0113 251 2844

Reversing Safety Systems

AUTOSOUND LTD
4 Lister Street, Dudley Hill, Bradford
BD4 9PQ
Tel: 01274 688990
Fax: 01274 651318
Web site: www.autosound.co.uk
E-mail: sales@autosound.co.uk

AVT SYSTEMS LTD
Unit 3, Tything Road, Arden Forest Trading
Estate, Alcester B49 6ES
Tel: 01789 400357
Fax: 01789 400359
E-mail: enquiries@avtsystems.co.uk
Web site: www.avtsystems.co.uk

BRIGADE ELECTRONICS plc
Brigade House, The Mills, Station Road,
South Darenth DA4 9BD
Tel: 0870 774 1500
Fax: 0870 774 1502
E-mail: sales@brigade-electronics.co.uk
Web site: www.brigade-electronics.co.uk,
www.bbs-tek.com

CARLYLE BUS & COACH LTD
Carlyle Business Park, Great Bridge Street,
Swan Village, West Bromwich B70 0X4
Tel: 0121 524 1200
Fax: 0121 524 1201
E-mail: admin@carlyleplc.co.uk

CLAN TOOLS & PLANT LTD
3 Greenhill Avenue, Giffnock, Glasgow
G46 6QX.
Tel: 0141 638 8040.
Fax: 0141 638 8881.

KELLETT (UK) LTD
8 Stevenson Way, Sheffield S9 3WZ.
Tel: 0114 261 1122.
Fax: 0114 261 1199.
E-mail: sales@kellett.co.uk

PLAXTON COACH SALES CENTRE
Ryton Road, Anston, Sheffield S25 4DL
Tel: 01909 551155
Fax: 01909 567994
E-mail: coaches@plaxtonlimited.co.uk
Web site: www.plaxtonlimited.co.uk

Roller Blinds - Passenger & Driver

CARLYLE BUS & COACH LTD
Carlyle Business Park, Great Bridge Street,
Swan Village, West Bromwich B70 0XA
Tel: 0121 524 1200
Fax: 0121 524 1201
E-mail: admin@carlyleplc.co.uk

HAPPICH V & I COMPONENTS LTD
Unit 30/31, Fort Industrial Park, Fort
Parkway, Castle Bromwich B35 7AR.
Tel: 0121 747 4400
Fax: 0121 747 4977
E-mail: sales@happich.co.uk
Web site: www.happich.co.uk

WIDNEY UK LTD
Plume Street, Aston, Birmingham B6 7SA
Tel: 0121 327 5500
Fax: 0121 328 2466
E-mail: richard@widney.co.uk

Roof-Lining Fabrics

AUTOMATE WHEEL COVERS LTD
California Mills, Oxford Road, Gomersal
BD19 4HQ
Tel: 01274 862700
Fax: 01274 851989
E-mail: sales@wheelcovers.co.uk
Web site: www.euroliners.com

AUTOMOTIVE TEXTILE INDUSTRIES
Unit 15 & 16, Priest Court, Springfield
Business Park, Grantham NG31 7BG
Tel: 01476 593050
Fax: 01476 593607
E-mail: sales@autotex.com
Web site: www.autotex.com

HAPPICH V & I COMPONENTS LTD
Unit 30/31, Fort Industrial Park, Fort
Parkway, Castle Bromwich B35 7AR.
Tel: 0121 747 4400
Fax: 0121 747 4977
E-mail: sales@happich.co.uk
Web site: www.happich.co.uk

Seat belts/restraint systems

*ABACUS TUBULAR PRODUCTS LTD
Abacus House, Highlode Industrial Estate,
Ramsey PE26 2RB
Tel: 01487 710700
Fax: 01487 710626
E-mail: info@abacus-tp.com

CARLYLE BUS & COACH LTD
Carlyle Business Park, Great Bridge Street,
Swan Village, West Bromwich B70 0X4
Tel: 0121 524 1200
Fax: 0121 524 1201
E-mail: admin@carlyleplc.co.uk

*ELITE SERVICES LTD
Unit 3/6, Adswood Industrial Estate,
Addswood Road, Stockport SK3 8LF
Tel: 0161 480 0617
Fax: 0161 480 3099

HATTS COACHWORKS & SERVICES
Foxham, Chippenham SN15 4NB
Tel: 01249 740444
Fax: 01249 740447
E-mail: adrian@hattstravel.co.uk
Web site: www.hattstravel.co.uk

*THE LAWTON MOTOR BODY BUILDING CO LTD
Knutsford Road, Church Lawton, Stoke-on-
Trent ST7 3DN
Tel: 01270 882056
Fax: 01270 883014
E-mail: sales@lawtonmotorbody.co.uk
Web site: www.lawtonmotorbody.co.uk

MTB EQUIPMENT LTD
Sixth Avenue, Zone Two, Deeside Industrial
Park, Deeside CH5 2LB
Tel: 0870 870 1282
Fax: 01244 289 818
E-mail: info@mtb-equipment.com
Web site: www.mtb-equipment.com

MULTIPART PSV
Pilling Lane, Chorley PR7 3EL.
Tel: 01257 225577.
Fax: 01257 225575.
E-mail: info@multipart.com
Web site: www.multipart.com

*NEXT BUS LTD
The Coach Yard, Vincients Road, Bumpers Farm Industrial Estate, Chippenham SN14 6QA
Tel: 01249 462462
E-mail: sales@next-bus.co.uk
Web site: www.next-bus.co.uk

*PARTLINE LTD
Dockfield Road, Shipley BD17 7AZ
Tel: 01274 531531
Fax: 01274 531088
E-mail: sales@partline.co.uk
Web site: www.partline.co.uk

PLAXTON
Plaxton Park, Cayton Low Road, Eastfield, Scarborough YO11 3BY
Tel: 01723 581500
Fax: 01723 5813238
E-mail: sales@plaxtonlimited.co.uk
Web site: www.plaxtonlimited.co.uk

PLAXTON COACH SALES CENTRE
Ryton Road, Anston, Sheffield S25 4DL
Tel: 01909 551155
Fax: 01909 567994
E-mail: coaches@plaxtonlimited.co.uk
Web site: www.plaxtonlimited.co.uk

Q'STRAINT
73-76 John Wilson Business Park, Whitstable CT5 3QU
Tel: 01227 773035
Fax: 01227 770035
E-mail: info@qstraint.co.uk
Web site: www.qstraint.com

SAFETEX LTD
Unit 16/17, Bookham Industrial Park, Church Road, Bookham KT23 3EV
Tel: 01372 451272
Fax: 01372 451282
E-mail: sales@safetex.com
Web site: www@safetex.com

SECURON (AMERSHAM) LTD
Winchmore Hill, Amersham HP7 0NZ.
Tel: 01494 434455.
Fax: 01494 726499.
E-mail: securon@securon.co.uk
Web site: www.securon.co.uk

*TRAMONTANA COACH DISTRIBUTORS
Chapelknowe Road, Carfin, Motherwell ML1 5LE
Tel: 01698 861790
Fax: 01698 860778
E-mail: wdt90@tiscali.co.uk

*UNWIN SAFETY SYSTEMS
Unwin House, The Horseshoe, Coat Road, Martock TA12 6EY
Tel: 01935 827740
Fax: 01935 827760
E-mail: sales@unwin-safety.co.uk
Web site: wwwunwin-safety.com

Seats/seat cushions & seat frames

*ABACUS TUBULAR PRODUCTS LTD
Abacus House, Highlode Industrial Estate, Ramsey PE26 2RB
Tel: 01487 710700
Fax: 01487 710626
E-mail: info@abacus-tp.com

ARDEE COACH TRIM LTD
Artnalivery, Ardee, Co Louth, Ireland
Tel: 00 353 41 685 3599
Web site: www.ardeecoachtrim.com

BERNSTEIN ENGINEERING LTD
Unit 1, Colne Way Court, Colne Way, Watford WD24 7NE
Tel: 01923 239996
Fax: 01923 252633

CAMIRA FABRICS LTD
Hopton Mills, Mirfield WF1 8HE
Tel: 01924 490591
Web site: www.camirafabrics.com

CARLYLE BUS & COACH LTD
Carlyle Business Park, Great Bridge Street, Swan Village, West Bromwich B70 0XA
Tel: 0121 524 1200
Fax: 0121 524 1201
E-mail: admin@carlyleplc.co.uk

CHAPMAN DRIVERS SEATING
68 Burners Lane, Kiln Farm, Milton Keynes MK11 3HD
Tel: 0845 838 2305
Fax: 0845 838 2909

COGENT PASSENGER SEATING LTD
Prydwen Road, Swansea West Industrial Estate, Swansea SA5 4HN
Tel: 01792 585444
Fax: 01792 588191
Web site: www.cogent.demon.co.uk
E-mail: seats@cogent.demon.co.uk

DUOFLEX LTD
Trimmingham House, 2 Shires Road, Buckingham Road Industrial Estate, Brackley NN13 7EZ
Tel: 01280 701366
Fax: 01280 704799
E-mail: sales@duoflex.co.uk
Web site: www.duoflex.co.uk

HAPPICH V & I COMPONENTS LTD
Unit 30/31, Fort Industrial Park, Fort Parkway, Castle Bromwich B35 7AR.
Tel: 0121 747 4400
Fax: 0121 747 4977
E-mail: sales@happich.co.uk
Web site: www.happich.co.uk

JBF SERVICES LTD
Southedge Works, Hipperholme, Halifax HX3 8EF
Tel: 01422 202840
Fax: 01422 206070
E-mail: jbfservices@aol.com

KAB SEATING LTD
Round Spinney, Northampton NN3 8RS
Tel: 01604 790500
Fax: 01604 790155

*THE LAWTON MOTOR BODY BUILDING CO LTD
Knutsford Road, Church Lawton, Stoke-on-Trent ST7 3DN
Tel: 01270 882056
Fax: 01270 883014
E-mail: sales@lawtonmotorbody.co.uk
Web site: www.lawtonmotorbody.co.uk

LUNAR SEATING LTD
Unit 3, Packhorse Place, Watling Street, Kensworth LU6 3QU
Tel: 01582 841535
Fax: 01582 841749
E-mail: sue@lunar-seating.co.uk

MAJORLINE ENGINEERING LTD
Baybridge Industrial Units, Baybridge Lane, Owslebury, Winchester SO21 1JN.
Tel: 01962 777077.
Fax: 01962 777661, 777667
E-mail: majorline@compuserve.com

MTB EQUIPMENT LTD
Sixth Avenue, Zone Two, Deeside Industrial Park, Deeside CH5 2LB
Tel: 0870 870 1282
Fax: 01244 289 818
E-mail: info@mtb-equipment.com
Web site: www.mtb-equipment.com

METRONET (REW) LTD
130 Bollo Lane, London W3 8BZ.
Tel: 020 7918 6666.
Fax: 020 7918 6599.
E-mail: fraser@r-e-w.co.uk
Web site: www.r-e-w.co.uk

*NEXT BUS LTD
The Coach Yard, Vincients Road, Bumpers Farm Industrial Estate, Chippenham SN14 6QA
Tel: 01249 462462
E-mail: sales@next-bus.co.uk
Web site: www.next-bus.co.uk

PHOENIX SEATING LTD
Unit 47, Bay 3, Second Avenue, Pensnett Estate, Kingswinford DY6 7UZ
Tel: 01384 296622

PLAXTON COACH SALES CENTRE
Ryton Road, Anston, Sheffield S25 4DL
Tel: 01909 551155
Fax: 01909 567994
E-mail: coaches@plaxtonlimited.co.uk
Web site: www.plaxtonlimited.co.uk

RESCROFT LTD
20 Oxleasow Road, East Moons Moat, Redditch B98 0RE
Tel: 01527 521300
Fax: 01527 521301
Web site: www.rescroft.com
E-mail: enquiries@rescroft.com

SCANDUS UK
Unit 21, Gainsborough Trading Estate, Rufford Road, Stourbridge DY9 7ND
Tel: 01384 443409
Fax: 01384 443 932
Web site: www.scandusuk.co.uk

TUBE PRODUCTS LTD
PO Box 13, Oldbury, Warley B69 4PF.
Tel: 0121 552 1511.
Fax: 0121 544 6026.

WOODBRIDGE FOAM UK LTD
Caxton Road, Elms Industrial Estate, Bedford MK41 0EJ.
Tel: 01234 211333.
Fax: 01234 272047

Trade Directory

Shelters/Street Furniture

*M BISSELL DISPLAY LTD
Unit 15, Beechwood Business Park, Burdock Close, Cannock WS11 7GB
Tel: 01543 502115
Fax: 01543 502118
E-mail: sales@bisselldisplay.com
Web site: www.bisselldisplay.com

BUS SHELTERS LTD
Dyffryn Business Park, Llantwit Major Road, Llandow CF71 7PY
Tel: 01446 795444
Fax: 01446 793344
E-mail: bus@shelters.demon.co.uk

CARMANAH UK
68 Basepoint Business Centre, Metcalf Way, Crawley RH11 7XX
Tel: 0870 345 9548 0208 323 8028
E-mail: info@carmanah.co.uk
Web site: www.carmanah.co.uk

*GABRIEL & COMPANY LTD
Abro Works, 10 Hay Hall Road, Tyseley, Birmingham B11 2AU
Tel: 0121 248 3333
Fax: 0121 248 3330
E-mail: contact@gabrielco.com
Web site: www.gabrielco.com

*MACEMAIN + AMSTAD
Boyle Road, Willowbrook Industrial Estate, Corby NN17 5XU
Tel: 01536 401331
Fax: 01536 401298
E-mail: enquiries@macemainamstad.com
Web site: www.macemainamstad.com

QUEENSBURY SHELTERS
Queensbury House, Fitzherbert Road, Farlington, Portsmouth PO6 1SE
Tel: 023 9221 0052
Fax: 023 9221 0059
Web site: www.queensbury.org

TRUEFORM ENGINEERING LTD
Unit 4, Pasadena Trading Estate, Pasadena Close, Hayes UB3 3NQ
Tel: 020 8561 4959
Fax: 020 8848 1397
E-mail: sales@trueform.co.uk
Web site: www..trueform.co.uk

WHITELEY ELECTRONICS
Victoria Street, Mansfield NG18 5RW
Tel: 01623 415600
E-mail: sales@whiteleyelectronics.com
Web site: www.whiteleyelectronics.com

Shock Absorbers/Suspension

ASHLEY BANKS LTD
5 King Street Estate, Langtoft, Peterborough PE6 9NF
Tel: 01778 560651
Fax: 01778 560721
E-mail: user@ashleybanks.fsnet.co.uk

*CRESCENT FACILITIES LTD
72 Willow Crescent, Chapeltown, Sheffield S35 1QS
Tel/fax: 0114 2451050
E-mail: cfl.chris@btinternet.com
Web site: www.cflparts.com

*DIRECT PARTS LTD
Unit 1, Churnet Court, Churnside Business Park, Harrison Way, Cheddleton ST13 7EF
Tel: 01538 361777
Fax: 01538 369100
E-mail: sales@direct-group.co.uk
Web site: www.direct-group.co.uk

ERENTEK LTD
Malt Kiln Lane, Waddington, Lincoln LN5 9RT
Tel: 01522 720065
Fax: 01522 729155
E-mail: sale@erentek.co.uk
Web site: www.erentek.co.uk

GLIDE RITE
Mill Lane, Passfield, Liphook GU30 7RP
Tel: 01428 751711
Web site: www.glide-rite.net

*HART BROTHERS (ENGINEERING) LTD
Soho Works, Soho Street, Oldham OL4 2AD
Tel: 0161 737 6791

IMEXPART LTD
Links 31, Willowbridge Way, Whitwood, Castleford WF10 5NP
Tel: 01977 553936
Fax: 01977 604684
E-mail: parts@imexpart.com
Web site: www.imexpart.com

KELLETT (UK) LTD
8 Stevenson Way, Sheffield S9 3WZ.
Tel: 0114 261 1122.
Fax: 0114 261 1199.
E-mail: sales@kellett.co.uk

MAJORLINE ENGINEERING LTD
Baybridge Industrial Units, Baybridge Lane, Owslebury, Winchester SO21 1JN.
Tel: 01962 777077.
Fax: 01962 777661, 777667
E-mail: majorline@compuserve.com

*MENTOR
Mentor Coach & Bus Ltd, Carlton House, Euroway Industrial Estate, Hellaby, Rotherham S66 8QL
Tel: 01709 700600
Fax: 01709 700007
E-mail: sales@mentorplc.com
Web site: www.mentorplc.com

MULTIPART PSV
Pilling Lane, Chorley PR7 3EL.
Tel: 01257 225577.
Fax: 01257 225575.
E-mail: info@multipart.com
Web site: www.multipart.com

*NEXT BUS LTD
The Coach Yard, Vincients Road, Bumpers Farm Industrial Estate, Chippenham SN14 6QA
Tel: 01249 462462
E-mail: sales@next-bus.co.uk
Web site: www.next-bus.co.uk

*PARTLINE LTD
Dockfield Road, Shipley BD17 7AZ
Tel: 01274 531531
Fax: 01274 531088
E-mail: sales@partline.co.uk
Web site: www.partline.co.uk

POLYBUSH
Clywedog Road South, Wrexham Industrial Estate, Wrexham LL13 9XS
Tel: 01978 664316
Fax: 01978 661190
E-mail: sales@polybush.co.uk
Web site: www.polybush.co.uk

ROADLINK INTERNATIONAL LTD
Strawberry Lane, Willenhall WV13 3RL
Tel: 01902 636210
Fax: 01902 606604
E-mail: sales@roadlink-international.co.uk
Web site: www.roadlink-international.co.uk

SHAWSON SUPPLY LTD
12 Station Road, Saintfield BT24 7DU
Tel: 028 9751 0994
Fax: 028 9751 0816
E-mail: shawsondiesel@btopenworld.com
Web site: www.shawsonsupply.com

*UNITEC
Parts Division, Denby Way, Hellaby, Rotherham S66 8HR
Tel: 01709 792000
Fax: 01709 792009
E-mail: parts@optare.com

Steering

*CRESCENT FACILITIES LTD
72 Willow Crescent, Chapeltown, Sheffield S35 1QS
Tel/fax: 0114 2451050
E-mail: cfl.chris@btinternet.com
Web site: www.cflparts.com

*DIRECT PARTS LTD
Unit 1, Churnet Court, Churnside Business Park, Harrison Way, Cheddleton ST13 7EF
Tel: 01538 361777
Fax: 01538 369100
E-mail: sales@direct-group.co.uk
Web site: www.direct-group.co.uk

HL SMITH TRANSMISSIONS LTD
Enterprise Business Park, Cross Road, Albrighton, Wolverhampton WV7 3BJ
Tel: 01902 373011
Fax: 01902 373608

IMEXPART LTD
Links 31, Willowbridge Way, Whitwood, Castleford WF10 5NP
Tel: 01977 553936
Fax: 01977 604684
E-mail: parts@imexpart.com
Web site: www.imexpart.com

IMPERIAL ENGINEERING
Delamare Road, Cheshunt EN8 9UD
Tel: 01992 6342555
Fax: 01992 630506
E-mail: sales@imperialengineering.co.uk
Web site: www.imperialengineering.co.uk

MAJORLINE ENGINEERING LTD
Baybridge Industrial Units, Baybridge Lane, Owslebury, Winchester SO21 1JN.
Tel: 01962 777077.
Fax: 01962 777661, 777667
E-mail: majorline@compuserve.com

Trade Directory

MULTIPART PSV
Pilling Lane, Chorley PR7 3EL.
Tel: 01257 225577.
Fax: 01257 225575.
E-mail: info@multipart.com
Web site: www.multipart.com

*NEXT BUS LTD
The Coach Yard, Vincients Road, Bumpers Farm Industrial Estate, Chippenham SN14 6QA
Tel: 01249 462462
E-mail: sales@next-bus.co.uk
Web site: www.next-bus.co.uk

*PARTLINE LTD
Dockfield Road, Shipley BD17 7AZ
Tel: 01274 531531
Fax: 01274 531088
E-mail: sales@partline.co.uk
Web site: www.partline.co.uk

PSS - STEERING & HYDRAULICS DIVISION
Folgate Road, North Walsham NR28 0AJ
Tel: 01692 406017
Fax: 01692 406957
E-mail: sales@pss.co.uk
Web site: www.pss.co.uk

ROADLINK INTERNATIONAL LTD
Strawberry Lane, Willenhall WV13 3RL
Tel: 01902 636210
Fax: 01902 606604
E-mail: sales@roadlink-international.co.uk
Web site: www.roadlink-international.co.uk

SHAWSON SUPPLY LTD
12 Station Road, Saintfield BT24 7DU
Tel: 028 9751 0994
Fax: 028 9751 0816
E-mail: shawsondiesel@btopenworld.com
Web site: www.shawsonsupply.com

*UNITEC
Parts Division, Denby Way, Hellaby, Rotherham S66 8HR
Tel: 01709 792000
Fax: 01709 792009
E-mail: parts@optare.com

*UNITEC LONDON
Unit 5, Gateway 25, Weston Avenue, West Thurrock RM20 3ZD
Tel: 01708 892440
Fax: 01708 862125
E-mail: london.service@optare.com

*UNITEC ROTHERHAM
Denby Way, Hellaby, Rotherham S66 8HR
Tel: 01709 535101
Fax: 01709 535103
E-mail: rotherham.service@optare.com

*UNITEC SCOTLAND
Unit 7, Cumbernauld Business Park, Ward Park Road, Cumbernauld G67 3JZ
Tel: 01236 726738
Fax: 01236 795651
E-mail: scotland.service@optare.com

ZF POWERTRAIN
Stringes Close, Willenhall WV13 1LE
Tel: 01902 366000
Fax: 01902 366504
E-mail: sales@powertrain.org.uk
Web site: www.powertrain.org.uk

Surveillance Systems

AUTOSOUND LTD
4 Lister Street, Dudley Hill, Bradford BD4 9PQ
Tel: 01274 688990
Fax: 01274 651318
Web site: www.autosound.co.uk
E-mail: sales@autosound.co.uk

AVT SYSTEMS LTD
Unit 3, Tything Road, Arden Forest Trading Estate, Alcester B49 6ES
Tel: 01789 400357
Fax: 01789 400359
E-mail: enquiries@avtsystems.co.uk
Web site: www.avtsystems.co.uk

CLAN TOOLS & PLANT LTD
3 Greenhill Avenue, Giffnock, Glasgow G46 6QX.
Tel: 0141 638 8040.
Fax: 0141 638 8881.

*CYBERLYNE COMMUNICATIONS LTD
Unit 5, Hatfield Way, South Church Enterprise Park, Bishop Auckland DL14 6XB
Tel: 01388 773761
Fax: 01388 773778
E-mail: k.brocklehurst@cyberlyne.co.uk
Web site: www.cyberlyne.co.uk

KELLETT (UK) LTD
8 Stevenson Way, Sheffield S9 3WZ.
Tel: 0114 261 1122.
Fax: 0114 261 1199.
E-mail: sales@kellett.co.uk

KNORR-BREMSE SYSTEMS FOR COMMERCIAL VEHICLES LTD
Douglas Road, Kingswood, Bristol BS15 8NL.
Tel: 0117 984 6100.
Fax: 0117 984 6101.
Web site: www.knorr-bremse.com

LOOK CCTV LTD
Look House, Aldon Road, Poulton-le-Fylde FY6 8JL
Tel: 01253 891222
Fax: 01253 891221
Web site: www.look-cctv.co.uk
E-mail: enquiries@look-cctv.co.uk

MAJORLINE ENGINEERING LTD
Baybridge Industrial Units, Baybridge Lane, Owslebury, Winchester SO21 1JN.
Tel: 01962 777077.
Fax: 01962 777661, 777667
E-mail: majorline@compuserve.com

MULTIPART PSV
Pilling Lane, Chorley PR7 3EL.
Tel: 01257 225577.
Fax: 01257 225575.
E-mail: info@multipart.com
Web site: www.multipart.com

PSV PRODUCTS
PO Box 166, Warrington WA4 5FG
Tel: 0870 062 4488
Fax: 0870 062 4499
E-mail: mike@psvproducts.com
Web site: www.psvproducts.com

WABCO AUTOMOTIVE UK LTD
Texas Street, Morley LS27 0HQ.
Tel: 0113 251 2510
Fax: 0113 251 2844

WEBASTO PRODUCT UK LTD
Webasto House, White Rose Way, Doncaster Carr DN4 5JH
Tel: 01302 322232
Fax: 01302 322231
E-mail: info@webastouk.com
Web site: www.webasto.co.uk

Tachographs

CHASSIS DEVELOPMENTS LTD
Groveburv Road, Leighton Buzzard LU7 8SL.
Tel: 01525 374151
Fax: 01525 370127

ERF MEDWAY LTD
Sir Thomas Longley Road, Medway City Estate, Rochester ME2 4QW.
Tel: 01634 711144.
Fax: 01634 711188.

THOMAS HARDIE – WIGAN
Lockett Road, Ashton-in-Makerfield WN4 8DE.
Tel: 01942 505124.
Fax: 01942 505119.

MAJORLINE ENGINEERING LTD
Baybridge Industrial Units, Baybridge Lane, Owslebury, Winchester SO21 1JN.
Tel: 01962 777077.
Fax: 01962 777661, 777667
E-mail: majorline@compuserve.com

MULTIPART PSV
Pilling Lane, Chorley PR7 3EL.
Tel: 01257 225577.
Fax: 01257 225575.
E-mail: info@multipart.com
Web site: www.multipart.com

*PARTLINE LTD
Dockfield Road, Shipley BD17 7AZ
Tel: 01274 531531
Fax: 01274 531088
E-mail: sales@partline.co.uk
Web site: www.partline.co.uk

PLAXTON
Plaxton Park, Cayton Low Road, Eastfield, Scarborough YO11 3BY
Tel: 01723 581500
Fax: 01723 5813238
E-mail: sales@plaxtonlimited.co.uk
Web site: www.plaxtonlimited.co.uk

PLAXTON COACH SALES CENTRE
Ryton Road, Anston, Sheffield S25 4DL
Tel: 01909 551155
Fax: 01909 567994
E-mail: coaches@plaxtonlimited.co.uk
Web site: www.plaxtonlimited.co.uk

SIEMENS VDO TRADING LTD
36 Gravelly Industrial Park, Birmingham B24 8TA
Tel: 0121 326 1234
Fax: 0121 326 1299
Web site: www.siemens-datatrack.com

*UNITEC LONDON
Unit 5, Gateway 25, Weston Avenue, West Thurrock RM20 3ZD
Tel: 01708 892440
Fax: 01708 862125
E-mail: london.service@optare.com

*UNITEC ROTHERHAM
Denby Way, Hellaby, Rotherham
S66 8HR
Tel: 01709 535101
Fax: 01709 535103
E-mail: rotherham.service@optare.com

*UNITEC SCOTLAND
Unit 7, Cumbernauld Business Park,
Ward Park Road, Cumbernauld G67 3JZ
Tel: 01236 726738
Fax: 01236 795651
E-mail: scotland.service@optare.com

WARD INTERNATIONAL CONSULTING LTD
Funtley Court, 19 Funtley Hill, Fareham
PO16 7UY
Tel: 01329 280280
Fax: 01329 221010
E-mail: info@wardint.co.uk
Web site: www.wardint.co.uk

Tachograph Calibrators

MAJORLINE ENGINEERING LTD
Baybridge Industrial Units, Baybridge Lane,
Owslebury, Winchester SO21 1JN.
Tel: 01962 777077.
Fax: 01962 777661, 777667
E-mail: majorline@compuserve.com

*MARSHALLS COMMERCIAL ENGINEERING LTD
Firbank Way, Leighton Buzzard LU7 4YP
Tel: 01525 375301
Fax: 01525 850967
Web site: www.mce-ltd.com

PLAXTON
Plaxton Park, Cayton Low Road, Eastfield,
Scarborough YO11 3BY
Tel: 01723 581500
Fax: 01723 5813238
E-mail: sales@plaxtonlimited.co.uk
Web site: www.plaxtonlimited.co.uk

PLAXTON COACH SALES CENTRE
Ryton Road, Anston, Sheffield S25 4DL
Tel: 01909 551155
Fax: 01909 567994
E-mail: coaches@plaxtonlimited.co.uk
Web site: www.plaxtonlimited.co.uk

SIEMENS VDO TRADING LTD
36 Gravelly Industrial Park, Birmingham
B24 8TA
Tel: 0121 326 1234
Fax: 0121 326 1299
Web site: www.siemens-datatrack.com

*UNITEC LONDON
Unit 5, Gateway 25, Weston Avenue,
West Thurrock RM20 3ZD
Tel: 01708 892440
Fax: 01708 862125
E-mail: london.service@optare.com

*UNITEC ROTHERHAM
Denby Way, Hellaby, Rotherham
S66 8HR
Tel: 01709 535101
Fax: 01709 535103
E-mail: rotherham.service@optare.com

*UNITEC SCOTLAND
Unit 7, Cumbernauld Business Park,
Ward Park Road, Cumbernauld G67 3JZ
Tel: 01236 726738
Fax: 01236 795651
E-mail: scotland.service@optare.com

VISECT LTD (TACH:TRAK)
PO Box 1478, Pill BS20 0DZ
Tel: 01275 372274
Fax: 01275 375091

Tachograph Chart Analysis Service

*IBPTS
43 Cage Lane, Felixstowe IP11 9BJ
Tel: 01394 672344
Fax: 01394 672344
E-mail: info@ibpts.com
Web site: www.ibpts.com

CHASSIS DEVELOPMENTS LTD
Grovebury Road, Leighton Buzzard
LU7 8SL.
Tel: 01525 374151.
Fax: 01525 370127.

SIEMENS VDO TRADING LTD
36 Gravelly Industrial Park, Birmingham
B24 8TA
Tel: 0121 326 1234
Fax: 0121 326 1299
Web site: www.siemens-datatrack.com

Tickets, Ticket Machines and Ticket Systems

ACT - APPLIED CARD TECHNOLOGIES
Langley Gate, Kington Langley,
Chippenham SN15 5SE
Tel: 01249 751 200
Fax: 01249 751 201
Email: info@card.co.uk
Web site: www.card.co.uk

ALMEX INFORMATION SYSTEMS
Metric House, Love Lane, Cirencester
GL7 1YG
Tel: 01285 651441
Fax: 01285 650633
E-mail: info@almex.co.uk
Web site: www.almex.co.uk

ATOS ORIGIN
4 Triton Square, Regents Place, London
NW1 3HG
Tel: 020 7830 4444
Fax: 020 7830 4445
Web site: www.atosorigin.co.uk

BEMROSEBOOTH LTD
Stockholm Road, Sutton Fields Industrial
Estate, Hull HU7 0XY
Tel: 01482 826343
Fax: 01482 371386
E-mail: lprecious@bemrosebooth.com
Web site: www.bemrosebooth.com

CANN PRINT
Block C, Unit 2, Crookedholm Commercial
Centre, Mainroad, Crookedholm, Kilmarnock
KA3 6JT
Tel/Fax: 01563 572440

CUBIC TRANSPORTATION SYSTEMS LTD
AFC House, Honeycrock Lane, Salfords,
Redhill RH1 5LA
Tel: 01737 782200
Fax: 01737 789759
Web site: www.cubic.com

DE LA RUE
De La Rue House, Jays Close, Viables,
Basingstoke RG22 4BS
Tel: 01256 605000
Fax: 01256 605004
Web site: www.delarue.com

*KEITH EDMONDSON TICKET ROLLS
Garden House, Tittensor, Stoke-on-Trent
ST12 9HQ
Tel: 01782 372305
Fax: 01782 351136
E-mail: kedmo.ticket@zoom.co.uk
Web site: www.ticketrolls.co.uk

*ELECTRONIC TICKET MACHINE SOFTWARE SERVICES (UK)
9 Dorset Avenue, Ferndown BH22 8HJ
Tel: 0844 800 9299
E-mail: info@etmss.com
Web site: www.etmss.com

JOHN GROVES TICKET SYSTEMS
Unit 5, Rennie Business Units, Factory
Place, Saltcoats KA21 5LZ
Tel: 01294 471133
Fax: 01294 471166
Web site: www.cambist.se

INIT
Broadway Business Centre, 32a Stoney
Street, The Lace Market, Nottingham
NG1 1LL
Tel: 0115 988 6916
Web site: www.init-ka.de

MARK TERRILL TICKET MACHINERY
5 De Grey Close, Lewes BN7 2JR.
Tel: 01273 474816
Fax: 01273 474816
E-mail: mark.terrill@ukonline.co.uk

PAYPOINT PLC
1 The Boulevard, Shire Park, Welwyn
Garden City AL7 1EL
Tel: 01707 60300
Email: grahambloye@paypoint.co.uk
Web site: www.paypoint.co.uk

SCAN COIN LTD
110 Broadway, Salford Quays M50 2UW
Tel: 0161 873 0500
Fax: 0161 873 0501
E-mail: sales@scancoin.co.uk
Web site: www.scancoin.co.uk

SCHADES LTD
Brittain Drive, Codnor Gate Business Park,
Ripley DE5 3RZ
Tel: 01773 748721
Fax: 01773 745601
Web site: www.schades.com
E-mail: sales@schades.co.uk

STUART MANUFACTURING CO LTD
Craft House, 135 Hayes Lane, Kenley
CR8 5JR
Tel: 020 8668 8107
Fax: 020 8668 8277
E-mail: sales@smco.co.uk
Web site: www.smco.co.uk

Trade Directory

*THOMAS AUTOMATICS CO LTD
Bishop Meadow Road, Loughborough
LE11 5RE
Tel: 01509 267611
Fax: 01509 266836
E-mail: sales@thomasa.co.uk
Web site: www.thomasa.co.uk

*TRANSPORT TICKET SERVICES LTD
Yew Tree Cottage, Newcastle, Monmouth
NP25 5NT
Tel/Fax: 01600 750650
E-mail: ttsservices@tiscali.com
Web site: www.ticket-machines.co.uk

*WAYFARER TRANSIT SYSTEMS LTD
10 Willis Way, Fleets Industrial Estate, Poole
BH15 3SS
Tel: 01202 339339
Fax: 01202 339369
E-mail: sales@wayfarer.co.uk
Web site: www.wayfarer.co.uk

Timetable Display Frames

*M BISSELL DISPLAY LTD
Unit 15, Beechwood Business Park,
Burdock Close, Cannock WS11 7GB
Tel: 01543 502115
Fax: 01543 502118
E-mail: sales@bisselldisplay.com
Web site: www.bisselldisplay.com

BROADWATER MOULDINGS LTD
Horham, Eye IP21 5JL.
Tel: 01379 384145.
Fax: 01379 384150

*GABRIEL & CO LTD
Abro Works, 10 Hay Hall Road, Tyseley,
Birmingham B11 2AU
Tel: 0121 248 3333
Fax: 0121 248 3330
E-mail: contact@gabrielco.com
Web site: www.gabrielco.com

Toilet Equipment

*BRADTECH LTD
Unit 3, Ladford Covert, Seighford, Stafford
ST18 9QL
Tel: 01785 282800
Fax: 01785 282558
E-mail: sales@bradtech.ltd.uk
Web site: www.bradtech.ltd.uk

CARLYLE BUS & COACH LTD
Carlyle Business Park, Great Bridge Street,
Swan Village, West Bromwich B70 0XA
Tel: 0121 524 1200
Fax: 0121 524 1201
E-mail: admin@carlyleplc.com

*ELSAN LTD
Bellbrook Park, Uckfield BN3 7RA
Tel: 01825 748200
Fax: 01825 761212
E-mail: sales@elsan.co.uk
Web site: www.elsan.co.uk

EXPRESS COACH REPAIRS LTD
Outgang Lane, Pickering YO18 7EL.
Tel: 01751 475215.

*THE LAWTON MOTOR BODY BUILDING CO LTD
Knutsford Road, Church Lawton,
Stoke-on-Trent ST7 3DN
Tel: 01270 882056
Fax: 01270 883014
E-mail: sales@lawtonmotorbody.co.uk
Web site: www.lawtonmotorbody.co.uk

PSV PRODUCTS
PO Box 166, Warrington WA4 5FG
Tel: 0870 062 4488
Fax: 0870 062 4499
E-mail: mike@psvproducts.com
Web site: www.psvproducts.com

SHADES TECHNICS
Marshgate Drive, Hertford SG13 7AJ
Tel: 01992 501683
Fax: 01992 501669
E-mail: sales@shades-technics.com
Web site: www.shades-technics.com

Transmission Overhaul

BUSS BIZZ
Goughs Transport Depot, Morestead,
Winchester SO21 1JD.
Tel: 01962 715555/66.
Fax: 01962 714868.

GARDNER PARTS LTD
Barton Hall, Hardy Street, Eccles,
Manchester M30 7WA.
Tel: 0161 278 9200
Fax: 0161 787 7549.

HL SMITH TRANSMISSIONS LTD
Enterprise Business Park, Cross Road,
Albrighton, Wolverhampton WV7 3BJ
Tel: 01902 373011
Fax: 01902 373608

*LH GROUP SERVICES LTD
Graycar Business Park, Barton Under
Needwood, Burton-on-Trent DE13 8EN
Tel: 01283 722600
Fax: 01283 722622
E-mail: lh@lh-group.co.uk
Web site: www.lh-group.co.uk

*MENTOR
Mentor Coach & Bus Ltd, Carlton House,
Euroway Industrial Estate, Hellaby,
Rotherham S66 8QL
Tel: 01709 700600
Fax: 01709 700007
E-mail: sales@mentorplc.com
Web site: www.mentorplc.com

METRONET (REW) LTD
130 Bollo Lane, London W3 8BZ.
Tel: 020 7918 6666.
Fax: 020 7918 6599.
E-mail: fraser@r-e-w.co.uk
Web site: www.r-e-w.co.uk

MULTIPART PSV
Pilling Lane, Chorley PR7 3EL.
Tel: 01257 225577.
Fax: 01257 225575.
E-mail: info@multipart.com
Web site: www.multipart.com

SHAWSON SUPPLY LTD
12 Station Road, Saintfield BT24 7DU
Tel: 028 9751 0994
Fax: 028 9751 0816
E-mail: shawsondiesel@btopenworld.com
Web site: www.shawsonsupply.com

*UNITEC
Parts Division, Denby Way, Hellaby,
Rotherham S66 8HR
Tel: 01709 792000
Fax: 01709 792009
E-mail: parts@optare.com

*UNITEC LONDON
Unit 5, Gateway 25, Weston Avenue,
West Thurrock RM20 3ZD
Tel: 01708 892440
Fax: 01708 862125
E-mail: london.service@optare.com

*UNITEC ROTHERHAM
Denby Way, Hellaby, Rotherham
S66 8HR
Tel: 01709 535101
Fax: 01709 535103
E-mail: rotherham.service@optare.com

*UNITEC SCOTLAND
Unit 7, Cumbernauld Business Park,
Ward Park Road, Cumbernauld G67 3JZ
Tel: 01236 726738
Fax: 01236 795651
E-mail: scotland.service@optare.com

*VOITH TURBO LTD
6 Beddington Farm Road, Croydon
CR0 4XB
Tel: 020 8667 0333
Fax: 020 8667 0403
E-mail: john.domigan@voith.com
Web site: www.voith.co.uk

*VOR TRANSMISSIONS LTD
Little London House, St Anne's Road,
Willenhall WV13 1DT
Tel: 01902 604141
Fax: 01902 603868
E-mail: vor@globalnet.co.uk
Web site: www.vor.co.uk

ZF POWERTRAIN
Stringes Close, Willenhall WV13 1LE
Tel: 01902 366000
Fax: 01902 366504
E-mail: sales@powertrain.org.uk
Web site: www.powertrain.org.uk

Tree Guards

*EAST LANCASHIRE COACHBUILDERS LTD (ELC)
Lower Philips Road, Whitebirk Industrial
Estate, Blackburn BB1 5UD
Tel: 01254 504150
Fax: 01254 504197
E-mail: john.horn@elcb.co.uk
Web site: www.elcb.co.uk

*GABRIEL & CO LTD
Abro Works, 10 Hay Hall Road, Tyseley,
Birmingham B11 2AU
Tel: 0121 248 3333
Fax: 0121 248 3330
E-mail: contact@gabrielco.com
Web site: www.gabrielco.com

Tyres

DUNLOP TYRES LTD
TyreFort, 88-98 Wingfoot Way, Birmingham
B24 9HY
Tel: 0121 306 6000
Web site: www.dunloptyres.co.uk

ZF Aftermarket Support

Your first and last call for ZF parts and service

Adtec Aerauto
Ireland
00 353 (0)46 9055126

Ecodrive
Scotland
0141 774 0808

Ecodrive
Northern England
North Wales
01204 701 812

Powertrain
Central and
Southern England
South Wales
01902 366 000

For ZF Service Solutions call:
0870 607 1231

Trade Directory

SNOWCHAINS EUROPRODUCTS
Borough Green TN15 8DG
Tel: 01732 884408
Web site: www.snowchains.co.uk

*****UNITEC LONDON**
Unit 5, Gateway 25, Weston Avenue,
West Thurrock RM20 3ZD
Tel: 01708 892440
Fax: 01708 862125
E-mail: london.service@optare.com

*****UNITEC ROTHERHAM**
Denby Way, Hellaby, Rotherham
S66 8HR
Tel: 01709 535101
Fax: 01709 535103
E-mail: rotherham.service@optare.com

*****UNITEC SCOTLAND**
Unit 7, Cumbernauld Business Park,
Ward Park Road, Cumbernauld G67 3JZ
Tel: 01236 726738
Fax: 01236 795651
E-mail: scotland.service@optare.com

Uniforms

ALLEN & DOUGLAS CORPORATE CLOTHING LTD
Compton Park, Wildmere Road, Banbury OX16 3EZ
Tel: 01295 228456
Fax: 01295 278972
E-mail: telesales@aandd.co.uk
Web site: www.aandd.co.uk

LEISUREWEAR DIRECT LTD
Harpur Hill Industrial Estate, Harpur Hill,
Buxton SK17 9JL
Tel: 01298 74737
Fax: 01298 71674
E-mail: jane@leisureweardirect.com
Web site: www.leisureweardirect.com

*****IMAGE FIRST CORPORATE CLOTHING LTD**
Exhibition House, Grape Street, Leeds
LS10 1BX
Tel: 0113 243 3855
Fax: 0113 242 1040
E-Mail: reception@image-first.co.uk
Web site: www.image-first.co.uk

*****HANDLEY COACH UNIFORMS**
Unit 3, Domestic Street, Holbeck, Leeds
LS11 9RT
Tel: 0113 245 7008
Fax: 0113 245 7009
E-mail: tor@tordesigns.com
Web-Site: www.tordesigns.com

RAINBOW CORPORATEWEAR
Gosforth Road, Derby DE24 8HU
Tel: 01332 342616
Fax: 01332 362328
www.rainbow-corporatewear.co.uk

TALISMAN
26 North Road, Yate BS37 7DA
Tel: 01454 335155
Fax: 01454 335133
E-mail: sales@talisman.ms.com
Web site: www.talisman.ms.com

Upholstery

AUTOMOTIVE TEXTILE INDUSTRIES
Unit 15 & 16, Priest Court, Springfield
Business Park, Grantham NG31 7BG
Tel: 01476 593050
Fax: 01476 593607
E-mail: sales@autotex.com
Web site: www.autotex.com

*****BLACKPOOL TRIM SHOPS LTD**
Brun Grove, Blackpool FY1 6PG
Tel: 01253 766762
Fax: 01253 798443
E-mail: sales@blackpooltrimshops.co.uk
Web site: www.blackpooltrimshops.co.uk

BRIDGE OF WEIR LEATHER CO LTD
Clydesdale Works, Bridge of Weir PA11 3LF.
Tel: 01505 612132.
Fax: 01505 614964.

*****CAMIRA FABRICS LTD**
Hopton Mills, Mirfield WF1 8HE
Tel: 01924 490591
Web site: www.camirafabrics.com

DUOFLEX LTD
Trimmingham House, 2 Shires Road,
Buckingham Road Industrial Estate,
Brackley NN13 7EZ
Tel: 01280 701366
Fax: 01280 704799
E-mail: sales@duoflex.co.uk
Web site: www.duoflex.co.uk

---

going green...
and blue, and purple, and orange and yellow and brown and...

- wool moquettes through to flat wovens
- seating fabric, wall & ceiling trims, anti-macassars and curtaining
- renowned for environmental best practice including green electricity and sustainable manufacturing
- conforms to crib 7 flammability standard
- custom made service available
- no minimum order
- offering a palette in hundreds of colourways

camira
fabric solutions for transport and contract interiors

Camira Fabrics, Hopton Mills, Mirfield, West Yorkshire, WF14 8HE, **T**: 01924 490591 **F**: 01924 495605 **www.camirafabrics.com**

Trade Directory

EXPRESS COACH REPAIRS LTD
Outgang Lane, Pickering YO18 7EL.
Tel: 01751 475215.

FIRTH FURNISHINGS LTD
PO Box 22, Flush Mills, Heckmondwike WF16 0EP.
Tel: 01924 406141.
Fax: 01924 401128.

*JOHN HOLDSWORTH & CO LTD
Shaw Lodge Mills, Halifax HX3 9ET
Tel: 01422 433000
Fax: 01422 433300
E-mail: sales@holdsworth.co.uk
Web site: www.holdsworth.co.uk

*THE LAWTON MOTOR BODY BUILDING CO LTD
Knutsford Road, Church Lawton, Stoke-on-Trent ST7 3DN
Tel: 01270 882056
Fax: 01270 883014
E-mail: sales@lawtonmotorbody.co.uk
Web site: www.lawtonmotorbody.co.uk

MARTYN INDUSTRIALS LTD
5 Brunel Way, Durranhill Industrial Esate, Carlisle CA1 3NQ
Tel: 01228 544000
Fax: 01228 544001
E-mail: enquiries@martyn-industrials.co.uk
Web site: www.martyn-industrials.com

METRONET (REW) LTD
130 Bollo Lane, London W3 8BZ.
Tel: 020 7918 6666.
Fax: 020 7918 6599.
E-mail: fraser@r-e-w.co.uk
Web site: www.r-e-w.co.uk

WIDNEY UK LTD
Plume Street, Aston, Birmingham B6 7SA.
Tel: 0121 327 5500.
Fax: 0121 328 2466.
E-mail: richard@widney.co.uk

Vacuum Systems

*SMART CENTRAL COACH SYSTEMS
5 Kings Acre House, 329 Kings Acre Road, Hereford HR6 8LP.
Tel: 01432 276380
Fax: 01432 351800
Web site: www.smartcoachsystems.co.uk
E-mail: info@smartcoachsystems.co.uk

Vehicle Washing & Washers

*BRADTECH LTD
Unit 3, Ladford Covert, Seighford, Stafford ST18 9QL
Tel: 01785 282800
Fax: 01785 282558
E-mail: sales@bradtech.ltd.uk
Web site: www.bradtech.ltd.uk

CRYSTALKLEEN LTD
8 Fifth Avenue, Hayes UB3 2ER
Tel: 020 8581 0599
Email: crystalkleen@blueyonder.co.uk

ATLANTIS INTERNATIONAL LTD
18 Weldon Road, Loughborough LE11 5RA
Tel: 01509 233770
Fax: 01509 210542
E-mail: peterspencer@atlantisint.co.uk
Web site: www.atlantisint.co.uk

MONOWASH (BRUSH REPLACEMENT SERVICE)
8 Contessa Close, Farnborough BR6 7ER.
Tel: 01689 860061.
Fax: 01689 861469

NATIONWIDE CLEANING & SUPPORT SERVICES LTD
Airport House, Purley Way, Croydon CR0 0XZ
Tel: 020 8288 3580
Web site: www.nationwidefm.com

*SMITH BROS & WEBB LTD
Britannia House, Arden Forest Industrial Estate, Alcester B49 6EX
Tel: 01789 400096
Fax: 01789 400231
E-mail: sbw@vehicle-washing-systems.co.uk
Web site: www.vehicle-washing-systems.co.uk

SOMERS TOTALKARE LTD
15 Forge Trading Estate, Mucklow Hill, Halesowen B62 8TR
Tel: 0121 585 2700
Fax: 0121 585 2725
E-mail: sales@somerstotalkare.co.uk
Web site: www.somerstotalkare.co.uk

*WINDOW CLEAN SERVICES
309 Cow Gate, Edinburgh EH1 1NA
Tel: 0131 556 5720
Fax: 0131 558 7377

Wheels, Wheeltrims & Covers

*ALCOA WHEEL PRODUCTS EUROPE
Industrieweg 135, 3583 PAAL, Belgium
Tel: 00 32 11 458464
E-mail: info.wheels@alcoa.com
Web site: www.alcoawheels.com

AUTOMATE WHEEL COVERS LTD
California Mills, Oxford Road, Gomersal BD19 4HQ
Tel: 01274 862700
Fax: 01274 851989
E-mail: sales@wheelcovers.co.uk
Web site: www.euroliners.com

HATCHER COMPONENTS LTD
Broadwater Road, Framlingham IP13 9LL.
Tel: 01728 723675.
Fax: 01728 724475.

J. HIPWELL & SON
427 Warwick Road, Greet, Birmingham B20 1JE.
Tel: 0121 706 7175.
Fax: 0121 706 0502

*THE LAWTON MOTOR BODY BUILDING CO LTD
Knutsford Road, Church Lawton, Stoke-on-Trent ST7 3DN
Tel: 01270 882056
Fax: 01270 883014
E-mail: sales@lawtonmotorbody.co.uk
Web site: www.lawtonmotorbody.co.uk

*MENTOR
Mentor Coach & Bus Ltd, Carlton House, Euroway Industrial Estate, Hellaby, Rotherham S66 8QL
Tel: 01709 700600
Fax: 01709 700007
E-mail: sales@mentorplc.com
Web site: www.mentorplc.com

*UNITEC
Parts Division, Denby Way, Hellaby, Rotherham S66 8HR
Tel: 01709 792000
Fax: 01709 792009
E-mail: parts@optare.com

Windows and Windscreens

AUTOGLASS COACH & BUS SERVICES
PO Box 343, Goldington Road, Bedford MK40 3BX
Tel: 01234 279572
Fax: 01234 279460
Tel: 01234 279559

BRITAX PMG LTD
Bressingby Industrial Estate, Bridlington YO16 4SJ
Tel: 01262 670161
Fax: 01262 605666
E-mail: info@britax-pmg.com
Web site: www.britax-pmg.com

CARLYLE BUS & COACH LTD
Carlyle Business Park, Great Bridge Street, Swan Village, West Bromwich B70 0XA
Tel: 0121 524 1200
Fax: 0121 524 1201
E-mail: admin@carlyleplc.co.uk

*CRESCENT FACILITIES LTD
72 Willow Crescent, Chapeltown, Sheffield S35 1QS
Tel/fax: 0114 2451050
E-mail: cfl.chris@btinternet.com
Web site: www.cflparts.com

*EAST LANCASHIRE COACHBUILDERS LTD (ELC)
Lower Philips Road, Whitebirk Industrial Estate, Blackburn BB1 5UD
Tel: 01254 504150
Fax: 01254 504197
E-mail: john.horn@elcb.co.uk
Web site: www.elcb.co.uk

EXPRESS COACH REPAIRS LTD
Outgang Lane, Pickering YO18 7EL
Tel: 01751 475215.

B HEPWORTH & CO LTD
Hepworth House, Brook Street, Redditch B98 8NF
Tel: 01527 61243
Fax: 01527 66836
Web site: www.b-hepworth.com
E-mail: bhepworth@b-hepworth.com

INDUSTRIAL & COMMERCIAL WINDOW CO LTD
Unit 2, Caldervale Industrial Estate, Horbury Junction, Wakefield WF4 5ER.
Tel: 01924 260106.
Fax: 01924 260152.

Trade Directory

*J W GLASS LTD
Units 6 & 7, Scropton Road, Hatton
DE65 5DT
Tel: 01283 520202
Fax: 01283 520022
E-mail: info@jwglass.co.uk
Web site: www.jwglass.co.uk

*THE LAWTON MOTOR BODY BUILDING CO LTD
Knutsford Road, Church Lawton,
Stoke-on-Trent ST7 3DN
Tel: 01270 882056
Fax: 01270 883014
E-mail: sales@lawtonmotorbody.co.uk
Web site: www.lawtonmotorbody.co.uk

*MENTOR
Mentor Coach & Bus Ltd, Carlton House, Euroway Industrial Estate, Hellaby, Rotherham S66 8QL
Tel: 01709 700600
Fax: 01709 700007
E-mail: sales@mentorplc.com
Web site: www.mentorplc.com

MULTIPART PSV
Pilling Lane, Chorley PR7 3EL.
Tel: 01257 225577.
Fax: 01257 225575.
E-mail: info@multipart.com
Web site: www.multipart.com

NEALINE WINDSCREEN WIPER PRODUCTS
Unit 1, The Sidings Industrial Estate, Birdingbury Road, Marton CV23 9RX
Tel: 01926 633256
Fax: 01926 632600

*PERCY LANE PRODUCTS LTD
Lichfield Road, Tamworth B79 7TL
Tel: 01827 63821
Fax: 01827 310159
E-mail: sales@percy-lane.co.uk
Web site: www.percy-lane.co.uk

PLAXTON COACH SALES CENTRE
Ryton Road, Anston, Sheffield S25 4DL
Tel: 01909 551155
Fax: 01909 567994
E-mail: coaches@plaxtonlimited.co.uk
Web site: www.plaxtonlimited.co.uk

*PSV GLASS
Hillbottom Road, High Wycombe
HP12 4HJ
Tel: 01494 533131
Fax: 01494 462675
E-mail: sales@psvglass.co.uk
Web site: www.psvglass.co.uk

*UNITEC
Parts Division, Denby Way, Hellaby, Rotherham S66 8HR
Tel: 01709 792000
Fax: 01709 792009
E-mail: parts@optare.com

*UNITEC LONDON
Unit 5, Gateway 25, Weston Avenue, West Thurrock RM20 3ZD
Tel: 01708 892440
Fax: 01708 862125
E-mail: london.service@optare.com

*UNITEC ROTHERHAM
Denby Way, Hellaby, Rotherham
S66 8HR
Tel: 01709 535101
Fax: 01709 535103
E-mail: rotherham.service@optare.com

*UNITEC SCOTLAND
Unit 7, Cumbernauld Business Park, Ward Park Road, Cumbernauld G67 3JZ
Tel: 01236 726738
Fax: 01236 795651
E-mail: scotland.service@optare.com

*VOLVO BUS AND COACH CENTRE
Belton Road West, Loughborough LE11 5HP
Tel: 01509 217777
Fax: 01509 239362
Web site: www.volvo.com

WIDNEY UK LTD
Plume Street, Aston, Birmingham B6 7SA.
Tel: 0121 327 5500.
Fax: 0121 328 2466.
E-mail: richard@widney.co.uk

INDUSTRY SERVICE PROVIDERS

Accident Investigation

KERNOW ASSOCIATES
18 Tresawla Court, Tolvaddon, Camborne TR14 0HF.
Tel/Fax: 01209 711870.
E-mail: 106472.3264@compuserve.com

Accountancy & Audit

BARRONS CHARTERED ACCOUNTANTS
Monometer House, Rectory Grove, Leigh on Sea SS9 2HN
Tel: 01702 481910
Fax: 01702 481911
E-mail: mail@barrons-bds.com
Web site: www.barrons-bds.com

Advertising Contractors

DECKER MEDIA LTD
Decker House, Lowater Street, Carlton, Nottingham NG4 1JJ
Tel: 0115 940 2406.
Fax: 0115 940 2407.
E-mail: sales@deckermedia.co.uk,
Web site: www.deckermedia.co.uk

Advisory Services

ADGROUP LTD
Ad House, East Parade, Harrogate HG1 5LT
Tel: 01423 526253
Fax: 01423 502522
E-mail: info@adbus.info
Web site: www.adbus.info

AD COACH SALES
Newbridge Coach Depot, Witheridge EX16 8PY
Tel: 01884 860787
Fax: 01884 860711
E-mail: ggoodwin@adcoachsales.co.uk
Web site: www.adcoachsales.co.uk

ADG TRANSPORT CONSULTANCY
Oak Cottage, Royal Oak, Machen CF83 8SN
Tel: 01633 441491
Fax: 01633 440591
E-mail: a.dgettins@btinternet.com

ANDY IZATT
10 Briton Court, St Thomas's Road, Spalding PE11 2TS
Tel: 01775 712542
E-mail: andy.izatt@btinternet.com
Web site: andy.izatt.btinternet.com

*AUSTIN ANALYTICS
Crown House, 183 High Street, Bottisham, Cambridge CB25 9BB
Tel: 01223 813151
Fax: 07005 946854
E-mail: john@j-austin.co.uk
Web site: www.analytics.co.uk

*CAREYBROOK LTD
PO Box 205, Southam CV47 0ZL
Tel: 01926 813938
Fax: 01926 814898
E-mail: cb.ltd@btinternet.com
Web site: www.careybrook.com

CAPOCO DESIGN
Stone Cross House, Chickgrove, Salisbury SP3 6NA
Tel: 01722 716722
Fax: 01722 716226

COLIN BUCHANAN
Newcombe House, 45 Notting Hill Gate, London W11 3PB
Tel: 020 7309 7000
Fax: 020 7309 0906
E-mail: london@cbuchanan.co.uk
Web site: www.cbuchanan.co.uk

COACH DIRECT
The Coach House, 22 South Street, Rochford SS4 1BQ
Tel: 0870 550 2069
Fax: 0870 070 2069
E-mail: info@coachdirect.co.uk
Web site: www.coachdirect.co.uk

Trade Directory

*ELECTRONIC TICKET MACHINE SOFTWARE SERVICES (UK)
9 Dorset Avenue, Ferndown BH22 8HJ
Tel: 0844 800 9299
E-mail: info@etmss.com
Web site: www.etmss.com

FCAV & CO
Brooklyn House, Coleford Road, Bream GL15 6EU
Tel: 01594 564552
Fax: 01594 564556
E-mail: info@fcav.co.uk
Web site: www.fcav.co.uk

GOSKILLS
Concorde House, Trinity Park, Solihull B37 7UQ
Tel: 0121 635 5520
Fax: 0121 635 5521
E-mail: info@goskills.org
Web site: www.goskills.org

*LEYLAND PRODUCT DEVELOPMENTS LTD
Aston Way, Leyland, Preston PR26 7TZ
Tel: 01772 435834
E-mail: sales@lpdl.co.uk
Web site: www.lpdl.co.uk

*MINIMISE YOUR RISK
11 Chatsworth Park, Telscombe Cliffs BN10 7DZ
Tel: 01273 580189
Fax: 01273 580189
E-mail: minimise@btconnect.com
Web site: www.minimiseyourrisk.co.uk

MVA
MVA House, Victoria Way, Woking GU21 1DD
Tel: 01483 755207
Web site: www.mva-group.com

*PROFESSIONAL TRANSPORT SERVICES
12 Silverdale, Stanford-le-Hope SS17 8BG
Tel: 01375 675262
Web site: www.proftranserv.co.uk
E-mail: enquiries@proftranserv.com

STEPHEN C MORRIS
PO Box 119, Shepperton TW17 8UX
Tel: 01932 232574
E-mail: buswriter@btinternet.com

SALTIRE COMMUNICATIONS
39 Lilyhill Terrace, Edinburgh EH8 7DR
Tel: 0131 652 0205
E-mail: gavin-booth@btconnect.com

TRANSPORTATION MANAGEMENT SOLUTIONS
PO Box 15174, Glasgow G3 6WB.
Tel: 0141 332 4733.
Fax: 0141 354 0076.
E-mail: tramsol@aol.com

WARD INTERNATIONAL CONSULTING LTD
Funtley Court, 19 Funtley Hill, Fareham PO16 7UY
Tel: 01329 280280
Fax: 01329 221010
E-mail: info@wardint.co.uk
Web site: www.wardint.com

Artwork

ADGROUP LTD
Ad House, East Parade, Harrogate HG1 5LT
Tel: 01423 526253
Fax: 01423 502522
E-mail: info@adbus.info
Web site: www.adbus.info

BEST IMPRESSIONS
15 Starfield Road, London W12 9SN
Tel: 020 8740 6443
Fax: 020 8740 9134
E-mail: talk2us@best-impressions.co.uk
Web site: www.best-impressions.co.uk

FIGUREHEAD DATA SYSTEMS
Felindre, Swansea SA5 7PP
Tel: 01792 883155
Fax: 01792 884934
E-mail: BusTimes@aol.com
Web site: www.bustimes.com

FWT
Whittington House, 764-768 Holloway Road, London N19 3JQ
Tel: 020 7281 2161
E-mail: sales@fwt.co.uk
Web site: www.fwt.co.uk

*TITAN BUS UK LTD
52 East Parade, Harrogate HG1 5LT
Tel: 01423 526253
Fax: 01423 502522
E-mail: info@titanbus.co.uk
Web site: www.titanbus.co.uk

TONY GREAVES GRAPHICS
19 Perth Mount, Horsforth, Leeds LS18 5SH
Tel/Fax: 0113 258 4795
E-mail: tony@greavesgraphics.fsnet.co.uk

HATTS COACHWORKS & SERVICES
Foxham, Chippenham SN15 4NB
Tel: 01249 740444
Fax: 01249 740447
E-mail: adrian@hattstravel.co.uk
Web site: www.hattstravel.co.uk

MCV BUS & COACH LTD
Sterling Place, Elean Business Park, Sutton CB6 2QE
Tel: 01353 773000
Fax: 01353 773001
E-mail: vernon.edwards@mcv-uk.com

*NEERMAN & PARTNERS
c/o 22 Larbre Crescent, Whickham, Newcastle-upon-Tyne NE16 5YG
Tel: 0191 488 6258
Fax: 0191 488 9158
Web site: www.neerman.net
E-mail: info@neerman.net

TIME TRAVEL UK
247 Bradford Road, Stanningley, Pudsey LS28 6QB
Tel: 0113 255 1188
E-mail: nick.baldwin@tinyworld.co.uk

*VETRO DESIGN
247 Bradford Road, Pudsey, Leeds LS28 6QB
Tel: 01132 551188
E-mail: nick@vetrodesign.co.uk

Auctioneers & Valuators

*MENTOR
Mentor Coach & Bus Ltd, Carlton House, Euroway Industrial Estate, Hellaby, Rotherham S66 8QL
Tel: 01709 700600
Fax: 01709 700007
E-mail: sales@mentorplc.com
Web site: www.mentorplc.com

Breakdown & Recovery Services

NB - Operator lists also indicate bus and coach operators able to provide breakdown and recovery services.

AD COACH SALES
Newbridge Coach Depot, Witheridge EX16 8PY
Tel: 01884 860787
Fax: 01884 860711
E-mail: ggoodwin@adcoachsales.co.uk
Web site: www.adcoachsales.co.uk

*BRITISH BUS SALES
Mike Nash, PO Box 534, Dorking RH5 5XB
Tel: 07836 656692
E-mail: nashionalbus1@btconnect.com
Web site: www.britishbussales.co.uk

BUZZLINES LTD
Unit G1, Lympne Industrial Park, Hythe CT21 4LR
Tel: 01303 261870
Fax: 01303 230093
Web site: www.buzzlines.co.uk

*COACH-AID
Unit 2, Brindley Close, Tollgate Industrial Estate, Stafford ST16 3SU
Tel: 01785 222666
E-mail: workshop@coach-aid.com
Web site: www.coach-aid.com

DRURY & DRURY
Unit 6, Cobbs Wood Industrial Estate, Brunswick Road, Ashford TN23 1EH.
Tel: 01303 610555.
Fax: 01303 610666.
E-mail: martinstrange@channelcommercials.co.uk

HATTS COACHWORKS & SERVICES
Foxham, Chippenham SN15 4NB
Tel: 01249 740444
Fax: 01249 740447
E-mail: adrian@hattstravel.co.uk
Web site: www.hattstravel.co.uk

LANTERN RECOVERY SPECIALISTS PLC
Lantern House, 39/41 High Street, Potters Bar EN6 5AJ
Tel: 0870 6090333
Fax: 01707 640450
Web site: www.lrs.uk.com
E-mail: bob@lrs.uk.com

THOMAS HARDIE – WIGAN
Lockett Road, Ashton-in-Makerfield WN4 8DE.
Tel: 01942 505124
Fax: 01942 505119

Trade Directory

MASS SPECIAL ENGINEERING LTD
Anston, Sheffield S25 4SD.
Tel: 01909 550480.
Fax: 01909 550486.

TRUCKALIGN CO LTD
VIP Trading Estate, Anchor & Hope Lane, London SE7 7RY
Tel: 020 8858 3781
Fax: 020 8858 3781

*UNITEC LONDON
Unit 5, Gateway 25, Weston Avenue, West Thurrock RM20 3ZD
Tel: 01708 892440
Fax: 01708 862125
E-mail: london.service@optare.com

*UNITEC ROTHERHAM
Denby Way, Hellaby, Rotherham S66 8HR
Tel: 01709 535101
Fax: 01709 535103
E-mail: rotherham.service@optare.com

*UNITEC SCOTLAND
Unit 7, Cumbernauld Business Park, Ward Park Road, Cumbernauld G67 3JZ
Tel: 01236 726738
Fax: 01236 795651
E-mail: scotland.service@optare.com

Coach Driver Agencies

DRIVER HIRE CANTERBURY
East Suite, Parsonage Office, Nackington, Canterbury CT4 7AD
Tel: 01227 479529
Fax: 01227 479531
E-mail: canterbury@driver-hire.co.uk

FRASER EAGLE MANAGEMENT SERVICES
Technology Management Centre, St James Square, Accrington BB5 0RE
Tel: 01254 357777
Fax: 01254 879461
E-mail: info@frasereagle.com
Web site: www.frasereagle.com

THE PENINSULA GROUP
Trematon Drive, St Peter's Way, Ivybridge PL21 0HT
Tel (office hrs): 01752 896471
Mobile/Direct: 07909 695438
Owner: Mike Yedermann **Touring Man:** Brian Madge
Associated companies: Peninsula Cars & Eastward Coaches (see operators section - Devon)

Cleaning services

TARA SUPPORT SERVICES LTD
32 Derby Road, Enfield EN3 4AW
Tel: 0845 450 0607
Fax: 0845 450 0608
E-mail: info@tarasupport.co.uk
Web site: www.tarasupport.co.uk

Coach Hire Brokers/Vehicle Rental

AVENTA
66B Victoria Road, Horley RH6 7PZ.
Tel: 01293 825001
Fax: 01293 825002
E-mail: info@aventa.co.uk
Web site: www.aventa.co.uk

COACH DIRECT
The Coach House, 22 South Street, Rochford SS4 1BQ
Tel: 0870 550 2069
Fax: 0870 070 2069
E-mail: info@coachdirect.co.uk
Web site: www.coachdirect.co.uk

COACHFINDER LTD
Woodbank House, 24 Matley Close, Newton, Hyde SK14 4UE
Tel: 0161 368 7877
Web site: www.coachfinder.uk.com

DAWSONRENTALS BUS AND COACH LTD
Delaware Drive, Tongwell, Milton Keynes MK15 8JH
Tel: 01908 218111
Fax: 01908 610156
E-mail: info@dawsongroup.co.uk
Web site: www.dawsongroup.co.uk

FRASER EAGLE MANAGEMENT SERVICES
Technology Management Centre, St James Square, Accrington BB5 0RE
Tel: 01254 357777
Fax: 01254 879461
E-mail: info@frasereagle.com
Web site: www.frasereagle.com

HAYWARD TRAVEL (CARDIFF)
2 Murch Crescent, Dinas Powys CF64 4RF
Tel: 029 2051 5551
Fax: 029 2051 5113
E-mail: haytvl@aol.com

*NEXT BUS LTD
The Coach Yard, Vincients Road, Bumpers Farm Industrial Estate, Chippenham SN14 6QA
Tel: 01249 462462
E-mail: sales@next-bus.co.uk
Web site: www.next-bus.co.uk

*TRAMONTANA COACH DISTRIBUTORS
Chapelknowe Road, Carfin, Motherwell ML1 5LE
Tel: 01698 861790
Fax: 01698 860778
E-mail: wdt90@tiscali.co.uk

*YORKSHIRE BUS & COACH SALES
254A West Ella Road, West Ella, Hull HU10 7SF
Tel: 01482 653302
Fax: 01482 653302
E-mail: craig.porteous@virgin.net

Coach Interchange & Parking Facilities

T & E DOCHERTY
40 Bank Street, Irvine KA12 0LP
Tel: 01294 278440
Web site: www.coach-hires.co.uk

SAMMYS GARAGE
Victoria Coach Station, Arrivals Hall, 3 Eccleston Place, London SW1W 9NF
Tel: 020 7793 7533/7730/8867

TOP LINE TRAVEL OF YORK LTD
23 Hospital Fields Road, Fulford Industrial Estate, York YO10 4EW
Tel: 01904 655585
Web site: www.toplinetravelofyork.co.uk

*TRAVELGREEN COACHES
Canda Lodge, Hampole Bank Lane, Skellow, Doncaster DN6 8LF
Tel: 01302 722227
Fax: 01302 727999
(also B&B accommodation)

VICTORIA COACH STATION LTD
164 Buckingham Palace Road, London SW1W 9TP
Tel: 020 7824 0000
Fax: 020 7824 0008
Web site: www.tfl.co.uk

Computer Systems/Software

ACIS
ACIS House, Knaves Beech Business Centre, Loudwater HP10 9QR
Tel: 01628 524900
Fax: 01628 523222
E-mail: enquiries@acis.uk.com
Web site: www.acis.uk.com

AUTOPRO SOFTWARE
1 Kingsmeadow, Norton Cross, Runcorn WA7 6PB
Tel: 01928 715962
Fax: 01928 714538
E-mail: sales@autoprouk.com
Web site: www.autoprosoftware.com

DISTINCTIVE SYSTEMS LTD
Amy Johnson Way, York YO30 4XT
Tel: 01904 692269
Fax: 01904 690810
E-mail: sales@distinctive-systems.com
Web site: www.distinctive-systems.com

*ELECTRONIC TICKET MACHINE SOFTWARE SERVICES (UK)
9 Dorset Avenue, Ferndown BH22 8HJ
Tel: 0844 800 9299
E-mail: info@etmss.com
Web site: www.etmss.com

FIGUREHEAD DATA SYSTEMS
Felindre, Swansea SA5 7PP
Tel: 01792 883155
Fax: 01792 884934
E-mail: BusTimes@aol.com
Web site: www.bustimes.com

Trade Directory

GRAMPIAN SOFTWARE
40 Carden Place, Aberdeen AB10 1UP
Tel: 01224 627600
Fax: 01224 627637
E-mail: info@grampian-software.co.uk
Web site: www.grampian-software.co.uk

JOHN GROVES TICKET SYSTEMS
Unit 5, Rennie Business Units, Factory Place, Saltcoats KA21 5LZ
Tel: 01294 471133
Fax: 01294 471166
Web site: www.cambist.se

INOVAS LTD
1 Glenbervie Business Park, Larbert, Falkirk FK5 4RB
Tel: 01324 682268
Fax: 01324 682269
Web site: www.inovas.co.uk
E-mail: info@inovas.co.uk

*OMNIBUS
Hollinwood Business Centre, Albert Street, Hollinwood, Oldham OL8 3QL
Tel: 0161 683 3100
Fax: 0161 683 3102
Web site: www.mnibus-systems.co.uk

*PROFESSIONAL TRANSPORT SERVICES
12 Silverdale, Stanford-le-Hope SS17 8BG
Tel: 01375 675262
Web site: www.proftranserv.co.uk
E-mail: enquiries@proftranserv.com

*ROEVILLE COMPUTER SYSTEMS
Station House, East Lane, Stainforth, Doncaster DN7 5HF
Tel: 01302 841333
Fax: 01302 843966
E-mail: sales@roeville.com
Web site: www.roeville.com

TAGTRONICS LTD
Suite 410, Daisyfield Business Centre, Appleby Street, Blackburn BB1 3BL
Tel: 01254 297732
Fax: 01254 698484
E-mail: info@tagtronics.co.uk
Web site: www.tagtronics.co.uk

TRANMAN SOLUTIONS
Thornbury Office Park, Midland Way, Thornbury BS35 2BS.
Tel: 01454 874000.
Fax: 01454 874001.
E-mail: enquire@tranman.co.uk

TRAVEL INFORMATION SYSTEMS
Grand Union House, 20 Kentish Town Road, London NW1 9NX
Tel: 020 7428 1288
Fax: 020 7267 2745
E-mail: enquiries@travelinfosystems.com
Web site: www.travelinfosystems.com

Consultants

ADG TRANSPORT CONSULTANCY
Oak Cottage, Royal Oak, Machen CF83 8SN
Tel: 01633 441491
Fax: 01633 440591
E-mail: a.dgettins@btinternet.com

*ANTAL INTERNATIONAL NETWORK
Kestrel House, 111 Heath Road, Twickenham, Middlesex TW1 1AF
Contact: Breen Coyne
Tel: 0870 770 1604
E-Mail: bcoyne@antal.com
Website: Currently under construction

*AUSTIN ANALYTICS
Crown House, 183 High Street, Bottisham, Cambridge CB25 9BB
Tel: 01223 813151
Fax: 07005 946854
E-mail: john@j-austin.co.uk
Web site: www.analytics.co.uk

AUTOPRO SOFTWARE
1 Kingsmeadow, Norton Cross, Runcorn WA7 6PB
Tel: 01928 715962
Fax: 01928 714538
E-mail: sales@autoprouk.com
Web site: www.autoprosoftware.com

AVENTA
66B Victoria Road, Horley RH6 7DZ.
Tel: 01293 825001.
Fax: 01293 825002.
E-mail: info@aventa.co.uk
Web site: www.aventa.co.uk

*BESTCHART LTD
6A Mims Yard, Down Road, Horndean, Waterlooville PO8 0YP
Tel: 023 9259 7707
Fax: 023 9259 1700
E-mail: info@bestchart.co.uk
Web site: www.bestchart.co.uk

*BORLAND, WINDER-DIXON LLP
Axe View, Axe Road, Drimpton, Beaminster DT8 3RJ
Tel: 01460 72769
E-mail: chris.borland@tiscali.co.uk

*CAREYBROOK LTD
PO Box 205, Southam CV47 0ZL
Tel: 01926 813938
Fax: 01926 814898
E-mail: cb.ltd@btinternet.com
Web site: www.careybrook.com

COACH DIRECT
The Coach House, 22 South Street, Rochford SS4 1BQ
Tel: 0870 550 2069
Fax: 0870 070 2069
E-mail: info@coachdirect.co.uk
Web site: www.coachdirect.co.uk

COLIN BUCHANAN
Newcombe House, 45 Notting Hill Gate, London W11 3PB
Tel: 020 7309 7000
Fax: 020 7309 0906
E-mail: london@cbuchanan.co.uk
Web site: www.cbuchanan.co.uk

CRONER CCH GROUP LTD
145 London Road, Kingston upon Thames KT2 6SR.
Tel: 020 8247 1261.
Fax: 020 8547 2638.
E-mail: info@croner.cch.co.uk

DCA DESIGN INTERNATIONAL
19 Church Street, Warwick CV34 4AB
Tel: 01926 499461
Fax: 01926 401134
Web site: www.dca-design.com/transport

*ELLIS INTERNATIONAL TRANSPORT CONSULTING LTD
61 Bodycoats Road, Chandlers Ford SO53 2HA
Tel: 023 8027 0447
Fax: 023 8027 6736
E-mail: info@ejtc.uk.ltd

*ELECTRONIC TICKET MACHINE SOFTWARE SERVICES (UK)
9 Dorset Avenue, Ferndown BH22 8HJ
Tel: 0844 800 9299
E-mail: info@etmss.com
Web site: www.etmss.com

*R W FAULKS FCIT
Penthouse J, Ross Court, Putney Hill, London SW15 3NY
Tel: 020 8785 1584
E-mail: rexfaulks@aol.com

FINANCIAL INSPECTION SERVICES LTD
PO Box 1075, Beaminster DT8 3YA.
Tel: 01460 74337.
Fax: 01460 72154.
E-mail: fininspect@aol.com

*LEYLAND PRODUCT DEVELOPMENTS LTD
Aston Way, Leyland, Preston PR26 7TZ
Tel: 01772 435834
E-mail: sales@lpdl.co.uk
Web site: www.lpdl.co.uk

*LEONARD GREEN ASSOCIATES
2 Short Clough Close, Reedsholme, Rawtenstall BB4 8PT
Tel: 01706 218539
Fax: 01706 218539
E-mail: lgreen@dsl-pipex.com

*IBPTS
43 Cage Lane, Felixstowe IP11 9BJ
Tel: 01394 672344
Fax: 01394 672344
E-mail: info@ibpts.com
Web site: www.ibpts.com

JACOBS BABTIE GROUP LTD
School Green, Shinfield, Reading RG2 9HL.
Tel: 0118 988 1555.
Fax: 0118 988 1653.

KERNOW ASSOCIATES
18 Tresawla Court, Tolvaddon, Camborne TR14 0HF.
Tel/Fax: 01209 711870.
E-mail: 106472.3264@compuserve.com

*NEERMAN & PARTNERS
c/o 22 Larbre Crescent, Whickham, Newcastle-upon-Tyne NE16 5YG
Tel: 0191 488 6258
Fax: 0191 488 9158
Web site: www.neerman.net
E-mail: info@neerman.net

*OMNIBUS
Hollinwood Business Centre, Albert Street, Hollinwood, Oldham OL8 3QL
Tel: 0161 683 3100
Fax: 0161 683 3102
Web site: www.mnibus-systems.co.uk

*THOMAS KNOWLES - TRANSPORT CONSULTANT
41 Redhills, Eccleshall ST21 6JW
Tel: 01785 859414
Fax: 01785 859414
E-mail: thmsknw@aol.com

MASS SPECIAL ENGINEERING LTD
Anston, Sheffield S25 4SD.
Tel: 01909 550480.
Fax: 01909 550486.

MAUN INTERNATIONAL
New Cross House, 8-10 Mansfield Road, Sutton in Ashfield NG17 4GR.
Tel: 01623 555621.
Fax: 01623 555671.

***MINIMISE YOUR RISK**
11 Chatsworth Park, Telscombe Cliffs BN10 7DZ
Tel: 01273 580189
Fax: 01273 580189
E-mail: minimise@btconnect.com
Web site: www.minimiseyourrisk.co.uk

MOTT MACDONALD
St Anne House, Wellesley House, Croydon CR9 2UL
Tel: 020 8774 2000
Fax: 020 8681 5706
E-mail: marketing@mottmac.com
Web site: www.mottmac.com

***PARRY PEOPLE MOVERS LTD**
Overend Road, Cradley Heath, Dudley B64 7DD
Tel: 01384 569171
Fax: 01384 637753
E-mail: jpmparry@aol.com
Website: www.parrytech.com

PRE METRO OPERATION LTD
21 Woodglade Croft, Kings Norton, Birmingham B38 8TD
Tel: 0121 243 9906
Fax: 0121 243 9906
E-mail: premetro@aol.com

***PROFESSIONAL TRANSPORT SERVICES**
12 Silverdale, Stanford-le-Hope SS17 8BG
Tel: 01375 675262
Web site: www.proftranserv.co.uk
E-mail: enquiries@proftranserv.com

***ROBERTSON TRANSPORT CONSULTING LTD**
Field House, Braceby, Sleaford NG34 0SZ
Tel: 01529 497254
E-mail: robertson@rtclincs.co.uk

SALTIRE COMMUNICATIONS
39 Lilyhill Terrace, Edinburgh EH8 7DR
Tel: 0131 652 0205
E-mail: gavin-booth@btconnect.com

***SPECIALIST TRAINING & CONSULTANCY SERVICES LTD**
6 Venture Court, Metcalfe Drive, Altham Industrial Estate, Accrington BB5 5TU
Tel: 0800 3283297
Fax: 01282 687091
E-mail: enquiries@specialisttraining.co.uk
Web site: www.specialisttraining.co.uk

***TAS PARTNERSHIP LTD**
Guildhall House, Guildhall Street, Preston PR1 3NU
Tel: 01772 204988
Fax: 01722 562070
E-mail: adrian.granto@tas-part.co.uk

TRANSPORTATION MANAGEMENT SOLUTIONS
PO Box 15174, Glasgow G3 6WB.
Tel: 0141 332 4733.
Fax: 0141 354 0076.
E-mail: tramsol@aol.com

TRANSPORT DESIGN INTERNATIONAL
12 Waterloo Road Estate, Bidford on Avon B50 4JH
Tel: 01789 490370
Fax: 01789 490592
E-mail:enquiries@tdi.uk.com
Web site: www.tdi.uk.com

VCA
No1, The Estate Office Centre, Eastgate Road, Bristol BS5 6XX
Tel: 0117 952 4126
Fax: 0117 952 4104
E-mail: paul.cooke@vca.gov.uk
Web site: www.vca.gov.uk

WARD INTERNATIONAL CONSULTING LTD
Funtley Court, 19 Funtley Hill, Fareham PO16 7UY
Tel: 01329 280280
Fax: 01329 221010
E-mail: info@wardint.co.uk
Web site: www.wardint.com

Driver Supply

WEBB'S
St Peters Farm, Middle Drove, Peterborough PE14 8JJ
Tel: 01945 430123
E-mail: webb-s-cant@fsbdial.co.uk

Driver Training

ADG TRANSPORT CONSULTANCY
Oak Cottage, Royal Oak, Machen CF83 8SN
Tel: 01633 441491
Fax: 01633 440591
E-mail: a.dgettins@btinternet.com

BUZZLINES LTD
Unit G1, Lympne Industrial Park, Hythe CT21 4LR
Tel: 01303 261870
Fax: 01303 230093
Web site: www.buzzlines.co.uk

COACH DIRECT
The Coach House, 22 South Street, Rochford SS4 1BQ
Tel: 0870 550 2069
Fax: 0870 070 2069
E-mail: info@coachdirect.co.uk
Web site: www.coachdirect.co.uk

***DATS (DAVE'S ACCIDENT & TRAINING SERVICES)**
13 Kingfisher Close, The Willows, Torquay TQ2 7TF
Tel: 07747 686789
E-Mail: daveboulter@btinternet.com
Web site: www.datservices.org

HATTS COACHWORKS & SERVICES
Foxham, Chippenham SN15 4NB
Tel: 01249 740444
Fax: 01249 740447
E-mail: adrian@hattstravel.co.uk
Web site: www.hattstravel.co.uk

***IBPTS**
43 Cage Lane, Felixstowe IP11 9BJ
Tel: 01394 672344
Fax: 01394 672344
E-mail: info@ibpts.com
Web site: www.ibpts.com

INOVAS LTD
1 Glenbervie Business Park, Larbert, Falkirk FK5 4RB
Tel: 01324 682268
Fax: 01324 682269
Web site: www.inovas.co.uk
E-mail: info@inovas.co.uk

***MINIMISE YOUR RISK**
11 Chatsworth Park, Telscombe Cliffs BN10 7DZ
Tel: 01273 580189
Fax: 01273 580189
E-mail: minimise@btconnect.com
Web site: www.minimiseyourrisk.co.uk

OMNIBUS TRAINING LTD
8 Lombard Road, London SW19 3TZ
Tel: 020 8543 4499
Fax: 020 8543 0011
E-mail: enquiries@omnibusltd.com

SKILLPLACE TRAINING
Acacia Avenue, Sandfields Estate, Port Talbot SA12 7DW.
Tel: 01639 899849

***SPECIALIST TRAINING & CONSULTANCY SERVICES LTD**
6 Venture Court, Metcalfe Drive, Altham Industrial Estate, Accrington BB5 5TU
Tel: 0800 3283297
Fax: 01282 687091
E-mail: enquiries@specialisttraining.co.uk
Web site: www.specialisttraining.co.uk

VOSA
Vehicle & Operator Services Agency, Commercial Projects Unit, Berkeley House, Croydon Street, Bristol BS5 0DA
Tel: 0117 954 3359
Fax: 0117 954 3496
E-mail: commercial.training@vosa.gov.uk

Exhibition/Event Organisers

COACH & BUS
PO Box 1359, Leamington Spa CV32 5GT.
Tel: 020 7240 5800.
Fax: 020 7240 5805.
E-mail: info@expom.co.uk
Web site: www.cpt-uk.org

***COACH DISPLAYS LTD**
21 The Poynings, Richings Park, Iver SL0 9DS
Tel: 01753 631170
Fax: 01753 655980
E-mail: info@coachdisplays.co.uk
Web site: www.coachdisplays.co.uk

***EXPO MANAGEMENT LTD**
Unit 3, Jepson Court, Tankred Close, Queensway, Leamington Spa CV31 3RZ
Tel: 01926 888123
Fax: 01926 888004
E-mail: info@expom.co.uk
Web site: www.expom.co.uk

MCI EXHIBITIONS LTD
Starley House, Eaton Road, Coventry CV1 2FH.
Tel: 0870 330 7834.
Fax: 0870 076 3292
E-mail: john@motorcycleshow.co.uk
Web site: www.motorcycleshow.co.uk

Trade Directory

Ferry Operators

*BRITTANY FERRIES GROUP TRAVEL
The Brittany Centre, Wharf Road,
Portsmouth PO2 8RU
Tel: 0870 901 2100
Fax: 0870 901 3100
E-mail: grouptravel@brittany-ferries.com
Web site: www.brittany-ferries.com/grouptravel

CALEDONIAN MACBRAYNE LTD
Head Office, The Ferry Terminal, Gourock
PA19 1QP
Tel: 01475 650100
Web site: www.calmac.co.uk

CONDOR FERRIES LTD
Condor House, New Harbour Road South,
Hamworthy, Poole BH15 4AJ
Tel: 01305 776883
Web site: www.condorferries.co.uk

DFDS SEAWAYS
Scandinavia House, Refinery Road,
Parkeston CO12 4QG
Tel: 08708 488 222
Web site: www.dfdsseaways.com

EUROTUNNEL
PO Box 2000, Folkestone CT18 8XY
Tel: 08702 430401
Fax: 01303 288909
Web site: www.eurotunnel.com

IRISH FERRIES LTD
Groups Department, Salt Island, Holyhead
LL65 1DR
Tel: 0151 236 6921
Web site: www.irishferries.ie
www.irishferries.com

ISLE OF MAN STEAM PACKET COMPANY
Imperial Buildings, Douglas IM1 2BY
Tel: 01624 661661
Tel: 01624 645618
E-mail: resesteam-packet.com
Web site: www.steam-packet.com

NORFOLKLINE
Norfolk House, Eastern Dock, Dover
CT16 1JA
Tel: 0870 870 1020
Web site: www.norfolkline.com

P&O FERRIES
Channel House, Channel View Road, Dover
CT17 9TJ
Tel: 08705 980444
Fax: 08707 625325
E-mail: groups@poferries.com
Web site: www.poferries.com

RED FUNNEL
Red Funnel Travel Centre, 12 Bugle Street,
Southampton SO14 2JY
Tel: 0870 444 8898
E-mail: post@redfunnel.co.uk
Web site: www.redfunnel.co.uk

*SEAFRANCE
Whitfield Court, Honeywood Close, Whitfield
CT16 3PX
Tel: 08705 301 301
Fax: 08700 644 775
E-mail: groups@seafrance.fr
Web site: www.seafrance.com

STENA LINE
Station Approach, Holyhead LL65 1DQ
Tel: 08705 20 44 02
E-mail: groups@stenaline.com
Web site: www.stenaline.co.uk/groups

SUPERFAST FERRIES
The Terminal Building, Port of Rosyth
KY11 2XP
Tel: 0870 234 221
Web site: www.superfast.com

TRANSMANCHE FERRIES
Newhaven-Dieppe
Tel: 0800 917 1201
Web site: www.transmancheferries.co.uk,
www.ldlines.com

WIGHTLINK ISLE OF WIGHT FERRIES
70 Broad Street, Portsmouth PO1 2LB
Tel: 0870 582 7744
Fax: 023 9285 5257
E-mail: sales@wightlink.co.uk
Web site: www.wightlink.co.uk

Finance/Leasing

AD COACH SALES
Newbridge Coach Depot, Witheridge
EX16 8PY
Tel: 01884 860787
Fax: 01884 860711
E-mail: ggoodwin@adcoachsales.co.uk
Web site: www.adcoachsales.co.uk

ARRIVA BUS AND COACH LTD
Lodge Garage, Whitehall Road West,
Gomersal BD19 4BJ.
Tel: 01274 681144.
Fax: 01274 651198.
Web site: www.arriva.co.uk
E-mail: busandcoachsales@arriva.co.uk

DAWSONRENTALS BUS AND COACH LTD
Delaware Drive, Tongwell, Milton Keynes
MK15 8JH
Tel: 01908 218111
Fax: 01908 610156
E-mail: info@dawsongroup.co.uk
Web site: www.dawsongroup.co.uk

HANSAR FINANCE LTD
Bridgeway House, Mellor Road, Cheadle
Hulme SK8 5AU
Tel: 0161 488 4000
Fax: 0161 488 4567
Web site: www.hansar.co.uk

*LHE FINANCE LTD
21 Headlands Business Park, Salisbury
Road, Ringwood BH24 3PB
Tel: 01425 474070
Fax: 01425 474090
E-mail: bhymers@lhefinance.co.uk
Web site: www.lhefinance.co.uk

MCV BUS & COACH LTD
Sterling Place, Elean Business Park, Sutton
CB6 2QE
Tel: 01353 773000
Fax: 01353 773001
E-mail: vernon.edwards@mcv-uk.com

NORTON FOLGATE FG PLC
50A St Andrew Street, Hertford SG14 1JA.
Tel: 01992 537735
Fax: 01992 537733

MISTRAL GROUP (UK) PLC
PO Box 130, Knutsford WA16 6AG
Tel: 0870 2415786
Fax: 0870 241 5784
E-mail: sales@mistral-group.com
Web site: www.mistral-group.com

ROADLEASE
Crossroads, Anston, Sheffield S25 7ES.
Tel: 01909 551177.
Fax: 01909 567994.
E-mail: roadlease@kirkbycoachandbus.com
Web site: www.roadlease.com

VOLVO FINANCIAL SERVICES
Wedgnock Lane, Warwick CV34 5YA
Tel: 01926 498888
Fax: 01926 410278

Graphic Design

ADGROUP LTD
Ad House, East Parade, Harrogate HG1 5LT
Tel: 01423 526253
Fax: 01423 502522
E-mail: info@adbus.info
Web site: www.adbus.info

BEST IMPRESSIONS
15 Starfield Road, London W12 9SN
Tel: 020 8740 6443
Fax: 020 8740 9134
E-mail: talk2us@best-impressions.co.uk
Web site: www.best-impressions.co.uk

FWT
Whittington House, 764-768 Holloway Road,
London N19 3JQ
Tel: 020 7281 2161
Fax: 020 7281 4117
E-mail: sales@fwt.co.uk
Web site: www.fwt.co.uk

HATTS COACHWORKS & SERVICES
Foxham, Chippenham SN15 4NB
Tel: 01249 740444
Fax: 01249 740447
E-mail: adrian@hattstravel.co.uk
Web site: www.hattstravel.co.uk

IMAGE & PRINT GROUP
Unit 9, Oakbank Industrial Estate, Garscube
Road, Glasgow G20 7LU
Tel: 0141 353 1900
Fax: 0141 353 8611

McKENNA BROTHERS LTD
McKenna House, Jubilee Road, Middleton,
Manchester M24 2LX
Tel: 0161 655 3244
Fax: 0161 655 3059
E-mail: info@mckennabrothers.co.uk
Web site: www.mckennabrothers.co.uk

*NEERMAN & PARTNERS
c/o 22 Larbre Crescent, Whickham,
Newcastle-upon-Tyne NE16 5YG
Tel: 0191 488 6258
Fax: 0191 488 9158
Web site: www.neerman.net
E-mail: info@neerman.net

*PLUM PUBLISHING
Suite 1, Cornerstone House, Stafford Park
13, Telford TF3 3AZ
Tel: 01952 204920
Web site: www.busandcoach.com

Trade Directory

*RH BODYWORKS
A140 Ipswich Road, Brome, Eye IP23 8AW
Tel: 01379 870666
Fax: 01379 872138
E-mail: mike.ball@rhbodyworks.co.uk
Web site: www.rhbodyworks.co.uk

TIME TRAVEL UK
247 Bradford Road, Stanningley, Pudsey LS28 6QB
Tel: 0113 255 1188
E-mail: nick.baldwin@tinyworld.co.uk

*TITAN BUS UK LTD
52 East Parade, Harrogate HG1 5LT
Tel: 01423 526253
Fax: 01423 502522
E-mail: info@titanbus.co.uk
Web site: www.titanbus.co.uk

*VETRO DESIGN
247 Bradford Road, Pudsey, Leeds LS28 6QB
Tel: 01132 551188
E-mail: nick@vetrodesign.co.uk

Hotels

CALOTELS HOTELS
88 Jordan Avenue, Stretton, Burton-on-Trent DE13 0JD
Tel: 01283 542455
Fax: 01283 542455

CIE TOURS INTERNATIONAL
Loveitts Farm, Brinklow CV23 0LG
Tel: 01788 833388
Fax: 01788 833710
E-mail: anne@ciegroups.freeserve.co.uk
Web site: www.cietours.co.uk

GRASSHOPPER INN
Moorhouse, Westerham TN16 2EU
Tel: 01959 563136
E-mail: info@grasshopperinn.co.uk
Web site: www.grasshopperinn.co.uk

STAGE HOTEL – LEICESTER
299 Leicester Road, (A5199) Wigston Fields, Leicester LE18 1JW
Tel: 0116 288 6161
Fax: 0116 281 1874

TRAVELPATH 3000
PO Box 32, Grantham NG31 7JA
Tel: 01476 570187
Fax: 01476 572718
E-mail: jon@travelpath-uk.com
Web site: www.travelpath3000.com

Insurance

BELMONT INTERNATIONAL LTD
Becket House, Vestry Road, Otford, Sevenoaks TN14 5EL
Tel: 01732 744700
Fax: 01732 744726
ite: www.belmontint.com
E-mail: sales@belmontint.com

R. L. DAVISON & CO LTD
Bury House, 31 Bury Street, London EC3A 5AH.
Tel: 020 7816 9876
Fax: 020 7816 9880

P J HAYMAN & CO LTD
Stansted House, Rowlands Castle PO9 6BR
Tel: 0845 6020 020
Web site: www.pjhayman.com

OMNI WHITTINGTONS
Arthur Castle House, 33 Creechurch Lane, London EC3A 5EB
Tel: 020 7709 9991
Fax: 020 7456 1225.

*RIGTON INSURANCE SERVICES LTD
Chevin House, Otley Road, Guiseley LS20 8BH
Tel: 01943 879539
Fax: 01943 875529
E-mail: enquiries@rigtoninsurance.co.uk
Web site: www.rigtoninsurance.co.uk

*TOWERGATE CHAPMAN STEVENS
Towergate House, 22 Wintersells Road, Wintersells Business Park, Byfleet KT14 7LF
Tel: 01932 331440
Fax: 01932 351238
E-mail: tcs@towergate.co.uk
Web site: www.towergate.co.uk

VOLVO INSURANCE SERVICES
Wedgnock Lane, Warwick CV34 5YA
Tel: 01926 401777.
Fax: 01926 407407.
Web site: www.volvo.com

WILLIS LTD
10 Trinity Square, London EC3P 3AX
Tel: 020 7488 8111
Fax: 020 7975 2884
E-mail: warren.dann@willis.com
Web site: www.willis.com

WILSURE INSURANCE BROKERS
9 Crusader Business Park, Stephenson Road West, Clacton on Sea CO15 4TN.
Tel: 01255 420564.
Fax: 01255 222764.
E-mail: info@wilsure.co.uk
Web site: www.wilsure.co.uk

WRIGHTSURE GROUP
799 London Road, West Thurrock RM20 3LH.
Tel: 01708 865553.
Fax: 01708 865100.
E-mail: info@wrightsure.com
Web site: www.wrightsure.com

Legal & Operations Advisers

*BORLAND, WINDER-DIXON LLP
Axe View, Axe Road, Drimpton, Beaminster DT8 3RJ
Tel: 01460 72769
E-mail: chris.borland@tiscali.co.uk

COACH DIRECT
The Coach House, 22 South Street, Rochford SS4 1BQ
Tel: 0870 550 2069
Fax: 0870 070 2069
E-mail: info@coachdirect.co.uk
Web site: www.coachdirect.co.uk

FREIGHT TRANSPORT ASSOCIATION
Hermes House, St John's Road, Tunbridge Wells TN4 9UZ.
Tel: 01892 526171
Fax: 01892 534989
E-mail: enquiries@fta.co.uk
Web site: www.fta.co.uk

*IBPTS
43 Cage Lane, Felixstowe IP11 9BJ
Tel: 01394 672344
Fax: 01394 672344
E-mail: info@ibpts.com
Web site: www.ibpts.com

KERNOW ASSOCIATES
18 Tresawla Court, Tolvaddon, Camborne TR14 0HF.
Tel/Fax: 01209 711870.
E-mail: 106472.3264@compuserve.com

*MINIMISE YOUR RISK
11 Chatsworth Park, Telscombe Cliffs BN10 7DZ
Tel: 01273 580189
Fax: 01273 580189
E-mail: minimise@btconnect.com
Web site: www.minimiseyourrisk.co.uk

*PROFESSIONAL TRANSPORT SERVICES
12 Silverdale, Stanford-le-Hope SS17 8BG
Tel: 01375 675262
Web site: www.proftranserv.co.uk
E-mail: enquiries@proftranserv.com

WARD INTERNATIONAL CONSULTING LTD
Funtley Court, 19 Funtley Hill, Fareham PO16 7UY
Tel: 01329 280280
Fax: 01329 221010
E-mail: info@wardint.co.uk
Web site: www.wardint.com

WEDLAKE SAINT
14 John Street, London WC1N 2EB.
Tel: 020 7405 9446.
Fax: 020 7242 9877.

Life Insurance & Pensions

WILSURE INSURANCE BROKERS
9 Crusader Business Park, Stephenson Road West, Clacton on Sea CO15 4TN.
Tel: 01255 420564.
Fax: 01255 222764.
E-mail: info@wilsure.co.uk
Web site: www.wilsure.co.uk

Livery Design

ADGROUP LTD
Ad House, East Parade, Harrogate HG1 5LT
Tel: 01423 526253
Fax: 01423 502522
E-mail: info@adbus.info
Web site: www.adbus.info

BEST IMPRESSIONS
15 Starfield Road, London W12 9SN
Tel: 020 8740 6443
Fax: 020 8740 9134
E-mail: talk2us@best-impressions.co.uk
Web site: www.best-impressions.co.uk

Trade Directory

DRURY & DRURY
Unit 6, Cobbs Wood Industrial Estate, Brunswick Road, Ashford TN23 1EH.
Tel: 01303 610555.
Fax: 01303 610666.
E-mail: martinstrange@channelcommercials.co.uk

TONY GREAVES GRAPHICS
19 Perth Mount, Horsforth, Leeds LS18 5SH
Tel/Fax: 0113 258 4795
E-mail: tony@greavesgraphics.fsnet.co.uk

HATTS COACHWORKS & SERVICES
Foxham, Chippenham SN15 4NB
Tel: 01249 740444
Fax: 01249 740447
E-mail: adrian@hattstravel.co.uk
Web site: www.hattstravel.co.uk

McKENNA BROTHERS LTD
McKenna House, Jubilee Road, Middleton, Manchester M24 2LX
Tel: 0161 655 3244
Fax: 0161 655 3059
E-mail: info@mckennabrothers.co.uk
Web site: www.mckennabrothers.co.uk

*NEERMAN & PARTNERS
c/o 22 Larbre Crescent, Whickham, Newcastle-upon-Tyne NE16 5YG
Tel: 0191 488 6258
Fax: 0191 488 9158
Web site: www.neerman.net
E-mail: info@neerman.net

*PLUM PUBLISHING
Suite 1, Cornerstone House, Stafford Park 13, Telford TF3 3AZ
Tel: 01952 204920
Web site: www.busandcoach.com

TIME TRAVEL UK
247 Bradford Road, Stanningley, Pudsey LS28 6QB
Tel: 0113 255 1188
E-mail: nick.baldwin@tinyworld.co.uk

*TITAN BUS UK LTD
52 East Parade, Harrogate HG1 5LT
Tel: 01423 526253
Fax: 01423 502522
E-mail: info@titanbus.co.uk
Web site: www.titanbus.co.uk

*VETRO DESIGN
247 Bradford Road, Pudsey, Leeds LS28 6QB
Tel: 01132 551188
E-mail: nick@vetrodesign.co.uk

Maps for the Bus Industry

BEST IMPRESSIONS
15 Starfield Road, London W12 9SN
Tel: 020 8740 6443
Fax: 020 8740 9134
E-mail: talk2us@best-impressions.co.uk
Web site: www.best-impressions.co.uk

FIGUREHEAD DATA SYSTEMS
Felindre, Swansea SA5 7PP
Tel: 01792 883155
Fax: 01792 884934
E-mail: BusTimes@aol.com
Web site: www.bustimes.com

FWT
Whittington House, 764-768 Holloway Road, London N19 3JQ
Tel: 020 7281 2161
Fax: 020 7281 4117
E-mail: sales@fwt.co.uk
Web site: www.fwt.co.uk

TONY GREAVES GRAPHICS
19 Perth Mount, Horsforth, Leeds LS18 5SH
Tel/Fax: 0113 258 4795
E-mail: tony@greavesgraphics.fsnet.co.uk

IMAGE & PRINT GROUP
Unit 9, Oakbank Industrial Estate, Garscube Road, Glasgow G20 7LU.
Tel: 0141 353 1900.
Fax: 0141 353 8611.
E-mail: alan@imageandprint.co.uk
Web site: www.imageandprint.co.uk

*OMNIBUS
Hollinwood Business Centre, Albert Street, Hollinwood, Oldham OL8 3QL
Tel: 0161 683 3100
Fax: 0161 683 3102
Web site: www.omnibus-systems.co.uk

PINDAR PLC
31 Edison Road, Aylesbury HP19 8TE
Tel: 01296 390100
Fax: 01296 381233
Web site: www.pindar.com

TIME TRAVEL UK
247 Bradford Road, Stanningley, Pudsey LS28 6QB
Tel: 0113 255 1188
E-mail: nick.baldwin@tinyworld.co.uk

*VETRO DESIGN
247 Bradford Road, Pudsey, Leeds LS28 6QB
Tel: 01132 551188
E-mail: nick@vetrodesign.co.uk

Marketing Services

ADG TRANSPORT CONSULTANCY
Oak Cottage, Royal Oak, Machen CF83 8SN
Tel: 01633 441491
Fax: 01633 440591
E-mail: a.dgettins@btinternet.com

AVENTA
66B Victoria Road, Horley RH6 7DZ.
Tel: 01293 825001.
Fax: 01293 825002.
E-mail: info@aventa.co.uk
Web site: www.aventa.co.uk

COACH DIRECT
The Coach House, 22 South Street, Rochford SS4 1BQ
Tel: 0870 550 2069
Fax: 0870 070 2069
E-mail: info@coachdirect.co.uk
Web site: www.coachdirect.co.uk

*CREATIVE MANAGEMENT DEVELOPMENT LTD
52 Okebourne Park, Liden, Swindon SN3 6AJ
Tel: 07771 732185
Fax: 01793 491786
E-mail: jowencmd@aol.com
Web site: www.cmd-training.co.uk

KERNOW ASSOCIATES
18 Tresawla Court, Tolvaddon, Camborne TR14 0HF.
Tel/Fax: 01209 711870.
E-mail: 106472.3264@compuserve.com

Mechanical Investigation

KERNOW ASSOCIATES
18 Tresawla Court, Tolvaddon, Camborne TR14 0HF.
Tel/Fax: 01209 711870.
E-mail: 106472.3264@compuserve.com

*UNITEC LONDON
Unit 5, Gateway 25, Weston Avenue, West Thurrock RM20 3ZD
Tel: 01708 892440
Fax: 01708 862125
E-mail: london.service@optare.com

*UNITEC ROTHERHAM
Denby Way, Hellaby, Rotherham S66 8HR
Tel: 01709 535101
Fax: 01709 535103
E-mail: rotherham.service@optare.com

*UNITEC SCOTLAND
Unit 7, Cumbernauld Business Park, Ward Park Road, Cumbernauld G67 3JZ
Tel: 01236 726738
Fax: 01236 795651
E-mail: scotland.service@optare.com

On-Bus Advertising

ADGROUP LTD
Ad House, East Parade, Harrogate HG1 5LT
Tel: 01423 526253
Fax: 01423 502522
E-mail: info@adbus.info
Web site: www.adbus.info

BEST IMPRESSIONS
15 Starfield Road, London W12 9SN
Tel: 020 8740 6443
Fax: 020 8740 9134
E-mail: talk2us@best-impressions.co.uk
Web site: www.best-impressions.co.uk

DECKER MEDIA LTD
Decker House, Lowater Street, Carlton, Nottingham NG4 1JJ
Tel: 0115 940 2406
Fax: 0115 940 2407
E-mail: sales@deckermedia.co.uk
Web site: www.deckermedia.co.uk

TIME TRAVEL UK
247 Bradford Road, Stanningley, Pudsey LS28 6QB
Tel: 0113 255 1188
E-mail: nick.baldwin@tinyworld.co.uk

*TITAN BUS UK LTD
52 East Parade, Harrogate HG1 5LT
Tel: 01423 526253
Fax: 01423 502522
E-mail: info@titanbus.co.uk
Web site: www.titanbus.co.uk

Printing/Publishing

*IAN ALLAN PRINTING LTD
Riverdene Business Park, Molesey Road, Hersham KT12 4RG.
Tel: 01932 266600
Fax: 01932 266601
E-mail: jonathan.bingham@ianallanprinting.co.uk
Web site: www.ianallanprinting.co.uk

BEMROSEBOOTH LTD
Stockholm Road, Sutton Fields Industrial Estate, Hull HU7 0XY
Tel: 01482 826343
Fax: 01482 371386
E-mail: lprecious@bemrosebooth.com
Web site: www.bemrosebooth.com

BEST IMPRESSIONS
15 Starfield Road, London W12 9SN
Tel: 020 8740 6443
Fax: 020 8740 9134
E-mail: talk2us@best-impressions.co.uk
Web site: www.best-impressions.co.uk

THE HENRY BOOTH GROUP
Stockholm Road, Sutton Fields Industrial Estate, Hull HU7 0XY
Tel: 01482 826343.
Fax: 01482 839767.
E-mail: mshanley@henrybooth.co.uk
Web site: www.henrybooth.co.uk

FIGUREHEAD DATA SYSTEMS
Felindre, Swansea SA5 7PP
Tel: 01792 883155
Fax: 01792 884934
E-mail: BusTimes@aol.com
Web site: www.bustimes.com

FWT
Whittington House, 764-768 Holloway Road, London N19 3JQ
Tel: 020 7281 2161
Fax: 020 7281 4117
E-mail: sales@fwt.co.uk
Web site: www.fwt.co.uk

TONY GREAVES GRAPHICS
19 Perth Mount, Horsforth, Leeds LS18 5SH
Tel/Fax: 0113 258 4795
E-mail: tony@greavesgraphics.fsnet.co.uk

IMAGE & PRINT GROUP
Unit 9, Oakbank Industrial Estate, Garscube Road, Glasgow G20 7LU
Tel: 0141 353 1900
Fax: 0141 353 8611
E-mail: alan@imageandprint.co.uk
Web site: www.imageandprint.co.uk

*MIDLAND COUNTIES PUBLICATIONS
4 Watling Drive, Hinckley LE10 3EY
Tel: 01455 254400
E-mail:midlandbooks@compuserve.com

PINDAR PLC
31 Edison Road, Aylesbury HP19 8TE
Tel: 01296 390100
Fax: 01296 381233
Web site: www.pindar.com

*PLUM PUBLISHING
Suite 1, Cornerstone House, Stafford Park 13, Telford TF3 3AZ
Tel: 01952 204920
Web site: www.busandcoach.com

TIME TRAVEL UK
247 Bradford Road, Stanningley, Pudsey LS28 6QB
Tel: 0113 255 1188
E-mail: nick.baldwin@tinyworld.co.uk

*TRANSPORT STATIONERY SERVICES
61 Bodycoats Road, Chandlers Ford SO53 2HA
Tel: 07041 471008
Fax: 07041 471009
E-mail: info@transportstationeryservices.co.uk

*VETRO DESIGN
247 Bradford Road, Pudsey, Leeds LS28 6QB
Tel: 01132 551188
E-mail: nick@vetrodesign.co.uk

Promotional Material

BEST IMPRESSIONS
15 Starfield Road, London W12 9SN
Tel: 020 8740 6443
Fax: 020 8740 9134
E-mail: talk2us@best-impressions.co.uk
Web site: www.best-impressions.co.uk

FWT
Whittington House, 764-768 Holloway Road, London N19 3JQ
Tel: 020 7281 2161
Fax: 020 7281 4117
E-mail: sales@fwt.co.uk
Web site: www.fwt.co.uk

MARKET ENGINEERING
23a Parsons Street, Banbury OX16 5LY
Tel: 01295 277050
Fax: 01295 297030
E-mail: contact@m-eng.com
Web site: www.marketengineering.com

*OMNIBUS
Hollinwood Business Centre, Albert Street, Hollinwood, Oldham OL8 3QL
Tel: 0161 683 3100
Fax: 0161 683 3102
Web site: www.mnibus-systems.co.uk

PINDAR PLC
31 Edison Road, Aylesbury HP19 8TE
Tel: 01296 390100
Fax: 01296 381233
Web site: www.pindar.com

*PLUM PUBLISHING
Suite 1, Cornerstone House, Stafford Park 13, Telford TF3 3AZ
Tel: 01952 204920
Web site: www.busandcoach.com

STEPHEN C MORRIS
PO Box 119, Shepperton TW17 8UX
Tel: 01932 232574
E-mail: buswriter@btinternet.com

TIME TRAVEL UK
247 Bradford Road, Stanningley, Pudsey LS28 6QB
Tel: 0113 255 1188
E-mail: nick.baldwin@tinyworld.co.uk

TONY GREAVES GRAPHICS
19 Perth Mount, Horsforth, Leeds LS18 5SH
Tel/Fax: 0113 258 4795
E-mail: tony@greavesgraphics.fsnet.co.uk

*VETRO DESIGN
247 Bradford Road, Pudsey, Leeds LS28 6QB
Tel: 01132 551188
E-mail: nick@vetrodesign.co.uk

Publications - Magazines & Books

*BRITISH BUS PUBLISHING LTD
16 St Margarets Drive, Telford TF1 3PH
Tel: 01952 255669
E-mail: bill@britishbuspublishing.co.uk
Web site: www.britishbuspublishing.co.uk

*BUSES
Ian Allan Publishing Ltd
Riverdene Business Park, Molesey Road, Hersham KT12 4RG.
Tel: 01932 266600
Fax: 01932 266601
Web site: www.busesmag.com

BUS & COACH BUYER
The Publishing Centre, 1 Woolram Wygate, Spalding PE11 1NU
Tel: 01775 711777
Fax: 01775 711777
E-mail: bcbsales@busandcoachbuyer.com

*BUS & COACH PRESERVATION
PO Box 636, Portsmouth PO2 9XR
Tel: 023 9265 5224
E-mail: presbus@aol.com

BUS USER
Bus Users UK, PO Box 320, Portsmouth PO5 3SD
Tel: 023 9281 4493
Fax: 023 9285 3080
Web site: www.bususers.org

COACH & BUS WEEK
3 The Office Village, Cygnet Park, Hampton, Peterborough PE7 8FD
Tel: 01733 293240
Fax: 0845 2802927
E-mail: jacqui.grobler@rouncymedia.co.uk
Web site: www.cbwnet.co.uk

CRONER CCH GROUP LTD
145 London Road, Kingston upon Thames KT2 6SR
Tel: 020 8247 1261
Fax: 020 8547 2638
E-mail: info@croner.cch.co.uk

JANES URBAN TRANSPORT SYSTEMS
163 Brighton Road, Coulsdon CR5 2YH
Tel: 020 8700 3700
Web site: www.janes.com/www.juts.janes.com

*PLUM PUBLISHING
Suite 1, Cornerstone House, Stafford Park 13, Telford TF3 3AZ
Tel: 01952 204920
Web site: www.busandcoach.com

ROUTE ONE
Expo Publishing, Suite 4, Century House, Towermead Business Park, Fletton, Peterborough PE2 9DY
Tel: 0870 241 8745
Fax: 0870 241 8891
E-mail: mike.morgan@route-one.net
Web site: www.route.one.net

SALTIRE COMMUNICATIONS
39 Lilyhill Terrace, Edinburgh EH8 7DR
Tel: 0131 652 0205
E-mail: gavin-booth@btconnect.com

STEPHEN C MORRIS
PO Box 119, Shepperton TW17 8UX
Tel: 01932 232574
E-mail: buswriter@btinternet.com

TRAMWAYS & URBAN TRANSIT/LRTA PUBLICATIONS
13A The Precinct, Broxbourne EN10 7HY
Web site: www.lrta.org

TIME TRAVEL UK
247 Bradford Road, Stanningley, Pudsey LS28 6QB
Tel: 0113 255 1188
E-mail: nick.baldwin@tinyworld.co.uk

*TRANSIT MAGAZINE
Quadrant House, 250 Kennington Lane, London SE11 5RD
Tel: 0845 270 7954
Fax: 0845 270 7961
E-mail: ed.transit@landor.co.uk
Web site: www.transitmagazine.co.uk

*VETRO DESIGN
247 Bradford Road, Pudsey, Leeds LS28 6QB
Tel: 01132 551188
E-mail: nick@vetrodesign.co.uk

Quality Management Systems

FTA VEHICLE INSPECTION SERVICE
Hermes House, St John's Road, Tunbridge Wells TN4 9UZ.
Tel: 01892 526171
Fax: 01892 534989
E-mail: enquiries@fta.co.uk
Web site: www.fta.co.uk

*OMNIBUS
Hollinwood Business Centre, Albert Street, Hollinwood, Oldham OL8 3QL
Tel: 0161 683 3100
Fax: 0161 683 3102
Web site: www.mnibus-systems.co.uk

*PROFESSIONAL TRANSPORT SERVICES
12 Silverdale, Stanford-le-Hope SS17 8BG
Tel: 01375 675262
Web site: www.proftranserv.co.uk
E-mail: enquiries@proftranserv.com

VCA
No1, The Estate Office Centre, Eastgate Road, Bristol BS5 6XX
Tel: 0117 952 4126
Fax: 0117 952 4104
E-mail: paul.cooke@vca.gov.uk
Web site: www.vca.gov.uk

VOSA COMMERCIAL PROJECTS UNIT
Berkeley House, Croydon Street, Bristol BS5 0DA
Tel: 0117 954 3359
Fax: 0117 954 3496
E-mail: commercial.training@vosa.gov.uk

Recruitment

*ANTAL INTERNATIONAL NETWORK
Kestrel House, 111 Heath Road, Twickenham, Middlesex TW1 1AF
Contact: Breen Coyne
Tel: 0870 770 1604
E-Mail: bcoyne@antal.com
Website: Currently under construction

Timetable Production

BEMROSEBOOTH LTD
Stockholm Road, Sutton Fields Industrial Estate, Hull HU7 0XY
Tel: 01482 826343
Fax: 01482 371386
E-mail: lprecious@bemrosebooth.com
Web site: www.bemrosebooth.com

BEST IMPRESSIONS
15 Starfield Road, London W12 9SN
Tel: 020 8740 6443
Fax: 020 8740 9134
E-mail: talk2us@best-impressions.co.uk
Web site: www.best-impressions.co.uk

FIGUREHEAD DATA SYSTEMS
Felindre, Swansea SA5 7PP
Tel: 01792 883155
Fax: 01792 884934
E-mail: BusTimes@aol.com
Web site: www.bustimes.com

FWT
Whittington House, 764-768 Holloway Road, London N19 3JQ
Tel: 020 7281 2161
Fax: 020 7281 4117
E-mail: sales@fwt.co.uk
Web site: www.fwt.co.uk

TONY GREAVES GRAPHICS
19 Perth Mount, Horsforth, Leeds LS18 5SH
Tel/Fax: 0113 258 4795
E-mail: tony@greavesgraphics.fsnet.co.uk

*IBPTS
43 Cage Lane, Felixstowe IP11 9BJ
Tel: 01394 672344
Fax: 01394 672344
E-mail: info@ibpts.com
Web site: www.ibpts.com

IMAGE & PRINT GROUP
Unit 9, Oakbank Industrial Estate, Garscube Road, Glasgow G20 7LU.
Tel: 0141 353 1900.
Fax: 0141 353 8611.
E-mail: alan@imageandprint.co.uk
Web site: www.imageandprint.co.uk

TIME TRAVEL UK
247 Bradford Road, Stanningley, Pudsey LS28 6QB
Tel: 0113 255 1188
E-mail: nick.baldwin@tinyworld.co.uk

*OMNIBUS
Hollinwood Business Centre, Albert Street, Hollinwood, Oldham OL8 3QL
Tel: 0161 683 3100
Fax: 0161 683 3102
Web site: www.mnibus-systems.co.uk

PINDAR PLC
31 Edison Road, Aylesbury HP19 8TE
Tel: 01296 390100
Fax: 01296 381233
Web site: www.pindar.com

*PROFESSIONAL TRANSPORT SERVICES
12 Silverdale, Stanford-le-Hope SS17 8BG
Tel: 01375 675262
Web site: www.proftranserv.co.uk
E-mail: enquiries@proftranserv.com

SOUTHERN VECTIS PLC
Nelson Road, Newport PO30 1RD.
Tel: 01983 812983.
E-mail: pwhite@southernvectis.com
Web site: www.southernvectis.com

TIME TRAVEL UK
247 Bradford Road, Stanningley, Pudsey LS28 6QB
Tel: 0113 255 1188
E-mail: nick.baldwin@tinyworld.co.uk

TRAVEL INFORMATION SYSTEMS
Grand Union House, 20 Kentish Town Road, London NW1 9NX
Tel: 020 7428 1288
Fax: 020 7267 2745
E-mail: enquiries@travelinfosystems.com
Web site: www.travelinfosystems.com

*VETRO DESIGN
247 Bradford Road, Pudsey, Leeds LS28 6QB
Tel: 01132 551188
E-mail: nick@vetrodesign.co.uk

Tour Wholesalers

ALBATROSS TRAVEL GROUP LTD
Albatross House, 14 New Hythe Lane, Larkfield ME20 6AB
Tel: 01732 879191
Fax: 01732 522968
E-mail: sales@albatross-tours.com
Web site: www.albatross-tours.com

BOTEL LTD
Botel House, 50 Northern Road, Wickersley, Rotherham S66 1EN
Tel: 01709 703535
Fax: 01709 703525
Web site: www.botel.co.uk

CI COACHLINES
Pools Lane, Highwood, Chelmsford CM1 3QL
Tel: 01245 248669
Fax: 01245 603534
E-mail: cicoachlines@btinternet.com

CIE TOURS INTERNATIONAL
Loveitts Farm, Brinklow CV23 0LG
Tel: 01788 833388
Fax: 01788 833710
E-mail: anne@ciegroups.freeserve.co.uk
Web site: www.cietours.co.uk

FJORD LINE
Norway House, Royal Quays, North Shields NE29 6EG
Tel: 0191 296 1313
Fax: 0191 296 1540
E-mail: fjordline.uk@fjordline.com
Web site: www.fjordline.com

*GREATDAYS TRAVEL GROUP
2 Stamford Park Road, Altrincham WA15 9EN
Tel: 0161 928 9966
Fax: 0161 928 1332
E-mail: sales@greatdays.co.uk
Web site: www.greatdays.co.uk

*GREATDAYS TRAVEL GROUP
10A Thurloe Place, London SW7 2RZ
Tel: 020 7584 0748
Fax: 020 7591 0375
E-mail: travel@greatdays.co.uk
Web site: www.greatdays.co.uk

INDEPENDENT COACH TRAVEL (WHOLESALING) LTD
South Quay Travel and Leisure Ltd, Studios 20/21, Colman's Wharf, 45 Morris Road, London E14 6PA
Tel: 020 7538 4627
Fax: 020 7538 8239
E-mail: aheaton@ictsqt.co.uk
Web site: www.ictsqt.co.uk

TRAVELPATH 3000
PO Box 32, Grantham NG31 7JA
Tel: 01476 570187
Fax: 01476 572718
E-mail: jon@travelpath-uk.com
Web site: www.travelpath3000.com

Tourist Venues/Refreshment Facilities

In this section we include brief directions and facilities, where available
Entries listed in county order

KENT

GRASSHOPPER INN
Moorhouse, Westerham TN16 2EU
Tel: 01959 563136
E-mail: info@grasshopperinn.co.uk
Web site: www.grasshopperinn.co.uk
on A25 near Westerham, Kent, close to M25 (jct 5 and 6); coffee, drinks, lunch dinner; large car park with coach bays

LEICESTERSHIRE

BELVOIR CASTLE
Grantham NG32 1PE
Tel: 01476 871004
Fax: 01476 871018
E-mail: mary@belvoircastle.com
Web site: www.belvoircastle.com
West of Grantham between A52 and A607, follow signposts. Castle tours. Group luncheon/light menus.

SURREY

GRASSHOPPER INN
Moorhouse, Westerham TN16 2EU
Tel: 01959 563136
E-mail: info@grasshopperinn.co.uk
Web site: www.grasshopperinn.co.uk
on A25 near Westerham, Kent, close to M25 (jct 5 and 6); coffee, drinks, lunch dinner; large car park with coach bays

SOMERSET

*THE JANE AUSTEN CENTRE
40 Gay Street, Bath BA1 2NT
Tel: 01225 443000
Fax: 01225 443018
Web site: www.janeausten.co.uk

Training Services

BUZZLINES LTD
Unit G1, Lympne Industrial Park, Hythe CT21 4LR
Tel: 01303 261870
Fax: 01303 230093
Web site: www.buzzlines.co.uk

COACH DIRECT
The Coach House, 22 South Street, Rochford SS4 1BQ
Tel: 0870 550 2069
Fax: 0870 070 2069
E-mail: info@coachdirect.co.uk
Web site: www.coachdirect.co.uk

*CREATIVE MANAGEMENT DEVELOPMENT LTD
52 Okebourne Park, Liden, Swindon SN3 6AJ
Tel: 07771 732185
Fax: 01793 491786
E-mail: jowencmd@aol.com
Web site: www.cmd-training.co.uk

*DATS (DAVE'S ACCIDENT & TRAINING SERVICES)
13 Kingfisher Close, The Willows, Torquay TQ2 7TF
Tel: 07747 686789
E-Mail: davepboulter@btinternet.com
Web site: www.datservices.org

GOSKILLS
Concorde House, Trinity Park, Solihull B37 7UQ
Tel: 0121 635 5520
Fax: 0121 635 5521
E-mail: info@goskills.org
Web site: www.goskills.org

*IBPTS
43 Cage Lane, Felixstowe IP11 9BJ
Tel: 01394 672344
Fax: 01394 672344
E-mail: info@ibpts.com
Web site: www.ibpts.com

MARKET ENGINEERING
23a Parsons Street, Banbury OX16 5LY
Tel: 01295 277050
Fax: 01295 297030
E-mail: contact@m-eng.com
Web site: www.marketengineering.com

*MINIMISE YOUR RISK
11 Chatsworth Park, Telscombe Cliffs BN10 7DZ
Tel: 01273 580189
Fax: 01273 580189
E-mail: minimise@btconnect.com
Web site: www.minimiseyourrisk.co.uk

OMNIBUS TRAINING LTD
8 Lombard Road, London SW19 3TZ
Tel: 020 8543 4499
Fax: 020 8543 0011
E-mail: enquiries@omnibusltd.com

*PROFESSIONAL TRANSPORT SERVICES
12 Silverdale, Stanford-le-Hope SS17 8BG
Tel: 01375 675262
Web site: www.proftranserv.co.uk
E-mail: enquiries@proftranserv.com

*SPECIALIST TRAINING & CONSULTANCY SERVICES LTD
6 Venture Court, Metcalfe Drive, Altham Industrial Estate, Accrington BB5 5TU
Tel: 0800 3283297
Fax: 01282 687091
E-mail: enquiries@specialisttraining.co.uk
Web site: www.specialisttraining.co.uk

*TRANSPORT & TRAINING SERVICES LTD
Warrington Business Park, Long Lane, Warrington WA2 8TX
Tel: 01925 243 500
Fax: 01925 243 000
E-mail:enquiries@transporttrainingservices.com
Web site:www.transporttrainingservices.com

Vehicle Certification

VCA
No1, The Estate Office Centre, Eastgate Road, Bristol BS5 6XX
Tel: 0117 952 4126
Fax: 0117 952 4104
E-mail: paul.cooke@vca.gov.uk
Web site: www.vca.gov.uk

section 2
Tendering & Regulatory Authorities

Tendering & Regulatory Authorities etc

PTAs   60
PTEs   60
Passenger Transport Regional Authorities   61
Transport Co-ordinating Officers   61
Traffic Commissioners   64
Office of Fair Trading   64
Department for Transport   64

Passenger Transport Authorities

Greater Manchester PTA:
PO Box 532, Town Hall, Manchester M60 2LA
Tel: 0161 234 3335
Fax: 0161 236 6459
Chmn: Cllr J. R. Jones. **Vice-Chmn**: Cllr A Brett

Merseyside PTA:
24 Hatton Garden, Liverpool L3 2AN
Tel: 0151 227 5181
Fax: 0151 236 2457
Chmn: Cllr Mark Dowd; **Vice-Chmn**: Cllr Hugh G. Lloyd;
Clerk: Steve Maddox; **Gen Man Mersey Tunnels**: John Gillard.
Operates with Merseyside PTE (qv) as Merseytravel.

South Yorkshire PTA:
PO Box 37, Regent Street, Barnsley S70 2PQ.
Tel: 01226 772848.
Web site: www.southyorks.org.uk
Chmn: Cllr J. M. Hoare; **Vice-Chmn**: Cllr M. Edgell;
Clerk/Treasurer: W J Wilkinson.

Tyne & Wear PTA:
Civic Centre, Newcastle upon Tyne NE99 2BN.
Tel: 0191 203 3209.
Fax: 0191 203 3180.
Chmn: Cllr T. D. Marshall; **Vice-Chairman & Monitoring Officer:** E. Holt; **Clerk**: K. G. Lavery; **Deputy Clerk & Treasurer:** D. Johnson; **Engineer**: J. Millar; **Legal advisor**: V. A. Dodds.

West Midlands PTA:
Room 120, Centro House, 16 Summer Lane, Birmingham B19 3SD.
Tel: 0121 214 7507
Fax: 0121 233 1841
Web site: www.wmpta.org.uk
E-mail for Councillors: ptateam@centro.org.uk
E-mail for Committee Team: ptateam@centro.org.uk
Chair: Cllr G Clarke **Vice-Chair**: Cllr P Allen
Clerk: Ms S Manzie **Deputy Clerk/Solicitor**: C Hinde **Treasurer**: Ms A Ridgewell
Head of Communications: Conrad Jones

West Yorkshire PTA:
Wellington House, 40-50 Wellington Street, Leeds LS1 2DE.
Tel: 0113 251 7272.
Fax: 0113 251 7373.
Chmn: Cllr J S King; **Vice-Chmn**: Cllr K Hussain
Clerk to the Authority: K T Preston, OBE.

Passenger Transport Executives

GMPTE

9 Portland Street, Manchester M60 1HX **Tel**: 0161 242 6000
Web site: www.gmpte.com
GMPTE is responsible to the Greater Manchester Passenger Transport Authority. The PTE is responsible for contracting socially necessary bus services and supporting the local rail service. It also owns the Metrolink light rail system on behalf of the Authority and is responsible for planning for the future of the Metrolink network.
GMPTE and the Authority are also committed to developing accessible transport, funding Ring and Ride, a fully accessible door to door transport service for people with mobility difficulties.
The PTE administers the concessionary fares scheme, which allows participants (pensioners, children and people with disabilities) either free or reduced rate travel. GMPTE owns and is responsible for the upkeep of bus stations and on-street infrastructure. It also provides information about public transport through telephone information lines, timetables, general publicity and Travelshops.

Interim Director General: David Leather
Deputy Director, General & Finance Director: Geoff Inskip
Strategy Director: Keith Howcroft
Projects Director: Michael Renshaw
Organisational Development Director: Urvashi Bramwell
Service Delivery Director: Denise Lennox

Merseyside Passenger Transport Authority and Executive (Merseytravel)

24 Hatton Garden, Liverpool L3 2AN **Tel**: 0151 227 5181
Fax: 0151 236 2457 **Web site**: www.merseytravel.gov.uk
Merseytravel ensures the availability of public transport in Merseyside, including financial support for the Merseyrail rail network and those bus services not provided for by the private sector.
It also promotes public transport by providing bus stations and infrastructure, comprehensive travel tickets and free travel with minimum restrictions for the elderly and those with mobility difficulties.
Merseytravel also owns and operates the Mersey ferries and Mersey tunnels.
Chair to PTA: Cllr M Dowd. **Vice-Chair to PTA**: Cllr H. Lloyd. **Chief Executive PTA & Director General PTE**: Neil Scales OBE. **Clerk to PTA:** Steve Maddox. **Director of Resources:** John Wilkinson. **Director of Resources**: Jim Barclay **Director of Operations:** Alan Stilwell

Nexus (Tyne & Wear PTE)

Nexus House, St James Boulevard, Newcastle upon Tyne NE1 4AX
Tel: 0191 203 3333 **Fax**: 0191 203 3180
Director General: Bernard Garner
Director, Metro: Mick Carbro
Web site: www.nexus.org.uk
Metro: www.tyneandwearmetro.co.uk
Nexus operates within the policies of the Tyne & Wear Passenger Transport Authority. Nexus owns and operates both the Tyne & Wear Metro system and the Shields Ferry (between North Shields and South Shields). Nexus ensures that bus services not operated commercially are provided where there is evidence of social need; operates a demand-responsive transport system, U-call; and organises the provision of special transport for those who can only use ordinary public transport with difficulty if at all. Nexus adminsters the Concessionary Travel scheme and provides comprehensive travel information and sales outlets for countywide season tickets, as well as related administrative support for the scheme.
Rolling Stock: 90 light rail cars. **Ferries**: MFs 'Pride of the Tyne' and 'Shieldsman'

South Yorkshire Passenger Transport Executive

PO Box 801, Exchange Street, Sheffield S2 5YT

Director General: Roy Wicks
Pass Services Director: David Brown
Tel: 0114 276 7575 **Fax**: 0114 275 9908
Web site: www.sypte.co.uk
The Executive is responsible to the South Yorkshire Passenger Transport Authority.

*Centro (West Midlands Passenger Transport Executive)

Centro House, 16 Summer Lane, Birmingham B19 3SD **Tel**: 0121 200 2787
Fax: 0121 214 7010
Web site: www.centro.org.uk
The Executive is responsible to the West Midlands Passenger Transport Authority
Director General: Geoff Inskip
Services Director: Robert Smith
Projects Director: Tom Magrath
Resources Director: Trevor Robinson
Member of Executive/Treasurer to PTA: Angie Rigwell
PTA Committee: Dan Essex, Marion Cheatham

West Yorkshire Passenger Transport Executive (Metro)

Wellington House, 40-50 Wellington Street, Leeds LS1 2DE
Tel: 0113 251 7272 **Fax**: 0113 251 7333
Web site: www.wymetro.com
WYPTE activities are conducted under the corporate name Metro. Metro is financed and supported by the West Yorkshire Passenger Transport Authority.
Director General: Kieran Preston, OBE **Dir Corp Sers**: Sheena Pickersgill **Dir Pass Sers**: John Henkel **Dir Projects**: John Carr

Passenger Transport Regional Authorities

Strathclyde Partnership for Transport (SPT)

Consort House, 12 West George Street, Glasgow G2 1HN
Tel: 0141 332 6811   **Fax**: 0141 332 3076
Web site: www.spt.co.uk
Dirof bus ops: Eric Stewart

Transport *for* London

Windsor House, 42-50 Victoria Street, London SW1H 0TL
Tel: 020 7941 4500
Web Site: www.tfl.gov.uk
Transport *for* London (T*f*L) took over most of the functions of London Transport from July 2000. It is under the control of the Mayor of London and Greater London Authority. TfL assumed control of London Underground Ltd in 2003.
Commissioner for Transport: Peter Hendy, CBE
Managing Director Surface Transport: David Brown
Director of Operations: Mike Weston
Coach Manager: Darek Podwiazka
Director of Road Safety Unit: Chris Lines
Director of the Congestion Charge: Malcolm Murray-Clark
Traffic Manager: Nick Morris
Managing Director for London Rail: Ian Brown
Head of London Trams: Phil Hewitt

T*f*L subsidiary companies:

London Buses Ltd
172 Buckingham Palace Road, London SW1W 9TN.
Tel: 020 7222 5600.
Director of Performance: Clare Kavanagh

Victoria Coach Station Ltd
164 Buckingham Palace Road, London SW1W 9TP.
Tel: 020 7730 3466. **Fax**: 020 7730 2589

London River Services Ltd
55 Broadway, London SW1H 0BD. **Tel**: 020 7222 5600.

London Underground Ltd
55 Broadway, London SW1H 0BD. **Tel**: 020 7222 5600
Managing Director: Tim O'Toole

Transport Co-ordinating Officers

Under the Transport Act 1978 the non-Metropolitan Counties were given power to co-ordinate public transport facilities in their areas. From 1 April 1996 Welsh Counties and Scottish Regions were replaced by new single-tier authorities. At the same time certain English Counties were replaced by new single-tier authorities. The major role is now to secure socially necessary services which are not provided commercially. The names of most of the responsible officers are set out below.

ENGLAND

Bedfordshire County Council - Chris Pettifer, Integrated Passenger Transport Manager, Integrated Passenger Transport Unit, Bedfordshire County Council, County Hall, Cauldwell Street, Bedford MK42 9AP
Tel: 01234 228881

Bracknell Forest Borough Council - R. Cook, Time Square, Bracknell RG12 1JD
Tel: 01344 424642.

Buckinghamshire - R. Slevin, County Passenger Transport Officer, County Hall, Aylesbury HP20 1YZ.
Tel: 01296 383751. **Fax**: 01296 383749.

Cambridgeshire - B. E. Jackson, Head of Passenger Transport, Department of Environment & Transport, Mailbox ET1015, Shire Hall, Castle Hill, Cambridge CB3 0AP.
Tel: 01223 717744. **Fax**: 01223 717789.

Cheshire - G. Goddard, County Transport Co-ordinator, Rivacre Business Centre, Mill Lane, Ellesmere Port CH66 3TL.
Tel: 01244 603218. **Fax**: 01244 603200.

*****Cornwall** - County Hall, Truro TR1 3AY
Tel: 01872 322003 **Fax**: 01872 323844
E-mail: enquiries@cornwall.gov.uk
Web site: www.cornwall.gov.uk

*****Cumbria County Council** - Lonsdale Building, The Courts, Carlisle CA3 8NA
Tel: 01228 606720 **Fax**: 01228 606755
E-mail: graham.whiteley@cumbriacc.gov.uk
Web site: www.cumbriacc.gov.uk

Derbyshire - T. M. Hardy, Public Transport Manager, County Hall, Matlock DE4 3AG
Tel: 01629 580000. **Fax**: 01629 585740.

*****Devon** - Bruce Thompson, Transport Co-ordination Service Manager, Matford Offices, County Hall, Exeter EX2 4QW
Tel: 01392 383244 **Fax**: 01392 382904
E-mail: bruce.thompson@devon.gov.uk
Web site: www.devon.gov.uk

*****Dorset** - Barry Thirlwall, Passenger Transport Manager, County Hall, Dorchester DT1 1XJ
Tel: 01305 224537 **Fax**: 01305 225166
E-mail: b.thirlwall@dorsetcc.gov.uk
Web site: www.dorsetcc.gov.uk

Durham - Adrian J White, Business Manager Public Transport, Environment Dept, County Hall, Durham DH1 5UQ.
Tel: 0191 383 3435 **Fax**: 0191 383 4096

*****East Riding of Yorkshire Council** - Passenger Services, The Offices, Beverley Depot, Annie Reed Road, Beverley HU17 0LF
Tel: 01482 395529 **Fax**: 01482 395090

East Sussex - N Smith, Group Manager (Passenger Transport), Transport & Environment, East Sussex County Council, County Hall, St Anne's Crescent, Lewes BN7 1UE.
Tel: 01273 482326. **Fax**: 01273 474361.
E-mail: nick.smith@eastsussexcc.gov.uk

Essex - J Pope, Group Manager, Passenger Transport, Highways & Transportation, County Hall, Chelmsford CM1 1QH
Tel: 01245 437506 **Fax**: 01245 496764
Web site: www.essexcc.gov.uk

Gloucestershire - Operations & Procurement Manager, Shire Hall, Bearland, Gloucester GL1 2TH
Tel: 01452 425968

Hampshire - K Wilcox, Head of Passenger Transport, Hampshire County Council, Environment Department, The Castle, Winchester SO23 8UD.
Tel: 01962 846997 **Fax**: 01962 845855
E-mail: keith.wilcox@hants.gov.uk

Hartlepool Borough Council – Ian Jopling, Transport Team Leader, Department of Neighbourhood Services, Bryan Hanson House, Hanson Square, Hartlepool TS24 7BT
Tel: 01429 284140 **Fax**: 01429 860830
E-mail: ian.jopling@hartlepool.gov.uk
Web site: www.hartlepool.gov.uk

Hertfordshire County Council Passenger Transport Unit, PO Box 99, Hertford SG13 8TJ
Tel: 01992 556725
Web site: www.intalink.org.uk

Tendering & Regulatory Authorities

Hull City Council
Web site: www.hullcc.gov

Isle of Wight Council - A A Morris, Transport Manager, Jubilee Stores, The Quay, Newport PO30 2EH
Tel: 01983 823710. Fax: 01983 823707.

Kent County Council - Julia Seaward, Head of Transport, Commercial Services, Kent County Council, Gibson Drive, Kings63Hill, West Malling ME19 4QG
Tel: 01622 605091 Fax: 01622 605084
E-mail: passenger.transport@kent.gov.uk
Web site: www.kentpublictransport.info

Lancashire - Stuart Wrigley, Head of Transport Policy, PO Box 9, Guild House, Cross Street, Preston PR1 8RD
Tel: 01772 534660. Fax: 01772 533833

Leicestershire - Tony Kirk, Group Manager (Public Transport), Department of Highways, Transportation & Waste Management, County Hall, Glenfield, Leicester LE3 8RJ
Tel: 0116 265 6270 Fax: 0116 265 7181
E-mail: tkirk@leics.gov.uk
Web site: www.leics.gov.uk

Lincolnshire - A R Cross, Head of Transport Services, 4th Floor, City Hall, Beaumont Fee, Lincoln LN1 1DN
Tel: 01522 553132 Fax: 01522 568735

Norfolk - Tracey Jessop, Head of Passenger Transport, Department of Planning & Transportation, County Hall, Martineau Lane, Norwich NR1 2SG
Tel: 01603 224368 Fax: 01603 222144

Northamptonshire - Sustainable Transport Manager, Northamptonshire County Council,Riverside House, Riverside Way, Bedford Road, Northampton NN1 5NX
Tel: 01604 236711

Northumberland - John Hodgson, Network Development Officer, Integrated Transport Unit, Community and Environmental Services Directorate, Northumberland County Council, County Hall, Morpeth NE61 2EF
Tel: 01670 534837 Fax: 01670 533086
E-mail: jhodgson@northumberland.gov.uk

North Yorkshire - R Owens, Passenger Transport Officer, County Hall, Northallerton DL7 8AH
Tel: 01609 780780, Ext 2870 Fax: 01609 779838

Nottinghamshire County Council - County Hall, West Bridgford, Nottingham NG2 7QP
Tel: 0115 982 3823 E-mail: enquiries@nottscc.gov.uk
Web site: www.nottinghamshire.gov.uk

Oxfordshire - R Helling, Public Transport Officer, Environmental Services, Speedwell House, Speedwell Street, Oxford OX1 1NE
Tel: 01865 815859 Fax: 01865 815085

Reading Borough Council – Mrs P Baxter, Civic Centre, Reading RG1 7TD
Tel: 0118 939 0813

Shropshire - K R Gallop, Principal Passenger Transport Officer, Environment Department, The Shirehall, Abbey Foregate, Shrewsbury SY2 6ND
Tel: 01743 253031 Fax: 01743 254382

Slough Borough Council - R Fraser, PO Box 570, Slough SL1 1FA

Somerset County Council - County Hall, The Crescent, Taunton TA20 1JS
Tel: 01823 356700 Fax: 01823 351356
E-mail: transport@somerset.gov.uk
Web site: www.somerset.gov.uk

Staffordshire - Charles Soutar, Head of Passenger Transport, Development Services Department, Riverway, Stafford ST16 3TJ
Tel: 01785 276735 Fax: 01785 276621

Suffolk - M Bradshaw, Public Transport Manager, Environment & Transport Department, Endeavour House, 8 Russell Road, Ipswich IP1 2BX
Tel: 01473 265050 Fax: 01473 216884
E-mail: mitchell.bradshaw@et.suffolkcc.gov.uk

Surrey County Council - A Teer, Group Manager Passenger Transport, Room 306, County Hall, Penrhyn Road, Kingston-on-Thames KT1 2DY
Tel: 020 8541 9371 Fax: 020 8541 9389
E-mail: alan.teer@surreycc.gov.uk
Web site: surreycc.gov.uk/passenger_transport

Warwickshire - K McGovern, Passenger Tranport Operations Manager, Warwickshire County Council, Environment & Economy Directorate, PO Box 43, Shire Hall, Warwick CV34 4SX
Tel: 01926 412930 Fax: 01926 418041
E-mail: passengertransport@warwickshire.gov.uk
Web site: www.warwickshire.gov.uk

West Berkshire Council - J Sherry, Market Street, Newbury
Tel: 01635 42400

West Sussex County Council - Mark Miller, Group Manager, Transport Co-ordination, Highways and Transport, The Grange, Tower Street, Chichester PO19 1RH
Tel: 01243 777811 Web site: www.westsussex.gov.uk

Wiltshire - I White, Passenger Transport Co-ordinator, Environmental Services Dept, County Hall, Trowbridge BA14 8JD
Tel: 01225 713322 Fax: 01225 713565

Royal Borough of Windsor & Maidenhead – E Mouser, Yorkstream House, St Ives Road, Maidenhead SL6 1RF
Tel: 01628 796732 Fax: 01628 796774

Wokingham - Roland Clausen-Thue, Transport, Environment Service, Shute End, Wokingham RG40 1WL
Tel: 0118 974 6468 Fax: 0118 974 6486

Worcestershire County Council - Passenger Transport Group, POBox 82, Pershore Lane, Worcester WR4 0AA
Tel: 01905 768411 Fax: 01905 768438
Web site: www.worcestershire.gov.uk

WALES

*Anglesey - Isle of Anglesey County Council,Highways & Transportation Service, Council Offices, Llangefni LL65 2UY
Tel: 01248 752457 Fax: 01248 724839
E-mail: dwrpl@anglesey.gov.uk Web site: www.anglesey.gov.uk

Blaenau Gwent - Blaenau Gwent County Borough Council, Municipal Offices, Civic Centre, Ebbw Vale NP3 6XB
Tel: 01495 350555. Fax: 01495 301255

Bridgend County Borough Council - D H Beynon, Transport Co-ordinating Manager, Transport & Engineering, Morien House, Bennet Street, Bridgend CF31 3SH
Tel: 01656 643643. Fax: 01656 668126
Web site: www.bridgend.gov.uk

*Caerphilly County Borough Council - Huw Morgan, Principal Passenger Transport Officer, Council Offices, Pontllanfraith, Blackwood NP12 2YW.
Tel: 01495 235089 Fax: 01495 235045
E-mail: morgash@caerphilly.gov.uk
Web site: www.caerphilly.gov.uk

Cardiff - Cardiff County Council, Traffic & Transportation Service, County Hall, Atlantic Wharf, Cardiff CF10 4UW

Carmarthenshire: Dir of Economic Development: Gerald Campbell Phillips. Carmarthenshire County Council, County Hall, Carmarthen SA31 1JP.
Tel: 01267 234567. Fax: 01267 230848.

Ceredigion: Cyngor Sir Ceredigion, County Council, County Hall, Market Street, Aberaeron SA46 0AT.
Tel: 01545 572501 Fax: 01545 571089

Conwy - Conwy County Borough Council, Bodlondeb, Conwy LL32 8DU.
Tel: 01492 574000, 592114. Fax: 01492 592114.

*Denbighshire - Denbighshire County Council, Transport & Infrastructure Department, Caledfryn, Smithfield Road, Denbigh LL16 3RJ.
Tel: 01824 706847 Fax: 01824 706970
Web site: www.denbighshire.gov.uk

Flintshire County Council - Directorate of Environment & Regeneration, County Hall, Mold CH7 6NG
Tel: 01352 704530 Fax: 01352 704540
Web site: www.flintshire.gov.uk

Gwynedd Council - M Cowban, Public Transport Officer, Council Offices, Shirehall 56, Caernarfon LL55 1SH.
Tel: 01286 679541 Fax: 01286 673324
E-mail: malcolmwaltercowban@gwynnedd.gov.uk

Merthyr Tydfil - Martin Haworth, Senior Transport Officer, Merthyr Tydfil County Borough Council, Civic Centre, Castle Street, Merthyr Tydfil CF47 8AN
Tel: 01685 726288 Fax: 01685 387982
E-mail: martin.howarth@merthyr.gov.uk

*Monmouthshire - Monmouthshire Passenger Transport Unit, County Hall, Cwmbran NP44 2XH
Tel: 01633 644644 **Fax**: 01633 644777 **E-mail**: passengertransportunit@monmouthshire.gov.uk

Neath Port Talbot - Neath Port Talbot County Borough Council, Civic Centre, Port Talbot SA13 1PJ .
Tel: 01639 763333. **Fax:** 01639 763444.

Newport - Dir. of Development/Transport: Brian Adcock, Newport County Borough Council, Civic Centre, Newport NP9 4UR.
Tel: 01633 244491. **Fax**: 01633 244721

Pembrokeshire County Council - M Hubert, Transport and Fleet Manager, County Hall, Haverfordwest SA61 1TP
Tel: 01437 764551 **Fax**: 01437 775008
E-mail: hubert.mathias@pembrokeshire.gov.uk

Powys - Transport Co-ordination Unit, County Hall, Llandrindod Wells LD1 5LG.
Tel: 01597 826260 **Fax**: 01597 826260.

*Rhondda Cynon Taf - Rhondda Cynon Taf County Borough Council, Corporate Transport Unit, Sardis House, Sardis Road, Pontypridd CF37 1DU
Tel: 01443 494816 **Fax** 01443 494875
Web site: www.rhonddacynontaff.gov.uk

*City & County of Swansea - Catherine Swain, Team Leader - Passenger Transport, Environment Department, County Hall, Oystermouth Road, Swansea SA1 3SN
Tel: 01792 636000 **Fax**: 01792 637260
E-mail: transportation.engineering@swansea.gov.uk
Web site: www.swansea.gov.uk

Torfaen - Torfaen County Borough Council, Civic Centre, Pontypool NP4 6YB.
Tel: 01495 762200. **Fax**: 01495 755513.

*Vale of Glamorgan Council - Dock Offices, Barry Docks, Barry CF63 4RT
Tel: 01446 704687 **Fax** 01446 704891
E-mail: planning&transport@valeofglamorgan.gov.uk
Web site: www.valeofglamorgan.gov.uk

Wrexham - Wrexham County Borough Council, Crown Buildings, Chester Street, Wrexham LL13 8BG
Tel: 01978 292000 **Fax**: 01978 292106

SCOTLAND

Aberdeen City - The Director, Environment & Infrastructure Services, Aberdeen City Council, St Nicholas House, Broad Street, Aberdeen AB10 1WL
Tel: 01224 523762. **Fax:** 01224 523764.
E-mail: rwaters@roads.aberdeen.net.uk.
Web site: www.aberdeencity.gov.uk

Aberdeenshire - R McKenzie, Public Transport Manager, Aberdeenshire Council, Woodhill House, Westburn Road, Aberdeen AB16 5GB.
Tel: 01224 664585 **Fax**: 01224 662005
E-mail: richard.mckenzie@aberdeenshire.gov.uk
Web site: www.aberdeenshire.gov.uk

Angus Council - L Millar, Transport Manager, Angus Council, St James House, St James Road, Forfar DD8 2ZD
Tel: 01307 461774 **Fax**: 01307 473711
E-mail: millarle@angus.gov.uk
Web site: www.angus.gov.uk/transport

Argyll and Bute Council - B D Blades, Public Transport Officer, Kilmory, Lochgilphead PA31 8RT
Tel: 01546 604360 **Fax**: 01546 604291
Web site: www.argyll-bute.gov.uk

*Clackmannanshire - Public Transport Officer, Development & Environment Services, Clackmannanshire Council, Kilncraigs, Greenside Street, Alloa FK10 1EB
Tel: 01259 450000

Dundee City - Mark Devine, Transport Officer, Dundee City Council, Planning & Transportation Department, Floor 16, Tayside House, Crichton Street, Dundee DD1 3RB.
Tel: 01382 433831. **Fax**: 01382 433313
E-mail: mark.devine@dundeecity.gov.uk.
Web site: www.dundeecity.gov.uk

Dumfries & Galloway - D Kirkpatrick, Team leader (Passenger Transport), Dumfries & Galloway Council, Militia House, English Street, Dumfries DG1 2HR.
Tel: 01387 260133 **Fax**: 01387 260383

East Ayrshire - East Ayrshire Council, London Road, Kilmarnock KA3 7BU.

East Dunbartonshire - East Dunbartonshire Council, PO Box 4, Civic Way, Kirkintilloch G66 4TJ.

East Lothian - Transport Planning Manager, Department of Planning, East Lothian Council, 25 Court Street, Haddington EH41 3HA.

East Renfrewshire - East Renfrewshire Council, Eastwood Park, Rouken Glen Road, Giffnock G46 6UG.

City of Edinburgh Council - Max Thomson, Public Transport Manager, City Development, 1 Cockburn Street, Edinburgh EH1 1BJ
Tel: 0131 469 3631. **Fax**: 0131 469 3635.
E-mail: max.thomson@edinburgh.gov.uk

Falkirk - Stephen Bloomfield, Public Transport Co-ordinator, Development Services, Falkirk Council, Abbotsfold House, David's Loan, Falkirk FK2 7YZ.
Tel: 01324 504723. **Fax**: 01324 504914.

Fife - Trond Haugen, Transportation Manager - Transportation Services, Fife Council, Fife House, North Street, Glenrothes KY7 5LT.
Tel: 01592 413106. **Fax**: 01592 413061
E-mail: trond.haugen@fife.gov.uk

Highland - Transport Officer, Highland Council, Glenurquhart Road, Inverness IV3 5NX.
Tel: 01463 702612. **Fax**: 01463 702606.

Inverclyde - Inverclyde Council, Municipal Buildings, Greenock PA15 1LY.

Midlothian - Brian Sharkie, Public Transport Manager, Midlothian Council, Fairfield House, 8 Lothian Road, Dalkeith EH22 3ZN.
Tel: 0131 271 3520. **Fax**: 0131 271 3537.
E-mail: brian.sharkie@midlothian.gov.uk

Moray - Peter Findlay, Public Transport Manager, Moray Council, Council Office, Academy Street, Elgin IV30 1LL
Tel: 01343 562541. **Fax**: 01343 545628.
E-mail: peter.findlay@moray.gov.uk.

North Ayrshire - North Ayrshire Council, Cunningham House, Irvine KA12 8EE.

North Lanarkshire - North Lanarkshire Council, Po Box 14, Civic Centre, Motherwell ML1 1TW
Tel: 01224 664580. **Fax**: 01224 662005.

Orkney - Orkney Islands Council, Council Offices, School Place, Kirkwall KW15 1NY.

Perth & Kinross - Andrew J Warrington, Public Transport Manager; The Environment Service, Pullar House, 35 Kinnoull Street, Perth PH1 5GD.
Tel: 01738 476530. **Fax**: 01738 476510.
E-mail: awarrington@pkc.gov.uk

Renfrewshire - Renfrewshire Council, North Building, Cotton Street, Paisley PA1 1WB.

Scottish Borders - B Young, Transport Policy Manager, Scottish Borders Council, Council Headquarters, Newtown St Boswells, Melrose TD6 0SA.
Tel: 01835 824000 **Fax**: 01835 823008

Shetland Islands - Ian Bruce, Service Manager - Transport Operations, Infrastructure Service Dept., Shetland Islands Council, Grantfield, Lerwick ZE1 0NT.
Tel: 01595 744872. **Fax**: 01595 744869.
E-mail: ian.bruce@sic.shetland.gov.uk

South Ayrshire - South Ayrshire Council, County Buildings, Wellington Square, Ayr KA7 1DR.

South Lanarkshire - South Lanarkshire Council, Council Offices, Almada Street, Hamilton ML3 0AA. *(No Public Transport responsibilities - see SPT)*

Stirling - Stirling Council, Council Headquarters, Viewforth, Stirling FK8 2ET.

West Dunbartonshire - West Dunbartonshire Council, Council Offices, Garshake Road, Dunbarton, G82 3PU. (No Public Transport responsibilities - see SPT)

Western Isles - Western Isles Council, Council Offices, Balivanich, Benbecula HS7 5LA.

*West Lothian - Roy Mitchell, Public Transport Manager, West Lothian Council, County Buildings, Linlithgow EH49 7EZ
Tel: 01506 775282. **Fax**: 01506 775265
E-mail: roy.mitchell@westlothian.gov.uk
Web site: www.westlothian.gov.uk

Traffic Commissioners

Web site: www.vosa.gov.uk

EASTERN TRAFFIC AREA
Terrington House, 13-15 Hills Road, Cambridge CB2 1NP
Tel: 01223 531060 **Fax**: 01223 309681
Traffic Commissioner: vacant
Deputy Traffic Commissioners: D. N. Stevens, R. C. Lockwood, M. J. Guy. **Area covered**: Leicestershire, Lincolnshire, Cambridgeshire, Norfolk, Suffolk, Essex, Bedfordshire, Northamptonshire, Hertfordshire, Buckinghamshire.

NORTH EASTERN TRAFFIC AREA
Hillcrest House, 386 Harehills Lane, Leeds LS9 6NF
Tel: 0870 606 0440 **Fax**: 0113 248 9607
Traffic Commissioner: Tom Macartney
Deputy Traffic Commissioners: M. Hinchcliffe, Ms L Perrett, P J Mulvenna
Area covered: Northumberland, Tyne & Wear, Co Durham, Yorkshire, Nottinghamshire
Web site: www.vosa.gov.uk

NORTH WESTERN TRAFFIC AREA
Hillcrest House, 386 Harehills Lane, Leeds LS9 6NF
Tel: 0870 606 0440 **Fax**: 0113 248 9607
Traffic Commissioner: Beverley Bell.
Deputy Traffic Commissioners: M Hinchcliffe, Ms L Perrett, P J Mulvenna
Area covered: Cumbria, Lancashire, Greater Manchester, Merseyside, Cheshire, Derbyshire.
Web site: www.vosa.gov.uk

SCOTTISH TRAFFIC AREA
J Floor, 3 Lady Lawson Street, Edinburgh EH3 9SE
Tel: 0131 200 4955 **Fax**: 0131 229 0682
Traffic Commissioner: Miss Joan Aitken
Deputy Traffic Commissioner: R H McFarlane
Area covered: Scotland

*SOUTH EASTERN & METROPOLITAN TRAFFIC AREA
Ivy House, 3 Ivy Terrace, Eastbourne BN21 4QT.
Tel: 01323 452403 **Fax**: 01323 721057
Traffic Commissioner: Philip Brown
Area covered: Greater London, Kent, Surrey, Sussex

WELSH TRAFFIC AREA
38 George Road, Birmingham B15 1PL
Tel: 0121 609 6832 **Fax**: 0121 456 4241
Traffic Commissioner: Nick Jones
Deputy Traffic Commissioners: A Jenkins, A L Maddrell, C R Seymour.
Area covered: Wales.

WEST MIDLAND TRAFFIC AREA
38 George Road, Birmingham B15 1PL
Tel: 0121 609 6832 **Fax**: 0121 456 4241
Traffic Commissioner: Nick Jones
Deputy Traffic Commissioners: A Jenkins, A L Maddrell, C R Seymour.
Area covered: Shropshire, Staffordshire, West Midlands, Warwickshire, Worcestershire, Herefordshire.

WESTERN TRAFFIC AREA
2 Rivergate, Bristol BS1 6EH
Tel: 0870 606 0440
Traffic Commissioner: Sarah Bell
Deputy Traffic Commissioners: Brig M. H. Turner, Mrs F. R. Burton, A. L. Maddrell.
Administrative Director: Tim Hughes.
Area covered: Cornwall, Devon, Somerset, Dorset, Hampshire, Wiltshire, Gloucestershire, Oxfordshire, Berkshire.

Office of Fair Trading

The Office of Fair Trading (OFT) plays a leading role in promoting and protecting consumer interests throughout the UK, while ensuring that businesses are fair and competitive. The tools to carry out this work are the powers granted to the OFT under consumer and competition legislation.
Address: Fleetbank House, 2-6 Salisbury Square, London EC4Y 8JX
Tel: 020 7211 8000 **Fax**: 020 7211 8800
Web site: www.oft.gov.uk
E-mail: enquiries@oft.gsi.gov.uk
Enquiries: 08457 22 44 99

Department for Transport

4/24 Great Minster House, 76 Marsham Street, London SW1P 4DR
Tel: 020 7944 3000
Web site: www.dft.gov.uk

Permanent Secretary: Robert Devereux
Director General, Railways & National Works: Dr Mike Mitchell

Executive Agencies: (includes:)
Driving Standards Agency (DSA)
Driver and Vehicle Licensing Agency (DVLA)
Highways Agency (HA)
Chief Executive: Archie Robertson
 Tel: 08457 50 40 30
Web Site: www.highways.gov.uk

Vehicle Certification
VCA
No1, The Estate Office Centre, Eastgate Road, Bristol BS5 6XX
Tel: 0117 952 4126
Fax: 0117 952 4104
E-mail: paul.cooke@vca.gov.uk
Web site: www.vca.gov.uk

Vehicle and Operator Services Agency (VOSA) (see also Driver Training A-Z Manufacturers section)
Web site: www.transportoffice.gov.uk

Advisory Non-Departmental Bodies: (includes:)

Commission for Integrated Transport
Chmn: Peter Hendy
Tel: 020 7944 8300
E-mail: cfit@dft.gsi.gov.uk

Disabled Persons Transport Advisory Committee
E-mail: dptac@dft.gsi.gov.uk

Executive Non-departmental Bodies: (includes:)
Health and Safety Commission
Health and Safety Executive

Tribunals
Traffic Areas

Public Corporations
Civil Aviation Authority
Transport for London

The Disabled Persons Transport Advisory Committee
Department for Transport
Great Minster House, 76 Marsham Street, London SW1P 4DR
Tel: 020 7944 8011
Minicom: 020 7944 3277
Fax: 020 7944 6998
E-mail: dptac@dft.gov.uk
Web site: www.dptac.gov.uk
Chair: Neil Betteridge

The Disabled Persons Transport Advisory Committee (DPTAC) is a statutory body established under Section 125 of the Transport Act 1985 to advise the Secretary of State for Transport on matters affecting the transport needs of disabled people. Membership is limited to a Chairman plus twenty members, at least half of whom must be disabled.

Mobility and Inclusion Unit
(address as above)
Tel: 020 7944 8021
Minicom: 020 7944 3277
Fax: 020 7944 6102
E-mail: miu@dft.gsi.gov.uk
Web site: www.dptac.gov.uk

Disability Rights Commission
Web site: www.drc-gb.org.uk

Rail Accident Investigation Branch
The Wharf, Stores Road, Derby DE21 4BA
Chief Inspector: Carolyn Griffiths
Tel: 01332 253300
Fax: 01332 253301
E-mail: enquiries@raib.gov.uk
Web site: www.raib.gov.uk

RAIB is the independent railway accident investigation organisation for the UK and is listed in LRB because its remit covers street tramways.

Do you want to keep your LITTLE RED BOOK up-to-date?
Buses magazine is now carrying updates every month.
See opposite title page for Subscription details

section 3
Organisations and Societies

British Operators Organisations	*68*
Institutions	*69*
International Associations	*69*
Other Organisations	*70*
First Aid and Sports Associations	*71*
Trade Organisations	*72*
Societies	*72*
Passenger Transport Museums	*77*

British Operators' Organisations

*ALBUM - ASSOCIATION OF LOCAL BUS COMPANY MANAGERS

The Association represents the professional views of the Executive Directors of those bus companies owned by district council and major independent operators on matters specifically affecting locally-owned bus company management and operations.
Chairperson: M Robson, Ipswich Buses Ltd, 7 Constantine Road, Ipswich IP1 2DL **Tel**: 01473 232600
Secretary: S Burd, Blackpool Transport Services Ltd, Rigby Road, Blackpool FY1 5DD **Tel**: 01253 473041

*COACH OPERATORS FEDERATION

Oakwood, Radway, Sidmouth EX10 8TW
Tel: 07768 846138 **Fax**: 01395 513508
E-mail: john.reece@virgin.net

*THE COACH TOURISM COUNCIL

10 Bermondsey Exchange, 179-181 Bermondsey St, London SE1 3UW
Tel: 0870 850 2839
E-mail: admin@coachtourismcouncil.co.uk
Web site: www.coachtourismcouncil.co.uk
The CTC's mission is to promote tourism and travel by coach.

COMMUNITY TRANSPORT ASSOCIATION

Highbank, Halton Street, Hyde SK14 2NY
Tel: 0870 774 3586 **Fax**: 0870 774 3581
Advice Service Tel: 0845 130 6195
E-mail: CTAUK@CommunityTransport.com
Web site: www.CommunityTransport.com
The community transport sector is vast. There are over 100,000 minibuses serving over 10 million passengers every year being operated for use by voluntary and community groups, schools, colleges and Local Authorities, or to provide door-to-door transport for people who are unable to use other public transport. This door-to-door transport is not limited to minibuses though; there are very many voluntary car schemes throughout the UK where volunteers will use their own cars to provide transport for individuals. Overcoming social exclusion is at the heart of what community transport has always been about. The CTA is committed to helping its members achieve this objective in their area both in terms of the direct support it can offer such as training, developmental support etc. but also by lobbying on behalf of the movement with government and other important agencies.

*CONFEDERATION OF PASSENGER TRANSPORT UK

34-43 Russell Street, London WC2B 5HA
Tel: 020 7240 3131 **Fax**: 020 7240 6565
E-mail: cpt@cpt-uk.org **Web site**: www.cpt-uk.org
The Confederation of Passenger Transport UK (CPT) is the trade association representing the UK's bus and coach operators and the light rail sector. CPT has wide responsibilities ranging from representation on government working parties (national, local, EU); establishing operating codes of practice; advising on legal, technical and mechanical standards; management of the Bonded Coach Holiday Scheme, a government recognised consumer travel protection scheme and Coachmarque, an industry quality standard; 24-hour Crisis Control service for members; organisation of industry events and the first point of contact for the media on transport and other related issues.

OFFICERS AND COUNCIL
President: Giles Fearnley
Immediate Past President: Alan Scoles
Chief Executive: Simon Posner
Manager, Chief Executive's Office: Miss L Tang
Finance Director: W Wright
Communications Director: J Major
Public Affairs Officer: C Nice
Director of Membership: Peter Gomersall
Director of Policy Development: S Salmon
Director of Coaching: S Barber
Technical Executive: C Copelin
Operations Executives: J Burch, S Smith
Fixed Track Executive: D Walmsley
Director, Government Relations, Northern Ireland: Karen Magill
The Ecos Centre, Broughshane Road, Ballymena, Co Antrim BT43 7QA
Tel: 0282 563 8938
Chair, CPT Northern Ireland: William Wright
Director of Government Relations, Scotland: Mrs M Rodger, 29 Drumsheugh Gardens, Edinburgh EH3 7RN
Tel: 0131 272 2150 **Fax**: 0131 272 2152
Director of Government Relations, Wales: J Pockett, 70 Hillside View, Craigwen, Pontypridd CF37 2LG
Tel: 01443 485814 **Fax**: 01443 485816

Regional Managers
East Midlands: Andrew Norman, 28 Coppice End Road, Allestree, Derby DE22 2TA
Tel: 01332 242169
London & Home Counties: Miss L Tang, 34-43 Russell Street, London WC2B 5HA
Tel: 020 7240 3131. **Fax**: 020 7240 6565
Northern: David Holding, Foxwood House, 6 The Dene, Chester Moor, Chester-le-Street DH2 3TB
Tel: 0191 388 7694 **Fax**: 0191 388 7694
North Western: Leonard Green, 2 Short Clough Close, Reedsholme, Rawtenstall BB4 8PT
Tel: 01706 218539 **Fax**: 01706 601485
Scotland: Sandra Mathieson, 29 Drumsheugh Gardens, Edinburgh EH3 7RN **Tel**: 0131 272 2150
Fax: 0131 272 2152
Wales: Ian McDonald, 46 Glyn Llwyfen Ewmlas, Llanbradach, Caerphilly CF83 3PN
Tel/Fax: 02920 862559
West Midlands: G Sutton, Drury House, 34-43 Russell St, London WC2B 5HA
Tel: 020 7240 3131
Fax: 020 7240 6565
South West: R Anderson, Heather Cottage, Smokey Cross, Haytor, Newton Abbot TQ13 9QU
Tel: 01364 661365 **Fax**: 01752 777931
Yorkshire: G Peach, Green Acres, 332 Barnsley Road, Flockton WF4 4AT
Tel: 01924 840767 **Fax**: 01924 849685

PASSENGER TRANSPORT EXECUTIVE GROUP

Wellington House, 40-50 Wellington Street, Leeds LS1 2DE
Tel: 0113 251 7204 **Fax**: 0113 251 7333
Web site: www.pteg.net
Chair: Roy Wicks
PTEG brings together and promotes the interests of the six

Passenger Transport Executives (PTEs) in England. Transport for London is an associate member.

Institutions

*THE CHARTERED INSTITUTE OF LOGISTICS & TRANSPORT

Logistics & Transport Centre, Earlstrees Court, Earlstrees Road, Corby NN17 4AX
Tel: 01536 740100 **Fax**: 01536 740101
E-mail: enquiry@ciltuk.org.uk.
Web site: www.ciltuk.org.uk
The Chartered Institute of Logistics and Transport (UK) is the professional body for individuals and organisations involved in all disciplines, modes and aspects of logistics and transport.

The Institute's 22,000 members have privileged access to a range of benefits and services, which support them, professionally and personally, throughout their careers and help connect them with world-wide expertise.

For further information and to join please contact Membership Services, Tel: 01536 740104 or visit the CILT(UK) web site above

*THE INSTITUTE OF THE MOTOR INDUSTRY

Fanshaws, Brickendon, Hertford SG13 8PQ
Tel: 01992 511521 **Fax**: 01992 511548
E-mail: imi@motor.org.uk
Web site: www.motor.org.uk
The Institute of the Motor Industry (IMI) is the professional association for individuals working in the retail motor industry and is the leading awarding body of vocational qualifications in the automotive sector. With some 25,000 members and 45,000 registered students at 350 assessment centres, the IMI is focused on improving professional standards through the recognition, qualification and development of individuals.

Qualifications offered by the Institute include NVQs/SVQs, technical certificates, vehicle sales awards, Quality Assured Awards and Certificate/Diploma in automotive retail management (ARMS).

The IMI governs the industry's Automotive Technician Accreditation (ATA) initiative, which has more than 4500 nationally-accredited technicians since launching in 2005.

OFFICERS AND VICE PRESIDENTS
Patron: HRH Prince Michael of Kent KCVO FIMI.
President: Garel Rhys CBE FIMI
Honorary Treasurer: Edward Clark FIMI.
Chairman of the council: Steve Nash FIMI
Chief Executive: Sarah Sillars FIMI
Company Secretary: Alan Tyrer FIMI

THE INSTITUTE OF TRANSPORT ADMINISTRATION

IOTA House, 7b St Leonards Road, Horsham RH13 6EH
Tel: 01403 242412 **Fax**: 01403 242413
E-mail: directors@iota.org.uk **Web site**: www.iota.org.uk
OFFICERS
President: D MacCuish
Trustees: Cllr G G Fiegel, J D Bailey, M Braid, I M Marshall
National Chairman: A Varney
National Chairman Elect: M Walker
National Vice Chairmen: T Dobson
National Treasurer: J Amos
Finance & General Purposes Chairman: J Amos
Membership/Training Chairman: A Whittington
External Affairs Chairman: G Fletcher
Director: J Miles

THE INSTITUTION OF MECHANICAL ENGINEERS

1 Birdcage Walk, London SW1H 9JJ
Tel: 020 7222 7899. **Fax**: 020 7222 4557
Web site: www.imeche.org.uk
Founded in 1847
Chief Executive: Sir Michael Moore KBE LVO
President 2006/7: W A Osborn MBE, CEng, FIMechE
Engineering Director: Dr Colin Brown C Eng FIMechE
Incorporates as the Automobile Division the former Institution of Automobile Engineers and as the Railway Division the former Institution of Locomotive Engineers.

*SOE

22 Greencoat Place, London SW1P 1PR
Tel: 020 7630 1111 **Fax**: 020 7630 6677
E-mail: soe@soe.org.uk **Web site**: www.soe.org.uk
The SOE is the umbrella professional body for those working in road transport and plant engineering. The IRTE is a professional sector within the SOE.

TRL LTD (TRANSPORT RESEARCH LABORATORY)

Address: Old Wokingham Road, Crowthorne RG45 6AU.
Tel: 01344 770007 **Fax**: 01344 770880
E-mail: enquiries@trl.co.uk
Web site: www.trl.co.uk

International Associations

*INTERNATIONAL ROAD TRANSPORT UNION (IRU)

Founded in 1948 in Geneva, the IRU is an international association of national road transport federations which has consultative status in the United Nations. One of its two Transport Councils is concerned with road passenger transport.
General Secretariat: IRU, Centre International, 3 Rue de Varembe, B.P.44, 1211 Geneva 20, Switzerland
Tel: 00 41 22 918 2700 **Fax**: 00 41 22 918 2741
E-mail: info@iru.org **Web site**: www.iru.org

*UITP, THE INTERNATIONAL ASSOCIATION OF PUBLIC TRANSPORT

President: Roberto Cavalieri (Italy)
Secretary General: Hans Rat
Offices: Rue Sainte Marie 6, B-1080 Bruxelles, Belgium
 Tel: 00 32 2 673 6100 **Fax**: 00 32 2 660 1072
Web site: www.uitp.org

WORLD ROAD ASSOCIATION (PIARC)

Hon Sec/Hon Treas: Room 914, Sunley Tower, Piccadilly Plaza, Manchester M1 4BE **Tel**: 0161 930 5579
E-mail: piarc.bnc@highways.gsi.gov.uk **Web site**: www.piarc.org
The Association is an international body with headquarters in Paris, administered by an elected President and other office bearers. Members are recruited from governments, local authorities, technical and industrial groups and private individuals whose interests are centred on roads and road traffic. The association is maintained by subscriptions from its members. International congresses are held every four years.

OFFICE BEARERS
President: O Michaud (Switzerland)
International Vice-Presidents: P Anguitas Salas (Chile), C Jordan (Australia), K Ghellab (Morocco)
Secretary General: J F Corte, PIARC, La Grande Arche, Paroi Nord, Niveau 8, 92055 La Defense Cedex, France
Tel: 00 33 1 47 96 81 21 **Fax:** 00 33 1 49 00 02 02

The British National Committee's role is to ensure adequate representation of British methods and experience on PIARC's international committees and Congresses, to disseminate the findings of those committees and generally look after British interests. The present officers of this committee are:
Patron: Minister for Transport.
UK President: Sir Richard Mottram KCB
UK Chairman: W J McCoubrey
Vice-Chairman: S Clarke
Hon Treasurer: C B Goodwillie
Hon Secretary/Hon Treasurer: M Neave

Other Organisations

ASSOCIATION OF TRANSPORT CO-ORDINATING OFFICERS (ATCO)

Web site: www.atco.org.uk
Chairman: John Hodgkins
Chairman, Bus Sub-Committee: David Neilson

The Association of Transport Coordinating Officers was formed in 1974 to bring together local authority officers whose work involved what were then new county council responsibilities for passenger transport.

ATCO members include senior staff directly concerned with strategic policy development and implementation for securing of passenger transport services for a wide range of public authorities. These include shire counties and unitary councils in England, Wales and Scotland, Passenger Transport Executives, TfL, the Isle of Man, the States of Jersey and Northern Ireland.

Through exchanging information and views the Association helps formulate policies and standards and promotes transport initiatives aimed at achieving better passenger transport services for all.

Members give advice to the Local Government Association and the Convention of Scottish Local Authorities. ATCO cooperates with the Community Transport Association and Passenger Transport Executive Group.

*BUS USERS UK

PO Box 2950, Stoke-on-Trent ST4 9EW
Tel: 01782 442855 **Fax:** 01782 442886
E-mail: enquiries@bususers.org **Web site:** www.bususers.org

Bus Users UK was formed in 1985 to bring together national and local organisations with an interest in bus services and concerned individual bus users to seek to give an effective voice to the consumer. It is actively involved in developing constructive dialogue between the users and providers of bus services. It publishes a quarterly newsletter – *Bus User*.
Life President: Caroline Cahm
Chairman: Gavin Booth
Secretary: Susan Dawson
Treasurer: Stephen Le Bras
Activity Officer in Wales: Barclay Davies, Bus Users UK Wales, c/o PTI Cymru, Leckwith Offices, Sloper Road, Cardiff CF11 8TB **Tel:** 029 2022 1370 **E-mail:** wales@bususers.org
***Bus User* Editor:** Stephen Morris, PO Box 119, Shepperton TW17 8UX
Tel: 01932 232574 **Fax:** 01932 246394
E-mail: editor@bususers.org
Operations Officer: Phil Tonks

BUSK

18 Windsor Road, Newport NP19 8NS
Tel: 01633 274944
E-mail: busk.beltupschoolkids@btopenworld.com

Formerly known for its Belt Up School Kids campaign, BUSK is now known through the European Union as an authority on vehicular safety for children and young people.

COACH DRIVERS CLUB

Unit 3, Jephson Court, Tancred Close, Queensway, Leamington Spa, Warwickshire CV31 3RZ
Tel: 01926 455266 **Fax:** 01926 888004
E-mail: barbara@expom.co.uk
Web site: www.coachdriversclub.com

Membership club for coach drivers, coaching and tourism. Offers accident cover, magazine, yearbook, members' website, legal advice.

*GOSKILLS

Concorde House, Trinity Park, Solihull B37 7UQ
Tel: 0121 635 5520 **Fax:** 0121 635 5521
Web site: goskills.org

GoSkills is the Sector Skills Council for passenger transport.

*LIGHT RAIL TRANSIT ASSOCIATION

c/o Haslams, 133 Lichfield Street, Walsall WS1 1SL
Tel/Fax: 01487 834000
Web site: www.lrta.org
E.mail: development@lrta.org

Founded in 1937 to advocate and encourage interest in light rail and modern tramways. Monthly magazine is Tramways & Urban Transit. Membership enquiries to:
Membership Secretary: Roger Morris
E-mail: membership@lrta.org
President: Michael Parker
Chairman: David F Russell
Deputy Chairman: Geoff Lusher
Editor in Chief, TAUT: Howard Johnston

LOCAL GOVERNMENT ASSOCIATION

Local Government House, Smith Square, London SW1P 3HZ
Tel: 020 7664 3000 **Fax:** 020 7664 3030
Web Site: www.lga.gov.uk

The Local Government Association was formed by the merger of the Association of County Councils, the Association of District Councils and the Association of Metropolitan Authorities in 1997. The LGA has just under 500 members, including all 238 shire district councils; 36 metropolitan district councils; 34 county councils; 46 new unitary authorities; 33 London authorities; and 22 Welsh authorities. In addition, the LGA represents police authorities, fire authorities and passenger transport authorities. The LGA provides the national voice for local communities in England and Wales; its members represent over 50 million people, employ more than 2 million staff and spend over £65 billion on local services.

Amongst the LGA's policy priorities is integrated transport; local authorities lead the way in encouraging the use of public transport and thereby reducing congestion, ill-health and environmental damage through a programme of partnerships between local authorities and other agencies.

President: Lord Ouseley
Chair: Sir Andy Bruce-Lockhart OBE (Conservative, Kent CC)
Vice-Chairs: Sir Jeremy Beecham (Labour, Newcastle), Peter Chalke (Conservative, Wiltshire)
Deputy Chairs:
 Ian Swithenbank CBE (Labour, Northumberland)
 Chris Clarke OBE (Liberal Democrat, Somerset)
 Chloe Lambert (Independent, Aylesbury Vale)
 Margaret Eaton OBE (Conservative, Bradford)
Chief Executive: Sir Brian Briscoe
Director of Economic & Environmental Policy: Sarah Wood
Director of Communications & Public Affairs:
 Oona Muirhead
Programme Manager, Planning: Lee Searles

LONDON TRAVELWATCH

6 Middle Street, London EC1A 7JA
Tel: 020 7505 9000 **Fax**: 020 7505 9003
Web site: www.londontravelwatch.org.uk
E-mail: info@londontravelwatch.org.uk
Formerly the London Transport Users Committee, London TravelWatch is the independent statutory body set up to represent the interests of the users of all transport for which the Greater London Authority and Transport for London is responsible for operating, providing, procuring and licensing. London TravelWatch is also the Rail Passengers Committee for London.
Chairperson: Brian Cooke, FInstTT
Chief Executive: Rufus Barnes

*ROAD OPERATORS' SAFETY COUNCIL (ROSCO)

Cowley House, Watlington Road, Oxford OX4 6GA
Tel: 01865 775552 **Fax**: 01865 775552
E-mail: rosco-oxford@supanet.com
Web site: www.rosco.org.uk
Chairman: Peter Shipp
Secretary: Tony Beetham

*THE ROYAL SOCIETY FOR THE PREVENTION OF ACCIDENTS

Edgbaston Park, 353 Bristol Road, Birmingham B5 7ST
Tel: 0121 248 2000. **Fax:** 0121 248 2001.
RoSPA promotes safety at work and in the home, at leisure and in schools, on (or near water) and on the roads, through providing information, publicity, training and consultancy.
 The Society works with central and local government, the caring services, the police and public and private sector organisations large and small. Some work is funded by grant and sponsorship, but most relies on the support of the Society's membership.
 The Society also produces and supplies a comprehensive selection of publications ranging from reference books to low-cost booklets for mass distribution.
Training Offered: Training courses cover practical skills and management training through to professional qualifications in Health and Safety.
Chief Executive: Tom Mullarkey

STATUS

c/o Michael Hughes, Manchester Metropolitan University, Chester Street, Manchester
M1 5GD
Tel: 0161 247 6242
Fax: 0161 247 6779
Web site: www.status.org.uk
E-mail: m.p.hughes@mmu.ac.uk
STATUS provides members, from all areas of the specialist road transport industry, with engineering development and test services, technical legislative consultancy and a range of general technical information.
 It is involved on behalf of its members in contributing to consultation documents, influencing transport related legislation and lobbying government departments and agencies.
 The organisation can call on a diverse range of personnel to help deal with more difficult problems. A primary benefit is the availability of telephone consultancy on technical or legislative matters.
 STATUS plays a prominent role in representing its members' interests on legislative matters and lobbies government agencies on behalf of members.
 A monthly newsletter is published, featuring industry related stories.

TRANSPORT 2000

Transport 2000, 1st Floor, The Impact Centre, 12-18 Hoxton Street, London N1 6NG
Tel: 020 7613 0743 **Fax**: 020 7613 5280.
Web site: www.transport2000.org.uk
E-mail: info@transport2000.org.uk
Transport 2000 is a campaign and research group that seeks greener, cleaner transport patterns through greater use of public transport, walking and cycling.
President: Michael Palin
Executive Director: Stephen Joseph

*TRANSPORT BENEVOLENT FUND

87A Leonard Street, London EC2A 4QS
Tel: 0870 0000 172/173 **Fax**: 0870 831 2882
Web site: www.tbf.org.uk
E-mail: help@tbf.co.uk
TBF is a Registered Charity (No 1058032) and was founded in 1923. Membership is open to most staff engaged in the public transport industry. Members pay £1 a week and in return are granted, at the discretion of the Trustees, cash help, convalescence, recuperation, a wide range of complementary medical treatments, legal advice, and medical equipment in times of need. Membership covers the employee and their partner and dependent children. Subject to age and length of membership, free membership may be awarded on leaving the industry. There are payroll deduction facilities in many companies.
Director: Chris Godbold
Senior Trustee: Ray Jordan (President)
Patrons: Sir Wilfrid Newton, CBE (Past Chairman, London Transport), Brian Souter (Stagecoach Group), Lew Adams OBE (BT Police Authority), Moir Lockhead OBE (FirstGroup), Peter Hendy CBE and Dave Wetzel (Transport for London), Phil White (National Express), Robert Crow (RMT), Graham Stevenson (T&GWU), Gerry Doherty (TSSA), Keith Norman (ASLEF), David Martin (Arriva), Keith Ludeman (Go-Ahead Group).

First Aid & Sports Accociations

COACH & BUS FIRST AID ASSOCIATION

President: J. Mackie, Commercial Director, First Aberdeen; 395 King Street, Aberdeen AB24 5RD
Hon Secretary: D A Crew, 11 Chertsey Road, Windlesham GU20 6EN.
 Tel: 01276 451977 **(Mobile)** 07721 457735
 E-mail: david.crew1@BTinternet.com
Membership of the Association is open to all companies in the passenger transport industry for a nominal annual subscription. The Association is purely a non profit making voluntary body administered by an executive committee comprising the elected

president, secretary and treasurer plus other members who meet four times per year.

CABFAA is supported by the Confederation of Passenger Transport. As no other representative body exists for the bus and coach industry to exchange views and be kept up to date on First Aid matters and legislation, it is hoped that all companies both large and small will give support to the Association.

NATIONAL PASSENGER TRANSPORT SPORTS ASSOCIATION

President: Ian Davies
Secretary: V Hills, 2 St Aidans Avenue, Grangetown, Sunderland SR2 9SF
Tel: 0191 567 2504 **Fax**: 0191 203 3177
E-mail: nptsasec@btinternet.com

The association organises inter-company sporting activities for the bus, coach, light rail and heavy rail industries. Currently 16 different sports are covered, each with competitions through the year, with trophies provided often by bus sponsors. A regular magazine is published. Corporate membership is provided to large transport undertakings. Furher information is available from the Secretary, address above.

Trade Organisations and Associations

BEAMA LTD

Offices: Westminster Tower, 3 Albert Embankment, London SE1 7SL. **Tel:** 020 7793 3000. **Fax:** 020 7793 3003.
The British Electrotechnical & Allied Manufacturers' Association.
Founded 1902. Incorporated 1905.
Objects: By co-operative action to promote the interests of the industrial, electrical and electronic manufacturing industries of Great Britain.
Director-General: A. A. Bullen

FEDERATION OF ENGINE REMANUFACTURERS

Director: Brian Ludford
Address: 49 New Stone Avenue, Wembury, Plymouth PL9 0JT
Tel: 01752 863681 **Web Site**: www.fer.co.uk.

FREIGHT TRANSPORT ASSOCIATION VEHICLE INSPECTION SERVICE

Address: Hermes House, St John's Road, Tunbridge Wells TN4 9UZ.
Tel: 01892 526171. **Web Site**: www.fta.co.uk.

The Freight Transport Association represents the interests of over 11,000 companies throughout the UK. FTA carries out over 100,000 vehicle inspections each year including many PSVs. The FTA Vehicle Inspection Service supports operators in maintaining their vehicles in a roadworthy condition - both mechanically and legally.

Further details from Alan Osborne, Head of Vehicle Inspection Services, FTA, Tunbridge Wells (01892 526171).
Publications: *Freight* (monthly journal), FTA Yearbook.
Chief Executive: Richard Turner.

*LOW CARBON VEHICLE PARTNERSHIP

17 Queen Anne's Gate, London SW1H 9BU
Tel: 020 7222 8000
E-mail: secretariat@lowcvp.org.uk
Web site: www.lowcvp.org.uk
The LowCVP is an action and advisory group providing a forum through which partners can work together towards shared goals and take the lead in the transition to a low-carbon future for road transport in the UK.
Bus Working Group Chmn: Bob Bryson (Alexander Dennis)

*MIRA LTD

Registered Office: MIRA Ltd, Watling Street, Nuneaton CV10 0TU
Tel: 024 7635 5000. **Fax**: 024 7635 5355.
MIRA an independent product engineering and technology centre and offers skills in innovation, problem-solving and consultancy.
Chairman: M Beasley
Executive Directors:
Managing Director: J. R. Wood.
Director of Finance & Company Secretary: C J N Phillipson.
Director of Engineering: G. Townsend

SOCIETY OF MOTOR MANUFACTURERS & TRADERS (SMMT)

Forbes House, Halkin Street, London SW1X 7DS.
Tel: 020 7235 7000
Web site: www.smmt.co.uk
E-mail: buscoachweb@smmt.co.uk

*THE VEHICLE BUILDERS & REPAIRERS ASSOCIATION LTD

Offices: Belmont House, Gildersome, Leeds LS27 7TW.
Tel: 0113 253 8333 **Fax**: 0113 238 0496
E-mail: vbra@vbra.co.uk **Web site**: www.vbra.co.uk
Director General: M Tagg
Journal Editor: Judi Barton

Societies

THE ASSOCIATION OF FRIENDS OF THE BRITISH COMMERCIAL VEHICLE MUSEUM TRUST

The Association was formed when The British Commercial Vehicle Museum was opened in 1983. Its aims are to support the full-time staff in matters of publicity, fund raising, maintenance and documentation of exhibits, work in the archives, organising rallies, etc. Facilities for members include a newsletter, free admission to the museum to undertake museum work and socialise with colleagues. New members are always welcome and special rates exist for families, students and senior citizens.
Hon Chairman: H Hatcher
Hon Secretary: A Pritchard
Hon Treasurer: A Pritchard
Members of the Committee: E Simister, D Lewis, J Gardner
Museum Manager: A Buchan
Address: The British Commercial Vehicle Museum, King Street, Leyland, Preston PR25 2LE **Tel**: 01772 451011

*ASTON MANOR ROAD TRANSPORT MUSEUM

Contact address: The Old Tram Depot, 208-216 Witton Lane, Aston, Birmingham B6 6QE
Phone: 0121 322 2298
Web site: www.amrtm.org.uk
Company limited by guarantee. Registered as a charity.
The museum is uniquely housed in a former depot of Birmingham's first-generation tramways. The display of commercial and passenger vehicles reflects the history of construction and operation in the West Midlands, and there are numerous displays of transport artefacts, tickets, notices and photographs. Joining as a Friend of the Museum gives entitlement to free entry and a quarterly newsletter. The museum is open on Saturdays, Sundays and Bank Holidays throughout the year, with a range of special events featuring a free heritage bus service to and from the city centre. Situated on Travel West Midlands bus services 7 and 11 and close to Aston railway station.
Further information from:
Chairman: Geoff Lusher, 86 Heritage Court, Warstone Lane, Jewellery Quarter, Birmingham B18 6HU

*BRITISH BUS PRESERVATION GROUP

25 Oldfield Road, Bexleyheath DA7 4DX
Membership enquiries: 51 Market Close, Shirebrook, Mansfield NG20 8AE
Tel: 07940 771439
Web site: www.bbpg.co.uk
E-mail: info@bbpg.co.uk
The BBPG was formed in 1990 and has been responsible for securing the future of more than 250 historic buses and coaches, many of which were saved at extremely short notice from being broken up. The society has more than 600 members, both individuals and preservation groups. The BBPG caters for all bus enthusiasts, whether or not they own a bus.
Chairman: Glyn Matthews.
General Secretary: Mike Lloyd.
Membership Secretary: Harry Glover

*BRITISH TROLLEYBUS SOCIETY

Formed as the Reading Transport Society in 1961, the present title was adopted in 1971, having acquired a number of trolleybuses for preservation from all over Britain. In 1969 it founded the Trolleybus Museum at Sandtoft, near Doncaster, where its vehicles are housed and regularly operate on mains power from the overhead wiring. West Yorkshire Transport Circle merged into the Society in January 1991. Currently membership stands at about 320. Members receive a monthly journal *Trolleybus* containing news and articles from home and abroad. Additionally members can subscribe to *Bus Fare* and *Wheels*, monthly magazines for motorbus operation in the Thames Valley and West Yorkshire areas respectively. Monthly meetings are also held in Reading, London and Bradford.
Chairman: G P Bilbe, 12 Belle Avenue, Reading RG6 7BL
Secretary: A. J. Barton, 2 Josephine Court, Southcote Road, Reading RG30 2DG.
Treasurer: R. V. Fawcett, 57 Sutcliffe Avenue, Earley RG6 7JN

*BUSES WORLDWIDE (BWW)

Web site: www.busesworldwide.org
E-mail: membership@busesworldwide.org
Established in 1982 to associate those particularly interested in bus operation in countries other than their own. Meetings are held, a bi-monthly magazine is published and visits abroad are organised.
Chairman: R Stedall

Membership Secretary: S. Guess, 37 Oyster Lane, Byfleet KT14 7HS
News Editor: N. R. Bartlett, 1 Hopping Jacks Lane, Danbury, Chelmsford CM3 4PN.
Features Editor: D. Corke, 8 Priestland Gardens, Berkhamsted HP4 2GT.

*CLASSIC BUS HERITAGE TRUST (INCORPORATING THE ROUTEMASTER HERITAGE TRUST)

The Classic Bus Heritage Trust aims to advance preservation of buses and coaches by fostering the interests of the general public. It is a Registered Charity.
Treasurer & Hon Sec: W. Ackroyd, 8 Twining Road, Ventnor, Isle of Wight PO38 1TX

*ESSEX BUS ENTHUSIASTS' GROUP

Web site: www.essexbus.org.uk
This group was formed in 1962, under its previous title, Eastern National Enthusiasts' Group. The present title was adopted in 1987 to reflect more fully the activities of the group. A monthly magazine is circulated to all members giving information on all aspects of First Essex Buses, Thamesway, Colchester and Southend and all other operators in Essex. Meetings are arranged on a regular basis whilst tours are also organised. A range of publications and photographs is also available. Membership is open to all over the age of 12.
Membership Secretary: Derek Stebbing, Conifers, Thorpe Road, Weeley, Clacton-on-Sea CO16 9JJ
  Tel: 01255 830732
  E-mail: derekstebbing@hotmail.com

*HISTORIC COMMERCIAL VEHICLE SOCIETY

The Society was founded in 1958 and four years later absorbed the Vintage Passenger Vehicle Society and the London Vintage Taxi Club. Its membership of over 4,000 owns more than 6,000 preserved vehicles. Activities include the organisation of rallies, among them the well known London to Brighton and Trans-Pennine runs. The club caters for all commercial vehicles over 20 years old.
OFFICERS
President: Lord Montagu of Beaulieu
Senior Exec Officer and Vice-President: M. Banfield, Iden Grange, Cranbrook Road, Staplehurst TN12 0ET
  Tel: 01580 892929. **Fax:** 01580 893227.
  E-mail: hcvs@btinternet.com **Web site**: www.hcvs.co.uk

*LEYLAND NATIONAL GROUP

Web site: www.leylandnationalgroup.org
E-mail: enquiries@leylandnationalgroup.org
Address: 27 Dukeshill Road, Bracknell RG42 2DU
Tel: 01344 640095
The Leyland National Group was formed in 1997 and has members throughout Great Britain and abroad. Although the group does not own any vehicles itself, some of its members are bus owners. There are more than 100 Leyland Nationals from a variety of operators preserved by group members. However, one does not need to own a bus to join the group, as membership is open to anyone with an interest in Leyland Nationals. The group also caters for those interested in the derivatives of the Leyland National; the Leyland-DAB, Leyland B21 and Leyland National bodied rail vehicles. Members receive a colour illustrated quarterly magazine, exclusive access to the members' only area on the group's website as well as other benefits. Please contact the Membership Secretary for more information about the group, the benefits of

membership and to receive a membership application form.
Chairman: Mick Berg
Secretary: David Layton
Address: 24 Patterson Court, Farnol Road, Dartford DA1 5DT
Tel: 01322 278050
E-mail: secretary@leylandnationalgroup.org
Treasurer: Mike Bellinger
Magazine Editor: Claire Barrett
Membership Secretary: Tim Wild
Address: 27 Dukeshill Road, Bracknell, RG42 2DU
Tel: 01344 640095
E-mail: membership@leylandnationalgroup.org

LINCOLNSHIRE VINTAGE VEHICLE SOCIETY

Road Transport Museum, Whisby Road, North Hykeham LN6 5TR Tel: 01522 500566/689497

The LVVS was founded in 1959 by local businessmen with the aim of forming a road transport museum. Charitable status was obtained some time ago, and with a capital grant from its local district council, it has now completed the first stage of its new museum project. Over 60 vehicles dating from the 1920s to the 1980s can be seen in the new exhibition hall with many more in the workshop. Opening times November–April Sundays 13.00-16.00. May–October Mon-Fri 12.00-16.00, Sun 10.00-16.00.
Chairman: S Milner
Hon Treasurer: J Child
Secretary: Mrs J Jefford

LONDON OMNIBUS TRACTION SOCIETY (LOTS)

Unit N305, Westminster Business Square, 1-45 Durham Street London SE11 5JH
Web site: www.lots.org.uk

Formed in 1964, LOTS has some 2,600 members and is the largest bus enthusiast society in the British Isles.

An Illustrated monthly newsletter is sent to all members. This covers all the current operators in the former London Transport area and includes General and Industry News, Route Developments, and Vehicle News for the former London Transport area as well as publicity, subsequent disposal information and service vehicles. Monthly meetings are usually held in central London featuring guest speakers, slide and film presentations during the year as well as the annual free bus rides from central London using vehicles of London interest.

Regular LOTS publications include fleet allocations and route working publications as well as the annual *London Bus and Tram Fleetbook*. A quarterly 64 page glossy magazine, the *London Bus Magazine (LBM)* has been produced for over 30 years.

Regular sales lists are produced and sent out to all members. An information service is also available to all members to answer those historical queries.

The Autumn Transport Spectacular (ATS) is held in London every year and is one of London's biggest transport sales.

*THE M & D AND EAST KENT BUS CLUB

42 St Albans Hill, Hemel Hempstead HP3 9NG
Web site: www.mdekbusclub.org.uk
E-mail: n.king112@btinternet.com

This club was formed in 1952 with the object of bringing together all those interested in road passenger transport in an area covering Kent and East Sussex. Facilities for members include a monthly news booklet (illustrated), information service, tours, meetings, vehicle photograph sales and vehicle preservation. A series of publications is also produced, including illustrated fleet histories.
Hon Chairman: J. V. Spillett
Hon Sec: P J Evans
Hon Editor: N D King
Hon Treasurer: N D King
Membership Officer: J. A. Fairley
Photographic Officer: B.Weeden
Sales Officer: to be appointed
Tours Officer: D. R. Cobb
Management Committee: N. D. King, R. A. Lewis, J. V. Spillett, P. J. Evans, D M Jones. Area Organisers in Ashford, Dover, Folkestone, Hastings, North-East Kent, Maidstone and the Medway Towns.

*NATIONAL TROLLEYBUS ASSOCIATION

15 Cambrian Crescent, Oulton Broad NR32 3HW
Web site: www.trolleybus.co.uk/nta

Formed in 1963, and incorporated in 1968 as The Trolleybus Museum Co Ltd. The vehicles and ancillary equipment collected by the NTA since its inception are now owned by the company, which is limited by guarantee and is a registered charity. Members receive *Trolleybus Magazine*, a printed and illustrated bi-monthly journal documenting all aspects of trolleybus operation past and present throughout the world.
Chairman: R. D. Helliar-Symons
Secretary: J. H. Ward
Treasurer: I Martin
Membership Secretary: I Martin
Enquiries: TMCMembSec@hotmail.com

*THE OMNIBUS SOCIETY

Website: www.omnibussoc.org.

The Omnibus Society was founded in 1929. Today it is a nationwide organisation with a network of provincial branches, offering a comprehensive range of facilities for those interested in the bus and coach industry. The Society has accumulated a wealth of information on public road transport. Members have the opportunity to receive and exchange data on every aspect of the industry including route developments, operational/traffic matters and fleet changes. Each branch has a full programme of activities and publishes its own Branch Bulletin to give local news of route changes, etc. A scheme exists whereby members subscribe to receive bulletins from branches other than that of which they are a member. A programme of indoor meetings is customary during winter, including film shows, invited speakers and discussions. In the summer months visits to manufacturers and tours to operators are featured.
OFFICERS
President: Giles Fearnley
Vice-Presidents: F P Groves, A W Mills, G Wedlake, T. F. McLachlan, K. W. Swallow, R. G. Westgate, Professor John Hibbs.
Chairman: B. Le Jeune.
Secretary: A. J. Francis, 185 Southlands Road, Bromley BR2 9QZ.
Treasurer: H. L. Barker, 31 High Street, Tarporley CW6 0DP.
Editor, Society's Publications: Cyril McIntyre
Members of the Council: I. D. Barlex, J. Hart, D. M. Persson, D. Roy, J Howie and nominations from each branch
Branch Officers:
Midland Branch: C R Warn, 11 The Meadows, Shawbury, Shrewsbury SY4 4HS
South Wales and West Branch: A J Armstrong, 16 Stanley Grove, Weston-super-Mare BS23 3EB
Northern Branch: Philip Battersby, 12 Crescent Lodge, Tile Crescent, Middlesbrough TS5 6SF.
North Western & Yorkshire Branch: P. Wilkinson, 10 Bradley Close, Timperley, Altrincham WA15 6SH

Scottish Branch: I. Allan, 10 Miller Avenue, Crossford, Dunfermline KY12 8PY

Essex & South Suffolk Group: J. L. Rugg, 86 Worthing Road, Laindon SS15 6JU

East Midland Group: A. Oxley, 4 Gordon Close, Attenborough, Nottingham NN4 9UF

Herts & Beds Group: R. C. Barton, 5 Viscount Court, Knights Field, Luton LU2 7LD

London Historical Research Group: D A Ruddom, 57 Bluebridge Road, Brookmans Park, Hatfield AL9 7UW

Provincial Historical Research Group: A E Jones, 8 Poplar Drive, Church Stretton S76 7BW

*THE PSV CIRCLE

15 Port Close, Lordswood, Chatham ME5 8DU

The Circle is an association of over 2000 members, interested in various ways in the vehicles used by the passenger transport industry on the roads of the United Kingdom and abroad. Membership is open to all over the age of 16, and in certain exceptional cases to those under this age. News Sheets, comprising nine regional sections, are published each month, together with numerous supplements and fleet histories which fully record information relating to operators, chassis builders and body constructors. There is no entrance fee. Annual subscriptions vary with the number of regional news sheets required, with a minimum for one area and graded additional payments according to members' requirements. Frequent meetings, mainly of a social nature, are held in London and several provincial towns.

HONORARY OFFICERS
Chairman: C. R. Costella
Secretary: J E Skilling
Treasurer: M D Bissex
Managing Editor: S Curl

The above with another eight members constitute the Committee of Management, and for convenience all mail other than editorial matters is handled at the above address.

*RIBBLE ENTHUSIASTS' CLUB

23 Richmond Road, Hindley Green, Wigan WN2 4ND
Tel: 01942 253497
E-mail: mjyat@msn.com
Web site: http://homepage.manx.net/JHL/REC/index.htm

Founded in 1954 by the late T. B. Collinge for the study of road transport past and present and in particular Ribble Motor Services and associated companies. Meetings are held and a monthly news sheet produced.

Life President: A E Chapman
Life Vice President: M. Shires
Vice President: C Bowles
Committee Chairman: D Bailey MBE
Secretary/Tours: M J Yates, 23 Richmond Road, Hindley Green, Wigan WN2 4ND
Treasurer: R A Harpum, 22 Woodside Road, Ferndown BH22 9LD
Records: S Blake, 23 Fairfield Road, North Shore, Blackpool FY1 2RA
Sales Dept: Mr & Mrs B Ashcroft, 11 Regent Road, Walton le Dale, Preston PR5 4QA
Sales Dept: Assistant: Mrs J Yates, 23 Richmond Road, Hindley Green, Wigan WN2 4ND
Archive: B Ashcroft, 11 Regent Road, Walton Le Dale, Preston PR5 4QA
Editor: R Kenyon, 18 Hatfield Road, Accrington BB5 6DF
Membership Sec: B Downham, 203 Brindle Road, Bamber Bridge, Preston PR5 6YL

*ROADS AND ROAD TRANSPORT HISTORY ASSOCIATION

Web site: www.rrtha.org.uk

Founded in 1992, the association promotes, encourages and co-ordinates the study of the history of roads and road transport, both passenger and freight. It aims to encourage those interested in a particular aspect of transport to understand their chosen subject in the context of developments in other areas and at other periods. It publishes a newsletter four times a year and holds an annual conference each autumn.

Membership is open to professional bodies/transport societies, museums and individuals.

President: Professor John Hibbs, OBE
Chairman: Garry Turvey, CBE
Hon. Secretary: Christopher Hogan, 124 Shenstone Avenue, Stourbridge DY8 3EJ **E-mail:** roadsandRTHA@aol.com

*ROUTEMASTER OPERATORS & OWNERS ASSOCIATION

23 Oakhurst Drive, Crewe, Cheshire CW2 6UE
Tel: 0870 720 2920 **E-mail:** grahamsteph1011@hotmail.co.uk
Web Site: www.routemaster.org.uk

The Routemaster Operators & Owners Association provides assistance, advice and news for operators, owners and enthusiasts of these vehicles. From the specification of a screw to a complete bus, the Association provides authoritative technical information. Bus rallies and events are organised and other selected events are supported each year. Members receive a quarterly news magazine and discounts on parts and accessories including a maintenance manual, owners handbook technical bulletins, suppliers handbook, badges and transfers, window sealing rubber and many other unique products. Large batches of Routemaster spares have been acquired from the London bus operators including mechanical units, electrical items and bodywork spares.

President: Colin Curtis OBE
Secretary: Graham Meadows
Chairman: Andrew Morgan, 45 Princess Diana Drive, St Albans, Herts AL4 0DZ
E-mail: andrewmorgan1368@tiscali.co.uk

*THE SAMUEL LEDGARD SOCIETY

C/O 58 Kirklees Drive, Farsley, Pudsey LS28 5TE
Tel: 0113 236 3695 **Fax:** 0113 259 1125
E-mail: rennison@mailcc.co.uk
Web site: wwwsamuelledgardsociety.org.uk

The Samuel Ledgard Society was formed in 1998 at the Rose & Crown Inn, Otley, during the second annual reunion of the devotees of this well-known bus company. Reunions are held twice yearly at Armley during April and Otley on or about October 14. A Christmas dinner is also part of the established calendar of events. The quarterly journal of the Society, *The Chat*, is published in March, June, September and December each year. Founding officers were Barry Rennison, Tony Greaves and Don Bate, all of whom have a wealth of knowledge about the Samuel Ledgard company. Membership is open to all with a subscription of £5 - contact any member of the Committee for details.

Hon President: Samuel Ledgard Mather AMIRTE (Retd)
COMMITTEE
Chairman: Barry Rennison, 58 Kirklees Drive, Farsley, Pudsey LS28 5TE
Vice-Chairman, Magazine Editor & Publicity Officer: Tony Greaves, 19 Perth Mount, Horsforth LS18 5SH
Treasurer: Bryan Whitham, 4 Airedale Drive, Horsforth LS18 4ER
Secretary & Membership: Margaret Rennison, 58 Kirklees Drive, Farsley, Pudsey LS28 5TE

*SCOTTISH TRAMWAY & TRANSPORT SOCIETY

PO Box 7342, Glasgow G51 4YQ
Founded in 1951 as the Scottish Tramway Museum Society, the Society claims to be 'Scotland's foremost tramway enthusiast organisation', publishing books and videos on tramways and other transport subjects and supporting the National Tramway Museum. Monthly meetings and newsletter.
Hon Chairman: B M Longworth
Gen Secretary: H. McAulay
E-mail: stts-glasgow@virgin.net
Hon Treasurer: A. Ramsay
Members of Committee: A Murray, N Bates, A Muir, B Quinn, F W B Mitchell, I Stewart

*SOUTH YORKSHIRE TRANSPORT MUSEUM

UNIT 9, Waddington Way, Aldwarke, Rotherham S65 3SH
Tel: 0114 255 3010
The Sheffield Bus Museum Trust was formed in 1987 with the purpose of co-ordinating the bus preservation movement in Sheffield and to establish a permanent museum. This was initially achieved at the former Sheffield Tramways Company's Tinsley Tram Depot but in 2007 the Trust moved its collection to new premises at Aldwarke, Rotherham. At the same time the museum was re-branded to the name above. The majority of the Trust's collection is local and extremely varied, ranging from a 1926 Sheffield tramcar to a 1985 Dennis Domino. In recent years the Museum Trust has benefited from Heritage Fund Lottery grants. The museum is an educational charity and promotes an ever-expanding schools visits programme. The museum is open to the public on a monthly basis from March to December.
Chairman: M W Greenwood
Membership Secretary: Dr. John Willis, 2 Pwll-Y-Waen, Ty'n-Y-Groes, Conwy LL32 8TQ.

*SOUTHDOWN ENTHUSIASTS' CLUB

Web site: www.southdownenthusiastsclub.org.uk
This club was founded in 1954 to bring together people interested in the vehicles, routes and history of Southdown Motor Services Ltd and now includes Stagecoach South (Hastings & District, South Coast Buses, Southdown, Hampshire Bus, Hants & Surrey, East Kent), Brighton & Hove, Eastbourne Buses and First Hampshire and Dorset. There is a monthly news publication and winter meetings. Membership is open to persons aged 14 years and over and details may be had from the Hon Secretary.
Hon Chairman: J Allpress, 9 Phoenix Way, Southwick, Brighton BN42 4HQ
Hon Secretary: N Simes, 11 High Cross Fields, Crowborough TN6 2SN
Hon Treasurer: D E Still, 12 Westway Close, Mile Oak, Portslade BN42 2RT
Hon Sales Officer: D Chalkley, 6 Valebridge Drive, Burgess Hill RH15 0RW
Hon News Sheet Editor: P Gainsbury, Park Cottage, Guestling TN35 4LT
Hon Publications Officer: J Smith, 1 Sackville Way, Worthing BN14 8BJ
Committee Member: J Barley, 84 Kipling Avenue, Brighton BN2 6UE.
Hon Photographic Officer: C Churchill, 53 Monks Close, Lancing BN15 9DB

*SWINDON VINTAGE OMNIBUS SOCIETY

10 Fraser Close, Nythe, Swindon SN3 3RP
Tel: 01793 526001
E-mail: davenicol@supanet.com
Preserved Daimler Weymann double deck, ex Swindon corporation society vehicle. Also Bristol RESL ECW ex-Thamesdown Transport.
Chairman: M. Naughton
Secretary: D. Nicol
Treasurer: D. Mundy

*THE TRANSPORT MUSEUM, WYTHALL
Birmingham & Midland Motor Omnibus Trust

The Transport Museum, Chapel Lane, Wythall B47 6JX
Web site: www.bammot.org.uk
E-mail: enquiries@bammot.org.uk
The Trust dates back to 1973, taking its present title in 1977, when it became a registered educational charity to establish and develop a regional transport museum.

Three large halls, the most recent built with the assistance of the Heritage Lottery Fund and opening in 2007, house a broad collection of around 100 buses, coaches, fire engines and battery-electric vehicles from all parts of the Midlands and beyond. Birmingham and the Black Country especially are featured, and the museum has a unique collection of buses and coaches designed, built and operated by Midland Red, a company which pioneered many technical innovations over a 50 year manufacturing period.

A museum archive to record the development of the bus and coach industry in the Midlands is also being established, with collections of photographs, uniforms, tickets, ticket equipment and street furniture.

Members receive the bi-monthly museum journal *Omnibus* containing details of museum developments. The museum is open to the public every weekend between March and the end of November. Special event days are held on some Sundays and holiday Mondays when vehicles are on display and historic bus services operate, including a link with Birmingham city centre. Also buses for hire - see West Midlands in Operators section.

*TRAMWAY & LIGHT RAILWAY SOCIETY

Web site: www.tramways.freeserve.co.uk
Founded in 1938, the Tramway & Light Railway Society caters for those interested in all aspects of tramways. Members receive *Tramfare*, a bi-monthly illustrated magazine. There are regular meetings throughout the country. The Society promotes tramway modelling, drawings, castings, and technical details are available to modellers. There are also comprehensive library facilities. For fuller details of the Society and of membership please write to the Membership Secretary.
HONORARY OFFICERS
President: P J Davis.
Vice-Presidents: E R Oakley, G. B. Claydon
Chairman: J R Prentice, 216 Brentwood Road, Romford RM1 2RP.
Secretary: G R Tribe, 47 Soulbury Road, Linslade, Leighton Buzzard LU7 7RW.
Membership Secretary: H J Leach, 6 The Woodlands, Brightlingsea CO7 0RY.

THE TRANSPORT TICKET SOCIETY

An association of students and collectors of passenger tickets and fare collection methods. Founded in 1946 the TTS now has some 500 members worldwide. An illustrated monthly Journal, and regular distributions of tickets, keep members up to date with both historical and recent developments in ticketing in all modes of transport. The TTS welcomes offers of obsolete tickets for distribution to members. Full details of membership together with a sample Journal will be sent on request to the TTS publicity officer, or visit the TTS website: www.transport-ticket.com.

Publicity Officer: Martin Rickitt, Bromes House, Isle Abbots, Taunton TA3 6RW. **Tel**: 01460 281228
   E-mail: mrickitt@hotmail.com
Chairman: John Tolson
Membership Secretary: David Randall
General Secretary: Patrick Geall
Treasurer: Graham Wootton.
Managing Editor: David Harman

THE TRANSPORT TRUST

202 Lambeth Road, London SE1 7JW
Tel: 020 7928 6464. **Fax**: 020 7928 6565.
   E-mail: hq@thetransporttrust.org.uk
   Web Site: www.thetransporttrust.org.uk
The national charity for the preservation and restoration of Britain's transport heritage.

Passenger Transport Museums

This list is in addition to those shown in the main Society section above

*ABBEY PUMPING STATION

Contact address: Corporation Road, Leicester LE4 5PX
Phone: 0116 299 5111
Fax: 0116 299 5125
Web site: www.leicester.gov.uk/museums, www.leicestermuseums.ac.uk

AMBERLEY WORKING MUSEUM

Contact address: Amberley, Arundel BN18 9LT
Phone: 01798 831370
Fax: 01798 831831
E-mail: office@amberleymuseum.co.uk
Web site: www.amberleymuseum.co.uk

ASTON MANOR ROAD TRANSPORT MUSEUM

(*See Societies section*)

BLACK COUNTRY LIVING MUSEUM TRANSPORT GROUP

Contact address: Tipton Road, Dudley DY1 4SQ
Phone: 0121 557 9643
Web site: wwww.bclm.co.uk

BRISTOL ROAD TRANSPORT COLLECTION

Contact address: William Staniforth, 37 Corbett Road, Birmingham B47 5LP (SAE please)
E-mail: william.staniforth@virgin.net

*BRITISH COMMERCIAL VEHICLE MUSEUM

Contact address: King Street, Leyland PR25 2LE
Phone: 01772 451011
Fax: 01772 451015

*CASTLE POINT TRANSPORT MUSEUM

Contact address: 105 Point Road, Canvey Island SS8 7TP
Phone: 01268 684272

CAVAN & LEITRIM RAILWAY

Contact address: Narrow Gauge Station, Station Road, Dromod, Co Leitrim, Ireland
Phone/fax: 00353 71 9638599
Web site: www.irish-railway.com
E-mail: info@irish-railway.com

COBHAM BUS MUSEUM - THE LONDON BUS PRESERVATION TRUST LTD

Contact address: Redhill Road, Cobham, Surrey, KT11 1EF
Phone/Fax: 01932 868665
Web site: www.lbpt.org
E-mail: cobhambusmuseum@aol.com

*COVENTRY TRANSPORT MUSEUM

Contact address: Millennium Place, Hales Street, Coventry CV1 1PN
Phone: 024 7623 4270
Fax: 024 7623 4284
E-mail: enquiries@transport-museum.com

DOVER TRANSPORT MUSEUM

Contact address: Willingdon Road, Port Zone White Cliffs Business Park, Whitfield, Dover CT16 2HJ
Phone: 01304 822409

*EAST ANGLIA TRANSPORT MUSEUM

Contact address: Chapel Road, Carlton Colville, Lowestoft NR33 8BL
Phone: 01502 518459
Fax: 01502 584658
E-mail: enquiries@eatm.org.uk
Web site: www.eatm.org.uk

GRAMPIAN TRANSPORT MUSEUM

Contact address: Alford AB33 8AE
Phone: 01975 562292
Fax: 01975 562180
E-mail: info@g-t-m.freeserve.co.uk
Web site: www.gtm.org.uk

IPSWICH TRANSPORT MUSEUM

Contact address: Old Trolleybus Depot, Cobham Road, Ipswich IP3 9JD
Phone: 01473 715666
E-mail: www.ipswichtransportmuseum.co.uk.html

*ISLE OF WIGHT BUS MUSEUM

Contact address: 28 Westmill Road, Newport PO30 5RG
Phone: 01983 526422
E-mail: nharris.westmill@tiscali.co.uk

Organisations and Societies

*KEIGHLEY BUS MUSEUM TRUST
Contact address: 47 Brantfell Drive, Burnley BB12 8AW
Phone: 01282 413179
E-Mail: shmdboard@aol.com
Web site: www.kbmt.org.uk

*LONDON TRANSPORT MUSEUM
Contact address: 39 Wellington Street, London WC2E 7BB.
Phone: 020 7379 6344; recorded information 020 7565 7299
E-mail: resourcedesk@ltmuseum.co.uk
Web site: www.ltmuseum.co.uk

MANCHESTER MUSEUM OF TRANSPORT
Contact address: Boyle Street, Cheetham, Manchester M8 8UW
Phone: 0161 205 2122
Fax: 0161 202 1110
E-mail: busmuseum@btconnect.com
Web site: www.gmts.co.uk or www.manchester.bus.museum

MIDLAND ROAD TRANSPORT GROUP — BUTTERLEY
Contact address: 21 Ash Grove, Mastin Moor, Chesterfield S43 3AW
Phone: Midland Road Transport Group — 01246 473619 Midland Railway 01773 747674, Visitor Information Line (01773) 570140.

*MUSEUM OF TRANSPORT
Contact address: Kelvin Hall, 1 Bunhouse Road, Glasgow G3 8DP
Phone: 0141 287 2720 (school bookings on 0141 565 4112/3)
Fax: 0141 287 2692

NATIONAL MUSEUM OF SCIENCE AND INDUSTRY
Contact address: Exhibition Road, London SW7 2DD
Phone: 0207 942 4105 or 01793 814466
E-mail: s.evans@nmsi.ac.uk

*THE NORTH OF ENGLAND OPEN AIR MUSEUM
Contact address: Beamish DH9 0RG
Phone: 0191 370 4000
Fax: 0191 370 4001
E-mail: museum@beamish.org.uk
Web site: www.beamish.org.uk

THE NATIONAL TRAMWAY MUSEUM
Crich, Matlock DE4 5DP
Tel: 01773 854321 **Fax**: 01773 854320
The Society was founded in 1955 to establish and operate a working tramway museum. The Museum is at Crich Tramway Village, Crich, near Matlock, in Derbyshire, and owns over 70 English, Irish, Scottish, Welsh and overseas tramcars. Members receive a copy of the Society's quarterly journal and can participate in the running of the museum.
Patron: HRH The Duke of Gloucester GCVO
Vice-Presidents: G. S. Hearse, W. G. S. Hyde, G. B. Claydon, D. J. H. Senior, A W Bond
Chairman: C. Heaton
Vice-Chairman: R T Pennyfather
Hon Secretary: I. M. Dougill
Hon Treasurer: P R Moore
Operations Superintendent: K. B. Hulme

NORTH WEST MUSEUM OF ROAD TRANSPORT
Contact address: The Old Bus Depot, 51 Hall Street, St Helens WA10 1DU
E-mail: general@hallstreetdepot.info
Web site: www.hallstreetdepot.info

*NOTTINGHAM TRANSPORT HERITAGE CENTRE
Contact address: Mere Way, Ruddington, Nottingham NG11 6NX
Phone: 0115 940 5705
E-mail: geoffrey.clark3@ntworld.com
Web site: http://www.nthc.co.uk

OXFORD BUS MUSEUM
Contact address: Station Yard, Long Hanborough OX29 8LA
Phone: 01993 883617 (Answerphone) or 01993 881662

*SCOTTISH VINTAGE BUS MUSEUM
Contact address: M90 Commerce Park, Lathalmond, Dumfermline, Fife KY12 OSJ
Phone: 01383 623380
Website: www.busweb.co.uk/svbm

THE TRANSPORT MUSEUM, WYTHALL
Birmingham & Midland Motor Omnibus Trust
(*See Societies section*)

*TRANSPORT MUSEUM SOCIETY OF IRELAND
Contact address: Howth Castle Demesne, Howth, Dublin 13, Ireland
Phone/Fax: 00 353 1 848 0831
E-mail: info@nationaltransportmuseum.org
Web site: www.nationaltransportmuseum.org

*TROLLEYBUS MUSEUM AT SANDTOFT
Contact address: Belton Road, Sandtoft, Doncaster DN8 5SX
Phone: 01724 711391
E-mail: enquiries@sandtoft.org
Web site: www.sandtoft.org

ULSTER FOLK & TRANSPORT MUSEUM
Contact address: Cultra, Holywood BT18 0EU
Phone: 028 9042 8428

WIRRAL TRANSPORT MUSEUM
Contact address: Pacific Road, Birkenhead L41 5HN
Phone: 0151 666 2756

section 4

British Isles Operators

Major Groups	80	Northumberland	154	Orkney	198
English Operators		Nottinghamshire, Nottingham	155	Perth & Kinross	199
Bedfordshire	81	Oxfordshire	158	Renfrewshire	200
Berkshire (West Berkshire,		Shropshire	159	Shetland	201
Bracknell Forest, Reading,		Somerset, Bath & North East		South Ayrshire	201
Slough, Windsor & Maidenhead,		Somerset/North Somerset	161	South Lanarkshire	201
Wokingham)	82	South Yorkshire	164	Stirling	202
Bristol	84	Staffordshire	167	West Dunbartonshire	202
Buckinghamshire, Milton Keynes	85	Suffolk	169	West Lothian	202
Cambridgeshire and		Surrey	171	Western Isles	203
Peterborough City	87	Tyne & Wear	174		
Cheshire, Halton and Stockport	89	Warwickshire	175	**Isle of Man Operators**	
Cornwall	91	West Midlands	176	Isle of Man	204
Cumbria	93	West Sussex	180		
Derbyshire	96	West Yorkshire, Bradford,		**Isles of Scilly Operators**	
Devon	99	Calderdale, Kirklees, Leeds,		Isle of Scilly	204
Dorset, Bournemouth, Poole	103	Wakefield	181		
Durham	105	Wiltshire	185	**Welsh Operators**	
East Sussex, Brighton & Hove	107	Worcestershire	188	Anglesey	205
East Riding of Yorkshire,				Blaenau Gwent	205
Kingston upon Hull	109	**Channel Islands Operators**		Bridgend	205
Essex	110	Alderney	189	Caerphilly	206
Gloucestershire	114	Guernsey	189	Cardiff	206
Greater Manchester, Bolton, Bury,		Jersey	189	Carmarthenshire	207
Oldham, Rochdale, Salford,				Ceredigion	207
Tameside, Wigan	116	**Scottish Operators**		Conwy	208
Hampshire	118	Aberdeen, City of	190	Denbighshire	208
Herefordshire	122	Aberdeenshire	190	Flintshire	209
Hertfordshire	123	Angus	191	Gwynedd	209
Isle of Wight	125	Argyll & Bute	191	Merthyr Tydfil	210
Kent	126	Borders	192	Monmouthshire	210
Lancashire, Blackburn with Darwen,		Clackmannanshire	192	Neath & Port Talbot	210
Blackpool, Wigan	130	Dumfries & Galloway	192	Newport	211
Leicestershire, City of Leicester,		Dundee, City of	193	Pembrokeshire	211
Rutland	133	East Ayrshire	194	Powys	211
Lincolnshire	135	East Lothian	194	Rhondda, Cynon, Taff	213
London	137	East Renfrewshire	194	Swansea	213
Merseyside area (St Helens,		Edinburgh, City of	194	Torfaen	214
Knowsley, Liverpool, Sefton,		Falkirk	195	Vale of Glamorgan	214
Wirral)	143	Fife	195	Wrexham	214
Middlesex	144	Glasgow, City of	196		
Norfolk	146	Highland	196	**Northern Ireland Operators**	
North Lincolnshire,		Inverclyde	197	Northern Ireland	217
North East Lincolnshire	148	Midlothian	197		
North Yorkshire, York	149	Moray	198	**Republic of Ireland Operators**	
Northamptonshire	153	North Ayrshire	198	Republic of Ireland	218
		North Lanarkshire	198		

Unitary authorities are included within the postal boundaries.

79

MAJOR GROUPS

*ARRIVA PLC
ADMIRAL WAY, DOXFORD INTERNATIONAL BUSINESS PARK, SUNDERLAND SR3 3XP
Tel: 0191 520 4000
Chairman (Non Exec): Sir Richard Broadbent **Chief Executive**: David Martin **Group Man Dir (Finance)**: Steve Lonsdale
Non Exec Dirs: Veronica Palmer OBE, Nick Buckles, Simon Batey, Steve Wiliams
***ARRIVA BUS & COACH**
Lodge Garage, Whitehall Road West, Gomersal, Cleckheaton BD19 4BJ
ARRIVA PASSENGER SERVICES
487 DUNSTABLE ROAD, LUTON LU4 8DS
Tel: 01582 587000
Man Dir UK Regional Bus: Mike Cooper **Eng Dir**: Mark Bowd

BLAZEFIELD GROUP
PROSPECT PARK, BROUGHTON WAY, STARBECK, HARROGATE HG2 7NY
Tel: 01423 884020
Web site: www.blazefieldholdings.com
Chmn: C Beaumont **Dirs**: Giles Fearnley, Stuart Wilde
Subsidiary companies: Burnley & Pendle, Harrogate & District Travel Ltd, Keighley & District Travel Ltd, Lancashire United, Yorkshire Coastliner Ltd.
Blazefield Holdings is part of Transdev Group

FIRST
395 KING STREET, ABERDEEN AB24 5RP
Tel: 01224 650100
Fax: 01224 650140
Website: www.firstgroup.com
Chmn: Martin Gilbert **DepChmn/Ch Exec**: Moir Lockhead
Fin Dir: Dean Finch **Dir, UK Bus**: Nicola Shaw
Ops Dir: David Kaye **Comm Dir**: Leon Daniels
Senior Independent Non-Exec Dir: David Dunn
Non Exec Dir: Jim Forbes
Dir International Development: David Leeder
UK Rail: Andrew Haines **Dep UK Bus Dir**: David Kaye
Non-exec Dirs: David Begg, John Sievwright
Non-Exec Employee Dir: Martyn Williams

THE GO-AHEAD GROUP PLC
3RD FLOOR, 41-51 GREY STREET, NEWCASTLE UPON TYNE NE1 6EE
Tel: 0191 232 3123
Fax: 0191 221 0315
E-mail: admin@go-ahead.com
Website: www.go-ahead.com
Ch Exec: Keith Ludeman **Non-Exec Chmn**: Sir Patrick Brown
Non-Exec Dirs: Christopher Collins, Rupert Pennant-Rea
Fleet: 3371 - 1157 double-deck bus, 542 single-deck bus, 532 coach, 94 articulated bus, 1046 minibus/midibus.
Ops incl: local bus services, excursions & tours, express
Livery: local fleet identity
Ticket System: various
Subsidiary companies:
BUS: Birmingham Coach Company, Brighton & Hove Bus & Coach Company, Go North East, London General, London Central, Metrobus, Oxford Bus Company, Solent Blue Line, Southern Vectis, Wilts & Dorset
RAIL: Southern Railway, South Eastern
PARKING: Meteor
AVIATION SUPPORT SERVICES: Aviance, Plane Handling

NATIONAL EXPRESS GROUP PLC
75 DAVIES STREET, LONDON W1K 5HT
Tel: 020 7529 2000
Fax: 020 7529 2100
E-mail: info@natex.co.uk
Website: www.nationalexpress.com
Ch Ex: Richard Bowker **Ch Ex (National Express Corporation, USA)**: Keith Stock **Man Dir (AirLinks)**: Bill Cahill
Finance Director: Adam Walker **Ch Ops Officer**: Ray O'Toole
Co Sec: Tony McDonald **Group Sales & Mktg Dir**: Frazer Smith
Group Customer Service Dir: David Bird **Project Dir**: Alex Perry
Eurolines Vice President: John Gilbert **Ch Exec National Express Coaches**: Paul Bunting
Subsidiary companies
Bus and coach: National Express (nationwide express coach network using coaches hired in from local operators under contract). National Express owns Travel West Midlands, Travel Dundee and Travel London, Alsa (Spain). Eurolines UK
Rail: C2C, Maintrain, Travel Midland Metro. One Railway
Overseas: National Express Corporation (USA) - Bauman, Crabtree-Harmaan, Durham Transportation, Robinson Bus, SSL, ATC, Forsythe & Associates, Intelitran, Multisystems, Stewart International; shareholding in Westbus.

STAGECOACH GROUP
10 DUNKELD ROAD, PERTH PH1 5TW
Tel: 01738 442111
Fax: 01738 643648
Web site: www.stagecoachgroup.com, www.megabus.com
Ch Exec: Brian Souter **Ch Exec (Rail)**: Ian Dobbs
Fin Dir: Martin Griffiths **Man Dir (UK bus)**: Les Warneford
Exec Dir (Rail): Graham Eccles **Non-Exec Chmn**: Robert Spiers
Reg Dir NW: Tom Wileman **Man Dir Scotland**: Robert Andrew
Non-Exec Dirs: Ann Gloag, Ewan Brown, Iain Duffin, Janet Morgan, Russell Walls
Fleet: 2589 double-deck bus, 1408 single-deck bus, 334 coach, 27 double-deck coach, 35 articulated bus, 1536 midibus, 855 minibus.
Livery: Stagecoach
Ticket system: ERG/Wayfarer
Overseas Division: Coach USA
Rail Division: South West Trains, Island Line, joint venture Virgin Rail Group, Sheffield Supertram (Sheffield).

TRANSDEV PLC
GARRICK HOUSE, STAMFORD BROOK GARAGE, 74 CHISWICK HIGH ROAD, LONDON W4 1SY
Tel: 020 8400 6052
Fax: 020 8400 6053
E-mail: information@transdevplc.co.uk
Web site: www.transdevplc.co.uk
Ch Exec: Francois Xavier Perin **Ch Op Officer**: C Beaumont
Fin Dir: P Gillespie **Corporate Sers Dir**: C Sellars
Subsidiary companies: Blazefield Holdings, Blackburn Borough Transport, Bournemouth Transport, shareholder partner with Nottingham council with Nottingham City Transport, Nottingham Express Transit (joint with NCT), London United, London Sovereign.

VEOLIA TRANSPORT UK LTD
37-41 OLD QUEEN STREET, LONDON SW1H 9JA
Tel: 0207 393 2700
Fax: 0207 393 2859
Web site: www.veolia-transport.info
Chmn: John O'Brien **Ch Op Off**: Steve McAleavy
Fin Dir: Michael Vermeulen **Man Dir, Midlands**: Steve Campbell
Man Dir, North East: Neil Wood
Subsidiary companies: Bebb Travel, Pullman Coaches, Longs Coaches, Hawkes Coaches, Shamrock Travel, Thomas of Barry, Dunn Line Holdings, Paul James Coaches

WELLGLADE LTD
MANSFIELD ROAD, HEANOR, DERBY DE75 7BG.
Tel: 01773 536309
Fax: 01773 536310
Subsidiary companies: Trent-Barton Ltd, Kinchbus Ltd, Nottinghamshire & Derbyshire Traction Co Ltd.

BEDFORDSHIRE

AtoB TRAVEL (LUTON) LTD

UNIT 54, BILTON WAY, LUTON
LU1 1UU
Tel: 01582 733333
Fax: 01582 733331
Web site: www.atobexec.com
Fleet: 50 - coach, minicoach, midicoach
Chassis: incl: Ford. Mercedes.
Bodies: incl: Ford. Mercedes.
Ops incl: school contracts, private hire
Livery: Silver

ARRIVA THE SHIRES & ESSEX LTD

487 DUNSTABLE ROAD, LUTON
LU4 8DS
Tel: 01582 587000/08701 201088
Web site: www.arrivabus.co.uk
Fleetname: Arriva the Shires & Essex.
Man Dir: Paul Woolmore
Fleet: 550 - double-deck bus, single-deck bus, coach, minibus.
Chassis: incl: 4 Optare
Bodies: incl: 4 Optare
Ops incl: local bus services, school contracts, excursions & tours, private hire, express.
Livery: Aquamarine and Cream.
Ticket System: Wayfarer 3, Prestige.

BARFORDIAN COACHES LTD

500 GOLDINGTON ROAD, BEDFORD
MK41 0DX
Tel: 01234 355440
Fax: 01234 355310
E-mail: info@barfordiancoaches.co.uk
Web site: www.barfordiancoaches.co.uk
Man Dir: P Bullard **Dir**: K Bullard **Ops Man**: K Hargreaves
Fleet: 24 - 5 double-deck bus, 1 single-deck bus, 12 coach, 2 double-deck coach, 1 midicoach, 1 minibus, 2 minicoach.
Chassis: 1 Bedford. 11 Bova. 4 Leyland. 1 MCW. 3 Mercedes. 2 Neoplan. 2 Toyota. 1 Volvo.
Bodies: 2 Alexander. 11 Bova. 1 Caetano. 1 Duple. 2 ECW. 1 Jonckheere. 1 MCW. 1 Mellor. 2 Neoplan. 1 Plaxton. 1 other.
Ops incl: local bus services, school contracts, excursions & tours, private hire, continental tours.
Livery: Orange/Yellow/White
Ticket System: Almex

CLASSIC COACHES

47 WELLINGTON STREET, LUTON
LU1 2QH
Tel: 01582 457008
Owner: R J Lush
Fleet: 7 - 5 coaches, 2 minibus.
Chassis: 2 DAF. 2 LDV. 2 Scania. 1 Volvo.
Bodies: 1 Berkhof. 1 Caetano. 2 LDV. 1 Plaxton. 2 Van Hool.
Ops incl: private hire, school contracts, excursions & tours, continental tours.
Livery: White

CEDAR COACHES

ARKWRIGHT ROAD, BEDFORD
MK42 0LE.
Tel: 01234 354054
Fax: 01234 219210
E-mail: nikki@cedarcoaches.co.uk
Web site: www.cedarcoaches.co.uk
Man Dir: Eric Reid **Co Sec**: Nichola Graham **Dirs**: Donna Reid, Kevin Reid
Fleet: 30 - 17 double-deck bus, 4 single-deck bus, 6 coach, 1 double-deck coach, 2 minicoach.
Chassis: Ayats. Bova. Irisbus. Iveco. Leyland. Scania. Volvo.
Bodies: Ayats. Beulas. Bova
Ops incl: local bus services, school contracts, excursions & tours, private hire.
Livery: Red/Yellow

CENTREBUS LTD

14 SEDGWICK ROAD, LUTON
LU4 9DT
Tel: 08707 444746
Web site: www.centrebus.co.uk
Man Dir: Peter Harvey **Ops Di**: Neil Harris
Fleet: 60 single-deck bus
Ops incl: local bus services
Livery: Blue/Orange
Ticket system: Wayfarer 3

*CHILTERN TRAVEL

THE COACH HOUSE, BARFORD
ROAD, BLUNHAM MK44 3NA
Tel: 01767 641400
Fax: 01767 641358
E-mail: chilterntravel@hotmail.com
Fleet: 17 - 3 single-deck bus, 12 coach, 2 minibus.
Chassis: 2 Bova. 2 Iveco. 3 Mercedes. 1 Neoplan. 3 Optare. 1 Renault. 3 Volvo.
Bodies: 2 Beulas. 2 Bova. 3 Mercedes. 1 Neoplan. 3 Optare. 2 other.
Ops incl: local bus services, private hire, continental tours, school contracts, excursions & tours.

CORPORATE COACHING

EAGLE HOUSE, EAGLE CENTRE
WAY, LUTON LU4 9US
Tel: 01525 715872
Fax: 01525 713020
E-mail: sales@corp-coach.co.uk
Web site: www.corp-coach.co.uk
Man Dir: Doreen Collins **Ops Dir**: Peter Collins
Fleet: 8 - 4 midicoach, 4 minicoach.
Chassis: 8 Mercedes-Benz.
Ops incl: private hire, express.
Livery: Blue/Silver

*DUNN-LINE GROUP

See Nottinghamshire

*EXPRESSLINES LTD

FENLAKE ROAD INDUSTRIAL
ESTATE, BEDFORD MK42 0HB
Tel: 01234 268704
Fax: 01234 272212
Dirs: Chris Spriggs, Richard Harris
Fleet: 15 - 4 midibus, 3 midicoach, 8 minicoach.
Chassis: 6 Ford Transit. 5 Mercedes-Benz. 4 Optare.
Bodies: 8 Optare. 7 other.
Ops incl: local bus services, school contracts, private hire.
Livery: Red/White/Silver
Ticket System: Wayfarer

*FLIGHTS HALLMARK

See West Midlands

GRANT PALMER PASSENGER SERVICES

UNIT 2, LAWRENCE WAY,
DUNSTABLE LU6 1BD
Tel: 01582 600844
Ops incl: local bus services

HERBERTS TRAVEL

UNIT 5, OLD ROWNEY FARM,
SHEFFORD SG17 5QH
Tel: 0845 0090 369
Fax: 01234 381117
Ops Dir: D S Dougall **Man Dir**: D M Dougall
Fleet Eng: S Myers
E-mail: booking@herberts-travel.co.uk
Web site: www.herberts-travel.co.uk
Fleet: 21 - 6 double-deck bus, 5 midibus, 4 midicoach, 1 minibus, 5 minicoach.
Chassis: 5 Ford Transit. 5 Leyland. 3 MCW. 4 Mercedes. 2 Optare. 1 Toyota. 1 Volvo.
Bodies: 4 Alexander. 1 Caetano. 2 ECW. 1 Leyland. 1 MCW. 4 Optare. 1 Plaxton. 6 other.
Ops incl: private hire, school contracts, local bus services.
Livery: White.
Ticket system: Wayfarer

*MARSHALLS COACHES

FIRBANK WAY, LEIGHTON
BUZZARD LU7 4YP
Tel: 01525 376077
Fax: 01525 850967
Recovery: 01525 375301
E-mail: info@marshalls-coaches.co.uk
Web site: www.marshalls-coaches.co.uk
Fleetname: MCE Ltd
Prop: G Marshall **Ops Man**: I White **Wkshp Man**: R Winters
Fleet: 28 - 3 double-deck bus, 22 coach, 2 double-deck coach, 1 midicoach.
Chassis: 3 Ayats. 4 Dennis. 3 Iveco. 2 Leyland. 1 Mercedes. 15 Volvo.
Bodies: 3 Ayats. 3 Beulas. 1 Caetano. 3 East Lancs. 5 Jonckheere. 1 Mercedes. 10 Plaxton.
Ops incl: private hire, school contracts, continental tours.
Livery: Blue/Multicoloured.

RED KITE COMMERCIAL SERVICES
UNIT 2, LEYS YARD, DUNSTABLE ROAD, TILSWORTH, LEIGHTON BUZZARD LU7 9PU
Tel: 01525 211441
Props: D. Hoar, R. H. Savage
Fleet: 18 - 15 double-deck bus, 3 coach.
Ops incl: local bus services, school contracts, excursions and tours, private hire, school contracts.
Livery: Red/Blue

*SAFFORD COACHES LTD
See Cambridgeshire

SHOREYS TRAVEL
119 CLOPHILL ROAD, MAULDEN MK45 2AE.
Tel: 01525 860694
Fax: 01525 861850.
E-mail: shoreystravel@talk21.com
Prop: E C J Shorey **Ptnrs**: D Shorey, G Shorey **Ch Eng**: D Bunker
Fleet: 8 - 7 double deck bus, 1 coach.
Chassis: 1 Iveco. 1 Leyland. 6 MCW.
Bodies: 1 Beulas. 6 MCW. 1 Leyland.
Ops incl: school contracts, private hire.
Livery: White/Green
Ticket System: Wayfarer.

*TATES COACHES
See Hertfordshire

THREE STAR COACH HIRE
6 HIGH TOWN ROAD, LUTON LU2 0DD
Tel: 01582 722626
Fax: 01582 484034
E-mail: sales@bookthisbus.com
Ops Man: Kevin Green
Fleet: 14 - 5 coach, 3 midicoach, 4 minibus, 2 minicoach.

Chassis: 2 Dennis. 1 MAN. 2 Volvo.
Bodies: incl: 9 Mercedes.
Ops incl: local bus services, school contracts, private hire.
Livery: Blue

VILLAGER MINIBUS (SHARNBROOK) LTD
SHARNBROOK UPPER SCHOOL, ODELL ROAD, SHARNBROOK MK44 1JL
Tel: 01234 781920
Fleet: 1 minibus
Chassis: 1 Ford
Ops incl: local bus services, private hire
Ticket system: printed book

BERKSHIRE
(WEST BERKSHIRE, BRACKNELL FOREST, READING, SLOUGH, WINDSOR & MAIDENHEAD, WOKINGHAM)

1ST CHOICE SCORPIO TRAVEL
67 WEST END COURT, WEST END LANE, STOKE POGES SL2 4NB
Tel: 01753 648435
Fax: 01753 644878
E-mail: admin@scorpiotravel.net
Web site: www.scorpiotravel.net
Ptnrs: Don Hughes, Gill Hughes.
Fleet: 1 coach
Chassis: Iveco
Body: Beulas
Ops incl: excursions & tours, private hire, continental tours.
Livery: Silver/Cerise/Teal

ALDERMASTON COACHES
ALDERMASTON RG7 5PP
Tel: 0118 971 3257
Fax: 0118 971 2722
Ptnrs: D. Arlott, T. Arlott, P. Arlott
Fleet: includes 1 midicoach, 1 minicoach.
Chassis: includes 4 Leyland.
Ops incl: private hire, school contracts.
Livery: White

BURGHFIELD MINI COACHES LTD
BURGHFIELD FARM, MILL ROAD, BURGHFIELD BRIDGE RG30 3SS
Tel/Fax: 0118 959 0719
E-mail: burghfield.coaches@virgin.net
Dir: Susan McCoud
Fleet: 38 - 30 minibus, 8 minicoach.
Chassis: Citroen. Dennis. Leyland. Mercedes-Benz. Optare. Renault.
Ops incl: local bus services, school contracts, private hire.

COURTNEY COACHES
TERRANOVA HOUSE, KILN LANE, BRACKNELL RG12 1NA
Tel: 01344 412302
Fax: 01344 868980/422278
E-mail: enquiries@courtneycoaches.com
Web site: www.courtneycoaches.com
Prop: Bill Courtney-Smith
Fleet: 37 - 5 double-decker bus, 11 coach, 3 double-deck, 4 single-deck bus, 14 minibus.
Chassis: 1 Ayats. 1 Iveco. 7 Leyland. 1 Marshall. 14 Mercedes. 1 Neoplan. 3 Optare. 2 Scania. 7 Volvo.
Ops incl: local bus services.
Livery: Orange/White.

FIRST IN BERKSHIRE
COLDBOROUGH HOUSE, MARKET STREET, BRACKNELL RG12 1JA
Tel: 01344 868688
Fax: 01344 868332
Web site: www.firstgroup.com
Comm Dir: Andrew Taylor
Fleet: 115 - 6 double-deck bus, 68 single-deck bus, 24 midibus, 17 coach.
Chassis: 6 Bluebird. 55 Dennis. 8 Mercedes. 33 Scania. 13 Volvo.
Bodies: 19 Alexander. 8 Berkhof. 6 Bluebird. 1 Irizar. 8 Mercedes. 10 Northern Counties. 43 Plaxton. 20 Wright.
Ops incl: local bus services, school contracts, express.
Livery: FirstGroup/Green Line
Ticket System: Wayfarer.

HAYWARDS COACHES
169 NEW GREENHAM PARK, THATCHAM RG19 6HN
Tel: 0118 547 4561

Fax: 01635 821128
Dir: Simon Weaver
Fleet: 24 - 18 coach, 6 double-deck coach.
Chassis: 8 Bova. 7 Scania. 9 Volvo.
Bodies: 8 Bova. 6 East Lancs. 7 Irizar. 3 Plaxton.
Ops incl: local bus services, school contracts
Livery: Electric Blue

HODGE'S COACHES (SANDHURST) LTD
100 YORKTOWN ROAD, SANDHURST GU47 9BH.
Tel: 01252 873131
Fax: 01252 874884.
E-mail: enquiries@hodges-coaches.co.uk
Web site: www.hodges-coaches.co.uk
Man Dir: P Hodge **Dir**: M Hodge, M Hodge
Fleet: 21 - 18 single-deck coach, 1 midicoach, 2 minicoach.
Chassis: 4 Bedford. 2 DAF, 1 MAN, 2 Toyota, 12 Volvo
Bodies: 10 Berkhof. 7 Caetano. 1 Duple. 3 Plaxton.
Ops incl: excursions & tours, private hire, continental tours, school contracts.
Livery: Blue/Gold

*HORSEMAN COACHES LTD
WHITLEY WOOD ROAD, READING RG2 8GG
Tel: 0118 975 3811
Fax: 0118 975 3515
E-mail: privatehire@horsemancoaches.myzen.co.uk
Man Dir: Keith Horseman **Ops Dir**: James Horseman **Ch Eng**: Derrick Holton
personnel: Anne Fletcher **Ser Man**: Trevor Underwood

82

Fleet: 59 - 50 coach, 9 midicoach.
Chassis: 1 Dennis. 4 Iveco. 9 Toyota. 45 Volvo.
Bodies: 4 Beulas. 3 Berkhof. 9 Caetano. 42 Plaxton. 1 UVG.
Ops incl: local bus services, school contracts, excursions & tours, private hire, continental tours.
Livery: multi-coloured

KINGFISHER MINI COACHES
357 BASINGSTOKE ROAD, READING RG2 0JA
Tel: 0118 931 3454
Prop: Kevin Pope
Fleet: 13 - 5 minibus, 8 minicoach
Chassis: incl. 6 Leyland. 4 Mercedes.
Ops incl: private hire. school contracts
Livery: White/Orange

MEMORY LANE VINTAGE OMNIBUS SERVICES
78 LILLIBROOKE CRESCENT, MAIDENHEAD SL6 3XQ
Tel: 01628 825050
E-mail: admin@memorylane.co.uk
Web site: www.memorylane.co.uk
Prop: M J Clarke
Fleet: 6 - 4 double-deck bus, 2 single-deck bus
Chassis: 5 AEC. 1 Bristol
Bodies: 1 ECW. 1 MCW. 4 Park Royal.
Ops incl: private hire
Livery: Original operators

*NEWBURY & DISTRICT
169 NEW GREENHAM PARK, NEWBURY RG19 6HN
Tel: 01635 33855
Fax: 01635 821128
Dir: Simon Weaver
Fleet: 3 single-deck bus.
Chassis: 3 Volvo.
Bodies: 3 Wright.
Ops incl: local bus services
Livery: White
Ticket System: Wayfarer 3

READING & WOKINGHAM COACHES
33 MURRAY ROAD, WOKINGHAM RG41 2TA
Tel: 0118 979 3983
Fax: 0118 979 4330
Props: Mark Way, Sharon Way.
Fleet: 10 - 8 coach, 2 minibus
Chassis: 1 Dennis. 1 Iveco. 1 Mercedes.

1 Setra. 1 Toyota. 5 Volvo.
Bodies: 1 Beulas. 2 Berkhof. 1 Caetano. 1 Ikarus. 1 Jonckheere. 1 Mercedes. 1 Setra. 2 Van Hool.
Ops incl: excursions & tours, private hire, school contracts, continental tours.
Livery: White

*READING HERITAGE TRAVEL
PO BOX 147, READING RG1 6PP
Tel: 07850 220151
Tran Man: M J Russell
Fleet: 1 double-deck bus.
Chassis: 1 AEC
Bodies: 1 Park Royal
Ops incl: private hire
Livery: Red/Cream
Ticket System: Almex

*READING TRANSPORT LTD
GREAT KNOLLYS STREET, READING RG1 7HH
Tel: 0118 959 4000
Fax: 0118 957 5379
Recovery: 0118 958 7625
E-mail: info@reading-buses.co.uk.
Web site: www.reading-buses.co.uk
Fleetname: Reading Buses, Newbury Buses, Goldline
Chmn: Tony Jones **Ch Exec Off**: James Freeman **Ops Dir**: Sam Simpson **Goldline Man**: Norman Fryer-Saxby **Newbury Man**: Paul Lightowler **Reading Buses Man**: Glynne Davies **Eng Man**: vacant **Personnel Man**: Caroline Anscombe
Fleet: 191 - 83 double-deck bus, 73 single-deck bus, 9 single-deck coach, 26 midibus.
Chassis: 27 DAF. 7 Dennis. 1 MAN. 41 Optare. 115 Scania.
Bodies: 1 Alexander. 62 East Lancs. 6 Irizar. 12 Omni. 58 Optare. 6 Plaxton. 3 Van Hool. 36 Wright.
Ops incl: local bus services, school contracts, excursions & tours, private hire, continental tours.
Livery: various brand liveries
Ticket System: Wayfarer TGX150

*TOP TRAVEL COACHES
See Hampshire

VINCE COACHES
AYRES HOUSE, AYRES LANE, BURGHCLERE RG20 9HG
Tel: 01635 278308

Prop: D. L. Vince
Fleet: 5 coaches
Chassis/Bodies: 2 Berkhof. 3 Dennis.
Ops incl: private hire, school contracts.

*WEAVAWAY TRAVEL
169 NEW GREENHAM PARK, NEWBURY RG19 6HN
Tel: 01635 820028
Fax: 01635 821128
Dir: Simon Weaver
Fleet: 33 - 4 single-deck bus, 22 coach, 6 double-deck coach, 1 minicoach.
Chassis: 8 Bova. 4 DAF. 4 Dennis. 1 Mercedes. 10 Scania. 6 Volvo.
Bodies: 3 Berkhof. 8 Bova. 9 East Lancs. 7 Irizar. 1 MCW. 1 Plaxton. 4 Van Hool.
Ops incl: school contracts, private hire.
Livery: Electric Blue

WHITE BUS SERVICES
NORTH STREET GARAGE, WINKFIELD SL4 4TP
Tel: 01344 88262
Fax: 01344 886403
E-mail: reception@whitebus.co.uk
Dir: D. E. Jeatt
Fleet: 12 - 3 single-deck bus, 9 coach.
Chassis: include DAF, Bedford.
Bodies: Duple. Optare. Plaxton. Van Hool.
Ops incl: local bus services, school contracts, private hire.
Livery: White/grey skirt.
Ticket System: Wayfarer Saver, Setright

*WINDSORIAN COACHES
373 HATTON ROAD, BEDFONT, FELTHAM TW14 9QS
Tel: 01753 860131
Fax: 020 8751 5054
Web site: www.windsoriancoaches.co.uk
Man Dir: Martin Cornell **Gen Man**: Gilbert Parsons
Fleet: 10 - 8 double-deck coach, 2 midicoach.
Chassis: 7 Dennis. 2 Mercedes. 1 Volvo.
Bodies: 2 Mellor. 8 Plaxton.
Ops incl: school contracts, excursions & tours, private hire, continental tours.
Livery: White/Blue

Berkshire

A/c	Air conditioning	✓	Replacement vehicle available
♿	Vehicles suitable for disabled	T	Toilet-drop facilities available
🍴	Coach(es) with galley facilities		Vintage vehicle(s) available
wc	Coach(es) with toilet facilities		Open top vehicle(s)
🔹	Seat belt-fitted vehicles		
R	Recovery service available (not 24 hr)		
R24	24hr recovery service		

BRISTOL

ABUS
104 WINCHESTER ROAD,
BRISLINGTON BS4 3NL
Tel: 0117 977 6126
E-mail: alan@abus.co.uk
Web site: www.abus.co.uk
Chmn/Man Dir: Alan Peters
Fleet: 20 - 17 double-deck bus, 3 midibus.
Chassis: 3 Bristol. 5 DAF. 1 Iveco.
8 Leyland. 2 Optare. 1 Scania.
Bodies: 7 Alexander. 3 ECW. 3 East Lancs.
6 Optare. 1 Reeve Burgess
Ops incl: local bus services
Livery: Cream/White/Maroon or Orange
Ticket System: Wayfarer 3

AZTEC COACH TRAVEL
6/8 EMERY ROAD, BRISLINGTON
BS4 5PF
Tel: 0117 977 0314.
Fax: 0117 977 4431.
Man Dir: I. Fortune. **Fleet Eng:** D. Harvey.
Ops Man: P. Rixon.
Fleet: 15 - 13 midicoach, 2 minibus.
Chassis: 1 Freight Rover. 14 Mercedes.
Bodies: 2 Optare. 7 Reeve Burgess.
4 Autobus Classique.
Ops incl: excursions & tours, private hire,
continental tours, school contracts.
Livery: White with diagonal red/orange
stripes.

BERKELEY COACH & TRAVEL
HAM LANE, PAULTON BS39 7PL
Tel: 01761 413196
Fax: 01761 416469
E-mail:
mail@berkeleycoachandtravel.co.uk
Web site:
www.berkeleycoachandtravel.co.uk
Fleet: 12 coach
Chassis: 12 Volvo
Bodies: 8 Plaxton. 4 Van Hool.
Ops incl: school contracts, private hire.
Livery: Silver/Blue

*BLAGDON LIONESS COACHES LTD
See Somerset

BLUE IRIS COACHES
25 CLEVEDON ROAD, NAILSEA
BS48 1EH
Tel: 01275 851121
Fax: 01275 856522
E-mail: tonys@blueiris.co.uk
Web site: www.blueiris.co.uk
Dirs: Philip Hatherall, Tony Spiller
Fleet: 15 - 2 single-deck bus, 7 single-deck
coach, 6 minicoach.
Chassis: 2 Mercedes. 6 Scania. 6 Toyota.
1 Volvo.
Bodies: 1 Alexander. 6 Caetano. 1 Carlyle.
6 Irizar. 1 Plaxton.
Ops incl: private hire, local bus services,
school contracts.
Livery: 2-tone Blue/White.
Ticket System: Setright

BRISTOL ELECTRIC RAILBUS LTD
HERON HOUSE, CHISWICK MALL,
LONDON W4 2PR
Tel: 020 8995 3000
Fax: 020 8994 6060
Dir: James Skinner
Fleet: 1 tram.
Chassis/Body: Parry/Clayton

BUGLERS COACHES
100 SCHOOL ROAD, BRISLINGTON
BS4 4NF
Tel: 0117 977 8759
E-mail: buglercoaches@yahoo.com
Web site: www.buglercoaches.co.uk
Dir: Gerald Creed
Fleet: 16 - 2 double-deck bus, 7 coach,
3 midicoach, 4 minibus
Chassis: Bristol, Dennis, Leyland, Mercedes,
Optare, Volvo
Bodies: Alexander, Plaxton, other
Ops incl: local bus services, private hire
Livery: Yellow/Red/White
(Subsidiary of Computer Village Group)

PETER CAROL PRESTIGE COACHING
BAMFIELD HOUSE, WHITCHURCH
BS14 0XD
Tel: 01275 839839
Fax: 01275 835604
E-mail: charter@petercarol.co.uk
Web site: www.luxurycoach.co.uk
Gen Man: Peter Collis
Fleet: 12 - 10 coach, 2 double-deck coach.
Chassis: 2 Bova. 2 DAF. 2 MAN. 4 Neoplan.
1 Scania. 1 Toyota.
Bodies: 1 Berkhof. 2 Bova. 2 Caetano.
4 Neoplan. 1 Noge. 2 Van Hool.
Ops incl: excursions & tours, private hire,
continental tours.
Livery: Dark Grey

*CLASSIC GOLD COACHES
74 COLERIDGE VALE ROAD, SOUTH
CLEVEDON BS21 6PG
Tel: 01275 870000
Fax: 01275 870087
Owner: A F Langson
Fleet: 7 - 1 double-deck bus, 1 coach,
1 midicoach, 4 minicoach
Ops incl: local bus services, school
contracts, excursions & tours, private hire

EAGLE COACHES
FIRECLAY HOUSE, NETHAM ROAD,
ST GEORGE BS5 9PJ
Tel: 0117 955 7130
Fax: 0117 941 1107
E-mail: any@eagle-coaches.co.uk
Web site: www.eagle-coaches.co.uk
Fleet: 15 - 2 double-deck bus, 11 coach,
1 midicoach, 1 minicoach
Chassis: 11 DAF. 1 Iveco. 1 Leyland.
1 Mercedes. 1 Scania.

Bodies: 2 Alexander. 1 Autobus. 1 Optare.
11 Van Hool.
Ops incl: school contracts, excursions &
tours, private hire
Livery: Yellow

EASTVILLE COACHES LTD
15 ASHGROVE ROAD, REDLAND
BS6 6NA
Tel: 0117 971 0657
Fax: 0117 971 5824.
Man Dir: T. Reece.
Fleet: 14 - 6 double-deck bus, 8 coach.
Chassis: 6 Bristol. 1 DAF. 7 Volvo.
Bodies: 6 ECW. 2 Plaxton. 6 Van Hool.
Ops incl: local bus services, school
contracts, private hire, continental tours.
Livery: Myosotis Blue/White.

*EUROTAXIS
CHERRY ORCHARD BARN, SISTON
HILL, BRISTOL BS30 5LT
Tel: 0871 250 5555
Fax: 0871 250 4444
Mobile: 07970 210220
E-mail: juan@eurotaxis.com
Web site: www.eurotaxis.com
Dirs: Juan Sanzo (**CoSec**), Keith Sanzo
(**Gen Man**), Anne Sanzo
Fleet: 115 - 4 double-deck bus,
15 single-deck bus, 25 coach, 20 midibus,
20 minicoach, 20 minibus, 20 minicoach.
Chassis: 100 Mercedes. 10 Optare.
15 Volvo.
Ops incl: local bus services, school
contracts, private hire, excursions & tours
Ticket system: Wayfarer 2

*EXPRESS TRANSPORT SERVICES
*See CLASSIC GOLD COACHES
above*

FIRST BRISTOL
ENTERPRISE HOUSE, EASTON
ROAD, BRISTOL BS5 0DZ
Tel: 0117 955 8211
Fax: 0117 955 1248
Web site: www.firstgroup.com
Man Dir: Tony Anthistle **Eng Dir:** Richard
Noble **Fin Dir:** Mike Gahan **Ops Dir:** Jenny
McLeod
Fleet: 314 - 133 double-deck bus, 44 single-
deck bus, 124 midibus, 13 minibus.
Chassis: 115 Dennis. 91 Leyland.
19 Mercedes. 89 Volvo.
Bodies: 29 Alexander. 8 East Lancs.
35 Leyland. 70 Northern Counties.
102 Plaxton. 30 Roe. 40 Wright.
Ops incl: local bus services, school
contracts.
Livery: First Bus Barbie 1+2
Ticket System: Wayfarer

GLENVIC OF BRISTOL LTD
THE OLD COLLIERY, STANTON
WICK, PENSFORD BS39 4BZ

Tel: 01761 490116
Fax: 0117 907 7032
Dirs: Paul Holvey, Philip Holvey
Ops Man/Comp Sec: Paul Holvey
Eng: Nick Reed
Fleet: 13 - 4 double-deck bus, 5 coach, 4 minicoach
Chassis: 2 LDV. 7 Leyland. 2 Mercedes-Benz. 2 Volvo.

*GRAHAM'S COACHES
wc 🎗 A/c 🔧

7 WYCK BECK ROAD, BRENTRY BS10 7JD
Tel/Fax: 0117 950 9398
Prop: Graham P Smith
Fleet: 8 - 5 double-deck bus, 3 midicoaches.
Chassis: 1 DAF. 2 Dennis. 2 Leyland. 1 Optare. 2 Volvo
Bodies: 2 Alexander. 2 Jonckheere. 1 Optare. 1 Van Hool.
Ops incl: private hire, school contracts.
Livery: White/Red/Maroon

ARNOLD LIDDELL COACHES 🎗

89 JERSEY AVENUE, BRISLINGTON BS4 4QX.
Tel: 0117 977 2011.
Prop: Michael. Liddell. **Gen Man**: Arnold. Liddell. **Fleet Eng**: Robert Liddell
Fleet: 2 - 1 coach, 1 midicoach.
Chassis: 1 Leyland. 1 Mercedes.
Ops incl: excursions & tours, school contracts.
Livery: Blue/White.

MARTINS SELF DRIVE MINICOACH HIRE 🎗

GRINDELL ROAD GARAGE, 1 GRINDELL ROAD, REDFIELD BS5 9PG.

Tel: 0117 955 1042.
Fax: 0117 939 3383.
Fleet: 12 - 12 minibus.
Chassis: 12 Ford Transit.
Ops incl: Self Drive Minicoach Hire.

*NORTH SOMERSET COACHES 🎗

COATES ESTATE, SOUTHFIELD ROAD, NAILSEA BS48 1JN
Tel/Fax: 01275 859123
Prop: Graham Clements.
Fleet: 2 coach.
Chassis: 1 Dennis. 1 Volvo.
Bodies: 1 Berkhof. 1 Plaxton.
Ops incl: school contracts, private hire.

PREMIER TRAVEL LTD
🎗 wc A/c R24 🔧 T

ALBERT CRESCENT, ST PHILIPS BS2 0SU
Tel: 0117 9300 5550
Fax: 0117 9300 5551
Man Dir: Glenn Bond
Fleet: 5 - 1 double-deck bus, 2 coach, 1 double-deck coach, 1 minicoach.
Chassis: 9 Bova. 1 DAF. 1 Freight Rover. 1 Leyland. 1 Volvo
Bodies: 1 Bova. 1 ECW. 2 Van Hool.
Ops incl: school contracts, continental tours, private hire.
Livery: White/Red with blue lettering.

SOUTH GLOUCESTERSHIRE BUS & COACH COMPANY
♿ 🎗 wc A/c 🔧

PEGASUS PARK, GYPSY PATCH LANE, PATCHWAY BS34 6QD
Tel: 0117 931 4340
Fax: 0117 979 9400
Man Dir: Roger Durbin **Gen Man**: Mike Owen **Wkshp Man**: Mark Wood **Sales Man**: Tony Laudie **Route Man**: Nathan Wrenn
Fleet: 99 - 26 double-deck bus. 26 single-deck bus. 22 coach. 1 double-deck coach. 9 midibus. 15 minibus.
Chassis: 10 Dennis. 35 Leyland. 15 Mercedes. 1 Toyota. 38 Volvo.
Bodies: 20 Alexander. 1 Caetano. 16 Northern Counties. 38 Plaxton. 6 Reeve Burgess. 12 Van Hool. 2 Wadham Stringer. 4 Wright.
Ops incl: local bus service, school contracts, excursions & tours, private hire, continental tours, express.
Livery: Blue/White.
Ticket system: Wayfarer 2

SOMERBUS LTD
See Somerset

*TURNERS COACHWAYS (BRISTOL) LTD
wc 🎗 A/c

59 DAYS ROAD, ST PHILIPS BS2 0QS
Tel: 0117 955 9086
Fax: 0117 955 6948
E-mail:
admin@turnerscoachways.co.uk
Web site:
www.turnerscoachways.co.uk
Man Dir: Tony Turner. **Private Hire Man**: Liz Venn **Traf Man**: Tony Harvey
Fleet: 31 - 30 coach, 1 minicoach.
Chassis: 7 Scania. 2 Setra. 1 Toyota. 20 Volvo.
Bodies: 2 Berkhof. 7 Irizar. 14 Jonckheere. 1 Optare. 2 Plaxton. 2 Setra. 2 Van Hool.
Ops incl: school contracts, private hire
Livery: Silver/Blue

BUCKINGHAMSHIRE, MILTON KEYNES

AUTODOUBLE LTD

90 HAINAULT AVENUE, GIFFARD PARK, MILTON KEYNES MK14 5PE.
Tel: 01908 281350.
Fleetname: Starlight.
Fin Dir/Sec: N. A Gibbard.
Traf Man/Dir: K. G. Gibbard.
Fleet: 5 - 1 coach, 1 midibus, 3 minicoach.
Chassis: 2 Bedford. 1 Bristol. 2 Ford Transit.
Bodies: 1 ECW. 1 Plaxton. 2 Dormobile. 1 Tricentrol.
Ops incl: private hire, school contracts.
Livery: White/Burgundy.

*BRAZIERS MINI COACHES

17 VICARAGE ROAD, WINSLOW MK18 3BE
Tel: 01296 712201
E-mail: pbrazier@btconnect.com
Web site: www.brazierscoaches.co.uk
Fleet: 3 minibus
Chassis: 3 LDV
Ops incl: private hire, school contracts

CAROUSEL BUSES LTD
🎗 🚌 🚍 A/c 🔧

1 HAYDEN HOUSE, BAKER STREET, HIGH WYCOMBE HP11 2RX
Tel: 01494 533436
E-mail: enquiries@carouselbuses.com
Web site: www.carouselbuses.com
Man Dir/Co Sec: S Burns **Fin Dir**: J Robinson
Fleet: 41 - 22 double-deck bus, 19 single-deck bus
Chassis: 1 AEC. 6 DAF. 10 Dennis. 3 Irisbus. 6 Leyland. 12 MCW. 3 Mercedes
Bodies: 3 East Lancs. 4 Leyland. 12 MCW. 3 Mercedes. 3 Northern Counties. 3 Optare. 1 Park Royal. 11 Plaxton. 1 Wright.
Ops incl: Local bus services, school contracts, private hire.
Livery: Red/Dark Red
Ticket system: Wayfarer 3

A/c	Air conditioning	🎗	Seat belt-fitted vehicles	🔧	Replacement vehicle available
♿	Vehicles suitable for disabled	R	Recovery service available (not 24 hr)	T	Toilet-drop facilities available
🍽	Coach(es) with galley facilities	R24	24hr recovery service	🚍	Vintage vehicle(s) available
wc	Coach(es) with toilet facilities			🚌	Open top vehicle(s)

*DRP TRAVEL A/c

1 THE MEADWAY, LOUGHTON, MILTON KEYNES MK5 8AN
Tel: 01908 394141
Web site: www.drptravel.co.uk
E-mail: drptravel@talktalk.net
Man: D R Pinnock
Fleet: 3 minibus
Chassis/Bodies: 1 Iveco. 1 Optare. 1 Renault
Ops incl: school contracts, private hire.

HOWLETTS COACHES

UNIT 2, STATION ROAD INDUSTRIAL ESTATE, WINSLOW MK18 3DZ
Tel: 01296 713201
Fax: 01296 715879
Prop: R. S. Durham
Fleet: 8 - 2 double-deck bus, 6 coach.
Chassis: 1 Bedford. 4 DAF. 2 MCW. 1 Setra.
Ops incl: private hire, continental tours, school contracts.
Livery: Brown/White.

LANGSTON & TASKER

23 QUEEN CATHERINE ROAD, STEEPLE CLAYDON MK18 2PZ
Tel/Fax: 01296 730347
Ptnrs: Mrs J Langston, Mrs M A Fenner
Man: J Langston **Ops Man**: A P Price
Fleet: 19 - 13 single-deck coach, 6 minibus.
Chassis: 1 Bedford. 4 Dennis. 1 Iveco. 2 Leyland. 4 Mercedes. 1 Toyota. 6 Volvo.
Bodies: 1 Autobus. 2 Caetano. 3 Duple. 2 Jonckheere. 3 Mercedes. 6 Plaxton. 1 Transbus. 1 Wadham Stringer.
Ops incl: local bus services, school contracts, private hire
Livery: White/Red
Ticket system: Wayfarer

*MAGPIE TRAVEL

BINDERS INDUSTRIAL ESTATE, CRYERS HILL, HIGH WYCOMBE HP15 6LJ
Tel: 01494 715381
E-mail: Martinpeterash@supanet.com
Prop: Martin Ash
Fleet: 18 - 3 single-deck bus, 9 coach, 1 midibus, 5 midicoach.
Chassis: 2 Dennis. 2 Leyland. 9 Mercedes. 5 Volvo.
Bodies: 1 Alexander. 2 Jonckheere. 1 Leyland. 1 Marshall/MCV. 1 Optare. 2 Plaxton. 5 Reeve Burgess. 1 Van Hool. 2 Wadham Stringer. 2 other.
Ops incl: local bus services, school contracts, private hire.
Livery: White/Black
Ticket System: Almex

MK METRO LTD

UNIT 3, ARDEN PARK, OLD WOLVERTON, MILTON KEYNES MK12 5RN
Tel: 01908 225100
Fax: 01908 313553
Gen Man: M Heywood
Fleet: 101 - double-deck bus, single-deck bus, midibus.
Chassis: DAF. Dennis. Mercedes. Optare. Scania. Volvo.
Bodies: Alexander. Caetano. Optare. Plaxton. Wright.
Ops incl: local bus services, school contracts
Livery: Blue/Yellow.
Ticket System: Wayfarer 3
Part of Arriva plc

*MOTTS COACHES AYLESBURY LTD

GARSIDE WAY, STOCKLAKE, AYLESBURY HP20 1BH
Tel: 01296 398300
Fax: 01296 398386
E-mail: info@mottstravel.com
Web site: www.mottstravel.com
Fleetname: Motts Travel
Man Dir: M R Mott **Ops Dir**: C J Mott **Eng Dir**: I Scutt **Tours Dir**: C Joel **Traf Man**: H Shanks
Fleet: 45 - 5 double-deck bus, 4 single-deck bus, 28 coach, 2 double-deck coach, 2 midibus, 4 midicoach
Chassis: 6 Leyland. 3 MCW. 4 Mercedes. 2 Neoplan. 2 Optare. 3 Scania. 25 Volvo.
Bodies: 1 Esker. 3 Irizar. 16 Jonckheere. 3 MCW. 2 Neoplan. 8 Plaxton. 1 Van Hool. 2 Sitcar.
Ops incl: local bus services, school contracts, excursions & tours, private hire, continental tours.
Livery: White/Yellow/Green.
Ticket System: Wayfarer.

PAYNES COACHES & CAR HIRE LTD

6 BALMER CUT, BUCKINGHAM INDUSTRIAL ESTATE, BUCKINGHAM MK18 1UL.
Tel: 01280 813108, 817761.
Dirs: J. V. & K. R. Jeffs.
Fleet: 14 - 12 coach, 2 minicoach.
Chassis: Bedford. Ford. Leyland.
Bodies: 4 Caetano. 1 Duple. 2 Jonckheere. 3 Leyland. 1 Mercedes. 2 Optare. 1 Plaxton.
Ops incl: local bus services, excursions & tours, private hire, express, continental tours.
Livery: Green/Cream.
Ticket System: Almex/Wayfarer.
Subsidiary of Jeffs Coaches, Helmdon

*RED ROSE TRAVEL LTD

BLINKING OWL GARAGE, OXFORD ROAD, AYLESBURY HP17 8TT
Tel: 01296 747926
Fax: 01296 612196
E-mail: chris@showbus.com.
Web site: www.redrosetravel.com
Fleet: 22 single-deck bus.
Chassis: 11 Dennis. 1 Leyland. 6 Mercedes. 4 Optare.
Ops incl: local bus services, school contracts, private hire.
Livery: Red/Yellow

SOULS COACHES LTD

R24

2 STILEBROOK ROAD, OLNEY MK46 5EA
Tel: 01234 711242
Fax: 01234 240130
Recovery: 07739 097775
E-mail: sales@souls-coaches.co.uk
Web site: www.souls-coaches.co.uk
Man Dir: David Soul **Sales Man**: Wendy Cheshire **Traf Man**: Neil McCormick **Wkshp Man**: Drew Blunt
Fleet: 45 - 44 coach, 1 minicoach
Chassis: 1 DAF. 9 Dennis. 6 Setra. 1 Toyota. 28 Volvo.
Bodies: 1 Caetano. 5 Jonckheere. 33 Plaxton. 6 Setra.
Ops incl: local bus services, school contracts, excursions & tours, private hire, continental tours.

*WOOTTENS

THE COACH YARD, LYCROME ROAD, LYE GREEN, CHESHAM HP5 3LG
Tel: 01494 774411
Fax: 01494 784597
E-mail: info@woottens.co.uk
Web site: www.woottens.co.uk
Dirs: N H Wootten, M M Wootten
Ops Man: M J Wootten
Traf Man: P Williams
Chief Eng: R A Gomm
Fleet: 25 - 4 double-deck bus, 3 single-deck bus, 18 coach.
Chassis: 2 Bristol. 4 Leyland. 1 Leyland National. 18 Volvo.
Bodies: 1 Alexander. 1 Berkhof. 2 ECW. 1 East Lancs. 2 Jonckheere. 2 Leyland. 14 Plaxton. 1 Van Hool. 1 Willowbrook.
Ops incl: local bus services, excursions and tours, continental tours, private hire, school contracts.
Livery: White with coloured swirls.
Ticket System: Wayfarer.

CAMBRIDGESHIRE, CITY OF PETERBOROUGH

*ANDREWS COACHES

20 CAMBRIDGE ROAD, FOXTON CB2 6SH
Tel: 01223 873002
Fax: 01223 873036
E-mail: andrewscoaches@aol.com
Web site: www.andrewscoaches.co.uk
Dirs: F Miller, J Miller **Ops Sup**: A Miller
Fleet: 5 coach
Chassis: 1 DAF. 4 Volvo.
Bodies: 1 Duple. 1 Irizar. 3 Plaxton.
Ops incl: private hire, school contracts

*C & G COACHES

R24

HONEYSOME LODGE, HONEYSOME ROAD, CHATTERIS PE16 6SB
Tel: 01354 692200
Fax: 01354 694433
Recovery: 07771 962 105
E-mail: info@candgcoaches.co.uk
Web site: www.candgcoaches.co.uk
Prtnrs: Mrs C Day, G Ellwood, R Day
Ops Man: C Smith
Fleet: 24 - 1 double-deck bus, 23 coach
Chassis: 3 Bedford. 1 Bova. 2 Leyland. 1 MCW. 1 Neoplan. 11 Scania. 5 Volvo.
Bodies: 2 Berkhof. 1 Bova. 2 Duple. 1 ECW. 8 Irizar. 1 MCW. 1 Neoplan. 8 Plaxton. 1 Van Hool.
Ops incl: school contracts, excursions & tours, private hire, continental tours
Livery: White/Red/Yellow

COLLINS COACHES

UNIT 4, CAMBRIDGE ROAD INDUSTRIAL ESTATE, CAMBRIDGE CB4 6AZ
Tel: 01223 420462
Fax: 01223 424739
E-mail: collinscoaches@sagehost.co.uk, office@collinscoaches.net
Ptnrs: C. R. Collins, R. T. Collins **Off Man**: Jacky Liptrot **Garage Man**: R D Curtis
Fleet: 19 - 3 coach, 3 midicoach, 13 minibus.
Chassis: 1 Bedford. 2 Dennis. 5 Ford Transit. 2 Freight Rover. 4 Iveco. 2 LDV.
Ops incl: excursions & tours, school contracts, private hire.
Livery: White/Orange

RON W DEW & SONS LTD

CHATTERIS ROAD, SOMERSHAM PE17 3DN.
Tel: 01487 740241.
Fax: 01487 740341.
E-mail: sales@dews-coaches.com
Web site: www.dews-coaches.com

Chmn: David Dew. **Ops Man:** Simon Dew.
Fleet: 10 - 3 single-deck bus, 7 single-deck coach.
Chassis: 2 Bedford, 1 DAF, 5 Scania, 2 Volvo.
Bodies: 2 Berkhof, 3 Irizar, 2 Van Hool.
Ops incl: local bus sevrices, excursions & tours, private hire, continental tours, school contracts.
Livery: Green/Grey.

EMBLINGS COACHES

BRIDGE GARAGE, GUYHIRN, WISBECH PE13 4ED.
Tel: 01945 450253.
Fax: 01945 450770
Man Dir: John Embling

*FENN HOLIDAYS

WHITTLESEY ROAD, MARCH PE15 0AG
Tel: 01354 653329
Fax: 01354 650647
E-mail: info@fennholidays.co.uk
Web site: www.fennholidays.co.uk
Man Dir: Peter Fenn **Dir**: Margaret Fenn
Off Man: Catherine Cross
Fleet: 4 coach
Chassis: 2 Bova. 2 Van Hool.
Bodies: 2 Bova. 2 Van Hool.
Ops incl: excursions & tours, private hire, continental tours
Livery: multicolour

FIRST CHOICE TRAVEL

9 LYTHEMERE, ORTON MALBORNE, PETERBOROUGH PE2 5NU.
Tel: 01733 753642.
Fleetname: First Choice.
Prop: D. Ely.
Fleet: 2 midibus.
Chassis: 1 Bedford. 1 Renault.
Bodies: 1 Marshall. 1 Wright.
Ops incl: local bus services, school contracts.
Livery: Maroon/Blue.
Ticket System: Setright.

*GRETTON'S COACHES

ARNWOOD CENTRE, NEWARK ROAD, PETERBOROUGH PE1 5YH
Tel: 01733 311008
Fax: 01733 319859
Prop: Roger Gretton
Fleet: 15 - 12 coach, 2 midicoach, 1 minicoach.
Chassis: 2 Bedford. 1 Mercedes. 12 Scania.
Ops incl: school contracts, excursions & tours, private hire.
Livery: Silver/Red/Maroon

GREYS OF ELY

41 COMMON ROAD, WITCHFORD, ELY CB6 2HY
Tel: 01353 662300
Fax: 01353 662412
E-mail: sales@greysofely.co.uk
Web site: www.greysofely.co.uk
Prop: D Grey **Co Sec**: R Grey
Ops Man: C Covill
Fleet: 15 - 11 double-deck coach, 1 midibus, 3 midicoach.
Chassis: 11 Dennis. 3 Mercedes. 1 Fiat.
Bodies: 2 Berkhof. 1 Caetano. 13 Plaxton. 2 Euro
Ops incl: school contracts, private hire
Livery: Cream/Green

DEREK HIRCOCKS COACHES

THE OLD BARN, SCHOOL ROAD, UPWELL PE14 9EW
Tel: 01945 773461.
Fleetname: Upwell & District.
Prop: D. Hircock. **Eng:** W. Hircock.
Sec: Ms. C. Hircock.
Fleet: 7 coach.
Chassis: 4 AEC. 3 Leyland.
Ops incl: excursions & tours, private hire, school contracts.
Livery: Red/White/Blue.

HUNTINGDON & DISTRICT

STUKELEY ROAD, HUNTINGDON PE29 6HG
Tel: 01480 453159
Web site: www.huntsbus.co.uk
Ops Man: T Mead
Fleet: 30 - 15 double-deck bus, 13 single-deck bus, 2 coach
Chassis: 2 Dennis. 15 Leyland. 13 Volvo.
Bodies: 11 Alexander. 3 ECW. 6 Northern Counties. 2 Plaxton. 8 Wright.
Ops incl: local bus services.
Livery: Blue/Cream
Subsidiary Companies: part of Cavalier Travel, Lincolnshire.

JANS COACHES

23 TOWNSEND, SOHAM CB7 5DD
Tel: 01353 721344
Fax: 01353 721341
E-mail: janscoaches@aol.com
Dirs: Roland Edwards, Janet Edwards, Stuart Edwards
Fleet: 8 - 3 double-deck bus, 3 coach, 1 double-deck coach, 1 minicoach.
Chassis: 1 Dennis. 1 Iveco. 1 Leyland. 2 MAN. 2 MCW. 1 Neoplan.
Bodies: 1 Berkhof. 2 MCW. 3 Neoplan. 1 Northern Counties. 1 Indcar.
Ops incl: excursions & tours, private hire, continental tours, school contracts.
Livery: White.

A/c	Air conditioning	♥ Seat belt-fitted vehicles	✓ Replacement vehicle available
♿	Vehicles suitable for disabled	R Recovery service available (not 24 hr)	T Toilet-drop facilities available
🍴	Coach(es) with galley facilities	R24 24hr recovery service	Vintage vehicle(s) available
wc	Coach(es) with toilet facilities		Open top vehicle(s)

Cambridgeshire

*MIL-KEN TRAVEL LTD

11 LYNN ROAD, LITTLEPORT, ELY CB6 1QG
Tel: 01353 860705
Fax: 01353 863222
E-mail: milken@btconnect.com
Web-site: www.milkentravel.com
Man Dir: Jason Miller **Fleet Eng**: Ian Martin
Gen Man: Mark Rogers
Fleet: 39 - 37 coach, 2 minibus.
Chassis: 2 DAF. 5 Dennis. 2 LDV. 30 Volvo.
Bodies: 1 Berkhof. 3 Duple. 3 Jonckheere. 25 Plaxton. 4 Van Hool. 3 other.
Ops incl: private hire, continental tours, excursions & tours, school contracts.

*NEAL'S TRAVEL LTD

102 BECK ROAD, ISLEHAM CB7 5QP
Tel: 01638 780066
Fax: 01638 780011
E-mail: sales@nealstravel.com
Web site: www.nealstravel.com
Dirs: Bridget Paterson, Graham Neal, Lionel Neal, Nancy Neal
Fleet: 19 - 9 coach, 1 midibus, 7 midicoach, 2 minibus.
Chassis: 1 Iveco. 1 MAN. 11 Mercedes. 6 Volvo.
Bodies: 1 Indcar. 3 Jonckheere. 2 Mercedes. 1 Neoplan. 3 Optare. 4 Plaxton. 2 Sunsundegui. 3 other.
Ops incl: local bus services, school contracts, private hire, excursions & tours, continental tours.
Livery: White/Blue, Silver/Blue
Ticket system: Wayfarer

D A PAYNE COACH HIRE

UNIT 2, FOUNDRY WAY, LITTLE END ROAD INDUSTRIAL ESTATE, EATON SOCON PE19 8JH.
Tel: 01480 473272.
Fax: 01480 211252
E-mail: david@dapayne.fsnet.co.uk
Web site: dapaynecoachhire.co.uk
Prop: D A Payne **Sec**: Mrs Carole Allen
Ops Man: R Wood
Fleet: 10 - 3 coach, 1 midibus, 1 midicoach, 2 minibus, 3 minicoach.
Chassis: include 3 Setra. 1 Toyota. 1 Volvo.
Bodies: include 1 Caetano. 1 Plaxton. 3 Setra..
Ops incl: school contracts, excursions & tours, private hire.

PETERBOROUGH TRAVEL CONSULTANTS

12 BUCKLAND CLOSE, NETHERTON, PETERBOROUGH PE3 9UQ
Tel: 01733 267025
Fax: 01733 267025
E-mail: petertravelcon@aol.com
Props: Mrs P C Greeves
Fleet: 3 - 2 coach, 1 midicoach.
Chassis: 1 DAF. 2 Setra.
Ops incl: excursions & tours, school contracts, private hire, continental tours.
Livery: Blue/White/Red

PLANET TRAVEL

PLANET HOUSE, MEADOW DROVE, EARITH PE17 3QE.
Tel: 01487 843333.
Fax: 01487 843285.
Prop: D. J. Collier. **Ch Eng**: B. Turnock.
Co Acct: M. Sloman. **Traf Man**: R. Birchenough. **Ops Man**: Mrs C. Stafford.
Fleet: 9 - 7 coach, 1 double-deck coach, 1 midicoach.
Chassis: 5 Bova. 1 Mercedes. 1 Scania. 2 Seddon.
Bodies: 1 Berkhof. 5 Bova. 2 Setra. 1 RH2000.
Ops incl: private hire, continental tours.

ROBINSON KIMBOLTON

19 THRAPSTON ROAD, KIMBOLTON PE28 0HW
Tel: 01480 860581
E-mail: robinsoncharles@btconnect.com
Web site: www.robinsonkimbolton.co.uk
Man Dir: Charles Robinson
Fleet: 9 - 8 coach, 1 minibus
Chassis: 7 Dennis. 1 Scania. 1 Toyota.
Bodies: 3 Berkhof. 1 Caetano. 1 Duple. 3 Plaxton. 1 Van Hool.
Ops incl: private hire, school contracts.
Livery: Cream/Brown/Red

*SAFFORD COACHES LTD

THE DRIFT, LITTLE GRANSDEN, SANDY SG19 3DW
Tel: 01767 677395
Fax: 01767 677742
E-mail: saffordscoaches@btconnect.com
Web site: www.saffordscoaches.co.uk
Dirs: Miss Tracey Gillett, Mrs Shirley Gillett.
Fleet: 12 - 1 single-deck bus, 11 coach.
Chassis: 1 Bova. 1 Mercedes. 10 Volvo.
Bodies: 1 Bova. 1 Caetano. 2 Jonckheere. 1 Mercedes. 7 Plaxton.
Ops incl: school contracts, excursions & tours, private hire, continental tours.
Livery: White with Blue/Yellow

SEARLES AUTO SERVICES

10 GREAT NORTH ROAD, THORNHAUGH PE8 6HJ
Tel: 01780 783016
Fax: 01780 783016
Dir: Frank Searle
Fleet: 4 1 coach, 3 minibus
Chassis: 1 Bova. 2 Iveco. 1 Mercedes.
Bodies: 1 Bova. 2 Carlyle. 1 Mercedes-Benz
Ops incl: school contracts, private hire

*SHAWS OF MAXEY

49 HIGH STREET, MAXEY PE6 9EF
Tel: 01778 342224
Fax: 01778 380378
Ptnrs: Jane Duffelen Richard Shaw, Christopher Shaw
Fleet: 25 - 1 single-deck bus, 20 coach, 3 midicoach, 1 minicoach.
Chassis: 3 Bedford. 1 Bova. 2 DAF. 1 Dennis. 2 Mercedes. 1 Optare. 1 Toyota. 14 Volvo.
Bodies: 1 Autobus. 1 Berkhof. 1 Bova. 1 Caetano. 5 Jonckheere. 13 Plaxton.

1 Optare. 2 other.
Ops incl: local bus services, school contracts, excursions & tours, private hire, continental tours.
Livery: Blue/White

*STAGECOACH CAMBRIDGE

100 COWLEY ROAD, CAMBRIDGE CB4 0DN
Tel: 01223 420544
Fax: 01223 420065
E-mail: cambridge.enquiries@stagecoachbus.com
Web site: www.stagecoachbus.com
Man Dir: Andy Campbell
Com Dir: Philip Norwell
Fleet: 242 - 119 double-deck bus, 54 single-deck bus, 8 coach, 48 midibus, 7 minibus, 6 open-top bus.
Chassis: 61 Dennis, 2 Ford Transit. 53 MAN. 7 Optare. 50 Transbus. 69 Volvo.
Bodies: 148 Alexander. 28 Northern Counties. 7 Optare. 9 Plaxton. 50 Transbus
Ops incl: local bus services.
Livery: Stagecoach
Ticket system: Wayfarer 3

TOWLERS COACHES LTD

CHURCH ROAD, EMNETH PE14 8AA
Tel: 01945 583645
Fax: 01945 583645
E-mail: joanne@towlerscoaches.fsnet.co.uk
Dirs: Mark Towler, Wendy Shepherd, Anton Towler, Joanne Walton
Fleet: 7 - 3 double-deck bus, 3 coach, 1 double-deck coach
Chassis: 1 Bova. 1 Bristol. 3 Leyland. 1 Scania. 1 LAG-EOS.
Bodies: 1 Bova. 1 Duple. 1 ECW. 1 East Lancs. 1 Jonckheere. 1 Plaxton. 1 LAG EOS.
Ops incl: school contracts, excursions & tours, private hire.
Livery: Green/Cream/Orange

*VICEROY OF ESSEX LTD

See Essex

WEBB'S

ST PETERS FARM, MIDDLE DROVE PE14 8JJ
Tel: 01945 430123
E-mail: webb-s-cant@fsbdial.co.uk
Prop: Barry Webb
Fleet: 3 - 1 midicoach,1 minicoach, 1 minibus.
Ops incl: local bus services

WHIPPET COACHES LTD
♿ wc 🚌 💺 R 🔧
CAMBRIDGE ROAD, FENSTANTON
PE18 9JB
Tel: 01480 463792
Web site: www.go-whippet.co.uk
Dirs: A. T. Lee, J. T. Lee, J. C. Lee,
P. H. Lee, M. H. Lee.
Fleet: 49 - 20 double-deck bus, 6 single-deck bus, 20 coach, 3 minibus.
Chassis: Bedford, Leyland, Scania, Volvo.
Bodies: Duple, East Lancs, Leyland,
Northern Counties, Park Royal, Plaxton,
Van Hool, Alexander.
Ops incl: local bus service, school contracts, excursions & tours, private hire, express.
Livery: Blue/Cream with logo.
Ticket System: Almex Eurofare.

W & M TRAVEL
♿ 💺 wc A/c 🔧
10 MAIN ROAD, PARSON DROVE,
WISBECH PE13 4LF
Tel: 01945 700492
Fax: 01945 700964
Recovery: 01945 700942
Dir: W Norman
Fleet: 6 - 3 single-deck bus, 3 coach
Chassis: Bedford. DAF. Dennis. Scania.
Bodies: Berkhof. Duple. Plaxton. Marcopolo
Ops incl: local bus services, school contracts, excursions & tours, private hire.

CHESHIRE, HALTON & STOCKPORT

ANGEL TRAVEL
♿ 💺 R24 🔧
108 GORSEY LANE, WARRINGTON
WA2 7RY
Tel: 07090 741550
Fax: 01925 445591
E-mail: angeltravelwarrington@yahoo.co.uk
Dir: Richard Keane
Fleet: 3 minibus.
Chassis: LDV. Mercedes.
Ops incl: school contracts, private hire, excursions & tours.
Livery: Blue/White

*ANTHONYS TRAVEL
wc 💺 A/c 🍴 🔧 T
8 CORMORANT DRIVE, RUNCORN
WA7 4UD
Tel: 01928 561460
Fax: 01928 561460
Emergency: 01928 576050
E-mail: anthonys@fsbdial.co.uk
Recovery: 07920 154240
E-mail: anthonys@fsbdial.co.uk
Web site: www.anthonys-travel.co.uk
Partners: Richard Bamber, Anne Bamber, Tony Bamber **Off Man**: Jodie Waring
Eng: Stephen Knight
Fleet: 17 - 9 single-deck coach, 1 minibus, 7 minicoach.
Chassis: 3 LDV. 1 MAN. 5 Mercedes. 5 Neoplan. 1 Optare. 2 Scania. 1 Setra.
Bodies: 1 Berkhof. 1 Irizar. 5 Mercedes. 5 Neoplan. 1 Optare. 1 Setra.
Ops incl: local bus services, school contracts, private hire, excursion & tours.
Livery: multi coloured
Ticket system: Setright/Wayfarer

ARROWEBROOK COACHES
THE OLD COACH YARD, WERVIN ROAD, CROUGHTON CH2 4DA
Tel: 01244 382444
Fax: 01244 379777
Prop: A. G. Parsons

Ops Incl: local bus services
Livery: White/Green.

*BARRATT'S COACHES LTD
wc 💺 🍴 🔧 A/c T
UNIT 15, MILLBANK WAY,
SPRINGVALE INDUSTRIAL ESTATE,
SANDBACH CW11 3GQ
Tel: 08450 625096
Fax: 08450 627728
E-mail: gilbarratt@tiscali.co.uk
Web site: www.barrattscoaches.co.uk
Dir: Gillian Barratt, D Bate
Fleet: 18 - coaches, double-deck coach, midibus, midicoach
Chassis: 1 Leyland. 1 Mercedes. 2 Neoplan. 14 Volvo.
Bodies: 1 Jonckheere. 1 Mercedes. 2 Neoplan. 8 Plaxton. 6 Van Hool.
Ops incl: local bus services, school contracts, private hire.
Livery: White.

BENNETT'S TRAVEL
ATHLONE ROAD, LONGFORD,
WARRINGTON WA2 8JJ
Tel/Fax: 01925 415299.
Prop.: B. A. Bennett, D. B. Bennett.
Ops incl: local bus services
Livery: White/Blue.

*A. & H. BOOTH LTD
See Greater Manchester

BOSTOCK'S COACHES
SPRAGG STREET GARAGE,
CONGLETON CW12 1QH
Tel: 01260 273108
Fax: 01260 276338
E-mail: bostocks@holmeswood.uk.com
Web site: www.holmeswood.uk.com
Dirs: J F Aspinall, M Aspinall, C H Aspinall, D E Aspinall, M F Aspinall, M J Forshaw
Ops Man: M E Bostock **Tours Man**: J. Bostock-Gibson **Ch Eng**: M Boniface
Fleet: 40 - 3 double-deck bus, 33 coach,
1 double-deck coach, 2 midicoach,
1 minicoach.
Chassis: 1 Ayats. 1 Bova. 7 DAF. 6 Dennis. 2 Iveco. 4 Leyland. 4 MAN. 9 Scania. 6 Volvo.
Bodies: 1 Ayats. 1 Beulas. 2 Berkhof. 1 Bova. 3 Caetano. 2 ECW. 1 East Lancs. 4 Ikarus. 1 Indcar.1 Irizar. 6 Marcopolo. 8 Plaxton. 9 Van Hool.
Ops incl: local bus services, excursions & tours, private hire, continental tours, school contracts.
Livery: Green
(Subsidiary of Holmwood Coaches, Lancashire)

H E BROWN & SONS
wc 💺 🔧
8 GREENFIELD ROAD,
GREENFIELD FARM INDUSTRIAL ESTATE, CONGLETON CW12 4TR
Tel: 01260 275281
Fax: 01260 280955
Fleetname: Browns Coaches.
Prop: Dennis Brown
Fleet: 5 - 3 coach, 1 double deck coach, 1 midibus.
Chassis: 1 Leyland. 1 Neoplan. 1 Optare. 1 Volvo. 1 Van Hool.
Bodies: 2 Duple. 1 Neoplan. 1 Optare. 1 Van Hool.
Ops incl: local bus services, school contract, private hire.
Livery: White/Red.
Ticket System: Setright.

CHESTERBUS ♿ 🚌
STATION ROAD, CHESTER CH1 3AD
Tel: 01244 347452
Fax: 01244 347453
E-mail: hyslop@chesterbus.co.uk
Web site: www.chesterbus.co.uk
Man Dir: S Hyslop **Eng Dir**: M J Ridge
Fin Dir: R W Pointon **Traf Man**: J R Lee
Fleet: 82 - 20 double-deck bus, 7 open-top bus, 14 single-deck bus, 36 midibus, 5 minibus.
Chassis: 8 BMC. 7 Daimler. 22 Dennis. 15 Leyland. 4 Marshall. 5 Optare. 6 Scania. 5 VW.

A/c	Air conditioning	💺	Seat belt-fitted vehicles	🔧	Replacement vehicle available
♿	Vehicles suitable for disabled	R	Recovery service available (not 24 hr)	T	Toilet-drop facilities available
🍴	Coach(es) with galley facilities	R24	24hr recovery service	🚌	Vintage vehicle(s) available
wc	Coach(es) with toilet facilities			🚌	Open top vehicle(s)

Bodies: 4 Alexander. 8 BMC. 5 Constable. 5 East Lancs. 11 Marshall. 19 Northern Counties. 5 Optare. 17 Plaxton. 2 Roe. 6 Wright.
Ops incl: local bus services, school contracts.
Livery: Blue/Cream
Ticket System: Wayfarer TGX

DOBSON'S BUSES LTD
WINCHAM PARK, CHAPEL STREET, WINCHAM, NORTHWICH CW9 6DA
Tel/Fax: 01606 350200
Man Dir: I P Dobson **Ch Eng**: P J Dobson **Ops Man**: R P Dobson **Co Sec**: R E Dobson
Fleet: 15 - 8 double-deck bus, 2 coach, 5 midibus
Chassis: 2 Daimler. 2 Dennis. 1 Iveco. 6 Leyland. 2 Mercedes. 2 Peugeot.
Bodies: include: 1 Duple. 1 Marshall. 1 Mellor. 2 Plaxton. 2 Peugeot.
Ops Include: local bus services, school contracts, private hire
Ticket system: Datafare

FIRST IN CHESTER & THE WIRRAL
669 NEW CHESTER ROAD, ROCK FERRY CH42 1PZ
Tel: 0151 645 8661
See Merseyside

JOHN FLANAGAN COACH TRAVEL
2 REDDISH HALL COTTAGES, BROAD LANE, GRAPPENHALL, WARRINGTON WA4 3HS
Tel: 01925 266115
Fax: 01925 261100
Recovery: 01925 266115
E-mail: admin@flanagancoaches.co.uk
Web site: www.flanagancoaches.co.uk
Props: John Flanagan, Janette Flanagan **Co Sec**: Sarah Ogden
Fleet: 7 - 3 coach, 1 midicoach, 3 minicoach
Chassis: 1 Dennis. 1 Ford. 3 Mercedes. 2 Volvo.
Bodies: 1 Berkhof. 1 Esker. 2 Mercedes. 1 UVG. 1 Van Hool. 1 other.
Ops incl: private hire, school contracts, excursions and tours.
Livery: Red/Black/White

*HALTON BOROUGH TRANSPORT LTD
MOOR LANE, WIDNES WA8 7AF
Tel: 0151 423 3333
Fax: 0151 424 2362
E-mail: enquiries@haltontransport.co.uk
Web site: www.haltontransport.co.uk
Fleetname: Halton Transport
Man Dir: Chris Adams **Eng Man**: Phil Matthews **Traf Man**: David Steadman
Fleet: 60 - 59 single-deck bus, 1 midibus
Chassis: 54 Dennis. 6 Leyland.
Bodies: 21 East Lancs. 6 Leyland. 33 Marshall/MCV.
Ops incl: local bus services.
Livery: Red/Cream.

Ticket System: Wayfarer III

HULME HALL COACHES LTD
1 STANLEY ROAD, CHEADLE HULME SK8 6PL
Tel: 0161 486 1187
Fax: 0161 482 8125
E-mail: hulmehallcoaches@talk21.com
Web site: www.hulmehallcoaches.co.uk
Man Dir: D. Herald **Tran Man**: C. J. O'Neill
Traf Man: I Johnson **Fl Eng**: P Henshall
Fleet: 12 - 7 double-deck bus, 1 single-deck bus, 3 coach, 1 midibus.
Chassis: 6 Bristol. 1 Iveco. 1 Leyland. 1 Leyland National. 3 Volvo.
Bodies: 7 ECW. 1 East Lancs. 1 Mellor. 3 Plaxton.
Ops incl: local bus services, school contracts, private hire.
Livery: Red/Cream
Ticket System: Wayfarer

HUXLEY COACHES
GREAVES LANE EAST, THREAPWOOD, MALPAS SY14 7AS
Tel: 01948 770661
Fax: 01948 770459
Prop: Fred Huxley
Fleet: 16 - 11 coach. 5 midibus.
Ops incl: local bus services, school contracts, excursions & tours, private hire, continental tours.
Livery: Cream/Yellow/Brown

*LE-RAD COACHES & LIMOUSINES
328 HYDE ROAD, WOODLEY SK6 1PF
Tel: 0161 430 2032
Recovery: 0770 314 5500
Prop: Derek & Jean Mycock
Fleet: 3 - 2 coach, 1 minicoach.
Chassis: 1 DAF. 1 Ford. 1 LDV.
Ops incl: private hire, excursions & tours

*ROY McCARTHY COACHES
THE COACH DEPOT, SNAPE ROAD, MACCLESFIELD SK10 2NZ
Tel: 01625 425060
Fax: 01625 619853
Senr Ptnr: A McCarthy **Ptnr**: M Lomas
Fleet: 10 coach.
Chassis: 1 Bedford. 2 Dennis. 1 MAN. 6 Volvo.
Bodies: 1 Berkhof. 1 Caetano. 8 Plaxton
Ops incl: school contracts, excursions & tours, private hire, continental tours.
Livery: Blue/Cream

MARPLE MINI COACHES
5 GROSVENOR ROAD, MARPLE SK6 6PR.
Tel: 0161 881 9111
Owner: G. W. Cross
Fleet: 2 minicoach

Chassis: Ford Transit, LDV.
Ops incl: school contracts, private hire.
Livery: White/Gold.

*MAYNE COACHES LTD
MARSH HOUSE LANE, WARRINGTON WA1 3AU
Tel: 01925 445588
Fax: 01925 232300
E-mail: warrington@mayne.co.uk
Web site: www.mayne.co.uk
Chmn/Man Dir: S B Mayne **Co Sec**: D Mayne **Gen Man**: R W Vernon **Asst Gen Man**: A Dykes **Traf Man**: J Drake **Ch Eng**: E Sutcliffe
Fleet: 31 - 5 double-deck bus, 26 coach.
Chassis: 2 Bova. 6 Leyland. 16 Scania. 7 Volvo.
Bodies: 2 Bova. 1 Duple. 5 East Lancs. 11 Irizar. 12 Plaxton.
Ops incl: local bus services, school contracts, private hire.
Livery: Red/Cream

MEREDITHS COACHES LTD
LYDGATE, WELL STREET, MALPAS SY14 8DE
Tel: 01948 860405
Fax: 01948 860162
E-mail: info@merediths.f9.co.uk
Web site: www.meredithscoaches.co.uk
Dirs: J K Meredith, Mrs M E Meredith, D J Meredith **Co Sec**: Mrs Kirin Meredith **Ch Eng**: C Bellis
Fleet: 16
Chassis: 1 Ford. 4 Leyland. 11 Volvo.
Bodies: 12 Plaxton. 2 Van Hool. 2 Wadham Stringer.
Ops incl: local bus services, school contracts, private hire.

*MILLMANS COACHES
STATION YARD, GREEN LANE, PADGATE, WARRINGTON WA1 4JR
Tel: 01925 813181
Fax: 01925 813181
Prop: Eric Millman
Fleet: 6 coach
Chassis: 2 DAF. 3 Leyland, 1 Volvo
Bodies: 1 Duple. 5 Plaxton.
Ops incl: local bus services, school contracts, private hire.
Livery: Blue/White

MOORE'S COACHES LTD
53 REES CRESCENT, HOLMES CHAPEL CW4 7NL.
Tel/Fax: 01477 537004
Dirs: D. M. Moore, J. C. Moore.
Fleet: 4 coach.
Chassis: 1 Dennis. 1 Scania. 1 Volvo. 1 Van Hool.
Bodies: 1 Jonckheere. 1 Plaxton. 2 Van Hool.
Ops incl: excursions & tours, private hire, express, continental tours, school contracts.
Livery: Moore's Coaches/Nat. Express.

NIDDRIE COACHES

THE GARAGE, LEVIN STREET,
MIDDLEWICH CW10 9AS
Tel: 01606 832343
Fax: 01606 833449
E-mail: niddries@aol.com
Man Dir: R I Niddrie **Sec**: Miss F J Niddrie
Fleet: 4 coach
Chassis: 1 Bedford. 2 DAF. 1 Scania.
Bodies: 3 Plaxton. 1 Van Hool
Ops incl: excursions & tours, private hire, continental tours, school contracts.
Livery: Silver/Maroon

SELWYNS TRAVEL SERVICES

CAVENDISH FARM ROAD, WESTON,
RUNCORN WA7 4LU
Tel: 01928 564515
Fax: 01928 591872
Recovery: 01928 572108
E-mail: sales@selwyns.co.uk
Web site: www.selwyns.co.uk
Man Dir: Selwyn A Jones **Gen Man**: Alan P Williamson **Co Sec/Acct**: Richard E Williams **Fleet Eng**: Cledwyn Owen
Fleet: 44 - 9 single-deck bus, 33 coach, 1 midibus, 1 minicoach.
Chassis: 31 DAF. 1 Caetano. 1 Dennis. 2 Mercedes. 1 Optare. 2 Volvo. 6 Tecnobus.
Bodies: 1 Caetano. 3 Ikarus. 2 Mercedes. 1 Optare. 6 Pantheon. 2 Plaxton. 27 Van Hool.
Ops incl: local bus services, school contracts, excursions & tours, private hire, express, continental tours.
Livery: White/Blue/Orange/Green
Ticket System: Wayfarer
See also Greater Manchester

SMITHS OF MARPLE LTD

72 CROSS LANE, MARPLE SK6 7PZ
Tel: 0161 427 2825
Fax: 0161 449 7731
E-mail: julie@smithsofmarple.fsnet.co.uk
Web site: www.smithsofmarple.fsnet.co.uk
Man Dir: Jason Hibbert. **Co Sec**: Julie Hibbert
Fleet: 6 - 1 double-deck bus, 3 coach, 2 midibus.
Chassis: 1 Bristol. 1 Irisbus. 2 Setra. 1 Toyota.
Bodies: 1 Beulas. 1 Caetano. 1 ECW. 1 Mellor. 2 Setra.
Ops incl: local bus services, school contracts, excursions & tours, private hire, continental tours.
Livery: White/Red, Green, Blue, Orange.

W A SHEARINGS LTD

BARLEYCASTLE LANE, APPLETON,
WARRINGTON WA4 4FR.
Tel: 01925 214600
Fax: 01925 262606
Ops Man: Chris Brown
See also W A Shearings Ltd, Greater Manchester.

JIM STONES COACHES

THE JAYS, LIGHT OAKS LANE,
GLAZEBURY, WARRINGTON
WA3 5LH
Tel/Fax: 01925 766465
E-mail: jimstones@ic24.net
Web site: www.jimstonescoaching.com
Ptnrs: J B Stones, Mrs J P Stones,
Gen Man: R Dyson
Fleet: 16 - single-deck bus.

Chassis: 12 Dennis. 4 Leyland.
Bodies: 1 DAB. 2 East Lancs. 13 Plaxton.
Ops incl: local bus services, school contracts
Livery: Blue/White
Ticket System: Almex, Wayfarer 3, Setright

WARRINGTON BOROUGH TRANSPORT LTD

WILDERSPOOL CAUSEWAY,
WARRINGTON WA4 6PT
Tel: 01925 634296
Fax: 01925 418382
Web site: www.warringtonboroughtransport.co.uk
Fleetname: Network Warrington
Man Dir: Nigel Featham **Fin Dir**: John Bannister **Ops Man**: Charlie Shannon
Eng Man: Damian Graham
Fleet: 115 - 34 double-deck bus, 69 midibus, 12 minibus.
Chassis: incl: Optare. Transbus. Volvo.
Bodies: incl: Wrightbus
Ops incl: local bus services, school contracts, private hire.
Livery: Red/Ivory
Ticket System: Wayfarer 3

WHITEGATE TRAVEL LTD

15 BEAUTY BANK, WHITEGATE,
NORTHWICH CW8 2BP
Tel: 01606 882760
Fax: 01606 883356
Owner: K. Prince
Fleet: 12 minibus
Chassis: 1 Ford Transit. 2 Freight Rover. 2 Iveco. 2 Mercedes. 5 Leyland DAF.
Ops incl: local bus services, school contracts, private hire.
Livery: Yellow/White

CORNWALL

CARADON RIVIERA TOURS

THE GARAGE, UPTON CROSS,
LISKEARD PL14 5AX
Tel: 01579 362226.
Fax: 01579 362220
Prop: John K. Deeble
Fleet: 39 - 6 single-deck bus, 28 coach, 1 midibus, 3 minicoach, 1 mincoach.
Chassis: 1 Bedford. 2 Bristol. 4 Dennis. 1 Freight Rover. 3 LDV. 26 Leyland. 2 MCW.
Bodies: 4 Alexander. 4 Duple. 4 East Lancs. 2 MCW. 4 Optare. 17 Plaxton. 1 UVG.

3 Wadham Stringer.
Ops incl: local bus services, school contracts, excursions & tours, private hire.
Livery: Cream/Blue.
Ticket System: Setright.

DAC COACHES LTD

RYLANDS GARAGE, ST ANNE'S
CHAPEL, GUNNISLAKE PL18 9HW
Tel: 01822 834571
Fax: 01822 833881

Recovery: 01822 833378
E-mail: dac.coaches@btconnect.com
Web site: www.daccoaches.co.uk
Dirs: Bernard Harding, Nick Smith
Fleet: 10 - 4 coach, 1 double-deck bus, 2 midibus, 3 minicoach.
Chassis: 1 Bedford. 1 Bristol. 1 Ford. 3 Mercedes. 1 Peugeot. 3 Volvo.
Bodies: Duple. ECW. 9 Plaxton. Van Hool.
Ops incl: local bus services, school contracts, excursions & tours, private hire, continental tours.
Livery: Blue/White/Red/Yellow.
Ticket System: Almex.

A/c	Air conditioning		Replacement vehicle available
	Vehicles suitable for disabled	T	Toilet-drop facilities available
	Coach(es) with galley facilities		Vintage vehicle(s) available
wc	Coach(es) with toilet facilities		Open top vehicle(s)
	Seat belt-fitted vehicles		
R	Recovery service available (not 24 hr)		
R24	24hr recovery service		

DARLEY FORD TRAVEL

DARLEY FORD, LISKEARD
PL14 5AS
Tel: 01579 362272
Fax: 01579 363425
Owner: Albert J Deeble
Fleet: 8
Chassis: 2 Scania. 6 Volvo.
Bodies: include 1 Berkhof.
Ops incl: private hire, excursions & tours, continental tours.
Livery: White

*FIRST IN DEVON & CORNWALL
See Devon

GROUP TRAVEL

DUNMERE ROAD GARAGE, BODMIN PL31 2QN
Tel: 01208 77989
Fax: 01208 77989
E-mail: grouptravel@btinternet.com
Web site: grouptravelcoachhire.com
Dirs: Dawn Moon, David Benny
Fleet: 21 - 7 coach, 13 midibus, 1 minicoach.
Chassis: 1 Autosan. 1 Leyland. 1 MAN. 2 Marshall. 10 Mercedes. 1 Optare. 4 Volvo.
Bodies: 1 Caetano. 1 Jonckheere. 2 Marshall/MCV. 5 Mellor. 1 Optare. 3 Plaxton. 4 Reeve Burgess. 2 Van Hool. 2 other.
Ops incl: local bus services, school contracts, excursions & tours, private hire
Livery: Silver/Turquoise + blue logo
Ticket system: Almex A90

*HOOKWAYS JENNINGS

LANSDOWNE ROAD, BUDE
EX23 8BN.
Tel: 01288 352359
Fax: 01288 352140
Recovery: 07850 038707
E-mail: barry@hookways.com
Web site: www.hookways.com
Man Dir: Alistair Gray **Dirs**: Kym Hookway, Sue Hookway, Jason Hookway, Martin Hookway **(Eng)**: Julie Hookway **(Sec)**
Fleet: 53 - 46 coach, 1 midicoach, 1 minibus, 1 minicoach, 4 multi-purpose vehices.
Chassis: 1 Leyland. 1 MAN. 3 Mercedes. 1 Scania. 4 VW. 43 Volvo
Bodies: 1 Irizar. 6 Jonckheere. 41 Plaxton. 1 Wright.
Ops incl: school contracts, excursions & tours, private hire, express, continental tours.
Livery: Yellow

HOPLEYS BUS & COACH

SUNIC, ROPE WALK, MOUNT HAWKE, TRURO TR4 8DW.
Tel: 01209 890268.
Fax: 01209 890268.
Ptnrs: B. Hopley, D. R. Hopley, N. A. Hopley.
Fleet: 5 - 1 double-deck bus, 2 single-deck bus, 2 coach.
Chassis: 1 Bedford. 1 Bristol. 3 Volvo.
Bodies: 1 Duple. 1 ECW. 1 Jonckheere. 1 Plaxton. 1 Wright.
Ops incl: local bus services, school contracts, excursions & tours, private hire.
Livery: Red/White/Grey.
Ticket System: Wayfarer 3.

LISKEARD & DISTRICT OMNIBUS COMPANY LTD

HIGHER ST LUKES, BOLVENTOR, LAUNCESTON PL15 7TP
Tel/Fax: 01566 86501
E-mail: cameldist@tesco.net
Ops Dir(Man): R Hobbs
Dir/Co Sec: C Hobbs
Fleet: 11 - 1 single-deck bus, 1 open-top bus, 9 minibus
Chassis: incl: 1 AEC. 2 LDV.
Bodies: incl: 7 Mercedes. 1 Weymann.
Ops incl: local bus services, private hire, school contracts.
Livery: White/Green
Ticket System: Almex

*MOUNTS BAY COACHES

4 ALEXANDRA ROAD, PENZANCE
TR18 4LY
Tel: 01736 363320
Fax: 01736 366985
E-mail: kathyoxenham@hotmail.com
Web site: www.mountsbaycoaches.co.uk
Dir: J M Oxenham
Fleet: 10 - 8 coach, 1 midicoach, 1 minibus.
Chassis: 2 Scania. 1 Toyota. 6 Volvo. 1 other.
Bodies: 1 Caetano. 8 Van Hool. 1 other.
Ops incl: school contracts, excursions & tours, private hire.
Livery: Blue/White

*OTS MINIBUS & COACH HIRE

48 FORE STREET, CONSTANTINE, FALMOUTH TR11 5AB
Tel: 01326 340703
Fax: 01326 340404
E-mail: salots@hotmail.com
Web site: www.otsfalmouth.co.uk
Prop: Stephen Moore
Fleet: 5 - 1 coach, 1 midicoach, 2 minibus, 1 minicoach.
Chassis: 1 Ford. 3 Mercedes. 1 Volvo.
Bodies: 2 Mercedes. 1 Optare. 1 Plaxton. 1 Van Hool.
Ops incl: local bus services, school contracts, excursions & tours, private hire.
Livery: White with Maroon/Blue
Ticket system: manual

PENMERE MINIBUS SERVICES

28 BOSMOOR ROAD, FALMOUTH TR11 4PU
Tel/Fax: 01326 314165
E-mail: enquiries@penmereminibus.co.uk
Web site: www.penmereminibus.co.uk
Man: Ben Moore

Fleet: 2 - 1 minibus, 1 minicoach.
Chassis: 2 Mercedes.
Ops incl: local bus services, school contracts, private hire.
Livery: Blue/Brown stripes.
Ticket system: Manual

PRIMROSE COACHES OF CORNWALL

2 MARKET SQUARE, HAYLE
TR27 4EA.
Tel: 01736 754788.
Fax: 01736 754788.
E-mail: wendy@primrose.co.uk
Web site: www.primrosecfreeserve.co.uk
Prop: J. W. Runnalls.
Ops. Man: W. J. Runnalls.
Fleet: 5 - 4 coach, 1 midicoach.
Chassis: 1 Bedford, 1 Setra, 1 Toyota.
Bodies: 1 Caetano, 1 Neoplan, 1 Plaxton, 1 Setra, 1 Van Hool.
Ops incl: excursions & tours, private hire, continental tours, local bus services, school contracts.

*ROSELYN COACHES

MIDDLEWAY GARAGE, ST BLAZEY ROAD, PAR PL24 2JA
Tel: 01726 813737
Fax: 01726 813739
Recovery: 01726 813737
E-mail: jonathanede@roselyncoaches.co.uk
Web site: www.roselyncoaches.co.uk
Dirs: Jonathan Ede, Karen Paramor **Ch Eng**: Graham Paramor **Ops Man**: Richard Moon **Gen Man**: John Stoneham
Fleet: 37 - 10 double-deck bus, 27 coach
Chassis: 1 Bova. 2 Bristol. 1 DAF. 1 Iveco. 8 Leyland. 24 Volvo.
Bodies: 1 Bova. 1 Caetano. 10 ECW. 1 Jonckheere. 16 Plaxton. 8 Van Hool.
Ops incl: school contracts, excursions & tours, private hire, continental tours.
Livery: Green/Gold

SUMMERCOURT TRAVEL

THE OLD COACH GARAGE, SUMMERCOURT TR8 5DR
Tel: 01726 861108
Fax: 01726 860093
Web site: www.summercourttravel.com
Ops incl: local bus services, private hire.
Livery: White

SUNSET COACHES

BRANE, PENZANCE TR20 8RB
Tel: 01736 810428
Props: Ian Topping
Fleet: 10 - 2 midibus, 1 midicoach, 6 minibus, 1 minicoach.
Chassis: 1 Iveco. 9 Mercedes.
Bodies: 2 Wadham Stringer. 8 other.
Ops incl: local bus services, school contracts, excursions & tours, private hire, continental tours.
Livery: Sky Blue
(part of Western Greyhound)

*TAVISTOCK COMMUNITY TRANSPORT

GREENLANDS, ST ANN'S CHAPEL, GUNNISLAKE PL18 9HW
Tel: 01822 833574
E-mail: keithp44@btinternet.com
Fleetname: Tavistock Country Bus
Chmn: K W Potter **Sec**: A Everitt
Fleet: 1 minibus
Chassis: Iveco
Body: G M Coachwork.
Ops incl: local bus services, private hire.
Livery: Red/White
Ticket System: Wayfarer

TILLEY'S COACHES

THE COACH STATION, WAINHOUSE CORNER, BUDE EX23 0AZ.
Tel: 01840 230244.
Man Dir: Paul Tilley
Fleet: 12 coaches
Chassis: incl: 1 Irisbus
Bodies: incl: 1 Indcar
Livery: White/Cream/Maroon.

TRELEY MOTORS

ST BURYAN, PENZANCE TR19 6DZ
Tel: 01736 810322
Chmn: J Ley **Ops Man**: A J Ley
Co Sec: A D Ley
Fleet: 2 - 1 coach, 1 minibus
Chassis/Body: 1 Dennis. 1 Mercedes.
Bodies: 1 Duple. 1 Olympus.
Ops incl: school contracts, excursions & tours, private hire
Livery: Blue/Cream

*TRURONIAN LTD

24 LEMON STREET, TRURO TR1 2LS
Tel: 01872 273453
Fax: 01872 222522
E-mail: enquiries@truronian.co.uk
Web site: www.truronian.com
Man Dir: Geoff Rumbles **Gen Man**: Graham Gilbert **Ops Man**: Andrew Watmore
Coaching Man: Alan Cleave **Fleet Eng**: Peter Worrall
Fleet: 60 - 4 double-deck bus, 35 single-deck bus, 13 coach, 3 articulated bus, 2 midibus, 2 minibus, 1 midicoach.
Ops incl: local bus services, school contracts, excursions & tours, private hire, express, continental tours.
Livery: Red/Silver.
Ticket System: Almex

*WESTERN GREYHOUND LTD

WESTERN HOUSE, ST AUSTELL STREET, SUMMERCOURT, NEWQUAY TR8 5DR
Tel: 01637 871871
Fax: 01872 510151
E-mail: enquiries@westerngreyhound.com
Web site: www.westerngreyhound.com
Man Dir: Mark Howarth **Co Sec**: Mari Howarth **Dir**: Robin Orbell **Ops Man**: Brian James **Eng Man**: Steve Harris
Fleet: 74 - 2 coach, 10 double-deck bus, 2 open-top bus, 55 midibus, 5 heritage.

Chassis: 3 AEC Routemaster. 2 Bristol. 2 Leyland. 55 Mercedes. 10 Volvo.
Bodies: 8 East Lancs. 2 Leyland. 55 Plaxton. 2 Van Hool.
Ops incl: local bus services, school contracts, excursions & tours, private hire.
Livery: Green/White
Ticket System: Wayfarer

WHEAL BRITON TRAVEL

MOOR COTTAGE, BLACKWATER, TRURO TR4 8ET
Tel: 01872 560281
Fax: 01872 560691
Prop: Stephen J Palmer
Fleet: 13 - 12 coach, 1 minibus.
Chassis: 2 Scania. 10 Volvo.
Bodies: 1 Jonckheere. 10 Plaxton. 1 Van Hool.
Ops incl: school contracts, excursions & tours, private hire, continental tours
Livery: Cream

F. T. WILLIAMS TRAVEL

DOLCOATH INDUSTRIAL PARK, DOLCOATH ROAD, CAMBORNE TR14 8RU
Tel: 01209 717152.
Fax: 01209 612511.
Prop: F. T. Williams.
Livery: White/Gold/Black.

CUMBRIA

D K & N BOWMAN

BURTHWAITE HILL, BURTHWAITE, WREAY, CARLISLE CA4 0RT
Tel: 01697 473262
Fax: 01697 474800
E-mail: enquiries@bowmans-coaches.co.uk
Web site: www.bowmans-coaches.co.uk
Ptnrs: David K Bowman, Nora Bowman
Fleet: 8 coach.
Chassis: 4 AEC. 1 Bedford. 1 MAN. 2 Scania.
Bodies: 1 Irizar. 1 Jonckheere. 5 Plaxton. 1 other.
Ops incl: school contracts, excursions and tours, private hire.
Livery: Ivory/Red

*S H BROWNRIGG

ENNERDALE HILL, EGREMONT CA22 2PN
Tel: 01946 822926
Fax: 01946 821919
Chmn: R J Cook
Dirs: Mr & Mrs D L Marshall, Mrs L Holliday
Fleet: 28 - 15 coach, 3 midibus, 10 minicoach
Chassis: 3 Ford. 4 Leyland. 9 Mercedes. 1 Scania. 1 Volkswagen. 10 Volvo.
Bodies: 1 Alexander. 17 Plaxton. 1 Van Hool. 2 Wright. 7 other.
Ops incl: local bus services, school contracts, private hire.
Livery: Purple/White

*CALDEW COACHES LTD

6 CALDEW DRIVE, DALSTON, CARLISLE CA5 7NS
Tel/Fax: 01228 711690
E-mail: caldewcoachesltd@aol.com
Web site: www.caldewcoaches.co.uk
Dirs: Hugh McKerrell, Ann McKerrell, Bill Rogers **Co Sec**: Mandy Rogers
Fleet: 11 - 2 single-deck bus, 1 midicoach, 4 minibus, 4 minicoach.
Chassis: 10 Mercedes. 1 Volvo.
Bodies: 10 Mercedes. 1 Van Hool.
Ops incl: school contracts, excursions & tours, private hire.
Livery: White/Red

A/c	Air conditioning	✔	Replacement vehicle available
	Vehicles suitable for disabled	T	Toilet-drop facilities available
	Coach(es) with galley facilities		Vintage vehicle(s) available
wc	Coach(es) with toilet facilities		Open top vehicle(s)
	Seat belt-fitted vehicles		
R	Recovery service available (not 24 hr)		
R24	24hr recovery service		

Cumbria

CARR'S COACHES
CONTROL TOWER, THE AIRFIELD, SILLOTH CA7 4NS
Tel: 01697 331276
Fax: 01769 33823
Prop: A J Markley **Ch Eng**: Fred Gill
Fleet: 9 - 4 coach, 2 midibus, 1 midicoach, 2 minibus.
Chassis: 1 Dennis. 3 Ford Transit. 1 Leyland. 2 Mercedes. 2 Scania.
Bodies: 2 Duple. 1 Optare. 2 Van Hool.
Ops incl: local bus services, school contracts, private hire.
Livery: Blue/White.

CLARKSON COACHWAYS LTD
UNIT 2B, ASHBURNER WAY, WALNEY ROAD INDUSTRIAL ESTATE, BARROW IN FURNESS LA14 5UZ
Tel: 01229 828022
Fax: 01229 828067
E-mail: info@clarksoncoachways.co.uk
Web site: www.clarksoncoachways.co.uk
Dirs: Susan Clarkson, Neil Clarkson
Fleet: 13 - 8 single-deck bus, 1 open-top bus, 3 midicoach, 1 minicoach. **Chassis**: 5 Dennis. 1 Ford. 1 Leyland. 3 MAN. 1 Mercedes-Benz.
Bodies: 1 Alexander. 4 Berkhof. 3 Caetano. 1 Crest. 1 Marcopolo. 1 Optare.
Ops incl: school contracts, excursions & tours, private hire.
Livery: two-tone Green

COAST TO COAST PACKHORSE
WEST VIEW, HARTLEY, KIRKBY STEPHEN CA17 4JH
Tel: 01768 371680
Fax: 01768 371680
E-mail: packhorse@cumbria.com
Web site: www.cumbria.com/packhorse
Operator: J. Bowman.
Fleet: 3 minibus.
Chassis: 2 Ford Transit. 1 Freight Rover.
Ops incl: local bus services, school contracts, private hire.

CUMBRIA COACHES LTD
ALGA HOUSE, BRUNEL WAY, DURRANHILL INDUSTRIAL ESTATE, CARLISLE CA1 3NQ.
Tel: 01228 404300.
Fax: 01228 404309.
Dir: Dennis Smith, H. Humble
Ops Man: S. Hall.
Fleet: 12 - 8 coach, 4 double-deck coach.
Chassis: 2 Neoplan. 2 Setra. 8 Volvo.
Bodies: 4 Duple. 2 Jonckheere. 2 Neoplan. 2 Plaxton. 2 Setra.
Ops incl: excursions & tours, private hire, express, continental tours, school contracts.

D & H TRAVEL LTD
66 STRAMONGATE, KENDAL LA9 4BD
Tel: 01539 730555
Fax: 01539 723181
Recovery: 07971 205314
Web site: www.dhtravel.co.uk
Dir: Derek Henderson
Ops Man: John Robinson
Fleet: 15 - 2 single-deck bus, 3 single-deck coach, 6 midibus, 2 midicoach, 2 minicoach
Chassis: 5 Ford. 9 Mercedes. 1 Scania.
Bodies: 2 Ikarus. 1 Jonckheere. 6 Plaxton.
Ops incl: excursions & tours, private hire, continental tours, school contracts, local bus services.
Livery: White

DAGLISH COACHES
BECK LEA, PASTURE ROAD, ROWRAH, FRIZINGTON CA26 3XN
Tel/Fax: 01946 861940
E-mail: daglish.coaches@bobertd.demon.co.uk
Web site: www.daglishcoaches.co.uk
Dir: R. Daglish
Fleet: 13 - 10 coach, 1 double-deck coach, 2 minibus.
Chassis: 3 DAF. 1 Ford Transit. 1 LDV. 4 Leyland. 1 Leyland National. 1 MAN. 1 MCW. 1 Scania.
Ops incl: excursions & tours, private hire, school contracts.
Livery: Yellow/Blue/Red

GRAND PRIX COACHES
MAIN STREET, BROUGH CA17 4AY
Tel: 01768 341328
Web site: www.grand-prix-services.com
E-mail: allison@fsbdial.co.uk
Dirs: Frank Allison, Gilbert Allison, Michael Allison
Fleet: 18 - 4 single-deck bus, 8 coach, 1 midicoach, 4 minibus, 1 minicoach.
Chassis: 1 Bedford. 1 Bristol. 1 Ford Transit. 2 Freight Rover. 1 LDV. 1 MCW. 2 Mercedes. 1 Renault. 4 Volvo.
Bodies: 1 Autobus. 4 Duple. 4 Leyland. 1 MCW. 2 Mercedes. 4 Plaxton. 2 Van Hool.
Ops incl: local bus services, school contracts, excursions & tours, private hire, continental tours.
Livery: White/Blue
Ticket System: Wayfarer 3

JOHN HOBAN TRAVEL LTD
22 KING STREET, WORKINGTON CA14 4DJ
Tel: 01900 603579
Fax: 01900 605528
E-mail: johnahoban@aol.com
Ptnrs: John Hoban, Allison Hoban
Fleet: 6 minicoach, 4 midicoach.
Chassis/Bodies: 10 Mercedes
Ops incl: local bus services, private hire

*IRVINGS COACH HIRE LTD
JESMOND STREET, CARLISLE CA1 2DE
Tel: 01228 521666
Fax: 01228 521792
E-mail: office@irvings-coaches.co.uk
Web site: www.irvings-coaches.co.uk
Man Dir: R Irving **Dir**: Miss A Irving
Tran Man: J Treasurer
Fleet: 10 - 9 coach, 1 midicoach.
Chassis: 2 DAF. 8 Volvo.
Bodies: 2 Bova. 1 Duple. 2 Plaxton. 1 Sunsundegui. 4 Van Hool.
Ops incl: excursions & tours, private hire, school contracts, express.
Livery: Orange/Black/White.

*K & B TRAVEL LTD
THE ASHES, CLIBURN, PENRITH CA10 3AL
Tel: 01768 865446
Fax: 01768 862715
E-mail: mail@kbtravel.co.uk
Web site: www.kbtravel.co.uk
Man Dir: G Lund **Dirs**: B Bainbridge (Co Sec), T Lund
Fleet: 15 - 10 coach, 1 minibus, 4 midibus.
Chassis: 5 MAN. 5 Mercedes. 4 Volvo.
Bodies: 1 Berkhof. 4 Mercedes. 5 Neoplan. 1 Optare. 4 Van Hool.
Ops incl: local bus services, excursions & tours, private hire, school contracts, continental tours.
Livery: Blue with Green lettering

*LADYBIRD TRAVEL
22 CLIFTON COURT, WORKINGTON CA14 3HR
Tel: 01900 61155
Fax: 01900 61155
E-mail: grahame.ladybird@virgin.net
Web site: www.ladybird-travel.com
Fleet: 12 - 9 coach, 1 midicoach, 2 minicoach.
Chassis: 4 DAF. 1 Dennis. 4 Iveco. 2 Optare. 1 Volvo.
Bodies: 4 Beulas. 2 Ikarus. 1 Marcopolo. 2 Optare. 1 Plaxton. 2 Van Hool.
Ops incl: excursions & tours, private hire, school contracts.
Livery: White with red/black stripes

LAKES SUPERTOURS
1 HIGH STREET, WINDERMERE LA23 1AF.
Tel: 01539 442751.
Fax: 01539 446026.
Dir: R. Minford, A. Dobson
Fleet: 9 minibus.
Chassis: 8 Renault. 1 Fiat.
Ops incl: excursions & tours.
Livery: White/Purple/Gold.

*MESSENGERS COACHES LTD
MEALSGATE STATION, MEALSGATE, WIGTON CA7 1JP
Tel: 01697 371111

Fax: 01697 371112
E-mail:
angie@messengerscoaches.co.uk
Web site:
www.messengerscoaches.co.uk
Dirs: Liam Walker, Angie Walker
Fleet: 10 coach
Chassis: 10 Volvo.
Bodies: 9 Plaxton. 1 Van Hool.
Ops incl: school contracts, excursions & tours, private hire, continental tours.

*MOUNTAIN GOAT LTD (incl PARK TOURS AND TRAVEL)

VICTORIA STREET, WINDERMERE
LA23 1AD
Tel: 015394 45161
Fax: 015394 45164
E-mail: enquiries@mountain-goat.com
Web site: www.mountain-goat.com
Dirs: Peter Nattrass, Stephen Broughton
Office Man: Sue Todd
Fleet: 16 minicoach
Chassis: 1 Ford Tourneo. 1 LDV.
14 Renault.
Ops incl: local bus services, excursions & tours, private hire, continental tours, school contracts.
Livery: Green/Red on White
Ticket system: Wayfarer

*NBM HIRE LTD

CROMWELL ROAD, PENRITH
CA11 7JW
Tel: 01768 890030
Fleet: coach, bus, minibus
Ops incl: excursions & tours, private hire, school contracts

REAYS COACHES LTD

STRAWBERRY FIELDS, SYKE PARK,
WIGTON CA7 9NE
Tel: 016973 49999
Fax: 016973 49900
E-mail: info@reays.co.uk
Web site: www.reays.co.uk
Dirs: C W Reay, N Reay
Ch Eng: J M McGill **Ops Man**: C W Reay
Co Sec: N Reay
Fleet: 33 - 5 single-deck bus, 17 coach,
1 double-deck coach, 5 midicoach,
4 minicoach.
Chassis: 10 DAF. 15 Mercedes. 2 Neoplan. 4 Scania. 2 Volvo.
Bodies: 6 Alexander. 10 Bova. 4 Irizar.
3 Mercedes. 2 Neoplan. 4 Optare. 4 Plaxton.
Ops incl: local bus services, school contracts, excursions & tours, private hire, continental tours.
Livery: White/Blue/Gold.

ROBINSONS COACHES

STATION ROAD GARAGE, APPLEBY
CA16 6TX
Tel: 01768 351424
Fax: 01768 352199
Prop: S E Graham
Fleet: 9 - 5 coach, 4 minibus.
Chassis: 1 DAF. 2 Dennis. 3 LDV.
1 Mercedes. 2 Volvo.
Bodies: include: 1 Mercedes. 1 Plaxton.
1 UVG. 2 Van Hool. 1 Wadham Stringer.
Ops incl: local bus services, school contracts, excursions & tours, private hire.
Livery: White/Green

SIMS TRAVEL

HUNHOLME GARAGE, BOOT,
HOLMROOK CA19 1TF
Tel: 019467 23227
Fax: 019467 23158
E-mail: simstravel@hotmail.com
Ptnrs: J Andrew Sim, D Peter Sim
Fleet: 9 - 6 coach, 2 midicoach, 1 minicoach.
Chassis: 3 Mercedes. 1 Neoplan. 5 Volvo.
Bodies: 1 Autobus. 1 Berkhof. 1 Mercedes.
1 Neoplan. 2 Plaxton. 2 Van Hool, 1 Other.
Ops incl: excursions & tours, private hire, school contracts.
Livery: White/Red/Maroon.

STAGECOACH NORTH WEST

BROADACRE HOUSE,
16-20 LOWTHER STREET,
CARLISLE
CA3 8DA
Tel: 01228 597222
Fax: 01228 597888
E-mail:
northwest.enquiries@stagecoachbus.com
Web site: www.stagecoachbus.com
Fleetname: Stagecoach
Cumbria/Lancaster/Lancashire
Man Dir: Chris Bowles **Eng Dir**: P W Lee
Ops Dir: D M Ashworth
Com Dir: C J Bowles
Fleet: 492 - 161 double-deck bus,
114 single-deck bus, 24 coach, 9 open-top bus, 73 midibus, 111 minibus.
Chassis: 1 Bristol. 91 Dennis. 67 Leyland.
16 MAN. 71 Mercedes. 2 Neoplan.
40 Optare. 204 Volvo.
Bodies: 306 Alexander. 4 Duple. 1 ECW.
10 Jonckheere. 20 Leyland. 2 Neoplan.
2 Northern Counties. 40 Optare. 2 Park Royal. 36 Plaxton. 69 Transbus.
Ops incl: local bus services, school contracts, excursions & tours, private hire, express.
Livery: Stagecoach - Blue/Red/Orange/White.
Ticket System: Wayfarer TGX

F W STAINTON & SON LTD

39 BURTON ROAD, KENDAL LA9 7LJ
Tel: 01539 720156.
Fax: 01539 740287.
Fleetname: Staintons Olympic Holidays.
Man Dir: R. S. Stainton. **Ops Man**:
C. J. Stainton. **Ch Eng**: I. M Stainton.
Fleet: 14 coach.
Chassis: 1 Mercedes, 7 Setra, 6 Volvo.
Ops incl: excursions & tours, private hire, continental tours.
Livery: Blue/Green/Silver.

STEVE'S OF AMBLESIDE LTD

GALAVA GATE, BORRANS ROAD,
AMBLESIDE LA22 0EN
Tel: 01539 433544.
Fax: 01539 432018.
Dir: S. A. Wise. **Sec**: Mrs E. Wise.
Fleet: 2 minibus.
Chassis: 1 Freight Rover. 1 Renault.
Ops incl: excursions & tours, private hire, school contracts. **Livery**: White.

*TITTERINGTON COACHES LTD

THE GARAGE, BLENCOW, PENRITH
CA11 0DG
Tel: 01768 483228
Fax: 01768 483680
Dirs: Ian Titterington, Paul Titterington, Colin Titterington
Fleet: 15 coach
Chassis: 1 Iveco. 1 Leyland. 1 MAN.
1 Mercedes. 11 Volvo.
Bodies: 1 Beulas. 1 Duple. 5 Jonckheere. 2 Neoplan. 4 Plaxton. 2 Van Hool.
Ops incl: excursions & tours, private hire, continental tours, school contracts
Livery: Mustard/White

TOWER COACHES

THE GARAGE, BURNFOOT, WIGTON
CA7 9HL
Tel: 01697 349600
Props: M D Sellars, Mrs T Sellars
Fleet: 5 - 2 coach, 2 midibus, 1 minibus.
Chassis: 1 DAF. 1 Leyland. 2 Mercedes.
1 Renault.
Bodies: 1 Alexander. 1 Holdsworth.
2 Plaxton. 1 Reeve Burgess.
Ops incl: local bus services, school contracts, private hire.
Livery: Dark Blue/Grey
Ticket System: Almex A

*THE TRAVELLERS CHOICE

See Lancashire

A/c	Air conditioning		Seat belt-fitted vehicles		Replacement vehicle available
	Vehicles suitable for disabled	R	Recovery service available (not 24 hr)	T	Toilet-drop facilities available
	Coach(es) with galley facilities				Vintage vehicle(s) available
wc	Coach(es) with toilet facilities	R24	24hr recovery service		Open top vehicle(s)

Cumbria

TUERS MOTORS LTD
R24

BRIDGE HOUSE, MORLAND,
PENRITH CA10 3AY
Tel: 01931 714224
Fax: 01931 714236
Fleet: 7 - 4 coach, 1 midicoach, 2 minicoach
Chassis: 1 AEC. 1 DAF. 1 Ford Transit.
1 Mercedes. 1 Toyota. 2 Volvo.
Bodies: 1 Caetano. 3 Plaxton. 2 Reeve Burgess. 1 Van Hool.
Ops incl: excursions & tours, private hire, school contracts, continental tours.
Livery: Cream/Red

WRIGHT BROS (COACHES) LTD
R24

CENTRAL GARAGE, NENTHEAD,
ALSTON CA9 3NP.
Tel: 01434 381200.
Fax: 01434 382089.
E-mail: wrightbros@btinternet.com
Chmn/Man Dir: J. G. Wright.
Dir: C. I. Wright.
Fleet: 12 - 10 coach, 2 double-deck coach.
Chassis: 5 Bedford. 2 Scania. 5 Volvo.
Bodies: 2 Jonckheere. 7 Plaxton. 2 Van Hool. 1 Ikarus.
Ops incl: local bus services, school contracts, private hire, continental tours.
Livery: Cream/Black/Gold.
Ticket System: Almex.

DERBYSHIRE

ANDREW'S OF TIDESWELL LTD
R24

ANCHOR GARAGE, TIDESWELL
SK17 8RB
Tel: 01298 871222
Fax: 01298 872412
E-mail: info@andrews-of-tideswell.co.uk
Web site: www.andrews-of-tideswell.co.uk
Dirs: R. B. Andrew, P. D. Andrew
Fleet: 18 - 2 double-deck bus, 11 coach, 2 double-deck coach, 2 midicoach, 1 minicoach.
Chassis: 2 Ford. 2 Leyland. 3 Mercedes. 1 Scania. 2 Setra. 8 Volvo.
Bodies: 2 Alexander. 3 Mercedes. 5 Plaxton. 2 Setra. 6 Van Hool.
Ops incl: excursions & tours, private hire, continental tours, school contracts
Livery: Cream/Ivory/Red flash.

ARRIVA DERBY LTD

ASCOT DRIVE, OFF LONDON ROAD, DERBY DE24 8ND
Tel: 01332 861500
Fax: 01332 861501
Fleetname: Arriva Serving Derby.
Prop: ARRIVA Midlands (*see Staffordshire*)
Man Dir: Catherine Mason
Fleet: 126 - 74 double-deck bus, 9 single-deck bus, 24 midibus, 19 minibus.
Chassis: 7 Daimler, 26 Dennis, 19 Mercedes, 3 Scania, 71 Volvo.
Bodies: Alexander, 31 East Lancs, Marshall, Northern Counties, Plaxton.
Ops incl: local bus services, school contracts, private hire.
Livery: Aquamarine/Cotswold Stone
Ticket System: Wayfarer II.

BAGNALLS COACHES

THE COACH STOP, GEORGE HOLMES WAY, SWADLINCOTE DE11 9DF
Tel: 01283 551964
Fax: 01283 552287
Dir/Ops Man: John Bagnall **Dir/Clerk**: Pat Bagnall **Dir/Ch Eng**: Karl Bagnall
Dir/Clerk: Gavin Bagnall
Fleet: 12 - single-deck bus, coach

Chassis: 12 Volvo
Bodies: 1 East Lancs. 1 Jonckheere. 1 Plaxton. 10 Van Hool.
Ops incl: local bus services, excursions & tours, private hire, school contracts.
Livery: various

BAKEWELL COACHES
24 MOORHALL, BAKEWELL
DE45 1FP
Tel: 01629 813995

BOWERS COACHES

ASPINCROFT GARAGE, CHAPEL-EN-LE-FRITH SK23 0NU
Tel: 01298 812204
Fax: 01298 816103
E-mail: kenny@bowerscoaches.co.uk
Web site: www.bowerscoaches.co.uk
Man Dir: Michael Bowers **Tran Man**: Kenny Duncan
Fleet: 34 - 7 single-deck bus, 6 coach, 19 midibus, 1 minibus. 1 van.
Chassis: 2 Dennis. 5 Leyland National. 1 MAN. 9 Mercedes. 10 Optare. 4 Scania. 1 Setra.
Bodies: 4 Alexander. 2 Irizar. 5 Leyland National. 10 Optare. 5 Reeve Burgess. 1 Setra. 3 Van Hool.
Ops incl: local bus services, school contracts, excursions & tours, private hire, continental tours.
(part of Centrebus)

*CLOWES COACHES

BARROWMOOR, LONGNOR
SK17 0QP
Tel: 01298 83292
Fax: 01298 83838
Dirs: George Clowes, Kathleen M Clowes
Fleet: 13 - 8 coach, 4 midibus, 1 minicoach
Chassis: 2 DAF. 1 MAN. 4 Mercedes. 2 Neoplan. 4 Scania.
Bodies: 4 Alexander. 2 Duple. 2 Irizar. 2 Neoplan. 2 Reeve Burgess. 1 Van Hool
Ops incl: local bus services, excursions & tours, private hire.
Livery: Cream/Green/Red
Ticket system: own

COX'S OF BELPER

GOODS ROAD, BELPER DE56 1UU
Tel: 01773 822395
Fax: 01773 821157
E-mail: coxsofbelper@lineone.net
Prop: Bernard Bembridge
Fleet: 6 - 2 coach, 1 midicoach, 1 minibus, 1 minicoach, 1 midibus.
Chassis: 1 LDV. 3 Mercedes. 2 Volvo
Bodies: 1 Carlyle. 1 Jonckheere. 1 Mercedes. 1 VanHool. 2 conversions
Ops incl: excursions & tours, private hire, school contracts.
Livery: White/Blue

CRESSWELL'S COACHES (GRESLEY) LTD

3 SHORTHEATH ROAD, MOIRA, SWADLINCOTE DE12 6AL
Tel: 01283 217215
Fax: 01283 550043
Recovery: 01283 217215
E-mail: info@cresswellscoaches.com
Web site: www.cresswellscoaches.com
Man Dir: David Cresswell **Dir**: Jean Raynor
Ch Eng: Steve Lloyd **Tran Man**: John Collins
Fleet: 19 - 13 coach, 6 minicoach
Chassis: 4 Iveco. 6 Mercedes. 1 Optare. 9 Volvo.
Bodies: 4 Beulas. 2 Jonckheere. 2 Marshall/MCV. 3 Mercedes. 1 Optare. 6 Plaxton. 1 Reeve Burgess.1 Van Hool.
Ops incl: local bus services, school contracts, excursions & tours, private hire, continental tours.
Ticket System: Wayfarer

CRISTAL HIRE COACHES OF SWANWICK

19 CROMWELL DRIVE, SWANWICK DE55 1DB.
Tel: 01773 604932.
Prop: A. Hunt. **Co Sec**: Mrs Christine Hunt.
Fleet: 2 coach.
Chassis: 1 Bova. 1 Leyland.
Ops incl: excursions & tours, private hire, school contract.

DAWSON'S MINICOACHES

10 HOLLAND CLOSE, MORTON
DE55 6HE
Tel: 01773 873149.
Prop: S. R. Dawson
Fleet: 4 - 2 minibus, 2 minicoach.
Chassis: 2 Ford Transit. 2 Freight Rover.
Ops incl: private hire, school contracts.
Livery: Grey/White/Blue stripe.

DERBY COMMUNITY TRANSPORT R24

MEADOW ROAD GARAGE,
MEADOW ROAD, DERBY DE1 2BH
Tel: 01332 380738
E-mail: derbyct@btinternet.com
Fleet: 28 minibus
Chassis: LDV. Mercedes.
Ops incl: local bus services, school contracts

K&H DOYLE

190 NOTTINGHAM ROAD, RIPLEY
DE55 3AY
Tel: 01773 745641
Prop. K Doyle.
Ops Incl: local bus services
Livery: Beige.

*TIM DRAPER'S GOLDEN HOLIDAYS

SEVERN SQUARE, ALFRETON
DE55 7BQ
Tel: 01773 590808
Fax: 01773 590816
E-mail: tim.draper@btconnect.com
Dirs: Tim Draper, Pam Draper, Clair Draper
Fleet: 10 - 1 double-deck bus, 6 coach, 1 midibus, 2 minibus.
Chassis: 1 DAF. 1 Iveco. 1 LDV. 1 MAN. 1 MCW. 2 Mercedes. 3 Volvo.
Bodies: 1 Beulas. 1 MCW. 2 Mercedes. 1 Noge. 2 Plaxton. 2 Van Hool.
Ops incl: excursions & tours, school contracts, private hire
Livery: White/Red/Yellow
Ticket System: Almex, Wayfarer 3, Setright

*DUNN-LINE GROUP

See Nottinghamshire

'E' COACHES OF ALFRETON

1 MANOR COURT, RIDDINGS
DE55 4DG
Tel: 01773 541222
Fax: 01629 825522
Owner: K. Bacon
Fleet: 5 - 2 midicoach, 3 minicoach.
Chassis: 3 Mercedes. 2 LDV.
Bodies: 2 Autobus. 3 Crest.
Ops incl: local bus service, school contract, excursions & tours, private hire.
Livery: Blue/White.

ENNIS COACHES

42 THE LIMES CLOSE, MATLOCK
DE4 3DT
Tel: 01629 582397
E-mail: enniscoaches@yahoo.co.uk
Web site: www.geocities.com/enniscoaches
Fleet: 9 — 5 coaches, 2 single-decker buses, 2 minicoaches.
Chassis: 5 Bova, 2 Leyland, 1 MCW, Mercedes-Benz
Bodies: 1 Advanced, 1 Alexander, 5 Bova, 1 Leyland National, 1 MCW
Ops incl: private hire, school contracts

*FELIX BUS SERVICES LTD

157 STATION ROAD, STANLEY
DE7 6FJ
Tel: 0115 932 5332
Fax: 0115 932 6096
Ops Man: Ian Middup
Fleet: 13 - 7 single-deck bus, 3 coach, 3 midibus.
Chassis: 2 Irisbus. 5 Leyland. 1 Mercedes. 2 Optare. 3 Scania.
Bodies: 5 Leyland. 2 Optare. 3 Plaxton. 3 Wright.
Ops incl: local bus services, school contracts, excursions & tours, private hire, continental tours.
Ticket system: Wayfarer TGX150

*FLIGHTS HALLMARK

See West Midlands

*GLOVERS COACHES LTD

MOOR FARM ROAD EAST,
ASHBOURNE DE6 1HD
Tel/Fax: 01335 300043
E-mail: gloverscoaches@btconnect.com
Web site: www.gloverscoaches.com
Dirs: Stephen Mason, Heather Mason
Fleet: 14 - 2 single-deck bus, 12 coach
Chassis: 2 Dennis. 3 Leyland. 9 Volvo.
Bodies: 2 Alexander. 12 Plaxton.
Ops incl: local bus serivces, school contracts, excursions & tours, private hire, continental tours.
Livery: Blue/Cream.

GOLDEN GREEN LUXURY TRAVEL

GOLDEN GREEN GARAGE,
LONGNOR SK17 0QP
Tel: 01298 83583.
Fax: 01298 83584
Props: John and Gill Worth
Fleet: 5 midicoach.
Chassis: 5 Mercedes.
Ops incl: school contracts, excursions & tours, private hire.

HARPUR'S COACHES

WINCANTON CLOSE, DERBY
DE24 8NB
Tel: 01332 757677
Fax: 01332 757259
E-mail: harpurscoaches@tiscali.co.uk
Web site: www.harpurscoaches.co.uk
Man Dir: Nick Harpur
Fleet: 27 - 10 double-deck bus, 4 single-deck bus, 13 coach.
Chassis: 1 AEC. 2 Leyland. 9 MCW. 11 Volvo.
Bodies: 7 MCW. 1 Park Royal. 15 Plaxton.
Ops incl: school contracts, excursions & tours, private hire.
Livery: Cream/Brown

HARRISON'S TRAVEL

154 SOMERCOTES HILL,
SOMERCOTES, ALFRETON
DE55 4HU
Tel: 01773 833337

G & J HOLMES (COACHES) LTD

124A MARKET STREET, CLAY
CROSS S45 9LY
Tel/Fax: 01246 863232.
Ops incl: local bus services

HENRY HULLEY & SONS LTD

DERWENT GARAGE, BASLOW
DE45 1RP
Tel: 01246 582246
Fax: 01246 583161
E-mail: www.hulleys-of-baslow.co.uk
Web site: info@hulleys-of-baslow.co.uk
Fleetname: Hulleys of Baslow
Dirs: P Eades, R W Eades
Fleet: 19 - 11 single-deck bus, 5 coach, 2 minibus, 1 minicoach.
Chassis: 9 Dennis. 1 Leyland. 3 MAN. 3 Mercedes. 1 Optare. 1 Scania. 1 Volvo.
Bodies: 1 Caetano. 1 Leyland. 1 Marshall/MCV. 6 Optare. 8 Plaxton. 1 Reeve Burgess. 1 Van Hool.
Ops incl: local bus services, school contracts, private hire.
Livery: Buses: Cream/Blue; Coaches: White/Blue
Ticket System: Wayfarer 3

LEANDER TRAVEL

7 WORDSWORTH AVENUE,
SWADLINCOTE DE11 0DZ
Tel/fax: 01283 213780
E-mail: pat@leandercoaches.co.uk
Web site: www.leandercoaches.co.uk
Fleetname: Leander Coaches
Prop: M. W. Bugden
Fleet: 4 coach, 1 minicoach.
Chassis: 3 DAF. 1 LDV. 1 Volvo.

A/c	Air conditioning		Seat belt-fitted vehicles
	Vehicles suitable for disabled	R	Recovery service available (not 24 hr)
	Coach(es) with galley facilities	R24	24hr recovery service
wc	Coach(es) with toilet facilities		
	Replacement vehicle available	T	Toilet-drop facilities available
			Vintage vehicle(s) available
			Open top vehicle(s)

Derbyshire

Ops incl: excursions & tours, private hire, school contracts, continental tours.

*JOHNSON'S TOURS
See Nottinghamshire

KINCHBUS LTD
MANSFIELD ROAD, HEANOR
DE75 7BG
Tel: 01775 536309
Web site: www.kinchbus.co.uk
Fleet: 35 - 8 double-deck bus, 9 single-deck bus, 18 minibus.
Chassis: 2 Dennis. 8 Leyland. 11 Mercedes. 11 Optare. 3 Volvo.
Ops incl: local bus services
Livery: Blue/Yellow
Ticket System: Wayfarer
Part of the Wellglade grop

LITTLE TRANSPORT LTD
HALLAM FIELDS ROAD, ILKESTON
DE7 4AZ
Tel: 0115 932 8581
Fax: 0115 932 5163
Recovery: 07919 020835
E-mail: enqiries@littletravel.co.uk
Web site: www.littlestravel.co.uk
Fleetname: Little's Travel
Dirs: Steve Wells, Paul Wright
Fleet: 20 - 11 double-deck bus, 9 coach
Chassis: 3 Bova. 4 DAF. 5 Leyland. 2 Leyland National. 1 MCW. 4 Scania. 1 Volvo.
Bodies: 3 Bova. 5 East Lancs. 1 Ikarus. 6 Leyland. 2 Leyland National. 3 Van Hool.
Ops incl: excursions & tours, private hire, school contracts, local bus services, continental tours.
Livery: White
Ticket system: Almex

MACPHERSON COACHES LTD
THE GARAGE, HILL STREET, DONISTHORPE DE12 7PL
Tel: 01530 270226
Web site: www.macphersoncoaches.co.uk
Man Dir: Neil MacPherson
Fleet: 15 - 1 single-deck bus, 9 coach, 3 midibus, 1 midicoach, 1 minicoach.
Chassis: 1 Dennis. 7 Mercedes. 7 Setra.
Bodies: 1 Alexander. 1 Jonckheere. 1 Mercedes. 3 Plaxton. 7 Setra. 1 Strachans.
Ops incl: local bus services, school contracts, excursions & tours, private hire, continental tours.
Livery: Cream/Red
Ticket System: Wayfarer.

*MYKANN COACH HIRE
29 WARREN DRIVE, LINTON, SWADLINCOTE DE12 6QP
Tel: 01283 762673
E-mail: mykanncoachhire@hotmail.com
Fleet: 2 coach
Chassis/bodies: 1 MAN. 1 Setra.
Bodies: 1 Jonckheere. 1 Setra.
Ops incl: private hire, school contracts.
Livery: Multi

NOTTS & DERBY TRACTION CO LTD
MANSFIELD ROAD, HEANOR
DE75 7BG
Fleet: 49 - 5 double-deck bus, 32 single-deck bus, 12 minibus.
Chassis: 18 Dennis. 5 Leyland. 12 Mercedes. 3 Optare. 11 Volvo.
Livery: Blue/Green
Ticket System: Almex
(Part of the Wellglade Group)

PARKERS COACHES
41 LABURNUM ROAD, NEWHALL, SWADLINCOTE DE11 0NR.
Tel: 01283 550015.
Prop: W. A. Parker.
Fleet: 2 minibus.
Chassis: Ford Transit.
Ops incl: school contracts, private hire.
Livery: Blue/White.

RINGWOOD LUXURY COACHES
SPEEDWELL GARAGE, CROMPTON ROAD, SPEEDWELL INDUSTRIAL ESTATE, STAVELEY S43 3PG
Tel/Fax: 01246 476366
Prop: David T Brockbank
Fleet: 6 - 2 midicoach, 4 minicoach
Chassis: 5 Mercedes.
Bodies: 1 Caetano. 4 Mercedes. 1 Sitcar
Ops incl: school contracts, private hire

SLACKS TRAVEL (K V & G L SLACK LTD)
THE TRAVEL CENTRE, LUMSDALE, MATLOCK DE4 5LB
Tel: 01629 582826
Fax: 01629 580519
E-mail: enq@slackscoaches.co.uk
Web site: www.slackscoaches.co.uk
Man Dir: G L Slack **Ch Eng**: R M Slack
Co Sec: D R Slack **Tran Man**: J Gough
Fleet: 19 - 15 coach, 2 midicoach, 2 minibus.
Chassis: 5 DAF. 3 Dennis. 2 Ford. 2 Ford Transit. 3 Iveco. 2 Mercedes. 1 Neoplan. 1 Scania. 1 Volvo.
Bodies: 1 Autobus. 3 Beulas. 1 Jonckheere. 1 Mercedes. 1 Neoplan. 5 Plaxton. 5 Van Hool.
Ops incl: excursions & tours, private hire, continental tours, school contracts

STAGECOACH EAST MIDLANDS
NEW STREET, CHESTERFIELD
S40 2LQ
Tel: 01246 222018
Fax: 01246 232205
Web site: www.stagecoachbus.com
Fleetname: Stagecoach East Midlands
Man Dir: Paul Lynch **Ops Dir**: Richard Kay
Eng Dir: John Taylor **Com Dir**: John Pope
Service Quality Man: John Curtis
Fleet: 502 - 193 double-deck bus, 76 single-deck bus, 33 single-deck coach, 126 midibus, 3 articulated coach, 71 minibus.
Chassis: 148 Dennis, 1 Ford, 117 Leyland, 71 Mercedes, 16 Optare, 2 Scania, 147 Volvo.
Bodies: 324 Alexander, 2 Duple, 15 ECW, 33 East Lancs, 13 Jonckheere, 33 Northern Counties, 17 Optare, 2 Park Royal, 58 Plaxton, 4 Van Hool, 1 Wadham Stringer.
Ops incl: local bus services, school contracts, private hire, express.
Livery: Stagecoach new.
Ticket System: ERG.

*TM TRAVEL LTD
FAN ROAD, STAVELEY S43 3PT
Tel: 01246 477331
Fax: 01246 281027
E-mail: info@tmtravel.co.uk
Web site: www.tmtravel.co.uk
Man Dir: T J Watts **Co Sec**: C M Watts
Ops Dir: P Hopkinson **Ops Man**: P Harding
Ch Eng: J Burton
Fleet: 86 - 26 double-deck bus, 17 single-deck bus, 10 coach, 1 double-deck coach, 30 midibus, 2 midicoach.
Chassis: 14 DAF. 3 Dennis. 20 Leyland. 1 MAN. 19 Mercedes. 11 Optare. 4 Scania. 12 Volvo.
Bodies: 8 Alexander. 6 ECW. 8 East Lancs. 1 Jonckheere. 1 Mellor. 9 Northern Counties. 12 Optare. 40 Plaxton. 1 Van Hool
Ops incl: local bus services, school contracts, excursions & tours, continental tours, private hire.
Livery: Cream/Red/Maroon.
Ticket System: Wayfarer TGX150

TRENTBARTON
MANSFIELD ROAD, HEANOR
DE75 7BG
Tel: 01773 536336
Tel: 01773 536333
Web site: www.trentbarton.co.uk
Chmn/Man Dir: B R King **Com Dir**: R F Morgan **Fin Dir**: G Sutton
Fleet: 286 - 279 single-deck bus, 7 coach.
Chassis: 51 Dennis. 8 Mercedes. 131 Optare. 75 Scania. 21 Volvo.
Bodies: 8 Irizar. 7 Northern Counties. 131 Optare. 72 Plaxton. 68 Wright.
Ops incl: local bus services.

VIKING TOURS & TRAVEL
UNIT 2, RYDER CLOSE, SWADLINCOTE DE11 9EU
Tel: 01283 217012
Fax: 01283 550685.
Fleetname: Viking
Gen Man: Graham Allen.
Ch Eng: Farrell Smith.
Fleet: 17 - 16 coach, 1 midicoach.
Chassis: 1 Bova, 1 MCW, 15 Volvo.
Bodies: 1 Bova. 1 ECW. 2 Jonckheere. 9 Plaxton. 4 Van Hool.
Ops incl: excursions & tours, private hire, express, continental tours, school contracts
Livery: Ocean Blue/Orange Band.

*WARRINGTON COACHES LTD
ILAM MOOR LANE, ILAM, ASHBOURNE DE6 2AZ
Tel: 01335 350204
Fax: 01335 350204
E-mail: info@warringtoncoaches.co.uk
Web site: www.warringtoncoaches.co.uk

Co Sec: L Boyton **Dirs**: K Warrington, M A Boydon
Fleet: 8 - 3 coaches, 3 mincoach, 2 midicoach
Chassis: 1 BMC. 2 Dennis. 3 LDV. 1 Mercedes. 1 Volvo.
Bodies: 1 BMC. 4 Plaxton. 3 other.
Ops incl: local bus services, school contracts, private hire

*P J WILDE & D A WARD

T/A ALBERT WILDE COACHES, 121 PARKSIDE, HEAGE, BELPER DE56 2AG
Tel/fax: 01773 856655
Dirs: Philip J Wilde, David Ward

Fleet: 5 coach.
Chassis: 4 DAF. 1 Leyland.
Ops incl: excursions & tours, school contracts.

*WOODWARD'S COACHES LTD

100 HIGH STREET EAST, GLOSSOP SK13 8QF
Tel: 01457 852651
Fax: 0156011 55430
E-mail: sales@woodwardscoaches.co.uk
Fleet: 6 - 5 coach, 1 minicoach
Ops incl: school contracts, excursions & tours, private hire.
Livery: Blue/White

YESTERYEAR MOTOR SERVICES

10 LADY GATE, DISEWORTH, DERBY DE74 2QF
Tel/fax: 01332 810774
E-mail: yesteryear10@hotmail.com
Prop: D. J. Moores
Fleet: 2 - 1 single-deck bus, 1 coach.
Chassis: Bedford, Leyland.
Bodies: Duple, ECW.
Ops incl: private hire.
Livery: Green/Cream.
Ticket System: Bell Punch.

DEVON

*A B COACHES LTD

WILLS ROAD, TOTNES INDUSTRIAL ESTATE, TOTNES TQ9 5XN
Tel: 01803 864161
Fax: 01803 864008
E-mail: abcoaches@btconnect.com
Web site: www.abcoaches.co.uk
Dirs: B T Smith, L Smith **Ch Eng**: N Buckley
Ops Man: M Chalk
Fleet: 11 coach.
Chassis: 3 DAF. 8 Dennis.
Bodies: 1 Bova. 7 Duple. 3 Van Hool.
Ops incl: local bus services, school contracts, excursions & tours, private hire.
Livery: Cream/Red

ALANSWAY COACHES LTD

KING CHARLES BUSINESS PARK, OLD NEWTON ROAD, HEATHFIELD, NEWTON ABBOT TQ12 6UT
Tel: 01626 833664
Fax: 01626 835648
Web site: www.alansway.co.uk
Man Dir: Ms A Ellison
Fleet: 18 minibus.
Chassis: 14 Ford Transit. 4 Iveco.
Ops incl: local bus services, school contracts, private hire.
Livery: Orange/White.
Ticket System: Setright.

AXE VALLEY MINI TRAVEL

BUS DEPOT, 26 HARBOUR ROAD, SEATON EX12 2NA
Tel/Fax: 01297 625959
Fleetname: AVMT
Prop: Mrs F. M. Searle **Traf Man**: J. R. Paddon.
Fleet: 9 - 5 double-deck bus, 4 midibus.

Chassis: 1 Dodge. 2 Iveco. 1 Leyland. 4 MCW. 1 Optare.
Bodies: 1 Leyland. 1 Reeve Burgess. 4 MCW. 2 Dormobile. 1 Optare.
Ops incl: local bus services.
Livery: Maroon/White.
Ticket System: Wayfarer.

AYREVILLE COACHES

202 NORTH PROSPECT ROAD, PLYMOUTH PL2 2PR
Tel: 01752 605450.
Fax: 01752 219366.
E-mail: ayrevillecoaches@tinyonline.co.uk
Owner: M. J. Buley.
Fleet: 6 - 3 midicoach, 3 minibus.
Chassis: 1 Ford, 1 Iveco, 4 Mercedes.
Bodies: 2 Carlyle, 1 Reeve Burgess, 1 Devon Conversion, 2 Pilcher Green.
Ops incl: private hire, school contracts.
Livery: White.

BURNHAM PARK COACHES

20 BURNHAM PARK ROAD, PLYMOUTH PL3 5QD
Tel: 01752 703412

*CARMEL COACHES

STATION ROAD, NORTHLEW, OKEHAMPTON EX20 3BN
Tel: 01409 221237
Fax: 01409 221226
E-mail: carmelcoaches@hotmail.com
Dirs: Tony Hazell, Michael Hazel
Fleet: 25 - 3 single-deck bus, 18 coach, 3 midicoach, 1 minicoach.
Chassis: 1 Albion. 4 Bova. 4 DAF. 5 Dennis. 5 Mercedes. 1 Optare. 4 Scania. 1 Toyota.
Bodies: 2 Autobus. 2 Berkhof. 4 Bova.

2 Caetano. 3 Duple. 3 Irizar. 1 Marcopolo. 1 Marshall/MCV. 1 Optare. 2 Plaxton. 1 UVG. 2 Van Hool. 1 other.
Ops incl: local bus services, school contracts, excursions & tours, private hire.
Livery: White
Ticket System: Almex

CLH TRAVEL

18 EUGENE ROAD, PAIGNTON TQ3 2PQ
Tel: 01803 668900
Tran Man: Geoff Wilkins

DAISH'S TRAVEL

PARKHILL ROAD, TORQUAY TQ1 2DY
Tel: 0870 902 1412
Web site: www.daishs.com
Fleet: 9 coach
Ops incl: excursions & tours, private hire, continental tours

*DARTLINE COACHES

LANGDONS BUSINESS PARK, CLYST ST MARY, EXETER EX5 1AF
Tel: 01392 872900
Fax: 01392 872909
E-mail: info@dartline-coaches.co.uk
Web site: www.dartlinecoaches.co.uk
Fleet: 28 - 20 coach, 3 midicoach, 5 minibus
Chassis: 5 DAF. 5 Dennis. 3 Optare. 11 Volvo.
Bodies: 1 Berkhof. 3 Bova. 2 Caetano. 8 Mercedes. 3 Optare. 8 Plaxton. 2 Van Hool
Ops incl: local bus services, school contracts, excursions & tours, private hire, continental tours, express.
Livery: White/Green
Ticket System: Almex.

A/c	Air conditioning	✓	Replacement vehicle available
	Vehicles suitable for disabled	T	Toilet-drop facilities available
	Coach(es) with galley facilities		Vintage vehicle(s) available
wc	Coach(es) with toilet facilities		Open top vehicle(s)
R	Recovery service available (not 24 hr)		
R24	24hr recovery service		

Derbyshire / Devon

DAWLISH COACHES LTD
[wc] [♿] [A/c] [R24] [🔑] [T]

SHUTTERTON INDUSTRIAL ESTATE, DAWLISH EX7 0NH
Tel: 01626 862525
Fax: 01626 867167
Web site: www.dawlishcoaches.com
Dir: John Weaver
Fleet: 34 - 28 coach, 2 midibus, 4 midicoach.
Chassis: 13 Bova. 2 Iveco. 5 Mercedes. 10 Volvo. 2 other.
Bodies: 2 Beulas. 2 Berkhof. 13 Bova. 1 Caetano. 2 Duple. 1 Plaxton. 9 Van Hool.
Ops incl: local bus services, school contracts, private hire.
Livery: Red/Blue/White
Ticket System: Setright

EAST TEIGNBRIDGE COMMUNITY TRANSPORT
THE MANOR HOUSE, OLD TOWN STREET, DAWLISH EX7 9AP
Tel: 01626 888890
Fax: 01626 889253
E-mail: etcta@lineone.net
Man: Jenny Connor **Coordinator**: Jan Green
Fleet: 3 minibus, 3 car.
Chassis: 1 Ford. 1 Ford Transit. 1 LDV. 1 Renault. 1 Fiat. 1 Volkswagen
Ops incl: school contracts, excursions and tours, private hire.

EASTWARD COACHES
[♿] [wc] [🍴] [🔑]

1 BARLANDS WAY, DOLTON, WINKLEIGH EX19 8QB
Tel: 01805 804659
Fax: 01805 804659
E-mail: eastwardcoaches@btopenworld.com
Props: Karen Wonnacott, Nick Woolacott
Tran Man: Mike Yedermann
Fleet: 6 - 5 coach, 1 minibus.
Chassis: 1 AEC. 2 Bedford. 1 DAF. 1 Ford. 1 Freight Rover.
Bodies: 1 Carlyle. 4 Plaxton. 1 Van Hool.
Ops incl: school contracts, excursions & tours, private hire.
Livery: White with Green/Red stripes

*FILERS TRAVEL LTD
[♿] [wc] [🍴] [A/c] [🔑]

SLADE LODGE, SLADE ROAD, ILFRACOMBE EX34 8LB
Tel: 01271 863819
Fax: 01271 867281
E-mail: filers@filers.co.uk
Web site: www.filers.co.uk
Dirs: Royston J Filer, Irene H Filer
Fleet: 20 - 12 coach, 2 midibus, 2 midicoach, 4 minibus.
Chassis: 2 Bova. 2 LDV. 2 MAN. 3 Mercedes. 1 Scania. 1 Volvo.
Bodies: 2 Bova. 1 Irizar. 2 Neoplan. 4 Plaxton. 1 Van Hool.
Ops incl: local bus services, excursions & tours, private hire, school contracts, continental tours.
Livery: White/Blue/Yellow
Ticket system: Almex

FIRST DEVON & CORNWALL LTD
[♿] [wc] [🚌] [♿]

THE RIDE, CHELSON MEADOW, PLYMOUTH PL9 7JT
Tel: 01752 495250
E-mail: firstdevonandcornwall@firstgroup.com
Web site: www.firstgroup.com
Fleetname: First
Man Dir: Marc Reddy **Fin Dir**: Chris Hayter
Eng Dir: Phil Pannell **Comm Dir**: Simon Newport **Gen Man (Devon)**: Steve Grigg
Gen Man (Cornwall): Chris Casson
Fleet: 322 - double-deck bus, single-deck bus, coach, open-top bus, midibus, minibus.
Chassis: 4 Bristol. 157 Dennis. 28 Leyland. 29 Mercedes. 19 Optare. 85 Volvo.
Bodies: 56 Alexander. 20 ECW. 18 East Lancs. 6 Marshall. 4 Northern Counties. 21 Optare. 1 Park Royal. 142 Plaxton. 9 Transbus. 5 Van Hool. 23 Wright. 17 other.
Ops incl: local bus services, school contracts, private hire, express.
Livery: First Group
Ticket System: Almex Optima.

GARRETT COACHES LTD
[wc] [♿] [A/c]

3 STOKES CLOSE, NEWTON ABBOT TQ12 3YY
Tel: 01626 366580
Fax: 01626 353733
E-mail: garrettcoach@tesco.net
Dir: P Garrett.
Fleet: 3 - 2 coach, 1 minibus.
Chassis/Bodies: 2 Bova. 1 Mercedes.
Ops incl: private hire, school contracts.
Livery: White

GOLD STAR COACHES
[♿] [♿]

18 WOODVILLE ROAD, TORQUAY TQ1 1LP
Tel/Fax: 01803 200080
Prop: E Stirk
Fleet: 9 minicoach
Chassis: 2 Ford Transit. 5 LDV. 2 Mercedes.
Ops incl: private hire, school contracts
Livery: Green/Cream

*GUSCOTT'S COACHES LTD [♿]
THE GARAGE, CROFT GATE, HALWILL EX21 5TL
Tel: 01409 221661
Fax: 01409 221435
Dirs: T Guscott, C D Guscott.
Fleet: 5 - 4 coach, 1 double-deck coach.
Chassis: 1 DAF. 1 Neoplan. 3 Volvo.
Bodies: 1 Duple. 1 Neoplan. 2 Plaxton.
Ops incl: local bus services, school contracts, private hire.
Livery: Cream/Blue/Red

*W L HEARD & SONS LTD
[♿] [wc] [A/c] [R] [🔑]

FORE STREET, HARTLAND, BIDEFORD EX39 6BD
Tel: 01237 441233
Fax: 01237 441789
E-mail: kmheard@aol.com
Fleet name: Heards Coaches
Dirs: D G Heard, B W Heard, G J Heard, J L Heard **Co Sec**: Miss K M Heard
Fleet: 18 coach
Chassis: 2 Dennis. 2 MAN. 1 Mercedes. 2 Scania. 11 Volvo.
Bodies: 1 Alexander. 1 Berkhof. 1 Caetano. 1 Duple. 2 Irizar. 1 Jonckheere. 1 Noge. 2 Van Hool. 8 other.
Ops incl: school contracts, excursions & tours, private hire, continental tours
Livery: Blue/White.

HARDY TOURS
WILDER ROAD, ILFRACOMBE EX34 9AF
Tel: 01271 866455/863426
Web site: www.hardystours.co.uk

*HEMMINGS COACHES LTD
[wc] [♿] [A/c] [🔑] [T]

POWLERS PIECE GARAGE, EAST PUTFORD, HOLSWORTHY EX22 7XW
Tel: 01237 451282
Fax: 01237 451920
E-mail: hemmingscoaches@aol.com
Props: Ken & Linda Hemmings.
Fleet: 13 - 11 coach, 2 midibus
Chassis: 1 Bova. 1 DAF. 1 Leyland. 3 MAN. 4 Mercedes. 1 Neoplan. 2 Toyota. 1 VW.
Bodies: 1 Berkhof. 1 Bova. 1 Leyland. 4 Mercedes. 1 Neoplan. 1 Noge. 4 other.
Ops incl: excursions & tours, private hire, continental tours, school contracts
Livery: White/Ruby

HILLS SERVICES LTD
[wc] [♿] [A/c] [🔑]

THE GARAGE, STIBB CROSS, LANGTREE, TORRINGTON EX38 8LH
Tel: 01805 601203
Fax: 01805 601476
Recovery: 01805 601102
E-mail: hills.servicesltd@btinternet.com
Dirs: David J Hearn, Mrs M E Hearn
Fleet: 27 - 14 coach, 3 midibus,10 minibus.
Chassis: 4 DAF. 2 Ford Transit. 10 LDV. 3 Mercedes. 9 Volvo.
Bodies: 1 Bova. 5 Jonckheere. 1 Mellor. 2 Plaxton. 2 Reeve Burgess. 6 Van Hool.
Ops incl: excursions & tours, private hire, school contracts.

*HOOKWAYS CLASSIC TOURS
[♿] [♿] [wc] [A/c] [R24] [🔑] [T]

16 WINNER STREET, PAIGNTON TQ3 3BJ
Tel: 01803 527959
Fax: 01803 522069
Tel: 07850 038707
E-mail: linn@hookways.com
Web site: www.hookways.com
Man Dir: Alistair Gray **Dirs**: Kym Hookway, Sue Hookway, Jason Hookway, Martin Hookway **(Eng)**, Julie Hookway **(Sec)**
Fleet: 53 - 46 coach, 1 midicoach,

Devon

1 minibus, 1 minicoach, 4 multi-purpose vehices.
Chassis: 1 Leyland. 1 MAN. 3 Mercedes. 1 Scania. 4 VW. 43 Volvo
Bodies: 1 Irizar. 6 Jonckheere. 41 Plaxton. 1 Wright.
Ops incl: school contracts, excursions & tours, private hire, express, continental tours.
Livery: Yellow

*HOOKWAYS GREENSLADES

PEEK HOUSE, ANHOE TRADING ESTATE, VENNY BRIDGE, EXETER EX4 8JN
Tel: 01392 469210
Fax: 01392 466036
Recovery: 07850 038707
E-mail: alistair@hookways.com
Web site: www.hookways.com
Man Dir: Alistair Gray **Dirs**: Kym Hookway, Sue Hookway, Jason Hookway, Martin Hookway **(Eng)**, Julie Hookway **(Sec)**
Fleet: 53 - 46 coach, 1 midicoach, 1 minibus, 1 minicoach, 4 multi-purpose vehices.
Chassis: 1 Leyland. 1 MAN. 3 Mercedes. 1 Scania. 4 VW. 43 Volvo
Bodies: 1 Irizar. 6 Jonckheere. 41 Plaxton. 1 Wright.
Ops incl: school contracts, excursions & tours, private hire, express, continental tours.
Livery: Yellow

*HOOKWAYS PLEASUREWAYS COACHES

THE GARAGE, MEETH EX20 3EP
Tel: 01837 810257
Fax: 01837 810066.
Recovery: 07850 038707
E-mail: lesley@hookways.com
Web site: www.hookways.com
Man Dir: Alistair Gray **Dirs**: Kym Hookway, Sue Hookway, Jason Hookway, Martin Hookway **(Eng)**, Julie Hookway **(Sec)**
Fleet: 53 - 46 coach, 1 midicoach, 1 minibus, 1 minicoach, 4 multi-purpose vehices.
Chassis: 1 Leyland. 1 MAN. 3 Mercedes. 1 Scania. 4 VW. 43 Volvo
Bodies: 1 Irizar. 6 Jonckheere. 41 Plaxton. 1 Wright.
Ops incl: school contracts, excursions & tours, private hire, express, continental tours.
Livery: Yellow

IVYBRIDGE & DISTRICT COMMUNITY TRANSPORT

DOURO COURT, BROOK ROAD, IVYBRIDGE PL21 0LS.
Tel: 01752 690444.
Fleetname: Ivybridge Ring & Ride.
Co-ordinator: Mrs S. Jenkins.
Chmn: I. Martin.
Fleet: 1 minibus. **Chassis/Body**: LDV.
Ops incl: local bus services, private hire.

*KINGDOM'S TOURS LTD

WESTFIELD GARAGE, EXETER ROAD, TIVERTON EX16 5NZ
Tel: 01884 252646
Fax: 01884 252646
E-mail: kingdoms-tours@supanet.com
Web site: www.kingdoms-tours.co.uk
Dirs: R. V. Kingdom, R. Kingdom, S. J. Kingdom.
Fleet: 24 - 12 coach, 4 midicoach, 5 minibus, 3 minicoach.
Chassis: 1 Ford. 3 Iveco. 1 MAN. 10 Mercedes. 6 Scania. 3 Volvo.
Bodies: 1 Beulas. 6 Irizar. 3 Mellor. 7 Mercedes. 1 Neoplan. 3 Van Hool. 3 other.
Ops incl: school contracts, excursions & tours, private hire, continental tours.

MID DEVON COACHES

STATION ROAD, BOW, CREDITON EX17 6JD
Tel/Fax: 01363 82200
E-mail: enquiries@mdcoaches.co.uk
Web site: www.mdcoaches.co.uk
Prop: K. J. Wills **Man**: Mrs L. A. Hamilton
Fleet: 22 - 18 single-deck coach, 2 minicoach, 2 minibus.
Chassis: 2 DAF. 3 Ford. 3 Ford Transit. 5 Leyland. 4 Scania. 2 Toyota. 2 Volvo.
Bodies: 2 Bova.. 2 Caetano. 1 Irizar. 2 Jonckheere. 10 Plaxton.
Ops incl: school contracts, excursions & tours, private hire, continental tours.
Livery: Green/Cream.

MOOR TO SEA

1 SOPHIA WAY, TOTNES ROAD, NEWTON ABBOT TQ12 1YW.
Tel/Fax: 01626 362002.
E-mail: moortosea@eurobell.co.uk
Owner/Operator: Robert Clifford.
Fleet: 1 midicoach.
Chassis: Volvo. **Body**: Plaxton.
Ops incl: private hire. **Livery**: White.

PARAMOUNT MINI-COACHES

6 VENN CRESCENT, HARTLEY, PLYMOUTH PL3 5PJ.
Tel: 01752 767255
Fax: 01752 767255
Prop: B. M. Couch
Fleet: 5 - 1 midicoach, 2 minibus, 2 minicoach.
Chassis: 2 Ford Transit. 1 Leyland. 2 Mercedes.
Ops incl: excursions & tours, private hire, school contracts.

 Touring Man: Brian Madge
Associated companies: Peninsula Drivers (see A-Z Driver Hire) Eastward Coaches (see above)

*PLYMOUTH CITYBUS LTD

1 MILEHOUSE ROAD, PLYMOUTH PL3 4AA
Tel: 01752 662271
Fax: 01752 567209
E-mail: md@plymouthbus.co.uk
Man Dir/Co Sec: J Ackroyd **Ops Dir**: P Smith **Fin Controller**: I Perring
Fleet: 172 - 19 double-deck bus, 89 single-deck bus, 13 coach, 1 open-top bus, 30 midibus, 20 minibus.
Chassis: 106 Dennis. 1 Leyland. 30 Mercedes. 35 Volvo.
Bodies: 24 Alexander. 6 East Lancs. 1 Leyland. 15 Mercedes. 113 Plaxton. 13 Transbus
Ops incl: local bus services, excursions & tours, private hire. continental tours, school contracts.
Livery: Red/White
Ticket system: Wayfarer TGX

*POWELLS COACHES

2 BARRIS, LAPFORD, CREDITON EX176PT
Tel: 01363 83468
Prop: James P Powell
Fleet: 7 coach
Chassis: 3 Leyland. 1 MAN. 1 Mercedes. 2 Volvo.
Bodies: 1 Duple. 1 Jonckheere. 1 Mercedes. 1 Neoplan. 2 Plaxton. 1 Van Hool.
Ops incl: school contracts, excursions & tours, private hire.

*OTTER COACHES

1 MILL STREET, OTTERY ST MARY EX11 1AB
Tel: 01404 812002
Tel: 01404 811128
Fleetname: Otter Coaches
Ptnrs: W M Down, A G Down, C P Down
Fleet: 11 coach
Chassis: 2 Bedford. 1 Bova. 5 Dennis. 1 Iveco. 1 MAN. 1 Toyota.
Bodies: 1 Beulas. 1 Bova. 4 Caetano. 3 Duple. 2 Plaxton.

RADMORES TRAVEL

4 WOODFORD CRESCENT, PLYMPTON PL7 4QY
Tel/Fax: 01752 335391
Owner: John Williams **Man**: Sarah Hale
Fleetname: Radmores Coaches
Fleet: 5 - 1 double-deck bus, 2 midibus, 2 midicoach.
Chassis: 1 DAF. 1 Ford Transit. 1 Iveco. 1 Toyota.
Bodies: 1 Caetano. 1 Mellor. 1 Reeve Burgess.
Ops incl: local bus services, school contracts, excursions & tours, private hire.
Livery: Red/Gold

A/c	Air conditioning
♿	Vehicles suitable for disabled
🍴	Coach(es) with galley facilities
WC	Coach(es) with toilet facilities
🌀	Seat belt-fitted vehicles
R	Recovery service available (not 24 hr)
R24	24hr recovery service
✓	Replacement vehicle available
T	Toilet-drop facilities available
🚌	Vintage vehicle(s) available
🚍	Open top vehicle(s)

Devon

RAYS COACHES
88 KINGS TAMERTON ROAD,
ST BUDEAUX PL5 2BW
Tel: 01752 369000

*REDWOODS TRAVEL
INDUSTRIAL PARK, HEMYOCK,
CULLOMPTON EX15 3SE
Tel: 01823 680288
Fax: 01823 681096
Recovery: 01823 680288
E-mail: info@redwoodstravel.com
Web site: www.redwoodstravel.com
Prop: Paul Redwood **Ops Man**: Jacquie Redwood **Ch Eng**: Garry Morrisy
Fleet: 22 - 17 coach, 4 minibus, 1 minicoach.
Chassis: 1 Iveco. 4 LDV. 3 MAN. 4 Scania. 10 Volvo.
Bodies: 1 Caetano. 1 Duple. 4 Irizar. 2 Jonckheere. 2 Noge. 10 Plaxton. 2 Van Hool.
Ops incl: school contracts, excursions & tours, private hire, continental tours
Livery: White/Red/Green (palm trees)

SEWARD COACHES
GLENDALE, DALWOOD,
AXMINSTER EX13 7EJ
Tel/Fax: 01404 881343.
Ops Man: Richard M Seward **Joint Ptnr**: Ivy Ann Seward **Sec**: Catherine Seward
Fleet: 21 - 3 single-deck bus, 9 coach, 6 midicoach, 3 minibus
Chassis: 2 Bova. 6 Dennis. 1 Iveco. 2 Leyland. 1 Toyota. 3 MAN. 4 Mercedes. 1 Renault. 1 BMC.
Bodies: 2 Berkhof. 2 Bova. 3 Caetano. 1 Irisbus. 1 Mercedes. 1 Optare. 4 Plaxton. 2 Transbus. 1 BMC.
Ops incl: local bus services, school contracts, private hire.
Livery: Cream/Orange/Green

H. & A. SLEEP
STATION ROAD, BERE ALSTON
PL20 7EW
Tel: 01822 840244.
Ptnrs: Mrs G. A. Sleep, R. G. Sleep.
Fleet: 6 coach.
Chassis: 4 Bedford. 2 Volvo.
Bodies: 3 Duple. 2 Plaxton. 1 Irizar.
Ops incl: local bus services, excursions & tours, private hire.
Livery: Maroon/Ivory.

*STAGECOACH SOUTH WEST
BELGRAVE ROAD, EXETER
EX1 2LB
Tel: 01392 439439
Tel: 01392 889727
Web site: www.stagecoachbus.com
Man Dir: C G Hilditch **Eng Dir**: M Horide
Ops Dir: R Stevens **Ops Man (Exeter)**: B George **Ops Man (Torbay)**: R MaAllister
Eng Man (Exeter): A Noel **Eng Man (Torbay)**: M Rundle **Customer Ser Man**: M Whittle **Resource Man**: G Bailey
Fleet: 304 - 108 double-deck bus, 13 single-deck bus, 6 coach, 3 open-top bus, 115 midibus, 59 minibus.
Chassis: 159 Dennis/Transbus. 14 Leyland.

22 Mercedes. 37 Optare. 16 Scania. 56 Volvo.
Bodies: 239 Alexander. 1 ECW. 3 Marshall. 11 Northern Counties. 37 Optare. 6 Plaxton. 2 Roe. 5 Wright.
Ops incl: local bus services, school contracts
Livery: Stagecoach UK bus livery - Blue/Red/Orange/White
Ticket System: Wayfarer 3.

*STREETS COACHWAYS LTD
THE OLD AERODROME,
CHIVENOR, BARNSTAPLE
EX31 4AY
Tel: 01271 815069
Fax: 01271 817333
E-mail: sandra@streetscoachways.co.uk
Dirs: Stephen Street, Harris Street, Sandra Popham
Ops incl: private hire, school contracts.

*TALLY HO! COACHES
STATION YARD INDUSTRIAL
ESTATE, KINGSBRIDGE TQ7 1ES
Tel: 01548 853081
Fax: 01548 853602
E-mail: info@tallyhocoaches.com
Web site: www.tallyhocoaches.com
Man Ptnr: Simon Wellington **Gen Man**: Steve Pengelly **Ch Eng**: Mark Drews
Fleet: 50 - 2 double-deck bus, 6 single-deck bus, 26 coach, 10 midibus, 2 midicoach, 4 minicoach.
Chassis: 2 DAF. 7 Dennis. 2 Ford Transit. 3 LDV. 17 Leyland. 11 Mercedes. 11 Renault. 4 Scania. 1 Toyota. 2 Volvo.
Bodies: 13 Alexander. 1 Caetano. 2 Duple. 2 East Lancs. 4 Irizar. 1 Marshall. 1 Mercedes. 2 Northern Counties. 15 Plaxton. 1 Reeve Burgess. 5 Van Hool. 2 Wadham Stringer. 1 other.
Ops incl: local bus services, school contracts, private hire.
Livery: White (coaches), Yellow (schoolbus), Red (bus)
Ticket system: Almex

*TAVISTOCK COMMUNITY TRANSPORT
See Cornwall

*TAW & TORRIDGE COACHES LTD
GRANGE LANE, MERTON,
OKEHAMPTON EX20 3ED
Tel: 01805 603400
Fax: 01805 603559
Recovery: 01805 603400
E-mail: enquiries@tawandtorridge.co.uk
Web site: www.tawandtorridge.co.uk
Man Dir: Tony Hunt **Dir/Ops Man**: Mark Hunt **Dir/Co Sec**: Linda Hunt **Dir**: Tracey Laughton **Fleet Eng/Dir**: Chris Laughton
Fleet: 39 - 30 coach, 2 midibus, 5 minibus, 2 midicoach
Chassis: 1 Bedford. 2 Bova. 1 Bristol. 6 Dennis. 1 Ford Transit. 4 LDV. 3 MAN. 1 Scania. 1 Toyota. 1 Van Hool. 19 Volvo.

Bodies: 2 Berkhof. 2 Bova. 1 Caetano. 3 Jonckheere. 2 Neoplan. 14 Plaxton. 2 Van Hool. 5 Wadham Stringer.
Ops incl: school contracts, excursions & tours, private hire, continental tours.
Livery: Miami Blue/Silver

TOTNES & DARTMOUTH RING & RIDE
C/O RED CROSS CENTRE,
BABBAGE ROAD, TOTNES TQ9 5JA.
Tel: 01803 867878.
Co-ordinator: L. Clark.
Fleet: 3 minibus.
Chassis: 2 Ford Transit. 1 Peugeot.
Ops incl: local bus services, school contracts, excursions & tours, private hire.

TOWN & COUNTRY COACHES
UNIT 8B, SILVERLANDS ROAD,
DECOY INDUSTRIAL ESTATE,
NEWTON ABBOT TQ12 5ND
Tel: 01626 201052
Tran Man: Geoff Wilkins

*TRATHENS TRAVEL SERVICES
BURRINGTON WAY, PLYMOUTH
PL5 3LS
Tel: 01752 794545/790565
Fax: 01752 777931
Chmn: D I Park **Dir**: John Bettinson
Fleet: 50 - 49/70/83-seat coach, double-deck coach, sleeper coach.
Ops incl: express, continental tours.
Livery: White with Red and Yellow lining; National Express: White.
(Subsidiary of Parks of Hamilton)

TURNERS TOURS
1 FORE STREET, CHULMLEIGH
EX18 7BT
Tel: 01769 580242
Fax: 01769 581281
E-mail: coaches@turnerstours.co.uk
Web site: www.turnerstours.co.uk
Dir: S Gilson
Fleet: 28 - coach, midibus, midicoach, minibus.
Chassis: 4 Dennis. 1 Dodge. 1 Freight Rover. 1 Mercedes. 21 Volvo.
Bodies: 4 Alexander. 1 Caetano. 5 Jonckheere. 2 Mercedes. 16 Plaxton.
Ops incl: local bus services, school contracts, excursions & tours, private hire, express, continental tours.
Livery: Cream.
Ticket System: Wayfarer.

*T. W. COACHES LTD
HACHE LANE, SOUTH MOLTON
EX36 3EH
Tel: 01769 572139
Fax: 01769 574182
E-mail: twcoaches@ukf.net
Dirs: C Tearall, N Williams **Eng**: R Bradshaw
Fleet: 16 coaches - 7 coach, 2 midibus, 6 midicoach, 1 minibus
Chassis: 3 Dennis, 13 Mercedes
Bodies: 1 Jonckheere. 1 Mellor,

6 Mercedes, 4 Optare, 3 Plaxton. 1 Setra.
Ops incl: local bus services, school contracts, excursions & tours, private hire, continental tours.
Livery: Blue
Ticket system: Almex

W A SHEARINGS
BARTON HILL WAY, TORQUAY TQ2 8JG
Tel: 01803 326016.
Fax: 01803 316059.
Depot Man: David Braund.
See also W A Shearings Ltd, Greater Manchester

WILLS MINI COACHES
2 LOWER UNION ROAD, KINGSBRIDGE TQ7 1EF
Tel/Fax: 01548 852140.
Man Dir: E. G. Wills. **Dir/Co Sec**: Mrs G. M. Wills.
Fleet: 5 minibus.
Chassis: 4 LDV. 1 Mercedes.
Ops incl: school contracts, private hire.

WOOD BROTHERS TRAVEL LTD
HAREWOOD GARAGE, BOSSELL ROAD, BUCKFASTLEIGH TQ11 0AL.
Tel: 01364 643870.
Fax: 01364 643870.
Livery: Yellow/White.

DORSET, BOURNEMOUTH, POOLE

*BARRY'S COACHES LTD
[wc] [🌀] [A/c]

9 CAMBRIDGE ROAD, GRANBY INDUSTRIAL ESTATE, WEYMOUTH DT4 9TJ
Tel: 01305 784850
Fax: 01305 782252
Fleet: 25 - 20 coach, 3 midicoach, 2 minicoach.
Man Dir: Mrs M Newsam **Fleet Eng**: Mr G Newsam **Co Sec**: Mrs M Hills
Chassis: 4 Dennis. 2 Iveco. 1 MAN. 9 Scania. 9 Volvo.
Bodies: 4 Berkhof. 2 Caetano. 1 Duple. 9 Irizar. 3 Jonckheere. 2 Neoplan. 2 Plaxton. 2 Van Hool.
Ops incl: school contracts, excursions & tours, private hire, continental tours.
Livery: White/Blue/Yellow

*BLUEBIRD COACHES (WEYMOUTH) LTD
[wc] [🌀] [🍴] [A/c] [R24] [✓] [T]

450 CHICKERELL ROAD, WEYMOUTH DT3 4DH
Tel: 01305 786262
Fax: 01305 766223
Recovery: 01305 786262/07771 561060
E-mail: martyn@bluebirdcoaches.com
Web site: www.bluebirdcoaches.com
Dirs: Martyn Hoare, Stephen Hoare
Fleet: 22 - 20 coach, 1 midicoach, 1 minibus.
Chassis: 7 DAF. 1 Mercedes. 2 Neoplan. 1 Volkswagen. 11 Volvo.
Bodies: 7 Bova. 1 Caetano. 3 Jonckheere. 2 Neoplan. 4 Plaxton. 5 Van Hool.
Ops incl: school contracts, excursions & tours, private hire, continental tours.
Livery: White/Blue/Orange

BOURNEMOUTH TRANSPORT LTD
[♿] [🚌] [🌀] [A/c] [T]

YEOMANS WAY, BOURNEMOUTH BH8 0BQ
Tel: 01202 636000
Fax: 01202 636001
E-mail: mail@yellowbuses.co.uk
Web site: www.yellowbuses.co.uk
Fleetname: Yellow Buses
Service Delivery Dir: D T Lott
Eng Dir: G Corrie **Fin Dir**: Mrs C Partridge.
Fleet: 118 - 65 double-deck bus, 36 single-deck bus, 14 coach, 3 open-top bus.
Chassis: 4 DAF. 55 Dennis. 4 Scania. 55 Volvo.
Bodies: 10 Alexander. 5 Caetano. 84 East Lancs. 5 Plaxton. 4 Van Hool. 10 Wright.
Ops incl: local bus services, school contracts, express.
Livery: bright Yellow
Ticket System: Wayfarer 3
(Part of the Transdev Group)

COACH HOUSE TRAVEL
[♿] [wc] [🌀] [🍴] [A/c]

16 POUNDBURY WEST INDUSTRIAL ESTATE, DORCHESTER DT1 2PG
Tel: 01305 267644
Fax: 01305 260608
Prop: Les Watts. **Ops Man**: John Woollen.
Co Sec: Sarah Fursy Taylor **Ch Eng**: Phillip Watts
Fleet: 17 - 8 coach, 3 single-deck bus, 2 midicoach, 4 minibus.
Chassis: 4 DAF. 3 Dennis. 2 Iveco. 4 Mercedes. 4 Volvo.
Bodies: 4 Berkhof, 1 Bova. 3 LDV. 4 Marshall. 4 Plaxton. 1 Van Hool.
Ops incl: local bus services, school contracts, excursions & tours, private hire, continental tours.
Livery: Red/White with red/blue stripes.

CROSS COUNTRY HIRE
[🌀]

64 DORCHESTER ROAD, UPTON, POOLE BH16 5NS
Tel/Fax: 01202 624031
Prop: William G Sykes
Fleet: 1 minicoach.
Chassis: Toyota. **Body**: Caetano.
Ops incl: excursions & tours, private hire.

*DAMORY COACHES
[wc] [🌀] [🚐] [A/c] [✓]

UNIT 1, CLUMP FARM, SHAFTESBURY LANE, BLANDFORD FORUM DT11 7TD
Tel: 01258 452545
Fax: 01258 451930
E-mail: igray@damorycoach.co.uk
Local Man: I Gray **Man Dir**: Alex Carter
Eng Dir: Geoff Parsons **Ops Dir**: Andrew Wickham **Fin Dir**: Matt Dolphin
Fleet: 44 - 8 double-deck bus, 8 single-deck bus, 13 coach, 9 midibus, 6 minicoach.
Chassis: 8 Bristol. 10 DAF. 6 LDV. 9 Optare. 11 Volvo.
Bodies: 8 ECW. 3 Ikarus. 2 Northern Counties. 9 Optare. 11 Plaxton. 5 Van Hool. 6 other.
Ops incl: local bus services, school contracts, excursions & tours, private hire, continental tours.
Livery: Turquoise/Maroon/White
Ticket system: Wayfarer
(Part of the Go-Ahead Group)

Devon / Dorset

A/c	Air conditioning	
♿	Vehicles suitable for disabled	
🍴	Coach(es) with galley facilities	
wc	Coach(es) with toilet facilities	
🌀	Seat belt-fitted vehicles	
R	Recovery service available (not 24 hr)	
R24	24hr recovery service	
✓	Replacement vehicle available	
T	Toilet-drop facilities available	
🚐	Vintage vehicle(s) available	
🚌	Open top vehicle(s)	

103

*DORSET COUNTY COUNCIL PASSENGER TRANSPORT SECTION

EDUCATION TRANSPORT GARAGE, GROVE TRADING ESTATE, DORCHESTER DT1 1ST
Tel: 01305 224540
Fax: 01305 225166
E-mail: kevinrclarke@dorsetcc.gov.uk
Local Man: K Clarke
Pass Tran Man: B Thirlwall
Fleet: 10 - six 70-seat, four 53-seat
Chassis: 2 Dennis. 2 Cummins. 6 Scania.
Bodies: 6 Irizar. 4 Plaxton
Ops incl: school contracts, affiliated school and youth organisation day excursions

*EXCELSIOR COACHES LTD

CENTRAL BUSINESS PARK, BOURNEMOUTH BH1 3SJ
Tel: 01202 652222
Fax: 01202 652223
E-mail: krobins@excelsior-coaches.com
Web site: www.excelsior-coaches.com
Man Dir: Ken Robins
Fleet: 25 - 19 coach, 2 midicoach, 4 minibus
Chassis: 6 Mercedes. 19 Volvo
Bodies: 5 Caetano. 2 Esker. 2 Jonckheere. 4 Mercedes. 9 Plaxton. 3 Sunsundegui.
Ops incl: excursions & tours, private hire, express, continental tours.
Livery: Cream

*MIKE HALFORD COACHES

KISEM, NORTH MILLS, BRIDPORT DT6 3AH
Tel/Fax: 01308 421106
Prop: M G Halford
Fleet: 7 - 3 midicoach, 4 minibus
Chassis: 7 Mercedes
Ops incl: local bus services, private hire, school contracts

*HOMEWARD BOUND TRAVEL

137 LYNWOOD DRIVE, WIMBORNE BH21 1UU
Tel: 01202 884491
Fax: 01202 885664
E-mail: enquiries@homewardboundtravel.co.uk
Web site: www.homewardboundtravel.co.uk
Prop: Louisa Fairhead
Fleet: 3 minicoach
Chassis: 3 Renault
Bodies: 3 other.
Ops incl: excursions & tours, private hire, continental tours.
Livery: Silver /Purple/Green

POWELLS COACHES

THORNFORD GARAGE, THORNFORD DT9 6QN
Tel: 01935 872390
Fleet: 3 coach
Ops incl: local bus services, excursions & tours, private hire.
Livery: Red/White.

RAMON TRAVEL

7 HARCOURT ROAD, BOSCOMBE BH5 2JG.
Tel: 01202 432690.
Fax: 01202 432690.
Owner/Ops: C. Rochester.
Fleet: 6 - 1 coach, 1 midicoach, 4 minibus.
Chassis: 1 Bedford. 4 Freight Rover.
Ops incl: excursions & tours, private hire, school contracts.

*ROADLINER PASSENGER TRANSPORT LTD

BANBURY ROAD, POOLE BH17 0GA
Tel: 01202 385055
Fax: 01202 690370
Recovery: 01202 385055
E-mail: mark.roadliner@btconnect.com
Web site: www.roadliner.biz
Fleetname: Roadliner
Man Dir: M Self **Dir**: Mrs J Self
Gen Man: M Towers **Ch Eng**: B Ling
Fleet: 13 - 1 single-deck bus, 7 coach, 2 double-deck coach, 2 midicoach, 1 minicoach
Chassis: 1 LDV. 1 Leyland. 2 Mercedes. 1 Optare. 6 Scania. 2 Volvo.
Bodies: 1 Beulas. 1 Concept. 2 East Lancs. 6 Irizar. 1 Leyland. 2 Optare.
Ops incl: local bus services, school contracts, excursions & tours, private hire, express, continental tours
Livery: Green/Black/Silver
Ticket system: Wayfarer

*SEA VIEW COACHES (POOLE) LTD

10 FANCY ROAD, POOLE BH12 4QZ
Tel: 01202 741439
Fax: 01202 740241
E-mail: info@seaviewcoaches.com
Web site: www.seaviewcoaches.com
Man Dir: D K Tarr **Dir**: D E Tarr
Co Sec: Mrs D Wigmore
Fleet: 26 - 18 coach, 4 minibus, 2 midicoach. 2 minicoach.
Chassis: 5 DAF. 4 Ford. 1 Iveco. 12 MAN. 4 Mercedes.
Bodies: 2 Ayats. 1 Beulas. 10 Noge. 3 Van Hool. 2 Sitcar.
Ops incl: school contracts, excursions & tours, private hire, continental tours.
Livery: Silver

*SHAFTESBURY & DISTRICT MOTOR SERVICES LTD

UNIT 2, MELBURY WORKSHOPS, CANN COMMON, SHAFTESBURY SP7 0EB
Tel/Fax: 01747 854359
E-mail: info@sdbuses.co.uk
Web site: www.sdbuses.co.uk
Dir: Roger Brown **Co Sec**: Liam Stacey
Fleet: 16 - 4 double-deck bus, 3 single-deck bus, 8 coach, 1 minicoach.
Chassis: 5 AEC. 1 Bristol. 1 DAF. 5 Leyland. 1 Optare. 1 Toyota. 2 Volvo.
Bodies: 1 Alexander. 1 Berkhof. 1 Caetano. 1 Duple. 1 Ikarus. 1 Jonckheere. 1 Leyland. 2 MCW. 1 Optare. 3 Park Royal. 3 Plaxton.
Ops incl: local bus services, school contracts, private hire.
Livery: Red
Ticket System: Wayfarer II

*SOVEREIGN COACHES

PINE LODGE, ROUSDON, LYME REGIS DT7 3RD
Tel: 01297 23000
Fax: 01297 22466
E-mail: sov_coaches@btinternet.com
Ptnrs: R A Keech, C M Keech, R C Keech
Fleet: 9 - 5 midicoach, 4 minicoach.
Chassis: 1 Irisbus. 1 Iveco. 5 Mercedes. 2 Toyota.
Bodies: 1 Autobus. 3 Mercedes. 1 Plaxton. 4 other.
Ops incl: school contracts, excursions & tours, private hire.
Livery: White

SURELINE

UNIT 17, TRADECROFT INDUSTRIAL ESTATE, PORTLAND DT5 2LN
Tel: 01305 823039
Fax: 01305 822936
Web site: www.surelinebuses.co.uk
Dir: David Beaman **Ops Dir**: Bill Landucci
Ops incl: local bus services

WILTS & DORSET BUS COMPANY LTD

TOWNGATE HOUSE, 2-8 PARKSTONE ROAD, POOLE BH15 2PR
Tel: 01202 680888/673555
Fax: 01202 670244
E-mail: enquiries-poole@wdbus.co.uk
Web site: www.wdbus.co.uk
Man Dir: A Carter **Ops Dir**: A Wickham
Eng Dir: G Parsons
Fleet: 344 - 132 double-deck bus (incl. convertible open-top) , 64 single-deck bus, 7 coach, 141 minibus.
Chassis: 25 Bristol. 96 DAF. 16 Leyland. 30 Mercedes. 156 Optare. 51 Volvo.
Bodies: 2 Duple. 35 ECW. 13 East Lancs. 30 Mercedes. 7 Northern Counties. 237 Optare. 11 Plaxton. 2 Roe. 3 Van Hool. 34 Wright.
Ops incl: local bus services, school contracts, private hire, express.
Livery: Red/White/Black Red/Blue
Ticket System: Wayfarer TGX
(Part of the Go-Ahead Group)

DURHAM

ALFA COACHES LTD
[wc] [galley] [seatbelt] [replacement]

17 RAMSGATE, STOCKTON-ON-TEES TS18 1BS.
Tel: 01642 678066
Fax: 01642 673462
Fleetname: Gladwin Tours
Man Dir: P. Sawbridge. **Man:** M. Gladwin.
Co Sec: P. Sawbridge. **Ops Man:** D. Squire
Fleet: 8 coach
Chassis: DAF
Bodies: 5 Ikarus. 3 Van Hool
Ops incl: excursions & tours, private hire, continental tours
Livery: Beige with Blue lettering

ALMAR TRAVEL
[wc] [galley] [seatbelt] [replacement]

7 GLENAVON AVENUE, SOUTH PELAW DH2 2JL.
Tel: 0191 388 6752.
Fax: 0191 388 1777.
Prop: A. Rogers.
Fleet: 3 - 2 coach, 1 minicoach.
Chassis: 1 Mercedes. 2 Volvo.
Bodies: 1 Carlyle. 1 Plaxton. 1 Van Hool.
Ops incl: excursions & tours, private hire, continental tours.
Livery: Brown/Orange.

BEST WAY TRAVEL [wc] [replacement]

21 CHARLTONS, SALTBURN TS12 3DA.
Tel: 01287 635573.
Co Sec: Ann Wakefield. **Business Man:** M. Wakefield. **Ops Man:** B. Wakefield.
Maintenance: C. Wakefield.
Fleet: 4 coach.
Chassis: 2 DAF. 2 Ford.
Ops incl: excursions & tours, private hire, continental tours, school contracts.
Livery: Bronze.

BROWNS OF DURHAM
[wc] [galley] [seatbelt] A/c [R24] [replacement] [T]

1 LEESFIELD DRIVE, MEADOWFIELD, DURHAM DH7 8NG
Tel: 0191 373 4200
Fax: 0191 378 0393
Recovery 0191 378 0393
E-mail: brownscoachesbv@aol.com
Dir: Ralph Brown
Fleet: 6 coach
Chassis: 1 Bova. 5 DAF.
Bodies: include LAG. EOS
Ops incl: excursions & tours, private hire, continental tours.

CLASSIC COACHES LTD
[wc] [galley] [seatbelt] A/c [replacement] [R] [T]

CLASSIC HOUSE, MORRISON ROAD, ANNFIELD PLAIN DH9 7RX
Tel: 01207 282288
Fax: 01207 282333
Recovery: 07736 178599
E-mail: sales@classic-coaches.co.uk
Web site: www.classic-coaches.co.uk
Man Dir: Ian Shipley
Fleet: 66 - 4 double-deck bus, 10 single-deck bus, 50 coach, 2 double-deck coach.
Chassis: 2 DAF. 1 Dennis. 4 MCW. 9 Mercedes. 12 Scania. 36 Volvo.
Bodies: 3 Berkhof. 7 Caetano. 12 Irizar. 4 MCW. 2 Neoplan. 26 Plaxton.
Ops incl: local bus services, school contracts, excursions & tours, private hire, continental tours
Livery: Red/Gold
Part of Tellings Golden Miller

COCHRANE'S [disabled] [seatbelt] [R24]

4 FARADAY ROAD, NORTH EAST INDUSTRIAL ESTATE, PETERLEE SR8 5AP.
Tel: 0191 586 2136.
Fax: 0191 586 5566.
Fleetname: Cochrane's Kelvin Travel.
Owner: I. P. Cochrane.
Fleet: 7 - 5 single-deck bus, 2 minicoach.
Chassis: 4 Bedford. 1 DAF. 1 Ford. 1 Freight Rover.
Bodies: 5 Plaxton. 2 others.
Ops incl: school contracts.
Livery: Orange/Black.
Ticket System: Setright.

COMPASS ROYSTON TRAVEL LTD
[wc] [galley] [seatbelt] [R24] [replacement] [T]

BOWESFIELD LANE INDUSTRIAL ESTATE, STOCKTON-ON-TEES TS18 3EG
Tel: 01642 606644
Fax: 01642 608617
Man Dir: G Walton **Trans Man:** M. Metcalfe
Fleet: 55 - double-deck bus, coach, midicoach.
Chassis: Bristol. Daimler. Ford. Leyland. Mercedes. Volvo.
Bodies: ECW. Jonckheere. Mercedes. Plaxton. Sunsundegui. Van Hool.
Ops incl: excursions & tours, private hire, express, continental tours, school contracts.
Livery: White with Red/Maroon stripe.
Associated with Procters Coaches, North Yorkshire

*DUNN-LINE (HOLDINGS) LTD
See Nottinghamshire

*DURHAM CITY COACHES LTD [wc] [seatbelt] A/c [replacement] [T]

BRANDON LANE, BRANDON, DURHAM DH7 8PG
Tel: 0191 378 0540
Fax: 0191 378 1985
E-mail: sales@durhamcitycoaches.co.uk
Web site: www.durhamcitycoaches.co.uk
Man Dir: Michael Lightfoot.
Co Sec: Christine Lightfoot
Ops Man: Malcolm Burnip
Fleet: 14 - 10 coach, 4 midicoach.
Chassis: 2 Bova. 4 Mercedes. 8 Volvo.
Bodies: 2 Bova. 3 Jonckheere. 4 Mercedes. 1 Optare. 3 Plaxton. 1 Van Hool
Ops incl: excursions & tours, private hire, continental tours, school contracts.
Livery: Black/Red/Gold

DURHAM TRAVEL SERVICES (DTS)

SEAHAM GARAGE INDUSTRIAL ESTATE, SEAHAM SR7 0PW
Tel: 0191 521 0202
Fax: 0191 521 0202
Subsidiary of Dunn-Line Holdings, part od Veolia Transport UK

*ENTERPRISE TRAVEL
[wc] [galley] [seatbelt] A/c [replacement] [T]

19 PINE GROVE, DARLINGTON DL3 8JF
Tel: 01325 286924
Fax: 01325 286924
E-mail: coachhire@aol.com
Web site: www.enterprisecoachhire.co.uk
Dirs: B.R.Brown, Mrs B. M. Brown
Fleet: 5 single-deck, 1 minicoach.
Chassis: 1 Bova, 1 DAF,1 MAN, 1 Mercedes-Benz,1 Setra, 1 Volvo.
Bodies: 1 Bova, 1 Caetano, 1 Mercedes-Benz, 1 Setra, 2 Van Hool.
Ops incl: Schools contracts, excursions & tours, private hire.
Livery: White with red/green reliefs

GARDINERS TRAVEL
[seatbelt] [wc] A/c [R] [replacement]

COULSON STREET, SPENNYMOOR DL16 7RS
Tel: 01388 814417
Fax: 01388 811466
E-mail: gardiners.travel@virgin.net
Man Dir: John Gardiner
Tran Man: Harry Revel
Fleet: 8 - 6 coach, 2 midibus.
Chassis: 1 Iveco. 1 Leyland. 2 Optare. 4 Volvo.
Bodies: 1 Beulas. 1 Jonckheere. 2 Optare. 3 Plaxton. 1 Van Hool.
Ops incl: local bus services, school contracts, excursions & tours, private hire, continental tours.
Livery: Cream/Maroon
Ticket system: AES

A/c	Air conditioning	
[disabled]	Vehicles suitable for disabled	
[galley]	Coach(es) with galley facilities	
[wc]	Coach(es) with toilet facilities	
[seatbelt]	Seat belt-fitted vehicles	
[R]	Recovery service available (not 24 hr)	
[R24]	24hr recovery service	
[replacement]	Replacement vehicle available	
[T]	Toilet-drop facilities available	
	Vintage vehicle(s) available	
	Open top vehicle(s)	

GARNETT'S COACHES

UNIT E1, ROMAN WAY INDUSTRIAL ESTATE, TINDALE CRESCENT, BISHOP AUCKLAND DL14 9AW.
Tel: 01388 604419.
Fax: 01388 609549.
Fleet Ops Man: Paul Garnett
Fleet: incl: coach
Chassis: incl: 4 Volvo.
Bodies: incl: 1 Sunsundegui.
Ops incl: excursions & tours, private hire, continental tours.
Livery: Yellow/Red/Black.

GRIERSONS COACHES

SEDGEFIELD ROAD GARAGE, FISHBURN, STOCKTON-ON-TEES TS21 4DD.
Tel: 01740 620209.
Fax: 01740 621243.
Prop: C. & D. Grierson.
Fleet: 20 - 5 double-deck bus, 6 single-deck bus, 4 coach, 1 midicoach, 4 minibus.
Chassis: 1 DAF. 1 Ford. 1 Ford Transit. 2 Freight Rover. 2 Mercedes. 1 Scania. 13 Volvo.
Bodies: 1 Carlyle. 3 Jonckheere. 2 Mercedes. 13 Plaxton. 1 Reeve Burgess. 1 Van Hool.
Ops incl: excursions & tours, private hire, express, continental tours.
Livery: Blue/Red.

HODGSONS COACHES

20 GALGATE, BARNARD CASTLE DL12 8BG.
Tel: 01833 630730.
Fax: 01833 630830.
Props: J. K. Hodgson, G. A. Hodgson.
Fleet: 6 - 2 coach, 1 midicoach, 3 minicoach.
Chassis: 1 Bedford. 1 Bova. 1 Leyland. 1 Mercedes.
Bodies: 1 Bova. 1 Plaxton. 1 Elme. 3 Concept Coach Craft.
Ops incl: local bus services, school contracts, excursions & tours, continental tours.

*HUMBLES COACHES

UP YONDER, ROBSON STREET, SHILDON DL4 1EB
Tel: 01388 772772
Fax: 01388 772211
E-mail: humblesholiday@tiscali.co.uk
Dirs: M Humble, P West
Ops Man: K Towler **Ch Eng:** R Naitby
Fleet: 7 - 2 coach, 2 midicoach, 3 minicoach
Chassis: incl. 3 LDV. 2 Volvo
Bodies: incl 2 Mercedes
Ops incl: school contracts, excursions & tours, private hire.
Livery: Champagne/Maroon

J & C COACHES

COACH DEPOT, GROAT DRIVE, AYCLIFFE INDUSTRIAL PARK, NEWTON AYCLIFFE DL5 6HY.
Tel: 01325 312728.
Fax: 01325 320385.
Snr Ptnr: J. N. Jones.
Ptnrs: A. Jones, N. Jones, D. Jones.
Fleet: 10 - 6 coach, 1 midicoach, 3 minicoach.
Chassis: 4 DAF. 1 Dennis. 1 Ford Transit. 1 Freight Rover. 2 Mercedes. 1 Setra.
Bodies: 4 Bova. 1 Duple. 1 Leyland. 2 Mercedes. 1 Setra.
Ops incl: school contracts, excursions & tours, private hire, continental tours.
Livery: various

JAYLINE BAND SERVICES LTD

UNIT 8A, KILBURN DRIVE, SEAVIEW INDUSTRIAL ESTATE, HORDEN SR8 4TQ
Tel: 0191 586 5787
Fax: 0191 586 5836
E-mail: jaylinetravel@hotmail.com
Web site: jaylinetravel.com
Prop: Jason Rogers **Dir:** Neil Tait
Fleet: 7 - 3 single-deck coach, 4 double-deck coach.
Chassis: 1 DAF. 5 Scania. 1 Volvo.
Bodies: 3 Berkhof. 1 Jonckheere. 3 Van Hool
Ops incl: private hire
Livery: Blue

*KINGSLEY COACHES LTD

See Tyne & Wear

*LEE'S COACHES LTD

MILL ROAD GARAGE, LITTLEBURN INDUSTRIAL ESTATE, LANGLEY MOOR DH7 8HE
Tel: 0191 378 0653
Fax: 0191 378 9086
E-mail: info@leescoaches.co.uk
Web site: www.leescoaches.co.uk
Dirs: Colin Lee, Jean Lee, Malcolm Lee
Fleet: 12 - 11 coach, 1 minicoach
Chassis: 1 Mercedes. 11 Volvo.
Bodies: 2 Berkhof. 4 Caetano. 1 Jonckheere. 1 Mercedes. 2 Plaxton. 2 Van Hool.
Ops incl: school contracts, excursions & tours, private hire, continental tours

MAUDES COACHES

REDWELL GARAGE, HARMIRE ROAD, BARNARD CASTLE DL12 8QJ
Tel: 01833 637341
Fax: 01833 631888
Prop: Stephen Maude
Fleet: 6 - 4 coach, 1 midicoach, 1 minicoach.
Chassis: 2 Mercedes. 4 Volvo.
Bodies: 1 Jonckheere. 2 Mercedes. 1 Plaxton. 2 Van Hool.
Ops incl: local bus services, school contracts, excursions & tours, private hire.
Livery: Red/White.

NORTON MINI TRAVEL

5 PLUMER DRIVE, NORTON TS20 1HF.
Tel: 01642 555832.
Owner: R. Spears.
Fleet: 2 minicoach.
Chassis: 1 Iveco, 1 Freight Rover.
Ops incl: private hire, school contracts.
Livery: White/Purple.

RICHARDSON COACHES

3 OXFORD ROAD, HARTLEPOOL TS25 5SS.
Tel/Fax: 01429 272235.
Man Dir/Ch Eng: T. Richardson.
Dir/Co Sec/Traf Man: D. Richardson.
Fleet: 8 coach.
Chassis: 1 DAF. 4 Leyland. 1 Mercedes. 1 Toyota. 1 Volvo.
Bodies: 1 Caetano. 1 Leyland. 1 Mercedes. 4 Plaxton. 1 Van Hool.
Ops incl: excursions & tours, private hire.
Livery: Green/Red/White.

ROBERTS TOURS

36 NORTH ROAD WEST, WINGATE TS28 5AP.
Tel: 01429 838268.
Fax: 01429 838228.
Web site: www.robertstours.co.uk
Dirs: T. G. Roberts, D Roberts, C. A. Harper.
Fleet: 14 coach, 1 midibus.
Chassis: 5 Bova. 5 DAF. 2 Leyland. 2 Volvo.
Bodies: 5 Bova. 8 Plaxton. 1 Wadham Stringer.
Ops incl: excursions & tours, private hire, express, school contracts.
Livery: Cream/Green.

*SCARLET BAND

WELFARE GARAGE, STATION ROAD, WEST CORNFORTH, FERRYHILL DL17 9LA
Tel: 01740 654247
Fax: 01740 656068
E-mail: sband@freeuk.com
Dirs: Arthur Blenkinsop, Nancy Blenkinsop
Tran Man: Andrew Dolan
Fleet: 20 - 5 coach, 15 midibus.
Chassis: 2 Dennis. 4 Leyland. 2 Mercedes. 11 Optare. 1 Volvo.
Bodies: 1 Marshall. 11 Optare. 6 Plaxton. 1 Van Hool. 1 Wright.
Ops incl: local bus services, school contracts, private hire.
Livery: White/Red/Yellow
Ticket System: Wayfarer

*SHERBURN VILLAGE COACHES

FRONT STREET, SHERBURN VILLAGE DH6 1QY
Tel: 0191 372 1531
Fax: 0191 372 1531
Prop: John Cousins.
Fleet: 7 - 2 coach, 3 midibus, 2 midicoach.
Chassis: 1 MAN. 4 Mercedes. 2 Volvo.
Bodies: 1 Autobus. 1 Berkhof. 1 Caetano. 3 Plaxton. 1 Wadham Stringer.
Ops incl: local bus services, excursions & tours, private hire.
Livery: Red/White
Ticket System: AES.

SNOWDON COACHES

SEASIDE LANE, EASINGTON
SR8 3TW.
Tel: 0191 527 0535.
Fax: 0191 527 3280.
Prop: A. Snowdon. **Man**: G. Parkin.
Ch Eng: J. R. Main. **Sec**: V. Dowson.
Fleet: 16 coach.
Chassis: 1 Bova. 1 MAN. 14 Volvo.
Bodies: 1 Bova. 14 Plaxton. 1 Van Hool.
Ops incl: private hire, school contracts.
Livery: White with Pink reliefs.

STAGECOACH TRANSIT

CHIRCH ROAD, STOCKTON
TS18 2HW
Tel: 01642 602112
Web site: www.stagecoachbus.com
Man Dir: John Conroy
Fleet: 207
Chassis: incl: Dennis. MAN. Mercedes. Scania. Volvo.
Bodies: Alexander. Leyland. Plaxton.
Ops incl: local bus services
Livery: Stagecoach

STANLEY BUSES & MINICOACHES

THE BUS STATION, STANLEY
DH9 OTD
Tel: 01207 237424.
Fax: 01207 233233.
Web site: www.minicoachhire.co.uk

TOWN & COUNTRY MOTOR SERVICES LTD

UNIT 2, HENSON ROAD, YARM ROAD BUSINESS PARK,
DARLINGTON DL1 4QD.
Tel: 01325 489966.
E-mail:
sales@townandcountrycoaches.co.uk
Web site:
www.townandcountrycoaches.co.uk
Fleetname: Town & Country.
Man Dir: Philip Notman
Fleet: 3 - 1 single-deck bus, 1 midibus, 1 midicoach.
Chassis: 2 Leyland. 2 Mercedes.
Bodies: 1 Duple. 1 Marshall, 1 Plaxton.
Ops incl: local bus services, school contracts, private hire.
Livery: White/Blue.
Ticket System: Almex.

Dir: Robert Scott
Fleet: 36 - 2 single-deck bus, 10 minibus, 14 minicoach, 7 taxi-bus
Ops incl: local bus services, private hire
Livery: White/Orange

*PAUL WATSON TRAVEL

BRIDGE HOUSE, MOOR ROAD,
STAINDROP DL2 3LF
Tel: 01833 660471

E-mail:
paul@pwatsontravel.fslife.co.uk
Web site: www.paulwatsontravel.co.uk
Prop: Paul Watson,
Fleet: 4 - 2 single-deck coach, 1 midicoach, 1 midibus.
Chassis: 1 Ford Transit. 1 Mercedes. 2 Volvo.
Ops incl: school contracts, excursions & tours, private hire, continental tours.
Livery: White

WEARDALE MOTOR SERVICES LTD

STANHOPE DL13 2YQ
Tel: 01388 528235
Fax: 01388 526080
Dirs: Messrs Gibson
Fleet: 30 - 11 double-deck bus, 4 single-deck bus, 10 coach, 3 minibus, 1 minicoach, 1 midibus.
Chassis: Bova. DAF. Iveco. Leyland. MAN. MCW. Mercedes. Neoplan. Optare. Scania. Volvo.
Bodies: Alexander. Berkhof. Bova. ECW. Ikarus. MCW. Mercedes. Neoplan. Optare. Plaxton. Roe.
Ops incl: local bus services, excursions & tours, school contracts, private hire, express, continental tours.
Livery: Red/White
Ticket System: Wayfarer

EAST SUSSEX, BRIGHTON & HOVE

BARCROFT TOURS & EVENTS

60 QUEENS ROAD, HASTINGS
TN34 1RE
Tel: 01424 200201
Fax: 01424 200206
Recovery: 07977 004371
E-mail: info@barcrofttours.co.uk
Web site: www.barcrofttours.co.uk
Dir: Peter Warren
Fleet: 5 - 3 coach, 1 minibus, 1 midicoach
Chassis: 1 Ford Transit. 3 Mercedes. 1 Toyota.
Bodies: incl: 1 Caetano. 3 Setra.
Ops incl: school contracts, excursions & tours, private hire, continental tours.

*BRIGHTON & HOVE BUS & COACH CO

43 CONWAY STREET, HOVE
BN3 3LT
Tel: 01273 886200

Fax: 01273 822073
E-mail: info@buses.co.uk
Web site: www.buses.co.uk
Fleetname: Brighton & Hove
Chmn: Keith Ludeman **Man Dir**:
Roger French OBE **Fin Dir**: Phil Woodgate
Eng Dir: Tony Griffiths **Ops Dir**: Paul Williams
Fleet: 278 - 201 double-deck bus, 64 single-deck bus, 9 coach, 4 open-top (convertible double-deck).
Chassis: 1 Bristol. 125 Dennis. 1 Optare. 124 Scania. 27 Volvo.
Bodies: 7 Alexander. 1 ECW. 161 East Lancs. 3 Irizar. 8 Marshall. 10 Optare. 67 Plaxton. 21 Wright.
Ops incl: local bus services, school contracts, excursions & tours, private hire, continental tours.
Livery: Red/Black/Cream (variations for Metro routes)
Ticket System: Wayfarer TGX

BRIGHTONIAN COACHES

3 THE AVENUE, BRIGHTON
BN2 4GF
Tel: 01273 696195

Props: Laurence R Walker, Susan M Walker
Fleet: 2 coach
Chassis: 2 Volvo.
Bodies: 1 Duple 1 Plaxton.
Ops incl: school contracts, private hire.
Livery: White

C & S COACHES

STATION ROAD, HEATHFIELD
TN21 8DF
Tel: 01435 866600
Fax: 01435 868264
E-mail: info@candscoaches.co.uk
Ptnrs: Chris Hicks, Geoff Shaw
Ch Eng: Paul Matthews
Fleet: 37 - incl 1 double-deck coach, 1 midicoach.
Chassis: 20 DAF. 2 Leyland. 6 Scania. 9 Volvo.
Bodies: 2 Jonckheere. 6 Plaxton. 1 Reeve Burgess. 28 Van Hool.
Ops incl: school contracts, private hire.
Livery: White with red/black/grey graphics

A/c	Air conditioning	✓	Replacement vehicle available
	Vehicles suitable for disabled	T	Toilet-drop facilities available
	Coach(es) with galley facilities		Vintage vehicle(s) available
WC	Coach(es) with toilet facilities		Open top vehicle(s)
R	Recovery service available (not 24 hr)		
R24	24hr recovery service		
	Seat belt-fitted vehicles		

Durham / East Sussex

*COASTAL COACHES
18 WEST POINT, NEWICK BN8 4NU
Tel: 01825 723024
E-mail: peterhjenkins@aol.com
Web-site: coastalcoaches.com
Fleetname: Coastal
Prop: Peter Jenkins **Ops Man**: Peter Lockhart
Fleet: 10 single-deck bus.
Chassis: 9 Dennis. 1 Transbus.
Bodies: 1 Alexander. 8 Plaxton. 1 Transbus.
Ops incl: local bus services
Livery: Green

*CUCKMERE COMMUNITY BUS LTD
THE OLD RECTORY, LITLINGTON, POLEGATE BN26 5RB
Tel: 01323 870920
Web site: www.cuckmerebus.freeuk.com
Chmn: Mrs B Smith **Organiser**: P Ayers
Hire Organiser: G Maynard
Sec: S de Angeli **Treasurer**: A Cottingham
Fleet: 6 minibus
Chassis: 6 Mercedes.
Bodies: 1 Alexander. 2 Mellor. 1 Mercedes. 2 Constable
Ops incl: local bus services, excursions, private hire.
Livery: Green/Cream
Ticket system: Wayfarer TGX150

EASTBOURNE BUSES LTD
BIRCH ROAD, EASTBOURNE BN26 6PD
Tel: 01323 416416
Fax: 01323 643034
E-mail: mailbox@eastbournebuses.co.uk
Web site: www.eastbournebuses.co.uk
Man Dir: Roger Bowker
Fleet: 5 - 13 double-deck bus, 42 single-deck bus
Chassis: 26 DAF. 6 Dennis. 7 Leyland. 10 Optare. 6 Volvo.
Ops incl: local bus services, school contracts
Livery: base Blue with branding.
Ticket System: Wayfarer

*L J EDWARDS COACH HIRE
BELLBANKS CORNER, MILL ROAD, HAILSHAM BN27 2AH
Tel: 01323 440622
Fax: 01323 442555
E-mail: info@ljedwards.co.uk
Web site: www.ljedwards.co.uk
Prop: L J Edwards
Fleet: 12 - 8 coach, 2 midicoach, 2 minicoach
Chassis: 6 Bova. 2 Iveco. 1 Mercedes. 2 Toyota. 1 Volvo.
Bodies: 1 Beulas. 6 Bova. 3 Caetano.

1 Indcar. 1 Mercedes.
Ops incl: excursions & tours, private hire, continental tours, school contracts.
Livery: White/Red

*EMPRESS COACHES LTD
10/11 ST MARGARETS ROAD, ST LEONARDS-ON-SEA TN37 6EH
Tel/Fax: 01424 430621
E-mail: info@empresscoaches.com
Web site: www.empresscoaches.com
Dir: Stephen Dine **Ch Eng**: Kelvin Bowen
Fleet: 10 - 1 coach, 2 midibus, 1 midicoach, 6 minibus.
Chassis: 1 Dennis. 2 Ford Transit. 2 Iveco. 1 Mercedes. 1 Optare. 1 Toyota. 1 CVE Omni.
Bodies: 1 Caetano. 1 Chassis Developments. 1 Devco. 1 Mellor. 2 Optare. 2 UVG. 1 Wadham Stringer.
Ops incl: school contracts, private hire.
Livery: Burgundy/Ivory

OCEAN COACHES
19 STONERY CLOSE, PORTSLADE BN41 2TD.
Tel/Fax: 01273 278385.
Web site: www.oceancoaches.net
E-mail: info@oceancoaches.net
Prop: Peter Woodcock.
Fleet: 1 coach.
Chassis: Volvo. **Body**: Ikarus.
Ops incl: private hire, school contracts.
Livery: Cream/Red.

*PAVILION COACHES
144 NEVILL AVENUE, HOVE BN3 7NH
Tel: 01273 732405
E-mail: nicky2168@hotmail.com
Web-site: www.pavilioncoaches.co.uk
Joint owners: Peter Hammer, Nicky Hammer
Fleet: 2 - double-deck bus, coach
Chassis: 1 Leyland. 1 Volvo.
Bodies: 1 Park Royal. 1 Plaxton
Ops incl: excursions & tours, private hire, continental tours

RAMBLER COACHES
WESTRIDGE MANOR, WHITWORTH ROAD, HASTINGS TN37 7PZ
Tel: 01424 754881
Fax: 01424 751815
Ptnrs: Colin Rowland, J. Goodwin.
Fleet: 38 - 5 single-deck bus, 26 coach, 1 midibus, 3 midicoach. 1 minicoach.
Chassis: 8 Bedford. 4 Dennis. 2 Leyland National. 5 Mercedes. 1 Scania. 18 Volvo.
Bodies: 5 Berkhof. 1 Duple. 2 Leyland National. 2 Optare. 17 Plaxton. 7 Van Hool. 1 Reeve Burgess. 1 Wadham Stringer. 1 Wright. 1 Hispano.
Ops incl: local bus services, school contracts, excursions & tours, private hire, continental tours.

Livery: White, Green/Black.
Ticket System: Wayfarer.

RENOWN COACHES
13 SEA ROAD, BEXHILL-ON-SEA TN40 1EE
Tel: 01424 211563
Fax: 01424 210744
Fleet: 18 - 4 double-deck bus, 4 single-deck bus, 10 coach
Chassis: 1 DAF. 1 Dennis. 11 Leyland. 1 Setra. 4 Volvo.
Bodies: 2 Caetano. 2 Duple. 6 Leyland. 1 Plaxton. 1 Reeve Burgess. 1 Setra. 4 Van Hool. 1 Wadham Stringer.
Ops incl: local bus services, school contracts, excursions & tours, private hire, continental tours.

STAGECOACH IN HASTINGS
BEAUFORT ROAD, SILVERHILL, ST LEONARDS ON SEA TN37 6PL
Tel: 01424 445600
Fax: 01424 435340
E-mail: enquiries.southeast@stagecoachbus.com
Web site: www.stagecoachbus.com/hastings
Man Dir: Paul Southgate **Ops Dir**: Neil Instrall **Eng Dir**: Keith Dyball
Fleet: 63 - 23 double-deck bus, 40 single-deck bus.
Chassis: 27 Dennis. 4 Leyland. 6 Scania. 26 Volvo
Bodies: 45 Alexander. 18 Northern Counties.
Ops incl: local bus services.
Livery: Stagecoach

SUSSEX PIONEER COACHES
3 THE AVENUE, BRIGHTON BN2 4GF.
Tel: 01273 696195.
Fax: 01273 696195.
Ptnrs: L. R. Walker, Mrs S. M. Walker.
Fleet: 3 coach.
Chassis: 3 Leyland.
Bodies: 1 Duple. 1 Plaxton. 1 Roe.
Ops incl: private hire.

*WISE COACHES LTD
74 HIGH STREET, HAILSHAM BN27 1AU
Tel: 01323 844321
E-mail: info@wisecoaches.co.uk
Web site: www.wisecoaches.co.uk
Fleet: 4 coach.
Chassis: 3 DAF. 1 Iveco.
Bodies: 1 Beulas. 1 Berkhof. 1 Ikarus. 1 Ovi.
Ops incl: excursions & tours, private hire, school contracts.
Livery: Red/Silver

EAST RIDING OF YORKSHIRE, CITY OF KINGSTON UPON HULL

*ABBEY COACHWAYS LTD

See North Yorkshire

ACKLAMS OF BEVERLEY

39 LADYGATE, BEVERLEY
HU17 8BX
Tel: 01482 887666
Fax: 01482 874949
Web site: www.acklams-coaches-beverley.co.uk
Prop: Paul Acklam
Fleet: 10 - 5 coach, 2 midicoach, 3 minicoach.
Chassis: 2 DAF. 3 Dennis. 2 LDV. 2 Mercedes.
Bodies: 1 Optare. 6 Plaxton.
Ops incl: local bus services, school contracts, private hire.
Livery: Red/Grey

ALPHA BUS & COACH CO

DAIRYCOATES INDUSTRIAL ESTATE, WILTSHIRE ROAD, HULL
HU4 6PA
Tel: 01482 353941
Fax: 01482 353771
Web site: www.dunn-line.com
Fleet: 37 - 13 double-deck bus, 9 single-deck bus, 12 coach, 1 midibus, 2 minibus.
Chassis: 8 Dennis. 1 Ford Transit. 10 MAN. 9 Mercedes. 9 Volvo.
Bodies: 4 East Lancs. 1 MCW. 9 Mercedes. 1 Optare. 8 Plaxton. 5 other.
Ops incl: local bus services, school contracts, private hire, continental tours.
Livery: Purple/Silver
Ticket system: Almex
(Subsidiary of Dunn Line Holdings, part of the Veolia Group)

R DRURY COACHES

CARTER STREET, GOOLE DN14 6SL
Tel/Fax: 01405 763440
Dirs: Roland Drury, Richard Drury
Fleet: 5 coach, 1 midicoach
Chassis: 1 Toyota. 5 Volvo.
Bodies: 1 Caetano. 5 Plaxton.
Ops incl: local bus services, school contracts, private hire.
Livery: White/Green/Yellow

*EAST YORKSHIRE MOTOR SERVICES LTD

252 ANLABY ROAD, HULL HU3 2RS
Tel: 01482 327142
Fax: 01482 212040
E-mail: admin@eyms.co.uk
Web site: www.eyms.co.uk
Chmn: P J S Shipp **Fin Dir**: P Harrison
Com Man: R Rackley **Ch Eng**: D Heptinstall
Co Sec: P A Leeman **Coaching Man**: A Bell
Fleet: 328 - 150 double-deck bus, 97 single-deck bus, 28 coach, 8 open-top bus, 43 midibus, 2 minibus.
Chassis: 2 AEC. 1 Bedford. 1 Bristol. 45 Dennis. 65 Leyland. 11 MAN. 26 Mercedes. 1 Neoplan. 13 Optare. 153 Volvo. 6 Enterprise. 4 ADL.
Bodies: 43 Alexander. 7 Berkhof. 9 Caetano. 3 Duple. 1 ECW. 1 East Lancs. 9 Leyland. 1 MCW. 2 Mercedes. 1 Neoplan. 75 Northern Counties. 32 Optare. 1 Park Royal. 101 Plaxton. 1 Willowbrook. 37 Wrightbus. 4 other.
Ops incl: local bus services, school contracts, excursion & tours, private hire, express, continental tours.
Livery: buses - Burgundy/Cream. coaches - Riviera Blue/Primrose
Ticket System: Wayfarer TGX150

FRODINGHAM COACHES

MIDDLE STREET SOUTH, DRIFFIELD YO25 6PY
Tel: 0870 4430473
Fax: 01482 212040
E-mail: alan@frodinghamcoaches.co.uk
Web site: www.frodinghamcoaches.co.uk
Chmn: P J S Shipp **Fin Dir**: P Harrison
Man: A Wilkinson
Fleet: 5 coach
Chassis: 1 MAN. 2 Mercedes. 1 Scania. 1 Volvo.
Bodies: 2 Mercedes. 1 Neoplan. 1 Plaxton. 1 Van Hool.
Ops incl: local bus services, school contracts, excursion & tours, private hire.
Livery: White/Blue/Grey
Part of East Yorkshire Motor Services

BEN JOHNSON COACHES

THE GRANGE, CATFOSS LANE, BRANDESBURTON YO25 8EJ.
Tel: 01964 542475.
Fax: 01964 543982
Prop: Ben Johnson.
Fleet: 8 - 7 coach, 2 minibus.
Chassis: 1 DAF, 2 LDV. 2 Leyland. 1 Setra. 2 Volvo.
Bodies: 4 Plaxton. 1 Setra. 1 Van Hool.
Ops incl: local bus services, school contracts, private hire.

MANOR TRAVEL

2 MANOR DRIVE, MAIN STREET, BEEFORD YO25 8BB.
Tel: 01262 488431.

NATIONAL HOLIDAYS

THE TRAVEL CENTRE, SPRINGFIELD WAY, ANLABY, HULL
HU10 6RJ
Tel: 01482 569006
Fax: 01482 569003
E-mail: info@national-holidays.co.uk
Web site: www.national-holidays.co.uk
Ch Exec: John Slatcher **Dir**: Graham Rogers **Ops Man**: Adrian Hutchinson
Fleet: 81 coach
Chassis: 81 Volvo.
Bodies: 29 Jonckheere. 40 Plaxton. 12 Van Hool.
Ops incl: excursions & tours, private hire, continental tours.
Livery: White
(Subsidiary company of of WA Shearings)

*PEARSON COACHES LTD

9 HEADLANDS ROAD, ALDBROUGH
HU11 4RR
Tel: 01964 527260
Fax: 01964 527774
E-mail: enquiries@pearsoncoaches.co.uk
Web site: www.pearsoncoaches.co.uk
Dirs: Mrs V Pearson, Mr C Pearson, Mr S Colley, Mrs G Sedgewick
Fleet: 10 - 5 coach, 2 midicoach. 3 minicoach.
ChassisBodies: 5 Mercedes. 5 Volvo.
Ops incl: local bus services, school contracts, excursions & tours, private hire.
Livery: Light Grey with Red/Burgundy stripe.
Ticket system: Wayfarer

COLLIN PHILLIPSON MINI-COACHES

1 HILLCREST, OUSEFLEET, GOOLE
DN14 8HP
Tel: 01405 704394
Prop: Collin Phillipson
Tran Man: Tracey Phillipson
Fleet: 1 minicoach
Chassis: 1 Mercedes
Bodies: 1 Excell
Ops incl: school contracts, private hire

STAGECOACH IN HULL

FOSTER STREET, HULL HU8 8BT
Tel: 01482 222333
Fax: 01482 217623
Web site: www.stagecoachbus.com
Dirs: as Stagecoach East Midland
Fleet: 132 - double-deck bus, single-deck bus, coach, midibus
Chassis: incl: 85 Dennis. 22 Volvo.
Bodies: incl: 22 Alexander. 28 Northern Counties. 14 Plaxton.
Ops incl: local bus services, express.
Livery: Stagecoach
Ticket system: Wayfarer 3.

SWEYNE COACHES

LONGSHORES, REEDNESS ROAD, SWINEFLEET DN14 8ER.
Tel: 01405 704263

A/c	Air conditioning	
	Vehicles suitable for disabled	
	Coach(es) with galley facilities	
WC	Coach(es) with toilet facilities	
	Seat belt-fitted vehicles	
R	Recovery service available (not 24 hr)	
R24	24hr recovery service	
	Replacement vehicle available	
T	Toilet-drop facilities available	
	Vintage vehicle(s) available	
	Open top vehicle(s)	

East Yorkshire

109

ESSEX

ANITA'S COACHES

ROOMS 4-5, AIRWAYS HOUSE, FIRST AVENUE, STANSTED AIRPORT CM24 1RY
Tel: 01279 661551
E-mail: anitas.coaches@virgin.net
Web site: www.anitascoaches.com
Dirs: E A S Wheeler, Mrs V A Wyatt
Fleet: 7 - 5 coach, 1 midicoach, 1 minicoach.
Chassis: 2 DAF. 1 MAN. 1 Mercedes. 3 Volvo.
Bodies: 2 Bova. 4 Caetano. 1 Plaxton
Ops incl: local bus services, school contracts, private hire, continental tours.

*APT COACHES LTD

UNIT 27, RAWRETH INDUSTRIAL ESTATE, RAWRETH LANE, RAYLEIGH SS6 9RL
Tel: 01268 783878
Fax: 01268 782656
E-mail: admin@aptcoaches.co.uk
Web site: www.aptcoaches.co.uk
Man Dir: Peter Thorn
Fleet: 13 - 12 coach, 1 miNicoach.
Chassis: 1 Bova. 1 Mercedes. 7 Scania. 1 Setra. 1 Toyota. 2 Volvo.
Bodies: 1 Bova. 2 Caetano. 4 Irizar. 1 Setra. 4 Van Hool. 1 other.
Ops incl: school contracts, private hire, continental tours
Livery: White/Pink

B J S TRAVEL

61A HIGH STREET, GREAT WAKERING SS3 0EF
Tel: 01702 219403
Fax: 01702 216472
Prop: Brian Snow
Fleet: 4 - 2 single-deck coach, 2 minicoach.
Chassis: 2 Mercedes. 1 Scania. 1 Volvo.
Bodies: 1 Berkhof. 1 Neoplan. 1 Reeve Burgess. 1 Other
Ops incl: school contracts, private hire.
Livery: White/Blue/Silver.

BLUE DIAMOND COACHES

37 HOLMES MEADOW, HARLOW CM19 5SG.
Tel: 01279 427524.
Fax: 01279 427525.
Prop: J. Robilliard. **Sec:** A. Robilliard.
Fleet: 4 - 1 coach, 2 minibus, 1 minicoach.
Chassis: 1 Bedford. 2 Freight Rover. 1 Toyota.
Bodies: 1 Caetano. 2 Carlyle. 1 Plaxton.
Ops incl: excursions & tours, private hire, continental tours, school contracts.
Livery: Blue/White.

BLUE TRIANGLE BUSES LTD

UNIT 3C, DENVER INDUSTRIAL ESTATE, RAINHAM RM13 9DD
Tel: 01708 631001/550743
Fax: 01708 522227
Web site: www.bluetrianglebuses.co.uk
Man Dir: Roger Wright
Fleet: 101 - 78 double-deck bus, 23 single-deck bus
Chassis: 8 AEC. 51 Dennis. 15 Leyland. 11 Leyland National. 23 MCW. 5 Volvo.
Bodies: 5 Alexander. 8 Caetano. 34 East Lancs. 6 Leyland. 23 MCW. 13 Park Royal. 20 Plaxton. 1 Saunders. 3 Weymann.
Ops incl: local bus services, excursions & tours
Livery: Red/Cream

*BORDACOACH

25B EASTWOOD ROAD, RAYLEIGH SS6 7JD
Tel: 01268 747608
Prop: D J Stubbington
Fleet: 1 coach.
Chassis: 1 Volvo
Ops incl: school contracts, excursions & tours, private hire.
Livery: White

BRENTWOOD COACHES

79 WASH ROAD, HUTTON, BRENTWOOD CM13 1DL.
Tel: 01277 233144.
Fax: 01277 201386.
Prop: A. J. Brenson. **Ch Eng:** K. Wright.
Sec: Mrs P. Alexander. **Traf Man:** B. Pierce.
Fleet: 30 - 15 double-deck bus, 14 coach. 1 midibus.
Chassis: Daimler, Volvo.
Bodies: Caetano, Jonckheere, Plaxton.
Ops incl: excursions & tours, private hire, school contracts, continental tours.
Livery: White/Brown/Orange/Yellow.
Ticket System: Almex.

BURTONS COLCHESTER COACHWAYS

38 MAGDALEN ROAD, COLCHESTER RM17 5HJ
Tel: 01206 544449
Tel: 01206 766345
E-mail: colchester@burtons-bus.co.uk
Web site: www.burtonscoaches.com
Fleetname: Harris
Man Dir: Paul Cooper **Fleet Eng:** Steve Legate
Fleet: 24 - 10 double-deck bus, 18 single-deck bus, 4 coach, 2 minibus
Chassis: 2 DAF. 16 Dennis. 3 Leyland. 2 Mercedes. 11 Volvo.
Bodies: 3 ECW. 12 East Lancs. 2 Ikarus. 9 Plaxton. 8 Transbus. 2 Van Hool.
Ops incl: local bus services, excursions & tours, school contracts, private hire, continental tours.
Livery: Blue/Yellow on White base

C I COACHLINES

POOLS LANE, HIGHWOOD, CHELMSFORD CM1 3QL
Tel: 01245 248669
Fax: 01245 603534
E-mail: cicoachlines@btopenworld.com
Props: S Lodge, I Lodge, C Ferrier
Fleet: 4 coach
Chassis: 1 Iveco. 3 Volvo
Ops incl: private hire, school contracts

C N ENTERPRISES LTD

9 BARTHOLOMEW DRIVE, HAROLD WOOD RM3 0WB
Tel/Fax: 01708 379700
E-mail: cnenterprise1@aol.com
ManDir: Colin Nossek **Dir:** Vena Nossek
Fleet: 1 coach.
Chassis: 1 Volvo.
Bodies: 1 Jonckheere.
Ops incl: excursions & tours, private hire.

*CEDRIC COACHES

1 THE AVENUE, WIVENHOE CO7 9AH
Tel: 01206 824363
Fax: 01206 822253
Web site: www.cedriccoaches.com
Dirs: Stephen Peck, Alan Short, Derek Hambling, Simon Osborne
Fleet: 23 - 10 double-deck bus, 1 single-deck bus, 10 coach, 1 double-deck coach. 1 minibus
Chassis: 3 Bova. 1 Bristol. 9 Leyland. 1 Mercedes. 2 Setra. 5 Volvo.
Bodies: 3 Bova. 10 ECW. 3 Jonckheere. 1 Plaxton. 2 Setra. 1 Van Hool.
Ops incl: local bus services, school contracts, private hire.
Livery: Orange/Red/Yellow/White
Ticket system: Wayfarer

CHADWELL HEATH COACHES

30 REYNOLDS AVENUE, CHADWELL HEATH RM6 4NT
Tel: 020 8590 7505
Fax: 020 8597 8883
Props: John Thompson, Lynn Thompson.
Fleet: 5 coach.
Chassis: 2 Leyland. 3 Volvo.
Bodies: 3 Berkhof. 1 Duple. 1 Plaxton.
Ops incl: excursions & tours, private hire, school contracts.
Livery: Country cream

CHARIOTS OF ESSEX LTD

THE COACH HOUSE, 1 ONE TREE HILL, STANFORD-LE-HOPE SS17 9NH
Tel: 01268 581444
Fax: 01268 581555
Man Dir: K T Flavin **Dir:** W J Collier
Fleet: 18 - 3 double-deck bus, 2 single-deck bus, 4 single-deck coach, 1 midicoach, 7 minibus, 1 minicoach.
Chassis: Bova. DAF. Freight Rover. Iveco. Mercedes. Toyota.
Bodies: Bova. Caetano. Marshall/MCV. MCW.
Ops incl: local bus services, school contracts, private hire, express.
Livery: Orange/Yellow
Ticket system: Wayfarer

*CLINTONA MINICOACHES

LITTLE WARLEY HALL LANE,
BRENTWOOD CM13 3HA
Tel: 01277 215526
Fax: 01277 200038
E-mail: enquiries@clintona.co.uk
Web site: www.clintona.co.uk
Fleet name: Clintona
Ptnrs: Robin Staines, Barbara Staines.
Fleet: 21 - 8 midibus, 6 midicoach,
1 minibus, 6 minicoach.
Chassis: 1 Ford Transit. 1 Iveco. 3 LDV.
16 Mercedes.
Ops incl: local bus services, school
contracts, private hire.
Livery: White/Blue.
Ticket System: Wayfarer 3

*COOKS COACHES

607 LONDON ROAD, WESTCLIFF-
ON-SEA SS0 9PE
Tel: 01702 344702
Fax: 01702 436887
E-mail: info@cookscoaches.co.uk
Web site: www.cookscoaches.com
Prop: W E Cook
Fleet: 11 - 10 coach, 1 minibus.
Chassis: 10 Bova. 1 LDV.
Bodies: 1 BMC. 10 Bova.
Ops incl: excursions & tours, private hire,
continental tours.
Livery: Red/White

*COUNTY COACHES

2 CRESCENT ROAD, BRENTWOOD
CM14 5JR
Tel: 01277 201505
Fax: 01277 225918
E-mail: enquiries@countycoaches.com
Web site: www.countycoaches.co.uk
Off Man: C A Jee **Tran Man**: R J Pratt
Fleet: 12 - 1 single-deck bus, 9 coach,
1 minicoach, 1 minibus.
Chassis: 1 Dennis. 2 MAN. 1 Mercedes.
1 Toyota. 7 Volvo.
Bodies: 2 Ayats. 1 Berkhof. 3 Caetano.
2 Duple. 1 Jonckheere. 1 Mercedes.1 Van
Hool. 1 other
Ops incl: excursions & tours, private hire,
school contracts.
Livery: Green/White

CROWN COACHES

35 DANDIES DRIVE, EASTWOOD,
LEIGH-ON-SEA SS9 5R4.
Tel/Fax: 01702 420201.
Owners: T. Cox, P. Cox.
Fleet: 8 - 3 coach, 1 midicoach, 4 minibus.
Chassis: 1 Bedford. 1 Bova. 1 DAF. 4 Iveco.
Bodies: 1 Bova. 4 Carlyle. 1 Duple. 1 Ikarus.
Ops incl: local bus services, excursions &
tours, private hire.
Livery: Silver/Red/Orange/Grey stripes.
Ticket System: Wayfarer.

*CRUSADER HOLIDAYS

CRUSADER BUSINESS PARK,
STEPHENSON ROAD WEST,
CLACTON-ON-SEA CO15 4HP
Tel: 01255 431777
Fax: 01255 222683
Recovery: 01255 431777
E-mail: info@crusader-holidays.co.uk
Web site: www.crusader-
holidays.co.uk
Man Dir: Michael Holden **Comm Dir**:
Michael Drinkwater **Gen Man**: David Mart
Ch Eng: Mark Brooke **Ops Man**: Barry
Jacobs
Fleet: 28 coach
Chassis/Bodies: 28 Setra
Ops incl: excursions & tours, continental
tours, private hire
Livery: White/Blue/Red

CUNNINGHAM CARRIAGE COMPANY

THE CARRIAGE HOUSE, FOBBING
ROAD, CORRINGHAM SS17 9BG
Tel: 01375 676578.
Fax: 01375 679719.
Prop: Pat Cunningham
Junior Ptnr: Sarah Cunningham
Fleet: 1 coach.
Chassis: 1 Scania.
Bodies: 1 Irizar.
Ops incl: private hire, express.
Livery: White
Ticket System: Setright.

*DOCKLANDS MINIBUSES LTD

See London

DONS COACHES DUNMOW LTD

PARSONAGE DOWNS, GREAT
DUNMOW CM6 2AT
Tel: 01371 872644
Fax: 01371 876055
Dirs: D T Hale, S D Harvey
Fleet: 16 - 2 double-deck bus, 10 coach,
2 midicoach, 2 minicoach.
Chassis: 1 Ayats. 6 Dennis. 2 Leyland.
2 Mercedes. 3 Neoplan. 2 Toyota.
Bodies: 2 Alexander. 1 Ayats. 2 Caetano.
2 Duple. 1 Marcopolo. 5 Neoplan. 3 Plaxton.
Ops incl: private hire, school contracts.

*EAST LONDON BUS GROUP

See London

EDS MINIBUS & COACH HIRE

257 PRINCESS MARGARET ROAD,
EAST TILBURY RM18 8SB
Tel/Fax: 01375 858049
Props: E Sammons, Mrs S Sammons
Fleet: 2 - 1 coach, 1 minibus.

Chassis/Body: MAN/Algarve
Ops incl: Private hire, excursions & tours

ENSIGN BUS CO LTD

JULIETTE CLOSE, PURFLEET
INDUSTRIAL PARK, PURFLEET
RM15 4YF
Tel: 01708 865656
Fax: 01708 864340
E-mail: sales@ensignbus.com
Web-site: www.ensignbus.com
Chmn: Peter Newman **Dirs**: Ross Newman
(**Sales**), Brian Longley (**Eng**), Steve
Newman (**City Sightseeing**) **Com Dir**: Gary
Nicholass **Eng Man**: Roger Jackson
Fleet (Purfleet): 36 - 24 double-deck bus,
8 single-deck bus, 1 coach, 4 open-top bus.
Chassis: 14 AEC. 1 Bristol. 2 Daimler.
6 Dennis. 12 MCW. 2 Volvo.
Bodies: 1 Ayats. 12 MCW. 1 Northern
Counties. 11 Park Royal. 6 UVG. 2 Craven.
1 Weymann.
Ops incl: local bus services, private hire.
Livery: Blue/Silver
Ticket System: Almex A90

EXCALIBUR COACH TRAVEL

44 MOUNTVIEW CRESCENT,
ST LAWRENCE BAY,
SOUTHMINSTER CM0 7NR
Tel: 01621 779980
Fax: 01621 778928
E-mail: info@excaliburcoach.co.uk
Web site: www.excaliburcoach.co.uk
Prop: Trevor Wynn
Fleet: 3 minibus.
Chassis: 1 Ford Transit. 1 LDV.
Ops incl: private hire, school contracts.

*EXCEL PASSENGER LOGISTICS LTD R24

AIRWAYS HOUSE, FIRST AVENUE,
STANSTED AIRPORT CM24 1RY
Tel: 01279 681800
Fax: 01279 682268
Recovery: 07770 873614
E-mail: mail@excelpl.co.uk
Web site: www.excelpl.co.uk
Man Dir: Graham Hayden **Fin Dir**: Lyn
Watson **Ops Dir**: Bill Hiron **Eng**: Carl
Johnson
Fleet: 54
Chassis: 2 Ayats. 10 Dennis. 12 Leyland.
4 MAN. 8 Mercedes. 11 Scania. 1 Scania.
6 Volvo.
Bodies: include: 2 Ayats. 5 Irizar. 1 Setra
Ops incl: local bus services, school
contracts

*FARGO COACHLINES

ALLVIEWS, SCHOOL ROAD, RAYNE,
BRAINTREE CM7 6SS
Tel/Fax: 01376 321817
E-mail:
fargocoachlines@btconnect.com

A/c	Air conditioning	▼ Seat belt-fitted vehicles	✓ Replacement vehicle available
♿	Vehicles suitable for disabled	R Recovery service available (not 24 hr)	T Toilet-drop facilities available
🍴	Coach(es) with galley facilities	R24 24hr recovery service	🚌 Vintage vehicle(s) available
wc	Coach(es) with toilet facilities		Open top vehicle(s)

Essex

Web site: www.fargocoachlines.co.uk
Prop: L J Smith
Fleet: 43 - 25 double-deck bus, 13 single-deck coach, 3 midicoach, 2 minicoach.
Chassis: incl: DAF, Scania.
Ops incl: private hire
Livery: White

FERRERS COACHES LTD

117B HULLBRIDGE ROAD, SOUTH WOODHAM FERRERS CM3 5LL
Tel: 01245 320456.
Dir: A. Read, G. Read.
Fleet: 4 - 2 coach, 2 minibus.
Chassis: 2 Dennis. 1 Ford Transit. 1 Freight Rover.
Ops incl: excursions & tours, private hire, school contracts.

FIRST ESSEX BUSES

RAINHAM BUS GARAGE, ALLBRIGHT INDUSTRIAL ESTATE, FERRY LANE, RAINHAM RM13 9BU
Tel: 01708 253000
Web site: www.firstgroup.com
Man Dir: R Dorr **Eng Dir:** S Little **Fin Dir:** M Dolphin **Div Man N Essex:** L Berry **Div Man S Essex:** C McCormick
Fleet: 341 - 42 double-deck bus, 272 single-deck bus, 1 open-top double-deck bus, 17 midibus, 9 midicoach.
Chassis: 1 Bristol. 204 Dennis. 17 Leyland. 54 Mercedes-Benz. 38 Scania. 27 Volvo.
Bodies: 36 Alexander. 12 ECW. 21 East Lancs. 16 Marshall/MCV. 37 Northern Counties. 28 Optare. 136 Plaxton. 17 Transbus. 38 Wright.
Ops incl: local bus service, school contracts.
Livery: First Group - White/Blue/Magenta
Ticket System: Wayfarer

*FORDS COACHES

THE GARAGE, FAMBRIDGE ROAD, ALTHORNE CM3 6BZ
Tel: 01621 740326
Fax: 01621 742781
E-mail: info@fordscoaches.co.uk
Web site: www.fordscoaches.co.uk
Prop: A A W Ford **Ch Eng:** A W Ford
Fleet: 16 - 1 single-deck bus, 10 coach, 3 double-deck coach, 2 midicoach
Chassis: 1 Ayats. 2 Bedford. 5 Dennis. 3 Iveco. 8 Leyland. 1 Optare. 2 Scania.
Bodies: 2 Alexander. 1 Ayats. 1 Beulas. 2 Berkhof. 2 Caetano. 1 Duple. 8 ECW. 1 Indcar. 1 Mellor. 1 Plaxton. 3 Van Hool.
Ops incl: local bus services, school contracts, excursions & tours, private hire.
Livery: White/Multi-colour stripe
Ticket system: Wayfarer

GATWICK FLYER LTD

DANES ROAD, ROMFORD RM7 0HL
Tel: 01708 730555
Fax: 01708 751231
Web site: www.gatwickflyer.co.uk
Fleetnames: Gatwick Flyer, Avon Coaches
Fleet: 15 - 6 coach, 9 minicoach.
Ops incl: private hire, express.

GENIAL TRAVEL

43 PEACE ROAD, STANWAY, COLCHESTER CO3 0HL.
Tel/Fax: 01206 571513
Prop: Trevor Brookes
Fleet: 1 coach.
Chassis: 1 DAF
Body: 1 Van Hool
Ops incl: excursions & tours, private hire.
Livery: White/Blue/Yellow.

PETER GODWARD COACHES

4 EDWIN HALL VIEW, SOUTH WOODHAM FERRERS CM3 5QL
Tel: 01268 591834
Fax: 01268 591835
Prop: Peter Godward
Fleet: 12 - 8 single-deck coach, 1 double-deck coach, 1 midibus, 2 minicoach.
Chassis: 1 Ford Transit. 1 Mercedes-Benz. 6 Irisbus. 6 Iveco. 1 LDV. 1 Scania.
Ops incl: school contracts, excursions & tours, private hire, express, continental tours.

*GOLDEN BOY COACHES

See Hertfordshire

GOODWIN'S COACHES

ALWYNN, LONDON ROAD, BLACK NOTLEY, BRAINTREE CM7 8QQ
Tel: 01376 321096
Prop: A. M. Goodwin. **Sec:** I. B. Goodwin.
Fleet: 6 - 5 coach, 1 minibus.
Chassis: 3 Bedford. 2 Volvo.
Bodies: 1 Berkhof. 4 Plaxton. 1 Crystal.
Ops incl: excursions & tours, private hire.
Livery: White/Blue/Grey stripes.

GRAHAM'S

19 CHURCH ROAD, KELVEDON CO5 9JH
Tel: 01376 570150.
Fax: 01376 570657
Prop: G. Ellis.
Livery: White/Blue.

HAILSTONE TRAVEL LTD

PLEASANT VIEW, DUNTON ROAD, LITTLE BURSTEAD CM12 9TZ
Tel: 01268 543543
Fax: 01268 543066
E-mail: info@hailstonetravel.co.uk
Web site: www.hailstonetravel.co.uk
Dirs: Mrs Tina Hailstone, Lawrence Hailstone
Fleet: midicoach, minicoach.
Chassis: Mercedes.
Ops incl: school contracts, private hire
Livery: White

*HEDINGHAM & DISTRICT OMNIBUSES LTD

WETHERSFIELD ROAD, SIBLE HEDINGHAM CO9 3LB
Tel: 01787 460621
Fax: 01787 462852
E-mail: services@hedingham.co.uk
Dirs: R J MacGregor, D R MacGregor
Fleet: 102 - 38 double-deck bus, 44 single-deck bus, 20 coach.
Chassis: 16 Bristol. 22 Dennis. 22 Leyland. 42 Volvo.
Bodies: 22 Alexander. 26 ECW. 1 East Lancs. 5 Leyland. 7 Northern Counties. 31 Plaxton. 3 Transbus. 1 Willowbrook. 3 Wright.
Ops incl: local bus services, school contracts, excursions & tours, private hire.
Livery: Red/Cream.
Ticket System: Wayfarer 3

IMPERIAL BUS CO LTD

FROG ISLAND, FERRY LANE, RAINHAM RM13 9YN
Tel: 01708 550320
Man Dir: M Biddell
Fleet: 37 - 27 double-deck bus, 9 single-deck bus, 1 coach.
Livery: Green.

*KINGS COACHES

364 LONDON ROAD, STANWAY, COLCHESTER CO3 8LT
Tel: 01206 210332
Fax: 01206 213861
E-mail: kings-coaches@fsbdial.co.uk
Web site: www.kings-coaches.co.uk
Prop: Andrew B Cousins
Fleet: 7 single-deck coach.
Chassis: 7 Bova.
Bodies: 7 Bova.
Ops incl: excursions & tours, private hire, continental tours.
Livery: Green/Cream

KIRBYS COACHES (RAYLEIGH) LTD

2 PRINCESS ROAD, RAYLEIGH SS6 8HR
Tel: 01268 777777
Fax: 01702 202555
Dir: Edward Kirby **Co Sec:** Elizabeth Kirby
Fleet: 9 coach.
Chassis/bodies: 9 Setra.
Ops incl: excursions & tours, private hire, continental tours.
Livery: Lilac/Turquoise

LINKFAST LTD T/A S&M COACHES

93 ROSEBERRY AVENUE, BENFLEET SS7 4JF.
Tel/Fax: 01268 795763.
Props: B. W. Smith (Ch Eng), W. N. May (Sec).
Fleet: 10 - 9 double-deck bus, 1 coach.
Chassis: Daimler, Leyland.
Bodies: ECW, Northern Counties, Park Royal, Plaxton.
Ops incl: school contracts, private hire.
Livery: Mixed.

LODGE COACHES

THE GARAGE, HIGH EASTER, CHELMSFORD CM1 4QT
Tel: 01245 231262
Fax: 01245 231825
E-mail: lodgecoaches@btconnect.com
Web site: www.lodgecoaches.co.uk
Dirs: R C Lodge, A D Lodge, C J Lodge.

Fleet: 10 - 10 coach, 1 midicoach, 3 minibus, 1 minicoach, 1 vintage
Chassis: 3 Bedford. 1 Ford Transit. 3 Mercedes. 8 Scania. 1 Toyota.
Bodies: 1 Caetano, 2 Carlyle, 3 Duple. 1 Plaxton. 7 Van Hool, 2 other.
Ops incl: local bus services, school contracts, excursions & tours, private hire, continental tours.
Livery: Blue/Cream

MIKES COACHES [wc] [seatbelt] [key]

THE GRANARY, PIPPS HILL ROAD NORTH, CRAYS HILL, BASILDON CM11 2UJ.
Tel: 01268 525900.
Fax: 01268 453654.
Ptnrs: M. Orphan, D. Orphan, P. Brown.
Fleet: 6 - 5 coach, 1 midicoach.
Chassis: 2 Bedford. 1 DAF. 3 Volvo.
Bodies: 5 Plaxton. 1 Van Hool.
Ops incl: local bus services, school contracts, private hire.

W. H. NELSON (COACHES) LTD

THE COACH STATION, BRUCE GROVE, WICKFORD SS11 8BZ.
Tel: 01268 767870
Fax: 01268 735307
E-mail: info@nibsbus.com
Web site: www.nibsbus.com
Fleetname: Nelsons Independent Bus Services.
Ops incl: local bus services, school contracts
Livery: Yellow.

OLYMPIAN COACHES LTD
[wc] [seatbelt] [key]

TEMPLE BANK, RIVER WAY, HARLOW CM20 2DY
Tel: 01279 868868.
Fax: 01279 868867
Web site: www.olympiancoaches.com
Dirs: C. Marino. **Co Sec**: Mrs D. K. Higgins.
Ops Dir: B. Gunton
Fleet: 40 - coach, minibus.
Ops incl: local bus services, school contracts, excursions & tours, private hire, continental tours.

P & M COACHES

74 CHURCHEND LANE, WICKFORD SS11 7JG.
Tel: 01268 763616.

PHILLIPS COACHES [wc] [seatbelt]

117B HULLBRIDGE ROAD, SOUTH WOODHAM FERRERS CM3 5LL.
Tel/Fax: 01245 323039.
Prop: L. Phillips.
Fleet: 3 - 2 coach, 1 minibus.
Chassis: 1 Freight Rover. 2 Volvo.
Bodies: Plaxton. Van Hool.
Ops incl: excursions & tours, private hire, school contracts.
Livery: Cream/Maroon.

REGAL BUSWAYS LTD [disabled]

ONGAR ROAD, CHELMSFORD CM1 3SR
Tel: 01702 291001
E-mail: info@regalbusways.com
Web site: www.regalbusways.com
Man Dir: Adrian McGarry **Ops Dir**: Lee Whitehead **Dir**: Mandy McGarry
Fleetname: Essex Pullman
Fleet: 14 - 4 double-deck bus, 9 single-deck bus, 1 double-deck coach
Chassis: 4 Dennis. 1 MCW. 3 Optare. 2 Transbus. 4 Volvo.
Bodies: 1 Alexander. 4 Marshall. 1 MCW. 3 Optare. 4 Plaxton. 2 Transbus.
Ops incl: local bus services, private hire, school contracts.
Livery: Maroon/Cream
Ticket system: ERG

RELIANCE LUXURY COACHES
[wc] [seatbelt] [A/C] [key] [T]

54 BROOK ROAD, BENFLEET SS7 5JF
Tel/Fax: 01268 758426
Props: Martyn J Titchen, Patricia M Titchen
Fleet: 4 - 1 double-deck bus, 3 single-deck coach
Chassis: 1 Leyland. 3 Scania.
Bodies: 1 other. 3 Van Hool.
Ops incl: tours, private hire, school contracts.
Livery: Yellow/White/Orange/Red.

STALLION COACHES
[galley] [seatbelt]

STACEYS FARM BUNGALOW, BROOMFIELD, CHELMSFORD CM1 7HF.
Tel/Fax: 01245 443500.
Ptnrs: D. A. Brewster, Miss J. C. Pinkerton.
Fleet: 2 midicoach.
Chassis: 1 Mercedes. 1 Toyota.
Bodies: 1 Caetano. 1 Reeve Burgess.
Ops incl: school contracts, private hire.

STAN'S COACHES [wc]

THE COACH-HOUSE, BECKINGHAM ROAD, GREAT TOTHAM, MALDON CM9 8DY.
Tel: 01621 891959.
Fax: 01621 891365.
Prop: S. J. Porter.
Fleet: 6 - 5 coach, 1 minibus.
Chassis: 1 Bedford. 3 Bova. 1 Mercedes. 1 Volvo.
Bodies: 3 Bova. 1 Duple. 1 Mercedes. 1 Plaxton.
Ops incl: excursions & tours, private hire, continental tours.
Livery: White with Blue/Grey stripes.

STANSTED TRANSIT [disabled]

BUILDING 155, SECOND AVENUE, STANSTED BUSINESS PARK, STANSTED AIRPORT CM24 1QZ
Tel: 01229 681786
Fleet: 33 - 5 double-deck bus, 22 single-deck bus, 6 midibus.
Chassis: 1 DAF, 12 Dennis, 1 Leyland National, 5 MCW. 7 Optare.
Bodies: 1 Alexander, 2 Caetano, 7 Leyland, 1 Leyland National, 5 MCW. 7 Optare. 7 Plaxton. 1 UVG. 2 Wright.
Ops incl: local bus services, school contracts, private hire.
Livery: White.
Ticket system: ERG.

STEPHENSONS OF ESSEX LTD
[wc] [seatbelt] [vintage] [key]

RIVERSIDE INDUSTRIAL ESTATE, SOUTH STREET, ROCHFORD SS4 1BS
Tel: 01702 541511
Fax: 01702 549461
Web site: www.stephensonsofessex.com
E-mail: sales@stephensonsofessex.com
Man Dir: Bill Hiron **Fin Dir**: Lyn Watson
Ops Man: Lee Shuttleworth **Wkshp Man**: Tony Wright
Fleet: 36 - 19 double-deck bus, 9 single-deck bus, 8 coach.
Chassis: 8 Dennis. 19 Leyland. 8 Volvo.
Bodies: 4 Alexander.14 ECW. 1 Leyland. 1 Northern Counties. 16 Plaxton.
Ops incl: local bus services, school contracts, private hire, express.
Livery: White/Green
Ticket System: Wayfarer 3

SWALLOW COACH CO LTD
[wc] [seatbelt] [R] [key]

RAINHAM HOUSE, MANOR WAY, RAINHAM RM13 8RE.
Tel: 01708 630555.
Fax: 01708 555135.
Chmn: D. R. Webb. **Man Dir**: K. I. Webb.
Sec: Mrs. S. D. Webb.
Fleet: 26 - 17 coach. 5 midicoach. 4 minicoach.
Chassis: 1 DAF. 1 Dennis. 1 Ford. 1 Ford Transit. 3 Freight Rover. 3 Leyland. 1 MAN. 2 Mercedes. 1 Setra. 1 Toyota. 11 Volvo.
Bodies: 5 Caetano. 1 Carlyle. 4 Jonckheere. 2 Mercedes. 6 Plaxton. 1 Setra. 2 Van Hool. **Ops incl**: Private hire.
Livery: Various.

T. F. MINI COACHES [seatbelt]

1 SCRATTONS TERRACE, RIPPLE ROAD, BARKING IG11 0TY.
Tel: 020 8593 6205.
Fax: 020 8592 7182.
Man Dir: T. Farrugia.
Fleet: 7 midicoach.
Chassis: 7 Renault.
Ops incl: excursions & tours, private hire, airport transfer.

A/C	Air conditioning	[key]	Replacement vehicle available
[disabled]	Vehicles suitable for disabled	T	Toilet-drop facilities available
[galley]	Coach(es) with galley facilities	R	Recovery service available (not 24 hr)
wc	Coach(es) with toilet facilities	[vintage]	Vintage vehicle(s) available
[seatbelt]	Seat belt-fitted vehicles	[opentop]	Open top vehicle(s)
R24	24hr recovery service		

Essex

TRUSTLINE SERVICES LTD
See Hertfordshire

***VICEROY OF ESSEX LTD**
12 BRIDGE STREET, SAFFRON WALDEN CB10 1BU
Tel: 01799 508010
Fax: 01799 506106
E-mail: enquiries@viceroycoaches.co.uk
Web site: www.viceroycoaches.co.uk
Dir: A R Moore **Ops Man**: A L Moore
Dir/Ch Eng: S A Moore
Fleet: 11 - 9 coach, 2 midicoach, 1 minicoach.
Chassis: 1 BMC. 1 Ford Transit. 1 Iveco. 1 MAN. 4 Mercedes. 1 Neoplan. 2 Scania.
Bodies: 1 BMC. 1 Hispano. 1 Indcar. 1 Irizar. 2 Mercedes. 1 Neoplan. 2 Plaxton. 1 Van Hool.
Ops incl: local bus services, school contracts, excursions & tours, private hire, continental tours.
Livery: White/Silver
Ticket System: Wayfarer 3

***WALDEN TRAVEL LTD**
126 THAXTED ROAD, SAFFRON WALDEN CB11 3BJ
Tel/Fax: 01799 516878
Man Dir: Peter Blanchard
Non-exec Dirs: John Wilson, David Grimmett, James Raynham
Fleet: 9 - 5 coach, 3 midibus, 1 minibus.
Chassis: 2 Dennis. 1 Ford. 1 Leyland. 3 Mercedes. 2 Volvo.
Bodies: 2 Duple. 1 Jonckheere. 6 Plaxton. 1 other.
Ops incl: local bus services, school contracts, excursions & tours, private hire.
Livery: White/Green
Ticket System: ERG

***WEST'S COACHES LTD**
See London

GLOUCESTERSHIRE

ALEXCARS LTD
LOVE LANE INDUSTRIAL ESTATE, CIRENCESTER GL7 1YG
Tel: 01285 653985
Fax: 01285 652964
E-mail: rod@alexcars.co.uk
Man Dir: Rod Hibberd **Dirs**: Jenny Jarvis, Barbara Hibberd **Tran Man**: Will Jarvis
Co Sec: Glyn Daye **Ch Eng**: Steve Hall
Fleet: 20 - 1 single-deck bus, 13 coach, 3 midicoach, 3 minicoach.
Chassis: 1 Bedford. 11 Dennis. 3 MAN. 2 Scania. 3 Toyota.
Bodies: 1 Berkhof. 5 Caetano. 1 Duple. 3 Irizar. 1 Noge. 3 Plaxton. 3 Wadham Stringer. 3 Marco Polo.
Ops incl: local bus services, school contracts, excursions & tours, private hire, continental tours.
Livery: Duo Blue
Ticket System: Almex

***BAKERS COACHES**
COTSWOLD BUSINESS VILLAGE, MORETON-IN-THE-MARSH GL56 0JQ
Tel: 0845 688 7707
Fax: 0845 688 7660
E-mail: enquiries@bakerscoaches.co.uk
Web site: www.bakerscoaches.co.uk
Dir: Mike Baker **Ops Man**: Dave Goodall
Fleet: 17 - 14 coach, 2 midicoach, 1 minibus.
Chassis: 2 Dennis. 2 Iveco. 3 Mercedes. 1 Scania. 2 Transbus. 7 Volvo.
Bodies: Alexander. Irizar. Plaxton.
Ops incl: local bus services, excursions & tours, school contracts, private hire, continental tours.
Livery: White/Red

K. W. BEARD LTD
VALLEY ROAD, CINDERFORD GL14 2PD
Tel: 01594 823031
Fax: 01594 825965
E-mail: beardscoaches.co@btconnect.com
Ch Eng: A Baker **Co Sec**: Mrs M Beard.
Fleet: 10 - 9 coach, 1 midicoach.
Chassis: 1 Bedford. 2 Bova. 1 DAF. 2 Leyland. 1 Mercedes. 1 Setra. 2 Volvo.
Bodies: 2 Bova. 1 Jonckheere. 4 Plaxton. 1 Setra. 1 Van Hool. 1 Onyx.
Ops incl: local bus services, school contracts, excursions & tours, private hire, continental tours.
Livery: White/Blue
Ticket System: Setright.

B. E. W. BEAVIS/BEAVIS HOLIDAYS
BUSSAGE GARAGE, BUSSAGE, STROUD GL6 8BA
Tel: 01453 882297
Fax: 01453 731019
E-mail: beavisholidays@btopenworld.com
Props/Ptnrs: Brian Beavis, Anita Baxter
Fleet: 8 - 5 coach, 1 midicoach, 1 minicoach, 1 minibus.
Chassis: 1 DAF. 4 Neoplan. 1 Scania. 1 Toyota. 1 Volkswagen.
Bodies: 1 Caetano, 1 Irizar, 4 Neoplan. 2 other.
Ops incl: excursions & tours, private hire, school contracts, continental tours.
Livery: Gold/Orange/Red/Yellow.

BENNETT'S COACHES
EASTERN AVENUE, GLOUCESTER GL4 7LP.
Tel: 01452 527809.
Fax: 01452 384448.
Prop: Peter Bennett
Fleet: 24 - 6 double-deck bus, 18 coach.
Chassis: incl: Bristol. DAF. Ford. Leyland. 4 Optare
Bodies: Duple. ECW. 4 Optare. Plaxton. Van Hool.
Ops incl: local bus services, excursions & tours, private hire, continental tours.
Livery: Blue/Grey/Orange.

***JAMES BEVAN (LYDNEY) LTD**
THE BUS STATION, HAMS ROAD, LYDNEY GL15 5PE
Tel/Fax: 01594 842859
E-mail: jamesbevancoaches@tiscali.co.uk
Man Dir: James Bevan
Ops Dir: J Zimmerman
Eng Dir: M Zimmerman
Fleet: 8 - 3 single-deck bus, 4 coach, 1 minibus
Chassis: 2 Dennis. 1 LDV. 1 Optare. 4 Volvo.
Bodies: 1 Optare. 2 Plaxton. 2 Sunsundegui. 2 Wadham Stringer.
Ops incl: local bus services, school contracts, excursions & tours, private hire, continental tours.
Livery: Silver
Ticket System: Wayfarer

***CASTLEWAYS LTD**
CASTLE HOUSE, GREET ROAD, WINCHCOMBE GL54 5PU
Tel: 01242 603715
Fax: 01242 604454
Man Dir: John Fogarty **Co Sec**: Mrs Rowena McCubbin **Ch Eng**: Trevor Wood
Fleet: 13 - 3 single-deck bus, 9 coach, 1 midicoach
Chassis: 1 Bova. 1 Dennis. 8 Mercedes. 1 Toyota. 2 Volvo.
Bodies: 1 Bova. 1 Caetano. 2 Mercedes. 2 Plaxton. 6 Setra. 1 Sunsundegui
Ops incl: local bus services, school contracts, private hire.
Livery: Black/Silver
Ticket System: Wayfarer

COTTRELLS COACHES
MILL END, MITCHELDEAN GL17 0HP
Tel: 01594 542224
Fax: 01594 542740
Fleet: 8 - 4 double-deck bus, 2 single-deck bus, 2 coach
Chassis: Dennis. Leyland. MCW. Volvo.
Bodies: Alexander. Duple. MCW.

EAGLE LINE TRAVEL
[WC] [A/C]

ANDOVERSFORD TRADING ESTATE, ANDOVERSFORD GL54 4LB
Tel: 01242 820535
Fax: 01242 820637
E-mail: brian@eaglelinetravel.co.uk
Web site: www.eaglelinetravel.co.uk
Man Dirs: Brian Davis Martin Davis Wayne Hodge **Ch Eng**: Tony Mezzone
Fleet: 22 - 10 coach, 2 double-deck coach, 2 midibus, 4 midicoach, 2 minicoach, 2 minibus.
Chassis: 2 DAF. 2 Dennis. 4 Ford Transit. 6 Mercedes. 1 Neoplan. 1 Scania. Setra. 1 Toyota. 5 Volvo.
Bodies: 2 Autobus. 2 Berkhof. 1 Caetano. 2 Mercedes. 4 Ford Transit. 1 Neoplan. 2 Plaxton. 6 Van Hool. 2 VW.
Ops incl: school contracts, excursions & tours, private hire, continental tours.
Livery: Dark Blue/Silver/Silver Blue

EBLEY COACHES LTD
[WC] [R24]

UNIT 27, NAILSWORTH MILLS ESTATE, AVENING ROAD, NAILSWORTH GL6 0BS
Tel/Fax: 01453 839333
Dirs: C C Levitt, G A Jones.
Fleet: 19 - 6 double-deck bus, 7 coach, 5 minibus, 1 minicoach.
Chassis: 6 Bristol. 5 DAF. 1 Leyland. 1 MAN. 6 Mercedes.
Bodies: 4 Alexander. 1 Duple. 6 ECW. 1 Plaxton. 2 Reeve Burgess. 5 Van Hool.
Ops incl: local bus services, school contracts, excursions & tours, private hire, continental tours.

*DAVID FIELD
[WC]

WHEATSTONE HOUSE, WATERY LANE, NEWENT GL18 1PY
Tel: 01531 820979
E-mail: dowfield@yahoo.co.uk
Web site: www.davidfieldtravel.co.uk
Prop/Ch Eng: David Field
Fleet: 9 - 4 coach, 1 midibus, 2 midicoach, 2 minicoach.
Chassis: 1 Bedford. 1 DAF. 1 Dennis. 2 Leyland. 2 Mercedes. 1 Setra. 1 Toyota.
Ops incl: school contracts, private hire.
Livery: Black/White

GRINDLES COACHES LTD
[WC]

4 DOCKHAM ROAD, CINDERFORD GL14 2DD.
Tel: 01594 822110.
Fax: 01594 823189.
Man Dir: P. R. Grindle. **Co Sec**: W. H. R. Grindle.
Fleet: 7 coach.
Chassis: 3 Bedford. 1 Bova. 3 DAF.
Bodies: 1 Bova. 5 Plaxton. 1 Van Hool.
Ops incl: local bus services, private hire.

*MARCHANTS COACHES
[WC] [A/C]

61 CLARENCE STREET GL50 3LB
Tel: 01242 257714
Fax: 01242 251360
E-mail: sales@marchants-coaches.com
Web site: www.marchants-coaches.com
Man Dir: Roger Marchant **Dir/Ops/Tran Man**: Richard Marchant **Ch Eng**: Russell Marchant **Co Sec**: Mrs Jean Ellis
Fleet: 24 -5 double-deck bus, 5 single-deck bus, 11 coach, 2 double-deck coach, 1 midicoach.
Chassis: 2 Bristol. 3 Leyland. 1 Mercedes. 2 Neoplan. 16 Volvo.
Bodies: 1 Alexander. 4 ECW. 4 Jonckheere. 2 Neoplan. 10 Plaxton. 3 Wright.
Ops incl: local bus services, school contracts, excursions & tours, private hire, continental tours.
Livery: Red/Gold
Ticket System: Wayfarer

ROVER EUROPEAN TRAVEL LTD
[WC] [A/C]

THE COACH HOUSE, HORSLEY, STROUD GL6 0PU
Tel: 01453 832121
Fax: 01453 832722
E-mail: rovereuropean@compuserve.com
Man Dir: David Hand **Dir**: Carol Hand
Fleet: 11 - 10 coach, 1 midicoach
Chassis: 7 Bova. 3 Dennis. 1 Toyota.
Bodies: 1 Berkhof. 7 Bova. 1 Caetano. 1 Plaxton. 1 Wadham Stringer.
Ops incl: school contracts, excursions & tours, private hire, continental tours.
Livery: Cream base with Light Blue/Dark Blue/Orange.

*STAGECOACH WEST
[T]

3RD FLOOR, 65 LONDON ROAD, GLOUCESTER GL1 3HF
Tel: 01452 418630
Fax: 01452 304857
Web site: www.stagecoachbus.com
Man Dir: I Manning **Eng Dir**: P Sheldon
Ops Dir: S Thomas
Fleet: 238 - 80 double-deck bus, 27 single-deck bus, 5 coach, 114 midibus, 12 minibus.
Chassis: 1 DAF. 10 Leyland. 1 MAN. 5 Mercedes. 50 Volvo.
Bodies: 144 Alexander. 7 Optare. 14 Plaxton
Ops incl: local bus services, school contracts.
Livery: multicolour
Ticket System: Wayfarer 3

*SWANBROOK TRANSPORT LTD

GOLDEN VALLEY, STAVERTON, CHELTENHAM GL51 0TE
Tel: 01452 712386
Fax: 01452 859217
E-mail: enquiries@swanbrook.co.uk
Web site: www.swanbrook.co.uk
Chmn: N Tee **Dirs**: D J Thomas, K J Thomas, K J West **Ch Eng**: G Hooper
Ops Man: M Bowle **Fleet Man**: J A Thomas
Fleet: 30 - 9 double-deck bus, 9 single-deck bus, 5 coach, 7 midibus.
Chassis: 2 Dennis. 4 Leyland. 6 MCW. 7 Mercedes. 6 Optare. 5 Volvo.
Bodies: 3 Alexander. 1 East Lancs. 2 Marshall. 6 MCW. 6 Optare. 10 Plaxton. 2 Wadham Stringer.
Ops incl: local bus services, school contracts, private hire.
Livery: Green/Purple
Ticket System: Wayfarer II

F R WILLETTS & CO (YORKLEY) LTD
[A/C]

DEAN RISE, MAIN ROAD, PILLOWELL GL15 4QY
Tel: 01594 562511
Fax: 01594 564373
Man Dir: Geoff Willetts **Sec**: Sue Willetts
Fleet: 6 - 4 coach, 1 minicoach, 1 minibus.
Chassis: 1 Dennis. 1 Leyland. 2 Mercedes. 1 Setra. 1 Volvo.
Bodies: 1 Mercedes. 4 Plaxton. 1 Setra.
Ops incl: local bus services, school contracts, excursions & tours, private hire.
Livery: Red
Ticket System: Setright

*MAL WITTS EXECUTIVE TRAVEL
[A/C]

1 YEW TREE COTTAGE, BRISTOL ROAD, HARDWICKE, GLOUCESTER GL2 4QZ
Tel/Fax: 01452 724072
E-mail: mal@malwittstravel.co.uk
Web site: www.malwittstravel.co.uk
Owners: Mal Witts, Lynn Witts
Fleet: 4 - 2 minicoach, 2 people carrier
Bodies: 2 Mercedes, 2 VW
Ops incl: private hire, continental tours, excursions & tours, school contracts

---

Gloucestershire

A/c	Air conditioning	
	Vehicles suitable for disabled	
	Coach(es) with galley facilities	
WC	Coach(es) with toilet facilities	
	Seat belt-fitted vehicles	
R	Recovery service available (not 24 hr)	
R24	24hr recovery service	
	Replacement vehicle available	
T	Toilet-drop facilities available	
	Vintage vehicle(s) available	
	Open top vehicle(s)	

GREATER MANCHESTER (BOLTON, BURY, OLDHAM, ROCHDALE, SALFORD, TAMESIDE, WIGAN)

ADLINGTON TAXIS AND MINICOACHES
LODGE FARM, SANDY LANE, HORWICH BL6 6RS
Tel: 01204 697577
E-mail: frank@fjohnson7.wanadoo.co.uk
Fleet: 5 - 2 single-deck bus, 1 coach, 2 midicoach.
Chassis: 1 Bedford. 2 Freight Rover. 2 Iveco.
Ops incl: local bus services, private hire.
Ticket System: Wayfarer

ASHALLS COACHES
UNIT 11, FROXMER STREET, GORTON M18 8EF
Tel: 0161 231 7777
Fax: 0161 231 7787
Web site: www.ashalls.co.uk
Prop: D S Ashall
Fleet: 20 - 6 double-deck bus, 4 single-deck bus, 8 single-deck coach, 2 midicoach.
Chassis: 15 Dennis. 2 Mercedes. 1 Scania. 2 Volvo.
Bodies: 2 Duple. 2 Mellor. 6 Northern Counties. 2 Plaxton. 2 Transbus. 6 Wadham Stringer
Ops incl: local bus services, private hire, school contracts.
Livery: Red
Ticket System: Wayfarer 2

BATTERSBY'S COACHES
73 BRIDGEWATER ROAD, WALKDEN M28 3AF
Tel/Fax: 0161 790 2842
Dirs: R W Griffiths, S. J. Griffiths
Fleet: 3 coach.
Chassis: 1 Leyland. 2 Setra.
Ops incl: private hire, school contracts.

*BLUEBIRD BUS & COACH
ALEXANDER HOUSE, GREENGATE, MIDDLETON M24 1RU
Tel: 0161 653 1900
Fax: 0161 653 6602
Web site: www.bluebirdbus.co.uk
Gen Man: Michael T G Dunstan
Fleet: 49 single-deck bus.
Chassis: 2 DAF. 40 Dennis. 7 MAN
Bodies: 28 Alexander. 3 Caetano. 9 East Lancs. 3 Marshall. 1 Optare. 2 Plaxton. 3 Wright.
Ops incl: local bus services.

*A & H BOOTH LTD
(with driver)
GROSVENOR GARAGE, 100 DOWSON ROAD, HYDE SK14 5BN
Tel: 0161 368 2413
Dirs: D Mycock, J Mycock
Fleet: 3 - 2 coach, 1 minicoach.
Chassis: 1 DAF. 1 Ford. 1 LDV.
Bodies: 1 Caetano. 1 Plaxton. 1 other.
Ops incl: private hire

R BULLOCK & CO (TRANSPORT) LTD
COMMERCIAL GARAGE, STOCKPORT ROAD, CHEADLE SK8 2AG
Tel: 0161 428 5265
Fax: 0161 428 9074
Web site: www.bullockscoaches.co.uk
Fleet: 59 - 33 double-deck bus, 6 single-deck bus, 19 coach, 1 minibus
Livery: Red/White.

BU-VAL BUSES LTD
UNIT 5, PARAGON INDUSTRIAL ESTATE, WALSDEN OL15 8QF
Tel: 01706 372787
Tel: 01706 372121
Man Dir: Martin Bull **Co Sec**: David Beames
Fleet: 20 midibus.
Chassis: 11 Dennis. 7 Marshall. 2 Optare.
Bodies: 2 Caetano. 7 Marshall/MCV. 2 Optare. 6 Plaxton. 2 Transbus. 1 UVG.
Ops incl: local bus services
Livery: White/Red
Ticket System: Wayfarer 386

LES BYWATER & SONS LTD
SPARTH BOTTOMS ROAD, ROCHDALE OL11 4HT.
Tel: 01706 648573.
Man Dir: M. T. Bywater. **Dir**: N. L. Bywater.
Fleet: 3 - 1 coach, 1 midicoach, 1 minibus.
Chassis: 1 Dennis. 2 Iveco.
Bodies: 1 Duple. 2 Robin Hood.
Ops incl: private hire, school contracts.
Livery: White/Blue/Black.

CARSVILLE COACHES
51A HIGHER ROAD, URMSTON M41 9AP
Tel: 0161 748 2698
Fax: 0161 747 2694
E-mail: janetcarsville@hotmail.com
Man Dir: Dave Dickson
Fleet: 13 - 2 double-deck bus, 10 coach, 1 midicoach.
Chassis: 1 Bedford. 2 Ford. 4 Scania. 3 Volvo.
Bodies: 1 Caetano. 1 East Lancs. 1 Leyland. 1 Marcopolo. 5 Plaxton. 1 Van Hool.
Ops incl: private hire, excursions & tours, school contracts.
Livery: White/Purple.

*COACH OPTIONS LTD
768 MANCHESTER ROAD, CASTLETON, ROCHDALE OL11 3AW
Tel: 01706 713966
Fax: 01706 759996
E-mail: coach.options@freeuk.com
Dirs: Paul Stone, Adrian Duffey
Fleet: 9 - 5 single-deck coach, 1 midicoach, 1 midibus, 2 minicoach

Chassis: 2 Bova. 2 DAF. 2 Ford Transit. 1 Iveco. 1 Mercedes. 2 Scania.
Ops incl: excursions & tours, private hire, continental tours, school contracts.
Livery: Blue

CROPPER COACHES
316 BURY ROAD, TOTTINGTON BL8 3DT
Tel: 01204 885322.
Prop: L. Donnell.
Fleet: 7 minibus.
Chassis: 5 Ford Transit. 1 Freight Rover.
Ops incl: private hire, school contracts.

DAM EXPRESS
GROVE HOUSE, 27 MANOR STREET, ARDWICK GREEN M12 6HE.
Tel: 0161 273 1234.
Fax: 0161 274 4141.
Fleetname: Don Travel.
Prop/Ops Man: D. Francis.
Sales Man: W. Lee. **Co Sec**: Miss T. Wilding.
Fleet: 3 - 1 coach, 2 double-deck coach.
Ops incl: excursions & tours, private hire, express, continental tours.

*ELLEN SMITH (TOURS) LTD
MANDALE PARK, CORPORATION ROAD, ROCHDALE OL11 4HJ
Tel: 01706 345000
Fax: 01706 345970
E-mail: p.targett@ellensmith.co.uk
Web site: www.ellensmith.co.uk
Man Dir: Paul Targett
Fleet: 6 - 4 coach, 2 minibus
Chassis: 2 Bova. 1 Iveco. 1 Mercedes. 2 VW.
Bodies: 1 Beulas. 2 Bova. 1 Mercedes.

*ELITE SERVICES LTD
UNITS 3/6, ADSWOOD ROAD INDUSTRIAL ESTATE, ADSWOOD ROAD, STOCKPORT SK3 8LF.
Tel: 0161 480 0617
Fax: 0161 480 3099
Dirs: Dave Nickson
Fleet: 21 - 2 double-deck bus, 17 coach, 2 double-deck coach.
Chassis: 1 Ayats. 1 Ford. 15 Scania. 2 Volvo.
Ops incl: excursions & tours, private hire, continental tours, school contracts.
Livery: White/Purple/Pink

*EXCEL PASSENGER LOGISTICS LTD
See Essex

*FINGLANDS COACHWAYS LTD wc ⓚ A/c

261 WILMSLOW ROAD, RUSHOLME, MANCHESTER M14 5LJ
Tel: 0161 224 3341
Fax: 0161 257 3154
E-mail: enquiry@finglands.co.uk
Web site: www.finglands.co.uk
Fleetname: Finglands
Chmn: P J S Shipp **Dirs**: D Shurden, P Harrison **Fleet Eng**: T Jenkins
Traff Man: F Walton
Fleet: 57 - 42 double-deck bus, 5 single-deck bus, 10 coach
Chassis: 4 Dennis. 48 Volvo. 5 other.
Bodies: 21 Alexander. 15 Northern Counties. 15 Plaxton. 1 Van Hool. 5 other.
Ops incl: local bus services, school contracts, private hire.
Livery: White/Orange/Brown/Gold
Ticket System: Wayfarer TGX150

FIRST IN MANCHESTER

WALLSHAW STREET, OLDHAM OL1 3TR
Tel: 0161 627 2929
Fax: 0161 627 5845
Fleetname: First
Man Dir: Ian Davies **Business Dir/Dep Man Dir**: Alan Pilbeam **Fin Dir**: Martin Wilson **Eng Dir**: Colin Stafford **Service Delivery Dir**: Robert Mason **Network Dir**: Simon Bennet
Fleet: 862 - 136 double-deck bus, 450 single-deck bus, 199 midibus, 34 articulated bus, 43 minibus.
Chassis: BMC. Dennis. Irisbus. Leyland. MCW. Mercedes. Optare. Scania. Volvo.
Bodies: BMC. ECW. East Lancs. Irisbus. Leyland. Marshall. Mercedes. Northern Counties. Optare. Scania. Transbus. Wright.
Ops incl: local bus services, school contracts, private hire.
Livery: First - Magenta/Blue & Grey/White
Ticket System: ERG TP4004

*FREEBIRD
ⓚ ● ¶ wc A/c ✂ R

REVERS STREET GARAGE, BURY BL8 1AQ
Tel: 0161 797 6633
Fax: 08712 773214
Recovery: 0161 797 6633
E-mail: info@freebirdcoaches.co.uk
Web site: www.freebirdcoaches.co.uk
Owner: Paul Dart **Man**: Rob Dart
Fleet: 15 - 9 coach, 2 midibus, 4 minibus.
Chassis: 1 DAF. 2 Dennis. 3 Ford. 2 Ford Transit. 3 Irisbus. 1 Iveco. 2 LDV. 2 Mercedes. 2 Volvo.
Bodies: 1 Beulas. 1 Berkhof. 1 Caetano. 1 Marcopolo. 2 Optare. 1 Plaxton. 1 Van Hool. 7 other.
Ops incl: private hire, school contracts
Livery: White

HAYTON'S EXECUTIVE TRAVEL LTD
wc ● ¶ A/c ✂ T

12 ACORN CLOSE, BURNAGE M19 2HS
Tel: 0161 223 3103
Fax: 0161 223 9528
Prop: Barry Hayton **Dir/Sec**: Barry A Hayton
Fleet: 17 - 3 double-deck bus, 3 single-deck bus, 10 coach, 1 midibus.
Chassis: 3 MAN. 1 Neoplan. 1 Optare. 1 Setra. 10 Volvo.
Bodies: 2 East Lancs. 2 Jonckheere. 1 Noge. 2 Optare. 4 Plaxton. 1 Setra. 4 Van Hool.
Ops incl: local bus services, school contracts, excursions & tours, private hire, express, continental tours.
Livery: White

HEALINGS INTERNATIONAL COACHES ● wc A/c

251 HIGGINSHAW LANE, ROYTON, OLDHAM OL2 6HW
Tel: 0161 624 8975
Fax: 0161 652 0320
Ptnrs: Philip Healing, Richard Healing
Fleet: 7 - 5coach, 1 midicoach, 1 minicoach.
Chassis: 1 DAF. 1 Mercedes. 1 Scania. 1 Toyota. 1 Volvo. 2 Duple425
Ops incl: school contracts, excursions & tours, private hire, continental tours.
Livery: White with coloured decals

*JONES EXECUTIVE COACHES LTD
● wc ¶ A/c ✂

THE COACH STATION, SHARP STREET, WALKDEN M28 3LX
Tel: 0161 790 9495
Fax: 0161 790 9400
Web site: www.jonesexecutive.co.uk
E-mail: simon@jonesexecutive.co.uk
Man Dir: Simon Jones
Fleet: 6 coach
Chassis: 1 Dennis. 1 Iveco. 2 Scania. 2 Volvo.
Bodies: 1 Beulas. 1 Irizar. 2 Plaxton. 2 Van Hool.
Ops incl: local bus services, private hire.
Livery: Blue

*LAMBS COACHES
● wc A/c ✂

2A BUXTON STREET, HAZEL GROVE, STOCKPORT SK7 4BB
Tel: 0161 483 5011
Fax: 0161 483 5011
E-mail: lambs139@aol.com
Web-site: www.lambscoaches.net
Dirs: Geoff Lamb, Graham Lamb
Fleet: 7 coach
Chassis: 3 DAF. 1 Mercedes. 2 Scania. 1 Volvo.
Bodies: 1 Mercedes. 6 Van Hool.
Ops incl: private hire, school contracts.
Livery: Blue/White

*LENDOR MINI COACHES
ⓚ ●

17 VALLEY CLOSE, MOSSLEY OL5 0NH
Tel/Fax: 01457 832845
Prop: Leonard E Glynn
Fleet: 6 minibus.
Chassis: 2 Ford Transit. 1 Iveco. 2 Mercedes. 1 Vauxhall.
Ops incl: private hire, school contracts

MARPLE MINI COACHES
● ✂

5 GROSVENOR ROAD, MARPLE SK6 6PR.
Tel: 0161 881 9111.
Owner: G. W. Cross.
Fleet: 2 minicoach.
Chassis: Ford Transit. LDV.
Ops incl: school contracts, private hire.
Livery: White/Gold.

*MAYNE OF MANCHESTER
ⓚ wc ● A/c ✂

1000 ASHTON NEW ROAD, CLAYTON M11 4PD
Tel (coaches): 0161 223 8111
Tel (buses): 0161 223 2035
E-mail: coaches@mayne.co.uk
Web site: www.mayne.co.uk
Fleetname: Mayne
Chmn/Man Dir: S B Mayne **Dirs**: A A Mayne, G R Thompson (**Gen Man**), **Dir**: D Mayne (**Co Sec**) **Ch Eng**: C Pannell **Comm Man**: A K Nuttall
Fleet: 59 - 22 double-deck bus, 19 single-deck bus, 18 coach.
Chassis: 3 Bova. 21 Dennis. 32 Scania. 3 Volvo.
Bodies: 3 Bova. 22 East Lancs. 9 Irizar. 5 Marshall. 5 Northern Counties. 6 Plaxton. 2 UVG. 7 Wright.
Ops incl: local bus services, school contracts, excursions & tours, continental tours.
Livery: Red/Cream
Ticket system: Wayfarer

METROLINK ⓚ

METROLINK, METROLINK HOUSE, QUEENS ROAD, MANCHESTER M8 0RY
Tel: 0161 205 8685
Fax: 0161 205 8699
Web site: www.gmpte.com
Man Dir: Phil Smith
Fleet: 28 - tram
Chassis: GEC Alstom
Bodies: Firema
Ops incl: tram service (part of Stagecoach)

DAVID PLATT COACHES & MINITRAVEL OF LEES

8 THE WOODS, GROTTON, SADDLEWORTH, OLDHAM OL4 4LP
Tel/Fax: 0161 633 4845
Props: David Platt

A/c	Air conditioning	✂	Replacement vehicle available
ⓚ	Vehicles suitable for disabled	T	Toilet-drop facilities available
¶	Coach(es) with galley facilities		Vintage vehicle(s) available
wc	Coach(es) with toilet facilities		Open top vehicle(s)
●	Seat belt-fitted vehicles		
R	Recovery service available (not 24 hr)		
R24	24hr recovery service		

Greater Manchester

Fleet: 2 - 1 coach, 1 minicoach.
Chassis: 1 Bedford. 1 Toyota.
Bodies: 1 Caetano. 1 Plaxton.
Ops incl: private hire.
Livery: Aqua/White

SELWYNS TRAVEL SERVICES

BUILDING 77, TERMINAL 2, MANCHESTER AIRPORT M90 1QX
Tel: 0161 489 5720
Fax: 0161 499 9157
E-mail: sales@selwyns.co.uk
Web site: www.selwyns.co.uk
Man Dir: Selwyn A Jones **Co Sec/Acct**: Richard E Williams **Fleet Eng**: Cledwyn Owen **Ops Man**: John Miller
Fleet: 18 - 7 coach, 2 midibus, 3 minicoach, 6 minicoach.
Chassis: 4 DAF. 1 Dennis. 9 Mercedes. 2 Optare. 2 Volvo.
Bodies: 1 Berkhof. 8 Mercedes. 2 Optare. 3 Plaxton. 4 Van Hool.
Ops incl: local bus services, school contracts, private hire.
Livery: White/Blue/Orange/Green
Ticket System: Wayfarer

SMITHS COACHES (MARPLE) LTD

72 CROSS LANE, MARPLE SK6 7PZ
Tel: 0161 427 2825.
Fax: 0161 449 7731.
Man Dir: J Hibbert
Fleet: 6 - 2 double-deck bus, 3 coach, 1 midibus.
Chassis: 2 Bristol. 2 Dennis. 1 Iveco. 1 Volvo.
Bodies: 1 Caetano. 2 ECW. 2 Neoplan.
Ops incl: local bus services, school contracts, excursions & tours, private hire, continental tours.
Livery: White/Orange-Rose.
(Part of the Elite Group)

SOUTH LANCS TRAVEL

UNIT 22/23, CHANTERS INDUSTRIAL ESTATE, ATHERTON M46 9BP
Tel: 01942 888893
Fax: 01942 894010
Man Dir: Martin Bott **Eng Dir**: D A Stewart
Tran Man: W Peach

Fleet: 50 - double-deck bus, single-deck bus, midibus.
Chassis: incl: 2 Optare
Bodies: incl: 2 Optare
Ops incl: local bus services, tram service, school contracts
Livery: Yellow/Blue
Ticket System: Wayfarer 3

STAGECOACH MANCHESTER

HEAD OFFICE, HYDE ROAD, MANCHESTER M12 6JS
Tel: 0161 273 3377
Fax: 0161 271 2594
E-mail: manchester.enquiries@stagecoachbus.com
Web site: www.stagecoachbus.com/manchester
Man Dir: M Threapleton **Ops Dir**: E Tasker.
Comm Dir: R A Cossins **Eng Dir**: D Roe
Ser Performance Man: A Wilson **Network Man**: J K Young **Mktng Man**: K Coventry
Personnel man: J E Crenigan
Fleet: 653 - 366 double-deck bus, 213 single-deck bus, 1 coach, 45 midibus, 33 minibus.
Chassis: 260 Dennis. 4 Iveco. 44 Leyland. 124 MAN. 33 Mercedes. 35 Scania. 158 Volvo.
Bodies: 443 Alexander. 20 Duple. 7 East Lancs. 1 Neoplan. 89 Northern Counties. 94 Plaxton. 4 other.
Ops incl: local bus services.
Livery: Blue/Orange/Red/White
Ticket System: ERG

STOTT'S TOURS (OLDHAM) LTD

144 LEES ROAD, OLDHAM OL4 1HT
Tel: 0161 624 4200.
Fax: 0161 628 2969.
Prop: A. Stott.
Ops incl: school contracts.
Livery: Cream/Red/Black.

VALES COACHES (MANCHESTER) LTD

49 BROUGHTON STREET, MANCHESTER M8 8AN
Tel: 0161 832 9445.
Fleetname: Vale of Manchester.
Dir: P. D. Green. **Dir/Sec**: G. L. Green
Fleet: 20 midibus.
Chassis: 20 Mercedes.
Bodies: 2 Alexander. 1 Carlyle. 13 Plaxton. 4 Reeve Burgess.
Ops incl: local bus services, school contracts, private hire.
Livery: Blue/Cream
Ticket System: Wayfarer 2

VIKING COACHES

DOCTOR FOLD FARM, DOCTOR FOLD LANE, BIRCH, HEYWOOD OL10 2QE.
Tel: 01706 368999.
Fax: 01706 620011.
E-mail: viking@coaches76.freeserve
Web site: www.coach-day-trips
Owners: A. Warburton, Ms A. Warburton.
Fleet: 4 coach.
Chassis: Volvo. Iveco.
Bodies: Beulas. Plaxton. Van Hool.
Ops incl: excursions & tours, private hire, continental tours, school contracts.
Livery: Viking Ship.

*W A SHEARINGS LTD

MIRY LANE, WIGAN WN3 4AG
Tel: 01942 244246
Fax: 01942 242518
Web site: www.washearings.com
Chmn: Bernard Norman **ChExec**: John Slatcher **Fin Dir**: David Newbold
Ops Dir (Transport): Jimmy King
Fleet: 252 coach
Chassis: 252 Volvo.
Bodies: 62 Jonckheere. 81 Plaxton. 6 Sunsundegui. 103 Van Hool.
Ops incl: excursions & tours, private hire, continental tours.
Livery: Blue or Gold

WRIGLEY'S COACHES LTD

4 FIDDLERS LANE, IRLAM M44 6QE
Tel: 0161 775 2414
Fax: 0161 775 1558
E-mail: sales@wrigleyscoaches.com
Web site: www.wrigleyscoaches.com
Man Dir: Colin Wrigley **Co Sec/Dir**: Lesley Wrigley **Ops Man**: Alan Grice
Fleet: 8 - 1 double-deck bus, 4 coach, 2 double-deck coach, 1 minicoach.
Chassis: 1 Leyland. 2 MAN. 1 Neoplan. 1 Setra. 1 Toyota. 2 Volvo.
Bodies: 1 Alexander. 1 Caetano. 3 Neoplan. 1 Plaxton. 1 Setra. 1 Van Hool.
Ops incl: private hire, school contracts.
Livery: Blue/White

HAMPSHIRE

*AIRLYNX TRAVEL

THE SYCAMORES, OAKLEY ROAD, SOUTHAMPTON SO16 4LJ
Tel: 023 8039 9078
Fax: 023 8077 7724
E-mail: us@airlynx.co.uk
Web site: www.airlynx.co.uk
Dirs: Steven Gear, Gary Gregory
Co Sec: Michael Rudder
Tran Man: Dominic Brown
Fleet: 11 - 1 single-deck bus, 1 coach, 11 minicoach
Chassis: 1 Dennis. 4 Ford Transit. 5 Mercedes. 1 Renault. 1 VW.
Ops incl: private hire, school contracts, local bus services.
Livery: Blue/Yellow

ALTONIAN COACHES

THE DEPOT, MILL LANE TRADING ESTATE, ALTON GU34 2QJ
Tel: 01420 84839
Fax: 01420 84803
Dirs: R Turner, S P Austen
Ops Man: M Jones **Ch Eng**: K Tillin
Fleet: 17 -11 coach, 3 midicoach, 2 minibus,

1 minicoach.
Chassis: 1 DAF. 9 Dennis. 1 Ford Transit. 1 Leyland. 1 Mercedes. 1 Optare. 1 Renault. 2 Setra.
Bodies: 1 Autobus. 1 Caetano. 3 Duple. 1 Irizar. 4 Neoplan. 1 Optare. 2 Plaxton. 1 Reeve Burgess. 2 Van Hool. 1 Wadham Stringer.
Ops incl: local bus services, school contracts, excursions & tours, private hire, continental tours.
Livery: Orange (cream lettering)

AMK CHAUFFEUR DRIVE LTD A/c

MILL LANE, PASSFIELD, LIPHOOK GU30 7RP
Tel: 01428 751675
Fax: 01428 751677
E-mail: info@amkxl.com
Web site: www.amkxl.com
Fleet: 78 - 65 minibus, 3 midibus, 10 minicoach.
Ops inc: local bus services, school contracts, excursions & tours, private hire.

*AMPORT & DISTRICT COACHES LTD
WC A/c

EASTFIELD HOUSE, AMESBURY ROAD, THRUXTON, ANDOVER SP11 8ED
Tel: 01264 772307
Fax: 01264 773020
E-mail: tedd@onetel.net
Dirs: P J Tedd, A M Tedd, N B Tedd
Fleet: 9 - 8 coach, 1 midicoach.
Chassis: 1 Mercedes. 2 Scania. 2 Setra. 4 Volvo.
Bodies: 2 Berkhof. 1 Optare. 4 Plaxton. 2 Setra.
Ops incl: private hire, continental tours, excursions & tours, express, school contracts.
Livery: White

*ANGELA COACHES LTD
WC A/c

OAKTREE HOUSE, LOWFORD, BURSLEDON SO31 8ES
Tel: 023 8040 3170
Fax: 023 8040 6487
E-mail: robert@angelacoaches.com
Web site: www.angelacoaches.com
Man Dir: M Pressley **Co Sec**: Mrs H M Pressley **Ops Dir**: R Pressley
Ch Eng: D Evans **Ops Man**: J Davies
Fleet: 9 - 3 coach, 1 midicoach, 5 minicoach.
Chassis: 2 Irisbus. 2 Iveco. 2 MAN. 1 Mercedes. 2 Toyota.
Bodies: 2 Beulas. 2 Caetano. 2 Indcar. 2 Neoplan. 1 other.
Ops incl: private hire, school contracts, excursions & tours, continental tours

*AVENSIS COACH TRAVEL LTD WC A/c T

29 PREMIER WAY, ABBEY PARK, ROMSEY SO51 9DQ

Tel: 01794 515260
Fax: 01794 512260
E-mail: info@avensiscoaches.co.uk
Web site: www.avensiscoaches.co.uk
Dirs: Graham Humby, Simon Humby
Gen Man: Zak la Gumina **Travel Cnsltnt**: Debbie Howarth, Scott McGow
Fleet: 8 coach.
Chassis: 6 Scania. 2 Volvo.
Bodies: 2 Berkhof. 6 Irizar.
Ops incl: excursions & tours, private hire, continental tours.
Livery: Yellow/Purple

BYNGS INTERNATIONAL COACHES WC A/c

1B ANGERSTEIN ROAD, NORTH END, PORTSMOUTH PO2 8HJ.
Tel: 023 9266 2223
Fax: 023 9267 8464
Dirs: Paul Grant, Trevor Grant. **Fleet Eng**: John Hampton.
Fleet: 40 - 1 single-deck bus, 37 coach, 1 midicoach, 1 minicoach.
Chassis: 10 Bova. 2 DAF. 2 Dennis. 4 Leyland. 4 Mercedes. 7 Scania. 1 Toyota. 10 Volvo.
Bodies: 10 Bova. 2 DAF. 2 Dennis. 4 irizar. 2 Jonckheere. 4 mercedes. 11 Plaxton. 7 Van Hool.
Ops incl: excursions & tours, private hire, school contracts.
Livery: Silver/Brown.

A. S. BONE & SONS

LONDON ROAD, HOOK RG27 9EQ
Tel: 01256 761388, 762106
Fleetname: Newnham Coaches
Man Dir: J. E. Bone. **Co Sec**: Mrs M. Bone.
Fleet: 5 - 3 double-deck bus, 2 single-deck bus.
Chassis: 1 Bristol. 2 Daimler. 2 Leyland National.
Ops incl: private hire.
Livery: Cream/Blue.

*BRIJAN TOURS LTD
 A/c R24

THE COACH STATION, UNITS 4/5, BOTTINGS INDUSTRIAL ESTATE, CULDRIDGE SO30 2DY
Tel: 01489 892942
Fax: 01489 789395
Recovery: 017711 435189
E-mail: sales@brijantours.com
Man Dir: Brian Botley **Co Sec**: Janet Botley
Ops Man: Brian Bedford
Fleet: 22 - 6 double-deck bus, 7 single-deck bus, 8 coach, 1 double-deck coach.
Chassis: 2 Bristol. 1 Iveco. 3 Leyland. 2 MCW. 9 Mercedes. 2 Scania. 3 Volvo.
Bodies: 2 Alexander. 3 Autobus. 3 ECW. 1 Irizar. 1 MCW. 1 Mellor. 1 Northern Counties. 1 Park Royal. 6 Plaxton. 2 Van Hool.
Ops incl: local bus services, school contracts, excursions & tours, private hire, continental tours
Livery: coaches: Cream/Grey/Burgundy. Buses: Blue or Red
Ticket system: Wayfarer

*CLEGG & BROOKING COACHES
WC A/c

WHITE HORSE SERVICE STATION, MIDDLE WALLOP, STOCKBRIDGE SO20 8DZ
Tel: 01264 781283
Fax: 01264 781679
E-mail: cleggandbrooking@btconnect.com
Dirs: Kevin Brooking, Jeanette Cook, John Cook
Fleet: 11 - 8 coach, 3 midicoach
Chassis: 1 Bova. 2 Dennis. 1 Mercedes. 4 Scania. 2 Toyota. 1 Volvo.
Bodies: 1 Alexander. 1 Berkhof. 1 Bova. 4 Caetano. 2 Irizar. 2 Plaxton
Ops incl: local bus services, private hire, school contracts.
Livery: Blue/Grey

*COLISEUM COACHES LTD WC galley A/c

BOTLEY ROAD GARAGE, WEST END, SOUTHAMPTON SO30 3JA
Tel: 023 8047 2377
Fax: 023 8047 6537
E-mail: info@coliseumcoaches.co.uk
Web site: www.coliseumcoaches.co.uk
Man Dirs: David Pitter (Sec), Kerry Pitter
Ch Eng: Dave Rowsell
Fleet: 12 coach
Chassis: 12 MAN
Bodies: 11 Neoplan. 1 Noge.

COOPERS COACHES

31-35 LAKE ROAD, WOOLSTON SO19 9EB
Tel: 023 8039 3393
Fax: 023 8044 4929.
Prop: Stephen Cooper
Fleet: 8 - 5 coach, 2 minibus, 1 midicoach.
Chassis: 1 DAF. 1 Ford Transit. 1 LDV. 1 Mercedes. 4 Volvo.
Bodies: 1 Caetano. 1 Ikarus. 2 Plaxton. 1 Van Hool. 1 Robin Hood.
Ops incl: local bus services, school contracts, private hire.
Livery: Cream/Pine/Burgundy

EASSONS COACHES LTD
WC A/c

44 WODEHOUSE ROAD, ITCHEN SO19 2EQ
Tel: 023 8044 8153
Fax: 023 8044 1635
Dirs: R. A. Easson, D. H. Easson.
Fleet: 10 - 7 coach, 2 midicoach, 1 minibus.
Chassis: 3 Mercedes. 1 Neoplan. 3 Setra. 2 Volvo. 1 Van Hool.
Bodies: 1 Mercedes. 1 Neoplan. 2 Plaxton. 3 Setra. 1 Van Hool. 2 Robin Hood.
Ops incl: excursions & tours, private hire, continental tours.
Livery: Cream/Khaki Brown.

A/c	Air conditioning	
	Vehicles suitable for disabled	
	Coach(es) with galley facilities	
WC	Coach(es) with toilet facilities	
	Seat belt-fitted vehicles	
R	Recovery service available (not 24 hr)	
R24	24hr recovery service	
	Replacement vehicle available	
T	Toilet-drop facilities available	
	Vintage vehicle(s) available	
	Open top vehicle(s)	

Hampshire

Hampshire

*EMSWORTH & DISTRICT MOTOR SERVICES LTD

THE BUS GARAGE, CLOVELLY ROAD, SOUTHBOURNE PO10 8PE
Tel: 01243 378337
Fax: 01243 389424
E-mail: caren@emsworthanddistrict.co.uk
Web site: www.emsworthanddistrict.co.uk
Dirs: Paul Lea, Caren Austin-Lea, Marion Lea, Joanne Lea
Fleet: 21 - 2 double-deck bus, 10 single-deck bus, 5 coach, 2 midicoach, 2 minibus
Chassis: Bedford. Dennis. Ford Transit. MAN. Mercedes. Optare.
Bodies: Alexander. Berkhof. Leyland. Mercedes. Optare. Reeve Burgess. Van Hool
Ops incl: local bus services, school contracts, excursions & tours, private hire
Ticket system: Wayfarer

FIRST HAMPSHIRE & DORSET LTD

226 PORTSWOOD ROAD, SOUTHAMPTON SO17 2BE
Tel: 023 8058 4321
Fax: 023 8067 1448
Web site: www.firstgroup.com
E-mail: hampshire-dorset.csc@firstgroup.com
Man Dir: Richard Soper **Dep Man Dir**: Marc Reddy **Eng Dir**: David Toy **Fin Dir**: Ian Stone **Ops Dir**: Mike Smith **Ops Man**: Chris Bainbridge **Ops Eng**: Mike Britten **Comm Man**: Kenneth Cobb
Fleet: 444 - 83 double-deck bus, 76 single-deck bus, 11 coach, 5 open-top bus, 179 midibus, 90 minibus.
Chassis: 7 Bristol. 177 Dennis. 36 Iveco. 32 Leyland. 67 Mercedes. 7 Optare. 26 Scania. 92 Volvo.
Bodies: 33 Alexander. 7 ECW. 26 East Lancs. 9 Leyland. 47 Marshall. 20 Northern Counties. 7 Optare. 124 Plaxton. 11 Roe. 1 Van Hool. 79 Wright. 80 other.
Ops incl: local bus services, school contracts, private hire

FLYGHT TRAVEL

3A SPUR ROAD, COSHAM PO6 3DY.
Tel: 023 9232 7703.
Fax: 023 9238 2900.
Chairm: J. Stewart. **Tran Man**: T. Byng.
Admin/Fin: Ms P. Stewart.
Fleet: 13 - 7 coach, 2 midibus, 1 midicoach, 2 minibus, 1 minicoach.
Chassis: 3 DAF. 2 MAN. 2 Mercedes. 1 Optare. 5 Scania.
Ops incl: excursions & tours, private hire, express, continental tours, school contracts.
Livery: White/Red Pegasus.

GEMINI TRAVEL SOUTHAMPTON LTD

MARCHWOOD INDUSTRIAL PARK, NORTH ROAD, MARCHWOOD SO40 4BL
Tel: 023 8066 0066
Fax: 023 8087 1308

Dirs: Ken Hatch, Mark Bennett
Gen Man: Nigel Smith
Fleet: 10 - 2 single-deck coach. 4 midicoach, 4 minibus.
Chassis: 4 LDV. 4 Mercedes. 2 Volvo.
Bodies: 3 Optare. 2 Plaxton. 5 other.
Ops incl: private hire, school contracts.
Livery: White/Blue

HERRINGTON COACHES LTD

MANOR FARM, SANDLEHEATH ROAD, ALDERHOLT, FORDINGBRIDGE SP6 3EG
Tel: 01425 652842
Props: A G Herrington, Mrs J Herrington
Fleet: 6 - 3 coach, 3 minibus.
Chassis: 1 Dennis. 3 Mercedes. 2 Volvo.
Bodies: 1 Crest. 1 Jonckheere. 2 Mercedes. 1 Plaxton. 1 Van Hool.
Ops incl: local bus services, school contracts, private hire.
Livery: Grey/Red.

HYTHE & WATERSIDE COACHES LTD

1A HIGH STREET, HYTHE SO45 6AG
Tel: 023 8084 4788
Fax: 023 8020 7284
E-mail: enquiries@watersidetours.co.uk
Web site: www.watersidetours.co.uk
Fleetname: Waterside Tours
Man Dir: Roy Barker **Dirs**: Pam Parker, Jackie Withey
Fleet: 7 - 4 coach, 1 minibus, 2 midicoach.
Chassis: 1 BMC. 1 Mercedes. 1 Toyota. 4 Volvo.
Bodies: 4 Berkhof. 1 Caetano. 2 other.
Ops incl: excursions & tours, private hire, continental tours, school contracts.
Livery: White/Burgundy/Gold.

LUCKETTS TRAVEL

BROADCUT, WALLINGTON, FAREHAM PO16 8TB
Tel: 01329 823755
Fax: 01329 823855
E-mail: info@lucketts.co.uk
Web site: www.lucketts.co.uk
Chmn: David Luckett **Joint Man Dirs**: Steven Luckett, Ian Luckett **Eng Dir**: Mark Jordan **Ops Man**: Tony Harper
Fleet: 33 - 29 coach, 2 double-deck coach, 2 minicoach.
Chassis: 1 DAF. 8 Dennis. 2 Neoplan. 18 Scania. 2 Toyota. 2 Volvo.
Bodies: 5 Berkhof. 1 Bova. 2 Caetano. 21 Irizar. 2 Neoplan. 4 Plaxton
Ops incl: excursions & tours, private hire, continental tours, school contracts.
Livery: Grey/White/Orange

*MARCHWOOD MOTORWAYS

200 SALISBURY ROAD, TOTTON SO40 3PE
Tel: 023 8066 3700
Fax: 023 8066 7762
Man Dir: A Carter **Ops Man**: A Hornby
Fleet: 48 - 22 single-deck bus, 18 coach, 3 double-deck coach, 3 midicoach, 2 minibus.
Bodies: 3 Caetano. 1 Duple. 7 Ikarus. 11 Optare. 10 Van Hool. 13 Wright. 7 other.
Ops incl: local bus services, school contracts, excursions & tours, private hire, continental tours.
Ticket system: Wayfarer
(Part of the Go-Ahead Group)

*MERVYN'S COACHES

THE NEW COACH HOUSE, INNERSDOWN, MICHELDEVER SO21 3BW
Tel/Fax: 01962 774574
Web site: www.mervynscoaches.com
Ptnrs: Mervyn Annetts, Carol Annetts, Linda Porter, James Annetts.
Fleet: 6 - 3 coach, 2 midicoach, 1 minicoach
Chassis: 5 Bedford. 1 Volvo.
Chassis: 1 Duple. 4 Plaxton. 1 other
Ops incl: local bus services, school contracts, excursions & tours, private hire.
Livery: Brown/Cream
Ticket System: Setright

JOHN PIKE COACHES

77 SCOTT CLOSE, WALWORTH INDUSTRIAL ESTATE, ANDOVER SP10 5NU.
Tel: 01264 334328.
Fax: 01264 334329.
Props: J. S. Pike, Jenny Pike, C. Pike, R. Pike.
Fleet: 15 - 4 double-deck bus, 5 coach, 2 midicoach, 4 minibus.
Chassis: Bristol. Ford Transit. Iveco. Mercedes. Volvo.
Bodies: Mercedes. Plaxton. ECW.
Ops incl: local bus services, school contracts, excursions & tours, private hire, continental tours.
Livery: White.
Ticket System: Setright.

PRINCESS COACHES LTD

PRINCESS COACHES GARAGE, BOTLEY ROAD, WEST END, SOUTHAMPTON SO30 3HA
Tel: 023 8047 2150
Fax: 023 8039 9944
E-mail: princesscoaches@aol.com
Web site: www.princesscoaches.com
Dirs: Y B Barfoot, D K Brown, P A Brown
Fleet: 16 - 12 coach, 2 double-deck coach, 1 minibus, 1 minicoach.
Chassis: 1 Ford. 14 Scania. 1 Toyota.
Bodies: 2 Berkhof. 1 Caetano. 8 Irizar. 4 Jonckheere. 1 other.
Ops incl: private hire, school contracts, continental tours.
Livery: White with multi-coloured flashes

SEAVIEW SERVICES LTD
See Isle of Wight

SOLENT BLUE LINE

BARTON PARK, EASTLEIGH
SO50 6RR
Tel: 023 8061 4459
Fax: 023 8061 4234
E-mail: enquiries@solentblueline.com
Web site: www.solentblueline.com
Man Dir: P J Stockley **Fin Dir**: A R Hiles
Ops Man: Alex Hornby **Comm Man**:
P C Curtis **Eng Man**: Steve Prewett
Fleet: 72 - 45 double-deck bus, 19 single-deck bus, 2 open-top bus, 6 midibus.
Chassis: 2 Bristol. 24 Dennis. 6 Iveco. 20 Leyland. 20 Volvo.
Bodies: 5 Alexander. 22 ECW. 18 East Lancs. 14 Leyland. 2 Marshall/MCV. 4 Mellor. 7 Northern Counties. 2 Reeve Burgess. 12 Transbus.
Ops incl: local bus services
Livery: Blue
Ticket System: Wayfarer 3
(Part of the Go-Ahead Group)

SOLENT COACHES LTD

BROOKSIDE GARAGE, CROW LANE, RINGWOOD BH24 3EA
Tel: 01425 473188
Fax: 01425 473669
Recovery: 0784 326 6720/1
E-mail: enquiries@solentcoaches.co.uk
Web site: www.solentcoaches.co.uk
Man Dir/Co Sec: John Skew
Dir/Ch Eng: Paul Skew.
Fleet: 9 - 7 coach, 1 minibus, 1 midicoach.
Chassis: 1 Mercedes. 6 Scania. 1 SETRA. 1 Toyota.
Bodies: 1 Caetano. 2 Irizar. 1 Mercedes. 1 Setra. 4 Van Hool.
Ops incl: excursions & tours, private hire, continental tours, school contracts.
Livery: White/Blue

STAGECOACH HAMPSHIRE

THE BUS STATION, FESTIVAL PLACE, CHURCHILL WAY, BASINGSTOKE RG21 7BE
Tel: 0845 121 0180
Web site:
www.stagecoachbus/com/hampshire
Man Dir: Andrew Dyer. **Eng Dir**: Richard Alexander. **Fin Dir**: Martin Stoggell.
Div Man: Matthew Callow.
Fleet: 150 - 47 double-deck bus. 86 single-deck bus. 17 minibus.
Chassis: 4 Bristol, 53 Dennis, 16 Leyland, 15 Mercedes, 2 Optare. 60 Volvo.
Bodies: 138 Alexander. 4 ECW. 2 Optare. Plaxton.
Ops incl: local bus services, school contracts.

Livery: Blue/Red/Orange
Ticket System: Wayfarer.

STAGECOACH HANTS & SURREY

HALIMOTE ROAD, ALDERSHOT GU11 1NJ
Tel: 01256 464501.
Man Dir: Andrew Dyer. **Eng Dir**: Richard Alexander. **Fin Dir**: Martin Stoggell. **Div Man**: Philip Medlicott.
Fleet: 80 - 13 double-deck bus, 43 single-deck bus, 24 minibus.
Chassis: 37 Dennis. 6 Leyland. 24 Mercedes. 13 Volvo.
Bodies: Alexander. Plaxton.
Ops incl: local bus services, school contracts.
Livery: Blue/Red/Orange
Ticket System: Wayfarer

*SUMMERFIELD COACHES LTD

247 ALDERMOOR ROAD, ALDERMOOR, SOUTHAMPTON SO16 5NU
Tel: 023 8077 8717
Fax: 023 8032 0327
E-mail: summerfield@tcp.co.uk
Dirs: Tracey Ralph, Colin Ralph
Tran Man: Dave Wheeler
Fleet: 9 - 6 coach, 2 minibus, 1 minicoach.
Chassis: 1 LDV. 1 MAN. 1 Mercedes. 1 Toyota. 4 Volvo.
Bodies: 1 Berkhof. 3 Caetano. 2 Leyland. 2 Plaxton. 1 other.
Ops incl: school contracts, private hire, excursions & tours, continental tours.
Livery: Green/Gold

*TEST VALLEY TRAVEL

See Wiltshire

*TOP TRAVEL COACHES

169 NEW GREENHAM PARK, BASINGSTOKE RG19 6HN
Tel: 01256 397270
Fax: 01635 821128
Dirs: Simon Weaver
Fleet: 33 - 4 double-deck bus, 2 coach bus, 6 double-deck coach, 1 minicoach.
Chassis: 8 Bova. 4 DAF. 4 Dennis. 1 Mercedes. 10 Scania. 6 Volvo.
Bodies: 3 Berkhof. 8 Bova. 9 East Lancs. 7 Irizar. 1 MCW. 1 Plaxton. 4 Van Hool.
Ops incl: school contracts, private hire
Livery: Electric Blue
(Subsidiary of Weavaway Travel, Berkshire)

UNI-LINK

Tel: 023 8059 5974
Web site: www.uni-link.info
Transp Sers Man: Alec Gore
Fleet: 20 - 5 double-deck bus, 15 single-deck bus
Chassis: Dennis. Mercedes. Scania.
Bodies: Alexander. Caetano. East Lancs. Mercedes. Scania.
Ops incl: local bus services
Livery: White/Blue
Services operated for Uni-Link by Minerva Accord

VISION TRAVEL INTERNATIONAL LTD

12 BUNTING GARDENS, COWPLAIN, WATERLOOVILLE PO8 9UN
Tel: 023 9235 9168
Fax: 023 9236 1253
Recovery: 023 9259 1940
E-mail: visiontravels@aol.com
Web site: www.visiontravel.co.uk
Dirs: Peter R Sharpe, David J Sharpe, Rebecca Simmons
Fleet: 13 - 11 coach, 1 midicoach, 1 minibus
Chassis: 2 DAF. 1 Leyland. 2 MAN. 2 Mercedes. 5 Scania.
Bodies: 5 Ikarus. 1 Leyland. 2 Mercedes. 1 Neoplan.
Ops incl: school contracts, excursions & tours, private hire, continental tours.

*WHEELERS TRAVEL LTD

UNIT 9, GROVE FARM, UPPDER NORTH DRIVE, HEDGE END, SOUTHAMPTON SO30 4BG
Tel: 023 8047 1800
Fax: 023 8047 0414
E-mail: sales@wheelerstravel.co.uk
Web site: www.wheelerstravel.co.uk
Dirs: D Wheeler, Lorraine Wheeler **Gen Man**: Paul Barker **Tran Man**: Keith Trenchard **Traff Man**: Nigel Taylor **Ch Eng**: Allan Cross
Fleet: 25 - 12 coach, 5 midicoach, 4 minibus, 4 disabled bus.
Chassis: 1 Ayats. 1 Bova. 4 Dennis. 2 Iveco. 1 MAN. 2 Scania. 1 Volvo.
Bodies: 1 Ayats. 1 Beulas. 3 Berkhof. 1 Bova. 2 Irizar. 2 Marcopolo. 2 Plaxton.
Ops incl: private hire, school contracts, continental tours.
Livery: Blue/Orange

Hampshire

A/c	Air conditioning
	Vehicles suitable for disabled
	Coach(es) with galley facilities
wc	Coach(es) with toilet facilities
	Seat belt-fitted vehicles
R	Recovery service available (not 24 hr)
R24	24hr recovery service
	Replacement vehicle available
T	Toilet-drop facilities available
	Vintage vehicle(s) available
	Open top vehicle(s)

HEREFORDSHIRE

BOWYER'S COACHES
QUARRY GARAGE, PETERCHURCH HR2 0TF.
Tel: 01981 550206.
Prop: Fernley C. Anning, Anthony H. Anning.
Fleet: 9 - 5 coach, 4 minibus.
Chassis: Bedford. LDV.
Ops incl: private hire, school contracts.
Livery: White/Red.

BROMYARD OMNIBUS COMPANY
STREAMHALL GARAGE, LINTON TRADING ESTATE, BROMYARD HR7 4QL
Tel: 01885 482782
Fax: 01885 482127
Prop: Martin Perry **Fleet Eng**: Michael Simcock
Fleet: 11 - 6 single-deck bus, 3 coach, 1 midibus, 1 minicoach.
Chassis: 1 Bedford. 2 Leyland. 2 Mercedes. 4 Optare. 1 Volvo. 1 Trojan.
Bodies: 2 Autobus. 1 Caetano. 1 Duple. 4 Optare. 2 Plaxton. 1 Trojan.
Ops incl: local bus services, school contracts, privte hire.
Livery: Red/Cream
Ticket System: Wayfarer Saver

COACH COMPANIONS LTD
MAGNOLIA HOUSE, 12 ST BOTOLPH'S GREEN, LEOMINSTER HR6 8ER
Tel: 01568 620279
Fax: 01568 616906
E-mail: enquiries@coachcompanions.co.uk
Web site: www.coachcompanions.co.uk
Dir: Richard Asghar-Sandys
Fleet: 1 midicoach.
Chassis: 1 Mercedes.
Bodies: 1 other.
Ops incl: private hire.
Livery: White

D R M BUS AND CONTRACT SERVICES
THE COACH GARAGE, BROMYARD HR7 4NT
Tel: 01885 483219
Prop: David R. Morris
Fleet: 9 single-deck bus
Chassis: 3 Scania. 6 Volvo.
Bodies: 2 Alexander. 3 East Lancs. 1 Leyland National. 3 Omnicity.
Ops incl: local bus services, school contracts.
Livery: Blue/Silver-White
Ticket System: Wayfarer 3

GOLDEN PIONEER TRAVEL
BRANDON, REDHILL, HEREFORD HR2 8BH
Tel: 01432 274307
Fax: 01432 275809

Prop: Bryan Crockett **Dir**:J Crockett.
Fleet: 5 coach, 1 minicoach.
Chassis: incl. 1 Scania. 1 Toyota.
Bodies: 2 Beulas. 1 Mercedes. 1 Van Hool.
Ops incl: school contracts, excursions & tours, private hire, continental tours.
Livery: Black/Gold/Red/Green

GOLD STAR TRAVEL
See Worcestershire

P. W. JONES COACHES
HILBROY GARAGE, BURLEY GATE, HEREFORD HR1 3QL
Tel: 01432 820214
Fax: 01432 820521
Recovery: 01432 820214
E-mail: coaches@p.w.jones.com
Owner: Philip W Jones
Fleet: 18 - 16 single-deck coach, 1 midicoach, 1 minicoach.
Chassis: 1 Bedford. 1 Bova. 13 Dennis. 1 MAN. 1 Mercedes. 1 Neoplan. 1 Toyota.
Bodies: 1 Bova. 1 Caetano. 1 Duple. 1 Marcopolo. 1 Neoplan. 14 Plaxton.
Ops incl: excursions & tours, private hire, continental tours, school contracts., express
Livery: White/Blue

*LUGG VALLEY PRIMROSE TRAVEL LTD
SOUTHERN AVENUE, LEOMINSTER HR6 0QX
Tel: 01432 344341
Fax: 01432 356206
Man Dir: Mrs E Sankey **Sec**: Mrs E Sankey
Ops Man: J E Hodges **Eng**: Paul Bird
Fleet: 26 - single-deck bus, coach.
Chassis: 1 BMC. 3 Dennis. 1 Marshall. 11 Optare. 2 Scania. 6 Volvo.
Bodies: 1 Berkhof. 1 BMC. 1 Carlyle. 2 Irizar. 1 Jonckheere. 11 Optare. 9 Plaxton.
Ops incl: local bus services, school contracts, excursions & tours, private hire, continental tours.
Livery: Cream
Ticket System: ERG

M & S COACHES OF HEREFORDSHIRE LTD
CROFTWELL HOUSE, KIMBOLTON, LEOMINSTER HR6 0HD
Tel: 01568 612803
Dir: Maurice Peruffo
Fleet: 7 - 4 midicoach, 3 minicoach.
Chassis: 4 Mercedes. 2 Toyota. 1 Volvo.
Bodies: 2 Caetano. 2 Mercedes. 1 Optare. 1 Van Hool. 1 other.
Ops incl: school contracts, private hire

NEWBURY COACHES
LOWER ROAD TRADING ESTATE, LEDBURY HR8 2DJ.
Tel: 01531 633483.
Fax: 01531633650.
Livery: Blue/White.

SARGANTS BROS LTD
MILL STREET, KINGTON HR5 3AL
Tel/Fax: 01544 230481
E-mail: mike@sargantsbros.com
Web site: www.sargantsbros.com
Prop: Michael Sargant
Fleet: 29 - 1 double-deck bus, 2 single-deck bus, 6 single-deck coach, 10 midibus, 1 midicoach, 9 minibus.
Chassis: 4 Bedford, 1 DAF, 1 Dodge, 4 Ford Transit, 1 LAG, 2 Leyland, 7 Mercedes, 4 Optare, 2 Renault, 1 Volvo, 2 Talbot.
Bodies: 1 Alexander, 2 Jonckheere, 7 Optare, 6 Plaxton, 2 Reeve Burgess, 2 PMT, 1 LAG, 1 Cymric, 2 Freeway, 4 Ford. 1 Renault.
Ops incl: local bus services, school contracts, private hire.
Livery: Red
Ticket System: Wayfarer

SMITHS MOTORS (LEDBURY) LTD
COACH GARAGE, HOMEND, LEDBURY HR8 1BA.
Tel: 01531 632953.
Dirs: F. W. B. Sterry, M. Sterry.
Fleet: 11 - 8 coach, 2 midicoach, 1 minibus.
Chassis: 3 Bedford. 1 Ford. 1 Iveco. 4 Leyland. 2 Mercedes.
Bodies: 1 Caetano. 3 Duple. 3 Plaxton. 2 Van Hool. 1 PMT. 1 Devon.
Ops incl: local bus services, continental tours.
Livery: White with Green/Blue/Red stripe.
Ticket System: Setright.

*STAGECOACH IN SOUTH WALES
See Torfaen

*YEOMANS CANYON TRAVEL LTD
21-23 THREE ELMS TRADING ESTATE, HEREFORD HR4 9PU
Tel: 01432 356201
Fax: 01432 356206
E-mail: nigelyeomans@aol.com
Dirs: N D & G H Yeomans **Sec**: S M T Yeomans **Traf Man**: N D Yeomans
Fleet: 35 - single-deck bus, coach, minibus.
Chassis: 2 BMC. 6 Dennis. 2 Ford Transit. 2 Leyland. 1 Neoplan. 6 Optare. 3 Scania. 13 Volvo.
Bodies: 2 Berkhof. 2 BMC. 1 Caetano. 2 Carlyle. 1 Duple. 1 Irizar. 2 Marcopolo. 1 Neoplan. 6 Optare. 13 Plaxton. 2 Van Hool. 1 Wadham Stringer.
Ops incl: local bus services, school contracts, excursions & tours, private hire, express, continental tours.
Livery: Cream
Ticket System: ERG

HERTFORDSHIRE

ABBEY TRAVEL LTD
WC 🎗 A/c

58 BURYMEAD ROAD, HITCHIN
SG5 1RT
Tel: 01462 421777/421888
Fax: 01462 421999
E-mail: rich@abbeytravel.co.uk
Web site: www.abbeytravel.co.uk
Man Dir: Peter Malyon **Dir**: Patricia Malyon
Co Man: Richard Window.
Co Sec: Leigh Featherstone
Fleet: 14 - 2 single-deck bus, 8 coach,
1 midibus, 2 minibus, 1 minicoach.
Chassis: 1 Dennis. 1 Ford Transit.
4 Mercedes. 1 Peugeot. 7 Volvo.
Bodies: 1 Berkhof. 1 Duple. 2 Jonckheere.
1 Mercedes. 4 Plaxton. 3 Reeve Burgess.
1 Van Hool. 1 Peugeot.
Ops incl: excursions & tours, private hire,
continental tours, school contracts.
Livery: White/Blue.

ALPHA PERSONALISED TRAVEL LTD 🎗
300 HIGH ROAD, LEAVESDEN
WD25 7EB
Tel/Fax: 01923 202052.
Chmn: G. Picton. **Man Dir**: D. Green.
Co Sec: J. Foster.
Fleet: 3 - 1 midicoach, 2 minibus
Chassis: 2 Ford Transit. 1 Toyota.
Bodies: 1 Caetano.
Ops incl: excursions & tours, private hire,
continental tours.
Livery: Blue/Orange/White.

*A R TRAVEL LTD
🎗 A/c R24 ✏

40 PERRY GREEN, HEMEL
HEMPSTEAD HP2 7ND
Tel: 01442 408093
Fax: 01442 389899
E-mail: artravelltd@hotmail.com
Web site: www.artravelltd.co.uk
Dir: Terry Hill
Fleet: 3 minibus
Chassis/bodies: 2 Mercedes. 1 VW.
Ops incl: excursions & tours, private
hire,school contracts.
Livery: White /Silver

*CANTABRICA COACH HOLIDAYS
🎗 WC A/c T

9 ELTON WAY, WATFORD
WD25 8HH
Tel: 01923 247444
Web site:
www.cantabricacoaches.co.uk
Dir: David Stewart
Fleet: incl single-deck coach
Chassis: Volvo.
Bodies: Berkhof
Ops incl: private hire, continental tours.
Livery: Blue/Red

*CHAMBERS COACHES (STEVENAGE) LTD
♿ 🎗 WC A/c

38 TRENT CLOSE, STEVENAGE
SG1 3RT
Tel: 01438 352920
Fax: 01462 486616
E-mail:
chamberscoaches@btconnect.com
Web site:
www.chamberscoaches.com
Dirs: C Chambers, M Chambers,
Mrs S Chambers **Co Sec**: Mrs D C Tidey.
Fleet: 22 - 17 single-deck coach,
3 midicoach, 2 minicoach
Chassis: Dennis. Ford. Leyland. Volvo.
Bodies: Caetano. Leyland. Marcopolo.
Transbus.
Ops incl: excursions & tours, school
contracts, private hire
Livery: White/Red/Blue

*GALLEON TRAVEL LTD
🎗 WC A/c R ✏

THE COACH HOUSE, FOXHOLES,
LONDON ROAD, HERTFORD
SG13 7NT
Tel: 01992 503393
Fax: 01992 503515
Recovery: 01992 503707
E-mail:
galleontravel@btopenworld.com
Web site: www.galleontravel.co.uk
Man Dir: Helen Bowden **Ops Dir**: Mark
Bowden **Priv Hire Dir**: Megan Baker
Gen Man: Steve Stapleton
Eng Man: Derek Collier
Business Man: James Doherty
Fleet: 37 - 7 double-deck bus, 20 single-
deck bus, 5 coach, 2 double-deck coach,
2 minibus
Chassis: 1 Ayats. 28 Dennis. 1 MAN.
3 Optare. 4 Scania.
Bodies: 2 Alexnder. 1 Ayats. 1 Berkhof.
1 Carlyle. 6 East Lancs. 3 Irizar. 2 Leyland.
4 Marshall. 14 Plaxton. 2 Transbus. 1 UVG.
Ops incl: local bus services, school
contracts, excursions & tours, private hire,
continental tours.
Livery: Yellow/Red/Blue (Bus), Maroon
(Coach)
Ticket system: Almex A90

*GOLDEN BOY COACHES LTD
WC 🎗 A/c ✏ T

JOHN TERENCE HOUSE,
GEDDINGS ROAD, HODDESDON
EN11 0NT
Tel: 01992 465747
Fax: 01992 450957
E-mail: sales@goldenboy.co.uk
Web site: www.goldenboy.co.uk
Joint Man Dirs: G A McIntyre, T P McIntyre
Tran Man: G Jaikens **Ch Eng**: P Murdoch
Fleet: 33 - 2 single-deck bus, 16 coach,
12 midicoach, 3 minicoach.
Chassis: 2 Dennis. 15 Mercedes. 16 Volvo.
Bodies: 2 Alexander. 2 Crest. 1 Euro.
1 Optare. 9 Plaxton. 2 Sitcar. 16 Van Hool.
Ops incl: local bus services, private hire,
school contracts.
Livery: Black/Red/Gold.
Ticket System: Wayfarer

GRAVES COACHES & MINIBUSES 🎗
134 WINFORD DRIVE DRIVE,
BROXBOURNE EN10 6PN
Tel/Fax: 01992 445556
E-mail: m.graves@btinternet.com
Prop: Michael Graves
Fleet: 2 -1 minicoach, 1 minibus
Chassis: 1 Mercedes. 1 Toyota.
Bodies: 1 Caetano. 1 Mercedes.
Ops incl: private hire, school contracts.

GROVE COACHES 🎗
101 MANDEVILLE ROAD,
HERTFORD SG13 8JL
Tel: 01992 583417
Fleetname: Pride of Hertford
Driver/operator: R A Bowers
Fleet: 1 coach.
Chassis: Volvo. **Body**: Plaxton.
Ops incl: private hire, school contracts.
LIvery: Brown/Orange

KENZIES COACHES LTD
WC 🎗 A/c

6 ANGLE LANE, SHEPRETH
SG8 6QH
Tel: 01763 260288
Fax: 01763 262012
Fleet: 25 coach.
Chassis: 2 Bedford. 1 Scania. 22 Volvo.
Bodies: 6 Plaxton. 19 Van Hool.
Ops incl: private hire, school contracts.

*LITTLE JIM'S 🎗
1 CASTLE STREET, BERKHAMSTED
HP4 2BQ
Tel: 01442 870029
Fax: 01442 877217
E-mail: littlejimbuses@aol.com
Prop: James H Petty
Fleet: 2 - 1 midibus, 1 midicoach.
Chassis: 2 Mercedes.
Bodies: 1 Plaxton. 1 Reeve Burgess..
Ops incl: local bus services, excursions &
tours, private hire, continental tours.
Livery: Variable.
Ticket System: Almex (manual)

A/c	Air conditioning	✏	Replacement vehicle available
♿	Vehicles suitable for disabled	T	Toilet-drop facilities available
🍽	Coach(es) with galley facilities		Vintage vehicle(s) available
WC	Coach(es) with toilet facilities		Open top vehicle(s)
🎗	Seat belt-fitted vehicles		
R	Recovery service available (not 24 hr)		
R24	24hr recovery service		

*MARSHALLS COACHES

FIRBANK WAY, LEIGHTON BUZZARD LU7 4YP
Tel: 01525 376077
Fax: 01525 850967
Recovery: 01525 375301
E-mail: info@marshalls-coaches.co.uk
Web site: www.marshalls-coaches.co.uk
Fleetname: MCE Ltd
Prop: G Marshall **Ops Man**: I White
Wkshp Man: R Winters
Fleet: 28 - 3 double-deck bus, 22 coach, 2 double-deck coach, 1 midicoach.
Chassis: 3 Ayats. 4 Dennis. 3 Iveco. 2 Leyland. 1 Mercedes. 15 Volvo.
Bodies: 3 Ayats. 3 Beulas. 1 Caetano. 3 East Lancs. 5 Jonckheere. 1 Mercedes. 10 Plaxton.
Ops incl: private hire, school contracts, continental tours.
Livery: Blue/Multicoloured.

*MASTER TRAVEL COACHES

9-12 PEARTREE FARM, WELWYN GARDEN CITY AL7 3UW
Tel: 01707 334040
Fax: 01707 334366
E-mail: mastertravel@btclick.com
Web site: www.master-travel.co.uk
Ptnrs: R J Goulden, S Goulden
Fleet: 20
Chassis: 1 BMC. 4 Dennis. 1 Ford Transit. 3 Iveco. 4 LDV. 3 Mercedes. 1 Neoplan. 1 Renault. 2 Scania.
Bodies: 1 Berkhof. 1 BMC. 2 Irizar. 2 Marcopolo. 3 Mercedes. 1 Neoplan. 1 Northern Counties. 1 Optare. 8 other.
Ops incl: school contracts, private hire, continental tours.
Livery: White/Blue, White

MINIBUS SERVICES

773 ST ALBANS ROAD, WATFORD WD25 9LA
Tel: 01923 219107
Fax: 01923 219108
E-mail: minibusservices@btconnect.com
E-mail: www.minibusservices.uk.com
Prop: Russell Crowson
Fleet: 5 - 1 coach, 2 minibus, 2 midicoach
Chassis: 1 Iveco. 1 LDV. 1 Mercedes. 1 Renault. 1 Volvo.
Bodies: include Plaxton
Ops incl: school contracts, private hire, excursions & tours

PARKSIDE TRAVEL

PARADISE WILDLIFE PARK, WHITE STUBBS LANE, BROXBOURNE EN10 7QA
Tel: 01992 444477
Fax: 01992 465441
Fleetname: Parkside Travel
Dirs: P C Sampson, G F Sampson
Fleet: 7 minibus.
Chassis: 7 Ford Transit.
Ops incl: school contracts, private hire.
Livery: Light Blue

*PROVENCE PRIVATE HIRE (P.P.H. COACHES)

HEATH FARM LANE, ST ALBANS AL3 5AE
Tel: 01727 864988
Fax: 01727 855275
E-mail: office@pphcoaches.com
Web site: www.pphcoaches.com
Dirs: A. K. Hayes, R. F. Hayes
Ch Eng: D. Higgins
Fleet: 30 - 2 double-deck bus, 20 coach, 2 double-deck coach, 2 minibus, 4 minicoach.
Chassis: 1 DAF. 4 Dennis. 1 Duple. 1 Ford Transit. 1 LDV. 3 Leyland. 1 MCW. 3 Mercedes. 10 Scania. 2 Toyota. 3 Volvo. 1 other.
Bodies: 3 Caetano. 1 Duple. 4 East Lancs. 6 Irizar. 1 MCW. 2 Optare. 21 Plaxton. 2 UVG. 1 Van Hool.
Ops incl: excursions & tours, private hire, continental tours, school contracts.
Livery: Yellow.

REG'S COACHES LTD

C/O FOXHOLES FARM, LONDON ROAD, HERTFORD SG13 7NT
Tel: 01992 586302
Fax: 01992 586302
E-mail: regscoaches@btconnect.com
Web site: www.regscoaches.co.uk
Man Dir: T Hunt **Dir**: Mrs B Hunt **Ch Eng**: W Parlow
Fleet: 15 - 2 single-deck bus, 12 coach, 1 midicoach.
Chassis: 9 Dennis. 1 Mercedes. 5 Volvo.
Bodies: 1 Optare. 10 Plaxton. 1 Transbus. 2 Van Hool. 1 Wright.
Ops incl: local bus services, school contracts, excursions & tours, private hire.
Livery: Black/Green/Orange
Ticket System: Wayfarer 2/Almex

REYNOLDS DIPLOMAT COACHES

285 LOWER HIGH STREET, WATFORD WD17 2HY
Tel: 01923 296877
Fax: 01923 210020
E-mail: enquiries@reynoldscoaches.com
Web site: www.reynoldscoaches.com
Props: Richard Reynolds, Susan Reynolds
Ops Dir: Christopher Barker
Fleet: 18 - 13 coach, 3 double-deck coach, 2 midibus.
Chassis: 1 MAN. 3 Mercedes. 3 Scania. 3 Setra. 7 Volvo.
Bodies: 1 Caetano. 7 Jonckheere. 3 Neoplan. 1 Optare. 3 Setra. 3 Van Hool.
Ops incl: excursions & tours, private hire, continental tours, school contracts.
Livery: Gold

RICHMOND'S COACHES

THE GARAGE, BARLEY, ROYSTON SG8 8JA
Tel: 01763 848226
Fax: 01763 848105
E-mail: postbox@richmonds-coaches.co.uk
Web site: www.richmonds-coaches.co.uk
Dirs: David Richmond, Michael Richmond, Andrew Richmond **Sales & Mktg Man**: Rick Ellis **Asst Ops Man**: Craig Ellis **Ch Eng**: Patrick Granville **Exc & Tours Man**: Natalie Richmond
Fleet: 26 - 19 single-deck coach, 1 midicoach, 6 midibus.
Chassis: 6 Bova. 2 DAF. 1 Dennis. 5 Mercedes. 2 Optare. 10 Volvo.
Bodies: 1 Berkhof. 6 Bova. 2 Optare. 4 Plaxton. 12 Van Hool. 1 other.
Ops incl: local bus services, school contracts, excursions & tours, private hire, express, continental tours.
Livery: Chocolate/Cream

SHIRE COACHES

PO BOX 862, ST ALBANS AL1 9BT
Tel: 01772 832519
Fax: 01727 832548
E-mail: shirecoaches@btconnect.com
Web site: www.shirecoaches.co.uk
Ptnrs: Lynda Maney, Michael Maney
Fleet: 10 coach - 8 coach, 2 minibus.
Chassis: 1 Ayats. 1 Ford. 1 Mercedes. 6 Scania. 1 Volvo.
Bodies: incl: 1 UVG
Ops incl: school contracts, excursions & tours, private hire, continental tours.
Livery: Purple/Silver

SMITH BUNTINGFORD

CLAREMONT, BALDOCK ROAD, BUNTINGFORD SG9 9DJ
Tel/Fax: 01763 271516
Prop: Graham H Smith **Fleet Eng**: Stewart C Smith
Fleet: 6 minicoach.
Chassis: 1 Ford Transit. 3 Mercedes. 1 Renault. 1 Vauxhall
Bodies: 1 Autobus. 1 Courtside. 1 Ford. 1 Mellor. 1 Stanford.
Ops incl: private hire, school contracts
Livery: White/Orange

SMITHS OF TRING

THE GARAGE, WIGGINTON HP23 6EJ
Tel: 01442 823163
Dirs: G. A. Smith (**Man Dir**), Mrs S. N. Smith, J. Smith.
Fleet: 8 - 6 coach, 1 midicoach, 1 minicoach. **Chassis**: 2 Mercedes. 6 Volvo.
Bodies: 2 Mercedes. 1 Plaxton. 1 Reeve Burgess.
Ops incl: local bus services, excursions & tours, private hire, continental tours.
Livery: Red/Cream.

SOUTH MIMMS TRAVEL LTD

WARRENGATE ROAD, NORTH MIMMS AL9 7TU
Tel: 01707 660664
E-mail: info@southmimmstravel.com
Web site: www.southmimmstravel.co.uk
Man Dir: S. J. Griffiths.
Fleet: 10 coach.
Chassis: incl: Dennis, MCW, Neoplan, Volvo.
Bodies: incl: Berkhof, Bova, MCW, Neoplan, Plaxton.

Ops incl: school contracts, excursions & tours, private hire, continental tours.
Livery: Red/Black/Gold

SULLIVAN BUSES LTD

FIRST FLOOR, DEARDS HOUSE,
ST ALBANS ROAD, POTTERS BAR
EN6 3NE
Tel: 01707 646803
Fax: 01707 646804
E-mail: admin@sullivanbuses.com
Web site: www.sullivanbuses.com
Man Dir: Dean Sullivan
Fleet: 36 - 26 double-deck bus, 10 single-deck bus
Chassis: 3 AEC. 11 Leyland. 9 MCW. 10 Transbus. 2 Volvo.
Bodies: 7 Caetano. 1 Carlyle. 2 East Lancs. 11 Leicester. 9 MCW. 3 Park Royal. 3 Plaxton.
Ops incl: local bus services
Livery: Red
Ticket system: Wayfarer TGX

*TATES COACHES

44 HIGH STREET, MARKYATE
AL3 8PA
Tel: 01582 840297
Fax: 01582 840014
E-mail: tates-coaches@fsbdial.co.uk
Web site: www.tates-coaches.co.uk
Dirs: Alan Tate (**Co Sec**), Tony Tate, Stephen Tate
Fleet: 10 - 1 single-deck bus, 8 coach, 1 midicoach
Chassis: 1 Bova. 2 DAF. 1 Dennis. 1 Mercedes. 1 Neoplan. 4 Scania.
Bodies: 1 Bova. 1 Caetano. 2 Hispano. 4 Irizar. 1 Neoplan. 1 Wadham Stringer.
Ops incl: school contracts, excursions & tours, private hire, continental tours.
Livery: Cream/Blue/Orange

TERRY'S COACHES

45 HOMEFIELD ROAD,
HEMEL HEMPSTEAD HP2 4BZ
Tel: 01442 265850
Dirs: Terry Bunyan, Shirley Bunyan.
Fleet: 5 - 1 midibus, 2 midicoach, 2 minicoach.
Chassis: 1 Iveco. 1 LDV. 2 Mercedes.
Bodies: 1 Leicester. 2 Optare. 2 other.
Ops incl: school contracts, private hire.
Livery: Blue/White

TIMEBUS TRAVEL

See London

TRUSTLINE

THE COACH HOUSE, FOXHOLES,
LONDON ROAD, HERTFORD
SG13 7NT
Tel: 01922 503343
Fax: 01992 503515
Recovery: 01922 503707
E-mail: trustlineservices@talk21.com
Man Dir: Helen Bowden **Ops Dir**: Mark Bowden **Fleet Eng**: Derek Collier **Admin Man**: V Chessman
Fleet: 20 - 5 double-deck bus, 15 single-deck bus
Chassis: 14 Dennis. 4 Leyland. 1 MAN. 1 MCW.
Ops incl: local bus services
Livery: Yellow/Red/Blue
Ticket System: Almex A90

UNICORN COACHES LTD

PO BOX 45, HATFIELD AL9 5LD
Tel: 01707 269003
Tel: 01707 260039
E-mail: stsunicorn@aol.com
Web site: www.unicorncoaches.com
Man Dir: Mrs J E Pleshette
Gen Man: S T Saltmarsh

Fleet: 2 minibus.
Chassis: 2 Ford Transit.
Ops incl: school contracts, private hire.
Livery: Red/White

UNO LTD

GYPSY MOTH AVENUE, HATFIELD
BUSINESS PARK, HATFIELD
AL10 9BS
Tel: 01707 255764
Web site: www.unobus.info
Man Dir: Bill Hilton
Fleet: 42 single-deck bus.
Chassis: 4 Bluebird, 8 DAF, 19 Dennis, 1 Leyland, 1 Marshall, 4 Mercedes, 3 Optare.
Bodies: 4 Bluebird, 1 Mercedes, 1 East Lancs, 1 Leyland, 5 Marshall, 2 Northern Counties, 4 Optare, 1 Reeve Burgess, 20 Wright.
Ops incl: local bus services, school contracts.
Livery: Pink/Purple.
Ticket System: Wayfarer 3 Inform.

LEN WRIGHT BAND SERVICES LTD

9 ELTON WAY, WATFORD WD2 8HH.
Tel: 01923 238611.
Fax: 01923 230134.
E-mail: lwbs1@aol.com
Web site: www.lenwright.co.uk
Ops Dir: L. Collins.
Fleet: 13 - 6 coach, 5 double-deck coach (all sleeper), 2 minibus.
Chassis: 1 Bova. 2 Mercedes. 4 Scania. 6 Volvo.
Bodies: 1 Bova. 2 Irizar. 2 Jonckheere. 2 Plaxton. 4 Van Hool. 2 Autobus.
Ops incl: specialist private hire.
Livery: Grey.

ISLE OF WIGHT

AWAY DAYS

56 WILTON ROAD, SHANKLIN
PO37 7BZ
Tel: 01983 862774
Fax: 01983 864315
E-mail: awaydays@supanet.com
Website: www.awaydaysiowco.uk
Props: Roy Townend, Hedda Townend
Fleet: 3 coach
Chassis: 2 Iveco. 1 Scania.
Bodies: 2 Beulas. 1 Berkhof.
Ops incl: school contracts, excursions & tours, private hire, continental tours.
Livery: White with orange lettering and multi-coloured kite.

GANGES COACHES

77 PLACE ROAD, COWES PO31 7AE
Tel: 01983 296666
Fax: 01983 296666
Prop: John Gange
Fleet: 9 - 4 coach, 3 midicoach, 1 minibus, 1 minicoach.
Chassis: 1 AEC. 1 Bedford. 1 Ford. 1 Leyland. 3 Mercedes. 1 Renault. 1 Peugeot/Talbot
Bodies: 2 Duple. 1 Mercedes. 3 Plaxton. 3 other.
Ops incl: private hire
Livery: Red/Cream and Blue/Cream

GRAND HOTEL TOURS LTD (KIM'S COACHES)

GRAND HOTEL, CULVER PARADE,
SANDOWN PO36 8QA.
Tel: 01983 402236.
Fax: 01983 406784.
Fleetname: Grand Tours.
Prop: R. J. H. & M. A. Hayter.
Sec: Mrs Marilyn Gerrard. **Traf Man**: G. Worrall. **Gen Man**: R. H. J. Hayter.
Fleet: 3 coach.
Chassis: DAF. Dennis. Scania.
Bodies: Duple. Van Hool. LAG.
Ops incl: excursions & tours, private hire.
Livery: Yellow/White.

A/C	Air conditioning		Seat belt-fitted vehicles		Replacement vehicle available
	Vehicles suitable for disabled	R	Recovery service available (not 24 hr)	T	Toilet-drop facilities available
	Coach(es) with galley facilities				Vintage vehicle(s) available
WC	Coach(es) with toilet facilities	R24	24hr recovery service		Open top vehicle(s)

Hertfordshire / Isle of Wight

ISLAND COACH SERVICES LTD

UNIT D10, SPITHEAD BUSINESS CENTRE, NEWPORT ROAD, SANDOWN PO36 9PH
Tel: 01983 408080
Fax: 01983 408808
Website: www.islandcoachservices.co.uk
E-mail: info@islandcoachservices.co.uk
Dir: R J Long **Tran Man**: D Draper
Fleet: 11 coach
Chassis: 1 DAF. 1 Dennis. 1 Mercedes. 8 Volvo.
Bodies: 2 Caetano. 2 Jonckheere. 1 Mercedes. 1 Neoplan. 3 Plaxton. 2 Van Hool.
Ops incl: excursions & tours, private hire, continental tours, school contracts.
Livery: Blue flash/White.

ISLE OF WIGHT COUNTY TRANSPORT DEPARTMENT

21 WHITCOMBE ROAD, NEWPORT PO30 1YS
Tel: 01983 823784.
Fax: 01983 825818.
Fleetname: Wightbus.
Tran Man: A. A. Morris. **Ops Man**: J. Lamb.
Fleet: 27 - 1 double-deck bus, 13 single-deck bus, 2 coach, 11 midibus.
Chassis: 13 Dennis. 1 Ford. 2 Leyland. 11 Mercedes.
Bodies: 2 Caetano. 1 Duple. 1 ECW. 1 Reeve Burgess. 15 Wadham Stringer. 1 Wright. 2 LCB. 1 Mellor. 1 Steedrive. 2 Withey.
Ops incl: local bus services, school contracts, excursions & tours, private hire.
Livery: White with Orange and Blue stripes.
Ticket System: Setright.

KARDAN TRAVEL LTD

490 NEWPORT ROAD, COWES PO31 8QU
Tel/Fax: 01983 520995
E-mail: info@kardan.co.uk
Web site: www.kardan.co.uk
Dir: R L Hodgson
Fleet: 5 coach
Chassis: 1 Leyland. 2 Setra. 2 Volvo.
Bodies: 3 Plaxton. 2 Setra.
Ops incl: private hire
Livery: Yellow/White

SEAVIEW SERVICES LTD
R24

SEAFIELD GARAGE, COLLEGE FARM ESTATE, FAULKNER LANE, SANDOWN PO36 9AZ
Tel: 01983 407070
Fax: 01983 407045
Recovery: 0773 923 7361
E-mail: mail@seaview-services.com
Web site: www.seaview-services.com
Chmn: P Robinson **Man Dirs**: A Robinson, Mrs M Robinson **Ops Man**: Karen Heathfield **Ch Eng**: Peter Brand
Co Tour Man: Mairi Robinson
Fleet: 11 - 10 coach, 1 min icoach.
Chassis: 2 Iveco. 1 Toyota. 8 Volvo.
Bodies: 2 Beulas. 2 Caetano. 7 Van Hool.
Ops incl: excursions & tours, private hire, continental tours, express, school contracts.
Livery: Green/Red

*THE SOUTHERN VECTIS OMNIBUS CO LTD
R24

NELSON ROAD, NEWPORT PO30 1RD
Tel: 01983 522456
Fax: 01983 524961
Recovery: 01983 821135
E-mail: v.gibbs@southernvectis.com
Web site: www.islandbuses.info
Man Dir: Alex Carter **Ops Dir**: Andrew Wickham **Fin Dir**: Matt Dolphin
Acting Eng Dir: Vernon Gibbs
Ops/Comm Man: Marc Morgan-Huws
Fleet: 94 - 54 double-deck bus, 26 single-deck bus, 2 coach, 10 open-top bus, 2 midibus.
Chassis: 4 Bristol. 28 Dennis. 2 Iveco. 24 Leyland. 7 Mercedes. 26 Volvo. 3 other.
Bodies: 4 ECW. 15 Leyland. 1 Marshall. 1 Mellor. 7 Mercedes. 28 Northern Counties. 28 Plaxton. 2 Transbus. 6 UVG. 3 other
Ops incl: local bus services, school contracts, excursions and tours, private hire.
Livery: Green/Red/Blue/Orange
Ticket system: Wayfarer
(Part of the Go-Ahead Group)

*WIGHTROLLER COACHES
R24

UNIT C7, SPITHEAD BUSINESS CENTRE, NEWPORT ROAD, SANDOWN PO36 9PH
Tel: 01983 404028
Fax: 01983 404772
E-mail: wightrollers@supanet.com
Web site: www.wightrollers.co.uk
Dirs: Patric Steele, Tracey Bryant, Geoff Bryant **Ch Eng**: Colin Steele
Fleet: 16 - 14 coach, 1 minibus, 1 minicoach
Chassis: 1 DAF. 3 Dennis. 2 MAN. 2 Mercedes. 1 Renault. 1 Setra. 6 Volvo.
Bodies: 5 Caetano. 4 Jonckheere. 3 Plaxton. 1 Renault. 1 Toyota. 2 Van Hool.
Ops incl: school contracts, excursions & tours, private hire, continental tours.

JOHN WOODHAMS VINTAGE TOURS

GROVE ROAD, RYDE PO33 3LH
Tel/Fax: 01983 812147
E-mail: vintagetours@btconnect.com
Web site: www.vintagetours.net
Prop: John Woodhams
Fleet: 2 midicoach.
Chassis: 2 Bedford.
Bodies: 2 Duple.
Ops incl: excursions & tours, private hire

KENT

ARRIVA SOUTHERN COUNTIES

INVICTA HOUSE, ARMSTRONG ROAD, MAIDSTONE ME15 6TX
Tel: 01622 697000
Fax: 01622 697001
Web site: www.arriva.co.uk
Man Dir: Heath Williams
Fleet: 153 - double-deck bus, single-deck bus, minibus, midibus, coach.
Chassis: 20 DAF. 60 Dennis. 1 Mercedes. 6 Optare. 10 Scania. 28 Volvo. 21 other.
Ops incl: local bus services, school contracts, excursions & tours, express, continental tours, private hire.
Livery: Blue/Cream.
Ticket System: Wayfarer 3 & TGX150

ASM COACHES

8 THE OAZE, WHITSTABLE CT5 4TQ
Tel: 01227 280254
Fax: 01227 280467
E-mail: asm.coaches@virgin.net
Props: Steven R Morrish, Alison Morrish.
Fleet: 2 minicoach
Chassis: 2 Mercedes.
Ops incl: school contracts, private hire, continental trips.
Livery: Purple/White

AUTOCAR BUS & COACH SERVICES LTD

64 WHETSTED ROAD, FIVE OAK GREEN, TONBRIDGE TN12 6RT
Tel: 01892 833830
Fax: 01892 836977
Dir: Eric Baldock **Fleet Eng**: Ray Tompsett
Fleet: 8 - 4 single-deck bus, 2 coach, 1 double-deck coach, 1 midicoach.
Chassis: 1 DAF. 1 Dennis. 4 Leyland. 1 Mercedes. 1 Scania.
Bodies: 1 Alexander. 1 Duple. 2 East Lancs. 2 Plaxton. 1 Wadham Stringer. Wright.
Ops incl: local bus services, school

contracts, private hire.
Livery: White/Purple (two shades)
Ticket System: Wayfarer 2

BRITANNIA COACHES

HOLLOW WOOD ROAD, DOVER
CT17 0UB
Tel: 01304 228111
Fax: 01304 215350
E-mail: enq@britannia-coaches.co.uk
Web site: www.britannia-coaches.co.uk.
Ptnrs: Barry Watson, Danny Lawson.
Fleet: 30 minicoach.
Chassis/bodies: 20 Mercedes. 10 Renault.
Ops incl: private hire, school contracts, excursions & tours.

BROWNS COACHES

OAKTREE COTTAGE, MANOR POUND LANE, BRABOURNE, ASHFORD TN25 5LG.
Tel: 01303 813555
Fax: 01303 812070
Prop: Patrick Browne
Fleet: 4 - 3 coach, 1 minibus.
Chassis: 1 LDV. . 3 Volvo.
Ops incl: school contracts, private hire

BUZZLINES

UNIT G1, LYMPNE INDUSTRIAL PARK, LYMPNE CT21 4LR
Tel: 01303 261870
Fax: 01303 230093
Recovery: 07767 475225
E-mail: sales@buzzlines.co.uk
Web site: www.buzzlines.co.uk
Dir: Mrs K Busbridge
Man Dir: N. P. Busbridge
Eng Man: D Lange
Ops Man: G Creasey
Fleet: 56 - 2 single-deck bus, 28 coach, 3 double-deck coach, 3 midicoach, 15 minbus, 5 people carrier.
Chassis: 1 Dennis. 4 Ford Transit. 11 Mercedes. 11 Neoplan. 8 Scania. 2 Seat. 7 Setra. 4 Toyota. 5 Volvo. 3 Volkswagen.
Bodies: 4 Caetano. 4 Ford Transit. 6 Irizar. 11 Neoplan. 7 Setra. 11 Mercedes. 5 Volvo. 3 Volkswagen. 2 Seat. 2 PTS.
Ops incl: local bus services, school contracts, excursions & tours, private hire, continental tours.
Livery: Metallic blue.

CENTRAL MINI COACHES

177 LOWER ROAD, DOVER
CT17 0RE.
Tel/Fax: 01304 823030.
Prop: P. Hull.
Fleet: 6 - 5 minibus, 1 minicoach.
Chassis: 3 Bedford. 1 Mercedes. 1 Renault.
Ops incl: private hire, school contracts.

*CHALKWELL COACH HIRE & TOURS

195 CHALKWELL ROAD, SITTINGBOURNE ME10 1BJ
Tel: 01795 423982
Fax: 01795 431855
E-mail: coachhire@chalkwell.co.uk
Web site: www.chalkwell.com
Fleet Name: Chalkwell
Man Dir: Clive Eglinton **Ops Man**: Roland Eglinton **Coach Reservations Man**: Steve Bolton
Fleet: 46 - 2 double-deck bus, 4 single-deck bus, 19 coach, 14 midibus, 5 midicoach, 2 minicoach.
Chassis: 17 Dennis. 1 LDV. 2 Leyland. 19 Mercedes. 2 Optare. 5 Volvo.
Bodies: 6 Alexander. 2 East lancs. 2 Jonckheere. 3 Optare. 17 Plaxton. 3 UVG. 6 Wadham Stringer. 4 Wright. 3 other.
Ops incl: local bus services
Livery: White/Red/Black
Ticket System: Almex A90

*CROSSKEYS COACHES

CROSSKEYS BUSINESS PARK, CAESARS WAY, FOLKESTONE CT19 4AL
Tel: 01303 272625
Fax: 01303 274085
E-mail: alan@crosskeys.uk.com
Web site: www.crosskeys.uk.com
Prop: Alan Johnson
Fleet: 24 - 2 single-deck bus, 19 coach, 3 minicoach.
Chassis: 9 Bova. 2 Leyland National. 3 Mercedes.
Bodies: 1 Jonckheere. 5 Plaxton. 1 Setra. 2 Van Hool.
Ops incl: school contracts, excursions & tours, private hire, continental tours.

ALAN DAWNEY HOLIDAYS

UNIT 6, TRANSIT WORKS, POWER STATION ROAD, HALFWAY, SHEERNESS ME12 3AD
Tel/Fax: 01795 662688
E-mail: dawneyholidays@aol.com
Dirs: Alan Dawney, Carole Dawney
Fleet: 9 - 3 coach, 6 minicoach.
Chassis: 1 MAN. 2 Volvo.
Bodies: include - 3 Caetano.
Ops incl: excursions & tours, private hire, continental tours.
Livery: White/Green/Yellow

EASTONWAYS LTD

MANSTON ROAD, RAMSGATE CT12 6HJ
Tel: 01843 588944
Fax: 01843 582300
E-mail: ele@eastonways.demon.co.uk
Web site: www.eastonways.demon.co.uk
Chmn/Co Sec E. L. Easton.

Man Dir: D. Austin **Dir**: Y. M. Easton.
Ops Man: S. Lee. **Eng**: E. Easton.
Fleet: 15 - 2 double-deck coach, 8 single-deck bus, 3 coach, 2 midicoach.
Chassis: 2 Bristol. 1 DAF. 1 Optare. 2 Toyota. 1 Volvo.
Bodies: 1 Caetano. 1 Duple. 2 Northern Counties. 8 Optare. 1 Van Hool.
Ops incl: local bus services, school contracts, private hire.
Livery: Coaches: Blue/Silver. Buses: Red.
Ticket System: Wayfarer.

*EUROLINK FOKESTONE

GREATWORTH, CANTERBURY ROAD, ETCHINGHILL, FOLKESTONE CT18 8BS
Tel: 01303 862767
Fax: 01303 862484
E-mail: eurolinkcoaches@btconnect.com
Ptnrs: Andy Williams, Lyn Williams
Fleet: 9 - 5 midicoach, 4 minicoach.
Chassis: 1 Ford Transit. 2 MAN. 4 Mercedes. 1 Renault. 1 Toyota.
Bodies: 3 Caetano. 1 Esker. 1 Mercedes. 1 Optare. 3 other.
Ops incl: school contracts, private hire.
Livery: White/Grey/Orange

FARLEIGH COACHES

ST PETERS WORKS, HALL ROAD, WOULDHAM, ROCHESTER ME1 3XL
Tel: 01634 201065.
Fax: 01634 660350.
Prop: D R Smith
Livery: White/Yellow/Red/Black.

FERRYMAN TRAVEL

RECTORY LANE NORTH, LEYBOURNE ME19 5HD.
Tel/Fax: 01732 843396
Fleet: 4 minibus.
Chassis: 3 DAF. 1 Ford Transit.
Ops incl: school contracts, excursions & tours, private hire, continental tours.

G & S TRAVEL

14 PYSONS ROAD, RAMSGATE CT12 6TS
Tel: 01843 591105.
Fax: 01843 596274.
E-mail: malc@pysons.freeserve.co.uk
Dirs: Shirley Rimmer, George Rimmer, Malcolm Wood **Ch Eng**: Robert Maunder
Fleet: 12 - 9 coach, 1 minibus, 2 midicoach.
Chassis: 1 LDV. 2 Toyota. 8 Volvo. 1 Van Hool
Bodies: 5 Caetano. 5 Plaxton. 1 Van Hool. 1 other.
Ops incl: school contracts, excursions & tours, private hire, continental tours.
Livery: White.

A/c	Air conditioning	![seat]	Seat belt-fitted vehicles	![key]	Replacement vehicle available
	Vehicles suitable for disabled	R	Recovery service available (not 24 hr)	T	Toilet-drop facilities available
	Coach(es) with galley facilities	R24	24hr recovery service		Vintage vehicle(s) available
wc	Coach(es) with toilet facilities				Open top vehicle(s)

127

GRIFFIN BUS
126 LONDON ROAD, DUNTON GREEN, SEVENOAKS

KENT COACH TOURS LTD
THE COACH STATION, MALCOLM SARGENT ROAD, ASHFORD TN23 6JW
Tel/Recovery: 01233 627330
Fax: 01233 612977
Web site: www.kentcoachtours.co.uk
Dirs: David Farmer, Ann Farmer, Andrew Farmer (**Co Sec**), Brian Farmer (**Ch Eng**)
Fleet: 13 - 1 single-deck bus, 7 coach, 5 minibus.
Chassis: 1 MAN. 5 Mercedes. 1 Optare. 7 Volvo
Bodies: 1 Optare. 12 Plaxton.
Ops incl: local bus services, school contracts, excursions & tours, private hire.
Livery: Blue
Ticket System: Wayfarer

KENT COUNTY COUNCIL
COMMERCIAL SERVICES, PASSENGER SERVICES, FORSTAL ROAD, AYLESFORD ME20 7HB
Tel: 01622 605935.
Fax: 01622 790338.
Tran Man: Kenneth Cobb **Ops Contr**: Roger Faunch. **Asst Ops Contr**: Mick Curd.
Fleet: 48 - 2 double-deck bus, 12 single-deck bus, 4 coach, 2 midibus, 1 midicoach, 27 minibus.
Chassis: 5 Dennis. 27 Iveco. 4 Leyland. 3 Mercedes. 4 Optare. 1 Volvo.
Bodies: 1 Alexander. 1 Caetano. 7 Leicester. 2 Leyland. 4 Optare. 6 Plaxton.27 Euromotive.
Ops incl: local bus services, school contracts, private hire.
Livery: Red on White.
Ticket System: Almex.

*THE KINGS FERRY TRAVEL GROUP
THE TRAVEL CENTRE, GILLINGHAM ME8 6HW
Tel: 01634 377577
Fax: 01634 370656
E-mail: sales@thekingsferry.co.uk
Web site: www.thekingsferry.co.uk
Chmn: P O'Neill **Man Dir**: S O'Neill
Dir: V Broster **Group Comm Man**: D Elford
Group Ops Man: I Fraser
Fleet: 77 - 1 double-deck bus, 3 single-deck bus, 55 coach, 7 double-deck coach, 1 open-top bus, 7 midicoach, 3 minicoach.
Chassis: 1 Bova. 2 DAF. 1 Daimler. 2 Dennis. 2 Iveco. 10 Mercedes. 1 Neoplan. 2 Optare. 29 Scania. 5 Setra. 12 Volvo.
Bodies: 2 Alexander. 17 Berkhof. 1 Bova. 1 Caetano. 1 Castrosua. 1 East Lancs. 3 Hispano. 2 Indcar. 8 Irizar. 3 Mercedes. 1 Neoplan. 10 Noge. 2 Optare. 1 Plaxton. 5 Setra. 5 Sunsundegui. 10 Van Hool. 4 other.
Ops incl: local bus services, school contracts, excursions & tours, private hire, continental tours.
Livery: Yellow with green stripe

KINGSMAN INTERNATIONAL TRAVEL
57 BRAMLEY AVENUE, FAVERSHAM ME13 8LP
Tel: 01795 531553
Fax: 01795 536798
E-mail: jonathanamancini@tiscali.co.uk
Prosp: J A Mancini, J Mancini
Fleet: 8 - 4 single-deck bus, 3 coach, 1 midicoach.
Chassis: 6 Mercedes. 3Neoplan.
Bodies: 4 Mercedes. 3 Neoplan. 2 Plaxton.
Ops incl: local bus services, excursions & tours, private hire, continental tours.

*LOGANS TOURS LTD
1 AND 2 THE COTTAGES, NORTHFLEET GREEN DA13 9PT
Tel: 01474 833876
E-mail: dave@loganstours.co.uk
Web site: www.loganstours.co.uk
Dir: David Logan
Fleet: 2 coach.
Chassis: 1 Dennis. 1 Raba.
Bodies: 1 Caetano. 1 Ikarus.
Ops incl: excursions & tours, private hire, continental tours
Livery: Pink/White

NEW ENTERPRISE COACHES
CANNON LANE, TONBRIDGE TN9 1PP.
Tel: 01732 355256.
Fax: 01732 357716.
Prop: Arriva Southern Counties.
Gen Man: Chris Lawrence.
Eng Man: Andy Weber.
Fleet: 24 - 5 double-deck bus, 2 single-deck bus, 17 coach.
Chassis: 8 DAF. 3 Leyland. 4 MCW. 3 Scania. 6 Volvo.
Bodies: 2 Caetano. 3 Duple. 4 MCW. 1 PMT. 11 Plaxton. 1 Reeve Burgess. 3 Van Hool.
Ops incl: local bus services, school contracts, excursions & tours, private hire, continental tours.
Livery: White/Red/Blue.
Ticket System: Wayfarer II.

*NU-VENTURE COACHES LTD
UNIT 2F, DEACON TRADING ESTATE, FORSTAL ROAD, AYLESFORD ME20 7SP
Tel: 01622 882288
Fax: 01622 718070
E-mail: nuventurecoachesltd@yahoo.co.uk
Web site: www.nu-venture.co.uk
Dir: D Quick **Co Sec**: N Kemp
Fleet: 28 - 11 double-deck bus, 14 single-deck bus, 3 coach.
Chassis: 10 Dennis. 13 Leyland. 1 MAN. 1 Mercedes. 2 Optare. 1 Scania
Bodies: 5 Alexander. 1 Caetano. 12 Leyland. 1 Marcopolo. 2 Marshall. 2 Optare. 1 Plaxton. 1 Reeve Burgess. 2 UVG. 1 Van Hool.
Ops incl: local bus services, school contracts, private hire, excursions & tours.
Livery: White/Blue
Ticket System: Wayfarer 3

*POYNTERS COACHES LTD
WYE COACH DEPOT, WYE TN25 5BX
Tel: 01233 812002
Fax: 01233 813210
Recovery: 07770 874631
E-mail: poyntercoaches@aol.com
Man Dir: B Poynter **Ch Eng**: B Poynter
Fleet: 15 - 1 double-deck bus, 8 single-deck bus, 5 coach, 1 double-deck coach.
Chassis: 2 DAF. 3 Dennis. 2 Leyland. 1 MAN. 7 Volvo.
Bodies: 4 Alexander. 1 Berkhof. 1 Bova. 1 Jonckheere. 2 Leyland. 2 Neoplan. 1 Optare. 2 Reeve Burgess. 1 Van Hool
Ops incl: local bus services, school contracts, excursions & tours, private hire, continental tours.
Livery: White
Ticket System: Wayfarer

R. K. F. TRAVEL
19 COBB CLOSE, STROOD ME2 3TY
Tel/Fax: 01634 715897.
Dir: Ray Fraser.
Fleet: 2 minibus.
Chassis: 1 LDV, 1 VW.
Ops incl: private hire.

*THE RAINHAM COACH CO
1A SPRINGFIELD ROAD, GILLINGHAM ME7 1YJ
Tel/Fax: 01634 852020
Recovery: 07850 657653
E-mail: info@rainhamcoach.co.uk
Web site: www.rainhamcoach.co.uk
Prop-Ptnrs: David Graham, Christine Graham **Ops Mans**: Alan Lorenston, Richard Graham
Fleet: 19 - 4 midicoach, 4 midibus, 15 minicoach.
Chassis/Bodies: 3 Ford Transit. 14 Mercedes. 1 Optare. 1 other.
Ops incl: school contracts, private hire, excursions & tours.
Livery: White

REDROUTE BUSES
GRANBY COACHWORKS, GROVE ROAD, NORTHFLEET DA11 9AX
Tel: 01474 353896
Web site: www.redroutebus.com
Fleet: 25 - 14 double-deck bus, 3 single-deck bus, 1 coach, 7 minibus.
Ops incl: local bus services
Livery: Red

REGENT COACHES
UNIT 16, ST AUGUSTINES BUSINESS PARK, WHITSTABLE CT5 2QJ
Tel: 01227 794345
Fax: 01227 795120
E-mail: info@regentcoaches.com

Web site: www.regentcoaches.co.uk
Ptnrs: Paul Regent, Kerry Regent **Tran Mans**: Colin MacDonald, Kenneth Bishop
Traff Assistant: Sam Regent **Fleet Eng**: Robert Wildish
Fleet: 25 - 8 minibus, 10 midicoach, 7 minicoach.
Chassis: 4 Iveco. 5 LDV. 12 Mercedes. 4 Renault.
Ops incl: local bus services, school contracts, private hire.
Livery: White/Red/Orange
Ticket system: Almex Electronic

SCOTLAND & BATES
wc A/c

HEATH ROAD, APPLEDORE
TN26 2AJ
Tel: 01233 758325.
Fax: 01233 758611.
E-mail: info@scotlandandbates.co.uk
Web site: www.scotlandandbates.co.uk
Ptnrs: D C R Bates, R M Bates, G A Bates.
Fleet: 17 coach.
Chassis: 1 Bedford. 16 Volvo.
Bodies: 6 Plaxton. 11 Van Hool.
Ops incl: local bus services, school contracts, private hire
Livery: Cream/Brown/Orange

SEATH COACHES

FIELDINGS, STONEHEAP ROAD,
EAST STUDDAL CT15 5BU
Tel/Fax: 01304 620825.
Owner: P. Seath.
Fleet: 4 coach.
Chassis: Ford. Iveco. Leyland. Volvo.
Bodies: Caetano. Plaxton.
Ops incl: school contracts, private hire.
Livery: Pink/White/Beige.

SPOT HIRE TRAVEL   A/c

STATION APPROACH, BEARSTED
RAILWAY STATION, MAIDSTONE
ME14 4PH
Tel: 01622 738932
Fax: 01622 630406
Prop: Roger Young
Fleet: 11 - 6 coach, 1 midicoach, 4 minicoach.
Chassis: 5 Mercedes. 6 Volvo.
Bodies: 2 Autobus. 1 Jonckheere. 2 Mercedes. 5 Plaxton. 1 Van Hool.
Ops incl: school contracts, private hire.
Livery: Cream

STAGECOACH IN EAST KENT & HASTINGS
 wc

BUS STATION, ST GEORGE'S LANE,
CANTERBURY CT1 2SY
Tel: 01227 828103
Fax: 01227 828150
Web site: www.stagecoachbus.com
Ch Exec: Brian Souter **Man Dir UK Bus**: L Warneford **Group Fin Dir**: M Griffiths
Co Sec: A Whitnall **Man Dir**: Paul Southgate **Ops Dir**: Neil Instrall **Eng Dir**: Jason Bush
Fleet: 302 - 143 double-deck bus, 45 single-deck bus, 17 coach, 45 midibus, 52 minibus.
Chassis: 48 Dennis. 3 Dodge. 1 Ford. 4 Ford Transit. 43 Leyland. 9 MAN. 52 Mercedes. 44 Scania. 106 Volvo.
Bodies: 182 Alexander. 4 Leyland. 7 Leyland. 74 Northern Counties. 40 Plaxton. 3 Wadham Stringer. 3 Wright.
Ops incl: local bus services, express.
Livery: Stagecoach (Blue,Orange,White,Red); National Express (White).
Ticket System: ERG/Wayfarer.

*STREAMLINE

WEST STATION APPROACH,
MAIDSTONE ME16 8RJ
Tel: 01622 750000
Fax: 01622 752978
Web site: www.streamlinetravel.co.uk
Fleet: 5 - 2 mincoach, 3 midicoach.
Chassis/Bodies: 1 Iveco. 4 Mercedes
Ops include: local bus services, excursions & tours, private hire, school contracts
Livery: Silver

*THOMSETT'S COACHES

50 GOLF ROAD, DEAL CT14 6QB
Tel/Fax: 01304 374731
E-mail: thomsettcoaches@fsmail.net
Prop: S. J. Thomsett
Fleet: 5 - 4 coach, 1 midicoach.
Chassis: 1 Bedford. 1 MAN. 3 Scania.
Bodies: 1 Caetano. 2 Plaxton. 2 Van Hool.
Ops incl: school contracts, private hire.

*TRACKS VEHICLE SERVICES LTD

THE FLOTS, BROOKLAND, ROMNEY
MARSH TN29 9TG
Tel: 01797 344164
Fax: 01797 344135
E-mail: info@tracks-travel.com
Web site: tracks-travel.com
Man Dir: Andrew Toms.
Fleet: 7 single-deck bus
Chassis: 1 DAF. 1 Scania. 5 Volvo.
Bodies: 1 Caetano. 1 Jonckheere. 5 Van Hool.
Ops incl: continental tours.

*TRAVELMASTERS
   wc A/c R24   T

DORSET ROAD INDUSTRIAL
ESTATE, DORSET ROAD,
SHEERNESS ME12 1LT
Tel: 01795 660066
Fax: 01795 660088
Recovery: 07850 848008
E-mail: sales.travel@btconnect.com
Dirs: T Lambkin, C Smith
Fleet: 23 - 4 double-deck bus, 2 single-deck bus, 10 coach, 2 double-deck coach, 2 midibus, 1 midicoach, 3 minibus.
Chassis: 1 Dennis. 2 Leyland. 5 Mercedes. 4 Scania. 11 Volvo.
Bodies: 2 Alexander. 2 ECW. 3 Mercedes. 2 Northern Counties. 5 Plaxton. 9 Van Hool.
Ops incl: school contracts, excursions & tours, private hire, continental tours.

VIKING MINICOACHES

UNIT 1, LYSANDER CLOSE,
PYSONS ROAD INDUSTRIAL
ESTATE, BROADSTAIRS CT10 2YJ
Tel/Fax: 01843 860876
Fax: 01843 866975
Prop: Paul Troke
Fleet: 7 - 2 midicoach, 5 minibus.
Chassis/bodies: 2 Iveco. 1 LDV. 2 Mercedes. 1 Renault. 1 Toyota. 1 Caetano
Ops incl: school contracts, private hire.

*WESTERHAM COACHES
See Surrey

The Grasshopper Inn
(A25) Moorhouse, Nr. Westerham, Kent
**13TH CENTURY TUDOR INN
WITH 21ST CENTURY HOSPITALITY**
Coffee, Drinks, Lunch or Dinner Stops
Kent/Surrey's Best Carvery
We welcome Coach Parties
Complimentary meal/refreshments for
the driver with each coach party.
Massive car park with coach bays. Situated South of
London, within 10 minutes of the M25 (jnct. 5 & 6)
Phone our friendly staff to make a booking.
Tel: 01959 563136
E-mail: info@grasshopperinn.co.uk
Website: www.grasshopperinn.co.uk

A/c	Air conditioning		Seat belt-fitted vehicles		Replacement vehicle available
	Vehicles suitable for disabled	R	Recovery service available	T	Toilet-drop facilities available
	Coach(es) with galley facilities	(not 24 hr)			Vintage vehicle(s) available
wc	Coach(es) with toilet facilities	R24	24hr recovery service		Open top vehicle(s)

LANCASHIRE (BLACKBURN, DARWEN, BLACKPOOL, WIGAN)

ADLINGTON TAXIS & MINICOACHES
See Greater Manchester

*ALFA TRAVEL
EUXTON LANE, EUXTON, CHORLEY PR7 6AF
Tel: 0845 130 5777
Fax: 0845 130 3777
E-mail: req@alfatravel .co.uk
Web site: www.alfatravel.co.uk
Fleetname: Alfa Travel
Man Dir: Paul Sawbridge **Fin Dir**: Peter Sawbridge **Head of Ops**: Neil McMurdy
Ops Man: Tom Smith
Fleet: 35 coach
Chassis: 6 DAF. 19 Dennis. 10 Volvo.
Bodies: 6 Ikarus. 29 Plaxton.
Ops incl: excursions & tours, private hire, continental tours.
Livery: Cream

J & F ASPDEN (BLACKBURN) LTD
LANCASTER STREET, BLACKBURN BB2 1UA.
Tel: 01254 52020.
Fax: 01254 57474.
Fleetname: Aspdens Coaches.
Fleet: 14 - 1 double-deck bus, 13 coach.
Chassis: 1 Bristol. 13 Leyland.
Bodies: 5 Duple. 1 Northern Counties. 8 Plaxton.
Ops incl: school contracts, excursions & tours, private hire, continental tours.
Livery: Yellow/Black.
Subsidiary of Holmeswood Coaches

*BATTERSBY SILVER GREY
THE COACH TRAVEL CENTRE, MIDDLEGATE, WHITE LUND BUSINESS PARK, MORECAMBE LA3 3PE
Tel: 01524 380000
Fax: 01524 380800
Recovery: 01524 380000
E-mail: richard@battersbys.co.uk
Chmn: J A Harrison **Co Sec**: M R Harrison
Ops Man: R Blaikie
Fleet: 34 - 4 single-deck bus, 24 coach, 6 midicoach.
Chassis: 4 Dennis. 6 Mercedes. 24 Volvo.
Bodies: 30 Plaxton. 4 Wadham Stringer.
Ops incl: local bus services, excursions & tours, private hire, continental tours, school contracts.
Livery: White

BLACKBURN BOROUGH TRANSPORT LTD
INTACK, BLACKBURN BB1 3JD.
Tel: 01254 51112
Fax: 01254 662637
E-mail: info@blackburntransport.co.uk
Web site: www.blackburntransport.co.uk
Fleetname: Blackburn Transport
Divisional Dir: Michael Morton **Fin Dir/Co Sec**: Ted Buckley **Fleet Eng**: Glenn Dearden **Fin Man**: Jan Lundie
Fleet: 109 - 59 double-deck bus. 20 single-deck bus. 30 midibus.
Chassis: 21 Dennis. 50 Leyland. 14 Optare. 23 Volvo.
Bodies: 6 Alexander. 34 ECW. 13 East Lancs. 9 Leyland. 8 Northern Counties. 15 Optare. 10 Plaxton. 1 Roe. 12 Wright.
Ops incl: local bus services, school contracts, private hire.
Livery: two-tone Green/Cream/Yellow
Ticket System: Almex Optima
(Part of the Transdev Group)

BLACKPOOL TRANSPORT LTD
RIGBY ROAD, BLACKPOOL FY1 5DD
Tel: 01253 473001
Fax: 01253 473101
E-mail: directors@blackpooltransport.com
Web site: www.blackpooltransport.com
Fleetname: MetroCoastlines
Man Dir: Steve Burd **Eng Dir**: Bill Gibson
Ops Dir: David Eaves **Fin Dir**: Allan Leach
Business Development Man: Liz Esnouf
Human Res Man: Annie Nancollis
Fleet: 229 - 72 double-deck bus, 39 single-deck bus, 46 midibus, 72 tram.
Chassis: 30 DAF. 18 Dennis. 48 Leyland. 55 Optare. 6 Volvo.
Bodies: 10 ECW. 44 East Lancs. 15 Northern Counties. 85 Optare. 3 Roe.
(also 8 Optare Solos jointly owned by Blackpool Borough Council and Lancashire County Council)
Ops incl: local bus services, tram services, school contracts, private hire.
Livery: Yellow plus route branded route colours.
Ticket System: Almex A90

*BRADSHAWS TRAVEL
46 WESTBOURNE ROAD, KNOTT END ON SEA, POULTON LE FYLDE FY6 0BS
Tel: 01253 810058
Fleet: 6 - 5 coach, 1 minibus.
Chassis: 1 Dennis. 3 Leyland. 1 Mercedes. 1 Volvo.
Bodies: 1 Berkof. 1 Duple. 3 Plaxton. 1 other
Ops incl: private hire, school contracts.
Livery: White.
Ticket System: Almex

BURNLEY & PENDLE
QUEENSGATE BUS DEPOT, COLNE ROAD, BURNLEY BB10 1HH
Tel: 01282 427778
Web site: www.burnleyandpendle.co.uk
Prop: Blazefield Holdings Ltd.
Chmn: Giles Fearnley. **Man Dir**: Stuart Wilde. **Dir (Lancs)**: George Scrymgeour.
Fleet: 72 - double-deck buses, single-deck buses.
Chassis: Dennis, Leyland, Mercedes-Benz, Optare, Volvo.
Bodies: Alexander, ECW, Northern Counties, Optare, Plaxton, Wright.
Livery: Red/Cream.
Ticket System: ERG.
Part of the Blazefield group which is owned by Transdev

*COACH OPTIONS
See Greater Manchester

COLRAY COACHES
14 PRESTBURY AVENUE, BLACKPOOL FY4 1PT
Tel: 01253 349481
Dirs: Geoffrey Shaw, V Shaw
Fleet: 4 - coach, midibus, midicoach.
Chassis: 1 Mercedes. 1 Setra. 2 Toyota. 1 Volvo.
Bodies: 1 Caetano. 1 Mercedes. 1 Plaxton. 1 Setra
Ops incl: excursions & tours, school contracts, private hire, continental tours.
Livery: White/Blue

*EAVESWAY TRAVEL LTD
BRYN SIDE, BRYN ROAD, ASHTON-IN-MAKERFIELD WN4 8BT
Tel: 01942 727985
Fax: 01942 271234
E-mail: operations@eavesweytravel.com
Web site: www.eavesweytravel.com
Man Dir: Mike Eaves **Dir**: Phil Rogers
Ops Man: Tim Presley
Fleet: 22 coach
Chassis: 19 DAF. 3 MAN.
Bodies: 22 Van Hool.
Ops incl: excursions & tours, private hire.
Livery: Silver/Blue/Green.

JOHN FISHWICK & SONS
GOLDEN HILL GARAGE, LEYLAND PR25 3LE.
Tel: 01772 421207.
Fax: 01772 622407.
E-mail: enquiries@fishwicks.co.uk
Web site: www.fishwicks.co.uk
Dir: J. C. Brindle. **Dir**: J. F. Hustler.
Ch Eng: J. Cave. **IT Man**: A Clenshaw
Coach Man: A Aldam.
Fleet: 47 - 7 double-deck bus, 31 single-deck bus, 8 coach, 1 minibus.
Chassis: 12 DAF. 4 Dennis. 5 EOS. 15 Leyland. 8 Leyland National. 2 Mercedes.
Bodies: 6 Alexander. 2 ECW. 8 Leyland. 9 Leyland National. 1 Plaxton. 1 Reeve Burgess. 7 Van Hool. 8 Wright.
Ops incl: local bus services, school contracts, excursions & tours, private hire, continental tours.
Livery: Green.
Ticket System: Wayfarer.

*FLIGHTS HALLMARK
See West Midlands

*FOCUS COACHES LTD

UNIT 4, LONGTON BUSINESS PARK, MUCH HOOLE, PRESTON PR4 5LE
Tel: 01772 616699
Fax: 01772 616677
E-mail: info@focuscoaches.co.uk
Web site: www.focuscoaches.co.uk
Man Dir: Darren J Critchley **Co Sec**: Lisa Lee
Fleet: 31 - 9 double-deck bus, 20 coach, 2 midicoach
Chassis: 1 Bova. 2 Mercedes. 7 Scania. 11 Volvo.
Bodies: 5 Alexander. 2 Bova. 2 East Lancs. 1 Esker. 3 Irizar. 2 Northern Counties. 5 Plaxton. 11 Van Hool.
Ops incl: school contracts, excursions & tours, private hire, continental tours.
Livery: White/Purple/Pink/Gold
Ticket System: Wayfarer/Almex

FRASER EAGLE

THE COACH HOUSE, SHUTTLEWORTH MEAD, BUSINESS PARK, PADIHAM BB12 7NG
Tel: 01254 231100
Fax: 01254 350575
Recovery: 01254 232700
E-mail: howard.tyrer@frasereagle.co.uk
Web site: www.frasereagle.com
Fleetname: Fraser Eagle Coaching
Dirs: Neil Atkins, Alan Dyson, Steve Ellis
Fleet: 18
Chassis: 8 DAF. 1 MAN. 2 Mercedes. 2 Scania. 5 Volvo.
Bodies: 3 Bova. 3 Neoplan. 12 Van Hool.
Ops incl: school contracts, excursions & tours, private hire, express, continental tours.
Livery: Green front/Blue rear/White slash with Eagle in middle.

*FREEBIRD

See Greater Manchester

GPD TRAVEL

27 HARTFORD AVENUE, HEYWOOD OL10 4XH
Tel: 01706 622297
Fax: 01706 361494
Web site: www.gpdtravel.freeserve.co.uk
E-mail: gary@gpdtravel.freeserve.co.uk
Props: Gary Dawson, Janine Dawson
Fleet: 7 - 3 coach, 2 minicoach, 2 midibus.
Chassis: 2 DAF. 4 Mercedes. 1 Volvo.
Bodies: 1 Autobus, 1 Caetano. 2 Plaxton.
Ops incl: school contracts, excursions & tours, private hire, continental tours.
Livery: Red/Gold stripes.

*G-LINE COACH TOURS

54 ST DAVIDS ROAD, ST ANNES FY8 1TS
Tel: 01253 725999
Fax: 01253 781843
Prop: Mr Bradshaw **Coach man**: Mr Nayler
Fleet: 10 coach
Chassis: 5 DAF. 1 Leyland. 4 Volvo
Bodies: 5 Plaxton. 5 Van Hool.
Ops incl: excursions & tours, private hire, continental tours.
Livery: Maroon/White/Gold

JEFF GRIFFITHS COACHES

22 MYERSCOUGH AVE, ST ANNES-ON-SEA FY8 2HY
Tel: 01253 714230
Fax: 01253 640560
E-mail: jeff-griffiths@comserve.com
Dir: Jeff Griffiths
Fleet: coach
Chassis: Volvo.
Bodies: Plaxton.
Ops incl: excursions & tours, private hire.
Livery: White

*RIGBY'S EXECUTIVE COACHES

THE COACH CENTRE, MOORFIELD DRIVE, MOORFIELD INDUSTRIAL ESTATE, ALTHAM, ACCRINGTON BB5 5WG
Tel: 01254 388866
Fax: 01254 232505
Man Dir: Derek Moorhouse **Eng Dir**: Mel Melling **Tran Man**: Andrew Knowles
Fleet: 20 coach
Bodies: Berkhof. Irizar. Mercedes. Plaxton. Van Hool.
Ops incl: school contracts, excursions & tours, private hire.
Livery: Orange

HEALINGS INTERNATIONAL COACHES

See Greater Manchester

HODDER MOTOR SERVICES LTD

3 ALDERFORD CLOSE, CLITHEROE BB7 2QP
Tel: 01200 422473
Fax: 01200 422590
E-mail: hodder@talk21.com
Dir: Paul Hodgson
Co Sec: Janice Hodgson.
Fleet: 1 coach
Chassis: Volvo.
Body: Jonckheere.
Ops incl: private hire, excursions & tours.
Livery: Green/Blue/White

HOLMESWOOD COACHES LTD

SANDY WAY, HOLMESWOOD, ORMSKIRK L40 1UB
Tel: 01704 821245
Fax: 01704 822090
E-mail: sales@holmeswood.uk.com
Web site: www.holmeswood.uk.com
Dirs: J F Aspinall, M Aspinall, D G Aspinall, C H Aspinall, M F Aspinall, M J Aspinall
Fleet: 134 - 18 double-deck bus, 97 coach, 2 double-deck coach, 1 midibus, 10 midicoach, 6 minicoach.
Chassis: 2 Ayats. 1 Bova. 18 DAF. 17 Dennis. 10 Irisbus/Iveco. 14 Leyland. 16 MAN. 2 Mercedes. 22 Scania. 32 Volvo.
Bodies: 5 Alexander. 1 Autobus. 2 Ayats. 4 Beulas. 7 Berkhof. 1 Bova. 8 Caetano. 3 ECW. 5 East Lancs. 9 Ikarus. 2 Irizar. 5 Jonckheere. 21 Marcopolo. 1 Neoplan. 4 Northern Counties. 25 Plaxton. 25 Van Hool. 6 Indcar.
Ops incl: local bus services, school contracts, excursions & tours, private hire, continental tours.
Livery: Green
Ticket system: Wayfarer

J & Y COACHES

9 MILLTHORNE AVENUE, CLITHEROE BB7 2LE.
Tel/Fax: 01200 426269.
Web site: www.uk-coachtours.co.uk
Ptnrs: J. Robinson, Yvonne Robinson.
Fleet: 1 coach. **Chassis/body**: Setra.
Ops incl: excursions & tours, private hire, continental tours.
Livery: Blue/White.

*JACKSONS COACHES

JACKSON HOUSE, BURTON ROAD, BLACKPOOL FY4 4NW
Tel: 01253 792222
Fax: 01253 792222
Ptnr: Paul Jackson
Fleet: 6 coach.
Chassis: 2 DAF. 2 Scania. 2 Volvo.
Bodies: i Irizar. 4 Plaxton. 1 Van Hool.
Ops incl: school contracts, private hire, excursions & tours, continental tours.
Livery: White/Blue.
Ticket System: Setright

*KIRKBY LONSDALE COACH HIRE LTD

OLD STATION YARD, WARTON ROAD, CARNFORTH LA5 9EU
Tel: 01524 733831
Fax: 01524 733821
Web site: www.klcoachhire.co.uk
E-mail: sutton@klch.bbfree.co.uk
Dirs: Mrs Jane Sutton, Stephen Sutton

Symbol	Meaning
A/c	Air conditioning
♿	Vehicles suitable for disabled
🍴	Coach(es) with galley facilities
WC	Coach(es) with toilet facilities
♥	Seat belt-fitted vehicles
R	Recovery service available (not 24 hr)
R24	24hr recovery service
🔑	Replacement vehicle available
T	Toilet-drop facilities available
🚌	Vintage vehicle(s) available
🚍	Open top vehicle(s)

Lancashire

Fleet: 20 - 4 coach, 12 midibus, 2 midicoach, 2 minicoach.
Chassis: 1 Bova. 3 DAF. 15 Mercedes. 1 Optare.
Bodies: 1 Alexander. 1 Bova. 1 Caetano. 1 Marshall/MCV. 3 Optare. 12 Plaxton. 1 Van Hool.
Ops incl: local bus services, school contracts, excursions & tours, private hire.
Livery: buses: Maroon/White coaches: White/Blue with maroon splats
Ticket System: Wayfarer TGX, Almex

LANCASHIRE UNITED
MANNER SUTTON STREET, BLACKBURN BB1 5DT.
Tel: 01254 260661
Web site: www.lancashireunited.co.uk
Prop: Blazefield Holdings Ltd
Man Dir: Stuart Wilde. **Dir (Lancs)**: George Scrymgeour.
Fleet: 131 - 45 double-deck buses, 68 single-deck buses, 18 minibuses.
Chassis: Dennis, Leyland, Mercedes-Benz, Optare, Volvo.
Bodies: Alexander, Berkhof, East Lancs, National, Northern Counties, Plaxton, Wright.
Livery: Blue/Cream.
Ticket System: ERG.
(Part of the Blazefield group which is owned by Transdev)

*LENDOR TAXIS & LUXURY MINICOACH TRAVEL
See Greater Manchester

McLAUGHLIN'S TOURS
UNIT 1A PORTAKABIN, FACTORY LANE, PENWORTHAM PR1 9TZ
Tel/Fax: 01772 749358
Prop: Anthony McLaughlin
Fleet: 7 - 4 coach, 3 minibus.
Chassis: 2 Leyland, 3 Volvo.
Bodies: 3 Mercedes.
Ops incl: local bus services, school contracts, excursions & tours, continental tours.
Livery: Blue/White/Yellow.
Ticket System: Almex

*NORTHERN BLUE
UNIT 7, DEAN MILL, PLUMBE STREET, BURNLEY BB11 3AG
Tel: 01282 456351
Fax: 01282 439386
E-mail: northernblue@btconnect.com
Web site: www.northernblue.co.uk
Man Dir: Philip Beaumont **Co Sec/Fin Dir**: Michael Robinson **Ch Eng**: Lee Welton
Fleet: 65 - 25 double-deck bus, 18 single-deck bus, 22 midibus
Chassis: 3 Dennis. 8 Leyland. 22 Optare. 18 Scania. 14 Volvo.
Bodies: 23 Alexander. 3 Duple. 1 ECW. 8 East Lancs. 4 Northern Counties. 22 Plaxton. 4 Plaxton
Ops incl: local bus services, school contracts, express, private hire.
Livery: Blue/White.
Ticket System: Wayfarer TGX

NORTH WEST COACHES & LIMOS
R24
HILLHOUSE INTERNATIONAL BUSINESS PARK, WEST ROAD, THORNTON CLEVELEYS FY5 4DQ
Tel: 01253 855000
Fax: 01253 859009
Recovery: 07850 500015
E-mail: stewart.farrel@tiscali.co.uk
Web site: www.northwestcoaches.co.uk
Owner/Operator: Stuart J Farrell
Ops Man: Paul Portisman
Head Fitter: John Keen
Fleet: 18 - 1 double-deck coach, 3 coach, 2 midibus, 5 midicoach, 7 minibus.
Chassis: 1 DAF. 1 Iveco. 5 Mercedes. 1 Neoplan. 8 Renault. 2 Volvo.
Ops incl: local bus services, excursions & tours, school contracts, private hire

OLYMPIA TRAVEL
44 ARGYLE STREET, HINDLEY WN2 3PH
Tel: 01942 522322
Fax: 01942 254666
E-mail: olympia@coach-hire.net
Web site: www.olympiatravel.co.uk
Props: Joseph Lewis, Shaun Lewis.
Fleet: 18 - 12 coach, 4 midicoach, 2 minibus.
Chassis: 1 Bedford. 6 Dennis. 1 Ford Transit. 1 LDV. 5 Volvo.
Bodies: 5 Duple. 2 Jonckheere. 2 Mercedes. 4 Plaxton. 1 Reeve Burgess.
Ops incl: local bus services, school contracts, private hire, continental tours.
Livery: White with blue stripes

*PRESTON BUS LTD
R24
221 DEEPDALE ROAD, PRESTON PR1 6NY
Tel: 01772 253671
Fax: 01772 555840
Recovery: 01772 253671
E-mail: peter.bell@prestonbus.co.uk
Web site: www.prestonbus.co.uk
Man Dir: Peter Bell **Ops Dir**: John Asquith
Eng Dir: Jack Hornby **Fin Dir**: Margaret Ingram
Fleet: 124 - 56 double-deck bus, 16 single-deck bus, 52 minibus.
Chassis: 18 Dennis. 45 Leyland. 52 Optare. 9 Scania.
Bodies: 12 Alexander. 1 ECW. 33 East Lancs. 21 Leyland. 5 Northern Counties. 52 Optare.
Ops incl: local bus services, school contracts.
Livery: Blue/Cream
Ticket System: Wayfarer TGX150

REDLINE COACHES
83 BISHAM AVENUE, LEYLAND PR5 3QE.
Tel: 01772 611612.
Fax: 01772 611613.
Prop: R. G. H. & S. R. Nuttall.

REEVES COACH HOLIDAYS
34 MONKS DRIVE, WITHNELL, CHORLEY PR6 8SG.
Tel/Fax: 01254 830545
E-mail: info@reevescoachholidays.com
Web site: www.reevescoachholidays.com
Prop: John E Reeves
Fleet: 1 coach.
Chassis/body: Setra.
Ops incl: excursions & tours, private hire, continental tours.
Livery: White/Purple/Red

ROBINSONS HOLIDAYS
PARK GARAGE, GREAT HARWOOD BB6 7SP
Tel: 01254 889900
Fax: 01254 884708
E-mail: sales@robinsons-holidays.co.uk
Web site: www.robinsons-holidays.co.uk
Dirs: D D Lord, J E Bannister (**Sec**), J McMillan **Ops Man**: C Skeen
Engineer: P Godwin **Off man**: B Cooke
Sales Man: G Holdsworth
Fleet: 17 - 15 coach, 2 minibus.
Chassis: 1 DAF. 4 MAN. 10 Volvo.
Bodies: 3 Jonckheere. 4 Noge. 7 Plaxton. 1 Van Hool.
Ops incl: excursions & tours, private hire, continental tours, school contracts.
Livery: Blue

ROSSENDALE TRANSPORT LTD
35 BACUP ROAD, RAWTENSTALL BB4 7NG
Tel: 01706 212337
Fax: 01706 229515
Web site: www.rossendalebus.co.uk
E-mail: info@rossendalebus.co.uk
Man Dir: Edgar Oldham **Comm Dir**: Barry Drelincourt
Fleet: 107 - 15 double-deck bus, 92 single-deck bus.
Chassis: 43 Dennis. 5 Leyland. 4 Mercedes. 23 Optare. 26 Volvo. 6 other.
Ops incl: local bus services, school contracts, private hire, express, continental tours.
Livery: White/Red/Cream.
Ticket System: Wayfarer TGX

SANDGROUNDER COACHES
28 WARWICK STREET, SOUTHPORT PR8 5ES
Tel: 01704 541194
Recovery: 07734 003464
E-mail: gerry@dohe.wanadoo.co.uk
Dirs: Gerald Doherty, John Fairbank
Fleet: 3 coaches.
Chassis: 2 DAF. 1 Mercedes.
Ops incl: school contracts, excursions & tours, private hire.

*THE TRAVELLERS CHOICE
♿ 💺 wc 🍴 A/c ✎ T

THE COACH & TRAVEL CENTRE, SCOTLAND ROAD, CARNFORTH LA5 9RQ
Tel: 01524 720033
Fax: 01524 720044
E-mail: info@travellerschoice.co.uk
Web site: www.travellerschoice.co.uk
Chmn: R Shaw **Man Dirs**: J Shaw, D Shaw **Co Sec**: P Shaw **Dir**: M Shaw
Fleet: 74 - coach, midicoach, minicoach.
Chassis: 13 Mercedes. 6 Scania. 55 Volvo.
Bodies: 4 Berkhof. 6 Caetano. 2 Esker. 1 Irizar. 30 Jonckheere. 8 Mercedes. 1 Optare. 89 Plaxton. 13 Sunsundegui.
Ops incl: school contracts, excursions & tours, private hire, continental tours, express.
Livery: White with blue/yellow/red stripe

*R S TYRER & SON wc 💺
168 CHORLEY ROAD, ADLINGTON, CHORLEY PR6 9LQ
Tel: 01257 480979
Fax: 01257 480951
Dirs: Gordon Buckle, Sylvia Buckle
Fleet: 10 - 2double-deck bus, 6 coach, 2 minicoach.
Chassis: DAF. MAN. Mercedes. Scania. Volvo.
Bodies: Plaxton. Van Hool.

Ops incl: excursions & tours, private hire, school contracts

TYRER OF ADLINGTON
♿ 💺 wc 🍴 A/c R24 ✎

THE COACH HOUSE, SHUTTLEWORTH MEAD, BUSINESS PARK, PADIHAM BB12 7NG
Tel: 01254 611123
Fax: 01254 350575
Recovery: 01254 232700
E-mail: howard.tyrer@fraseragle.co.uk
Web site: www.tyrercoaching.com
Chmn: Alan Dyson **Dir**: Kevin Dean
Principal: Howard Tyrer
Fleet: 13 - 11 coach, 1 midicoach.
Chassis: 10 DAF. 2 Mercedes.
Bodies: 1 Neoplan. 1 Plaxton. 10 Van Hool.
Ops incl: school contracts, excursions & tours, private hire, express, continental tours.
Livery: White with Blue/Red lettering

VISCOUNT CENTRAL COACHES LTD
💺 wc A/c ✎

6 DEAN MILL, PLUMBE STREET, BURNLEY BB11 2AG
Tel: 01282 439371

Fax: 01282 421386
Web site: www.viscountcentral.co.uk
Man Dir: Philip Beaumont
Fleet: 10 - 7 coach, 1 minicoach.
Chassis: 3 Iveco. 1 Toyota. 4 Volvo.
Bodies: 3 Beulas. 1 Caetano. 4 Van Hool.
Ops incl: private hire

YELLOW ROSE COACHES
💺 wc

WEST LEA, DIXON'S FIELD, CRAG BANK, CARNFORTH LA5 9JN
Tel: 01524 735853
E-mail: www.yellowrosecoaches.co.uk
Web site: yellowrosecoaches@tiscali.co.uk
Dirs: G Brocken(**Co Sec**), Mrs C M Brocken **Fleet Eng**: C R Ardis
Fleet: 5 - 2 coach, 1 midicoach, 1 minibus, 1 minicoach.
Chassis: 1 MAN. 2 Mercedes. 2 Volvo.
Bodies: 1 Caetano. 1 Mellor. 1 Mercedes. 2 Van Hool.
Ops incl: excursions & tours, private hire, school contracts.
Livery: Yellow/White
Ticket System: Almex.

LEICESTERSHIRE, CITY OF LEICESTER, RUTLAND

*ADBEY TRAVEL wc 💺
RMC YARD, THURMASTON FOOTPATH, HUMBERSTONE LANE, LEICESTER LE4 9JU
Tel: 0116 246 1755
Fax: 0116 246 1755
Man Dir: Bryan A Garratt **Tran Man**: Pauline Garratt **Eng**: Paul Garratt
Fleet: 7 coach
Chassis: Bova. DAF. Leyland. Volvo.
Bodies: Bova. Duple. Ikarus. Leyland.
Ops incl: school contracts, excursions & tours, private hire.
Livery: White/Red/Green

ARRIVA MIDLANDS ♿
PO BOX 613, LEICESTER LE4 8BT
Tel: 0116 264 0400
Fax: 0116 260 5605
Web site: www.arriva.co.uk
Man Dir: Catherine Mason **Fin Dir**: John Barlow **Eng Dir**: Richard Dyball **Ops Dirs**: Stuart McIntosh, John Marrow **Eng Dir**: Jason Chalk
Fleet: 650 - double-deck bus, single-deck bus, coach, midibus.
Chassis: 46 DAF. 58 Dennis. 21 Leyland. 99 Mercedes. 58 Scania. 49 Volvo.
Bodies: Alexander. ECW. East Lancs. Leicester. Leyland. Northern Counties.

Optare. Plaxton. Reeve Burgess.
Ops incl: local bus services, school contracts, private hire, express.
Livery: Aquamarine/Cotswold Stone
Ticket System: Wayfarer

ASMAL COACHES
70 KEDLESTONE ROAD, LEICESTER LE5 5HW
Tel/Fax: 0116 249 0443
Man Dir: Mehboob M. Asmal.

AUSDEN CLARK LTD
wc 🍴 💺 ✎

DYSART WAY, LEICESTER LE1 2JY
Tel: 0116 262 9492
Fax: 0116 251 5551
Man Dir: Paul Ausden-Clark.
Fleet: 60 - 44 coach, 8 double-deck coach, 8 minicoach.
Chassis: incl: Irizar. Mercedes. Scania.
Ops incl: local bus services, school contracts, excursions & tours, private hire, continental tours.

BAILISS TOURS wc 💺 T
21 ODSTONE ROAD, BARTON-IN-THE-BEANS CV13 0DF.
Tel: 01455 290253.
Fax: 01455 292700.
Prop: G. Treadwell.
Fleet: 1 coach. **Chassis**: DAF. **Body**: Duple.
Ops incl: excursions & tours, private hire, continental tours.
Livery: Blue/Cream.

*CONFIDENCE BUS & COACH LTD 💺 🚌
30 SPALDING STREET, LEICESTER LE5 4PH
Tel: 0116 276 2171
Fax: 0116 276 2171
E-mail: confidencebus@btclick.com
Web site: www.confidencebus.co.uk
Man Dir: K M Williams **Ch Eng**: M Crawford
Fleet: 32 - 20 double-deck coach, 12 coach.
Chassis: 1 AEC. 27 Leyland. 4 Volvo.
Bodies: 1 Duple. 13 ECW. 2 East Lancs. 1 Optare. 1 Park Royal. 10 Plaxton. 3 Roe. 1 Van Hool.
Ops incl: school contracts, private hire.
Livery: Buses: Grey/Black, Coaches: Red/Black
Ticket System: Setright

A/c	Air conditioning	✎	Replacement vehicle available
♿	Vehicles suitable for disabled	T	Toilet-drop facilities available
🍴	Coach(es) with galley facilities	🚌	Vintage vehicle(s) available
wc	Coach(es) with toilet facilities		Open top vehicle(s)
💺	Seat belt-fitted vehicles		
R	Recovery service available (not 24 hr)		
R24	24hr recovery service		

COUNTY MINI COACHES
31 EDENHURST AVENUE,
LEICESTER LE3 2PH.
Tel/Fax: 0116 289 7205.
Owner: F. Bradshaw.
Fleet: 3 - 2 midicoach, 1 minibus.
Chassis: 1 DAF. 1 Freight Rover. 1 Iveco.
Ops incl: school contracts, private hire.

COUNTRY HOPPER
213 MELBOURNE ROAD, IBSTOCK
LE67 6NQ
Tel: 01530 260888

*DUNN-LINE GROUP
See Nottinghamshire

FIRST MIDLANDS
ABBEY PARK ROAD, LEICESTER
LE4 5AH.
Tel: 0116 251 6691.
Fax: 0116 253 8270.
Man Dir: Kevin Bellfield **Eng Dir:**
C. Stafford. **Fin Dir:** J. Hollis.
Gen Man Ops: C. Lara.
Fleet: 116 - double-deck bus, single-deck bus, coach, midibus, minibus.
Chassis: Bristol. Dennis. Mercedes. Optare. Scania. Volvo.
Bodies: 8 Alexander. 71 East Lancs. 10 Marshall. 20 Northern Counties. 19 Optare. 3 Plaxton. 11 Wright.
Ops incl: local bus services, school contracts, excursions & tours, private hire, express, continental tours.
Livery: Multicoloured.
Ticket System: Wayfarer 3

HYLTON & DAWSON
18 CHESTNUT ROAD, GLENFIELD,
LEICESTER LE3 8DB
Tel: 0116 233 0222
Fax: 0116 233 1011
E-mail: hyltonadrian@yahoo.co.uk
Web site: www.hyltonanddawson.co.uk
Prop: A. E. Hylton.
Fleet: 3 coach.
Chassis: 2 Bedford. 1 Dennis.
Bodies: 3 Duple.
Ops incl: school contracts, private hire.
Livery: Maroon/Cream/Grey.

PAUL JAMES COACHES
UNIT 5, GRANGE FARM BUSINESS
PARK, GRANGE ROAD,
HUGGLESCOTE LE67 2BT
Tel: 01530 832399
Fax: 01530 836128
E-mail: info@pauljamescoaches.co.uk
Web site:
www.pauljamescoaches.co.uk
Gen Man: Wayne Smith
Fleet: 35 - single-deck bus, coach, midibus.
Chassis: incl: 3 Bedford. 2 Bova. 1 Dennis. 2 Leyland. 6 Mercedes. 6 Optare. 1 Setra. 6 Volvo
Bodies: incl: 5 Alexander. 1 Autobus. 2 Bova. 6 Optare. 10 Plaxton. 2 Van Hool.
Ops incl: excursions & tours, private hire, local bus services, school contracts, continental tours.

Livery: Ivory
Ticket System: Wayfarer 3
(Part of the Veolia Group)

MACPHERSON COACHES LTD
See Derbyshire

*NESBIT BROS LTD
BURROUGH ROAD, SOMERBY,
MELTON MOWBRAY LE14 2PP
Tel: 01664 454284
Fax: 01664 454106
Dirs: I Foster, J Townsend
Fleet: 13 coach.
Chassis: 13 Volvo.
Bodies: 7 Plaxton. 6 Van Hool
Ops incl: school contracts, private hire

*NIGEL JACKSON TRAVEL
5 NEW ZEALAND LANE,
QUENIBOROUGH LE7 3FU
Tel: 0116 260 0839
Fax: 0116 276 1969
Prop: N Jackson
Fleet: 7 - 3 double-deck bus, 2 coach, 1 midicoach, 1 minibus
Chassis: 1 Dennis. 1 Leyland. 2 MCW. 1 Scania. 2 Toyota.
Bodies: 1 Alexander. 2 Caetano. 1 Duple. 2 MCW. 1 Plaxton
Ops incl: school contracts, private hire
Livery: coaches White, buses Blue/Red

ROBERTS COACHES LTD
THE LIMES, MIDLAND ROAD,
HUGGLESCOTE LE67 2FX
Tel: 01530 817444
Fax: 01530 817666
E-mail: info@robertscoaches.co.uk
Web site: www.robertscoaches.co.uk
Man Dir: Jonathan Hunt
Fleet: 26 - 11 double-deck bus, 10 coach, 3 open-top bus, 1 minibus, 1 minicoach.
Chassis: 1 LDV. 2 Leyland. 10MCW. 1 Mercedes. 3 Scania. 9 Volvo.
Bodies: 2 East Lancs. 2 Jonckheere. 10 MCW. 1 Plaxton. 8 Van Hool. 2 other.
Ops incl: local bus services, school contracts, excursions & tours, private hire, continental tours
Livery: Gold.

SCHOFIELD TRAVEL LTD
PRINCE WILLIAM ROAD,
LOUGHBOROUGH LE11 OGU.
Tel: 01509 611045
Fax: 01509 611012
Man Dir: E. B. Mee. **Dir/Ch Eng:**
K. W. Greasley. **Gen Man:** R. A. Schofield.
Fleet: 6 - 4 coach, 2 midicoach.
Chassis: 1 Bedford. 2 Bova. 2 DAF. 1 Ford.
Bodies: 2 Bova. 4 Plaxton.
Ops incl: school contracts, private hire, express.
Livery: Blue/Pale Grey.

TRAVEL-WRIGHT
64 ROCKHILL DRIVE,
MOUNTSORREL LE12 7DT.
Tel: 0116 230 2887.
Fax: 0116 230 2223.
E-mail: trwright@demon.co.uk
Dir: C. Wright.
Fleet: 5 minibus.
Chassis: 1 DAF. 2 Mercedes. 2 VW.
Bodies: 2 Crystals. 2 VW. 1 Advanced.
Ops incl: private hire, school contracts.

WEST END/RUTLAND TRAVEL
COACH & BUS CENTRE, DIXON
DRIVE, LEICESTER ROAD, MELTON
MOWBRAY LE13 0BS
Tel: 01664 563498
Fax: 01664 568568
Fleetname: Romdrive
Man Dirs: John Penniston, Peter Penniston
Fleet: 23 - 1 single-deck bus, 11 coach, 8 midibus, 2 minibus, 1 minicoach.
Chassis: 1 Dennis. 11 Mercedes. 1 Scania. 3 Setra. 4 Volvo.
Bodies: 4 Alexander. 2 Jonckheere. 5 Mercedes. 7 Plaxton. 1 Reeve Burgess. 3 Setra. 1 Wadham Stringer.
Ops incl: local bus services, school contracts, excursions & tours, private hire, continental tours.
Livery: Red/Blue/White
Ticket System: Wayfarer 3

WIDE HORIZON
48 COVENTRY ROAD, BURBAGE,
HINCKLEY LE10 2HP
Tel: 01455 615915
Fax: 01455 230767
Ptnrs: Reg Clarke, Jon Clarke.
Fleet: 16 - 9 double-deck bus, 7 coach
Chassis: 1 Bova. 3 DAF. 1 Dennis. 1 Leyland. 1 MAN. 1 Mercedes. Neoplan. 1 Scania. 1 Volvo.
Bodies: 2 Berkhof. 1 Bova. 2 Plaxton. 2 Setra.
Ops incl: local bus services, excursions & tours, school contracts, private hire, continental tours.
Livery: White

PAUL S WINSON COACHES LTD
ROYAL WAY, LOUGHBOROUGH
LE11 5XR
Tel: 01509 232354
Fax: 01509 265110
Recovery: 01509 237999
Web site: www.winsoncoaches.co.uk
E-mail: sales@winsoncoaches.co.uk
Chmn: Paul Winson **Ch Eng:**
Paul B Winson **Dir:** Mrs M A Winson
Ops Man: Anthony J Winson
Fleet: 28 - 6 double-deck bus, 18 coach, 4 minibus.
Chassis: 4 Bova. 1 DAF. 3 Dennis. 6 Leyland. 7 Mercedes. 8 Volvo.
Bodies: 1 Autobus. 4 Bova. 1 Caetano. 3 Jonckheere. 2 Northern Counties. 12 Plaxton. 3 Roe.
Ops incl: local bus services, school contracts, excursions & tours, private hire, continental tours.

Livery: Red/White/Blue.
Ticket system: Wayfarer

WOODS COACHES LTD
💺 wc A/c R 🔧 T

211 GLOUCESTER CRESCENT,
WIGSTON LE18 4YH
Tel: 0116 278 6374
Fax: 0116 247 7819
E-mail: sales@woods-coaches.co.uk
Web site: woods-coaches.com

Chmn: Mark Wood **Man Dir**: Kevin Brown
Mktg Exec: Alison Trunkfield
Eng Dir: Ian Trigg
Fleet: 32 - 14 single-deck bus, 18 midibus.
Chassis: 18 Mercedes. 14 Volvo.
Bodies: 8 Alexander. 1 Caetano. 1 Duple.
1 Marshall. 1 Mellor. 1 Mercedes.
19 Plaxton.
Ops incl: local bus services, excursions &
tours, private hire, continental tours.
Livery: Blue base – orange/yellow/white
relief
Ticket System: Wayfarer.

LINCOLNSHIRE

*BRYLAINE TRAVEL LTD ♿
291 LONDON ROAD, BOSTON
PE21 7DD
Tel: 01205 364087
Fax: 01205 359504
Man Dir: Brian W Gregg **Dir**: Elaine R
Gregg **Co Sec**: Susan E Bradshaw
Eng Dir: Brian P Gregg
Ops Dir: Malcolm P Wheatley
Fleet: 37 - 9 double-deck bus, 18 single-
deck bus, 10 midibus.
Chassis: 3 BMC. 6 DAF. 4 Dennis.
6 Leyland. 1 MCW. 1 Mercedes. 10 Optare.
3 Scania.
Ops incl: local bus services

J W CARNELL LTD
72 BRIDGE ROAD, SUTTON
BRIDGE PE12 9UA.
Tel: 01406 350482.
Fax: 01406 350600.
E-mail: carnellcoaches@ukonline.co.uk
Dirs: John Grindwood, Mervyn Emmet
Fleet: 22 - 3 double-deck bus, 16 coach,
2 midicoach, 1 minicoach.
Chassis: 2 Bedford. 1 Bova. 2 DAF.
5 Leyland. 1 MAN. 3 MCW. 2 Toyota
6 Volvo.
Bodies: 1 Bova. 3 Caetano. 8 Duple.
3 MCW. 6 Plaxton. 1 Van Hool.
Ops incl: local bus services, school
contracts, excursions and tours.
Livery: Silver/Red/Orange.
Ticket system: Setright.

*CAVALIER CONTRACTS LTD ♿
198 SEAGATE ROAD, LONG
SUTTON PE12 9AD
Tel: 01406 362518
Fax: 01406 362418
E-mail: dennis@cavaliertravel.co.uk
Web site: www.cavaliertravel.co.uk
Fleetname: Cavalier Travel, Huntingdon &
District

Man Dir: Dennis Upton **Fin Dir**: Chris Boor
Fleet: 80 -28 double deckbus, 35 single
deck bus, 5 coach, 12 minibus
Ops incl: local bus services, school
contracts, private hire
Ticket system: Wayfarer

CROPLEY COACHES
♿ wc A/c 💺 🔧

MAIN ROAD, FOSDYKE, BOSTON
PE20 2BH
Tel: 01205 260226
Fax: 01205 260246
Web site: www.cropleycoach.co.uk
E-mail: enquiries@cropleycoach.co.uk
Dirs: J R Cropley, Mrs S R Cropley
Fleet: 12 coach.
Chassis: 1 Setra, 11 Volvo.
Bodies: 1 Jonckheere. 7 Plaxton. 1 Setra.
3 Sunsundegui
Ops incl: school contracts, excursions &
tours, private hire, continental tours.
Livery: White

*DELAINE BUSES LTD ♿
8 SPALDING ROAD, BOURNE
PE10 9LE
Tel: 01778 422866
Fax: 01778 425593
Web site: www.delainebuses.com
Chmn: I Delaine-Smith **Man Dir**: A Delaine-
Smith **Dirs**: M Delaine-Smith,
K Delaine-Smith **Sec**: Mrs B P Tilley
Fleet: 20 - 15 double-deck bus, 5 single-
deck bus.
Chassis: 1 Leyland. 19 Volvo.
Bodies: 1 Duple. 17 East Lancs. 2 Wright.
Ops incl: local bus services
Livery: Light/Dark Blue Blue/Ivory.
Ticket System: Almex A90

*DUNN-LINE (HOLDINGS) LTD
See Nottinghamshire

EAGRE COACHES LTD
wc 🍴 💺 A/c

CROOKED BILLET STREET,
MORTON, GAINSBOROUGH
DN21 3AG
Tel: 01427 612098
Fax: 01427 811340
Ch Eng: M Thrower **Tours Man**: Ann Lee
Fleet: 8 coaches
Chassis: incl: Irisbus. MAN.
Bodies: incl: Beulas. Noge. Marcopolo.
Ops incl: excursions & tours, private hire,
continental tours
Livery: Multicolours
(Subsidiary of Wilfreda Beehive, South
Yorkshire)

*W H FOWLER & SONS (COACHES) LTD
🚌 💺 wc A/c 🔧

155 DOG DROVE SOUTH,
HOLBEACH DROVE, SPALDING
PE12 0SD
Tel: 01406 330232
Fax: 01406 330923
E-mail: andrew@fowlerstravel.com
Web site: www.fowlerstravel.com
Fleetname: Fowlers Travel
Man Dir: John Fowler **Co Sec**:
Jackie Fowler **Dir**: Andrew Fowler
Fleet: 19 - 7 double-deck bus, 2 single-deck
bus, 9 coach, 1 open-top bus.
Chassis: 2 DAF. 3 Leyland. 1 Mercedes.
13 Volvo.
Bodies: 3 Alexander. 1 Duple.
2 Jonckheere. 4 Marshall. 11 Plaxton.
Ops incl: local bus services, school
contracts, excursions & tours, private hire.
Livery: Cream/Orange
Ticket System: Wayfarer

Lancashire / Lincolnshire

A/c	Air conditioning	💺	Seat belt-fitted vehicles	🔧	Replacement vehicle available
♿	Vehicles suitable for disabled	R	Recovery service available (not 24 hr)	T	Toilet-drop facilities available
🍴	Coach(es) with galley facilities			🚌	Vintage vehicle(s) available
wc	Coach(es) with toilet facilities	R24	24hr recovery service		Open top vehicle(s)

Lincolnshire

*GRAYSCROFT BUS SERVICES LTD
15A VICTORIA ROAD, MABLETHORPE LN12 2AF
Tel: 01507 473236
Fax: 01507 477073
Recovery: 01507 473236
E-mail: grayscroftltd@btinternet.com
Dirs: C W Barker, N Barker, N W Barker, C S Barker
Fleet: 19 - 6 double-deck bus, 2 single-deck bus, 9 coach, 2 midibus.
Chassis: 2 Leyland. 2 Mercedes. 1 Optare. 12 Volvo.
Bodies: 2 Alexander. 1 Caetano. 4 East Lancs. 1 Hispano. 3 Jonckheere. 2 Mercedes. 1 Optare. 2 Plaxton. 3 Van Hool.
Ops incl: local bus services, school contracts, excursions & tours, private hire, express
Livery: White/Blue
Ticket system: Setright/Wayfarer

PHIL HAINES COACHES
RALPHS LANE, FRAMPTON WEST, BOSTON PE20 1QU.
Tel/Fax: 01205 722359.
Props: N. A. & F. E. Haines.

*HODSON COACHES LTD
CHAPEL LANE, NAVENBY LN5 0ER
Tel: 01522 810262
Fax: 01522 810793
E-mail: sales@hodsoncoaches.co.uk
Web Site: www.hodsoncoaches.co.uk
Dirs: S Carter, J Carter.
Fleet: 12 - 5 coach, 1 midibus, 1 midicoach, 2 minibus, 3 minicoach.
Chassis: 8 Mercedes. 4 Setra
Bodies: 1 Esker. 4 Mercedes. 3 Optare. 4 Setra.
Ops incl: local bus services, school contracts, excursions & tours, private hire, express, continental tours.
Livery: Cream/Purple
Ticket system: Almex

*HORNSBY TRAVEL SERVICES LTD
See North Lincolnshire

F HUNT COACH HIRE LTD
2/3 WEST STREET, ALFORD LN13 9DG
Tel/Fax: 01507 463000
E-mail: hunts@hunttravel.fsnet.co.uk
Web site: www.hunts-coaches.co.uk
Fleetname: Hunts Travel
Dirs: Michael Hunt, Charles Hunt, Dave Eales
Fleet: 19 - 1 double-deck bus, 5 single-deck bus, 10 coach, 3 midibus.
Chassis: 3 Dennis. 1 Leyland. 3 Mercedes. 1 Optare. 11 Volvo.
Bodies: 2 Alexander. 3 Mercedes. 1 Optare. 10 Van Hool. 3 Wright.
Ops incl: local bus services, school contracts, excursions & tours, private hire, express, continental tours.
Livery: White/Red/Grey
Ticket System: Almex

R KIME & CO LTD
3 SLEAFORD ROAD, FOLKINGHAM, SLEAFORD NG34 0SB
Tel: 01529 497251
Fax: 01529 497554
Fleetname: Kimes Coaches.
Man Dir: Paul Brown
Fleet: 20 - 10 double-deck bus, 6 single-deck bus, 3 coach, 1 midicoach.
Chassis: 4 DAF. 12 Leyland. 1 Mercedes. 3 Volvo.
Bodies: 2 Alexander. 12 Leyland. 3 Northern Counties. 1 Optare. 2 Plaxton.
Ops incl: local bus services, school contracts, excursions & tours, private hire.
Livery: Cream/Green
Ticket System: Almex

SLEAFORDIAN COCHES
PRIDE PARKWAY, EAST ROAD, SLEAFORD NG34 7EH
Tel: 01529 303333
Fax: 01529 303324
Fleetname: Sleafordian
Fleet: 21 - 4 double-deck bus, 12 coach, 3 midibus, 1 minibus.
Chassis: Leyland. Mercedes. Neoplan. Optare. Renault. Volvo.
Bodies: Leyland. Neoplan. Optare. Plaxton. Renault. Van Hool.
Ops incl: private hire.
Livery: White/Orange
(part of Sleafordian Taxi Co Ltd)

STAGECOACH LINCOLNSHIRE
PO BOX 15, DEACON ROAD, LINCOLN LN2 4JB
Tel: 01522 522255
Fax: 01522 538229
Web site: www.stagecoachbus.com
Man Dir: Gary Nolan **Eng&Ops Dir**:
Fleet: 272 - 100 double-deck bus, 145 single-deck bus, 4 open-top bus, 20 midibus, 3 minibus.
Chassis: incl: DAF. Dennis. Mercedes. Optare. Renault. Scania. 80 Volvo.
Bodies: incl: Alexander. East Lancs. Optare. Plaxton. Wright.
Ops incl: local bus services, school contracts
Livery: Green/Yellow/White; Blue/Yellow/Red
Ticket System: Almex.
Part of Stagecoach

MEMORY LANE COACHES
ELM HOUSE, OLD BOLINGBROKE, SPILSBY PE23 4HF
Tel: 01790 763394
Prop: John R Dorey
Fleet: 5 - 3 coach, 2 midicoach.
Chassis: 2 Bedford. 1 Iveco. 1 Leyland. 1 Mercedes.
Bodies: 1 Carlyle. 3 Duple. 1 Plaxton.
Ops incl: school contracts, private hire.
Livery: White/Green/Red.

*MILLMAN COACHES
See North Lincolnshire

*PC COACHES OF LINCOLN LTD
R24
17 CROFTON ROAD, LINCOLN LN3 4NL
Tel: 01522 533605
Fax: 01522 560402
Recovery: 07970 886605
E-mail: enquiries@pccoaches.co.uk
Web site: www.pccoaches.co.uk
Man Dir: Peter Smith **Off Man**: Miss Sarah Smith **Admin Man**: Mrs Linda Longmate
Wkshp Man: Duncan Longmate
Fleet: 50 - 13 double-deck bus, 2 single-deck bus, 27 coach, 4 midibus, 1 midicoach, 2 minibus, 1 minicoach.
Chassis: 1 Ford. 2 LDV. 2 Mercedes. 3 Optare. 42 Scania.
Bodies: 1 Autobus. 2 Berkhof. 13 East Lancs. 16 Irizar. 1 Jonckheere. 3 Optare.
6 Plaxton. 2 Van Hool. 1 Wright. 5 other.
Ops incl: local bus services, school contracts, private hire, excursions & tours, continental tours.
Livery: White/Maroon/Red

*PULFREYS COACHES
THE BUS STATION, WHARF ROAD, GRANTHAM NG31 6EE
Tel: 01476 564144
Dlr: Andrew Pulfrey.
Fleet: 3 - 2 coach, 1 midicoach.
Chassis: 1 Dennis. 1 Iveco. 1 Mercedes.
Bodies: 1 Beulas. 2 Plaxton.
Ops incl: local bus, school contracts, excursions & tours, private hire, continental tours.
Livery: Blue/White
Ticket System: Wayfarer

ROY PHILLIPS
69 STATION ROAD, RUSKINGTON NG34 9DF
Tel: 01526 832279
Prop: R Phillips.
Fleet: 6 coach.
Chassis: 1 Leyland. 5 Volvo.
Bodies: 3 Plaxton. 3 Van Hool.
Ops incl: private hire, school contracts.

SMITHS COACHES, CORBY GLEN
THE GREEN, CORBY GLEN NG33 4NR.
Tel: 01476 550285.
Fax: 01476 550032.
Ptnrs: H. J. and Mary J. Smith.
Fleet: 7 - 5 coach, 1 double-deck coach, 1 minibus.
Chassis: 1 Bedford. 1 Bova. 1 Ford. 1 Freight Rover. 2 MAN. 1 Mercedes.
Bodies: 1 Bova. 1 Carlyle. 1 Duple. 2 MAN. 1 Neoplan. 1 Plaxton.
Ops incl: excursions & tours, private hire, continental tours, school contracts.
Livery: Blue/White.

TRAVELPATH 3000
PO BOX 32, GRANTHAM NG31 7JA
Tel: 01476 570187
Fax: 01476 572718
E-mail: info@travelpath-uk.com
Web site: www.travelpath3000.com

Ops Man: Jon Brown
Ops incl: continental tours

*TRANSLINC

A/c 🪑 ♿

JARVIS HOUSE, 157 SADLER ROAD, LINCOLN LN6 3RS
Tel: 01522 503400
Fax: 01522 503406
E-mail: logistics@translinc.co.uk
Web site: www.translinc.co.uk
Man Dir: Brian West **Sales & Mktg Dir**: John Soulby **Dir of Logistics**: Carole Smith
Ops Man: Tricia Wilson
Fleet: 193 - 18 coach, 19 midibus, 136 minibus, 20 minicoach (8 seats & under)
Chassis: 16 Citroen. 2 DAF. 10 Dennis. 8 Fiat. 104 Iveco. 7 LDV. 20 Mercedes. 2 Optare. 13 Renault. 2 Scania. 4 Toyota. 1 VW. 4 Volvo.
Ops incl: local bus services, school contracts, excursions & tours, private hire, express.

LONDON

This section includes those operators in the London postal areas, as well as operators who have asked to appear under this heading. Other operators within Greater London with a non-London postal address, eg Kingston, Surrey; Bromley, Kent; Enfield, Middlesex, etc, may be found under their respective postal counties.

AA, KNIGHTS OF THE ROAD

WC 🪑 R ✏

WREN ROAD, SIDCUP DA14 4NA
Tel: 020 8309 7741
Prop: J. V. H. Knight. **Ch Eng**: D. Knight
Fleet: 10 - 6 coach, 2 double-deck coach, 2 minicoach.
Chassis: 6 DAF. 2 Mercedes. 2 Volvo.
Bodies: 6 Bova. 2 Jonckheere. 2 Mercedes.
Ops incl: excursions & tours, private hire, continental tours, school contracts.
Livery: Cream/Beige.

AIRLINKS

HEATHROW COACH CENTRE, SIPSON ROAD, WEST DRAYTON UB7 0HN
Tel: 020 8990 6300
Fax: 020 8997 3626
Man Dir: Bill Cahill. **Fin Dir**: Richard Smith.
Dir of Eng: Steve Perks.
Fleet: 329 - includes 19 double-deck bus.
Chassis: 76 DAF. 54 Dennis. 3 MAN. 57 Mercedes. 16 Scania. 12 Toyota. 111 Volvo.
Bodies: 14 Alexander. 32 Berkhof. 15 Caetano. 6 Cobus. 17 East Lancs. 8 Jonckheere. 2 LDV. 11 Frank Guy. 16 Mercedes. 2 Northern Counties. 6 Optare. 99 Plaxton. 13 UVG. 32 Van Hool. 36 Wright.
Ops incl: local bus services, excursions & tours, private hire, express.
Livery: Various.
Subsidiary of National Express

ANDERSON TRAVEL LTD /LONDON MINI-COACHES

🪑 WC 🍴 A/c ✏

178A TOWER BRIDGE ROAD, LONDON SE1 3LS
Tel: 020 7403 8118
Fax: 020 7403 8421
E-mail: sales@andersontravel.co.uk
Web site: www.andersontravel.co.uk

Comm Man: Keith Payne
Fleet: 24 - 17 coach, 4 midicoach, 3 minibus
Chassis: 12 Bova. 10 Mercedes. 2 Toyota.
Bodies: 12 Bova. 2 Caetano. 5 Mercedes. 5 Setra.
Ops incl: excursions & tours, private hire, continental tours.
Livery: White/Green, Silver/Red

ANGEL MOTORS (EDMONTON) LTD

1 CONSTABLE CRESCENT, LONDON N15 4QZ
Tel: 020 8808 2000
Fax: 020 8808 0008
Fleet: 19 - 17 coach, 2 minicoach.
Livery: White/Blue/Yellow.

ARRIVA LONDON

♿ 🚌

16 WATSONS ROAD LONDON N22 7TZ
Tel: 020 8271 0200
Web site: arrivabus.co.uk
Man Dir: Mark Yexley
Fleet: 1460 - incl: double-deck bus, single-deck bus, 157 articulated bus.
Chassis: incl: DAF. Dennis. Mercedes. Volvo.
Bodies: incl: Alexander. Mercedes. Plaxton. Wright
Ops incl: local bus services, excursions & tours, private hire.
Livery: Red

BACK ROADS TOURING CO LTD 🪑 A/c ✏

14A NEW BROADWAY, LONDON W5 2XA.
Tel: 020 8566 5312
Fax: 020 8566 5457
E-mail: info@backroadstouring.co.uk
Web site: www.backroadstouring.co.uk

Man Dir: Bruce Cherry **Fin Dir**: Erika Harcz
Ops Dir: Alex Newmann
Fleet: 22 minibus.
Chassis/Bodies: 16 Mercedes. 6 Renault
Ops incl: excursions & tours, private hire, continental tours.
Livery: White

*BIG BUS COMPANY 🚌

GROSVENOR GARDENS HOUSE, 35-37 GROSVENOR GARDENS, LONDON SW1W 0BS
Tel: 020 7233 8722
Fax: 020 7233 8766
E-mail: info@bigbustours.com
Web site: www.bigbustours.com
Fleet: 72 open-top bus.
Chassis: 14 Dennis. 42 Leyland. 16 MCW.
Ops incl: local bus services, private hire, excursions & tours.
Livery: Maroon/Cream
Ticket system: Almex

BLUEWAYS GUIDELINE COACHES LTD

WC 🍴 🪑 A/c

49 WINDERS ROAD, LONDON SW11 3HE
Tel: 020 7228 3515
Fax: 020 7228 0290
E-mail: blueways@clara.co.uk
Web site: www.bluewaysguideline.co.uk
Dirs: Philip Bruton, Janet Bruton, Thomas McKechnie.
Fleet: 6 - 4 coach. 2 minicoach.
Chassis: 1 Mercedes. 3 Scania. 2 Toyota
Bodies: 2 Caetano. 3 Irizar. 1 Mercedes.
Ops incl: excursions & tours, private hire, continental tours, school contracts.
Livery: 2 White/two-tone Blue, 2 White, 2 England sponsors.

Symbol	Meaning	Symbol	Meaning
A/c	Air conditioning	🪑	Seat belt-fitted vehicles
♿	Vehicles suitable for disabled	R	Recovery service available (not 24 hr)
🍴	Coach(es) with galley facilities	R24	24hr recovery service
WC	Coach(es) with toilet facilities	✏	Replacement vehicle available
		T	Toilet-drop facilities available
		🚐	Vintage vehicle(s) available
		🚌	Open top vehicle(s)

Lincolnshire / London

BRENTONS OF BLACKHEATH

GREENWICH HIGH ROAD, LONDON SE10 8JL
Tel: 020 820 2020
Fax: 020 692 4932
E-mail: davee@brentonsofblackheath.co.uk
Web site: www.brentonsofblackheath.co.uk
Prop: C Clark **Coach Man**: D Eaton
Ch Eng: I Powell
Fleet: 14 - 11 coach, 1 midicoach, 2 minicoach.
Chassis: 2 Dennis. 5 Leyland. 3 Mercedes. 5 Volvo.
Bodies: 1 Berkhof 2 Duple. 3 Mercedes. 7 Plaxton. 1 Van Hool.
Ops incl: private hire, school contracts, excursions and tours.
Livery: Red/Cream/Grey

BRYANS OF ENFIELD

19 WETHERLEY ROAD, ENFIELD EN2 0NS.
Fax: 020 8366 0062.
Owner: B. Nash.
Fleet: 6 - 3 double-deck bus, 1 single-deck bus, 1 coach, 1 double-deck coach.
Chassis: 1 AEC. 1 DAF. 2 Daimler. 1 Leyland. 1 MCW.
Bodies: 1 ECW. 2 MCW. 2 Park Royal. 1 Van Hool.
Ops incl: school contracts, private hire.
Livery: Red.

CENTAUR TRAVEL MINICOACHES

188 HALFWAY STREET, SIDCUP DA15 8DJ.
Tel: 020 8300 3001.
Fax: 020 8302 5959.
Man Dir: M. Sims. **Ch Eng**: R. Raison.
Ops Man: Kay Priestley.
Fleet: 14 - 2 midicoach, 5 minibus, 7 minicoach.
Chassis: 7 Freight Rover. 2 Mercedes. 5 Renault.
Ops incl: private hire, school contracts.

*CALL-A-COACH
See Surrey

*CAVALIER TRAVEL SERVICES

ASH COURT, LANC "C", PHOENIX DISTRIBUTION PARK, PHOENIX WAY, HESTON TW5 9NB
Tel: 0845 125 9379
Fax: 0845 833 2295
E-mail: bookings@caviliercoaches.com
Web site: www.caviliercoaches.com
Dirs: Andrew W Pagan, Denise H Pagan
Fleet: 12 - 7 double-deck coach, 2 midicoach, 2 minibus. 1 people carrier.
Chassis: 3 Iveco. 4 Mercedes. 2 Neoplan. 1 Scania. 1 Toyota.
Bodies: 3 Beulas. 1 Caetano. 1 Esker. 1 Irizar. 2 Neoplan. 3 Optare.
Ops incl: private hire
Livery: White, White/Blue

*CHALFONT LINE LTD
See Middlesex

CHERRY BRIAR LTD

SUPREME HOUSE, STOUR WHARF, STOUR ROAD, LONDON E3 2NT
Tel: 020 8985 8888
Fax: 020 8936 8444
Man Dir: Clifford Humphreys **Ops Man/Co Sec**: Helen Humphreys **Ch Eng**: B Raif.
Fleetname: Channel Coachways
Fleet: 5 - 4 coach. 1 midicoach.
Chassis: Scania. Toyota.
Bodies: Caetano. Irizar.
Ops incl: school contracts, excursions & tours, private hire, continental tours.
Livery: White/Red/Blue.

*CLARKES OF LONDON

KANGLEY BRIDGE ROAD, LONDON SE26 5AT
Tel: 020 8778 6697
Fax: 020 8778 0389
E-mail: info@clarkescoaches.co.uk
Web site: www.clarkescoaches.co.uk
Man Dir: Mrs D Newman **Comm Dir**: J Devacmaker **Fin Dir**: S Reeve
Fleet: 51 - 46 coach, 5 minicoach.
Chassis: 22 Setra. 23 Scania . 5 Toyota. 1 Volvo.
Bodies: 5 Caetano. 23 Irizar. 1 Jonckheere. 22 Setra
Ops incl: excursions & tours, private hire, express, continental tours.
Livery: Green/Silver.

COLLINS COACHES LTD

UNIT 6, WATERSIDE TRADING CENTRE, TRUMPERS WAY, LONDON W7 2QD
Tel: 020 8843 2145
Fax: 020 8843 2375
E-mail: collinscoaches@aol.com
Web site: www.collins-coaches.co.uk
Man Dir: Eric Collins **Sec**: Pauline Collins
Dir: Alfred Collins
Fleet: 9 coach.
Chassis: 9 Volvo.
Bodies: 4 Jonckheere. 4 Plaxton. 1 Van Hool.
Ops incl: private hire, school contracts.
Livery: Red/White.

CONISTON COACHES LTD

88 CONISTON ROAD, BROMLEY BR1 4JB.
Tel/Fax: 020 8460 3432
Web site: www.conistoncoaches.co.uk
Dir: Richard Smock
Fleet: 5 coach
Chassis: 5 Volvo
Bodies: 1 Caetano. 4 Plaxton.
Ops incl: excursions & tours, private hire, continental tours, school contracts.
Livery: White/Red.

*COUNTY COACHES
See Essex

DAVID CORBEL OF LONDON LTD

6 CAMROSE AVENUE, EDGWARE HA8 6EG
Tel: 020 8952 1300.
Fax: 020 8952 8641
E-mail: corbeloflondon@aol.com
Dir: Robert Whelan
Fleet: 9 coach
Chassis: 4 Dennis. 1 Setra. 4 Volvo.
Bodies: 4 Plaxton. 1 Setra. 4 UVG.
Ops incl: school contracts, private hire.
Livery: Pink/Blue.

CROWN COACHES

68 CANON ROAD, BICKLEY BR1 2SP
Tel: 020 8313 3020
Fax: 020 8464 2375
Fleet: 5 - 4 coach, 1 minibus.
Chassis: incl: 1 Ford Transit.
Bodies: incl: 2 Mercedes. 1 Setra. 1 Van Hool.
Ops incl: excursions & tours, private hire, continental tours.

CROYDON TRAMLINK

TRAMTRACK CROYDON LTD, COOMBER WAY, CROYDON CR0 4TQ
Tel: 020 8665 9695
Web site: www.tfl.gov.uk/trams
Ops Dir: John Ryman
Head of Safety: C Tomlinson
Fleet: 24 Tram
Chassis/bodies: Bombardier
Ops incl: local tram services
Livery: Red/White

CRYSTALS COACHES LTD

HORTENSIA ROAD, LONDON SW10 0QP.
Tel: 020 7376 3015
Fax: 020 7376 3019
Ops Man: G. Betts.
Fleet: 30 - 15 minibus, 15 minicoach.
Chassis: Ford Transit. Freight Rover. Mercedes.
Ops incl: local bus services, school contracts, private hire.

DANS MINI-BUS HIRE LTD

ROYAL FOREST COACH HOUSE, 109 MAYBANK ROAD, LONDON E18 1EZ.
Tel: 020 8505 8833.
Fax: 020 8519 1937.
Man Dir: D. J. Brown. **Dir**: S. A. Brown.
Fleet: 43 mini/midicoaches
Chassis: 19 Ford Transit. 24 Mercedes
Bodies: 24 Mercedes. 7 Optare. 5 Reeve Burgess. 1 Ford
Ops incl: school contracts, excursions & tours, private hire, continental tours.

*DAVIAN COACHES LTD
1-3 BECKET ROAD, EDMONTON, LONDON N18 3PN
Tel: 020 8807 1515
Fax: 020 8807 2323
Dirs: J H Heaps, J R Heaps, D K Wardle, J A Wardle (**Co Sec**) **Gen Man**: D J Bee
Ops Man: R A Candlish
Ch Eng: A D Wilson-Kelsey
E-mail: daviancoaches@btconnect.com
Web site: www.daviancoaches.co.uk
Fleet: 23 - 11 coach, 12 minicoach
Chassis: 1 Bedford. 1 BMC. 1 Iveco. 10 LDV. 2 Mercedes. 5 Scania. 3 Volvo.
Bodies: 1 BMC. 1 Duple. 4 Irizar. 4 Plaxton. 13 other.
Ops incl: excursions & tours, school contracts, private hire, continental tours.
Livery: White

*DOCKLANDS MINIBUSES LTD
FACTORY ROAD, LONDON E16 2EW
Tel: 020 7474 8130
E-mail: enquiries@go-ahead-london.com
Web site: www.go-ahead-london.com
Fleetname: Docklands
Ch Exec: John Trayner **Eng Dir**: Phil Margrave **Fin Dir**: Paul Reeves.
Ops Dir: David Cutts
Fleet: 29 midibus
Chassis: 29 Dennis
Bodies: 29 Marshall/MCV
Ops incl: local bus services
(part of the Go Ahead Group)

EALING COMMUNITY TRANSPORT LTD
97 BOLLO LANE, LONDON W3 8QN
Tel: 020 8753 7810
Web site: www.ectgroup.co.uk
Pass Ops Dir: Anna Whitty
Fleet: 28 - 13 single-deck bus, 15 minibus
Ops incl: local bus services
Livery: Red/Yellow

*EAST LONDON BUS GROUP
2 CLEMENTS ROAD, ILFORD IG1 1BA
Tel: 020 8477 7200
CEO: Nigel Barrett **Ch Fin Off**: Paul Cox **Eng Dir**: Peter Sumner **Ser Perf Dir**: Richard Franklin **HR Dir**: Sarah Rennie
Fleet: 1276 - 941 double-deck bus, 262 single-deck bus, 73 articulated bus
Chassis: 10 AEC. 7 DAF. 1168 Dennis. 73 Mercedes. 16 Scania. 2 Volvo.
Bodies: 1170 Alexander. 73 Mercedes. 7 Optare. 10 Park Royal. 16 Wright.
Ops incl: local bus services

P & J ELLIS LTD
UNIT 3, RADFORD ESTATE, OLD OAK LANE, LONDON NW10 6UA
Tel: 020 8961 1141
Fax: 020 8965 5995
E-mail: enquiries@pjellis.co.uk
Web-site: www.pjellis.co.uk
Dir: Matthew Ellis
Fleet: 12 coach.
Chassis: 12 Volvo.
Bodies: 12 Jonckheere.
Ops incl: excursions & tours, private hire, continental tours.

ELTHAM EXECUTIVE CHARTER LTD
21-23 CROWN WOODS WAY, LONDON SE9 2NL
Tel: 020 8850 2011
Fax: 020 8850 5210
E-mail: enquiries@eec-minicoaches.co.uk
Web site: www.eec-minicoaches.co.uk
Dirs: Ray Lawrence, Jill Lawrence, Fiona Lawrence
Fleet: 6 - 3 midicoach, 1 minibus, 2 minicoach
Chassis: 1 Ford. 5 Iveco.
Bodies: 3 Indcar. 1 Optare. 2 other
Ops incl: private hire.
Livery: White with blue&gold graphics

EMPRESS MOTORS LTD
3 CORBRIDGE CRESCENT, LONDON E2 9DS.
Tel: 020 7739 5454
Fax: 020 7729 0237
E-mail: info@empresscoaches.co.uk
Web site: www.empresscoaches.co.uk
Fleetmane: Empress of London
Man Dir: P D Stanton **Co Sec**: T A Stanton
Dir: L M R Stanton **Op Mans**: J C Stanton, M E Stanton
Fleet: 18 - 13 coach, 3 midicoach, 2 minibus.
Chassis/Bodies: 1 Caetano. 1 Jonckheere. 1 Mercedes. 1 Optare. 13 Plaxton. 1 Toyota.
Ops incl: private hire.
Livery: Cream/Maroon.

EXCALIBUR COACHES
1A BRABOURN GROVE, LONDON SE15 2BS
Tel: 020 7358 1441
Fax: 020 7358 1661
E-mail: garbyzacca@aol.com
Web site: www.excaliburcoaches.com
Man Dir: Garby Zacca **Ch Eng**: C Patel
Fleet: 12 coach.
Chassis: 2 Iveco. 10 Scania.
Bodies: 2 Beulas. 10 Irizar.

Ops incl: excursions & tours, private hire, express, continental tours, school contracts.
Livery: Blue

FIRST LONDON & BERKSHIRE
3RD FLOOR, MACMILLAN HOUSE, PADDINGTON STATION, LONDON W2 1TY
Tel: 020 7298 7300
Fax: 020 7706 8789
Web site: www.firstgroup.co.uk
Man Dir: Adrian Jones.
Fleet: 1204 - 699 double-deck bus, 12 single-deck bus, 476 midibus, 15 minibus, 2 open-top bus.
Chassis: 59 AEC. 924 Dennis. 21 Leyland. 24 MCW. 24 Mercedes. 149 Volvo.
Bodies: 67 Alexander. 3 Carlyle. 49 East Lancs. 1 Leyland. 450 Marshall. 30 MCW. 14 Mercedes. 89 Northern Counties. 59 Park Royal. 429 Plaxton. 2 Reeve Burgess. 11 Wright.
Ops incl: local bus services, school contracts, private hire.
Livery: Red with Yellow/Grey stripes.
Ticket System: Prestige (TfL).

*FLIGHTS HALLMARK
See West Midlands

FOREST COACHES
THE COACH HOUSE, NELSON STREET, LONDON E6 2QA.
Tel: 020 8472 5954.
Fax: 020 8472 6098.

*FORESTDALE COACHES LTD
68 VINEY BANK, COURTWOOD LANE, FORESTDALE, ADDINGTON CR0 9JT
Tel/Fax: 020 8651 1359
Chmn/Man Dir: V Holub
Co Sec: Mrs P R Holub
Fleet: 1 coach.
Chassis/Body: Bova.
Ops incl: excursions & tours, private hire
Livery: Red/Gold

GOLDENSTAND (SOUTHERN) LTD
13 WAXLOW ROAD, LONDON NW10 7NY
Tel: 020 8961 9974/5
Fax: 020 8961 9949
Web site: www.goldenstand.co.uk
Chmn: J Chivrall **Sec**: J Kemp
Fleet: 8 - 5 coach, 3 minibus.
Chassis: 3 LDV. 5 Scania.
Bodies: 5 Jonckheere. 3 Leyland
Ops incl: school contracts, private hire, excursions & tours
Livery: Red/White

A/c	Air conditioning	
	Vehicles suitable for disabled	
	Coach(es) with galley facilities	
wc	Coach(es) with toilet facilities	
	Seat belt-fitted vehicles	
R	Recovery service available (not 24 hr)	
R24	24hr recovery service	
	Replacement vehicle available	
T	Toilet-drop facilities available	
	Vintage vehicle(s) available	
	Open top vehicle(s)	

THE GOLD STANDARD

94A HORSENDEN LANE NORTH, GREENFORD UB6 7QH
Tel: 020 8795 0075.
Fax: 020 8900 9630.
E-mail: paul@luxuryminicoaches.co.uk
Web site: www.luxuryminicoach.co.uk
Prop: Paul Grant
Fleet: 1 minicoach.
Chassis: Optare.
Ops incl: excursions & tours, private hire.

*A GREEN COACHES LTD

357A HOE STREET, WALTHAMSTOW, LONDON E17 9AP
Tel: 020 8520 1138
Fax: 020 8520 1139
E-mail: agreencoaches357@aol.com
Man Dir: Keith Richards **Tran Man**: Janis Grover
Fleet: 5 coach
Chassis: 1 Scania. 4 Volvo
Ops incl: private hire, school contracts.

*HEARNS COACHES

801 KENTON LANE, HARROW WEALD HA3 6AH
Tel: 020 8954 0444
Fax: 020 8954 5959
E-mail: ged@hearns-coaches.co.uk
Web site: www.hearns-coaches.co.uk
Prop: R J Hearn **Ops Man**: Ged Newham
Ch Eng: Dave Berry
Contracts Man: Dave Sharpe
Fleet: 38 - 34 coach, 3 minibus, 1 midicoach.
Chassis: 1 Leyland. 8 Mercedes. 2 Neoplan. 9 Scania. 11 Setra. 3 Volvo.
Ops incl: private hire, school contracts, excursions & tours, continental tours

*JOHN HOUGHTON LUXURY MINI COACHES

2 ELGAR AVENUE, EALING, LONDON W5 3JU
Tel: 020 8567 0056
Fax: 020 8567 5781
E-mail: jrhoughton@connectfree.co.uk
Web site: www.luxury-mini-coaches.co.uk
Man Dir: John Houghton **Co Sec**: Marlene Houghton
Fleet: 3 minicoach.
Chassis/bodies: 3 Mercedes.
Ops incl: private hire.

HOUNSLOW MINI COACHES

2 VINEYARD ROAD, HIGH STREET, FELTHAM TW13 4HQ.
Tel: 020 8890 8429
Fax: 020 8893 1736
Web site: www.hounslowminicoaches.co.uk
E-mail: hounslowminicoaches@btconnect.com

Fleet: 19 - 3 midicoach, 4 minibus, 4 minicoach, 8 people carrier.
Chassis: 2 Ford Transit, 1 Iveco. 5 LDV. 7 Mercedes. 1 Toyota.
Bodies: 1 Caetano. 3 Mellor. 4 Mercedes. 5 Optare. 3 other.
Ops incl: school contracts, private hire.

HOUSTON'S OF LONDON

83 GLADESMORE ROAD, LONDON N15 6TL.
Tel/Fax: 020 8800 4576.
Prop: H. Jones.
Fleet: 2 coach. **Chassis**: Leyland.
Ops incl: school contracts, excursions & tours, private hire.

IMPACT OF LONDON

7-9 WADSWORTH ROAD, GREENFORD UB6 7JZ
Tel: 020 8579 9922
Fax: 020 8840 4880.
E-mail: info@impactgroup.co.uk
Web site: www.impactgroup.co.uk
Dir: A Hill **Gen Man**: A. Palmer.
Engs: H Louis, L. Singh.
Fleet: 44 - 14 coach, 20 midicoach, 10 minibus.
Chassis: 2 Bova. 2 Dennis. 10 LDV. 20 Mercedes. 10 Volvo.
Bodies: 7 Berkhof. 2 Bova. 1 Caetano. 2 Mellor. 24 Mercedes. 3 Optare. 3 Plaxton. 2 Van Hool.
Ops incl: excursions & tours, private hire, express, continental tours, school contracts.
Livery: White.

INTERNATIONAL COACH LINES LTD

19 NURSERY ROAD, THORNTON HEATH CR7 8RE.
Tel: 020 8684 2995.
Fax: 020 8689 3483.
Dir: Mrs S. Bailey.
Fleet: 18 - 3 double-deck bus, 1 single-deck bus, 10 coach, 4 minicoach.
Ops incl: excursions & tours, private hire, express, continental tours.
Livery: Blue/White.

*THE KINGS FERRY

See Kent

LEWIS TRAVEL UK PLC

2-10 DENHAM STREET, LONDON SE10 0RY
Tel: 020 8858 0031
Fax: 020 8858 7631
E-mail: sales@lewistravel.co.uk
Dir: T Legnor-Lewis **Gen Man**: J Harpic
Fleet: 29 - 20 coach, 4 midibus, 3 minibus, 2 minicoach.
Chassis: 1 Ayats. 1 Bova. 4 DAF. 3 Dennis. 4 Mercedes. 2 Neoplan. 2 Scania. 1 Setra. 6 Transbus. 6 Volvo.
Bodies: 1 Ayats. 1 Bova. 1 Duple. 4 Ikarus. 3 Irizar. 1 Jonckheere. 2 Mercedes. 1 Neoplan. 7 Plaxton. 1 Setra. 4Transbus. 3 Van Hool.
Ops incl: local bus services, school contracts, excursions & tours, private hire, continental tours.
Livery: incl. Red

LINK LINE COACHES LTD

1 WROTTESLEY ROAD, LONDON NW10 5XA.
Tel: 020 8965 2221.
Fax: 020 8961 3680.
E-mail: info@linkline-coaches.co.uk
Web site: wwwlinkline-coaches.co.uk
Man Dir: T. J. Russell.
Fleet: 10 - 7 single-deck bus, 3 coach.
Chassis: 6 Dennis. 1 Mercedes. 3 Volvo.
Bodies: 8 Caetano. 1 Optare. 1 Plaxton.
Ops incl: private hire, continental tours, school contracts.
(Subsidiary of Tellings Golden Miller)

THE LITTLE BUS COMPANY

HOME FARM, ALDENHAM ROAD, ELSTREE WD6 3AZ
Tel: 020 8953 0202
Fax: 020 8953 9553
E-mail: enquiry@littlebus.co.uk
Web site: www.littlebus.co.uk
Fleet: includes single deck coach, midicoach, minibus, minicoach
Chassis: LDV. Leyland. Mercedes.
Bodies: Mercedes.
Prop: Jeremy Reese
Fleet: 7 minibus.
Chassis: 5 LDV. 2 Ford Transit.
Ops incl: school contracts, private hire.

LONDON BUSES LTD t/a EAST THAMES BUSES

ASH GROVE, MARE STREET, LONDON E8 4RH
Tel: 020 7241 7220.
Fax: 020 7241 7239.
Fleet Name: East Thames Buses.
Man Dir: Alan Barrett
Fin Dir: David Bowen. **Eng. Dir**: Gary Filbey. **Gen Man**: Norman Priestly.
Fleet: 128 - 77 double-deck bus. 51 single-deck bus.
Chassis: 12 DAF, 15 Dennis. 10 Optare. 14 Scania. 77 Volvo.
Bodies: 40 East Lancs. 10 Optare. 21 Plaxton. 3 Wright.
Ops incl: local bus services.
Livery: Red.
Ticket System: Prestige
(Part of Transport for London)

*LONDON CENTRAL BUS CO LTD

18 MERTON HIGH STREET, LONDON SW19 1DN
Tel: 020 8545 6100
Fax: 020 8545 6101
E-mail: enquiries@go-ahead-london.com
Web site: www.go-ahead-london.com
Fleet Name: London Central
Ch Exec: John Trayner **Eng Dir**: Phil Margrave **Fin Dir**: Paul Reeves.
Ops Dir: David Cutts
Fleet: 622 - 429 double-deck bus, 130 single-deck bus, 63 articulated bus.
Chassis: 3 AEC. 6 DAF. 163 Dennis. 63 Mercedes. 387 Volvo.
Bodies: 189 Alexander. 20 Marshall. 10 Northern Counties. 3 Park Royal. 269 Plaxton. 62 Wright. 69 other.

Ops incl: local bus services, school contracts, private hire.
Livery: Red
(part of the Go Ahead Group)

*LONDON GENERAL TRANSPORT SERVICES LTD

18 MERTON HIGH STREET, LONDON SW19 1DN
Tel: 020 8545 6100
Fax: 020 8545 6101
E-mail: enquiries@go-ahead-london.com
Web site: www.go-ahead-london.com
Fleet Name: London General
Ch Exec: John Trayner **Eng Dir**: Phil Margrave **Fin Dir**: Paul Reeves.
Ops Dir: David Cutts
Fleet: 719 - 516 double-deck bus, 172 single-deck bus, 31 articulated bus.
Chassis: 5 AEC. 240 Dennis. 31 Mercedes. 443 Volvo.
Bodies: 173 Alexander. 52 East Lancs. 17 Marshall/MCV. 30 Noge. 5 Park Royal. 200 Plaxton. 211 Wright. 31 other.
Ops incl: local bus services, school contracts, private hire.
Livery: Red
(part of the Go Ahead Group)

*LONDON UNITED BUSWAYS LTD
See Middlesex

LUXURY MINI COACH

94A HORSENDEN LANE, GREENFORD UB6 7QH
Tel: 020 8795 0075.
Fax: 020 8900 9630.
E-mail: paul@luxuryminicoach.co.uk
Web site: www.luxuryminicoach.co.uk
Dir: Paul Grant
Fleet: minicoaches.
Ops incl: private hire.

*MARTINS COACHES

THE GAS WORKS, 709 OLD KENT ROAD, LONDON SE15 1JZ
Tel: 020 7732 1000
Fax: 020 7732 1011
E-mail: info@martinscoachesco uk
Web site: www.martinscoaches.co.uk
ManDir: Steve Martin
Fleet: 21 - 10 coach, 10 midicoach, 1 minibus
Chassis: 11 Mercedes. 10 Transbus.
Bodies: 11 Plaxton. 10 Transbus.
Ops incl: school contracts, excursions & tours, private hire, continental tours.
Livery: White/Purple

*MARSHALLS COACHES
R24
FIRBANK WAY, LEIGHTON BUZZARD LU7 4YP
Tel: 01525 376077
Fax: 01525 850967
Recovery: 01525 375301
E-mail: info@marshalls-coaches.co.uk
Web site: www.marshalls-coaches.co.uk
Fleetname: MCE Ltd
Prop: G Marshall **Ops Man**: I White
Wkshp Man: R Winters
Fleet: 28 - 3 double-deck bus, 22 coach, 2 double-deck coach, 1 midicoach.
Chassis: 3 Ayats. 4 Dennis. 3 Iveco. 2 Leyland. 1 Mercedes. 15 Volvo.
Bodies: 3 Ayats. 3 Beulas. 1 Caetano. 3 East Lancs. 5 Jonckheere. 1 Mercedes. 10 Plaxton.
Ops incl: private hire, school contracts, continental tours.
Livery: Blue/Multicoloured.

*METROBUS
See West Sussex

*METROLINE
See Middlesex

M&M COACHLINES
See Middlesex

M T P CHARTER COACHES
39 GROSVENOR ROAD, LONDON E11 2EW
Tel/Fax: 020 8989 0211
Prop: M Powis
Fleet: 2 - 1 coach, 1 mdnicoach.
Chassis/bodies: 1 Setra. 1 Caetano.
Ops incl: private hire, excursions & tours, continental tours.
Livery: White

NEW BHARAT COACHES LTD
1A PRIORY WAY, SOUTHALL UB2 5EB
Tel: 020 8574 6810
Fax: 020 8813 9555
E-mail: admin@newbharat.co.uk
Web site: www.newbharat.co.uk
Dir: Surjit Singh Dhaliwal
Ch Eng: Alan Littlemore
Fleet: 4 coach
Chassis: 4 Volvo
Ops incl: school contracts, excursions & tours, private hire, express, continental tours.
Livery: Red/Yellow/Blue on white base.

NEWBOURNE COACHES
R24
FIRBANK WAY, LEIGHTON BUZZARD LU7 4YP
Tel: 020 7837 6663
Fax: 01525 850967

Web site: www.marshalls-coaches.co.uk
E.mail: info@marshalls-coaches.co.uk
Props: G R Marshall, S J Marshall
Ops Man: Ian White **Ch Eng**: Nick Aris
Fleet: 22 - 20 coach, 1 double-deck coach, 1 midicoach.
Chassis: 4 Dennis. 6 Iveco. 1 Mercedes. 1 Neoplan. 10 Volvo.
Bodies: 6 Beulas. 1 Ikarus. 6 Jonckheere. 1 Mercedes. 1 Neoplan. 7 Plaxton.
Ops incl: private hire, school contracts, local bus services.
Livery: Blue/Multicoloured.
(part of Marshalls Coaches)

THE ORIGINAL LONDON TOUR

JEWS ROW, LONDON SW18 1TB
Tel: 020 8877 1722
Fax: 020 8877 1968
E-mail: info@theoriginaltour.com
Web site: www.theoriginaltour.com
Man Dir: Bob Scowen
Fleet: 94 - 24 double-deck bus, 70 open-top bus.
Chassis: 2 Dennis. 13 Leyland. 41 MCW. 14 Volvo.
Bodies: 13 Alexander. 41 MCW. 2 Northern Counties. 14 Transbus.
Ops incl: local bus services.
Livery: Red/Cream
Ticket system: Almex/Wayfarer
Subsidiary of Arriva

REDWING COACHES

10 DYLAN ROAD, LONDON SE24 0HL
Tel: 020 7733 1124
Fax: 020 7733 5194
E-mail: redwing@redwing-coaches.co.uk.
Web site: www.redwing-coaches.co.uk.
Man Dir: vacant **Ops Man**: Barry Nunn
Gen Man: John Fowler **Ch Eng**: Robbie Hodgekiss **Reservations**: Jef Johnson
Fleet: 45 - 43 coach, 2 midicoach.
Chassis: 20 Iveco. 11 Mercedes. 14 Setra.
Bodies: 20 Beulas. 11 Caetano. 14 Setra
Ops incl: excursions & tours, private hire, continental tours.
Livery: Red/Cream
Part of Addison Lee

ROUNDABOUT BUSES

25 OLDFIELD ROAD, BEXLEYHEATH DA7 4DX
Tel: 020 8302 7551
E-mail: info@roundaboutbuses.co.uk
Web site: www.roundaboutbuses.co.uk
Man Dir: Glyn Matthews.
Fleet: 6 - 1 single-deck bus, 1 minibus.
Chassis: 1 AEC. 2 Iveco. 5 Leyland.
Bodies: 3 ECW. 1 Marshall. 1 Park Royal. 1 Roe. 1 Robin Hood.
Ops incl: local bus services, school contracts.

A/C	Air conditioning
	Vehicles suitable for disabled
	Coach(es) with galley facilities
WC	Coach(es) with toilet facilities
	Seat belt-fitted vehicles
R	Recovery service available (not 24 hr)
R24	24hr recovery service
	Replacement vehicle available
T	Toilet-drop facilities available
	Vintage vehicle(s) available
	Open top vehicle(s)

Livery: Green/Cream.
Ticket System: Wayfarer.

SILVERDALE LONDON LTD

UNIT 3, RADFORD ESTATE, OLD OAK LANE, LONDON NW10 6UA
Tel: 020 8961 1812
Fax: 020 8961 5677
Email: silverdalelondon@aol.com
Web site: www.silverdalelondon.com
Dir: Robert Green **Tran Man:** Richard Cassell
Fleet: 14 - coach, midibus.
Chassis: 1 Dennis. 1 MAN. 2 Mercedes. 10 Volvo.
Bodies: 10 Caetano. 1 Marcopolo. 2 Optare. 1 Plaxton.
Ops incl: school contracts, excursions & tours, private hire, express, continental tours.
Livery: White/Red
(part of the Silverdale Tours, Nottinghamshire)

SOUTHGATE & FINCHLEY COACHES LTD

231A COLNEY HATCH LANE, LONDON N11 3DG
Tel: 020 8368 0040
Fax: 020 8361 1934
Web site: www.coaches.org.uk
Man Dir: M. P. Rice. **Dirs:** Mrs V. M. Rice (**Co Sec**), P. M. Rice, Mrs E. B. Scrivens.
Fleet: 23 coach.
Chassis: 23 V.olvo.
Bodies: 23 Plaxton
Ops incl: school contracts, excursions and tours, private hire
Livery: Yellow/Blue/Orange

TELLINGS GOLDEN MILLER COACHES LTD

ENSIGN CLOSE, HEATHROW AIRPORT, HOUNSLOW TW6 2PQ
Tel: 020 8757 4700
Fax: 020 8757 4718
E-mail: sales@telling.co.uk
Web site: www.tellingsgoldenmiller.co.uk
Chmn: Stephen Telling **Group Ops Dir:** Richard Telling **Fin Dir/Co Sec:** Basil Taylor
Ops Dir: Paul Cowell **Eng Man:** Ian Foster
Fleet: 75 - 58 coach, 14 minicoach, 3 minicoach.
Chassis: 2 Iveco. 15 Mercedes. 3 Setra. 2 Toyota. 53 Volvo.
Bodies: 2 Beulas. 6 Caetano. 3 Mercedes. 59 Plaxton. 3 Setra. 2 Van Hool.
Ops incl: school contracts, excursions & tours, private hire, express, continental tours.
Livery: White/Blue/Yellow

TIMEBUS TRAVEL

7 BOLEYN DRIVE, ST ALBANS AL1 2BP
Tel: 01727 866248
Web site: www.timebus.co.uk
Fleetname: Timebus
Prop: David Pring
Fleet: 12 - 8 double-deck bus, 2 single-deck bus, 2 open-top bus
Chassis: 11 AEC. 1 Leyland.
Bodies: 2 MCW. 9 Park Royal. 1 other.
Ops incl: private hire
Livery: Red with grey lining

TOMORROWS TRANSPORT

GIBBS STORAGE, GIBBS ROAD, LONDON N18 3PU
Tel: 020 8807 4555
Fax: 020 8807 4603
Prop: V A Daniels
Fleet: 3 - 2 coach, 1 midicoach
Chassis: 1 DAF. 1 Leyland. 1 Toyota.
Bodies: 1 Caetano. 1 Duple. 1 Van Hool.
Ops incl: private hire

TRAVEL LONDON LTD

301 CAMBERWELL NEW ROAD, LONDON SE5 0TF
Tel: 020 7805 3500
Fax: 020 7805 3510
Web site: www.travellondonbus.co.uk
Man Dir: Paul McGowan **Ops Dir:** Bill Weatherley **Eng Dir:** Steve Hamilton
Fin Dir: Ross Hanley
Fleet: 433 - 198 double-deck bus, 223 single-deck bus, 12 midibus
Chassis: Dennis. Optare. Mercedes. Volvo.
Bodies: Alexander. Wright. East Lancs. Plaxton. Caetano.
Ops incl: local bus services
Livery: Red (London), Red and white (Surrey CC)
Ticket system: Wayfarer, Almex
(Subsidiary of National Express Group)

WESTBUS COACH SERVICES LTD

27A SPRING GROVE ROAD, HOUNSLOW TW3 4BE
Tel: 020 8572 6348
Fax: 020 8570 2234
Recovery: 020 8572 6348
E-mail: reservations@westbus.co.uk
Web site: www.westbus.co.uk
Gen Man: Tim Miles **Ops Man:** Chris Shaw
Ch Eng: Graham Bessant
Chassis: 15 DAF. 4 Mercedes. 2 Setra. 5 Volvo.
Bodies: 2 Berkhof. 1 Hispano. 5 Plaxton. 2 Setra. 1 Sitcar. 15 Van Hool.
Ops incl: private hire, continental tours, excursions & tours, school contracts.

Livery: Red/Cream
(Part of the Comfort Delgro Corporation)

*WEST'S COACHES LTD

198/200 HIGH ROAD, WOODFORD GREEN IG8 9EF
Tel: 020 8504 9747
Fax: 020 8559 1085
Dirs: R L West, E J M West, M M West
Ch Eng: P Faux
Fleet: 17- 15 coach, 1 open-top bus, 1 midibus.
Chassis: 1 AEC. 2 DAF. 3 Dennis. 1 Iveco. 1 MCW. 9 Volvo
Bodies: 1 Beadle. 2 Caetano. 2 Marcopolo. 1 MCW. 9 Plaxton. 2 UVG.
Ops incl: excursions & tours, private hire, school contracts, continental tours.
Livery: White/Red/Blue

WESTWAY COACH SERVICES

7A RAINBOW INDUSTRIAL ESTATE, STATION APPROACH, RAYNES PARK, LONDON SW20 0JY
Tel: 020 8944 1277.
Fax: 020 8947 5339.
E-mail: david@westway-coaches.co.uk
E-mail:
www.westwaycoachservices.com
Prop: David West.
Gen Man: Arthur Richardson.
Fleet: 16 - 7 coach, 7 double-deck coach, 2 midicoach.
Chassis: 2 Mercedes. 14 Volvo
Bodies: 6 Jonckheere. 1 Plaxton. 6 Van Hool. 2 other.
Ops incl: school contracts, excursions & tours, private hire, continental tours.
Livery: Blue/Red

*WINGS LUXURY TRAVEL LTD

47 WALLINGFORD ROAD, UXBRIDGE UB8 2XS
Tel: 020 8573 8388
Fax: 020 8573 7773
Web site: www.wingstravel.co.uk
E-mail: info@wingstravel.co.uk
Chmn: F L Gritt **Gen Man:** W Gritt
Ops Man: S Hughes
Fleet: 16 - 8 midicoach, 8 minicoach
Chassis/Bodies: 16 Mercedes
Ops Incl: school contracts, excursions and tours, private hire
Livery: White

MERSEYSIDE (ST HELENS, KNOWSLEY, LIVERPOOL, SEFTON, WIRRAL)

A1A LTD
373 CLEVELAND STREET,
BIRKENHEAD CH41 4JW
Tel: 0151 650 1616
Fax: 0151 650 0007
Web site: www.a1atravel.co.uk
Props: John and Barbara Ashworth
Fleet: 26 - 7 single-deck bus, 8 midibus, 11 minibus.
Chassis: 7 Dennis. 8 LDV. 1 Mazda. 5 Mercedes. 1VW.
Ops incl: local bus services, school contracts, private hire.
Livery: White/Blue

*A.2.B TRAVEL UK LTD
PRENTON WAY, NORTH CHESHIRE TRADING ESTATE, PRENTON CH43 3DU
Tel: 0151 609 0600
Fax: 0151 609 0601
Dirs: G Evans, D Evans
Fleet: 26 - 2 single-deck coach, 2 midbus, 12 midiicoach, 10 minibus
Chassis: 1 Dennis. 4 Ford. 6 Ford Transit. 10 Freight Rover. 2 Iveco. 1 MAN. 1 Mercedes. 1 Renault.
Bodies: 1 Beulas. 1 Caetano. 2 Mercedes. 1 Plaxton.
Ops incl: school contracts, private hire, excursions & tours.
Livery: White/Blue

AINTREE COACHLINE
11 CLARE ROAD, BOOTLE L20 9LY.
Tel: 0151 922 8630.
Fax: 0151 933 6994.
Livery: Red/Cream.
Owns Helms of Eastham.

ARRIVA NORTH WEST AND WALES
73 ORMSKIRK ROAD, AINTREE L9 5AE.
Tel: 0151 522 2880
Fax: 0151 525 9556
Web site: www.arriva.co.uk
Man Dir: Bob Hind
Eng Dir: Malcolm Gilkerson
Fleet: 1325 - 181 double-deck bus, 890 single-deck bus, 2 coach, 10 open-top bus, 234 midibus, 8 minibus.
Chassis: 1 Bristol. 135 DAF. 553 Dennis. 74 Leyland. 4 MCW. 104 Mercedes. 15 Neoplan. 10 Optare. 98 Scania. 331 Volvo.
Bodies: 89 Alexander. 5 Carlyle. 9 ECW. 136 East Lancs. 5 Ikarus. 8 Leyland. 64 Marshall. 4 MCW. 1 Mellor. 15 Neoplan. 194 Northern Counties. 10 Optare. 471 Plaxton. 2 Van Hool. 2 Wadham Stringer. 2 UVG. 308 Wright.
Ops incl: local bus services, school contracts.

Livery: Arriva Blue/Cream
Ticket System: Wayfarer TGX150GB

G. ASHTON COACHES
WATERY LANE, ST HELENS WA9 3JA
Tel: 01744 733275
Fax: 01744 454122
Prop: George Ashton
Fleet: 8 coach
Chassis/bodies: 1 Ford. 4 Scania. 2 Duple. 1 Caetano.
Ops incl: excursions & tours, private hire, continental tours.

AVON COACH AND BUS COMPANY
10 BROOKWAY, NORTH CHESHIRE TRADING ESTATE, PRENTON CH43 3DT.
Tel: 0151 608 8000.
Fax: 0151 608 9955.
Props: Larry Smith, George Lewis
Ops Man: George Lewis
Fleet: 10 - 7 double-deck bus, 2 single-deck bus, 1 coach.
Chassis: 1 Bedford. 2 Daimler. 4 Leyland. 2 Leyland National. 1 Volvo.
Bodies: incl 3 Plaxton
Ops incl: local bus services, school contracts, excursions & tours, private hire.
Livery: Cream with Blue and Gold stripe.
Ticket System: Wayfarer.

BLUELINE COACHES
54 STATION ROAD, MAGHULL L31 3DB.
Tel/Fax: 0151 526 8888.
Prop: C. P. Carr.
Fleet: 12 - 3 coach, 4 midicoach, 5 minicoach.
Ops incl: private hire, school contracts.

CUMFY COACHES
49 MILL LANE, SOUTHPORT PR9 7PL.
Tel: 01704 227321.
Fax: 01704 505781.
Prop: M. R. Vickers. **Admin**: Mrs P. Lyon.
Fleet: 12 - 1 midicoach, 3 minibus, 8 minicoach.
Chassis: 1 Bedford. 3 Dodge. 1 Iveco. 1 Mercedes. 5 Renault.
Bodies: 1 Duple. 1 Wright. 3 Reeve Burgess. 6 van conversions.
Ops incl: excursions & tours, private hire, school contracts.

FIRST IN CHESTER & THE WIRRAL
659 NEW CHESTER ROAD, ROCK FERRY CH42 1PZ
Tel: 0151 645 8661
Web site: www.firstgroup.com
Area Ops Man: Peter Walch
Fleet: 203 double-deck bus, single deck bus, coach, midibus.
Ops incl: local bus services

*FIVE STAR GROUP TRAVEL
SNAPE GATE, FOXS BANK LANE, WHISTON, PRESCOTT L35 3SS
Tel: 0151 481 0000
Fax: 0151 493 9999
Web site: www.fivestartravel.co.uk
Prop: Phil Riley
Fleet: 3 coach.
Chassis: 3 DAF
Bodies: 3 Bova.
Ops incl: excursions & tours, private hire, continental tours.
Livery: White

FORMBY COACHWAYS LTD
38 STEPHENSON WAY, FORMBY L37 8EG
Tel: 01704 834448
Fax: 01704 878820
Fleetname: Freshfield Coaches.
Man Dir: K W Bradley **Sec**: D A Bradley
Fleet: 1 minicoach.
Chassis/bodies: Mercedes.
Ops incl: school contracts, private hire.
Livery: Green/Silver

HAPPY AL'S COACHES
40 CLEVELAND STREET, BIRKENHEAD L41 8EQ
Tel: 0151 653 0053
Fax: 0151 670 0509
E-mail: dan@happyals.com
Web site: www.happyals.com
Fleetname: Happy Al's
Owner: T. A. Cullinan. **Ops Man**: M. Cullinan
Fleet: 51 - 39 double-deck bus, 3 single-deck bus, 8 coach, 1 double-deck coach.
Chassis: 20 Bristol. 3 DAF. 5 Dennis. 14 Leyland. 6 Leyland National. 1 Neoplan. 3 Volvo.
Bodies: 5 Alexander. 2 ECW. 2 Ikarus. 14 Leyland. 6 Leyland National. 1 Neoplan. 2 Optare. 4 Van Hool. 3 others.
Ops incl: local bus services, school contracts, excursions & tours, private hire, express, continental tours.
Livery: Multi-coloured.
Ticket System: Wayfarer 3.

A/C	Air conditioning	◆	Seat belt-fitted vehicles
♿	Vehicles suitable for disabled	R	Recovery service available (not 24 hr)
🍴	Coach(es) with galley facilities	R24	24hr recovery service
WC	Coach(es) with toilet facilities		
🔧	Replacement vehicle available	T	Toilet-drop facilities available
		🚌	Vintage vehicle(s) available
			Open top vehicle(s)

HARDINGS TOURS LTD
♿ 🍴 WC A/c 🔑

60 ST JOHNS ROAD, HUYTON
L36 5SY
Tel: 0151 489 1228
Fax: 0151 480 2030
Web site: www.hardingstours.co.uk
Man Dir: Selwyn A Jones **Ops Man**: Ken Pickavance **Fleet Eng**: Cledwyn Owen
Fleet: 13 - 11 coach, 1 minibus, 1 minicoach
Chassis: 1 Caetano. 2 Mercedes. 8 Scania. 2 Volvo.
Bodies: 1 Berkhof. 1 Caetano. 7 Irizar. 2 Mercedes. 2 Van Hool.
Ops incl: school contracts, excursions & tours, private hire, continental tours.
Livery: White/Red/Orange/Yellow.

LIVERPOOL CITY COACHES/CITY BUS ♿
99-103 STANHOPE STREET, LIVERPOOL L8 5RE.
Tel: 0151 708 6201.
Fax: 0151 708 7201.
Prop: J. Bleasdale.
Fleet: 13 - 2 double-deck bus, 6 single-deck bus, 2 coach, 1 midibus, 2 minibus.
Chassis: 2 Bristol. 1 Ford Transit. 1 Freight Rover. 4 Leyland. 5 Leyland National.
Bodies: 2 ECW. 1 Leyland. 5 Leyland National. 1 Optare. 2 Plaxton.
Ops incl: local bus services, private hire.
Livery: Blue/White.
Ticket System: Wayfarer.

MAYPOLE COACHES
♿ WC R24 🔑 T

SPENCERS LANE, MELLING
L31 1HB
Tel: 0151 547 2713
Fax: 0151 548 2849

Prop: John Donnelly
Fleet: 23 - 10 double-deck bus, 10 coach, 2 midicoach, 1 minibus.
Chassis: 10 Leyland. 2 Mercedes. 1 Optare. 10 Volvo.
Bodies: 5 Ikarus. 2 Jonckheere. 10 Leyland. 2 Mercedes. 1 Optare. 2 Van Hool.
Ops incl: school contracts, excursions & tours, private hire, express, continental tours.
Livery: White.
Ticket System: ERG

GAVIN MURRAY & ELLISONS COACHES
WC 🍴 ♿ A/c 🔑 T

QUEENS GARAGE, 61 BOUNDARY ROAD, ST HELENS WA10 2LX.
Tel: 01744 22882.
Fax: 01744 24402.
Dirs: A. Magowan, M. Magowan.
Fleet: 10 coach.
Chassis: 6 Bova. 3 Mercedes. 1 Volvo.
Bodies: 6 Bova. 3 Neoplan. 1 Van Hool.
Ops incl: private hire.
Livery: White/Red/Yellow.

DAVID OGDEN COACHES
WC ♿ A/c R24 🔑 T

BAXTERS LANE, SUTTON, ST HELENS WA9 3DH
Tel/Recovery: 01744 606176
Fax: 01744 850903
E-mail: ogdenssutton@btconnect.com
Web site: www.davidogdenholidays.co.uk
Dirs: David Ogden, Carol Ogden.
Fleet: 19 - 2 single-deck bus, 14 coach, 3 minibus.
Chassis: 16 DAF. 2 Ford Transit. 1 Mercedes.
Bodies: 3 Ikarus. 3 Plaxton. 10 Van Hool.
Ops incl: excursions & tours, private hire, express, continental tours.
Livery: Red/White/Blue.

STAGECOACH MERSEYSIDE
GILMOSS GARAGE, EAST LANCASHIRE ROAD, LIVERPOOL L11 0BB
Tel: 0151 330 6204
Web site: www.stagecoachbus.com
Fleet: 173 - includes single-deck bus, double-deck bus.
Ops incl: local bus services.

*SUPERTRAVEL OMNIBUS LTD
♿ ♿ A/c 🔑

STC HOUSE, SPEKE HALL ROAD, SPEKE L24 9HD
Tel: 0151 486 3994
Fax: 0151 448 1216
Man Dir: Graham Bolderson.
Fleet: 38 - 24 single-deck bus, 2 coach, 1 midibus, 6 midicoach, 1 minibus, 4 minicoach.
Chassis: 12 Dennis. 12 Mercedes. 13 Optare. 1 Renault.
Bodies: 2 Alexander. 2 Mellor. 7 Mercedes. 15 Optare. 11 Plaxton. 1 other.
Ops incl: local bus services, school contracts, private hire.
Ticket system: Wayfarer

MIDDLESEX

ALLIED COACHLINES LTD
WC ♿ A/c

THE BULLS BRIDGE CENTRE, NORTH HYDE GARDENS, HAYES UB3 4QT
Tel: 020 8573 2626
Fax: 020 8561 6636
E-mail: sales@alliedcoachlines.co.uk
Web site: www.alliedcoachlines.co.uk
Dirs: R & R Charles
Fleet: 7 coach.
Chassis: 5 Mercedes. 2 Setra.
Bodies: 5 Mercedes. 2 Setra.
Ops incl: private hire.

ARON COACHLINES LTD
♿ WC ♿

THE BULLS BRIDGE CENTRE, NORTH HYDE GARDENS, HAYES UB3 4QT
Tel: 020 8569 2949
Fax: 020 8561 2829

E-mail: sales@aroncoachlines.co.uk
Web site: www.aroncoachlines.co.uk
Dirs: S. Robinson, R. Charles
Fleet: 6 - 4 coach, 2 minibus.
Chassis: 6 Mercedes.
Bodies: 6 Mercedes.
Ops incl: private hire.

ASHFORD LUXURY COACHES
♿ A/c 🔑

373 HATTON ROAD, FELTHAM TW14 9QS
Tel: 020 8890 6394
Fax: 020 8751 5054
Web site: www.ashfordluxurycoaches.co.uk
Man Dir: Martin Cornell
Fleet: 10 - 1 single-deck bus, 6 coach, 2 midicoach, 1 minicoach.
Chassis: 7 Dennis. 3 Mercedes.
Bodies: 3 Mellor. 7 Plaxton.
Ops incl: private hire, school contracts, local bus services.

BEECHES TRAVEL ♿
23 POWDER MILL LANE, TWICKENHAM TW2 6EE.
Tel/Fax: 020 8898 7048.
Prop: C. Miller.
Fleet: 4 minicoach.
Chassis: Ford Transit. Freight Rover.
Ops incl: school contracts, excursions & tours, private hire.
Livery: White/Yellow.

BESSWAY TRAVEL ♿ A/c
16 TINTERN WAY, WEST HARROW HA2 0SA.
Tel: 020 8422 3128.
Prop: Michael Heffernan.
Fleet: 6 - 1 coach, 3 midicoach, 2 minicoach.
Chassis: 1 Dennis. 5 Mercedes.
Bodies: 5 Autobus. 1 UVG.
Ops incl: private hire, school contracts.

CABIN COACHES
[wc] [galley] [A/c] [replacement]
1 PARSONAGE CLOSE, HAYES
UB3 2LZ
Tel: 020 8573 1100
Fax: 020 8573 8604
E-mail: cabincoaches@aol.com
Props: P Martin
Fleet: 5 - 4 coach, 1 midicoach.
Chassis: 1 Dennis. 1 Mercedes. 1 Scania. 2 Setra.
Bodies: 1 Duple. 1 Mercedes. 2 Setra. 1 Van Hool.
Ops incl: excursions & tours, school contracts, private hire.
Livery: White

*CALL-A-COACH
See Surrey

*CAVALIER TRAVEL SERVICES
See London

CARAVELLE COACHES
9 CHESTNUT AVENUE, EDGWARE
HA8 7RA
Tel/Fax: 020 8952 4025
Dir: H Lawrence.
Fleet: 2 - 1 midibus, 1 minibus.
Chassis: 1 Iveco. 1 Mercedes.
Ops incl: school contracts, private hire.

CHALFONT COACHES OF HARROW LTD
[seat belt] [wc] [R] [replacement]
200 FEATHERSTONE ROAD,
SOUTHALL UB2 5AQ
Tel: 020 8843 2323
Fax: 020 8574 0939
E-mail: chalfont.coaches@btopenworld.com
Web site: www.chalfontcoaches.co.uk
Man Dir: C J Shears **Dirs**: I Shears, M Shears **Ops Man**: P Williams
Ch Eng: R Arents **Co Sec**: G Shears
Fleet: 18 - 15 coach, 1 midicoach, 2 minibus.
Chassis: 2 LDV. 1 Mercedes. 15 Volvo.
Bodies: 3 Autobus. 15 Van Hool.
Ops incl: school contracts, excursions & tours, private hire, express, continental tours.
Livery: Mauve/White

*CHALFONT LINE LTD
[disabled] [seat belt] [A/c]
4 PROVIDENCE ROAD, WEST
DRAYTON UB7 8HJ
Tel: 01895 459540
Fax: 01895 459549
E-mail: info@chalfont-line.co.uk
Web site: www.chalfont-line.co.uk
Chmn: T J Reynolds **Man Dir**: R Chadija
Dir: M Kerr **Tran Man**: Lynn Young
Fleet: 84 minibus.
Chassis: 64 DAF. 6 Ford Transit. 8 Mercedes. 6 Renault.
Ops incl: school contracts, excursions & tours, private hire, continental tours.
Livery: White/Green

CUMFI-LUX COACHES [wc]
69 CORWELL LANE, HILLINGDON
UB8 3DE.
Tel: 020 8561 6948
Fax: 020 8569 3809.
Prop: N. R. Farrow (**Traf Man**).
Sec: Mrs T. K. Lovell.
Fleet: 3 - 1 coach, 1 minibus, 1 minicoach.
Chassis: 2 Mercedes. 1 Scania
Ops incl: excursions & tours, private hire.
Livery: Orange/White (coach); White (minibuses).

FALCON TRAVEL [wc] [seat belt] [A/c]
123 NUTTY LANE, SHEPPERTON
TW17 0RQ
Tel: 01932 787752
Fax: 01932 785521
Fleet: 6 - 5 coach, 1 midicoach.
Chassis: 1 Mercedes. 5 Volvo.
Bodies: 5 Van Hool. 1 other.
Ops incl: private hire, school contracts.
Livery: White/Black/Crimson

THE GOLD STANDARD
[wc] [galley] [seat belt]
94A HORSENDEN LANE NORTH,
GREENFORD UB6 7QH.
Tel: 020 8795 0075.
Fax: 020 8900 9630.
Owner/driver: P. Grant.
Fleet: 1 minicoach.
Chassis: Mercedes. **Body**: Soroco.
Ops incl: excursions & tours, private hire, continental tours.

HAMILTON OF UXBRIDGE
[wc] [galley] [seat belt] [A/c]
589-591 UXBRIDGE ROAD, HAYES
END UB4 8HP
Tel: 01895 232266
Fax: 01895 810454.
Ops Man: D. L. Bennett.
Fleet: 10 - 8 coach, 2 double-deck coach.
Chassis: 10 MAN.
Bodies: 5 Ayats. 4 Noge. 1 Marco Polo
Ops incl: private hire, express, continental tours.

*HEARNS COACHES
See London

HOUNSLOW COMMUNITY TRANSPORT [disabled] [seat belt]
9 MONTAGUE ROAD, HOUNSLOW
TW3 1JY.
Tel: 020 8572 8204.
Fax: 020 8572 0997
E-mail: haightim@aol.com
Ch Officer: Tim Haigh
Flt Co-ord: Steve Cann
Fleet: 9 minibus

HOUNSLOW MINI COACHES
See London

VIC HUGHES & SON LTD
[disabled] [seat belt] [replacement]
61 FERN GROVE, FELTHAM
TW14 9AY
Tel: 020 8831 0770
Fax: 020 8831 0660
Man Dir: V B Hughes.
Co Sec: Mrs V. Hughes. **Dir**: K. Hughes.
Fleet: 21 - 4 midicoach, 5 minibus, 12 ambulance.
Chassis: Ford, Mercedes.
Ops incl: school contracts, excursions & tours, private hire.
Livery: White/Black.

*J & D EUROTRAVEL
[disabled] [wc] [seat belt] [A/c] [replacement]
58 WEALD LANE, HARROW WEALD
HA3 5EX
Tel: 020 8861 1829
Fax: 020 8424 2585
E-mail: jdetravel@aol.com
Man Dir: J T Thomas
Fleet: 10 - 3 coach, 3 midicoach, 2 minibus, 2 minicoach.
Ops incl: school contracts, excursions & tours, private hire, express, continental tours.

LEOLINE TRAVEL
[wc] [seat belt] [galley] [A/c]
UPPER SUNBURY ROAD, HAMPTON
TW12 2DW
Tel: 020 8941 3370
Fax: 020 8941 3372
E-mail: daveleoline@aol.com
Web site: www.leolinetravel.co.uk
Prop: David Baker **Ops Man**: Judy Dale
Fleet: 6 - 5 coach, 1 minibus.
Chassis: 1 Iveco. 1 Toyota. 4 Volvo.
Bodies: 1 Beulas. 1 Caetano. 2 Jonckheere. 2 Van Hool.
Ops incl: excursions & tours, private hire, school contracts.
Livery: Dark Blue/Orange

LONDON SOVEREIGN [disabled]
BUSWAYS HOUSE, WELLINGTON
ROAD, TWICKENHAM TW2 5NX
Tel: 020 8400 6600
Web site: www.sovereignlondonbuses.co.uk
Man Dir: Nigel Stevens
Fleet: 100 - double-deck bus, single-deck bus.
Ops Incl: local bus services, private hire
Livery: TfL
Part of the Transdev Group

*LONDON UNITED BUSWAYS LTD [disabled] [open top] [A/c]
BUSWAYS HOUSE, WELLINGTON
ROAD, TWICKENHAM TW2 5NX
Tel: 020 8400 6605
Fax: 020 8943 2688
E-mail: customer@lonutd.co.uk
Web site: www.lonutd.co.uk

A/c	Air conditioning	[seat belt] Seat belt-fitted vehicles	[replacement] Replacement vehicle available
[disabled]	Vehicles suitable for disabled	R Recovery service available (not 24 hr)	T Toilet-drop facilities available
[galley]	Coach(es) with galley facilities		[vintage] Vintage vehicle(s) available
wc	Coach(es) with toilet facilities	R24 24hr recovery service	[open top] Open top vehicle(s)

Middlesex

Man Dir: Nigel Stevens **Fin Dir**: Richard Casling **Human Res Dir**: Karen Fuller
Eng Dir: Les Birchley **Ops Dir**: Paul Matthews **Com Man**: Steffan Evans
Fleet: 781 - 420 double-deck bus, 361 single-deck bus.
Chassis: 503 Dennis. 88 Scania. 190 Volvo.
Bodies: 235 Alexander. 128 East Lancs. 400 Plaxton. 3 Reeve Burgess. 15 other.
Ops Incl: local bus services, private hire
Livery: Red
Ticket system: Oyster
(Part of the Transdev Group)

LUXURY MINI COACH

94A HORSENDEN LANE, GREENFORD UB6 7AH
Tel: 020 8795 0075.
Fax: 020 8900 9630.
Web site: www.luxuryminicoach.co.uk
Dir: Paul Grant
Fleet: minicoaches.
Ops incl: private hire.

M&M COACHLINES

33 HITHERWELL DRIVE, HARROW WEALD HA3 6JD
Tel: 020 8863 2085
Fax: 020 8861 6175
Prop: M C Burcombe **Sec/Prop**: Mrs M M Burcombe **Ch Eng**: N Bassett
Fleet: 1 coach.
Chassis: Scania.
Body: Berkhof.
Ops incl: private hire, excursions & tours, continental tours.

*METROLINE TRAVEL LTD

66 COLLEGE ROAD, HARROW HA1 1BE
Tel: 020 8218 8888
Fax: 020 8218 8899
E-mail: info@metroline.co.uk
Web site: www.metroline.co.uk
Chief Exec Off: Jaspal Singh **Ch Op Officer**: Sean O'Shea **Fin Dir**: David Donelly **Eng Dir**: Russell Hargrave
Fleet: 1226 - 777 double-deck bus, 441 single-deck bus, 1 open-top bus, 7 midibus.
Chassis: 3 AEC. 867 Dennis. 11 MAN. 2 MCW. 7 Optare. 336 Volvo.
Bodies: 199 Alexander. 6 East Lancs. 76 Marshall. 2 MCW. 13 Northern Counties. 7 Optare. 3 Park Royal. 920 Plaxton.
Ops incl: local bus services, school contracts, private hire.
Livery: Red/Blue.
Ticket System: Wayfarer (London Buses spec)
(part of Comfort DelGro Corporation)

NCP CHALLENGER

TWICKENHAM TRADING ESTATE, RUGBY ROAD, TWICKENHAM TW1 1DU
Tel: 020 8892 5830
Fax: 0 20 8744 3893
Web site: www.ncpchallenger.co.uk
Head of Public transport: Matt Larkin
Ops incl: local bus services
Livery: Red/Yellow
Ticket System: Wayfarer
(Subsidiary of National Car Parks Ltd)

SUNBURY COACHES

204A CHARLTON ROAD, SHEPPERTON TW17 0RG.
Tel: 01932 785153.
Fax: 01932 761923.
Dir: P. Jones.
Fleet: 5 coach.
Chassis: Irisbus, Leyland, Volvo.
Bodies: Berkhof, Beulas, Jonckheere.
Ops incl: excursions & tours, private hire.
Livery: White/Turquoise.

TELLINGS GOLDEN MILLER COACHES LTD
See London

VENTURE TRANSPORT (HENDON) (1965) LTD

307 PINNER ROAD, HARROW HA1 4HG.
Tel: 020 8427 0101.
Fax: 020 8427 1707.
Ops incl: private hire
Subsidiary of Hearns Coaches

WESTBUS COACH SERVICES LTD
See London

*WILTAX BUSES LTD
See Surrey

*WINGS LUXURY TRAVEL LTD
See London

NORFOLK

*AMBASSADOR TRAVEL (ANGLIA) LTD

R24

JAMES WATT CLOSE, GAPTON HALL INDUSTRIAL ESTATE, GREAT YARMOUTH NR31 0NX
Tel: 01493 440350
Fax: 01493 440367
E-mail: lindsay@ambassador-travel.co.uk
Chmn: R H Green **Man Dir**: M Green
Ops Man: B Picton
Dep Ops Man: M Pleasants
Fleet: 45 - 1 double-deck bus, 10 single-deck bus, 34 coach
Chassis: 5 Leyland. 4 Optare. 4 Scania. 32 Volvo.
Bodies: 2 Caetano. 5 ECW. 4 Jonckheere. 1 Leyland. 4 Optare. 25 Plaxton. 2 Sunsundegui. 2 Van Hool.
Ops incl: local bus services, school contracts, private hire, express, excursions & tours.
Livery: White.
Ticket System: Setright/Almex/Wayfarer

ANGLIAN COACHES LTD
See Suffolk

CHENERY TRAVEL

THE GARAGE, DICKLEBURGH, DISS IP21 4NJ
Tel: 01379 741221
Fax: 01379 740728
Recovery: 01379 741656
E-mail: julia@chenerytravel.co.uk
Web site: www.chenerytravel.co.uk
Dir: Mrs P Garnhem
Gen Man: Mrs J M McGraffin
Fleet: 20 coach.
Chassis: 1 Bedford. 1 Leyland. 18 Setra.
Bodies: 1 Duple. 1 Plaxton. 18 Setra.
Ops incl: school contracts, excursions & tours, private hire, express, continental tours.
Livery: Silver/Blue.

*COACH SERVICES LTD

1A HOWLETT WAY, THETFORD IP24 1HZ
Tel: 01842 821509
Fax: 01842 766581
E-mail: info@coachservicesltd.co.uk
Prop: A Crawford **Tran Man**: R Matin
Fleet: 27 - 1 double-deck bus, 21 coach, 3 midibus, 2 minibus.
Chassis: 1 AEC. 2 Bova. 3 DAF. 1 LDV. 1 Leyland. 2 Mercedes. 3 Optare. 3 Scania. 2 Transbus. 9 Volvo.
Bodies: 1 Routemaster. 2 Bova. 3 Irizar. 2 LDV. 7 Jonckheere. 3 Optare. 4 Plaxton. 1 Transbus. 3 Van Hool.
Ops incl: local bus services, school contracts, excursions & tours, private hire, continental tours
Ticket System: Almex

*CRUSADER HOLIDAYS
See Essex

D-WAY TRAVEL
See Suffolk

*A. W. EASTONS COACHES LTD

THE OLD COACH HOUSE, STRATTON STRAWLESS, NORWICH NR10 5LR
Tel: 01603 754253
Fax: 01603 754133

E-mail:
admin@eastonsholidays.co.uk
Web site: www.eastonsholidays.co.uk
Dirs: Robert Easton, Derek Easton
Fleet: 11 - 1 single-deck bus, 10 coach.
Chassis: 2 Bova. 3 DAF. 1 Dennis. 1 Iveco. 4 Volvo.
Bodies: 1 Beulas. 2 Bova. 1 Duple. 1 Optare. 6 Van Hool.
Ops incl: local bus services, excursions & tours, school contracts, private hire, continental tours.
Livery: Purple
Ticket System: Almex

EUROSUN COACHES
wc 🍽 💺 A/c 🔧 T

THORPE MARKET ROAD, UNIT 1, GREENWAYS, SOUTH REPPS NR11 8NQ.
Tel: 01263 834483
Fax: 01263 834482
E-mail:
eurosuncoaches@hotmail.com
Web site: www.eurosun.net
Ch Eng: Adam Goffin **Sales & Mktg Man**: Tony Porter **Dirs**: Phil Overy, Jack Overy
Fleet: 19 - 16 coach, 3 double-deck coach.
Chassis: 7 DAF. 4 Leyland. 3 MAN. 2 Mercedes. 5 Neoplan.
Bodies: 3 Bova. 2 Leyland. 5 Neoplan. 6 Plaxton. 2 Van Hool. 1 other.
Ops incl: school contracts, excursions & tours, private hire, continental tours.
Livery: Red and Gold

FARELINE COACH SERVICES
See Suffolk

FIRST EASTERN COUNTIES BUSES LTD
♿ 💺 🚌 A/c

ROUEN HOUSE, ROUEN ROAD, NORWICH NR1 1RB
Tel: 01603 760076
Fax: 01603 615439
E-mail: contactus.fec@firstgroup.com
Web site: www.firstgroup.com
Man Dir: Peter Iddon **Fin Dir**: David Marshall **Ops/Com Dir**: Philip Seago
Fleet: 325 - 69 double-deck bus, 216 single-deck bus, 40 coach.
Chassis: 3 AEC. 121 Dennis. 44 Leyland. 60 Scania. 97 Volvo.
Bodies: 67 Alexander. 2 Duple. 5 ECW. 2 East Lancs. 11 Leyland. 3 Marshall. 10 Northern Counties. 3 Park Royal. 183 Plaxton. 1 Roe. 79 Wright.
Ops incl: local bus services, private hire, express.
Livery: First Group
Ticket System: Wayfarer 3

*FREESTONES COACHES LTD 💺 wc A/c R24 🔧 T
GREEN LANE, BEETLEY, DEREHAM NR20 4DL

Tel: 01362 860236
Fax: 01362 860276
Dir: Mrs Gloria Feeke **Ops Man**: Robert Tibbles **Co Sec**: Gary Feeke
E-mail:
freestonescoachesltd@tiscali.co.uk
Fleet: 11 - 2 single-deck bus, 8 coach, 1 minibus.
Chassis: 2 DAF. 1 Iveco. 2 Leyland. 1 Scania. 4 Volvo.
Bodies: 1 Beulas. 2 Optare. 2 Plaxton. 5 Van Hool.
Ops incl: local bus services, excursions & tours, school contracts, private hire, continental tours.
Livery: Silver

GRANGEWOOD TRAVEL 💺
GRANGEWOOD, CHAPEL ROAD, POTTER HEIGHAM NR29 5LS.
Tel: 01692 670944.
Prop: Phil Burgin.
Fleet: 1 minibus.
Chassis: 1 Toyota.
Ops incl: private hire.

D&H HARROD (COACHES) LTD 💺 wc A/c
BUS STOP, CASTLE ROAD, WORMEGAY, KING'S LYNN PE33 0SG
Tel: 01553 840492
Fax: 01553 841318
E-mail:
harrod.coaches@eidosnet.co.uk
Web site:
www.harrodcoachesltd.co.uk
Man Dir: David Reeve **Co Sec**: Jennifer Reeve **Ch Eng**: Derek Harrod.
Fleet: 12 coach
Chassis: 3 Dennis. 1 Iveco. 8 Volvo.
Bodies: 4 Jonckheere. 1 Plaxton. 3 Van Hool. 2 Wadham Stringer. 2 other.
Ops incl: local bus services, school contracts, excursions & tours, private hire, continental tours.
Livery: White

*KONECTBUS LTD ♿
7 JOHN GOSHAWK ROAD, DEREHAM NR19 1SY
Tel: 01362 851210
Fax: 01362 851215
E-mail: enquiries@konectbus.co.uk
Web site: www.konectbus.co.uk
Dirs: Julian Patterson, Steve Challis
Fleet: 33 - 5 double-deck bus, 28 single-deck bus.
Chassis: 4 DAF. 5 VDL. 1 Leyland National. 23 Optare.
Bodies: 1 Leyland National. 27 Optare. 5 Wright.
Ops incl: local bus services
Livery: Blue/Yellow/Grey
Ticket System: Almex A90

*MATTHEWS COACHES
💺 wc A/c 🔧

WESTGATE STREET, SHOULDHAM, KING'S LYNN PE33 0BN
Tel: 01366 347220
Fax: 01366 347293
E-mail:
john@matthewscoaches.co.uk
Man Dir: John Lloyd
Fleet: 6 - 5 coach, 1 minibus
Chassis: 2 DAF. 3 Dennis. 1 LDV.
Bodies: 1 Berkhof. 1 Leyland. 2 Plaxton. 2 Van Hool.
Ops incl: local bus servcies, school contracts, excursions & tours, private hire.
Livery: White/Blue
Ticket system: Setright

*NORFOLK GREEN
HAMLIN WAY, KINGS LYNN PE31 6HA
Tel: 01553 776980
Fax: 01553 770891
E-mail: enquiries@norfolkgreen.co.uk
Web site: www.norfolkgreen.co.uk
Man Dir: Ben Colson **Dir**: Keith Shayshutt
Fleet Eng: Nigel Firth **Ops Man**: Richard Pengelly **Accountant**: Simon Carr
Fleet: 44 - 8 single-deck bus, 29 midibus, 7 minibus
Chassis: 6 Dennis. 17 Mercedes. 21 Optare.
Bodies: 10 Alexander. 21 Optare. 13 Plaxton.
Ops incl: local bus services, school contracts
Livery: two-tone Green
Ticket System: Wayfarer TGX

PEELINGS COACHES
💺 wc 🍽 A/c 🔧

THE GARAGE, CLAY HILL, TITTLESHALL, KING'S LYNN PE32 2RQ
Tel/Fax: 01328 701531
E-mail:
jr@peelingscoaches.fsnet.co.uk
Prop: Jonathan Joplin **Ch Eng**: Jonathan Sayer
Fleet: 6 - coach.
Chassis: 1 Bedford. 1 DAF. 1 Dennis. 1 Van Hool. 2 Volvo.
Bodies: 4 Plaxton. 2 Van Hool.
Ops incl: local bus services, school contracts, excursions & tours, private hire, express.
Livery: White
Ticket System: Setright

*REYNOLDS COACHES OF CAISTER 💺 wc 🍽 A/c 🔧
THE GARAGE, ORMESBY ROAD, CAISTER-ON-SEA NR30 5QJ
Tel: 01493 720312
Fax: 01493 721512
E-mail:
reynolds.coaches@gtyarmouth.co.uk
Man Dir: C J Reynolds **Dir**: Mrs J D Reynolds **Co Sec**: Mrs G E Reynolds

---

A/c	Air conditioning	💺	Seat belt-fitted vehicles	🔧	Replacement vehicle available
♿	Vehicles suitable for disabled	R	Recovery service available (not 24 hr)	T	Toilet-drop facilities available
🍽	Coach(es) with galley facilities	R24	24hr recovery service	🚌	Vintage vehicle(s) available
wc	Coach(es) with toilet facilities				Open top vehicle(s)

Fleet: 16 - coach, midicoach, minicoach.
Chassis: 1 Bedford. 1 DAF. 6 Dennis.
1 Ford Transit. 1 Iveco. 1 MAN. 1 Mercedes.
1 Scania. 3 Volvo.
Bodies: 1 Beulas. 1 Caetano. 1 Neoplan.
7 Plaxton. 1 Reeve Burgess. 4 Van Hool.
Ops incl: school contracts, excursions &
tours, private hire, continental tours.
Livery: Blue/Grey/Yellow.

SANDERS COACHES

HEATH DRIVE, HEMPSTEAD ROAD
INDUSTRIAL ESTATE, HOLT
NR25 6ER
Tel: 01263 712800
Fax: 01263 710920
Website: www.sanderscoaches.com
Dir: Charles Sanders
Fleet: 85 - 8 double-deck bus,
24 single-deck bus, 36 coach, 14 midibus,
2 minicoach, 1 minibus.
Chassis: 10 Bedford. 43 DAF. 7 Dennis.
4 Leyland. 17 Mercedes. 2 Setra. 2 Volvo.
Bodies: 3 Duple. 4 ECW. 17 Ikarus.
2 Neoplan. 4 Northern Counties. 14 Optare.
20 Plaxton. 7 Reeve Burgess. 2 Setra.
12 Van Hool.
Ops incl: local bus services, school
contracts, excursions & tours, private hire,
continental tours.
Livery: Yellow/Blue/Orange
Ticket System: Wayfarer 3

H SEMMENCE & CO LTD

34 NORWICH ROAD, WYMONDHAM
NR18 0NS
Tel: 01953 602135

Fax: 01953 605867
E-mail: sales@semmence.co.uk
Web site: www.semmence.co.uk
Chairm: R H Green **Man Dir**: Sean Green
Co Sec: Mark Green **Tran Man**: Brian
Lafferty **Eng Man**: Kevin Hughes
Fleet: 30 - 26 coach, 4 minicoach.
Chassis: 15 Dennis. 4 Mercedes. 1 Scania.
10 Volvo.
Ops incl: local bus services, school
contracts, excursions & tours, express,
private hire
Livery: White
Ticket System: Wayfarer
(Subsidiary of Ambassador Travel)

*SIMONDS COACH & TRAVEL

ROSWALD HOUSE, OAK DRIVE,
DISS IP22 4GX
Tel: 01379 647300
Fax: 01379 647350
E-mail: martyn@simonds.co.uk
Web site: www.simonds.co.uk
Man Dir: M S Simonds **Dirs**: D O Simonds,
R S Simonds **Eng Dir**: A Tant
Fleet: 40 - 8 single-deck bus, 34 coach,
5 minibus, 1 minicoach.
Chassis: 1 DAF. 4 MAN. 6 Mercedes.
2 Transbus. 27 Volvo.
Bodies: 1 Alexander. 4 Marshall/MCV.
1 Optare. 14 Plaxton. 2 Transbus. 28 Van
Hool.
Ops incl: local bus services, school
contracts, excursions & tours, private hire,
continental tours.
Livery: White with Green/Red/Gold leaves
Ticket system: Wayfarer/Setright

*SPRATTS COACHES LTD

THE GARAGE, WRENINGHAM,
NORWICH NR16 1AZ
Tel: 01508 489262
Fax: 01508 489404
E-mail: sprattscoaches@aol.com
Web site: www.sprattscoaches.co.uk
Dirs: Richard Spratt, Christine Bilham
Ops Man: Mark Benham
Fleet: 11 - 8 coach, 2 midicoach, 1 minibus.
Chassis: 1 Bedford. 1 Bova. 2 MAN.
1 Mercedes. 5 Scania. 1 Volvo.
Bodies: 2 Berkhof. 1 Bova. 1 Caetano.
1 Duple. 6 Van Hool.
Ops incl: private hire, school contracts.
Livery: White

*SUNBEAM COACHES LTD

WESTGATE STREET, HEVINGHAM,
NORWICH NR10 5NH
Tel/Fax: 01603 754211
E-mail: sunbeamcoaches@aol.com
Dirs: G M Coldham, J M Cole
Ch Eng: G J Coldham
Fleet: 7 - 6 coach, 1 minicoach.
Chassis: 2 Dennis. 2 MAN. 1 Toyota.
2 Volvo.
Bodies: 1 Caetano. 2 Neoplan. 3 Plaxton.
1 Van Hool.
Ops incl: school contracts, private hire,
excursions & tours.
Livery: White with Orange/Blue/Yellow

NORTH & NORTH EAST LINCOLNSHIRE

APPLEBYS COACHES

CONISHOLME, LOUTH LN11 7LT
Tel: 01472 355 964
E-mail: sales@expertcoaches.co.uk
Web site:
www.applebyscoaches.co.uk
Fleet: 14 coach
Ops incl: excursions & tours, continental
tours.
(Subsidiary of L F Bowen Ltd, Staffordshire)

EMMERSON COACHES LTD

BLUESTONE LANE, IMMINGHAM
DN40 2EL.
Tel: 01469 578166
Fax: 01469 575278
Web site:
www.emmersoncoaches.ukf.net
Dirs: Alan Brumby, O. M. Stocks,
Allen Stocks.
Fleet: 12 - 11 coach, 1 minibus.
Chassis: 1 Bedford. 1 DAF. 1 Ford. 2 MAN.
3 Mercedes. 1 Scania. 3 Volvo.
Bodies: 2 Duple. 1 Ikarus. 1 Jonckheere.

2 Mercedes. 4 Plaxton. 1 other.
Ops incl: school contracts, private hire.
Livery: Cream with orange and brown
stripes.

BEN GEORGE TRAVEL LTD

BRICKHILLS, BROUGHTON, BRIGG
DN20 0BZ
Tel: 01652 654681
Fax: 01652 350396
Dirs: S & J Easton
Fleet: 31 - 5 double-deck bus, 7 coach,
1 double-deck coach, 1 midicoach,
3 minibus.
Chassis: 3 AEC. 3 Bedford. 1 Bristol.
1 Daimler. 1 Dennis. 2 Leyland. 2 MAN.
3 Mercedes. 1 Neoplan.
Bodies: 1 Alexander. 3 Duple.
1 Jonckheere. 2 Leyland. 3 Mercedes.
1 Neoplan. 3 Plaxton.
Ops incl: local bus services, school
contracts, excursions & tours, private hire,
continental tours.
Livery: Red/White/Blue

EXPERT COACH SERVICES LTD

2 PASTURE STREET, GRIMSBY
DN31 1QD
Tel: 01472 350650
Fax: 01472 351926
E-mail: sales@expertcoaches.co.uk
Web site: www.expertcoaches.co.uk
Man Dir: L A Harniess **Dir**: C J Cator
Fleet: 2 coach
Chassis: 2 Scania.
Bodies: 1 Berkhof. 1 Plaxton.
Ops incl: excursions & tours, private hire,
continental tours.
Livery: Blue/White.

HOLLOWAY COACHES LTD

COTTAGE BECK ROAD,
SCUNTHORPE DN16 1TP.
Tel: 01724 282277, 281177.
Fax: 01724 289945.
Dirs: F. S. Holloway (**Man Dir**),
P. A. Holloway.
Fleet: 14 - 7 double-deck bus, 6 coach,
1 minicoach.
Chassis: 1 Bedford. 2 Dennis. 11 Leyland.

Bodies: 7 Alexander. 6 Plaxton. 1 other.
Ops incl: excursions & tours, express.
Livery: Red/White/Blue.

*HORNSBY TRAVEL SERVICES LTD

[icons] wc A/c T

51 ASHBY HIGH STREET,
SCUNTHORPE DN16 2NB
E-mail: office@hornsbytravel.co.uk
Man Dir: R Hornsby **Gen Man:** N Hornsby
Fleet: 30 - 4 double-deck bus, 17 single-deck bus, 9 coach, 1 minibus
Chassis: 1 BMC. 4 DAF. 13 Dennis. 2 Leyland. 2 MCW. 2 Plaxton. 1 Vauxhall. 2 Volvo.
Bodies: 3 Alexander. 1 BMC. 2 MCW. 19 Plaxton. 1 Transbus. 4 Wright. 1 other.
Ops incl: local bus services, excursions & tours, private hire, school contracts
Livery: Silver/Blue.
Ticket System: Almex

*MILLMAN COACHES

[icons] wc

17 WILTON ROAD, HUMBERSTON, GRIMSBY DN36 4AW
Tel: 01472 210297
Fax: 01472 595915
E-mail: enquiries@millmancoaches.co.uk
Web site: www.millmancoaches.co.uk
Ptnrs: Marjorie Millman, David Millman, Amanda J Millman
Fleet: 9 - 6 single-deck coach, 2 midicoach, 1 minibus.
Chassis: 2 Cummins. 1 Dennis. 2 Leyland. 1 Mercedes. 3 Volvo.
Bodies: 2 Duple. 2 Jonckheere. 1 Mercedes. 4 Plaxton.
Ops incl: private hire, school contracts.
Livery: White/Blue/Yellow

*RADLEY COACH TRAVEL

[icons] wc A/c

50 WRAWBY STREET, BRIGG DN20 8JB
Tel: 01652 653583
Fax: 01652 656020
E-mail: radleytravel@aol.com
Web site: www.radleytravel.co.uk
Owner: Kevin Radley.
Fleet: 2 coach
Chassis: 2 Scania.
Bodies: 2 Irizar.
Ops incl: excursions & tours, private hire, continental tours.
Livery: Gold/Maroon

*SHERWOOD TRAVEL

[icons] wc A/c

19 QUEENS ROAD, IMMINGHAM DN40 1QR
Tel: 01469 571140
Fax: 01469 574937
E-mail: enquiries@sherwoodtravel.co.uk
Web site: www.sherwoodtravel.co.uk
Dirs: Stuart Oakland, Mrs Jane Oakland, Mrs Lucy Oakland
Fleet: 10 - 4 coach, 2 minicoach, 4 minibus.
Chassis: 1 Dennis. 1 Ford Transit. 6 Mercedes. 3 Scania
Ops incl: school contracts, excursions & tours, private hire.

SOLID ENTERTAINMENTS

[wc]

46 WELLOWGATE, GRIMSBY DN32 0RA.
Tel: 01472 349222.
Fax: 01472 362275.
Prop: S. J. Stanley.
Fleet: 2 - 1 coach, 1 minibus.
Chassis: 1 Scania.
Bodies: 1 Irizar.
Ops incl: excursions & tours, private hire, continental tours.
Livery: Black.

NORTH YORKSHIRE, YORK

*ABBEY COACHWAYS LTD

[icons] A/c

MEADOWCROFT GARAGE, LOW STREET, CARLTON DN14 9PH
Tel: 01405 860337
Fax: 01405 869433
Dirs: Mrs L E Baker, S J Stockdale.
Fleet: 5 coaches.
Chassis: 1 Scania. 4 Volvo.
Ops incl: school contracts, private hire

G. ABBOTT & SONS

[icons] wc A/c R24

AUMANS HOUSE, LEEMING, NORTHALLERTON DL7 9RZ
Tel: 01677 422858/422571
Fax: 01677 424971
Fleetname: Abbotts of Leeming
Ptnrs: David C Abbott, Clifford G Abbot.
Fleet: 61 - 1 double-deck bus, 3 single-deck bus, 50 coach, 6 midibus, 1 minicoach.
Chassis: 2 Bedford. 6 DAF. 6 Ford Transit. 1 Iveco. 10 Leyland. 3 Optare.
Bodies: 1 Caetano. 6 Duple. 10 Irizar. 3 Optare. 20 Park Royal. 10 Van Hool.
Ops incl: local bus services, school contracts, excursions & tours, private hire, express, continental tours.

H ATKINSON & SONS (INGLEBY) LTD

[icons] wc ℏ A/c T

NORTHALLERTON DL6 3LN
Tel: 01609 882222
Fax: 01609 882222
E-mail: h.atkinson@eurotelonline.com
Web site: www.atkinsoncoaches.co.uk
Dirs: D Atkinson, R Atkinson
Co Sec: M T Atkinson
Fleet: 12 - 1 double-deck bus, 9 coach, 1 double-deck coach, 1 midicoach
Chassis: 3 Irisbus.1 Leyland. 2 Setra. 6 Volvo.
Bodies: 2 Beulas. 2 Berkhof. 2 Jonckheere. 1 Leyland. 1 Marcopolo. 1 Plaxton. 2 Setra. 1 other.
Livery: Maroon/Cream

BALDRY'S COACHES

[icons] R T

LEYLANDII, SELBY ROAD, HOLME-ON-SPALDING-MOOR YO43 4HB.
Tel: 01430 860992.
Prop: A. Baldry.
Fleet: 9 - 8 coach, 1 midicoach.
Chassis: 1 AEC. 1 Bedford. 5 Ford.
Ops incl: school contracts, excursions & tours, private hire.
Livery: Two-tone Green.

Symbol	Meaning
A/c	Air conditioning
♿	Vehicles suitable for disabled
🍴	Coach(es) with galley facilities
wc	Coach(es) with toilet facilities
●	Seat belt-fitted vehicles
R	Recovery service available (not 24 hr)
R24	24hr recovery service
✔	Replacement vehicle available
T	Toilet-drop facilities available
🚌	Vintage vehicle(s) available
🚍	Open top vehicle(s)

149

BEECROFT COACHES

POST OFFICE, FEWSTON HG3 1SG.
Tel/Fax: 01943 880206.
Prop: D. Beecroft.
Fleet: 6 - 3 coach, 1 midicoach, 2 minibus.
Chassis: 1 DAF. 1 Dodge. 2 Freight Rover. 1 Scania. 1 Volvo.
Bodies: 1 Alexander. 1 Bova. 3 Carlyle. 1 Duple. 1 Plaxton. 1 Van Hool.
Ops incl: local bus services, school contracts, excursions & tours, private hire, continental tours.
Livery: Green/Orange/White.

BIBBY'S OF INGLETON

NE0W ROAD, INGLETON LA6 3NU.
Tel: 01524 241330
Fax: 01524 242216
E-mail: bibbys_travel@talk21.com
Man Dir: P Bibby **Co Sec:** Mrs S Holcroft
Ch Eng: M Stephenson.
Fleet: 22 - 17 coach, 5 minibus.
Chassis: 17 DAF. 3 LDV. 3 Mercedes.
Bodies: 6 Ikarus. 3 LDV. 2 Mercedes. 4 Plaxton. 7 Van Hool. 1 Ovi.
Ops incl: school contracts. excursions & tours, private hire, continental tours.
Livery: Blue/Grey/Red with white stripes.

*BOTTERILLS

HIGH STREET GARAGE, THORNTON DALE YO18 7QW
Tel: 01751 474210
E-mail: botterills@hotmail.com
Web site: www.botterills.org
Fleet: 4 minibus
Chassis/bodies: 4 Mercedes
Ops incl: local bus services, school contracts, private hire.
Livery: White

*BURRELLS (BARNARD CASTLE COACHES)

SOUTH VIEW GARAGE, NEWSHAM, RICHMOND DL11 7RA
Tel: 01833 621302
Fax: 01833 621431
E-mail: qlburrell@hotmail.com
Dirs: Alan Burrell, Mrs Sandra Burrell
Fleet: 5 - 4 coach, 1 minibus.
Chassis: 1 Beluga. 4 Volvo.
Bodies: 1 Mercedes. 1 Plaxton. 3 Van Hool
Ops incl: school contracts, excursions & tours, private hire, express, continental tours.
Livery: Yellow/White

*EDDIE BROWN TOURS LTD

BAR LANE, ROECLIFFE, YORK YO51 9LS
Tel: 01423 321248
Fax: 01423 326213
Fax: 07736 692702
E-mail: enquiries@eddiebrowntours.com
Web site: www.eddiebrowntours.com
Dirs: Philip Brown, Mrs Deidre Brown
Gen Man: Peter Joyce
Fleet: 44 - 1 single-deck bus, 35 coach, 8 midicoach
Chassis: 4 Dennis. 7 Mercedes. 2 Scania. 2 Setra. 1 Toyota. 28 Volvo.
Bodies: 2 Autobus. 1 Caetano. 1 Carlyle. 1 Duple. 28 Plaxton. 1 Reeve Burgess. 2 Setra. 8 Van Hool.
Ops incl: local bus services, school contracts, excursions & tours, private hire, continental tours.
Livery: White/Orange/Red/Maroon
Ticket system: Wayfarer

CHARTER COACH LTD

THE CONTROL TOWER OFFICES, THE AIRFIELD, TOCKWITH YO26 7QF
Tel: 01423 359655.
Fax: 01423 359459.
E-mail: expert.coaches@btinternet.com
Dir: Antoni LaPilusa.

*COASTAL AND COUNTRY COACHES

THE GARAGE, FAIRFIELD WAY, STAINSACRE INDUSTRIAL ESTATE, WHITBY YO22 4PU
Tel: 01947 602922
Fax: 01947 600830
E-mail: enquiries@coastalandcountry.co.uk
Web site: www.coastalandcountry.co.uk
Fleet: 20 - 1 double-deck bus, 2 single-deck bus, 13 coach, 1 open-top bus. 1 midicoach, 2 minibus, 1 vintage
Chassis: 1 Bedford. 1 Bristol. 3 Leyland. 5 Mercedes. 10 Volvo.
Bodies: 1 Duple. 1 ECW. 1 Jonckheere. 2 Mercedes. 12 Plaxton. 3 Van Hool.
Ops incl: local bus services, school contracts, excursions & tours, private hire.
Livery: White/Blue.
Ticket system: Wayfarer

COLLINS COACHES

CLIFFE SERVICE STATION, YORK ROAD, CLIFFE, SELBY YO8 6NN
Tel: 01757 638591
Fax: 01757 630196
E-mail: collins@coaches.hotmail.co.uk
Web site: www.collinscoaches.co.uk
Prop: Alan Collins.
Fleet: 5 - 4 coach, 1 midicoach
Chassis: 1 Mercedes. 4 Volvo.
Ops incl: school contracts, private hire.
Livery: White

*COUNTRYSIDE BUS SERVICES

SOUTH GOWLAND, GOWLAND LANE, CLOUGHTON, SCARBOROUGH YO13 0DU
Tel: 01723 870790
Fax: 01273 870790
Tran Man: Piers Turner
Ptnr: Mrs Jasmin M Turner.
Fleet: 2 minicoach.
Chassis/bodies: 2 LDV
Ops incl: local bus services, school contracts.
Livery: Yellow/Blue

JOHN DODSWORTH (COACHES) LTD

WETHERBY ROAD, BOROUGHBRIDGE YO5 9HS.
Tel: 01423 322236.
Fax: 01423 324682.
Dir: John Dodsworth.
Fleet: 17 - 10 coach, 2 midicoach, 1 minicoach.
Chassis: 3 Mercedes. 12 Volvo.
Bodies: 10 Plaxton. 2 Reeve Burgess. 1 Onyx.
Ops incl: excursions & tours, private hire, continental tours, school contracts.
Livery: Cream/Orange.

FIRST YORK

7 JAMES STREET, YORK YO10 3HH
Tel: 01904 883000
Fax: 01904 883056
Web site: www.firstgroup.com
Fleet: 100 - 12 double-deck bus, 86 single-deck bus, 2 midibus, articulated bus.
Chassis: 98 Volvo, 2 Optare
Bodies: 12 Alexander. 2 Optare. 86 Wright.
Ops incl: local bus services, school contracts.
Livery: Grey/Magenta/Blue.
Ticket System: Wayfarer.

*R HANDLEY & SONS LTD

NORTH ROAD, MIDDLEHAM, NEAR LEYBURN DL8 4PJ
Tel: 01969 623216
Fax: 01969 624546
Dirs: Mark Anderson, Jean Anderson
Fleet: 14 - 9 coach, 5 minicoach.
Chassis: 1 Ford Transit. 1 LDV. 4 Leyland. 3 Mercedes. 3 Scania. 2 Volvo.
Bodies: 1 Berkhof. 2 Mercedes. 7 Plaxton. 2 Van Hool. 2 other.
Ops incl: local bus services, private hire, school contracts, excursions & tours.
Livery: Black/White/Grey

*HARGREAVES COACHES

BRIDGE HOUSE, HEBDEN, SKIPTON BD23 5DE
Tel: 01756 752567
Fax: 01756 753768
E-mail: hargreaves.coaches@ukonline.co.uk
Prop: Andrew C Howick
Fleet: 7 - 3 coach, 1 double-deck coach, 2 midicoach, 1 minibus.
Chassis: 1 LDV. 2 MAN. 3 Mercedes. 1 Scania.
Bodies: 1 Berkhof. 1 Leyland. 3 Neoplan. 2 Plaxton.

HARROGATE & DISTRICT TRAVEL LTD

PROSPECT PARK, BROUGHTON WAY, STARBECK, HARROGATE HG2 2NY
Tel: 01423 884020
Fax: 01423 885670

Web site:
www.harrogateanddistrict.co.uk
www.the36.co.uk
Fleetname: Harrogate & District.
Chmn: G R Fearnley **Man Dir**:
Dave Alexander
Fleet: 66 - 8 double-deck bus, 45 single-deck bus, 13 coach.
Chassis: 13 Dennis. 6 Leyland. 47 Volvo.
Bodies: 7 Alexander. 4 Northern Counties. 13 Plaxton. 42 Wright.
Ops incl: local bus services, school contracts.
Livery: Red/Cream.
Ticket System: Wayfarer 3
Part of the Blazefield group which is owned by Transdev

HOPWOOD COACHES
A/c

22 MAIN STREET, ASKHAM BRYAN YO23 3QU
Tel: 01904 707394
Dirs: P Hopwood, Mrs D A Hopwood, R C Baker, Mrs A J Baker
Fleet: 3 coach.
Chassis: 3 Dennis.
Bodies: 2 Duple. 1 Plaxton.
Ops incl: school contracts, private hire.

INGLEBY'S LUXURY COACHES LTD
A/c R T

24 HOSPITAL FIELDS ROAD, FULFORD ROAD, YORK YO10 4DZ
Tel: 01904 637620
Fax: 01904 612944
Dir: C Ingleby **Fleet Eng**: R Atkinson
Ops: A Evans
Fleet: 12 - 8 coach, 2 midicoach, 2 minibus.
Chassis: 1 Bova. 1 Dennis. 4 Mercedes. 6 Volvo.
Bodies: 1 Bova. 2 Mercedes. 2 Plaxton. 1 Sitcar. 6 Van Hool.
Ops incl: private hire.
Livery: Blue/Cream

J. R. TRAVEL
wc R24 T

36 CALF CLOSE, HAXBY YO3 3NS.
Tel: 01904 766233.
Ptnrs: R. Flatt, J. Smith.
Fleet: 10 - 3 double-deck bus, 3 coach, 4 double-deck coach.
Chassis: 3 Daimler. 3 Mercedes. 4 Neoplan.
Bodies: 1 East Lancs. 2 Neoplan. 2 Northern Counties. 2 Plaxton. 3 Taz.
Ops incl: local bus services, school contracts, excursions & tours, private hire, continental tours.
Livery: White with green/red stripes.
(associated with Compass Royston Travel, Durham)

KINGS LUXURY COACHES
wc

FERRY ROAD, MIDDLESBROUGH TS2 1PL.
Tel: 01642 243687.

Prop: K. E. King.
Fleet: 5 - 2 double-deck bus, 3 coach.
Chassis: 2 Scania. 3 Setra.
Bodies: 1 Jonckheere. 3 Setra. 1 Van Hool.
Ops incl: private hire, continental tours.
Livery: Yellow/White.

METRO COACHES
THE CONIFERS, DARLINGTON RD, STOCKTON-ON-TEES TS21 1PE
Tel: 07970 826115
E-mail: info@coachiremiddlesbrough.co.uk

PERRY'S COACHES
wc A/c

RICCAL DRIVE, YORK ROAD INDUSTRIAL PARK, MALTON YO17 6YE.
Tel: 01653 690500
Fax: 01653 690800
Web site: www.perrystravel.com
E-mail: info@perrystravel.com
Ptnrs: D J Perry (**Gen Man/Ch Eng**) Mrs A Holtby (**Co Sec**)
Fleet: 19 - 11 coach, 6 midicoach, 2 minicoach.
Chassis: 1 Dennis. 7 Mercedes. 1 Toyota. 9 Volvo.
Bodies: 1 Caetano. 2 Crest. 1 Jonckheere. 9 Plaxton. 3 Van Hool. 2 Sitcar.
Ops incl: local bus services, school contracts, excursions & tours, private hire, continental tours.
Livery: Red/White.

PROCTERS COACHES (NORTH YORKSHIRE) LTD
♿ wc A/c

TUTIN ROAD, LEEMING BAR INDUSTRIAL ESTATE, LEEMING BAR, NORTHALLERTON DL7 9UJ
Tel: 01677 425203
Fax: 01677 426550
E-mail: enquiries@procterscoaches.co.uk
Web site: www.procterscoaches.co.uk
Man Dir: Kevin Procter **Fleet Eng**: Philip Kenyon **Tran Man**: Andrew Fryatt
Fleet: 56 - 31 coach, 1 double-deck coach, 2 midicoach, 22 minibus.
Chassis: 1 DAF. 5 Dennis. 1 Ford Transit. 1 Leyland. 13 Mercedes. 9 Optare. 1 Setra. 1 Van Hool. 23 Volvo.
Bodies: 1 Alexander. 1 Autobus. 5 Berkhof. 3 Jonckheere. 1 Mercedes. 9 Optare. 29 Plaxton. 1 Setra. 3 Transbus. 2 Van Hool. 1 Wright.
Ops incl: local bus services, school contracts, private hire, continental tours.
Livery: White
Ticket System: Wayfarer 3

*RELIANCE MOTOR SERVICES ♿

RELIANCE GARAGE, YORK ROAD, SUTTON-ON-FOREST, YORK YO61 1ES
Tel/Fax: 01904 768262
Prop: John H Duff

Fleet: 10 - 4 double-deck bus, 4 single-deck bus, 1 coach, 1 midicoach.
Chassis: DAF. Mercedes. Volvo.
Bodies: Alexander. East Lancs. Optare. Van Hool. Wright.
Ops incl: local bus services, school contracts, private hire.
Livery: Cream/Green
Ticket System: Wayfarer TGX

RONDO TRAVEL
wc A/c

LEVENS HALL PARK, LUND LANE, KILLINGHALL, HARROGATE HG3 2BG
Tel: 01423 526800
Fax: 01423 527800
E-mail: sales@rondotravel.co.uk
Web site: www.rondotravel.co.uk
Man Dir: J D Bullock **Duty Man**: M A Wilson **Traff Man**: N T Chatterton
Fleet: 3 coach
Chassis: 1 Scania, 2 Setra
Bodies: 2 Setra, 1 Van Hool
Ops incl: private hire, excursions & tours, continental tours.
Livery: Red/Gold.

SCARBOROUGH & DISTRICT
♿ 🚌 wc R T

BARRY'S LANE, SCARBOROUGH YO12 4HA
Tel: 01723 500064
Fax: 01723 370064
E-mail: sd@eyms.co.uk
Web site: www.eyms.co.uk
Chmn: P J S Shipp **Fin Dir**: P Harrson
Com Man: R Rackley
Eng&Ops Man: R Graham
Ops incl: local bus services, school contracts, excursions & tours, private hire, express, continental tours.
Livery: Burgundy/Cream
Ticket system: Wayfarer TGX150
A division of East Yorkshire Motor Services Ltd

SIESTA INTERNATIONAL HOLIDAYS
wc A/c

158 LINTHORPE ROAD, MIDDLESBROUGH TS1 3RB
Tel: 01642 227711
Fax: 01642 225067
Web site: www.siestaholidays.co.uk
Dir: Paul R Herbert **Co Sec**: Julie Marsh
Fleet Man: Brian Watson
Fleet: 14 - 3 coach, 10 double-deck coach, 1 minibus.
Chassis: 1 DAF. 1 Ford Transit. 12 Scania.
Bodies: 12 Berkhof. 1 Bova.
Ops incl: excursions & tours, private hire, continental tours.
Livery: Blue.

A/c	Air conditioning	✓	Replacement vehicle available
♿	Vehicles suitable for disabled	T	Toilet-drop facilities available
🍽	Coach(es) with galley facilities	🚌	Vintage vehicle(s) available
wc	Coach(es) with toilet facilities		Open top vehicle(s)
	Seat belt-fitted vehicles		
R	Recovery service available (not 24 hr)		
R24	24hr recovery service		

North Yorkshire

*JOHN SMITH & SONS LTD
R24

THE AIRFIELD, DALTON, THIRSK
YO7 3HE
Tel: 01845 577250
Fax: 01845 577752
E-mail: admin@johnsmithandsons.net
Web site: www.johnsmithandsons.net
Dirs: A N Smith, J Smith, T G Smith, I Smith (**Ops Man**) **Sec**: B White
Fleet: 23 - 1 double-deck bus, 2 single-deck bus, 11 coach, 4 midibus, 2 midicoach, 1 minibus, 2 minicoach.
Chassis: 1 Bedford. 14 DAF. 1 Ford. 2 Ford Transit. 3 Leyland. 2 Mercedes. 2 Neoplan.
Bodies: 1 Duple. 1 Mercedes. 3 Neoplan. 8 Plaxton. 1 Reeve Burgess. 2 UVG. 6 Van Hool.
Ops incl: local bus services, school contracts, excursions & tours, private hire, continental tours.
Livery: Green/Cream/Gold/Black
Ticket system: Wayfarer

*STEPHENSONS OF EASINGWOLD LTD

MOOR LANE INDUSTRIAL ESTATE, THOLTHORPE, YORK YO61 1SR
Tel: 01347 838990
Fax: 01347 830189
E-mail: sales@stephensonsofeasingwold.co.uk
Web site: www.stephensonsofeasingwold.co.uk
Dirs: Harry Stephenson, David Stephenson
Fleet: 37 - 6 double-deck bus, 7 single-deck bus, 24 coach
Chassis: 3 DAF. 4 Leyland. 1 Leyland National. 1 MCW. 1 Scania. 27 Volvo.
Bodies: 1 Caetano. 2 Duple. 4 leyland. 1 Leyland National. 1 MCW. 2 Optare. 22 Plaxton. 1 Van Hool. 2 Wright. 1 other.
Ops incl: local bus services, school contracts, excursions & tours, private hire.
Livery: Cream
Ticket system: Wayfarer

STEVE STOCKDALE COACHES (t/a Validford Ltd)

76 GREEN LANE, SELBY YO8 9AW
Tel: 01757 703549
Fax: 01757 210956
Dirs: S. Stockdale, J. Stockdale
Dir/Co Sec: Julie O'Neill
Fleet: 6 - 2 double-deck bus, 4 coach
Chassis: 2 Bedford. 2 Bristol. 2 Leyland.
Bodies: 2 Alexander. 2 Duple. 2 Plaxton.
Ops incl: local bus services, school contracts, private hire.
Livery: Red/White.
Ticket System: Almex.

*THORNES INDEPENDENT LTD

THE COACH STATION, HULL ROAD, HEMINGBROUGH, SELBY YO8 6QG
Tel: 01757 630777
Fax: 01757 630666
Man Dir: P Thornes **Ch Eng**: S Cotton
Co Sec: C Thornes **Ops Man**: L J Thornes
Fleet: 15 - 2 double-deck bus, 1 single-deck bus, 6 coach, 1 midicoach, 1 minicoach, 4 heritage coach
Chassis: 1 Bedford. 1 Bristol. 1 DAF. 2 Dennis. 1 Ford Transit. 1 Leyland. 1 Beadle.1 Mercedes. 1 Seddon. 5 Volvo.
Bodies: 1 Beadle. 1 Dormobile. 1 Duple. 3 East Lancs. 1 Harrington. 1 Optare. 7 Plaxton.
Ops incl: local bus services, school contracts, excursions & tours, private hire, continental tours
Livery: Blue/Grey/Red
Ticket System: Wayfarer Saver

*TOP LINE TRAVEL OF YORK LTD

23 HOSPITAL FIELDS ROAD, FULFORD INDUSTRIAL ESTATE, YORK YO10 4EW
Tel: 01904 655585
Fax: 01904 655587
E-mail: toplinetravel@aol.com
Web site: www.toplinetravelofyork.co.uk, www.yorktourbuses.co.uk
Fleetname: York City Sightseeing.

Man Dir: Peter Dew
Dir/Co Sec: Susan Dew.
Ops Supt: Tom Richardson.
Fleet: 18 - 6 double-deck bus, 1 single-deck bus, 11 open-top bus.
Chassis: 1 DAF. 3 Dennis. 4 Leyland. 10 MCW.
Bodies: 1 Alexander. 5 East Lancs. 10 MCW. 1 Optare. 1 Wright.
Ops incl: local bus services, school contracts, private hire.
Livery: Blue/Yellow (Top Line), Red (City Sightseeing), Green(Guide Friady),
Ticket System: Almex A90

WINN BROS
8 MILL HILL CLOSE, BROMPTON DL6 2QP.
Tel: 01609 773520.
Fax: 01609 775234.

WISTONIAN COACHES
PLANTATION GARAGE, CAWOOD ROAD, WISTOW YO8 0XB.
Tel: 01757 269303.
Props: John Firth, Gordon Firth.
Fleet: 3 coach, 1 midicoach.
Chassis: 1 Bedford. 3 Volvo.
Bodies: 4 Plaxton.
Ops incl: school contracts, private hire.
Livery: Cream, Red/Orange/Yellow stripes.

YORKSHIRE COASTLINER LTD
BUS STATION, RAILWAY STREET, MALTON YO17 7NR.
Tel: 01653 692556.
Fax: 01653 695341.
Web site: www.yorkshirecoastliner.co.uk
Prop: Blazefield Holdings Ltd.
Ops Man: Brian Kneeshaw.
Fleet: 19 - 12 double-deck bus, 7 single-deck bus.
Chassis: 26 Volvo.
Bodies: 11 Alexander. 1 Northern Counties. 3 Plaxton. 13 Wright.
Ops incl: local bus services.
Livery: Cream/Blue.
Ticket System: Wayfarer 3
(Part of the Blazefield group which is owned by Transdev)

NORTHAMPTONSHIRE

ALEC HEAD
♿ WC 🪑 🚌 A/c R24 🔧 T
LUTTON, PETERBOROUGH
PE8 5NE
Tel: 01832 272546
Fax: 01832 273077
Web site:
www.alecheadcoaches.co.uk
Ptnrs: A M Head, Mrs J Head, Mrs S J Johns
Fleet: 39 - 7 double-deck bus, 10 single-deck bus, 15 coach, 4 double-deck coach, 1 open-top bus, 1 midicoach, 1 minicoach.
Chassis: 24 Bedford. 7 Dennis. 4 Iveco. 1 Leyland. 2 MAN. 2 Mercedes. 7 Scania. 1 Toyota. 5 Volvo.
Bodies: 7 Alexander. 4 Ayats. 1 Caetano. 2 Marcopolo. 4 MCW. 2 Neoplan.
Ops incl: local bus services, school contracts, excursions & tours, private hire, continental tours.

*GEOFF AMOS COACHES LTD
♿ WC 🪑 🍴 A/c 🔧 T
THE COACH STATION, WOODFORD ROAD, EYDON, DAVENTRY
NN11 3PL
Tel: 01327 260522
Fax: 01327 262883
E-mail: sales@geoffamos.co.uk
Web site: www.geoffamos.co.uk
Fin Dir: Shirley Smith **Tran Man/Dir:** Brian Amos **Ops Man:** Brian Ellard **Ch Eng:** Kevin Wilson
Fleet: 24 - 9 double-deck bus, 7 single-deck bus, 7 coach, 1 minicoach
Chassis: 4 Dennis. 10 Leyland. 4 MAN. 1 Mercedes. 1 Optare. 4 Volvo.
Bodies: 2 Berkhof. 1 Caetano. 7 ECW. 5 Marshall. 1 Mercedes. 2 Northern Counties. 1 Optare. 2 Plaxton. 3 Sunsundegui.
Ops incl: local bus services, school contracts, private hire, continental tours.
Livery: buses: Yellow, coaches: Metallic
Ticket system: Wayfarer

BASFORDS COACHES LTD
WC 🪑 🔧
HIGH STREET, GREENS NORTON
NN12 8BA.
Tel: 01327 350493.
Dirs: J. V. & K. R. Jeffs.
Fleet: 15 - 3 double-deck bus, 12 single-deck bus.
Chassis: 3 Bedford. 1 Ford. 3 Leyland. 8 Volvo.
Bodies: 6 Caetano. 4 Duple. 2 Jonckheere. 3 Leyland National.
Ops incl: school contracts, excursions & tours, private hire, continental tours.
Livery: Red/White/Green.
Ticket System: Bellgraphic.

(Subsidiary of Jeffs Coaches Ltd)

*L F BOWEN T/A YORKS COACHES
WC A/c 🪑 🔧 T
SHORT LANE, COGENHOE NN7 1LE
Tel: 01604 890210
Fax: 0870 990 9524
Recovery: 01604 890210
E-mail: yorksta@yorks-travel.co.uk
Web site: www.yorkstravel.com
Fleetname: Yorks Coaches
Chmn: A H Moseley **Ch Exec:** K Lower
Man Dir (coaching): R Lyng **Eng Man:** D Hoy **Group Ops Man:** N G Tetley
Fleet: 28 - 25 coach, 1 midicoach, 2 minibus.
Chassis: 3 Dennis. 2 Iveco. 2 LDV. 9 MAN. 1 Neoplan. 3 Scania. 3 Setra. 1 Toyota. 4 Volvo.
Bodies: 2 Beulas. 1 Caetano. 3 Irizar. 5 Marcopolo. 1 Neoplan. 7 Noge. 3 Plaxton. 3 Setra. 1 Van Hool. 2 other.
Ops incl: local bus services, excursions & tours, school contracts, private hire, express, continental tours.
Livery: Silver
Ticket System: Almex

BRITTAINS COACHES LTD
SOUTHBRIDGE, COTTON END, NORTHAMPTON NN4 8BS.
Tel: 01604 765708.
Fax: 01604 700481.
Dirs: W. J. Cunningham, Mrs P. M. Brittain, Mrs J. Cunningham.
Co Sec: Miss C. Brittain. **Off Man:** M. Kelly.
Fleet: 7 - 3 double-deck bus, 4 coach.
Chassis: 3 Bristol. 2 DAF. 2 Scania.
Bodies: 3 Alexander. 2 Caetano. 2 Van Hool.
Ops incl: private hire.
Livery: White with Black lettering.

*BUCKBY'S COACHES
🪑 WC A/c 🔧
3 FOX STREET, ROTHWELL, KETTERING NN14 6AN
Tel: 01536 710344
Tel: 01536 712244
Recovery: 07887945564
Prop: Minesh Uka.
Fleet: 10 - 1 double-deck bus, 1 single-deck bus, 6 coach, 1 double-deck coach, 1 minicoach.
Chassis: 1 Bedford. 2 Dennis. 1 Mercedes. 6 Volvo.
Bodies: 1 Duple. 1 East Lancs. 1 Jonckheere. 7 Plaxton.
Ops incl: local bus services, school contracts, excursions & tours, private hire, continental tours.

*COUNTRY LION (NORTHAMPTON) LTD
♿ WC 🪑 A/c
87 ST JAMES MILL ROAD, NORTHAMPTON NN5 5JP
Tel: 01604 754566
Fax: 01604 755800
Dirs: J S F Bull, A J Bull
Fleet: 40 - 8 coach, 2 single-deck bus, 22 coach, 8 midicoach
Chassis: 6 Dennis. 6 Irisbus. 4 Leyland National. 8 Mercedes. 2 Scania. 14 Volvo.
Bodies: 1 Alexander. 6 Beulas. 1 East Lancs. 2 Irizar. 1 Jonckheere. 3 Northern Counties. 1 Optare. 19 Plaxton. 1 Van Hool. 4 Wadham Stringer
Ops incl: local bus services, school contracts, excursions & tours, continental tours, private hire.
Livery: White or Gold

FIRST NORTHAMPTON
♿ WC 🪑 🔧
ST JAMES' ROAD, NORTHAMPTON
NN5 5JD
Tel: 01604 751431.
Man Dir: I. Humphreys **Fin Dir:** A Bhimani
Fleet: 75 - 42 double-deck bus, 24 single-deck bus, 5 coach, 4 minibus.
Chassis: 3 Bristol. 9 MCW. 4 Renault. 6 Scania. 45 Volvo.
Bodies: Alexander, East Lancs, Northern Counties, Wright.
Ops incl: local bus services, school contracts, private hire.
Livery: Cream/Red.
Ticket System: Wayfarer 3

GOODE COACHES
WC 🪑 A/c
47 BURFORD AVENUE, BOOTHVILLE, NORTHAMPTON
NN3 6AF
Tel: 01604 862700
Prop: David Goode **Tran Man:** Andrew Wall
Fleet: 4
Chassis: 4 Leyland.
Bodies: 3 Plaxton. 1 Van Hool.
Ops incl: school contracts, private hire.
Livery: Cream/Maroon.

*JCS COACHES
WC 🪑 A/c
2 THE JAMB, CORBY NN17 1AY
Tel: 01536 202660
Fax: 01536 406299
E-mail: jambtravel@yahoo.co.uk
Props: Jackie Burton, Michael Burton
Fleet: 5 - 4 coach, 1 midicoach.
Chassis: 2 Bova. 2 DAF. 1 Mercedes.
Bodies: 2 Bova. 1 Caetano. 1 Ikarus. 1 Marshall.
Ops incl: excursions & tours, private hire.

A/c	Air conditioning	🔧	Replacement vehicle available
♿	Vehicles suitable for disabled	T	Toilet-drop facilities available
🍴	Coach(es) with galley facilities	🪑	Seat belt-fitted vehicles
WC	Coach(es) with toilet facilities	R	Recovery service available (not 24 hr)
		R24	24hr recovery service
		🚐	Vintage vehicle(s) available
		🚌	Open top vehicle(s)

153

J. R. J. COACHES

24 STALBRIDGE WALK, CORBY NN18 0DT.
Tel: 01536 200317.
Fax: 01536 394387.
Prop: J. D. Judge.
Fleet: 6 - 3 coach, 1 midicoach, 2 minibus.
Chassis: 1 Bedford. 1 Ford Transit. 1 Mercedes.
Bodies: 1 Caetano. 1 Carlyle. 1 Duple. 1 Mercedes.
Ops incl: local bus services, school contracts, excursions & tours, private hire.

*JEFFS COACHES LTD

STATION ROAD, HELMDON, BRACKLEY NN13 5QT
Tel: 01295 768292
Fax: 01295 760365
E-mail: admin@jeffscoaches.com
Web site: www.jeffscoaches.com
Ch Exec: Kevin Lower **Man Dir**: Bob Lyng
Ops Man: Sarah Bayliss **Sales Man**: Fred Eaton **Contracts Man**: Eddie Rainbow
Wkshp Man: Clive Faulkner
Fleet: 58 - 8 double-deck bus, 1 single-deck bus, 47 coach, 2 midicoach.
Fleet: 4 Dennis. 6 Iveco. 8 Leyland . 2 Toyota. 38 Volvo.
Bodies: 6 Beulas. 23 Caetano. 8 Jonckheere. 8 Leyland. 9 Plaxton. 2 Van Hool. 2 other.
Ops incl: school contracts, excursions & tours.
Livery: White /Red/Green/Silver

MARTINS COACHES

6 HAZEL ROAD, KETTERING NN16 7AL.
Prop: G. H. Martin.

R B TRAVEL

ISHAM ROAD, PYTCHLEY NN4 1EW
Prop: Roger Bull
Tel/Fax: 01536 791066
Fleet: 10 coach
Chassis: 6 DAF. 4 MAN.
Bodies: 2 Plaxton. 8 Van Hool.

*RODGER'S COACHES LTD

102 KETTERING ROAD, WELDON NN17 3JG
Tel: 01536 200500
Fax: 01536 407407
E-mail: rodgerscoaches@hotmail.com
Props: James Rodger, Linda Rodger
Fleet: 14 - 7 double-deck bus, 7 single-deck bus.
Chassis: 1 DAF. 1 Dennis. 1 Leyland. 1 Scania. 10 Volvo.
Bodies: 2 Alexander. 2 East Lancs. 1 Ikarus. 4 Jonckheere. 2 Northern Counties. 2 Van Hool.
Ops incl: private hire, excursions & tours, continental tours.
Livery: White/Red

SOUL BROTHERS

See: Buckinghamshire

*STAGECOACH EAST

ROTHERSTHORPE AVENUE, NORTHAMPTON NN4 8UT
Tel: 01604 662266
Fax: 01604 662260
E-mail: eastenquiries@stagecoachbus.com
Web site: www.stagecoachbus.com
Man Dir: vacant at Jly07 **Ops Dir**: Michelle Hargreaves **Eng Dir**: Keith Dyball
Fleet: 305 - 102 double-deck bus, 13 single-deck bus, 26 coach, 102 midibus, 62 minibus.
Chassis: 1 Bristol. 124 Dennis. 32 Leyland. 9 Mercedes. 53 Optare. 5 Scania. 81 Volvo
Bodies: 99 Alexander. 1 ECW. 5 East Lancs. 31 Northern Counties. 53 Optare. 116 Plaxton.
Ops incl: local bus services, school contracts.
Livery: Stagecoach Group
Ticket System: ERG

NORTHUMBERLAND

*ADAMSON'S COACHES

8 PORLOCK TOWER, NORTHBURN CHASE, CRAMLINGTON NE23 3TT
Tel/Fax: 01670 734050
Recovery: 07721 633351
E-mail: adamsonscoaches@btconnect.com
Prop: Allen Mullen **Ch Eng**: Paul Mullen
Co Sec: Mrs Wendy Mullen
Fleet: 4 coach
Chassis: 4 DAF
Bodies: 4 Van Hool
Ops incl: excursions & tours, private hire
Livery: Cream

*HENRY COOPER

See Tyne & Wear

*CRAIGGS TRAVEL EUROPEAN

1 CENTRAL AVENUE, AMBLE, MORPETH NE65 0NQ
Tel/Fax: 01665 710614
E-mail: classicalholiday@tiscali.co.uk
Web site: www.coachhireandholidays.co.uk
Props: J Craiggs, I C Craiggs
Co Sec: L C Craiggs **Eng**: I C Craiggs
Fleet: 4 coach.
Chassis: 1 DAF. 2 Setra. 1 Volvo.
Bodies: 2 Plaxton. 2 Setra.
Ops incl: excursions & tours, private hire, continental tours, school contracts.
Livery: Red

*GO NORTH EAST

See Tyne & Wear.

HILLARYS COACHES

20 CASTLE VIEW, PRUDHOE NE42 6NG
Tel/Fax: 01661 832560
Props: L Hillary, V Hillary
Fleet: 5 - 1 coach. 3 midicoach, 1 minibus.
Chassis/Bodies: 1 DAF. 1 MAN. 3 Mercedes.
Ops incl: local bus services, school contracts, excursions & tours, private hire.

LONGSTAFF'S COACHES

UNIT 107, AMBLE INDUSTRIAL ESTATE, AMBLE, MORPETH NE65 0PE
Tel: 01665 713300
Fax: 01665 710987
Man Dir: Frederick Longstaff
Co Sec: Alison Longstaff
Ops Man: Frederick Longstaff
Fleet: 9 - 7 coach, 1 midicoach
Chassis: 1 Leyland. 1 Mercedes. 1 Neoplan. 7 Volvo
Bodies: 1 Jonckheere. 1 Neoplan. 3 Plaxton. 3 Van Hool. 1 other
Ops incl: local bus services, excursions & tours, private hire, continental tours, school contracts.
Livery: Blue/Cream/Yellow.

ROWELL COACHES

3B DUKES WAY, PRUDHOE NE42 6PQ
Tel: 01661 832316
Fax: 01661 834485
E-mail: sales@rowellcoaches.co.uk
Web site: www.rowellcoaches.co.uk
Dirs: Mrs Gardiner, Mrs B Gardiner
Fleet: 10 coach
Chassis: 6 Bova. 4 Duple.
Ops incl: school contracts, excursions & tours, private hire.
Livery: White

SERENE TRAVEL

86A FRONT STREET EAST, BEDLINGTON NE22 5AB.
Tel: 01670 829636.
Fax: 01670 827961.

Web site:
www.yell.co.uk/sites/serenetravel
Man Dir: Mrs C. E. Fielding. **Flt Eng:** G. J. Balsdon. **Co Sec:** D. A. Fielding.
Fleet: 17 - 7 single-deck bus, 6 coach, 2 midicoach, 2 minibus.
Chassis: 1 AEC. 2 Bedford. 1 Ford Transit. 1 Iveco. 3 Leyland. 6 Leyland National. 2 MCW. 1 Volvo.
Bodies: 2 Carlyle. 2 Duple. 6 Leyland National. 2 Optare. 4 Plaxton. 1 Burlingham.
Ops incl: local bus services, school contracts, excursions & tours, private hire, express.
Livery: Blue/Cream.
Ticket System: Wayfarer II.

*TRAVELSURE
R24

25 MAIN STREET, SEAHOUSES NE68 7RE.
Tel: 01665 720907
Fax: 01665 721381
E-mail: travelsure@travelsure.co.uk
Web site: www.travelsure.co.uk
Owner: Barrie Patterson **Dir:** Karen Patterson

Fleet: 28 - 2 double-deck bus, 2 single-deck bus, 13 coach, 5 midibus, 4 midicoach, 4 minibus.
Chassis: 2 Bova. 4 DAF. 4 Dennis. 2 Iveco. 2 LDV. 4 Leyland. 3 MCW. 4 Mercedes. 2 Scania. 1 Volvo.
Bodies: 2 Beulas. 1 Berkhof. 2 Bova. 1 Caetano. 1 Duple. 1 East Lancs. 1 Esker. 1 Irizar. 5 Plaxton. 2 Setra. 1 Transbus. 2 Van Hool. 8 other.
Ops incl: local bus services, school contracts, excursions & tours, private hire, continental tours.
Livery: Blue.
Ticket System: Wayfarer.

TYNEDALE GROUP TRAVEL

TOWNFOOT GARAGE, HALTWHISTLE NE49 0EJ.
Tel: 01434 322944.
Fax: 01434 322955.
E-mail: admin@tynedalegrouptravel.co.uk
Web site: www.tynedalegrouptravel.co.uk
Ptnr: Andy Sinclair.

Fleet: 6 - 1 single-deck coach, 3 midibus, 2 midicoach.
Chassis: 5 Mercedes. 1 Volvo.
Bodies: 4 Plaxton, 1 Van Hool, 1 other.
Ops incl: local bus servcices, school contracts, excursions & tours, private hire, continental tours.

TYNE VALLEY COACHES LTD

ACOMB, HEXHAM NE46 4QT
Tel: 01434 602217
Fax: 01434 604150
Dirs: H. D. Weir, K. M. Weir.
Fleet: 18 - 1 single-deck bus, 17 coach.
Chassis: 1 DAF. 13 Leyland. 4 Volvo.
Bodies: 6 Duple. 1 Optare. 10 Plaxton. 1 Van Hool.
Ops incl: local bus services, school contracts, private hire
Livery: Blue/Silver
Ticket System: AES

NOTTINGHAMSHIRE, NOTTINGHAM

BAILEY'S COACHES LTD

EEL HOLE FARM, LONG LANE, WATNALL NG16 1HY.
Tel: 0115 968 0141
Fax: 0115 968 1101.
Dirs: T. Bailey (**Gen Man & Traf Man**), Mrs J. Bailey (**Sec**).
Ch Eng: G. Payne.
Fleet: 10 - 2 double-deck bus, 6 coach, 2 double-deck coach.
Chassis: Bristol. DAF. Duple. Volvo.
Bodies: 10 Duple. 3 Others.
Ops incl: local bus services, school contracts, excursions & tours, private hire, continental tours.
Livery: White with Yellow/Brown/Orange stripes.

BUTLER BROTHERS COACHES

60 VERNON ROAD, KIRKBY IN ASHFIELD NG17 8ED
Tel: 01623 753260
Fax: 01623 754581
E-mail: butlerscoaches@btconnect.com
Dirs: Robert Butler, Anita Butler, James Butler.
Fleet: 9 - 1 double-deck bus, 7 coach, 1 midicoach.
Chassis: 2 DAF. 3 Dennis. 1 Leyland.

2 MAN. 1 Volvo.
Bodies: 1 Berkhof. 2 Caetano. 1 East Lancs. 2 Plaxton. 3 Van Hool.
Ops incl: school contracts, excursions & tours, private hire, continental tours.
Livery: Dual Blue
Ticket System: Wayfarer

*DUNN-LINE (HOLDINGS) LTD

BEECHDALE ROAD, BEECHDALE, NOTTINGHAM NG8 3EU
Tel: 0115 916 9000
Fax: 0115 942 0578
E-mail: scot.dunn@dunn-line.com
Web site: www.dunn-line.com
Dirs: R A Dunn, A S Dunn, J T Moore, B K Geldart (**Co Sec**)
Fleet: 230 - 54 double-deck bus, 22 single-deck bus, 66 coach, 1 double-deck coach, 1 open-top bus, 82 midibus, 4 minibus.
Chassis: 1 Bova. 1 DAF. 6 Dennis. 4 Leyland National. 5 MAN. 23 MCW. 42 Mercedes. 43 Optare. 9 Scania. 3 Transbus. 93 Volvo.
Bodies: 24 Alexander. 1 Bova. 16 Caetano. 1 Duple. 1 ECW. 19 East Lancs. 3 Irizar. 4 MCV/Marshall. 23 MCW. 4 Mellor. 3 Mercedes. 3 Northern Counties. 44 Optare. 68 Plaxton. 5 Sunsundegui. 3 Transbus. 8 Van Hool.
Ops incl: local bus services, school contracts, private hire, express, continental tours.
(part of the Veolia Group)

GOSPEL'S COACHES

27 ASCOT DRIVE, HUCKNALL NG15 6JA
Tel: 0115 963 3894
Dirs: T Gospel, G Gospel, G T Gospel
Fleet: 4 - 2 double-deck bus, 2 coach.
Chassis: 2 Leyland. 2 Volvo.
Bodies: 1 Alexander. 1 Northern Counties. 2 Plaxton.
Ops incl: excursions & tours, private hire, school contracts.
Livery: White/Blue.

HENSHAWS COACHES

57 PYE HILL ROAD, JACKSDALE NG16 5LR
Tel: 01773 607909
Prop: Paul Henshaw
Fleet: 6 - 5 coach, 1 midicoach
Chassis: Bova, DAF, Leyland, MAN, Mercedes
Bodies: Bova, Duple, Hispano, Noge, Van Hool.
Ops incl: excursions & tours, private hire, school contracts, continental tours.
Livery: Cream/Orange/Brown

A/c	Air conditioning		Seat belt-fitted vehicles		Replacement vehicle available
	Vehicles suitable for disabled	R	Recovery service available (not 24 hr)	T	Toilet-drop facilities available
	Coach(es) with galley facilities	R24	24hr recovery service		Vintage vehicle(s) available
wc	Coach(es) with toilet facilities				Open top vehicle(s)

Northumberland / Nottinghamshire

Nottinghamshire

*JOHNSON BROS TOURS
R24

GREEN ACRE, GREEN LANE, HODTHORPE, WORKSOP S80 4XR
Tel: 01909 721847
Fax: 01909 722886
E-mail: enquiries@johnsonstours.co.uk
Web site: www.johnsonstours.co.uk
Chmn: Tony Johnson **Dis**: Lee Johnson, Antony Johnson, Scott Johnson
Co Sec: Colleen Johnson
Fleet: 109 - 65 double-deck bus, 2 single-deck bus, 30 coach, 2 double-deck coach, 5 midibus, 2 midicoach, 1 minibus, 2 minicoach.
Chassis: 2 Bedford. 2 Bova. 30 Bristol. 4 DAF. 1 Ford. 3 Irisbus. 1 MAN. 30 MCW. 5 Mercedes. 5 Neoplan. 1 Optare. 5 Scania. 10 Volvo.
Bodies: 3 Beulas. 2 Berkhof. 3 Bova. 2 Irizar. 3 Jonckheere. 2 Optare. 3 Van Hool.
Ops incl: local bus services, school contracts, excursions & tours, private hire, continental tours.
Livery: Blue/Yellow fade

JUMBO MINI COACHES
338 THE WELLS ROAD, NOTTINGHAM NG3 3AA.
Tel: 0115 958 4730.
Owner: J. Talbot.
Fleet: 2 minibus. **Chassis**: 2 LDV.
Ops incl: school contracts, private hire.
Livery: White/Blue.

K & S COACHES
21 CLIFTON GROVE, MANSFIELD NG18 4HY.
Tel/Fax: 01623 656768.
Prop: K. & Sue Burnside.
Fleet: 4 - 1 midicoach, 3 minicoach.
Chassis/bodies: Ford Transit. Mercedes. Renault. Talbot.
Ops incl: school contracts, excursions & tours, private hire.
Livery: White/Red/Grey.

KETTLEWELL (RETFORD) LTD
GROVE STREET, RETFORD DN22 6LA
Tel: 01777 860360
Fax: 01777 710351
Chmn: A J Kettlewell **Man Dir**: P C Kettlewell **Dir**: C C Kettlewell **Senior Officer**: M Burton **Ops Man**: T Bradley
Fleet: 18 - 2 double-deck coach, 15 coach, 1 minicoach.
Chassis: 1 Leyland. 1 Mercedes. 2 Neoplan. 12 Scania. 1 Volvo.
Bodies: 1 East Lancs. 10 Irizar. 1 Jonckheere. 1 Mercedes. 2 Neoplan. 1 Plaxton.
Ops incl: school contracts, excursions & tours, private hire, continental tours.
Livery: White/Yellow.

MARSHALLS OF SUTTON-ON-TRENT
11 MAIN STREET, SUTTON-ON-TRENT NG23 6PF.
Tel: 01636 821138
Fax: 01636 822227
Web site: www.marshallscoaches.co.uk
Prop: J. A. Marshall. **Flt Eng**: P. J. Marshall
Ops Man: K G Tagg
Fleet: includes double-deck bus, single-deck bus, coach, midibus, midicoach.
Chassis: Dennis. Leyland. MAN. Mercedes. Optare. Transbus. Volvo.
Bodies: Alexander. Berkhof. Caetano. East Lancs. Northern Counties. Optare. Plaxton. Transbus. Van Hool.
Ops incl: local bus services, school contracts, excursions & tours, private hire, continental tours.
Livery: Blue/Cream.
Ticket System: Almex

MAUN CRUSADER TOURS
NEW CROSS HOUSE, 8-10 MANSFIELD ROAD, SUTTON-IN-ASHFIELD NG17 4GR.
Tel: 01623 555621.
Fax: 01623 555671.
Dirs: R. A. Read (**Gen Man/Traf Man**), N. G. Barks (**Sec**). **Ch Eng**: S. Palmer.
Fleet: 17 - 8 double-deck bus, 8 single-deck bus. 1 midicoach.
Chassis: 3 DAF, 1 Daimler. 5 Dennis. 2 Leyland. 1 MAN. 1 Mercedes. 4 Integral.
Bodies: 1 Alexander. 1 Caetano. 6 Duple. 1 East Lancs. 1 Jonckheere. 1 Marco Polo. 4 Northern Counties. 1 Plaxton. 1 SC.
Ops incl: private hire, continental tours, school contracts.
Livery: Multi-coloured.

C. W. MOXON LTD
MALTBY ROAD, OLDCOTES, WORKSOP S81 8JN.
Tel: 01909 730345.
Fax: 01909 733670.
Web site: www.moxons-tours.co.uk
Fleetname: Moxons Coaches.
Dirs: Mrs L. Marlow, Mrs M. Moxon, **Co Sec**: Mrs J. Holder, **Ch Eng**: M. Marlow.
Fleet: 15 - 3 double-deck bus, 12 coach.
Chassis: 2 Bedford. 3 Bristol. 7 DAF. 2 Leyland. 1 Iveco.
Bodies: 2 Bova. 1 Duple. 3 MCW. 5 Plaxton. 3 Van Hool. 1 Eos.
Ops incl: excursions & tours, private hire, continental tours, school contracts.
Livery: Cream/Red.

*NOTTINGHAM CITY TRANSPORT
LOWER PARLIAMENT STREET, NOTTINGHAM NG1 1GG
Tel: 0115 950 5745
Fax: 0115 950 4425
E-mail: shiela.swift@nctx.co.uk, info@nctx.co.uk
Web site: www.nctx.co.uk
Chmn: Brian Parbutt **Man Dir**: Mark Fowles **Eng Dir**: Barry Baxter **Fin Dir/Co Sec**: Rob Hicklin **Mktg & Comms Dir**: Nicola Tidy **Comm Man**: Barrie Burch **Fleet Eng**: Farrell Smith
Fleet: 335 - 161 double-deck bus, 74 single-deck bus, 5 articulated bus, 95 midibus
Chassis: 54 Dennis. 108 Optare. 149 Scania. 23 Volvo.
Bodies: 114 East Lancs. 51 Scania. 54 Transbus. 5 Wright.
Ops incl: local bus services
Livery: Multi-Branded
Ticket system: Almex

NOTTINGHAM EXPRESS TRANSIT
LAWRENCE HOUSE, TALBOT STREET, NOTTINGHAM NG1 5NT
Tel: 0115 915 6600
Web site: www.thetram.net, www.nottinghamcity.gov.uk, www.nottinghamexpresstransitco.uk, www.netphasetwo.com
Concession Co: Arrow Light Rail (Bombardier, Carillion, Transdev, Nottingham City Transport, Inisfree, CDC Projects)
Commercial Manager: Colin Lea
Fleet: 15 tram
Chassis/bodies: Bombardier
Ops incl: tram service
Livery: Green/White

PATRON TRAVEL
GLEBE COTTAGE, 1 FOSSE WAY, FLINTHAM NG23 5LH
Tel: 01636 525725
Fax: 01636 525731
Prop: Ron Todd
Fleet: 3 - 1 double-deck bus, 2 coach.
Chassis: 1 Leyland. 2 Volvo
Bodies: 1 Alexander. 2 Jonckheere.
Ops incl: continental tours, private hire, school contracts.
Livery: Cream

PEGASUS COACHWAYS LTD
GROVE STREET, RETFORD DN22 6LA.
Tel: 01777 860360.
Fax: 01777 710351.
Chmn: A. J. Kettlewell. **Man Dir**: P. C. Kettlewell. **Dir**: C. C. Kettlewell.
Tours Man: M. Burton
Fleet: 9 coach
Chassis: 9 Scania.
Bodies: 9 Irizar.
Ops incl: excursions and tours, continental tours.
Livery: White/Yellow

REDFERN COACHES (MANSFIELD) LTD
R24

LINDLEY STREET, MANSFIELD NG18 1QE
Tel: 01623 27653
Fax: 01623 25787
E-mail: enquiries@johnsontours.co.uk
Web site: www.johnsontours.co.uk
Fleet: 29 - 18 double-deck bus, 4 single-deck bus, 4 coach, 1 midibus, 1 midicoach, 1 minicoach.
Chassis: 18 Bristol. 1 Ford. 1 Freight Rover. 1 Scania. 2 Volvo.
Bodies: include 2 Irizar.
Ops incl: local bus services, excursions & tours, private hire, express, continental tours, school contracts.
Livery: Green/Faded Green/Gold
(Subsidiary of Johnsons Tours)

*SHARPE & SONS (NOTTINGHAM) LTD

UNIT 10, CANALSIDE INDUSTRIAL PARK, CROPWELL BISHOP, NOTTINGHAM NG12 3BE
Tel: 0115 989 4466
Fax: 0115 989 4666
E-mail: trevor.sharpe@sharpesofnottingham.com
Web site: www.sharpesofnottingham.com
Man Dir: Trevor Sharpe
Ops Dir: James Sharpe
Fleet: 20 - 1 double-deck bus, 3 single-deck bus, 16 coach, 1 double-deck coach.
Chassis: 2 Leyland. 1 Leyland National. 17 Volvo.
Bodies: 1 Alexander. 2 Leyland. 1 Leyland National. 16 Van Hool.
Ops incl: local bus services, school contracts, private hire, continental tours, excursions & tours.
Livery: Silver Blue/Navy Blue

*SILVERDALE TOURS LTD

LITTLE TENNIS STREET SOUTH, NOTTINGHAM NG2 4EU
Tel: 0115 912 1000
Fax: 0115 912 1558
E-mail: info@silverdaletours.co.uk
Web site: www.silverdaletours.co.uk
Dir: Shaun Doherty
Fleet: 39 - 6 double-deck bus, 3 single-deck bus, 26 coach, 2 double-deck coach, 2 midicoach
Chassis: 2 Ayats. 2 DAF. 3 Leyland National. 2 Mercedes. 30 Volvo.
Bodies: 5 Beulas. 19 Caetano. 3 Jonckheere. 3 Leyland National. 8 Plaxton. 1 Van Hool.
Ops incl: local bus services, private hire, express, school contracts, continental tours.
Livery: Yellow/Red/Black

*SKILLS HOLIDAYS

BELGRAVE ROAD, NOTTINGHAM NG6 8LY
Tel: 0115 977 0080
Fax: 0115 977 7436
E-mail: pete.hallam@skillsholidays.co.uk
Web site: www.skillsholidays.co.uk
Man Dir: Nigel Skill **Fin Dir:** Simon Skill
Comm Dir: Roy Fitch **Ops Dir:** Pete Hallam
Fleet: 38 - 4 double-deck bus, 30 coach, 2 midibus, 2 midicoach.
Chassis: 2 MAN. 4 MCW. 18 Mercedes. 13 Volvo.
Bodies: 7 Jonckheere. 4 MCW. 1 Plaxton. 16 Setra. 6 Van Hool. 4 other.
Ops incl: school contracts, excursions & tours, private hire, continental tours.
Livery: Green

SPENCERS COACHES

20 THORNHILL DRIVE, BOUGHTON, NEWARK NG22 9JG
Tel: 01623 860394
Dir: R Spencer.
Fleet: 2 midicoach.
Chassis: 2 Mercedes.
Bodies: 2 Plaxton
Ops incl: school contracts, private hire
Livery: Cream/Green

F T TAGG COACHES

QUARRY YARD, SUTTON-IN-ASHFIELD NG17 1BQ
Tel/Fax: 01623 554458
E-mail: ft.taggcoaches@virgin.net
Props: F T Derbyshire, Mrs D J Derbyshire
Fleet: 3 coach.
Chassis: 1 DAF. 1 MAN. 1 Scania.
Bodies: 1 Irizar. 2 Van Hool.
Ops incl: excursions & tours, private hire, continental tours.
Livery: White with red and blue

*TRANSIT EXPRESS TRAVEL

UNIT 7, EVANS BUSINESS PARK, RADMARSH ROAD, LENTON, NOTTINGHAM NG7 2GN
Tel: 0115 970 2900
Fax: 0115 970 5515
E-mail: garycrosby@hotmail.com
Prop: Gary M Crosby
Fleet: 8 - 4 coach, 2 midicoach, 2 minicoach.
Chassis: 1 Bedford. 2 Ford. 2 Ford Transit. 2 Leyland. 1 MAN.
Bodies: 1 Caetano. 1 Duple. 2 Plaxton. 1 Reeve Burgess. 3 other.
Ops incl: private hire.
Livery: Blue/White

*TRAVEL WRIGHT LTD

BRUNEL BUSINESS PARK, JESSOP CLOSE, NEWARK NG24 2AG
Tel: 01636 703813
Fax: 01636 674641
E-mail: info@travelwright.fsnet.co.uk
Web site: www.travelwright.co.uk.
Fleet: 29 - 1 double-deck bus, 3 single-deck bus, 17 coach, 5 midibus, 3 midicoach.
Chassis: 6 Dennis. 9 MAN. 5 Mercedes. 2 Neoplan. 2 Optare. 1 Scania. 4 Volvo.
Bodies: 2 Berkhof. 6 Caetano. 4 Mercedes. 3 Neoplan. 2 Optare. 10 Plaxton. 2 Van Hool.
Ops incl: local bus services, school contracts, excursions & tours, private hire, continental tours.
Livery: Cread/Red
Ticket System: Wayfarer

UNITY COACHES

BECK GARAGE, CLAYWORTH DN22 9AG.
Tel: 07777 817556.
Ptnrs: F. Marriott, Mrs J. Marriott.
Livery: Blue/Grey/Cream.

*WALLIS COACHWAYS

100 GRILLINGTON ROAD, BILSTHORPE NG22 8SP
Tel: 01623 870655
Fax: 01623 870655
Prop: Stephen Wallis
Fleet: 2 - 1 midibus, 1 midicoach.
Chassis/Bodies: 1 Mercedes. 1 Toyota
Ops incl: school contracts, private hire
Livery: White
Ticket system: Almex

Nottinghamshire

- A/c — Air conditioning
- Vehicles suitable for disabled
- Coach(es) with galley facilities
- WC — Coach(es) with toilet facilities
- Seat belt-fitted vehicles
- R — Recovery service available (not 24 hr)
- R24 — 24hr recovery service
- Replacement vehicle available
- T — Toilet-drop facilities available
- Vintage vehicle(s) available
- Open top vehicle(s)

OXFORDSHIRE

BAKERS COMMERCIAL SERVICES
UNIT 5A, ENSTONE BUSINESS PARK, ENSTONE OX7 4NP
Tel: 01608 677415/6
Fax: 01608 677150
E-mail: enquiries@bakerscoaches.co.uk
Web site: www.bakerscoaches.co.uk
Prop: Mike Baker **Ops Man**: Dave Goodall
Ch Eng: Dave Nappin
Fleet: 12 - 11 coach, 1 minibus, 2 minicoach.
Chassis: 6 Dennis. 3 Mercedes. 5 Volvo.
Bodies: 1 Berkhof. 1 Caetano. 11 Plaxton.
Ops incl: local bus services, school contracts, excursions & tours, private hire, continental tours.
Livery: Red on White.

BANBURYSHIRE ETA LTD
UNIT 17, BEAUMONT BUSINESS CENTRE, BEAUMONT CLOSE, BANBURY OX16 7TN
Tel: 01295 263777
Fax: 01295 273086
E-mail: bcta@msn.com
Fleetname: Cherwell District Dial-A-Ride
Fleet: 3 minibus
Chassis/Bodies: 2 Mercedes. 1 Peugeot
Ops incl: local bus services, private hire

BLUNSDON'S COACH TRAVEL
73 GROVE ROAD, BLADON OX20 1RJ
Tel: 01993 811320
Fax: 01993 811416
E-mail: blunsdons-coaches@merlyn73.wanadoo.co.uk
Dirs: Merlyn H Blunsdon, Michael A Blunsdon
Fleet: 5 coach
Chassis: 5 Dennis.
Bodies: 2 Neoplan. 3 Plaxton
Ops incl: private hire, school contracts, excursions & tours
Livery: White with Red/Green.

CHARLTON-ON-OTMOOR SERVICES
THE GARAGE, CHARLTON-ON-OTMOOR OX5 2UQ.
Tel: 01865 331249.
Fax: 01865 316189.

*CHENEY COACHES LTD
THORPE MEAD, BANBURY OX16 4RZ
Tel: 01295 254254
Fax: 01295 271990
E-mail: travel@cheneycoaches.co.uk
Web site: www.cheneycoaches.co.uk
Chmn: G W Peace **Man Dir**: M R Peace
Co Sec: S A Peace **Dir**: A G Peace

Fleet Eng: Tony Piotrowski
Fleet: 45 - 1 double-deck bus, 34 coach, 1 midicoach, 9 minibus.
Chassis: 2 DAF. 1 Dennis. 7 Ford Transit. 1 LDV. 2 Mercedes. 1 Neoplan. 4 Scania. 23 Volvo. 3 other.
Bodies: 1 Berkhof. 4 Caetano. 11 Jonckheere. 2 Mercedes. 1 Neoplan. 7 Plaxton. 10 Van Hool.
Ops incl: school contracts, private hire

*GRAYLINE COACHES
STATION APPROACH, BICESTER OX26 6HU
Tel: 01869 246461
Fax: 01869 240087
E-mail: sales@grayline.co.uk
Web site: www.grayline.co.uk
Dirs: A Gray, B Gray **Gen Man**: P Gray
Traff Man: S Gray **Fleet Eng**: G Willoughby
Fleet: 16 - 8 coach, 8 midicoach.
Chassis: 1 Bedford. 3 Dennis. 5 Iveco. 1 MAN. 3 Mercedes. 3 Optare.
Bodies: 5 Beulas. 1 Mercedes. 1 Neoplan. 3 Optare. 5 Plaxton. 1 Reeve Burgess
Ops incl: school contracts, local bus services, private hire, continental tours.
Livery: White/Red/Blue
Ticket System: Wayfarer

HEYFORDIAN TRAVEL LTD
MURDOCK ROAD, BICESTER OX26 4PP.
Tel: 01869 241500.
Fax: 01869 360011.
E-mail: info@heyfordian.co.uk
Web site: www.heyfordian.co.uk
Dir: Graham Smith
Fleet: 85 - 4 double-deck bus, 70 coach, 2 double-deck coach, 3 minibus. 3 minicoach.
Chassis: 8 Bova. 8 DAF. 2 Dennis. 27 Leyland. 1 MAN. 4 Optare. 20 Scania. 15 Volvo.
Bodies: 7 Alexander. 8 Bova. 4 Caetano. 31 Jonckheere. 2 Neoplan. 4 Optare. 25 Plaxton. 4 Van Hool.
Ops incl: local bus services, school contracts, excursions & tours, private hire, continental tours.
Livery: White/Red/Orange/Black.
Ticket System: Wayfarer.

McLEANS COACHES
UNIT 5, TWO RIVERS INDUSTRIAL ESTATE, STATION LANE, WITNEY OX28 6BH.
Tel: 01993 771445.
Fax: 01993 779556
Dirs: Roger Alder, Mark Hepden
Fleet: 18 - 14 coach. 4 midicoach.
Chassis: MAN. Mercedes. Neoplan. Volvo.
Bodies: incl. Sunsundegui
Ops incl: local bus services, school contracts, excursions & tours, private hire.
Livery: White/Red.

*OXFORD BUS COMPANY
COWLEY HOUSE, WATLINGTON ROAD, OXFORD OX4 6GA
Tel: 01865 785410
Fax: 01865 711745
E-mail: info@oxfordbus.co.uk
Web site: www.oxfordbus.co.uk
Man Dir: Philip Kirk **Dir/Gen Man**: Louisa Weeks **Eng Dir**: Ray Woodhouse
Fin Dir/Comm Dir: Helen Le Fevre
Fleet: 150 - 21 double-deck bus, 87 single-deck bus, 39 coach, 3 midibus.
Chassis: 24 Dennis. 38 Mercedes. 12 Scania. 76 Volvo.
Bodies: 20 Alexander. 12 Irizar. 6 Jonckheere. 50 Plaxton. 24 Wright.
Ops incl: local bus services, express.
Livery: various
Ticket System: Wayfarer

*OXFORD INTERNATIONAL
169 NEW GREENHAM PARK, BASINGSTOKE RG19 6HN
Tel: 01865 770778
Fax: 01635 821128
Dirs: Simon Weaver
Fleet: 33 - 4 single-deck bus, 22 coach, 6 double-deck coach, 1 minicoach.
Chassis: 8 Bova. 4 DAF. 4 Dennis. 1 Mercedes. 10 Scania. 6 Volvo.
Bodies: 3 Berkhof. 8 Bova. 9 East Lancs. 7 Irizar. 1 MCW. 1 Plaxton. 4 Van Hool.
Ops incl: school contracts, private hire
Livery: Electric Blue

PEARCES PRIVATE HIRE
TOWER ROAD INDUSTRIAL ESTATE, BERINSFIELD, WALLINGFORD OX10 7LN
Tel: 01865 340560.
Fax: 01865 341582.
Props: Clive Pearce, Martin Pearce.
Fleet: 12 - 8 coach, 2 midicoach, 2 minicoach.
Chassis: 1 Bova. 6 Dennis. 2 Mercedes. 1 Scania. 2 Toyota.
Bodies: 1 Bova . 2 Caetano. 2 Neoplan. 6 Plaxton. 1 Van Hool.
Ops incl: school contracts, excursions and tours, private hire.
Livery: Yellow/White

*PLASTOWS COACHES
134 LONDON ROAD, WHEATLEY OX33 1JH
Tel: 01865 872270
Fax: 01865 875066
E-mail: plastowscoaches@btconnect.com
Web site: www.plastows.co.uk
Fleet: 9 coach.
Chassis: 9 Volvo.
Ops incl: private hire, school contracts.

*STAGECOACH IN OXFORDSHIRE

HORSPATH ROAD, COWLEY
OX4 2RY
Tel: 01865 772250
Fax: 01865 405500
E-mail:
oxford.enquiries@stagecoachbus.com
Web site:
www.stagecoachbus.com/warwickshire
Man Dir: Martin Sutton **Service Delivery Dir**: Paul O'Callaghan
Fleet: 176 - 38 double-deck bus, 57 single-deck bus, 5 coach, 25 double-deck coach, 21 minibus, 30 midibus.
Chassis: 49 Dennis. 44 MAN. 33 Mercedes. 25 Neoplan. 18 Optare. 5 Scania. 32 Volvo.
Bodies: 106 Alexander. 5 Caetano. 25 Neoplan. 18 Optare. 21 Plaxton. 1 UVG.
Ops incl: local bus services, express, school contracts.
Livery: Stagecoach corporate
Ticket system: Wayfarer 3

TAPPINS COACHES

COLLETT ROAD, DIDCOT OX11 7ET
Tel: 01235 819393
Fax: 01235 816464
Recovery: 01235 819393
E-mail: coaches@tappins.co.uk
Web site: www.tappins.co.uk
Man Dir: G Smith
Fleet: 69 - 1 double-deck bus, 3 single-deck bus, 50 coach, 1 double-deck coach, 2 minicoach, 12 open top double-deck bus.
Chassis: 12 Leyland. 1 Neoplan. 2 Toyota. 54 Volvo.
Bodies: 11 Alexander. 2 Caetano. 1 East Lancs. 1 MCW. 1 Neoplan. 28 Plaxton. 25 Van Hool.
Ops incl: school contracts, excursions & tours, private hire, express, continental tours.
Livery: Orange/Black
(Subsidiary of HeyfordianTravel)

WORTHS MOTOR SERVICES LTD

ENSTONE, CHIPPING NORTON
OX7 4LQ
Tel: 01608 677322
Fax: 01608 677298
E-mail:
worths.coaches@ukonline.co.uk
Web site: www.worthscoaches.co.uk
Dirs: Richard Worth, Paul Worth
Ch Eng: Mike Florey
Fleet: 23 - 2 double-deck bus, 3 single-deck bus, 18 coach.
Chassis: 2 Dennis. 2 Leyland. 1 Mercedes. 18 Volvo.
Bodies: 1 Berkhof. 2 Jonckheere. 1 Mercedes. 2 Northern Counties. 17 Plaxton.
Ops incl: local bus services, school contracts, continental tours, private hire.
Livery: Silver/Blue
Ticket System: Wayfarer 3.

SHROPSHIRE

ASTONS OF NEWPORT

STATION GARAGE, NEWPORT
TF10 7EN
Tel/Fax: 01952 811285
Dirs: E. H. Aston, J. E. Aston, P. T. H. Aston
Fleet: 4 - 1 single-deck bus, 2 coach, 1 minibus.
Chassis: 2 Bedford. 1 Ford Transit. 1 Renault
Bodies: 1 Duple. 1 Northern Counties. 1 Plaxton. 1 Ford.
Ops incl: school contracts, private hire.

*BOULTONS OF SHROPSHIRE LTD

SUNNYSIDE, CARDINGTON,
CHURCH STRETTON SY6 7JZ
Tel: 01694 771226
Fax: 01694 771296
Dirs: M Boulton, G Boulton
Fleet: 17 - 6 single-deck bus, 6 coach, 5 midicoach.
Chassis: 6 Bova. 1 BMC. 5 Mercedes
Bodies: 1 BMC. 6 Bova. 5 Mercedes
Ops incl: local bus services, school contracts, excursions & tours, private hire, continental tours.
Livery: Cream/Orange/Brown
Ticket System: Microfare

A T BROWN (COACHES) LTD

81 TRENCH ROAD, TELFORD
TF2 6PF
Tel: 01952 605331
Fax: 01952 608011
E-mail: atbrowncoaches@aol.com
Web site: www.atbrowncoaches.co.uk
Dirs: Nina Macleod, Ewen Macleod
Fleet: 12 - 10 coach, 2 midicoach
Chassis: 9 DAF. 1 Dennis. 2 Mercedes.
Bodies: 1 Autobus. 3 Caetano. 1 Ikarus. 5 Plaxton. 2 Van Hool.
Ops incl: school contracts, private hire, excursions & tours.
Livery: Sky Blue/Navy

*BUTTERS COACHES LTD

LEWELLYN ROBERTS WAY, (OFF MAER LANE), MARKET DRAYTON
TF9 1QS
Tel: 01630 658470
Fax: 01630 658490
E-mail: butterscoaches@hotmail.com
Dirs: Erica Mackintosh, Lesley Mackintosh, Barry Managh.
Fleet: 10 - 9 coach, 1 minibus.
Chassis: 6 DAF. 1 Dennis. 1 LDV. 1 Leyland. 1 Volvo.
Bodies: 1 Jonckheere. 7 Van Hool. 2 other.
Ops incl: local bus services, school contracts, excursions & tours, private hire.
Livery: Blue lettering on White

CARADOC COACHES

UNIT 3, CROSSWAYS INDUSTRIAL
ESTATE, CHURCH STRETTON
SY6 6PQ
Tel/Fax/Recovery: 01694 724522
Prop: G Gough
Fleet: 9 - 2 coach, 2 midicoach, 4 minibus, 1 minicoach
Chassis: 1 Iveco. 4 LDV. 1 Leyland. 1 Mercedes. 1 Toyota. 1 Volvo.
Bodies: 1 Caetano. 1 Mercedes. 3 Plaxton. 4 other.
Ops incl: local bus services, school contracts, excursions & tours, private hire.

*COURTESY TRAVEL

2 WOODFIELD AVENUE,
SHREWSBURY SY3 8HT
Tel/Fax: 01743 358209
E-mail: courtesy@tiscali.co.uk
Prop: John Amies.
Fleet: 2 - 1 minicoach, 1 midicoach.
Chassis: 1 LDV. 1 Mercedes.
Bodies: 1 Autobus. 1 other.
Ops incl: excursions & tours, private hire.
Livery: Blue/White

A/c	Air conditioning
	Vehicles suitable for disabled
	Coach(es) with galley facilities
wc	Coach(es) with toilet facilities
	Seat belt-fitted vehicles
R	Recovery service available (not 24 hr)
R24	24hr recovery service
	Replacement vehicle available
T	Toilet-drop facilities available
	Vintage vehicle(s) available
	Open top vehicle(s)

*ELCOCK REISEN

THE MADDOCKS, MADELEY, TELFORD TF7 5HA
Tel: 01952 585712
Fax: 01952 582577
Man Dir: J C Elcock **Dirs**: J H Prince, J D Ashley **Ops Man**: Mark Perkins
Gen Man: Pete Taylor
Fleet: 35 - 28 coach, 4 midicoach, 3 minicoach.
Chassis: 7 Mercedes. 28 Volvo.
Bodies: 2 Autobus. 2 Esker. 31 Plaxton.
Ops incl: school contracts, excursions & tours, private hire, continental tours.
Livery: Silver/Red/Gold

*HAPPY DAYS COACHES

See Staffordshire

HOLMES GROUP TRAVEL

CHAPEL HOUSE, 6 STAFFORD ROAD, NEWPORT TF10 7LY
Tel: 01952 820477
Fax: 01952 270607
Fax: 07831 258084
Dir: C Holmes
Fleet: 3 - coach
Chassis: includes 1 Mercedes, 1 Volvo.
Bodies: 1 Mercedes. 1 Plaxton.
Ops incl: excursions & tours, private hire.
Livery: White with flag emblem

HORROCKS

IVY HOUSE, BROCKTON, LYDBURY NORTH SY7 8BA.
Tel: 01588 680364
Prop: A P Horrocks
Fleet: 9 - 2 double-deck bus, 2 single-deck bus, 5 midibus.
Chassis: 1 Bedford. 1 Bristol. 1 Daimler. 1 Dodge. 1 LDV. 4 Mercedes. 1 Volvo.
Ops incl: school contracts, private hire
Livery: White/Blue

*LAKESIDE COACHES LTD

THE COACH CENTRE, ELLESMERE BUSINESS PARK, ELLESMERE SY12 0EW
Tel: 01691 622761
Fax: 01691 623694
E-mail: mailbox@lakesidecoaches.co.uk
Web site: www.lakesidecoaches.co.uk
Dirs: J R Davies, D Davies **Man**: N N Hall
Fleet: 19 - 15 coach, 3 midibus, 1 midicoach
Chassis: 1 DAF. 3 Dennis. 2 Mercedes. 3 Toyota. 11 Volvo.
Bodies: 5 Caetano. 1 Mercedes. 1 Optare. 11 Plaxton. 1 Van Hool.
Ops incl: excursions & tours, private hire, school contracts.
Livery: Green/White

LONGMYND TRAVEL LTD

THE COACH DEPOT, LEA CROSS, SHREWSBURY SY5 8HX
Tel: 01743 861999
Fax: 01743 861901
E-mail: info@longmyndtravel.co.uk
Dirs: T G Evans, F J Evans, V Sheppard-Evans, D M Sheppard.
Fleet: 22 - 19 coach, 2 midicoach, 1 minibus
Chassis: 2 DAF. 1 Iveco. 1 Mercedes. 1 Toyota. 17 Volvo.
Bodies: 1 Berkhof. 2 Bova. 2 Caetano. 16 Jonckheere.
Ops incl: school contracts, private hire.
Livery: Red/White

MYTTON TRAVEL

MYTTON DINGLE, STIPERSTONES, MINSTERLEY SY5 0LZ
Tel: 01743 791309/ 01588 520358
Prop: D J Bradbury
Fleet: 8
Chassis: 2 Ford Transit . 4 LDV. 1 Freight Rover. 1 Mercedes.
Ops incl: school contracts, private hire.
Livery: White with yellow/red stripes

M &B COACHES & MINIBUSES

UNIT 22, HADLEY PARK INDUSTRIAL ESTATE, TELFORD TF1 2PY
Tel: 01952 251125
Fax: 01952 619619
Mobile: 07812 178163
Prop: Brian Bull
Fleet: 6 - 5 midicoach. 1 coach
Chassis: 1 Dennis. 1 DAF. 4 Mercedes.
Bodies: 1 Duple. 1 LDV. 3 Mercedes. 1 Robin Hood.
Ops incl: school contracts, private hire.
Livery: Red (metallic) with gold and silver letters

M & J TRAVEL

COACH GARAGE, NEWCASTLE, CRAVEN ARMS SY7 8QL.
Tel: 01588 640273.
Prop: W. M. Price.
Fleet: 13 - 7 coach, 1 midicoach, 5 minibus.
Chassis: 4 Bedford. 2 Dennis. 1 Toyota. 1 Talbot.
Bodies: 1 Caetano. 2 Duple. 4 Plaxton.
Ops incl: school contracts, excursions & tours, private hire, continental tours.
Livery: White/Black/Gold.
Ticket System: Setright.

*M P MINICOACHES

14 REDBURN CLOSE, KETLEY GRANGE TF2 0EE
Tel: 01952 415607
Fax: 01952 619188
Dir: Mark Perkins
Fleet: 3 minicoach.
Chassis: 3 Mercedes.
Bodies: 3 other
Ops incl: school contracts, private hire.
Livery: Two-tone Blue

*MINSTERLEY MOTORS SERVICES LTD

STIPERSTONES, MINSTERLEY, SHREWSBURY SY5 0LZ
Tel: 01743 791208
Fax: 01743 790101
E-mail: minsterleymotors@i12.com
Web site: www.minsterley-motors.co.uk
Man Dir: John Jones
Fleet: 32 - 7 single-deck bus, 23 coach, 2 midicoach.
Chassis: 5 Bedford. 1 Dennis. 2 Mercedes. 9 Scania. 15 Volvo.
Bodies: 8 Berkhof. 3 Duple. 6 Jonckheere. 2 Mercedes. 1 Sunsundegui. 4 Wright.
Ops incl: local bus services, school contracts, excursions & tours, private hire, continental tours.
Livery: Blue/Dark Blue/White
Ticket system: Wayfarer

*N.C.B. MOTORS LTD

EDSTASTON GARAGE, WEM SY4 5RF
Tel: 01939 232379
Fax: 01939 234892
E-mail: mail@ncb-motors.co.uk
Web site: www.ncb-motors.co.uk
Dirs: Derek Brown, Paul Brown
Fleet: 10 coach
Chassis: 10 Volvo.
Bodies: 5 Jonckheere. 4 Plaxton. 1 Van Hool
Ops incl: private hire, school contracts.
Livery: Brown/Cream

*OWENS COACHES LTD

36 BEATRICE STREET, OSWESTRY SY11 1QG
Tel: 01691 652126
Fax: 01691 670047
Recovery: 01691 839944
Dir: Michael Owen **Co Sec**: Joyce Horton
Ops Man: Peter Worthy
Fleet: 21 - 4 single-deck bus, 14 coach, 1 midicoach, 2 minibus.
Chassis: 2 Ayats. 1 DAF. 2 Dennis. 1 Irisbus. 1 Iveco. 3 MAN. 3 Mercedes. 2 Toyota. 6 Volvo.
Bodies: 2 Ayats. 2 Berkhof. 1 BMC. 3 Caetano. 1 Jonckheere. 1 Marcopolo. 1 Mercedes. 1 Noge. 7 Plaxton. 1 UVG. 1 Wright.
Ops incl: local bus services, excursions & tours, private hire, continental tours, school contracts.

R & B TRAVEL

PLEASANT VIEW, KNOWLE, LUDLOW SY8 3NE.
Tel/Fax: 01584 890770.
Prop: A T Radnor, L Radnor.
Fleet: 11 - midibus,
Chassis: 2 Bedford. 2 Leyland DAF. 1 Ford Transit. 2 VW. 1 Iveco. 2 Volvo.
Bodies: Duple. Optare. Plaxton. Robin Hood. Wright.
Ops incl: Local bus services, school contracts, private hire, excursions & tours.
Livery: Silver/Red/Orange/White

RIVERSIDE COACHES [R]
HEATH HILL, DAWLEY TF4 2JU
Tel: 01952 505490
Fax: 01952 505590
Prop: K H Pollen
Fleet: 13 - included 2 double-deck buses, 1 double-deck coach
Chassis: includes - Bristol. Ford. Volvo.
Ops Incl: private hire, school contracts
Livery: Blue/Silver and Blue/White

SHROPSHIRE COUNTY COUNCIL
INTEGRATED TRANSPORT UNIT,
107 LONGDEN ROAD,
SHREWSBURY SY3 9DS.
Tel: 01743 245300
Fax: 01743 253279
E-mail: peter.ralphs@shropshire-cc.gov.uk

Web site: www.shropshireonline.gov.uk
Fleetname: Fleet Operations
Ch Exec: Carolyn Downs
Gen Man Transp: Adrian Millard
Fleet Ops Off: Peter Ralphs.
Fleet: 55 - 1 single-deck bus, 51 minibus, 2 midicoach, 1 midibus.
Chassis: 1 Ford Transit. 30 Iveco. 13 LDV. 8 Mercedes. 1 Optare. 2 Renault.
Ops incl: local bus services, school contracts.
Livery: White
Ticket system: Almex

WORTHEN TRAVEL
[wc] [A/c] [R24] [T]
STATION ROAD, LITTLE MINSTERLEY SY5 0BW
Tel: 01743 792622
Fax: 01743 791053

Recovery: 01743 792622
E-mail: jackie@worthentravel.freeserve.co.uk
Prop: D A Pye **Gen Man:** C L Robinson
Sec: J Davies
Fleet: 20 - 2 single-deck bus, 15 coach, 3 minibus.
Chassis: 5 DAF. 1 Ford Transit. 7 other.
Bodies: 3 Caetano. 4 Leyland. 3 Van Hool.
Ops incl: local bus services, school contracts, excursions & tours, private hire, express, continental tours.
Livery: White/Blue
Ticket system: Wayfarer 2

SOMERSET (ALSO BATH & N E SOMERSET, N SOMERSET)

A1 TRAVEL
80 HIGHFIELD ROAD, YEOVIL BA21 4RJ
Tel/Fax: 01935 477722
Web site: www.a1travelservices.com
Dir: Ian Watson
Fleet: 5 - 2 midibus, 3 minibus.
Chassis: 1 Ford. 2 Freight Rover. 2 LDV. 1 Mercedes. 1 Setra.
Bodies: include 1 Plaxton. 1 Setra.
Ops incl: school contracts, private hire.

*ARLEEN COACH HIRE & SERVICES LTD
14 BATH ROAD, PEASEDOWN ST JOHN, BATH BA2 8DH
Tel: 01761 434625
Fax: 01761 436578
E-mail: arleen.coach-hire@virgin.net
Web site: www.arleen.co.uk
Dir: A W Spiller **Co Sec:** Mrs M K Spiller
Dir: A A Spiller **Ops Man:** J C Spiller
Ch Eng: K T Spiller
Fleet: 23 - 20 single-deck bus, 3 minicoach.
Chassis: 2 Bedford. 3 DAF. 2 Dennis. 1 Ford. 1 LDV. 2 Leyland. 2 MAN. 6 Mercedes. 2 Neoplan. 2 Volvo.
Bodies: 1 Berkhof. 3 Duple. 6 Mercedes. 5 Plaxton. 3 Van Hool. 1 Wadham Stringer. 2 other.
Ops incl: school contracts, excursions & tours, private hire.
Livery: Red/White/Blue

AXE VALE COACHES
BIDDISHAM, AXBRIDGE BS26 2RD
Tel: 01934 750321
Fax: 01934 750334
Ptnrs: A L Bailey, C P Bailey (**Ops**), J Bailey
Ch Eng: J Bailey
Fleet: 12 - 10 coach, 1 midicoach, 1 minibus.
Chassis: 7 Bova. 2 DAF. 1 Ford. 1 LDV. 1 Mercedes.
Bodies: incl: 7 Bova. 1 Leyland. 3 Plaxton.
Ops incl: local bus services, school contracts, excursions & tours, private hire, express, continental tours.
Livery: White
Ticket system: Setright

BAKERS COACHES
[wc] [R24]
8 BUCKLAND ROAD, YEOVIL BA21 5EA.
Tel: 01935 428401.
Fax: 01935 410423
Recovery: 01935 428401
Dirs: S Baker, A Palmer
Fleet: 13 - 9 coach, 1 midicoach, 3 minibus.
Chassis: 1 Bova. 6 DAF. 1 Mercedes.
Bodies: 1 Bova. 1 Jonckheere. 2 Van Hool.
Ops incl: school contracts, excursions & tours, private hire, continental tours.
Livery: Red/White

BAKERS DOLPHIN COACH TRAVEL
48 LOCKING ROAD, WESTON-SUPER-MARE BS23 3DN

Tel: 01934 635635.
Fax: 01934 641162.
E-mail: coach.hire@bakersdolphin.com
Web site: www.bakersdolphin.com
Chmn: John Baker **Man Dir:** Tim Newcombe **Ch Eng:** Mark Vearncombe
Mktg Dir: Amanda Harrington **Ops Dir:** Max Fletcher **Ops Man:** Chris Rubery
Fin Controller: Steve Hunt
Fleet: 75 - 68 single-deck coach, 3 double-deck coach, 1 midicoach, 2 minibus, 1 minicoach
Chassis: 4 Bedford. 1 Bova. 1 Dennis. 5 Iveco. 2 LDV. 15 Leyland. 2 Mercedes. 45 Volvo.
Bodies: 5 Beulas. 1 Bova. 3 Jonckheere. 2 LDV. 1 Mercedes. 1 Optare. 34 Plaxton. 28 Van Hool.
Ops incl: local bus services, excursions & tours, private hire, express, continental tours, school contracts.
Livery: Blue/White/Green/Yellow.
Ticket System: Setright

BATH BUS COMPANY
1 PIERREPONT STREET, BATH BA1 1LB.
Tel: 01225 330444.
Fax: 01225 330727.
E-mail: hq@bathbuscompany.com
Web site: www.bathbuscompany.com
Chmn: Peter Newman **Man Dir:** Martin Curtis. **Dir:** Dr. Mike Walker. **Eng Dir:** Collin Brougham-Field. **Co Sec/Dir:** Rob Bromley. **Com Dir:** Keith Tazewell.
Fleet: 11 double-deck bus, 7 single-deck bus, 3 minibus.
Chassis: 1 AEC, 6 Bristol, 6 Dennis, 3 Leyland-DAB, 3 Leyland, 3 MCW. 4 Mercedes.

A/c	Air conditioning	● Seat belt-fitted vehicles	✔ Replacement vehicle available
♿	Vehicles suitable for disabled	R Recovery service available (not 24 hr)	T Toilet-drop facilities available
🍴	Coach(es) with galley facilities	R24 24hr recovery service	Vintage vehicle(s) available
wc	Coach(es) with toilet facilities		Open top vehicle(s)

Bodies: 1 Alexander. 6 ECW. 1 Leyland. 3 MCW. 1 Park Royal. 3 Plaxton. 6 Wright.
Ops incl: local bus services, excursions & tours, private hire.
Livery: Red/Primrose.
Ticket System: Wayfarer/BBC punch system.
Subsidiary of Ensignbus

*BERRY'S COACHES (TAUNTON) LTD

CORNISHWAY WEST, NEW WELLINGTON ROAD, TAUNTON TA1 5NA
Tel: 01823 331356
Fax: 01823 322347
E-mail: info@berryscoaches.co.uk
Web site: www.berryscoaches.co.uk
Dirs: S A Berry, P I Berry
Fleet: 30 - 25 coach, 5 double-deck coach.
Chassis: 30 Volvo.
Bodies: 3 Jonckheere. 7 Plaxton. 20 Van Hool.
Ops incl: local bus services, school contracts, excursions & tours, private hire, express, continental tours.
Livery: White/Red/Orange
Ticket system: Setright

*BLAGDON LIONESS COACHES LTD

MENDIP GARAGE, BLAGDON BS40 7TL
Tel: 01761 462250
Fax: 01761 463237
Recovery: 01761 462250
Dir: T M Lyons **Gen Man:** M A Lyons
Fleet: 3 - 2 coach, 1 minibus
Chassis: 1 Bova. 1 Leyland. 1 Mercedes
Bodies: 1 Bova. 2 Plaxton.
Ops incl: local bus services, excursions & tours, private hire, school contracts.
Livery: White
Ticket System: Wayfarer

BLUE IRIS COACHES
See Bristol

*CENTURION TRAVEL LTD

WEST ROAD GARAGE, WELTON, MDSOMER NORTON, RADSTOCK BA3 2TP
Tel: 01761 417392
Fax: 01761 417369
E-mail: coach-hire@centuriontravel.co.uk
Web site: www.centuriontravel.co.uk
Man Dir: Martin Spiller
Fleet: 23 - 17 coach, 1 minibus, 4 minicoach.
Chassis: 2 Bedford. 2 Bova. 4 DAF. 3 Dennis. 6 Mercedes. 1 Scania. 2 Volvo. 1 Ford limo.
Bodies: 1 Autobus. 1 Berkhof. 2 Bova. 1 Caetano. 3 Duple. 1 Esker. 1 Irizar. 2 Jonckheere. 1 Marcopolo. 1 Mercedes. 3 Optare. 2 Plaxton. 2 Van Hool
Ops incl: school contracts, private hire, continental tours, excursions & tours.
Livery: Red/Cream/Burgundy

CLAPTON COACHES

1 HAYDON ESTATE, RADSTOCK BA3 3RD
Tel: 01761 431936
Fax: 01761 431935
E-mail: claptonholidays@btconnect.com
Dirs: S C Lippet, M C Lippet, C Higgs
Fleet: 12 - 6 coach, 6 minicoach.
Bodies: 2 Beulas. 4 Bova.
Ops incl: excursions & tours, private hire, continental tours.
Livery: Lilac

COOKS COACHES

VICTOR HOUSE, GREENHAM BUSINESS PARK, WELLINGTON TA21 0LR
Tel: 01823 672247
Fax: 01823 673101
E-mail: landylines@aol.com
Web site: www.cookscoaches-somerset.co.uk
Man Dir: Paul Landymore
Ops Dir: Nigel Billinger.
Fleet: 60 - 21 single-deck bus, 1 coach, 8 midicoach, 12 midibus, 14 minibus, 4 minicoach.
Chassis: 1 Dennis. 1 Iveco. 16 LDV. 21 Mercedes. 21 Optare.
Bodies: 4 Alexander. 3 Autobus. 1 Berkhof. 21 Optare. 9 Plaxton. 2 UVG. 1 Wadham Stringer.
Ops incl: local bus services, school contracts, private hire.
Livery: White with Red/Blue
Ticket System: Almex Optima
(Part of Stagecoach)

COOMBS TRAVEL

SEARLE CRESCENT, WESTON-SUPER-MARE BS23 3YX
Tel: 01934 428555
Fax: 01934 428559
E-mail: coombscoaches@aol.com
Man Dir: B. F. Coombs **Ops Man:** Mrs J Carroll **Sec:** Mrs M Lillie **Traf Man:** C Winser **Ch Eng:** J. J. Ellis
Fleet: 38 - 1 double-deck bus, 14 coach, 4 midibus, 1 midicoach, 6 minibus, 12 minicoach.
Chassis: 3 Dennis. 10 Ford Transit. 6 LDV. 3 Leyland. 6 Mercedes. 8 Scania. 1 Toyota.
Bodies: 1 Autobus. 3 Irizar. 10 Plaxton. 3 Van Hool
Ops incl: local bus services, school contracts, excursions & tours, private hire.
Livery: Yellow/White

FIRST SOMERSET & AVON LTD

OLDMIXON CRESCENT, WESTON-SUPER-MARE BS24 9AY
Tel: 01934 620122
Fax: 01934 415859
Recovery: 0117 955 4442
Web site: www.firstgroup.com
Man Dir: Tony Anthistle **Fin Dir:** Mike Gahan
Fleet: 460 - 85 double-deck bus, 10 articulated single-deck bus, 106 single-deck bus, 8 coach, 124 midibus, 127 minibus.
Ops incl: local bus services, school contracts, excursions & tours, express, private hire.
Livery: First
Ticket System: Wayfarer

HUTTON COACH HIRE

95 MOORLAND ROAD, WESTON-SUPER-MARE BS23 4HS
Tel: 01934 618292
Fax: 01934 641362
E-mail: hutton-coach-hire.co.uk
Owner: John Lawrence **Man:** Wendy Dover
Fleet: 4 - 2 coach, 1 minibus, 1 midicoach.
Chassis: 1 Dennis. 1 MAN. 1 Mercedes. Volvo.
Ops incl: private hire, school contracts.
Livery: Maroon with orange/green logo

NITEFLIGHT BUS LEASING

THE BUS DEPOT, TWEED ROAD, CLEVEDON BS21 6RR
Tel/Fax: 01275 876543
Fax: 01275 340280
E-mail: chris@niteflitebussing.co.uk
Web site: www.niteflitebusleasing.co.uk
Owner: M D C Langson
Fleet: 9 - 1 coach, 8 double-deck coach.
Bodies: 2 Berkhof. 1 Irizar. 1 Jonckheere. 1 Neoplan. 4 Van Hool.
Ops incl: continental tours, private hire
Livery: Blue

*QUANTOCK MOTOR SERVICES LTD

UNIT 13A, TAUNTON TRADING ESTATE, NORTON FITZWARREN TA2 6RX
Tel: 01823 251140
Fax: 01823 251833
E-mail: sales@quantockmotorservices.co.uk
Web site: www.quantockmotorservices.co.uk
Dirs: Steve A Morris, Liz Ranson **Fleet Eng:** Paul Smith **Ops Man:** Jonathan Pratt
Fleet: 21 - 4 double-deck bus, 4 single-deck bus, 8 single-deck coach, 5 open-top bus.
Chassis: 2 AEC. 4 Bristol. 2 DAF. 2 Dennis. 8 Leyland. 2 Volkswagen.
Bodies: 4 ECW. 2 East Lancs. 5 Plaxton. 2 Van Hool. 10 other.
Ops incl: local bus services, private hire, school contracts, excursions & tours.
Livery: Red with Gold lettering
Ticket system: Wayfarer 3

*RIDLERS LTD

JURY ROAD GARAGE, DULVERTON TA22 9EJ
Tel: 01398 323398
Fax: 01398 324398
E-mail: info@ridlers.co.uk
Web site: www.ridlers.co.uk
Dirs: G Ridler, S Ridler
Chassis: 1 Bedford. 4 Dennis. 1 Iveco.

Ops Man: M E Jamieson
Fleet: 15 - 14 coach, 1 midicoach.
3 Leyland. 5 Scania. 1 Toyota.
Bodies: 1 Berkhof. 1 Caetano. 5 Duple.
2 Irizar. 4 Plaxton. 2 Van Hool.
Ops incl: local bus services, school contracts, express, continental tours, private hire
Livery: White/Red/Silver.
Ticket system: Almex

D. W. SKELTON
90 BROADWAY, CHILTON POLDEN
TA7 9EQ.
Tel: 01278 722066.
Fax: 01278 722608.
Fleetname: Skelton Tours.
Prop: D. W. Skelton.
Fleet: 3 coach.
Chassis: 1 Ford. 2 MAN.
Bodies: 1 Neoplan. 1 Plaxton. 1 MAN.
Ops incl: excursions & tours, private hire, continental tours.
Livery: Black/Green/Gold.

SMITH'S COACHES (B.E. & G.W. SMITH)
BYFIELDS, PYLLE BA4 6TA.
Tel: 01749 830126
Fax: 01749 830888
Prop: Graham Smith
Fleet: 14 coach.
Chassis: 3 Bedford. 3 Leyland. 8 Volvo.
Bodies: 14 Plaxton.
Ops incl: school contracts, private hire.
Livery: Maroon/Cream

SOMERBUS LTD
64 BROOKSIDE, PAULTON,
BRISTOL BS39 7YR
Tel/Fax: 01761 415456
Web site: www.somerbus.co.uk
E-mail: somerbus@tinyworld.co.uk
Man Dir: Tim Jennings
Fleet: 5 - 1 single-deck bus, 4 midibus.
Chassis: 1 Dennis. 2 Mercedes. 2 Optare.
Bodies: 1 Marshall. 3 Optare. 1 other.
Ops incl: local bus services, school contracts
Livery: Orange/White
Ticket system: Wayfarer

*SOUTH WEST COACHES LTD/SOUTH WEST TOURS LTD
SOUTHGATE ROAD, WINCANTON
BA9 9EB
Tel: 01963 33124
Fax: 01963 31599
E-mail: info@southwestcoaches.co.uk

Web site: www.southwestcoaches.co.uk
Man Dir: A M Graham **Co Sec**: S Graham
Comm Dir: S Caine **Eng Man**: K Jeffrey
Traff Man: J A Hiscock **Tours Man**: D Green
Fleet: 72 - 11 single-deck bus, 34 coach, 8 midibus, 2 midicoach, 17 minibus.
Chassis: 3 Bedford. 1 BMC. 1 DAF. 3 Dennis. 1 Ford. 10 Ford Transit. 2 LDV. 13 Leyland. 10 Mercedes. 4 Optare. 5 Setra. 2 VW. 17 Volvo.
Bodies: Alexander. Berkhof. BMC. Caetano. Duple. East Lancs. Jonckheere. Leyland. Mercedes. Optare. Plaxton. Setra. Van Hool.
Ops incl: local bus services, school contracts, excursions & tours, private hire, continental tours.
Livery: White with Red/Blue stripes
Ticket System: Paycell/Wayfarer

STONES OF BATH
LOWER BRISTOL ROAD, BATH
BA2 3DR
Tel: 01225 422267
Fax: 01225 442209
E-mail: stonescoaches@compuserve.com
Senior Ptnr: D G Stone, **Ops Man**: C G Stone, **Ch Eng**: S M Stone, **Sec/Fin**: Mrs N R Russell
Fleet: 13 - 10 double-deck coach, 3 midicoach
Chassis: DAF. Neoplan. Scania. Toyota.
Bodies: Bova. Irizar. Neoplan. Van Hool.
Ops incl: excursions & tours, school contracts, private hire, continental tours.
Livery: Cream/Red

*TAYLORS COACH TRAVEL LTD
PLOT 10, BRYMPTON WAY, LYNX
WEST TRADING ESTATE, YEOVIL
BA20 2HP
Tel: 01935 427177
Fax: 01935 423177
E-Mail: taylorscoachtravel@tintinhull.fsword.co.uk
Web site: www.taylorscoachtravel.co.uk
Man Dir: D D J Elliott
Co Sec: Mrs T R Elliott **Eng Dir**: D Porter
Ops Dir: M D Kirkland
Fleet: 46 - 34 coach, 7 midicoach, 5 minibus.
Chassis: 2 Autosan. 2 Bova. 4 BMC. 3 DAF. 3 Dennis. 4 Irisbus. 4 Iveco. 2 LDV. 6 Leyland. 1 Mercedes. 15 Volvo.
Bodies: 2 Autosan. 3 Alexander. 4 BMC.

2 Bova. 2 Duple. 3 Indcar. 2 Leyland.
1 Mercedes. 10 Plaxton. 1 Reeve Burgess.
12 Van Hool. 1 Wadham Stringer. 3 Vehixel.
Ops incl: local bus services, private hire, school contracts, excursions & tours, continental tours
Livery: Burgundy/White/Yellow/Gold
Ticket system: Wayfarer

TRAVELINE
SUMMERLAND CAR PARK,
MINEHEAD TA24 5BN.
Tel: 01643 704774, 821883.
Fax: 01643 821883.
Dirs: D. C. & P. A. Grimmett.
Fleet: 1 coach. **Chassis/Body**: Bova.
Ops incl: excursions & tours, private hire, continental tours.

*VISTA COACHWAYS
9 GRAITNEY CLOSE, CLEEVE,
BRISTOL BS49 4NJ
Tel: 01934 832074
Web site: www.vistacoach.co.uk
Prop: T P Jones
Fleet: 2 midibus
Chassis: 2 Iveco
Bodies: 2 Mellor
Ops incl: local bus services
Livery: Cream with green/red
Ticket system: Wayfarer

*WEBBER BUS
BRUE AVENUE, BRIDGWATER
TA6 5LT
Tel: 01278 452086
Fax: 01278 455250
Web site: www.webberbus.com
Man Dir: Tim Webber
Ops Dir: David Webber
Fleet: 38 - 25 coach, 3 midicoach, 7 minibus, 3 midibus.
Chassis: incl: 2 Bova. 1 DAF. 5 Ford Transit. 5 Irisbus. 2 LDV. 4 Optare.
Bodies: incl: 2 Bova. 4 Optare. 11 Plaxton. 4 Van Hool.
Ops incl: local bus services, school contracts, excursions & tours, private hire
Ticket system: Wayfarer

A/c	Air conditioning
♿	Vehicles suitable for disabled
🍽	Coach(es) with galley facilities
wc	Coach(es) with toilet facilities
💺	Seat belt-fitted vehicles
R	Recovery service available (not 24 hr)
R24	24hr recovery service
✔	Replacement vehicle available
T	Toilet-drop facilities available
🚌	Vintage vehicle(s) available
🚍	Open top vehicle(s)

SOUTH YORKSHIRE

ANDERSON COACHES LTD
4 HOLLY BANK AVENUE, SHEFFIELD S12 2BL
Tel: 0114 239 9231
Fax: 01709 364750
Fleet: 5 - 3 coach, 2 minibus.
Chassis: 2 Dennis. 1 Ford Transit. 1 LDV. 1 Neoplan.
Ops incl: excursions & tours, private hire.

ASHLEY TRAVEL LTD
t/a GRANT & McALLIN
8A STATION ROAD, MOSBOROUGH, SHEFFIELD S19 5AD.
Tel: 0114 251 1234.
Fax: 0114 251 1900.
Dirs: R. Atack (**Gen Man/Traf Man**), T. F. Atack (**Ch Eng/Sec**).
Fleet: 3 coach.
Chassis: 1 Bedford. 2 Volvo.
Bodies: 3 Plaxton.
Ops incl: excursions & tours, private hire.
Livery: Turquoise/Blue/White.

BARNSLEY & DISTRICT TRACTION CO
WAKEFIELD ROAD, BARNSLEY S71 1NU
Tel: 01226 299288
Fax: 01226 779079
Gen Man: K Allison
Fleet: 43 single-deck bus.
Chassis: 19 DAF. 24 Volvo.
Bodies: 23 Alexander. 1 East Lancs. 19 Optare.
Ops incl: local bus services.

BILLIES COACHES LTD
C/O W GORDON & SONS, CHESTERTON ROAD, EASTWOOD TRADING ESTATE, ROTHERHAM S65 1SU
Tel: 01709 363913
Fax: 01709 830570
Dir: D Gordon
Fleet: 1 coach
Chassis/Bodies: 1 Bova
Ops Incl: school contracts, excursions & tours, private hire
Livery: Red/ivory

BUCKLEYS
STONEHAVEN, GATEHOUSE LANE, AUCKLEY, DONCASTER DN9 3EJ
Tel: 01302 770379.
Man Dir: Richard Buckley.
Fleet: 2 double-deck coach.
Chassis/Bodies: Mercedes/Neoplan.
Ops incl: excursions & tours.

BURDETTS COACHES LTD
8 STATION ROAD, MOSBOROUGH, SHEFFIELD S20 5AD
Tel: 0114 248 2341
Fax: 0114 247 5733
Dir: F. Burdett

Fleet: 12 coach.
Chassis: 2 Leyland. 10 Volvo.
Bodies: 2 Plaxton. 10 Van Hool.
Ops incl: private hire

BYRAN COACHES LTD
31 SUSSEX STREET, SHEFFIELD S4 7YY
Tel/Fax: 0114 270 0060
Dir/Owner: Julie Scott **Dir:** Dennis Heaton
Fleet: 6 - 3 minibus, 3 minicoach.
Chassis: 1 Ford. 4 Mercedes.
Bodies: include 1 Setra.
Ops incl: school contracts, excursions & tours, private hire.
Livery: White/Jade/Black.

CLARKSONS HOLIDAYS
See West Yorkshire

COOPERS TOURS LTD
R24
ALDRED CLOSE, NORWOOD INDUSTRIAL ESTATE, KILLAMARSH S21 2JH
Tel: 0114 248 2859.
Fax: 0114 248 3867.
E-mail: sales@cooperstours.co.uk
Web site: www.cooperstours.co.uk
Dirs: Alan Cooper, Graham Cooper.
Fleet: 8 coach.
Chassis: 1 AEC. 2 Leyland. 1 MAN. 3 Volvo.
Bodies: 2 Berkhof. 4 Plaxton. 2 Van Hool.
Ops incl: excursions & tours, private hire, continental tours.
Livery: Yellow/White.

COSY COACHES
5 MEYNELL WAY, KILLAMARSH, SHEFFIELD S21 1HG
Tel: 0114-248 9139
E-mail: enquiries@cosycoach.co.uk
Web site: www.cosycoach.co.uk
Fleet: 1 Bedford/Duple vintage coach

ELLENDERS COACHES
71 HURLFIELD AVE, SHEFFIELD S12 2TL.
Tel: 0114 264 1837.
Ptnrs: Mrs P. J. D. Ellender, C. S. Ellender.
Fleet: 2 coach.
Chassis: Volvo. **Bodies:** Jonckheere.
Ops incl: excursions & tours, private hire, continental tours, school contracts.

EXPRESSWAY COACHES
DERWENT WAY, WATH ON DEARNE, ROTHERHAM S63 6EX
Tel: 01709 877797
Fax: 01709 879919
E-mail: expresswaycoaches@btconnect.com
Web site: www.expresswaycoaches.co.uk
Dirs: Peter Regan, Liam Regan

Fleet: 15 - 4 coach 5 midicoach, 6 minibus.
Chassis: 1 MAN. 12 Mercedes. 2 Volvo.
Bodies: 1 Neoplan. 1 Noge. 2 Plaxton. 2 Transbus. 9 Other.
Ops incl: private hire, continental tours, school contracts, excursions & tours.
Livery:)range/Yellow/White

FIRST SOUTH YORKSHIRE
MIDLAND ROAD, ROTHERHAM S61 1TF.
Tel: 01709 566000
Fax: 01709 566063
E-mail: enquiries@firstgroup.com
Web site: www.firstgroup.com
Man Dir: Bob Hamilton **Eng Dir:** John Clayton **Comm Dir:** Brandon Jones
Ops Dir: Dennis Hajdukiewicz
Fleet: 623 - 151 double-deck bus, 318 single-deck bus, 112 midibus, 42 minibus.
Chassis: 111 Dennis. 30 Mercedes. 12 Optare. 12 Scania. 458 Transbus.
Bodies: 164 Alexander. 134 Northern Counties. 12 Optare. 113 Plaxton. 200 Wright.
Ops incl: local bus services
Livery: FirstGroup corporate livery
Ticket System: Wayfarer 3

L. FURNESS & SONS
THOMPSON HILL, HIGH GREEN, SHEFFIELD S30 4JU.
Tel: 0114 284 8365.
Ptnrs: G. Furness, A. Furness.
Ch Eng: P. Hayes.
Fleet: 8 - 7 coach 1 minicoach.
Chassis: 3 DAF. 3 Ford. 1 Leyland. 1 Mercedes.
Bodies: 1 Duple. 7 Plaxton.
Ops incl: excursions & tours, private hire.
Livery: Red/Cream.

*GEE-VEE TRAVEL
173 DONCASTER ROAD, BARNSLEY S70 1UF
Tel: 01226 287403
Fax: 01226 284783
Owner: G Clark
Fleet: 13 - 12 coach, 1 minibus.
Chassis: 12 DAF. 1 Mercedes.
Bodies: 12 Bova. 1 Mercedes.
Ops incl: excursions & tours, private hire, continental tours.

W GORDON & SONS
EASTWOOD TRADING ESTATE, CHESTERTON ROAD, ROTHERHAM S65 1SU
Tel: 01709 363913
Fax: 01709 830570
Dir: D Gordon
Fleet: 16 coach
Chassis: 2 Dennis. 1 Mercedes. 12 Volvo.
Bodies: incl: 15 Plaxton
Ops incl: school contracts, excursions & tours, private hire, express.
Livery: Red/Ivory

GRAYS LUXURY TRAVEL
30-32 SHEFFIELD ROAD, HOYLAND COMMON S74 0DQ.
Tel: 01226 743109.
Fax: 01226 749430.
E-mail: stephen@grays-travel.co.uk
Web site: www.grays-travel.co.uk
Man Dir: S. Gray. **Ch Eng**: P. Winter.
Fleet: 10 - 7 coach 1 midicoach, 1 minibus, 1 minicoach.
Chassis: 1 Bova. 6 DAF. 2 Dennis. 1 Toyota.
Bodies: 1 Berkhof. 1 Caetano. 2 Duple. 6 Plaxton.
Ops incl: excursions & tours, private hire, school contracts.
Livery: White/Blue/Yellow.

HAGUES COACHES
C/O W GORDON & SONS, CHESTERTON ROAD, EASTWOOD TRADING ESTATE, ROTHERHAM S65 1SU
Tel: 01709 382912
Fax: 01709 382570
Ops incl: excursions & tours.

HEATON'S OF SHEFFIELD
46 CANTERBURY CRESCENT, FULWOOD, SHEFFIELD S10 3RX
Tel/Fax: 0114 230 9184
Fleet: 10 - 4 coach, 2 midicoach, 4 minicoach.
Chassis: 1 Ford. 4 Mercedes. 5 Setra.
Bodies: 4 Mercedes. 1 Plaxton. 5 Setra.
Ops incl: school contracts, excursions & tours.
Livery: White.

HOGG EUROPEAN COACHES
50 DOVERCOURT ROAD, SHEFFIELD S2 1UA.
Tel: 0114 272 0895.
Prop: A. Hogg.
Fleet: 1 coach.
Chassis: DAF. **Body**: Moseley.
Ops incl: excursions & tours, continental tours.
Livery: Blue/Blue.

ISLE COACHES
97 HIGH STREET, OWSTON FERRY DN9 1RL
Tel: 01427 728227.
Props: J. & C. Bannister.
Ch Eng: E. Scotford. **Sec**: Jill Bannister.
Fleet: 12 - 2 double-deck bus, 3 single-deck bus, 6 coach 1 minibus.
Chassis: 2 Daimler. 1 Ford. 4 Leyland. 3 Leyland National. 1 Mercedes. 1 Volvo.
Bodies: 1 Alexander. 1 Duple. 3 Leyland National. 4 Plaxton. 1 Reeve Burgess. 1 Roe. 1 Van Hool.
Ops incl: local bus services, excursions & tours, private hire.
Livery: Blue/Cream.
Ticket System: Almex.

JEMS TRAVEL
23 STANWOOD CRESCENT, STANNINGTON S6 5JA
Tel: 0800 298 1938.
Fax: 0114 233 5329.
E-mail: info@jemstravel.co.uk
Prop: Malcolm S Mallender.
Fleet: 1 minibus.
Chassis: 1 LDV
Bodies: 1 other
Ops incl: school contracts, private hire.

*JOHNSON'S TOURS
See Nottinghamshire

K. M. MOTORS LTD
WILSON GROVE, LUNDWOOD, BARNSLEY S71 5JS
Tel: 01226 245564
Fax: 01226 213004
Man Dir: Keith Meynell
Fleet: 10 - 8 coach, 1 minicoach, 1 midicoach.
Chassis/bodies: incl: 2 Bova. 1 Mercedes. 4 Scania.
Ops incl: excursions & tours, continental tours, private hire.
Livery: Gold/Maroon/White.

LADYLINE
47 BERNARD STREET, RAWMARSH S62 5NR.
Tel: 01709 522422.
Fax: 01709 525558.
Owner: C. B. Goodridge.
Fleet: 6 coach.
Chassis: 2 AEC. 3 Bova. 1 DAF.
Bodies: 3 Bova. 1 Caetano. 2 Plaxton.
Ops incl: local bus services, school contracts, excursions & tours, private hire, continental tours.
Livery: Blue/White.

LEON MOTOR SERVICES LTD
FINNINGLEY DN9 3DE.
Tel: 01302 770273.
Fax: 01302 770483.
Traf Man: E. McGuinness.
Fleet: 38 - 19 double-deck bus, 10 single-deck bus, 9 coach.
Chassis: Dennis, Leyland.
Bodies: Alexander, Duple, East Lancs, ECW, Northern Counties, Plaxton, Optare, Van Hool.
Ops incl: local bus services, excursions & tours, express, continental tours.
Livery: Blue/Cream.
Ticket System: Almex, A90
Subsidiary of Mass Transit

MALCYS
27 BOYNTON ROAD, SHIRECLIFFE, SHEFFIELD S5 7HJ
Tel: 0800 298 1938
Fax: 0114 242 0885
E-mail: malcystravel@aol.com
Dir: Malcolm S Mallender

Fleet: 2 minibus.
Chassis: 1 Iveco. 1 LDV.
Bodies: 1 Mellor. 1other.
Ops incl: school contracts, excursions & tours, private hire.

WALTER MARTIN COACHES
57 OLD PARK AVENUE, GREENHILL, SHEFFIELD S8 7DQ
Tel: 0114 274 5004
Prop: John Martin, June Martin.
Fleet: 3 coach.
Chassis: 3 Volvo.
Ops incl: excursions & tours, private hire.

MARTINS COACHES
58 ARUNDEL ROAD, CHAPELTOWN, SHEFFIELD S35 2RD.
Tel: 0114 246 0111.

MASS TRANSIT
HOUGHTON ROAD, THE NORTH ANSTON TRADING ESTATE, ANSTON, SHEFFIELD S25 4JJ.
Tel: 01909 550480.
Fax: 01909 550486.
E-mail: masseng@aol.com
Man Dir: M. Strafford.
Fleet: 45 double-deck bus.
Chassis: 3 Dennis, 42 Leyland.
Bodies: 3 Alexander. 42 Leyland.
Ops incl: local bus services, school contracts, private hire.
Livery: Red/White/Green.
Ticket System: Wayfarer.
Also offers a complete maintenance/ refurbishment service to bus and coach operators.

MAYFIELD COACHES
172 AUGHTON ROAD, AUGHTON, SHEFFIELD S26 3XE
Tel: 0114 287 2622
Fax: 0114 287 5003
E-mail: info@mayfieldstravel.co.uk
Web site: www.mayfieldstravel.co.uk

MOSLEYS TOURS
LEES HALL ROAD, THORNHILL LEES, DEWSBURY WF12 9EQ.
Tel: 01226 382243.
Fax: 01924 458465.
Dirs: A. Gath-Bragg, J. R. Bragg.
Gen Man: P. R. Emerton.
Fleet: 3 - 2 coach, 1 midicoach.
Chassis: 1 Dennis, 1 Leyland, 1Volvo.
Ops incl: school contracts, private hire, continental tours, excursions and tours, express
Livery: Grey/Cream

A/c	Air conditioning		Seat belt-fitted vehicles		Replacement vehicle available
	Vehicles suitable for disabled	R	Recovery service available (not 24 hr)	T	Toilet-drop facilities available
	Coach(es) with galley facilities				Vintage vehicle(s) available
WC	Coach(es) with toilet facilities	R24	24hr recovery service		Open top vehicle(s)

South Yorkshire

NIELSEN TRAVEL SERVICE

23 WINN GROVE, MIDDLEWOOD, SHEFFIELD S6 1UW
Tel/Fax: 0114 234 2961
E-mail: niel@nielsentravel.co.uk
Web site: www.nielsenstravel.co.uk
Fleet: 2 minibus
Chassis: 2 Mercedes.
Ops incl: school contracts, private hire, excursions & tours

COLLIN PHILLIPSON

1 HILLCREST, OUSEFLEET, GOOLE DN14 8HP.
Tel: 01405 704394.
Prop: C. Phillipson.
Traf Man: Miss T. Phillipson.
Fleet: 1 minicoach.
Chassis: Mercedes.
Bodies: Autobus Classique.
Ops incl: excursions & tours, private hire.
Livery: White.

*JOHN POWELL TRAVEL LTD

R24

UNIT 2, 6 HELLABY LANE, HELLABY, ROTHERHAM S66 8HN
Tel: 01709 700900
Fax: 01709 701521
Recovery: 0870 6008787
E-mail: ian@johnpowelltravel.co.uk
Co-dirs: John Powell, Pauline Powell, Ian Powell, Jane Powell **Off Man:** Lynn Oliver **Ch Eng:** Ian Slater
Fleet: 10 - 8 double-deck bus, 2 minicoach
Chassis: 1 BMC. 1 Dennis. 8 Volvo.
Bodies: 1 BMC. 1 Duple. 8 Plaxton.
Ops incl: school contracts, excursions & tours, private hire
Livery: Blue/Orange/Red

ROEVILLE TOURS LTD

APEX HOUSE, CHURCH LANE, ADWICK-LE-STREET DN6 7DY.
Tel: 01302 330330.
Fax: 01302 330204.
Dirs: W. A. & S. M. Scholey. **Ch Eng:** N. G. Haxby. **Gen Man:** P. G. Haxby.
Fleet: 7 - 1 double-deck bus, 4 coach 2 minibus. Also nine taxis able to carry disabled passengers.
Chassis: 1 AEC. 1 DAF. 2 Ford. 1 Leyland. 1 Mercedes. 1 Scania.
Bodies: 1 Duple. 1 Mercedes. 3 Plaxton. 1 Reeve Burgess. 1 Roe.
Ops incl: local bus services, excursions & tours, private hire, continental tours.
Livery: Green/Blue/White.
Ticket System: Almex.
Subsidiary of Wilfreda Beehive.

ROYLES TRAVEL

114 TUNWELL AVENUE, SHEFFIELD S5 9FG
Tel: 0114 245 4519
Fax: 0114 257 8585
E-mail: info@roylestravel.co.uk
Web site: www.roylestravel.co.uk
Ptnrs: Ricky Eales, Roy Eales.
Fleet: 2 coach.

Chassis: 1 Bova. 1 Iveco.
Bodies: 1 Beulas. 1 Bova.
Ops incl: excursions & tours.

SLEIGHTS COACHES

87 STATION STREET, SWINTON S64 8PZ.
Tel: 01709 584561.
Fax: 01709 582016.
Owner: J. Sleight.
Fleet: 3 coach.
Chassis: DAF. **Bodies:** Jonckheere.
Ops incl: excursions & tours, private hire, continental tours, school contracts.
Livery: Orange/Cream

*STAGECOACH YORKSHIRE

UPPER SHEFFIELD ROAD, BARNSLEY S70 4PP
Tel: 01226 202555
Fax: 01226 282313
Web site: www.stagecoachbus.com
Man Dir: Paul Lynch **Eng Dir:** Joe Gilchrist
Ops Dir: Sue Hayes **Comm Dir:** Rupert Cox
Fleet: 551 – 66 double-deck bus, 157 single-deck bus, 37 coach, 2 double-deck coach, 1 open-top bus, 242 midibus. 46 minibus.
Chassis: 6 BMC. 16 DAF. 125 Dennis. 61 MAN. 2 MCW. 7 Mercedes. 40 Optare. 48 Scania. 46 Transbus. 232 Volvo.
Bodies: Alexander. BMC. East Lancs. Hispano. Jonckheere. Marshall/MCV. MCW. Mercedes. Northern Counties. Optare. Plaxton. Reeve Burgess. Transbus. Wright.
Ops incl: local bus services, school contracts, excursions & tours, private hire, express, continental tours.
Livery: Stagecoach
Ticket system: Wayfarer

STAGECOACH SUPERTRAM

NUNNERY DEPOT, WOODBURN ROAD, SHEFFIELD S9 3LS
Tel: 0114 275 9888
Fax: 0114 279 8120
Web site: www.supertram.com
Man Dir: A Morris
Fleet: 25 tramcars
Chassis/bodies: Siemens
Ops incl: tram services.
Livery: White/Orange/Red

SWIFTS HAPPY DAYS TRAVEL

HAPPY DAYS, THORNE ROAD, BLAXTON DN9 3AX
Tel/Fax: 01302 770999
Ptnrs: S J Swift, J E Swift
Fleet: 3 coach.
Chassis: 3 DAF.
Bodies: 3 Van Hool.
Ops incl: private hire.
Livery: Red/White/Blue

*TRAVELGREEN COACHES

R24

CANDA LODGE, HAMPOLE BALK LANE, SKELLOW, DONCASTER DN6 8LF
Tel: 01302 722227
Fax: 01302 727999
Recovery: 07836 292816
Owner: David Green
Fleet: 7 - 1 double-deck bus, 2 midicoach, 4 minicoach.
Chassis: 1 AEC. 6 Mercedes.
Bodies: 2 Esker. 2 Mercedes. 2 Optare. 1 Park Royal.
Ops incl: excursions & tours, private hire
Livery: Maroon/White
(Overnight parking - see Parking Facilities, A-Z section)

*WILFREDA BEEHIVE

APEX HOUSE, CHURCH LANE, ADWICK-LE-STREET DN6 7AY
Tel: 01302 330330
Fax: 01302 330204
E-mail: sales@wilfreda.co.uk
Web site: www.wilfreda.co.uk
Chmn: W A Scholey **Man Dir:** Mrs S M Scholey **Dirs:** P G Haxby, N G Haxby
Ops Man: I Kaye **Ch Eng:** P Whitaker
Fleet: 38 - 6 double-deck bus, 1 single-deck bus, 13 coach, 12 midibus, 1 midicoach, 5 minicoach.
Chassis: 4 BMC. 2 Bristol. 1 Daimler. 2 MAN. 8 Mercedes. 1 Neoplan. 1 Optare. 8 Scania
Bodies: 2 Beulas. 4 BMC. 2 East Lancs. 6 Irizar. 5 Mercedes. 1 Neoplan. 11 Optare. 3 Plaxton
Ops incl: local bus services, school contracts, excursions & tours, private hire, continental tours.
Livery: Blue
Ticket System: Wayfarer TGX150

WILKINSONS TRAVEL

2 REDSCOPE CRESCENT, KIMBERWORTH PARK, ROTHERHAM S61 3LX
Tel: 01709 553403
Fax: 01709 550550
Owner: M. D. Wilkinson.
Fleet: 9 - 2 coach 3 minibus, 4 minicoach.
Chassis: AEC. Volvo.
Bodies: Berkhof. Duple. Ikarus. Jonckheere.
Ops incl: excursions & tours, private hire, continental tours, school contracts.

WILLIAMSONS OF ROTHERHAM

19 VICTORIA STREET, CATCLIFFE S60 5SJ.
Tel: 01709 366856.
Fax: 01709 828241.
Prop: P. Williamson.
Fleet: 3 coach.
Chassis: 1 Bedford. 1 DAF. 1 Leyland.
Bodies: 1 Duple. 1 Leyland. 1 Van Hool.
Ops incl: school contracts, excursions & tours, private hire, continental tours.
Livery: White.

*WILSON'S COACHES
[wc] [seatbelt] [galley] [replacement]

PLOT 5, BANKWOOD LANE INDUSTRIAL ESTATE, ROSSINGTON, DONCASTER DN11 0PS.
Tel: 01302 866193
Recovery: 07836 757618
Fleet: 3 coach.
Chassis: 3 Volvo.
Bodies: 1 Berkhof. 2 Van Hool.
Ops incl: excursions & tours, private hire.

STAFFORDSHIRE

ACE TRAVEL [seatbelt]
10 BIDDULPH PARK, IRONSTON ROAD, BURNTWOOD WS7 8LG.
Tel: 01543 279068.
Prop: G. E. Elson.
Fleet: 1 midicoach. **Chassis**: Toyota.
Ops incl: excursions & tours, private hire, continental tours, school contracts.

ARRIVA MIDLANDS LTD
[disabled] [seatbelt] [R] [replacement]

DELTA WAY, CANNOCK WS11 3XB.
Tel: 01543 466123.
Fax: 01543 570900.
Web site: www.arriva.co.uk
Fleetname: Arriva Serving the North Midlands.
Man Dir: Catherine Mason **Fin Dir**: M. G. Doyle. **Eng Dir**: B. J. Baxter. **Com Dir**: K. J. Belfield. **Ops Dir**: J. Morrow.
Fleet: 386 - 19 double-deck bus, 289 single-deck bus, 78 midibus.
Chassis: 38 DAF. 151 Dennis. 44 Leyland. 78 Mercedes. 2 Optare. 24 Scania. 49 Volvo.
Bodies: Alexander. Carlyle. ECW. East Lancs. Leyland. Marshall. Northern Counties. Optare. Plaxton. Reeve Burgess. Wright.
Ops incl: local bus services, school contracts.
Livery: Aquamarine/Cotswold Stone.
Ticket System: Wayfarer 3.

*BAKERS COACHES
[disabled] [wc] [A/c] [seatbelt] [replacement] [T]

THE COACH TRAVEL CENTRE, PROSPECT WAY, VICTORIA BUSINESS PARK, BIDDULPH ST8 7PL
Tel: 01782 522101
Fax: 01782 522363
E-mail: sales@bakerscoaches.com
Web site: www.bakerscoaches.com
Man Dir: Philip Baker **Fleet Eng**: Steve Marsh **Ops Man**: David Machin
Fleet: 42 - 8 single-deck bus, 18 coach, 14 midibus, 2 midicoach.
Chassis: 6 DAF. 16 Mercedes. 7 Scania. 13 Volvo.
Bodies: 1 Alexander. 2 Berkhof. 3 Caetano. 4 Irizar. 4 Optare. 20 Plaxton. 7 Wright. 1 other.
Ops incl: local bus services, school contracts, excursions & tours, private hire, continental tours.

BENNETTS TRAVEL (CRANBERRY) LTD
CRANBERRY, COTES HEATH ST21 6SQ.
Tel: 01782 791468
Prop/Gen Man: J. P. McDonnell.
Fleet: 27
Chassis: Bedford. Ford Transit. Leyland. Mercedes.
Bodies: Mercedes. Plaxton.
Ops incl: local bus services, excursions & tours, private hire.
Livery: Blue/White

*L F BOWEN LTD
[wc] [seatbelt] [galley] [A/c] [replacement] [T]

104 MARINER, LICHFIELD ROAD INDUSTRIAL ESTATE, TAMWORTH B79 7UL
Tel: 01827 300000
Fax: 01827 300009
E-mail: coachhire@bowenstravel.com
Web site: www.bowenstravel.com
Chmn: A R Moseley **Ch Exec**: Kevin Lower
Man Dir: Bob Lyng **Group Ops Man**: Nick Tetley **Traff Man**: Tony York
Group Ch Eng: David Hoy
Fleet: 39 - 27 coach, 2 midicoach, 10 minibus
Chassis: 10 MAN, 15 Scania, 2 Toyota. 10 Volkswagen. 2 Volvo.
Bodies: 15 Irizar, 2 Marcopolo. 8 Noge, 2 Plaxton.
Ops incl: school contracts, private hire, express, continental tours, excursions & tours.
Livery: Silver/sun emblem

TERRY BUSHELL TRAVEL
[wc] [galley] [seatbelt] [A/c]

13 DERBY STREET, BURTON-ON-TRENT DE14 2LA
Tel/Fax: 01283 538242
Prop: Terry Bushell
Fleet: 4 - 3 coach, 1 minicoach.
Chassis: 2 Volvo. 2 Mercedes.
Bodies: 1 Jonckheere. 1 Mercedes. 1 Neoplan. 1 Van Hool.
Ops incl: excursions & tours, private hire, continental tours.
Livery: Red/Gold/Orange

*CLOWES COACHES
See Derbyshire

COPELAND TOURS (STOKE-ON-TRENT) LTD
[disabled] [wc] [seatbelt] [opentop] [R24] [replacement] [T]

UTTOXETER ROAD, MEIR, STOKE-ON-TRENT ST3 6HE.
Tel: 01782 324466
Fax: 01782 319401
Recovery: 01782 324466
E-mail: mb@copelandtours.co.uk
Web site: www.copelandtours.co.uk
Chmn/Man Dir: J E M Burn
Dir: Mrs P Burn **Ch Eng**: J C Burn
Co Sec: J E M Burn
Fleet: 26 - 1 single-deck bus, 22 coach, 2 midibus, 1 midicoach.
Chassis: 1 AEC. 14 DAF. 1 Dennis. 7 Leyland. 1 MAN. 2 Mercedes.
Bodies: 1 Duple. 1 Jonckheere. 1 Marshall. 17 Plaxton. 4 Van Hool. 2 Wadham Stringer.
Ops incl: local bus services, school contracts, excursions & tours, private hire, express, continental tours.
Livery: Blue-Blue/Orange.
Ticket System: Wayfarer.

CRUSADE TRAVEL LTD
[seatbelt] [wc]

THE COACHYARD, PINFOLD LANE, PENKRIDGE ST19 5AS
Tel/Fax: 01785 714124
E-mail: enquiries@crusade-travel.com
Web site: www.crusade-travel.com
Dir: J P McDonnell
Co Sec: Mrs J McDonnell
Fleet: 6 - 3 coach, 1 midicoach, 2 minibus.
Chassis: 1 Dennis. 2 Mercedes. 1 Toyota. 2 Volvo.
Bodies: 1 Caetano. 1 Jonckheere. 1 Plaxton. 1 Van Hool. 2 Central Conversions.
Ops incl: school contracts, private hire.

D & G COACH AND BUS LTD [disabled] [seatbelt]

MOSSFIELD ROAD, OFF ANCHOR ROAD, LONGTON ST3 5BW
Tel: 01782 332337
Fax: 01782 337864
E-mail: dreeves@dgbus.co.uk
Man Dir: D Reeve **Fleet Eng**: M Johnson
Depot Eng: K Mitchell
Fleet: 49 - 14 coach, 35 midibus.
Chassis: 10 Dennis. 1 Ford. 33 Mercedes. 5 Optare.
Bodies: 7 Alexander. 2 Carlyle. 3 East

Symbol	Meaning
A/c	Air conditioning
[disabled]	Vehicles suitable for disabled
[galley]	Coach(es) with galley facilities
wc	Coach(es) with toilet facilities
[seatbelt]	Seat belt-fitted vehicles
R	Recovery service available (not 24 hr)
R24	24hr recovery service
[replacement]	Replacement vehicle available
T	Toilet-drop facilities available
[vintage]	Vintage vehicle(s) available
[opentop]	Open top vehicle(s)

South Yorkshire / Staffordshire

Lancs. 1 Marshall. 6 Optare.12 Plaxton.
2 Reeve Burgess. 1 Wadham Stringer.
4 Wright. 11 other.
Ops incl: local bus services, school contracts.
Livery: Cream/Blue
Ticket system: Wayfarer

D H CARS OF DENSTONE LTD

9 HAWTHORN CLOSE, DENSTONE, UTTOXETER ST14 5HB
Tel: 01889 590819
Fax: 01889 591888
Dir: Donald Handley **Sec**: Alison Williams
Fleet: 2 - 1 coach, 1 midicoach.
Chassis: 1 Bova. 1 Mercedes.
Bodies: 1 Bova. 1 Van Conversions.
Ops incl: private hire
Livery: White

D R M MINIBUS & COACH TRAVEL R24

43 HIGH STREET, CHASE TERRACE WS7 8LR.
Tel: 01543 410223 (day),
01543 276655 (night).
Fax: 01543 416223.
Prop: D. R. Morgan.
Fleet: 8 - 6 coach, 2 minibus.
Chassis: 3 Bedford. 1 DAF. 1 Ford Transit. 1 Freight Rover. 1 Leyland. 1 Volvo.
Bodies: 3 Duple. 2 Plaxton. 1 LAG.
Ops incl: school contracts, excursions & tours, private hire, express, continental tours.
Livery: White/Silver.

*DUNN-LINE GROUP

See Nottinghamshire

EAGLE TRAVEL R24

3A NEWPORT ROAD, STAFFORD ST16 2HH
Tel: 01785 220777
Fax: 01785 220666
Recovery: 07931 828762
E-mail: mikegilmore@btconnect.com
Dirs: M W Gilmore, D E Kaminski
Fleet: 11 - 3 coach, 3 midibus, 5 minibus.
Chassis: 1 DAF. 4 LDV. 3 Mercedes. 1 Talbot. 2 Volvo.
Bodies: incl: 3 Alexander. 2 Duple. 1 LAG.
Ops incl: private hire, school contracts.
Livery: Gold eagle/Burgundy and Gold stripes and lettering

FIRST IN NORTH STAFFORDSHIRE

ADDERLEY GREEN GARAGE, DIVIDY ROAD, STOKE-ON-TRENT ST3 0AJ
Tel: 01782 592500
Fax: 01782 592541
Man Dir: Michael Branigan
Fleet: 490 (274 in Staffs)

*HAPPY DAYS COACHES R24

GREYFRIARS COACH STATION, GREYFRIARS WAY, STAFFORD ST16 2SH
Tel: 01785 229797
Fax: 01785 229791
Recovery: 01785 229797
E-mail: neil@happydayscoaches.co.uk
Web site: www.happydayscoaches.co.uk
Man Dir: B V Austin **Dirs**: N G Austin, R A Austin.
Fleet: 26 - 23 coach, 3 minicoach.
Chassis: 3 Mercedes. 1 Mercedes. 8 Scania. 14 Volvo.
Bodies: 3 Irizar. 1 Neoplan. 10 Plaxton. 12 Van Hool.
Ops incl: excursions & tours, private hire, express, school contracts.
Livery: rising sun motif

HOLLINSHEAD COACHES LTD

WHARF ROAD, BIDDULPH ST8 6AQ.
Tel: 01782 512209.
Man Dir: David Haydon
Fleet: 10 coach
Chassis: 1 DAF. 2 Leyland. 7 Volvo.
Ops incl: school contracts, excursions & tours, private hire

*JOSEPHS MINI COACHES

171 CRACKLEY BANK, CHESTERTON, NEWCASTLE-UNDER-LYME ST5 7AB
Tel: 01782 564944
Dir: Joseph Windsor
Fleet: 2 minicoach.
Chassis/bodies: 2 Mercedes.
Ops incl: private hire
Livery: White

*LEONS COACH TRAVEL LTD

DOUGLAS HOUSE, TOLLGATE, BEACONSIDE, STAFFORD ST16 3EE
Tel: 01785 244575
Fax: 01785 258444
Web site: www.leons.co.uk
Man Dir: L H Douglas **Co Sec**: S Douglas
Dirs: R L Douglas, A Douglas
Fleet: 26 - 23 coach, 2 midicoach, 1 minicoach.
Chassis: 6 Bova. 3 Ford. 8 Scania. 3 Setra. 3 Volvo.
Bodies: 5 Berkhof. 6 Bova. 3 Irizar. 6 Plaxton. 3 Setra.
Ops incl: excursions & tours, school contracts, private hire, continental tours.
Livery: Red/Yellow/Orange/Purple

MOORLAND BUSES

WESTON SERVICE STATION, WESTON COYNEY ST3 6QB.
Tel: 01782 334202.
Prop: A Titterton.
Ops incl: local bus services
Livery: Blue/White.

PARAGON TRAVEL LTD R24

THE GARAGE, SPATH ST14 5AE
Tel: 01889 569899
Fax: 01889 563518
Recovery: 01889 569899
E-mail: phil@paragontravel.co.uk
Web site: www.paragontravel.co.uk
Dir: P L Smith **Ops Man**: www.paragontravel.co.uk
Fleet: 14 coach
Chassis: 1 Leyland. 1 Mercedes. 2 Scania. 10 Volvo
Bodies: 1 Alexander. 3 Jonckheere. 4 Plaxton. 6 Van Hool.
Ops incl: local bus services, school contracts, excursions & tours, continental tours, private hire.
Livery: White with Blue/Red lettering.
Ticket system: Setright

PARRYS INTERNATIONAL TOURS LTD

LADYWOOD GREEN, CHESLYN HAY WS6 7QX
Tel: 01922 414576.
Fax: 01922 413416
E-mail: info@parrys-international.co.uk
Web site: www.parrys-international.co.uk
Man Dir: David Parry
Fleet: 11 coach.
Chassis: 11 Neoplan.
Bodies: 11 Neoplan.
Ops incl: excursions & tours
Livery: Red/Gold

PLANTS LUXURY TRAVEL

167 TEAN ROAD, CHEADLE ST10 1LS
Tel: 01538 753561
Fax: 01538 757025
E-mail: julie.plant@plantsluxurytravel.co.uk
Web site: www.plantsluxurytravel.co.uk
Ptnrs: T J Plant, M P Plant
Fleet: 6 - 1 coach, 2 midicoach, 3 minicoach.
Chassis: 1 LDV. 5 Mercedes.
Bodies: 2 Optare. 2 Onyx. 2 Unvi.
Ops incl: private hire, excursions & tours, school contracts.
Livery: Silver with Burgundy/Gold/Mustard stripes

F PROCTER & SON LTD

DEWSBURY ROAD, FENTON ST4 2HS.
Tel: 01782 846031.
Fax: 01782 744732.
Dirs: R Walker, J Walker.
Fleet: 16
Chassis: 2 Bova. 5 DAF. 1 Iveco. 6 Leyland. 2 Scania.
Ops incl: local bus services, school contracts, excursions & tours, private hire.
Livery: Blue/White
Ticket System: Wayfarer

*ROBIN HOOD TRAVEL LTD
wc 🪑 🍴 A/c

HIGHWAY GARAGE,
MACCLESFIELD ROAD, LEEK
ST13 8PS
Tel: 01538 306618
Fax: 01538 306079
Web site: www.robinhoodtravel.co.uk
Dirs: R Eyre, Mrs M Eyre
Fleet: 10 - 8 single-deck bus, 2 midicoach.
Chassis: incl: 6 Bova
Bodies: incl: 1 Caetano. 1 Mercedes.
Ops incl: school contracts, excursions & tours, private hire, continental tours

*SHIRE TRAVEL INTERNATIONAL LTD
wc 🪑 A/c 🔧

UNIT 4:02 CANNOCK ENTERPRISE CENTRE, WALKERS RISE,
HEDNESFORD WS12 0QU
Tel/Fax: 01543 871605
E-mail: hire@shiretravel.co.uk
Web site: www.shiretravel.co.uk
Dir: Robert Garrington
Fleet: 10 - 3 single-deck bus, 2 midicoach, 5 minibus.
Chassis: incl: 1 Scania. 2 Setra.
Bodies: incl: 1 Irizar. 2 Setra.
Ops incl: private hire, school contracts, excursions & tours, continental tours.
Livery: White with England flag

*STANWAYS COACHES
🪑 wc 🍴 A/c R 🔧

THE OLD GASWORKS,
HARDINGSWOOD ROAD,
KIDSGROVE ST7 1EF
Tel: 01782 786232
Fax: 01782 786040
E-mail: stanwayscoaches@yahoo.co.uk

Dirs: D Elliot, P Richman, D Finney
Fleet: 10 - 1 double-deck bus, 7 coach, 1 midicoach, 1 minibus.
Chassis: 2 DAF. 2 Dennis. 1 Iveco. 3 Scania. 1 Setra. 1 Volvo.
Bodies: 1 Berkhof. 2 Duple. 1 ECW. 1 Irizar. 2 Jonckheere. 1 Setra. 1 Van Hool.
Ops incl: excursions & tours, private hire, school contracts.

*STODDARDS LTD
🪑 wc A/c 🔧

GREENHILL GARAGE, LEEK ROAD,
CHEADLE ST10 1JF
Tel: 01538 752253
Fax: 01538 750375
Chmn: D Stoddard **Man Dir**: Miss J Stoddard **Transp Dir**: P Stoddard
HSE Dir: P H Stoddard
Fleet: 6 - 2 single-deck bus, 4 coach.
Chassis: 6 DAF
Bodies: 6 Bova.
Ops incl: excursions & tours, private hire, school contracts.
Livery: Silver/Blue

*SWIFTSURE TRAVEL
wc 🍴 A/c 🪑 🔧

3 GUILD STREET, BURTON-UPON-TRENT DE14 1NA.
Tel: 01283 512974
Fax: 01283 516728
E-mail: info@swiftsure-travel.co.uk
Web site: www.swiftsure-travel.co.uk
Man Dir: Richard Hackett **Co Sec**: Kathleen Hackett **Dirs**: Brian Kershaw, Julian Peddle
Fleet: 7 - 4 coach, 2 midicoach, 1 minibus.
Chassis: 1 Bova. 2 DAF. 1 LDV. 1 Mercedes. 1 Scania. 1 Toyota.
Bodies: 1 Bova. 1 Caetano. 1 Irizar. 1 Optare. 2 Van Hool. 1 other.
Ops incl: excursions & tours, express, private hire, continental tours.
Livery: White/Blue/Green

*WARRINGTON COACHES
See Derbyshire

WARSTONE MOTORS LTD
THE GARAGE, LANDYWOOD WS6 6AD.
Tel: 01922 414141.
Fleetname: The Green Bus Service.
Dir: G. Martin
Fleet: 25 - 3 double-deck bus, 18 single-deck bus, 4 minibus.
Chassis: Leyland, Mercedes.
Bodies: Alexander. Carlyle. Duple. East Lancs. Massey. Roe.
Ops incl: local bus services.
Livery: Green/Cream.
Ticket System: Wayfarer.

WINTS COACHES
🪑 wc 🍴 A/c

MONTANA, WETTON ROAD,
BUTTERTON ST13 7ST
Tel/Fax: 01538 304370
Props: Andrew Wint, Maxine Wint.
Fleet: 10 - 8 coach, 2 minicoach.
Chassis: 1 DAF. 1 Dennis. 6 Mercedes. 1 Optare. 1 Volvo.
Bodies: 1 Bova. 6 Mercedes. 1 Neoplan. 1 Optare. 1 Plaxton.
Ops incl: school contracts, excursions & tours, private hire, continental tours.

J. P. A. WORTH R24
GOLDEN GREEN GARAGE,
LONGNOR SK17 0QP.
Tel: 01298 83583.
Fleet: 2 - 1 midicoach, 1 minicoach.
Chassis: 1 Leyland. 1 Mercedes.
Ops incl: school contracts, private hire.

SUFFOLK

ANGLIAN BUS & COACH LTD
♿ 🪑

BECCLES BUSINESS PARK,
BECCLES NR34 7TH
Tel: 01502 711109
Fax: 01502 711161
E-mail: andrew@angliancoaches.co.uk
Web site: www.anglianbus.co.uk
Fleet: 55 - 5 double-deck bus, 8 single-deck bus, 9 single-deck coach, 33 minibus.
Chassis: 2 Leyland. 36 Mercedes. 9 Optare. 8 Volvo.
Bodies: 1 ECW. 3 East Lancs. 7 Mercedes.
1 Northern Counties. 9 Optare. 31 Plaxton. 1 Van Hool. 2 Wadham Stringer.
Ops incl: local bus services, school contracts.
Livery: Yellow with blue stripes
Ticket System: Wayfarer 3

IAN BALDRY PUBLIC TRANSPORT SERVICES
🚌

43 CAGE LANE, FELIXSTOWE
IP11 9BJ
Tel: 01394 672344
E-mail: ic.baldry@talk21.com
Man Dir: Ian Baldry

*BEESTONS (HADLEIGH) LTD ♿ wc 🪑 A/c R24 🔧
LONG BESSELS, HADLEIGH
IP7 5DB
Tel: 01473 823243
Fax: 01473 823608
Recovery: 07769 978191
E-mail: info@beestons.co.uk
Web site: www.beestons.co.uk
Man Dir: P R Munson **Co Sec**: S J Munson
Ops Man: T Munson **Ch Eng**: G Griggs
Fleet: 42 - 9 double-deck bus, 5 single-deck bus, 15 coach, 1 double-deck coach, 12 minibus.
Chassis: 5 Leyland. 10 Mercedes.

A/c	Air conditioning	🔧	Replacement vehicle available
♿	Vehicles suitable for disabled	T	Toilet-drop facilities available
🍴	Coach(es) with galley facilities	🚐	Vintage vehicle(s) available
wc	Coach(es) with toilet facilities	🚌	Open top vehicle(s)
🪑	Seat belt-fitted vehicles		
R	Recovery service available (not 24 hr)		
R24	24hr recovery service		

2 Optare. 14 Scania. 11 Volvo.
Bodies: 2 Alexander. 5 East Lancs.
1 Leyland. 1 Northern Counties. 2 Optare.
11 Plaxton. 15 Van Hool. 2 Wright. 3 other.
Ops incl: local bus services, school contracts, excursions & tours, private hire, continental tours.
Livery: coach - Gold/Black, bus - Blue/White
Ticket System: Wayfarer 3

BURTONS COACHES LIMITED

DUDDERY HILL, HAVERHILL
CB9 8DR
Tel: 01440 420512
Fax: 01440 713287
E-mail: hire@burtons-bus.co.uk
Web site: www.burtoncoaches.com
Fleetname: Burtons
Chmn: Stephen Telling **Man Dir**: Paul Cooper **Fleet Eng**: Steve Legate
Fleet: 66 - 9 double-deck bus, 16 single-deck bus, 30 coach, 10 midibus, 1 midicoach.
Chassis: 3 Bova. 16 Dennis. 1 Iveco. 3 Leyland. 10 Mercedes. 33 Volvo.
Bodies: 5 Alexander. 1 Beulas. 3 Bova. 15 Caetano. 3 ECW. 3 East Lancs. 36 Plaxton
Ops incl: local bus services, school contracts, excursions & tours, private hire, express, continental tours.
Livery: Blue/Yellow on white base.
Ticket system: Almex A90

H C CHAMBERS & SON LTD

HIGH STREET, BURES CO8 5AB
Tel: 01787 227233
Fax: 01787 227042
Recovery: 07770 886834
E-mail: info@chamberscoaches.co.uk
Web site: www.chamberscoaches.co.uk
Fleet: 25 - 13 double-deck bus, 2 single-deck bus, 7 coach, 3 minibus
Chassis: 3 DAF. 4 Leyland. 2 MAN. 3 Mercedes. 13 Volvo.
Bodies: 5 Alexander. 4 East Lancs. 2 Jonckheere. 4 Marshall. 4 Northern Counties. 2 Plaxton. 4 Van Hool.
Ops incl: local bus services, excursions & tours, private hire.
Livery: Red
Ticket System: Wayfarer

D-WAY TRAVEL

GREENWAYS, THE STREET, EARSHAM, BUNGAY NR35 2TZ
Tel: 01986 895375
Fax: 01986 891110
E-mail: david@dwaytravel.com
Web site: www.dwaytravel.com
Prop: David Thompson
Fleet: 8 - 6 coach, 1 minibus, 1 midicoach.
Chassis: 1 Ford Transit. 6 MAN. 1 Mercedes.
Bodies: incl: 6 MAN. 1 Robin Hood.
Ops incl: school contracts, excursions & tours, private hire.

*FARELINE BUS & COACH SERVICES

OLD ROSES, SYLEHAM ROAD, WINGFIELD, EYE IP21 5RF
Tel: 01379 668151
Mobile: 07850 940445
Prop: Jeff Morss
Fleet: 1 coach
Chassis: 1 Bedford.
Body: 1 Plaxton
Ops incl: local bus services, school contracts, excursions & tours, private hire.
Livery: Blue/Cream
Ticket System: Setright Mk 3

*FORGET-ME-NOT (TRAVEL) LTD

CHAPEL ROAD, OTLEY, IPSWICH
IP6 9NT
Tel: 01473 890268
Fax: 01473 890748
E-mail: sales@forgetmenot-travel.co.uk
Web site: www.forgetmenottravel.co.uk
Fleetname: Soames
Dirs: A F Soames, Mrs M A Soames
Ch Eng: A M Soames
Fleet: 17 - 16 coach, 1 midicoach.
Chassis: 1 Mercedes. 16 Volvo.
Bodies: 1 Optare. 12 Plaxton. 4 Van Hool.
Ops incl: private hire, school contracts.
Livery: three-tone Blue

*GALLOWAY EUROPEAN COACHLINES

DENTERS HILL, MENDLESHAM, STOWMARKET IP14 5RR
Tel: 01449 766323
Fax: 01449 766241
Dirs: David Cattermole, J Miles, R Stedman, A Kemp, R Smith, R Abbott, G Calver, I Stocker
Fleet : 42 - 3 double-deck bus, 7 single-deck bus, 25 coach, 2 minicoach, 5 minibus.
Chassis: 28 DAF. 2 Dennis. 1 Iveco. 3 Leyland. 7 Mercedes. 1 Scania.
Bodies: 1 Beulas. 1 Caetano. 3 Ikarus. 1 MCW. 1 Plaxton. 1 UVG. 23 Van Hool. 3 Wright. 2 other.
Ops incl: local bus services, school contracts, excursions & tours, private hire, express, continental tours.
Ticket System: Wayfarer.

*GEMINI TRAVEL

UNIT 20, STERLING COMPLEX, FARTHING ROAD, IPSWICH IP1 5AP
Tel: 01473 462721
Fax: 01473 462731
E-mail: info@geminiofipswich.co.uk
Web site: www.geminiofipswich.co.uk
Man Dir: E Nicholls **Co Sec**: K Nicholls
Tran Man: S Middlemas
Fleet: 7 - 4 midicoach, 1 minibus, 2 minicoach
Chassis: 1 BMC. 6 Mercedes.
Bodies: 1 BMC. 3 Optare. 2 Plaxton.
Ops incl: excursions & tours, private hire, school contracts, continental tours
Livery: Red/White

HARLEQUIN TRAVEL

77 LANERCOST WAY, IPSWICH
IP2 9DP
Tel: 01473 407408
E-mail: paul.lewis80@ntlworld.com
Web site: www.harlequin-travel.co.uk
Dirs: P D Lewis, Mrs L M Lewis
Fleet: 3 - 2 midicoach, 1 minibus.
Chassis: 2 Mercedes. 1 Peugeot
Bodies: incl: 1 Autobus. 1 Plaxton.
Ops incl: school contracts, private hire
Livery: Maroon/White

*IPSWICH BUSES LTD

7 CONSTANTINE ROAD, IPSWICH
IP1 2DL.
Tel: 01473 232600
Fax: 01473 232062
E-mail: info@ipswichbuses.co.uk
Web site: www.ipswichbuses.co.uk
Fleet: 98 - 28 double-deck bus,1 open-top bus, 54 single-deck bus, 15 midibus.
Chassis: 7 DAF. 28 Dennis. 12 Leyland. 39 Optare. 9 Scania. 3 Volvo.
Bodies: 2 Alexander. 8 ECW. 41 East Lancs. 41 Optare. 1 Roe. 6 Scania Omnicity
Ops incl: local bus services, school contracts, private hire.
Livery: White/Green/Cream
Ticket System: Wayfarer TGX150

*LAMBERT'S COACHES (BECCLES) LTD

UNIT 4A, MOOR BUSINESS PARK, BECCLES NR34 7TQ
Tel: 01502 717579
Fax: 01502 711209
E-mail: office@lambertscoaches.co.uk
Web site: www.lambertscoaches.co.uk
Man Dir: D M Reade **Dir**: Miss L K Reade
Fleet: 7 coach.
Chassis: 4 DAF. 3 Volvo.
Bodies: 2 Plaxton. 5 Van Hool.
Ops incl: private hire, school contracts.
Livery: Blue/White

*MIL-KEN TRAVEL LTD

GRASSMERE, BURY ROAD, KENTFORD, NEWMARKET CB8 7PZ
Tel: 01638 750201
Fax: 01638 750439
E-mail: milkenkentford@btconnect.com
Web site: www.milkentravel.com
Gen Man: Mark Rogers **Man Dir**: Jason Miller **Fleet Man**: Ian Martin
Fleet: 39 - 37 coach, 2 minibus.
Chassis: 2 DAF. 5 Dennis. 2 LDV. 30 Volvo.
Bodies: 1 Berkhof. 3 Duple. 3 Jonckheere. 25 Plaxton. 4 Van Hool. 3 other.
Ops incl: private hire, excursions & tours, continental tours, school contracts.

MINIBUS & COACH HIRE

LINGS FARM, BLACKSMITHS LANE, FORWARD GREEN, EARL STONHAM IP14 5ET.
Tel: 01449 711117.
Fax: 01449 711977.
Owner: Mrs L. J. Eustace.

Fleet: 11 - 3 coach, 8 minibus.
Chassis: 3 Bedford, 1 Iveco. 6 LDV.
1 Nissan.
Bodies: Plaxton.
Ops incl: local bus services, school contracts, excursions & tours, private hire.

MULLEYS MOTORWAYS LTD

STOW ROAD, IXWORTH IP31 2JB.
Tel: 01359 230234
Fax: 01359 232451
E-mail: enquiries@mulleys.co.uk
Web site: www. mulleys.co.uk
Dir/Co Sec: Jayne D Munson
Dir: David J Munson
Fleet: 39 - 4 double-deck bus, 26 coach, 2 double-deck coach, 3 midicoach, 4 midibus.
Chassis: 4 Iveco. 8 Leyland. 4 Mercedes. 7 Scania. 4 Setra. 12 Volvo.
Bodies: 1 Alexander. 3 Beulas. 2 Duple. 4 ECW. 11 Jonckheere. 11 Plaxton. 4 Setra. 6 Van Hool. 2 Indcar. 1 Euro Coach.
Ops incl: local bus services, school contracts, excursions & tours, private hire.
Livery: Orange/Silver.
Ticket System: Wayfarer.

B R SHREEVE & SONS LTD

BELLE COACHES, RIVERSIDE ROAD, LOWESTOFT NR33 0TU
Tel: 01502 564384
Fax: 01502 532009
E-mail: info@bellecoaches.co.uk
Web site: www.bellecoaches.co.uk
Fleetname: Belle Coaches.
Dirs: Ken Shreeve, Robert Shreeve, John Shreeve **Co Sec**: Sue Speed
Tran Man: Alan White
Tours Man: David Dickinson
Fleet: 41 - 38 coach, 3 midicoach
Chassis: 2 Bedford. 4 DAF. 3 MAN. 2 Mercedes. 11 Scania. 10 Setra. 1 Toyota. 8 Volvo.
Bodies: 3 Berkhof. 1 Caetano. 1 Duple. 11 Plaxton. 13 Setra. 11 Van Hool. 1 other.
Ops incl: local bus services, school contracts, excursions & tours, private hire, continental tours.
Livery: Blue/Yellow

*SQUIRRELL'S COACHES

OLD MILL GARAGE, HITCHAM, IPSWICH IP7 7NF
Tel/Fax: 01449 740582
E-mail: squirrells@btconnect.com
Fleet: 7 - 5 coach, 2 midicoach.
Chassis: 1 Leyland. 2 Mercedes. 4 Volvo.
Bodies: 1 Autobus. 1 Reeve Burgess. 5 Van Hool.
Ops incl: school contracts, private hire.

THOMPSON'S REMOVALS & COACH HIRE

DORMICK HOUSE, NEW STREET, FRAMLINGHAM IP13 9RF.
Tel: 01728 723403.
Prop: M. A. Rogers, D. J. Rogers (**Sec**).
Fleet: 3 coach.
Chassis: 1 Ford. 2 Volvo.
Bodies: 1 Duple. 2 Jonckheere.
Ops incl: local bus services, excursions & tours, private hire, continental tours.
Livery: Blue/White.

SURREY

ARRIVA SURREY & WEST SUSSEX

FRIARY BUS STATION, GUILDFORD GU1 4YP
Tel: 01483 505693
Fleetname: Arriva serving Guildford & West Surrey.
Acting Man Dir: Kevin Hawkins
Eng Dir: I. Tarran. **Fin Dir**: Ms E. Limm.
Gen Man: R. Thornton.
Fleet: 59 - 3 double-deck bus, 56 single-deck bus.
Chassis: 29 DAF. 39 Dennis.
Bodies: East Lancs. Plaxton. Wright.
Ops incl: local bus services.
Livery: Aquamarine and Stone.
Ticket System: Wayfarer 3

*BANSTEAD COACHES LTD

1 SHRUBLAND ROAD, BANSTEAD SM7 2ES
Tel: 01737 354322
Fax: 01737 371090
E-mail: sales@bansteadcoaches.co.uk
Web site: www.bansteadcoaches.co.uk
Dirs: D C Haynes, C J Haynes, M C Haynes.

Fleet: 16 coach.
Chassis: 1 Bedford. 11 Dennis. 3 Mercedes. 1 Volvo.
Bodies: 4 Berkhof. 1 Caetano. 3 Mercedes. 8 Plaxton.
Ops incl: school contracts, private hire.

BUSES4U

EAST SURREY RURAL TRANSPORT PARTNERSHIP, TANDRIDGE DISTRICT COUNCIL, STATION ROAD EAST, OXTED RH8 0BT
Tel: 01730 815518
Web site: www.buses4u.org.uk

*CALL-A-COACH

CAPRI HOUSE, WALTON-ON-THAMES KT12 2LY
Tel: 01932 223838
Fax: 01932 269109
E-mail: callacoach@aol.com
Web-site: call-a-coach.org
Prop: Arthur Freakes
Fleet: 9 - 4 coach, 1 midicoach, 4 minicoach.
Chassis: 2 Bova. 1 DAF. 4 LDV.
Bodies: 1 Mercedes. 1 Van Hool.
Ops incl: school contracts, excursions & tours, private hire.

Livery: White

CARS INTERNATIONAL A. C. T.

4 WYCHWOOD CLOSE, ASH GU12 6RA.
Tel: 01252 328774.
Fax: 01252 332337.
Prop: G. Hawkins. **Traf Man**: J. Baker.
Fleet: 3 coach.
Chassis: 1 Leyland. 2 Setra.
Bodies: 1 Leyland. 2 Setra.
Ops incl: excursions & tours, private hire, continental tours, school contracts.

CHEAM COACHES

11 FREDERICK CLOSE, CHEAM SM1 2HY
Tel: 01372 742527
Fax: 01372 742528
E-mail: cheamco@aol.com
Web site: www.cheamcoaches.co.uk
Props: Michael Mower, Lise Cyr-Mower
Fleet: 6 - 2 coach, 4 minibus.
Chassis: 4 Mercedes. 1 Setra. 1 Volvo.
Bodies: 1 Jonckheere. 4 Mercedes. 1 Setra.
Ops incl: private hire, school contracts.

A/c	Air conditioning		Seat belt-fitted vehicles
	Vehicles suitable for disabled	R	Recovery service available (not 24 hr)
	Coach(es) with galley facilities	R24	24hr recovery service
wc	Coach(es) with toilet facilities		Replacement vehicle available
		T	Toilet-drop facilities available
			Vintage vehicle(s) available
			Open top vehicle(s)

Surrey

*CHIVERS COACHES LTD
13A ROSS PARADE, WALLINGTON SM6 8QG
Tel: 020 8647 6648
Fax: 020 8647 6649
E-mail: chivlyn@aol.com
Dirs: Lynne Lucas, Melanie Chivers
Fleet: 4 - 2 coach, 1 midicoach, 1 minibus.
Chassis: 1 LDV. 1 Mercedes. 2 Volvo.
Bodies: incl: 2 Van Hool.
Ops Incl: private hire, school contracts.
Livery: White with blue graphics

COUNTRYBUS
UNIT 3CA, CANAL BRIDGE INDUSTRIAL ESTATE, BYFLEET ROAD, ADDLESTONE KT15 3JE
Tel: 01932 853020
Web site: www.countrybus.info
Dir: James MacNamara
Fleet: 5 - 2 double-deck bus, 2 single-deck bus, 1 coach.
Chassis: 1 Dennis. 2 Leyland. 1 MCW. 1 Volvo.
Bodies: 1 Duple. 1 Leyland. 1 MCW. 1 Volvo. 1 Wright.
Ops incl: school contracts, private hire, excursions & tours
Livery: Green, Orange/White

COUNTRYLINER COACH HIRE LTD
GB HOUSE, WESTFIELD ROAD, GUILDFORD GU1 1RR
Tel: 01483 506919
Fax: 01483 306395
E-mail: info@countryliner-coaches.com
Web site: www.countryliner-coaches.co.uk
Dirs: R Hodgetts, R Belcher, B King
Gen Man: N Hatcher **Ops Mans**: M Lambley, M Chadwick, J Rees
Fleet: 40 - 5 double-deck bus, 21 single-deck bus, 10 coach, 2 double-deck coach, 1 midibus, 1 midicoach.
Chassis: 2 DAF. 19 Dennis. 6 Leyland. 5 Mercedes. 1 Neoplan. 2 Optare. 5 Volvo.
Bodies: 1 Alexander. 1 Caetano. 1 Duple. 5 ECW. 1 Ikarus. 1 Neoplan. 2 Optare. 21 Plaxton. 2 Van Hool. 5 other.
Ops incl: local bus services, school contracts, excursions & tours, private hire.
Livery: Green/White.
Ticket System: Wayfarer 2

*CRUISERS LTD
UNIT M, KINGSFIELD BUSINESS CENTRE, REDHILL RH1 4DP
Tel: 01737 770036
Fax: 01737 770046
E-mail: info@cruisersltd.co.uk
Web site: www.cruisersltd.co.uk
Dir: M J Walter
Fleet: 35 - 3 single-deck bus, 3 coach, 6 midicoach, 2 minicoach, 20 minibus.
Chassis: Dennis, LDV, Mercedes, Volvo.
Bodies: Optare, Plaxton
Ops incl: local bus services, school contracts, private hire.
Livery: metallic various

*EPSOM COACHES GROUP
BLENHEIM ROAD, EPSOM KT19 9AF
Tel: 01372 731700
Fax: 01372 731740
Recovery: 01372 731727
E-mail: enquiries@epsomcoaches.com
Web site: www.epsomcoaches.com
Fleetname: Epsom Coaches, Quality Line
Chmn: Roy Richmond **Man Dir**: Andrew Richmond **Comm Dir**: Steve Whiteway **Ch Eng**: Peter Mabbott **Bus Services Man**: Graham Wernham **Coach Services Man**: Melanie Mackie **Mktg Man**: Alistair Scott **Training Man**: Terry Torch
Fleet: 86 - 10 double-deck bus, 56 single-deck bus, 17 coach, 3 minibus.
Chassis: 38 Dennis. 1 Iveco. 9 Mercedes. 21 Optare. 15 Setra.
Bodies: 22 Alexander. 16 East Lancs. 1 Indcar. 9 Mercedes. 21 Optare. 15 Setra
Ops incl: local bus services, excursions & tours, private hire, express, continental tours.
Livery: Coach: Red/Cream. Bus: Red
Ticket system: Wayfarer

*FARNHAM COACHES
ODIHAM ROAD, FARNHAM GU10 5AE
E-mail: sales@farnhamcoaches.co.uk
Web site: www.farnhamcoaches.co.uk
Ops incl: school contracts, private hire
Livery: Red/Cream
(Fleet etc - see Safeguard Coaches)

*G J TRAVEL LTD
STATION APPROACH, GUILDFORD STREET, CHERTSEY KT16 9BQ
Tel: 01932 560196
Fax: 01460 66967
Dirs: StephenAdams, Barbara M Adams.
Fleet: 6 - 2 minibus, 4 midicoach.
Chassis: 1 Leyland. 5 Mercedes.
Bodies: 2 Autobus. 1 Leyland. 2 Mercedes. 1 Optare.
Ops incl: private hire.
Livery: Red/Blue on White

GALES COACHES LTD
SPRINGFARM ROAD, CAMELSDALE, HASLEMERE GU27 3RH.
Tel: 01428 643837.
Fax: 01428 658809.
Dir: J. P. Pirard. **Co Sec**: R. L. Pirard.
Fleet: 5 - 3 coach, 2 midicoach.
Chassis: 1 Mercedes. 1 Toyota. 3 Volvo.
Bodies: 1 Caetano. 3 Jonckheere. 1 Plaxton.
Ops incl: private hire, school contracts.
Livery: White/Red/Gold.

*HARDINGS COACHES
WELLWOOD, WELLHOUSE LANE, BETCHWORTH RH3 7HH
Tel: 01737 842103
Fax: 01737 842831
E-mail: sales@hardings-coaches.co.uk
Fleet: 13 - 6 coach, 3 midicoach, 4 minicoach.
Chassis: 1 MAN. 5 Mercedes. 2 Scania. 4 Volvo.
Bodies: 2 Berkhof. 2 Autobus. 1 Caetano. 3 Esker. 2 Irizar. 3 Plaxton.
Ops incl: private hire

HARWOOD COACHES
51 ELLESMERE ROAD, WEYBRIDGE KT13 0HW.
Tel: 01932 842073, 227272.
Prop: G. A. Harwood.
Fleet: 5 coach.
Chassis: 2 Bedford. 3 Volvo.
Bodies: 2 Duple. 3 Van Hool.
Ops incl: private hire.
Livery: Beige/Red/Brown.

HILLS
129 BURWOOD ROAD, HERSHAM KT12 4AN
Tel: 01932 254795
Fax: 01932 222671
Dir: D Hill
Fleet: 6 - 4 coach, 1 minicoach, 1 minibus.
Chassis: 1 DAF. 1 Iveco. 1 Mercedes. 1 Toyota. 2 Volvo.
Bodies: 1 Beulas. 1 Bova. 1 Caetano. 1 Mercedes.
Ops incl: school contracts, private hire

K-VALLEY MINI-COACHES
WOODPECKERS, CARLTON ROAD, WOKING GU21 4HE.
Tel: 01483 769462.
Mobile: 0771 368 1207.
Fax: 01483 769462.
Prop: F. E. Trotman.
Fleet: 1 minibus.
Chassis/body: DAF.
Ops incl: private hire.

MAYDAY TRAVEL
SUITE 7, UNIT 8, MILL LANE TRADING ESTATE, MILL LANE, CROYDON CR0 4AA
Tel: 020 8680 5111
Web site: www.coachhirelondon.co.uk
Fleet: coach, midibus, minibus.
Ops incl: private hire, excursions & tours.
Livery: Silver/White/Blue

M&E COACHES
11 VAUX CRESCENT, HERSHAM KT12 4HE.
Tel: 01932 244664.
Prop/Gen Man: M. W. Oram.
Sec: Mrs A. E. Oram.
Fleet: 3 coach.
Chassis: 1 MAN. 2 Mercedes.
Ops incl: school contracts, excursions & tours, private hire.
Livery: Blue/White.

MERTON COMMUNITY TRANSPORT
JUSTIN PLAZA 3, SUITE 3, LONDON ROAD, MITCHAM CR4 4BE
Tel: 020 8648 7727
E-mail: mertonct@ukonline.co.uk

PICKERING COACHES
wc 🔖 R24 🔑
12 HAYSBRIDGE COTTAGES, WHITE WOOD LANE, SOUTH GODSTONE RHG 8JN.
Tel/Fax: 01342 843731.
Props: R. Pickering, Ms D. Pickering.
Fleet: 5 coach.
Chassis: Volvo.
Bodies: 2 Duple. 1 Jonckheere. 2 Plaxton.
Ops incl: private hire, school contracts.

*SAFEGUARD COACHES LTD ♿ 🔖 wc 🍴 🚌 A/c 🔑
GUILDFORD PARK ROAD, GUILDFORD GU2 7TH
Tel: 01483 561103
Fax: 01483 455865
E-mail: sales@safeguardcoaches.co.uk
Web site: www.safeguardcoaches.co.uk
Man Dir: Andrew Halliday **Ops Man**: Chris West **Non Exec Dirs**: E G Newman, C Newman, D K Newman, J Newman, T Hunter
Fleet: 36 - 5 single-deck bus, 27 coach, 2 midibus, 2 midicoach.
Chassis: 1 AEC. 6 Dennis. 2 MAN. 5 Mercedes. 4 Optare. 3 Setra. 15 Volvo.
Bodies: 1 Carlyle. 1 Hispano. 1 Mercedes. 2 Neoplan. 1 Northern Counties. 5 Optare. 17 Plaxton. 3 Setra. 4 Van Hool. 1 other.
Ops incl: local bus services, school contracts, private hire.
Livery: Red/Cream.
Ticket System: Almex A90

SKINNERS OF OXTED
🔖 wc 🍴 A/c
15 BARROW GREEN ROAD, OXTED RH8 0NJ
Tel: 01883 713633
Fax: 01883 730079
E-mail: info@skinnerstravel.co.uk
Web site: www.skinnerstravel.co.uk
Dirs: Stephen Skinner, Deborah Skinner.
Fleet: 14 - 11 coach, 1 midicoach, 2 minicoach.
Chassis: 2 Dennis. 1 MCW. 2 Mercedes. 1 Neoplan. 6 Setra. 2 Volvo.
Bodies: 2 Duple. 1 Neoplan. 2 Optare. 2 Plaxton. 1 Reeve Burgess. 6 Setra.
Ops incl: excursions & tours, private hire, school contracts, continental tours.

SOUTH COAST MOTOR SERVICES LTD 🚌 🚌
PO BOX 1029, CROYDON CR9 6AA
Tel: 0701 0708 767
Fax: 0701 0709 767
E-mail: enquiries@southcoastmotorservices.co.uk
Web site: www.southcoastmotorservices.co.uk
Dirs: Peter Staveley, Alan Elliott, Tim Baker, Graham Burtenshaw, Tim Robbins
Fleet: 3 - 1 double-deck, 1 open-top bus, 1 coach
Chassis: 3 Leyland
Ops incl: private hire, excursions & tours
Livery: Green/Cream

SUNRAY TRAVEL LTD
🔖 A/c 🔑
79 ASHLEY RD, EPSOM KT18 5BN
Tel: 01372 740400
Web site: www.sunraytravel.co.uk
Fleetname: Go Sunray.com
Dir: Noel Millier
Fleet: 7 - 4 bus, 3 coach
Chassis: 3 Dennis. 1 Leyland. 3 Volvo
Bodies: include: 2 Alexander. 2 Carlyle. 4 Plaxton
Ops incl: local bus services, school contracts, excursions & tours, private hire, continental tours.
Livery: Blue with yellow/orange/red sun rays

*SURELINE COACHES
🔖 wc A/c
UNIT 8, MARTLANDS INDUSTRIAL ESTATE, SMARTS HEATH LANE, MAYFORD GU22 0RQ
Tel: 01483 234649
Fax: 01483 236464
E-mail: sureline@btclick.com
Prop: John McCracken
Fleet: 12 - 8 coach, 2 midicoach, 2 minibus.
Chassis: 6 Bova. 2 LDV. 2 Mercedes. 1 Setra. 1 Volvo.
Bodies: 6 Bova. 1 Plaxton. 1 Setra. 4 other.
Ops incl: excursions & tours, private hire, school contracts, continental tours.
Livery: White with red lettering

*SUTTON COMMUNITY TRANSPORT
♿ 🔖 A/c
HALLMEAD DAY CENTRE, ANTON CRESCENT, COLLINGWOOD ROAD, SUTTON SM1 2NT
Tel: 020 8644 6001
Fax: 020 8644 2247
Web site: www.suttonct.co.uk
Ch Exec: Turner Duff **Ops Man**: Malcolm Sailing **Chmn**: P Hewitt **Dirs**: D Mason, P Bloxham, Judith Pratt, Tony Pattison, Inger Wilson, Pam Wilson, Lal Hussain MBE
Fleet: 15 minibus.
Chassis/bodies: Ford Transit. Iveco. VW. LDV. Mercedes. Optare.
Ops incl: school contracts, excursions & tours, private hire.
Livery: White with purple logo

TELLINGS GOLDEN MILLER COACHES LTD
See Middlesex

EDWARD THOMAS & SON 🔖 A/c
442 CHESSINGTON ROAD, WEST EWELL KT19 9EJ
Tel: 020 8397 4276
Fax: 020 8397 5276
E-mail: edwardthomasandson@btconnect.com
Owner: Ivan Thomas **Ch Eng**: Manny Seager **Ops Man**: Neil Seager
Acc: Sharman Grey
Fleet: 24 - 4 double-deck bus, 20 coach
Chassis: Leyland. Volvo.
Ops incl: local bus services, school contracts, private hire.
Livery: Green/Cream

TRINGWOOD TRAVEL
🔖 A/c
TRINGWOOD, 28 NEW ZEALAND AVENUE, WALTON ON THAMES KT12 1PT
Tel: 01932 242900.
Fax: 01932 252829.
E-mail: tringwood.travel@virgin.net
Props: Jean Bell
Fleet: 1 minicoach.
Chassis: 1 Mercedes
Ops incl: excursions & tours, private hire.
Livery: White/Green/Gold.

*W H MOTORS
See West Sussex.

*WESTERHAM COACHES
wc 🔖 A/c
15 BARROW GREEN ROAD, OXTED RH8 0NJ
Tel: 01883 713633
Fax: 01883 730079
Ptnrs: Stephen Skinner, Deborah Skinner.
Fleet: 15 - 11 coach, 3 midicoach, 1 minicoach.
Chassis: 4 Dennis. 1 MCW. 3 Mercedes. 6 Setra. 1 Volvo.
Bodies: 2 Duple. 1 MCW. 1 Mercedes. 2 Neoplan. 1 Optare. 1 Plaxton. 1 Reeve Burgess. 6 Setra.
Ops incl: excursions & tours, private hire, school contracts, continental tours.

*WILTAX BUSES LTD
♿ 🔖 wc 🍴 🚌 A/c 🔑
UNIT 4A, CANAL BRIDGE INDUSTRIAL ESTATE, BYFLEET ROAD, NEW HAW, ADDLESTONE KT15 3JE
Tel: 01932 856655
Fax: 01932 858101
E-mail: info@wiltax.co.uk

A/c	Air conditioning	🔖 Seat belt-fitted vehicles	🔑 Replacement vehicle available
♿	Vehicles suitable for disabled	R Recovery service available (not 24 hr)	T Toilet-drop facilities available
🍴	Coach(es) with galley facilities	R24 24hr recovery service	🚌 Vintage vehicle(s) available
wc	Coach(es) with toilet facilities		🚌 Open top vehicle(s)

Surrey

Web site: www.wiltax.co.uk
Gen Man: Martijn Gilbert **Ops Man**: Sean O'Sullivan **Comm Man (Coach & Bus Charter)**: Neil Glaskin
Fleet: 24 - 12 double-deck bus, 4 single-deck bus, 6 coach, 1 midicoach, 1 minibus.
Chassis: 4 DAF. 3 Dennis. 1 LDV. 6 Leyland. 2 MCW. 1 Mercedes. 7 Volvo.

Bodies: 3 Alexander. 1 ECW. 1 Jonckheere. 1 Leyland. 2 MCW. 1 Northern Counties. 3 Optare. 1 Park Royal. 11 Plaxton
Ops incl: local bus services, school contracts, private hire, excursions & tours
Livery: Orange (Buses), Silver (Coaches)
Ticket System: Almex A90

TYNE & WEAR

*A & J COACHES OF WASHINGTON
6 SKIRLAW CLOSE, GLEBE VILLAGE, WASHINGTON NE38 7RE
Tel: 0191 417 2564
Fax: 0191 415 4672
Recovery: 07702 068 063
E-mail: jean@ajcoaches.fsnet.co.uk
Dir: Ian Ashman **Co Sec**: Jean Ashman
Fleet: 1 coach
Chassis: 1 Volvo
Bodies: 1 Plaxton
Ops incl: school contracts, private hire.
Livery: Blue/White

A LINE COACHES
UNIT 1, PELAW INDUSTRIAL ESTATE, GATESHEAD NE10 0UW
Tel/Fax: 0191 495 2424
E-mail: les@a-linecoaches.co.uk
Web site: www.a-linecoaches.co.uk
Ptnrs: D C Annis, L B Annis **Sec**: Mrs S Reay **Wkshp**: B Jennings, S King
Fleet: 8 - 2 single-deck bus, 2 coach, 4 midibus.
Chassis: 1 DAF. 4 Dennis. 1 Leyland. 1 Mercedes. 1 Optare.
Bodies: 1 Duple. 1 Leyland. 1 Mellor. 1 Optare. 2 Plaxton. 1 Van Hool. 1 Wright.
Ops incl: local bus services, school contracts, excursions & tours, private hire, continental tours.
Livery: Red/White
Ticket System: AES 2000

ALTONA COACH SERVICES & TRAVEL CONSULTANT
UNIT K4, SKILLION BUSINESS CENTRE, GREEN LANE, FELLING NE10 0QW.
Tel: 0191 469 2193.
Fax: 0191 469 3025.
Fleetname: Altona Travel.
Prop: A. C. Hunter. **Ops Man**: A. I. Hunter.
Office Man: R. Dudding.
Fleet: 9 - 5 coach, 2 midicoach, 2 minicoach.
Chassis: 1 DAF. 1 Dennis. 2 Mercedes. 1 Toyota. 3 Volvo.
Bodies: 2 Caetano. 2 Duple. 1 LAG. 2 Plaxton. 1 Robin Hood. 1 Bus Craft Impala.

Ops incl: excursions & tours, private hire, continental tours.
Livery: Two tone Blue and Orange.

ARRIVA NORTH EAST
ADMIRAL WAY, DOXFORD INTERNATIONAL BUSINESS PARK, SUNDERLAND SR3 3XP
Tel: 0191 520 4200
Fax: 0191 520 4222
Web site: www.arriva.co.uk
Man Dir: vacant as at June 07 **Eng Dir**: J Greaves **Fin Dir**: Sue Richardson
Ops Dir: I McInroy **Comm Dir**: Liz Esnouf
Fleet: 650 - 117 double-deck bus, 326 single-deck bus, 8 coach, 199 minibus.
Chassis: DAF. Dennis. Iveco. Leyland. MCW. MAN. Mercedes. Optare. Scania. Transbus. Volvo.
Bodies: Alexander. ECW. East Lancs. Ikarus. Leyland. MCW. Mercedes. Northern Counties. Optare. Plaxton. Transbus. Van Hool. Wright.
Ops incl: local bus services, school contracts, private hire, express.
Livery: Aquamarine/Stone
Ticket System: Wayfarer 3

*CAMPBELLS COACHES
37 MORPETH AVENUE, SOUTH SHIELDS NE34 0SF
Tel: 0191 455 4295
Prop: Gordon Campbell
Fleet: 1 coach
Chassis: 1 Bedford
Body: 1 Duple
Ops incl: excursions & tours, private hire
Livery: Orange/Cream

*COACHLINERS OF TYNESIDE
16 BRANDLING COURT, SOUTH SHIELDS NE34 8PA
Tel/Fax: 0191 427 1515
Prop: John Dorothy
Fleet: 2 midicoach
Chassis: 2 Mercedes.
Bodies: 2 Plaxton.
Ops incl: school contracts, excursions & tours, private hire.
Livery: White with red stripes

*HENRY COOPER COACHES
LANE END GARAGE, ANNITSFORD NE23 7BD
Tel: 0191 250 0260
Fax: 0191 250 1820
E-mail: ggpam@tiscali.co.uk
Ptnrs: Graham Greaves
Fleet: 7 single-deck bus
Chassis: 1 Leyland. 7 Volvo.

DERWENT COACHES LTD
MORRISON ROAD, ANNFIELD PLAIN DH9 7RX
Tel: 0191 488 7248.
Fax: 01207 281333.
E-mail: derwentc@aol.com
Man Dir: I. Shipley. **Dir**: A. Fox.
Comm Exec: D. Allan.
Garage Foreman: B. Thurgood.
Fleet: 10 coach.
Chassis: Volvo.
Bodies: 5 Plaxton. 5 Van Hool.
Ops incl: local bus services, school contracts, excursions & tours, private hire, express, continental tours.
Livery: White, Red & Blue.
Ticket System: Almex.

*ERB SERVICES LTD
HANNINGTON PLACE, BYKER, NEWCASTLE UPON TYNE NE6 1JU
Tel: 0191 224 0002
Fax: 0191 224 0030
E-mail: sales@erb.entadsl.com
Web site: www.erbservices.co.uk
Man Dir: Edmund Brown **Dirs**: Edmund Brown(jnr), David R Brown
Fleet: 13 - 1 single-deck bus, 3 coach, 2 midicoach, 7 minibus
Chassis: 1 Dennis. 1 Ford. 9 Mercedes. 2 Volvo.
Bodies: 1 Jonckheere. 7 Mercedes. 1 Neoplan. 2 Optare. 1 Van Hool. 1 other
Ops incl: school contracts, excursions & tours, private hire
Livery: White

*GO NORTH EAST

117 QUEEN STREET, GATESHEAD
NE8 2UA
Tel: 0191 420 5050
Fax: 0191 420 0225
E-mail: customerservices@gonortheast.co.uk
Web site: www.simplygo.co.uk
Man Dir: Peter Huntley **Ops Dir**: K Carr
Fin Dir: G C McPherson
Comm Dir: M P Harris
Fleet: 644 - 140 double-deck bus, 339 single-deck bus, 18 coach, 4 articulated bus, 143 minibus.
Chassis: 70 DAF. 220 Dennis. 20 Leyland. 26 Optare. 128 Scania. 26 Transbus. 154 Volvo.
Bodies: 16 Alexander. 13 Cetano. 30 East Lancs. 27 Marshall/MCV. 92 Northern Counties. 38 Optare. 132 Plaxton. 68 Transbus. 187 Wright. 41 other.
Ops incl: local bus services, school contracts, express.
Livery: Red/Blue/Yellow
Ticket System: Wayfarer 3

*JIM HUGHES COACHES LTD

WEAR STREET, LOW SOUTHWICK, SUNDERLAND SR5 2BH
Tel: 0191 548 9600
Fax: 0191 549 3728
Man Dir: James Hughes **Dir**: Valerie Hughes **Co Sec**: Jean Fisher **Ch Eng**: Stephen McGuinness
Fleet: 6 coach
Chassis: 6 Volvo.
Bodies: 3 Plaxton. 3 Van Hool.
Ops incl: excursions & tours, private hire, continental tours

*KINGSLEY COACHES

UNIT 20, PENSHAW WAY, PORTOBELLO INDUSTRIAL ESTATE, BIRTLEY DH3 2SA
Tel: 0191 492 1299
Fax: 0191 410 9281
E-mail: accounts@kingsleycoaches.co.uk
Dirs: David Kingsley (senior), David Kingsley (junior), Mrs Eileen Kingsley (Co Sec)
Fleet: 26 - 13 double-deck bus, 3 single-deck bus, 2 double-deck coach, 7 coach, 2 minibus.
Chassis: 1 Freight Rover. 5 Leyland. 2 MAN. 14 MCW. 1 Mercedes. 1 Optare. 1 Scania. 1 Volvo.
Bodies: 1 Berkhof. 1 Duple. 2 Marshall/MCV. 14 MCW. 1 Mercedes. 1 Optare. 4 Plaxton. 2 Van Hool.
Ops incl: school contracts, excursions & tours, private hire
Livery: Blue/White.
Ticket System: Wayfarer 3

PRIORY MOTOR COACH CO LTD

59 CHURCHWAY, NORTH SHIELDS NE29 0AD.
Tel: 0191 257 0283.
Man Dir: S. H. Lee. **Eng**: G. Hatley.
Fleet: 8 coach.
Chassis: Bedford.
Bodies: 2 Duple. 6 Plaxton.
Ops incl: excursions & tours, private hire, school contracts.

REDBY BUS & COACH

STRATTONS GARAGE, HENDON ROAD, SUNDERLAND SR2 8NT
Tel: 0191 514 2294
E-mail: jean@redbycoaches.com
Man Dir: Jean Stratton **Dir**: Neil Stratton
Fleet: double-deck bus, single-deck bus, coach, double-deck coach, open-top bus, midibus, midicoach, minicoach, minibus.
Chassis: Dennis. Ford Transit. Mercedes. Scania. Volvo.
Bodies: Alexander. Caetano. Jonckheere. Leyland. Mercedes. Optare. Plaxton.
Ops incl: local bus services, excursions & tours, school contracts, private hire, express, continental tours.
Livery: White/Red/Black

ROWLANDS GILL TAXIS & COACHES

1 THORNLEY VIEW, ROWLANDS GILL NE39 1QL
Tel: 01207 543118
Prop: David Murphy
Fleet: 7 - 2 midibus, 2 minibus, 1 midicoach, 2 minicoach.
Chassis: 5 Ford Transit. 1 LDV. 1 Mercedes.
Ops incl: shool contracts, private hire

*STAGECOACH NORTH EAST

WHEATSHEAF, SUNDERLAND SR5 1AQ
Tel: 0191 567 5251
Fax: 0191 566 0202
E-mail: infonortheast@stagecoachbus.com
Web site: www.stagecoachgroup.com
Man Dir: John Conroy
Ops Dir: Nigel Winter **Eng Dir**: David Kirsopp **Com Dir**: Robin Knight
Fleet: 555 - 71 double-deck bus, 279 single-deck bus, 2 double-deck coach, 5 open-top bus, 189 midibus, 9 minibus.
Chassis: 209 Dennis. 7 Leyland. 163 MAN. 9 Mercedes. 2 Scania. 157 Volvo. 10 other.
Bodies: 463 Alexander. 2 Jonckheere. 46 Northern Counties. 34 Plaxton. 10 other
Ops incl: local bus services, school contracts.
Livery: White/Blue/Orange/Red
Ticket System: ERGsystem4000

WARWICKSHIRE

CATTERALLS OF SOUTHAM

74 COVENTRY STREET, SOUTHAM CV47 0EA
Tel: 01926 813840/3192
Fax: 01926 813915
Recovery: 01926 817442
E-mail: paul@travelcatteralls.co.uk
Web site: www.travelcatteralls.co.uk
Dir: Paul Catterall **Tran Man**: Stan Griffin
Eng: Paul Rhodes **Garage Man**: Dave Ould
Operations (Tours): Maureen Allison
Admin: Richard Wilderspin
Fleet: 20 - 16 coach, 3 double-deck coach, 1 midicoach
Chassis: 3 MAN. 2 Mercedes. 2 Scania. 13 Volvo.
Bodies: 1 Irizar. 3 Jonckheere. 1 Marcopolo. 2 Noge. 10 Plaxton. 1 Setra. 2 Van Hool.
Ops incl: local bus services, school contracts, excursions & tours, private hire, continental tours.
Livery: Blue/Yellow stripes on White

CHAPEL END COACHES

WILSON HOUSE, 3 OASTON ROAD, NUNEATON CV11 6JX
Tel: 024 7635 4588
Fax: 024 7635 6406
Web site: www.chapelendcoaches.co.uk
E-mail: cecoaches@ukonline.co.uk
Chmn: Malcolm Wilson **Man Dir**: Ian Wilson **Dir/Sec**: Mrs Tracey Wilson
Fleet: 12 coaches.

A/c	Air conditioning	✓	Replacement vehicle available
♿	Vehicles suitable for disabled	T	Toilet-drop facilities available
🍴	Coach(es) with galley facilities	🚌	Vintage vehicle(s) available
WC	Coach(es) with toilet facilities		
💺	Seat belt-fitted vehicles		Open top vehicle(s)
R	Recovery service available (not 24 hr)		
R24	24hr recovery service		

Chassis: 2 Dennis. 1 Scania. 9 Volvo.
Bodies: 4 Caetano. 4 Plaxton. 4 Van Hool.
Ops incl: local bus services, excursions & tours, private hire, continental tours, school contracts.
Livery: White/Red/Black

L. S. COURT LTD

RED HILL, FILLONGLEY CV7 8DA
Tel: 01676 540282
Fax: 01676 541110
Dirs: G Purchase, Mrs J Purchase.
Co Sec: J Purchase **Ch Eng**: D Purchase
Fleet: 14 - 2 double-deck bus, 1 single-deck bus, 7 coach, 3 midicoach, 1 minibus
Chassis: 1 Bedford. 1 Iveco. 3 Leyland. 2 MCW. 4 Mercedes. 3 Scania.
Bodies: 1 Beulas. 1 Jonckheere. 2 MCW. 4 Mercedes. 3 Plaxton. 3 Reeve Burgess. 1 Van Hool.
Ops incl: local bus services, school contracts, private hire.

*MIKE DE COURCEY TRAVEL LTD

See West Midlands.

MARTIN'S OF TYSOE

20 OXHILL ROAD, MIDDLE TYSOE CV35 0SX
Tel: 01295 680642.
Prop: Martin Thomas.

SKYLINERS LTD

19 BOND STREET, NUNEATON CV11 4NX.
Tel: 024 7632 5682
Fax: 024 7635 4626
E-mail: haydn@skyliners.co.uk
Dir: Haydon J. Dawkins
Fleet: 1 double-deck coach.
Body: Neoplan.
Ops incl: excursions & tours, private hire, continental tours.

*STAGECOACH IN WARWICKSHIRE

RAILWAY TERRACE, RUGBY CV21 3HS
Tel: 01788 562036
Fax: 01788 566094
E-mail: warksenquiries@stagecoachbus.com
Web site: www.stagecoachbus.com/warwickshire
Man Dir: Phil Medlicot **Eng Dir**: Mike Bishop
Fleet: 187 - 41 double-deck bus, 40 single-deck bus, 5 coach, 68 midibus, 33 minibus.
Chassis: 1 AEC. 53 Dennis. 16 Leyland. 6 MCW. 5 Mercedes. 28 Optare. 5 Scania. 73 Volvo.
Bodies: 114 Alexander. 3 ECW. 5 Jonckheere. 6 MCW. 2 Northern Counties. 28 Optare. 1 Park Royal. 16 Plaxton. 7 Transbus. 5 other.
Ops incl: local bus services, school contracts, private hire, express
Livery: Stagecoach
Ticket System: ERG

WEST MIDLANDS

ADAMS TOURS

75 SANDBANK, BLOXWICH WS3 2HL
Tel: 01922 406469
Fax: 01922 406469
Ptnr: David Adams
Fleet: 8 - 4 coach, 2 midicoach, 2 minibus.
Chassis: 4 DAF. 4 Mercedes.
Bodies: 2 Autobus. 1 Mellor. 1 Plaxton. 4 Van Hool.
Ops incl: private hire, school contracts, excursions & tours
Livery: Cream/Green/Orange

B B COACHES LTD

22 VICTORIA AVENUE, HALESOWEN B62 9BL
Tel: 0121 422 4501
Fax: 0121 602 2040
Dirs: Barbara, Mick
Fleet: 2 coach.
Chassis: 2 Volvo
Bodies: 2 Plaxton
Ops incl: excursions & tours, private hire.

BEACON COACHES

24 CHICHESTER GROVE, CHELMSLEY WOOD B37 5RZ.
Tel: 0121 783 2221
Fax: 0121 680 2582
E-mail: enquiries@beaconcoaches
Web site: www.beaconcoaches.co.uk
Fleet: 6 - 2 double-deck coach, 1 midicoach, 1 minicoach, 2 minibus.
Chassis: 1 MAN, 2 Scania, 1 Toyota. LDV.

Bodies: 3 Jonckheere.
Ops incl: excursions & tours, private hire, school contracts, continental tours.
Livery: White /Red/Grey.

*L F BOWEN LTD

See Staffordshire

GO WEST MIDLANDS (THE BIRMINGHAM COACH COMPANY LTD)

CROSS QUAYS BUSINESS PARK, HALLBRIDGE WAY, TIPTON ROAD, TIVIDALE, OLDBURY B69 3HY
Tel: 0121 557 7337
Fax: 0121 520 4999
Man Dir: Philip Kirk **Ops Dir**: Nigel Eggleton
Fleet: 229 - single-deck bus, coach.
Chassis: 20 DAF. 159 Dennis. 4 Leyland. 17 Mercedes. 10 Optare. 7 Scania. 16 Volvo.
Ops incl: local bus services, school contracts, private hire, express.
Part of the Go-Ahead Group

BIRMINGHAM INTERNATIONAL COACHES

10 FORTNUM CLOSE, TILE CROSS, BIRMINGHAM B33 0JT
Tel/Fax: 0121 783 4004
E-mail: birminghamintl@btconnect.com
Web site: www.birminghaminternationalcoaches.co.uk
Dirs: A Watkiss, M Watkiss, N Watkiss

Co Sec: M Watkiss
Fleet: 10 - 9 coach, 1 midicoach.
Chassis: incl: 9 Bova.
Bodies: incl: 1 Caetano.
Ops incl: excursions & tours, private hire, continental tours, school contracts.
Livery: Dark Silver/Red

CENTRAL CONNECT/ZAK'S BUS & COACH SERVICES

ZAK'S DEPOT, SHADY LANE, GREAT BARR, BIRMINGHAM B44 9ER
Tel: 0121 360 2862
Fax: 0121 360 2862
Recovery: 07973 939103
E-mail: e-mail@zaksbuses.com
Web site: www.zaksbuses.com
Man Dir: Matt Lawton **Fin Dir**: Chris Hart
Snr Ops Man: Steve Elms **Ch Eng**: Graham Woodall
Fleet: 46 - 24 single-deck bus, 14 coach, 12 minibus.
Chassis: 30 Dennis. 9 LDV. 1 MAN. 1 Neoplan. 1 Setra. 8 Volvo.
Bodies: 4 Caetano. 1 Duple. 1 Neoplan. 2 Plaxton. 1 Setra. 6 Van Hool.
Ops incl: local bus services, school contracts, excursions & tours, private hire, express, continental tours
Livery: various
Ticket System: Wayfarer TGX
(Subsidiary of Flights Hallmark)

*COURTESY TRAVEL

See Shropshire

*DEN CANEY COACHES LTD

THE COACH STATION, STONE HOUSE LANE, BARTLEY GREEN, BIRMINGHAM B32 3AH
Tel: 0121 427 2078
Fax: 0121 427 8905
E-mail: enquiry@dencaneycoaches.co.uk
Web site: www.dencaneycoaches.co.uk
Man Dir: D Stevens **Dir**: M Stevens
Ch Eng: A Doggett **Ops Man**: J Clarke
Administrator: Mrs D Johnston
Fleet: 9 coach
Chassis: 1 Dennis. 1 Leyland. 2 Toyota. 7 Volvo
Ops incl: private hire, school contracts

CHAUFFEURS OF BIRMINGHAM

CREST HOUSE, 7 HIGHFIELD ROAD, EDGBASTON, BIRMINGHAM B15 3ED.
Tel: 0121 456 3355.

CLARIBEL COACHES

10 FORTNUM CLOSE, TILE CROSS, BIRMINGHAM B33 0JT
Tel: 0121 789 7878
Fax: 0121 785 0967
Dirs: A Watkiss, M Watkiss, N Watkiss, M Watkiss
Fleet: 21 - 1 double-deck bus, 20 single-deck bus.
Chassis: 14 DAF. 1 Dennis. 6 Optare.
Ops incl: local bus services, school contracts, private hire, excursions & tours
Livery: Blue/White.
Ticket System: Wayfarer 3

*N N CRESSWELL

See Worcestershire

*DAIMLER

99 SAREHOLE ROAD, BIRMINGHAM B28 8ED
Tel: 0121 778 2837
Fax: 0121 702 2843
E-mail: roy@daimlertours.wanadoo.co.uk
Prop: Roy Picken
Fleet: 1 coach
Chassis/Body: 1 Neoplan
Ops incl: excursions & tours
Livery: White/Burgundy

*MIKE DE COURCEY TRAVEL LTD

ROWLEY DRIVE, COVENTRY CV3 4FG
Tel: 024 7630 2656
Fax: 024 7663 9276
E-mail: contactus@traveldecourceytravel.com
Web site: www.traveldecourcey.com
Fleetname: Travel De Courcy
Man Dir: Mike de Courcey **Co Sec**: A de Courcey **Dir**: B de Courcey **Gen Man**: Bob Wildman **Fleet Eng**: Neville Collins **Ops Man**: John Bowns **Services Man**: Nick Rossiter **Co Sec**: A de Courcey **Acc Man**: Dee Jones
Fleet: 68 - 25 double-deck bus, 28 single-deck bus, 12 coach, 2 midibus, 1 minibus.
Chassis: 1 Daimler. 4 Dennis. 1 LDV. 1 Leyland. 1 Leyland National. 25 MAN. 21 MCW. 2 Mercedes. 13 Volvo.
Bodies: 4 Caetano. 2 Carlyle. 5 Jonckheere. 1 Leyland. 1 Leyland National. 3 Marcopolo. 25 Marshall/MCV. 21 MCW. 4 Northern Counties. 3 Van Hool.
Ops incl: local bus services, school contracts, private hire.
Livery: White/Blue/Orange.
Ticket System: Wayfarer 2 & TGX

DIRECT COACH TOURS

68 BERKELEY ROAD EAST, HAY MILLS, BIRMINGHAM B25 8NP
Tel: 0121 772 0664.
Fax: 0121 773 8649.
Tours Man: Brian Bourne.
Fleet: 7 - 6 coach, 1 midicoach.
Chassis: 1 Toyota. 6 Volvo.
Bodies: 1 Caetano. 6 Plaxton.
Ops incl: excursions & tours, private hire.

ENDEAVOUR COACHES LTD

30 PLUME STREET, ASTON, BIRMINGHAM B6 7RT
Tel: 0121 326 4994
Fax: 0121 326 4999
Dirs: J Mitchell, G Mitchell, D Mitchell
Fleet: single-deck coach, midibus.
Chassis: 1 Bova. 1 DAF. 1 MAN. 5 Volvo.
Bodies: 1 Bova. 1 Marcopolo. 2 Plaxton. 5 Van Hool.
Ops incl: excursions and tours, school contracts, express.

*EUROLINERS

1631 BRISTOL ROAD SOUTH, REDNAL, BIRMINGHAM BH45 9UA
Tel: 0121 453 5151
Fax: 0121 453 5504
E-mail: info@euroliners.co.uk
Web site: www.euroliners.co.uk
Prop: T Armstrong **Gen Man**: G Styles
Fleet: 16 - 4 coach, 2 midicoach, 10 minicoach.
Chassis: 4 LDV. 12 Mercedes.
Bodies: 1 Esker. 10 Mercedes. 3 Optare. 2 other.
Ops incl: local bus services, school contracts, private hire, continental tours.

*FLIGHTS HALLMARK LTD

BEACON HOUSE, LONG ACRE, NECHELLS, BIRMINGHAM B7 5JJ
Tel: 0121 322 2222
Fax: 0121 322 2718
Recovery: 0121 322 2710
E-mail: sales@flightshallmark.com
Web site: www.flightshallmark.com
Chmn: John Gunn **Ch Exec**: Kim Taylor
Man Dir: Simon Dunn **Dir**: Geoff Flights
Eng Man: Dave Russell **Bus Dev Man**: Anthony Goozee **Com Man**: Ian Pollard
Ops Mans: Paul Williams (coach), Steve Elms (bus)
Fleet: 232 - 20 double-deck bus, 170 single-deck bus, 30 single-deck coach, 12 midicoach.
Chassis: 5 DAF. 69 Dennis. 6 LDV. 5 MAN. 10 Mercedes. 5 Optare. 2 Toyota. 100 Volvo.
Bodies: 10 Alexander. 3 Caetano. 2 Jonckheere. 2 MCW. 6 Mercedes. 6 Neoplan. 5 Optare. 190 Plaxton. 2 Sunsundegui. 1 Van Hool. 15 Wright.
Ops incl: local bus services, school contracts, excursions & tours, private hire, express, continental tours.
Ticket system: Wayfarer, ERG

GLIDER TRAVEL

13 HILLSIDE, BROWNHILLS WS8 7AE.
Tel/Fax: 01543 375801.
Owner: S. J. Mealey.
Fleet: 1 coach.
Chassis: Volvo. **Body**: Jonckheere.
Ops incl: excursions & tours, private hire.
Livery: Cream/Red.

*GOODE'S COACHWAYS

150 CRANKHALL LANE, WEDNESBURY WS10 0ED
Tel: 0121 556 0706
Fax: 0121 505 1619
E-mail: info@goodebus.com
Web site: www.goodebus.com
Dirs: Philip W Goode, Keith Goode
Fleet: 11 - 8 single-deck bus, 1 midicoach, 1 minibus, 1 minicoach.
Chassis: 2 Mercedes. 8 Volvo. 1 Toyota. .
Bodies: 5 Jonckheere. 1 Mercedes. 2 Optare. 2 Plaxton. 1 Van Hool.
Ops incl: excursions & tours, private hire, continental tours.

GRAY'S TRAVEL OF COVENTRY

12 MONMOUTH CLOSE, MOUNT NOD, COVENTRY CV5 7JA.
Tel/Fax: 024 7647 4481.
Prop: E. Gray.
Fleet: 3 coach. **Chassis**: Bedford.
Ops incl: local bus services, school contracts, private hire.
Livery: Name Black with Red shadow; Black/Red stripes.
Ticket System: Setright.

*HARDINGS INTERNATIONAL

See Worcestershire

A/c	Air conditioning	
	Vehicles suitable for disabled	
	Coach(es) with galley facilities	
wc	Coach(es) with toilet facilities	
	Seat belt-fitted vehicles	
R	Recovery service available (not 24 hr)	
R24	24hr recovery service	
	Replacement vehicle available	
T	Toilet-drop facilities available	
	Vintage vehicle(s) available	
	Open top vehicle(s)	

West Midlands

J. R. HOLLYHEAD INTERNATIONAL
32 CROSS STREET, WILLENHALL WV13 1PG.
Tel: 01902 607364.
Fax: 01902 609772.
Owner: J. R. Hollyhead.
Fleet: 5 coach.
Chassis: 2 Bova. 3 Volvo.
Bodies: 2 Bova. 3 Plaxton.
Ops incl: excursions & tours, private hire, express, continental tours.
Livery: White.

*JOHNSONS COACH & BUS TRAVEL
wc A/c T

LIVERIDGE HOUSE, LIVERIDGE HILL, HENLEY-IN-ARDEN B95 5QS
Tel: 01564 797000
Fax: 01564 797050
E-mail: info@johnsonscoaches.co.uk
Web site: www.johnsonscoaches.co.uk
Dirs: P G Johnson, J R Johnson **Co Sec**: J M Johnson
Fleet: 60 - 23 single-deck bus, 34 coach, 3 minicoach.
Chassis: Bova. Mercedes. Toyota.
Bodies: Bova. East Lancs. Optare.
Ops incl: local bus services, school contracts, excursions & tours, private hire, continental tours.
Livery: Blue/Yellow
Ticket system: Wayfarer
Bodies: 28 Bova. 1 Irizar. 1 Leyland. 2 Mercedes. 8 Plaxton.
Ops incl: school contracts, excursions & tours, private hire, continental tours.
Livery: Yellow/Blue/White.
Ticket System: Setright.

*JOSEPHS MINI COACHES
See Staffordshire

KEN MILLER TRAVEL
wc A/c R24

10 CHURCHILL ROAD, SHENSTONE WS14 0LP
Tel: 01827 60494
Fax: 01827 60494
Recovery: 07976 303951
E-mail: ken.m.travel@amserve.net
Fleetname: Ken Miller Recovery
Prop: Ken Miller
Fleet: 2 single-deck bus, 2 minibus.
Chassis: LDV. Volvo.
Ops incl: school contracts, private hire, express, continental tours.
Livery: Blue/Silver
Ticket system: Wayfarer.

KINGSNORTON COACHES
wc

40 BISHOPS GATE, NORTHFIELD, BIRMINGHAM B31 4AJ
Tel: 0121 550 8519
Fax: 0121 501 6554
Web site: www.kingsnortoncoaches.co.uk
Props: Richard Egan, Malcolm Stanley
Fleet: 15 - 2 coach, 13 minibus.
Ops incl: school contracts, excursions & tours, private hire.

KINGSWINFORD COACHWAYS
wc R24

HIGH STREET, PENSNETT, BRIERLEY HILL DY6 8XB
Tel: 01384 401626
Fax: 01384 401580
Recovery: 07831 148222
Dir: C J Wood **Ch Eng**: R J Lamsdale
Ops Man: B A J Probert
Fleet: 9 - 7 coach, 1 midibus, 1 midicoach.
Chassis: 3 Bedford. 4 Volvo.
Ops incl: school contracts, private hire, excursions & tours.
Livery: White/Yellow/Green.

*LAKESIDE COACHES LTD
See Shropshire

LUDLOWS OF HALESOWEN LTD
wc

COOMBS ROAD, HALESOWEN B62 8AA.
Tel: 0121 559 7506.
Fax: 0121 561 4503.
Dirs: Mrs P. C. Ludlow, A. S. Ludlow.
Fleet: 32 - 22 single-deck bus, 7 coach, 2 minibus, 1 minicoach.
Chassis: 8 Dennis. 11 Leyland National. 2 Mercedes. 5 Scania. 4 Volvo. 2 Irizar.
Bodies: 2 Duple. 11 Leyland National. 2 Plaxton. 3 Van Hool. 9 Wright.
Ops incl: local bus services, school contracts, private hire.
Livery: Base White and multi-colour.
Ticket System: Wayfarer 3

MEADWAY PRIVATE HIRE LTD
MEADWAY COACHES, 28-32 BERKELEY ROAD, HAY MILLS, BIRMINGHAM B25 8NG
Tel: 0121 773 8389
Fax: 0121 693 7171
Fleet: single-deck bus, coach, midicoach, minibus.
Chassis: Bedford. Dennis. Leyland. Mercedes. Transbus. Volvo.
Bodies: Caetano. Leyland. Mercedes. Plaxton. Transbus.
Ops incl: private hire, school contracts.

*NASH COACHES LTD
wc R24

83 RAGLAN ROAD, SMETHWICK B66 3TT
Tel: 0121 558 0024
Fax: 0121 558 0907
E-mail: info@nashscoaches.co.uk
Web site: www.nashscoaches.co.uk
Dirs: I F Powell, L P K Powell, G S Powell
Fleet: 9 - 8 coach, 1 midicoach.
Chassis: 4 Mercedes. 2 Scania. 1 Toyota. 2 Volvo.
Bodies: 1 Berkhof. 1 Caetano. 1 Neoplan. 3 Setra. 3 Van Hool.
Ops incl: excursions & tours, private hire, express, continental tours, school contracts.

*NATIONAL EXPRESS LTD
wc A/c

ENSIGN COURT, 4 VICARAGE ROAD, BIRMINGHAM B15 3ES
Tel: 0121 625 1122
Fax: 0121 456 1397
E-mail: reception@nationalexpress.com
Web site: www.nationalexpress.com
Ch Exec: Paul Bunting
Chassis: Bova. DAF. MAN. Marshall. Mercedes. Neoplan. Scania. Volvo.
Bodies: Berkhof. Bova. Caetano. Irizar. Jonckheere. Marshall/MCV. Mercedes. Neoplan. Plaxton. Van Hool.
Ops incl: express.
Livery: Red/White/Blue.
Ticket System: Pre-sale, Wayfarer.

NEWBURY TRAVEL
wc

NEWBURY LANE, OLDBURY B69 1HF
Tel: 0121 552 3262
Fax: 0121 552 0230
E-mail: newburytravel@aol.com
Web site: www.newburytravel.co.uk
Man Dir: David Greenhouse
Ch Eng: Chris Phillips
Fleet: 11 - 5 coach, 3 midicoach, 3 minicoach.
Chassis: 1 Ford Transit. 2 LDV. 3 Mercedes. 5 Volvo.
Bodies: 1 Berkhof. 3 Mercedes. 4 Van Hool.
Ops incl: school contracts, private hire.
Livery: White

NORTH BIRMINGHAM BUSWAYS LTD
R

38 WOOD LANE, ERDINGTON, BIRMINGHAM B24 9QL
Tel: 0121 377 8554.
Fax: 0121 377 7456
Web site: www.northbhambusways.co.uk
Chmn: Patrick Lane **Fin Dir**: Ken Daniels.
Ops Dir: David Wall. **Eng Man**: Les Watts.
Admin Man: Andrew Moore.
Fleet: 29 - 23 double-deck bus. 3 single-deck bus. 1 trainer. 1 recovery vehicle. 1 exhibition.
Chassis: 22 Leyland, 4 Dennis.
Bodies: 8 East Lancs. 2 Alexander. 15 Northern Counties. 1 Reeve Burgess.
Ops incl: local bus services, school contracts, private hire.
Livery: Green/Cream.
Ticket System: Wayfarer.

*PRE METRO OPERATIONS LTD
21 WOODGLADE CROFT, KINGS NORTON, BIRMINGHAM B38 8TD
Tel: 0121 243 9906
Fax: 0121 243 9906 or 01384 569171
E-mail: premetro@aol.com
Web site: www.premetro.co.uk
Dirs: John P M Parry MBE, Geoffrey J Lusher, Philip R Evans, Alan K Wenban-Smith **Co Sec**: Philip R Evans
Fleet: 2 - 1 tram, 1 ominbus.
Chassis: 1 Mercedes. 1 PPM.
Bodies: 1 Mercedes. 1 other.
Ops incl: tram service

West Midlands

Livery: Green/Yellow/Blue
Ticket system: manual

*PROSPECT COACHES WEST LTD

81 HIGH STREET, LYE, STOURBRIDGE DY9 8NG
Tel: 01384 895436
Fax: 01384 898654
E-mail: sales@prospectcoaches.co.uk
Web site: www.prospectcoaches.co.uk
Man Dir: Geoffrey Watts **Dir**: Roslynd A D Hadley **Ops Man**: D Price **Personnel Man**: Nathan Hadley
Fleet: 30 coach.
Chassis: 3 DAF. 23 Dennis. 1 Neoplan. 3 Volvo
Bodies: 3 Duple. 1 Neoplan. 26 Plaxton.
Ops incl: school contracts, private hire.
Livery: Silver

HARRY SHAW

MILL HOUSE, MILL LANE, BINLEY, COVENTRY CV3 2DU.
Tel: 024 7665 0650
Fax: 024 7663 5684
E-mail: john@harryshaw.co.uk
Web site: www.harryshaw.co.uk
Fleet: 15 coach
Chassis: 1 Scania, 3 Setra, 11 Volvo
Ops incl: local bus services, excursions & tours, school contracts, private hire, continental tours.
Livery: Orange

SHEN CARE VOLUNTARY TRANSPORT

330 GREEN MEADOW ROAD, SELLY OAK, BIRMINGHAM B29 4EE.
Tel/Fax: 0121 476 1816.
Man: J. McKernan.
Fleet: 5 minibus.
Chassis: 1 Ford Transit. 1 Iveco. 3 Leyland.
Services for elderly/less abled.

SILVERLINE LANDFLIGHT LTD

ARGENT HOUSE, VULCAN ROAD, SOLIHULL B91 2JY
Tel: 0121 711 7799
Fax: 0121 709 0556
E-mail: silverline@landflight.co.uk
Web site: www.landflight.co.uk
Man Dir: Malcolm Breakwell **Co Sec**: Jim Fell **Bus Dev Dir**: Danny Matthews.
Ops Dir: Richard Knott **Eng Man**: Roger Nolan
Fleet: 13 - 2 single-deck bus, 6 coach, 5 midicoach.
Chassis: 4 MAN. 2 Mercedes. 2 Neoplan. 2 Optare. 1 Scania. 4 Toyota.
Bodies: 4 Caetano. 1 Irizar. 2 Neoplan. 2 Noge. 4 Optare.
Ops incl: local bus services, excursions & tours, private hire, continental tours.
Livery: Silver/Blue

T. N. C. COACHES

257 CHESTER ROAD, CASTLE BROMWICH B36 0ET
Tel: 0121 747 5722
Fax: 0121 747 5722
Dirs: N T Cunningham, K M Cunningham.
Fleet: 5 - 2 coach, 3 minibus.
Chassis: 1 DAF. 1 Leyland. 3 LDV.
Bodies: Duple. Van Hool.
Ops incl: school contracts, excursions & tours, private hire.

*TERRYS COACH HIRE

21 PANDORA ROAD, WALSGRAVE, COVENTRY CV2 2FU
Tel/Fax: 024 7636 2975
E-mail: enquiries@terrys-coaches.co.uk
Web site: www.terrys-coaches.co.uk
Prop: T C Hall **Coach Man**: L Hall **Eng**: J Hall **Co Sec**: S G Hall **Ser Man**: R Bradiul
Fleet: 10 - 2 single-deck bus, 8 coach
Chassis: 2 Dennis. 5 MAN. 5 Volvo.
Bodies: 1 Neoplan. 4 Plaxton. 5 other.
Ops incl: excursions & tours, private hire, continental tours, school contracts.
Livery: Gold/green motif

*THE TRANSPORT MUSEUM, WYTHALL

See Worcestershire

*TRAVEL WEST MIDLANDS

51 BORDESLEY GREEN, BIRMINGHAM B9 4BZ
Tel: 0121 254 7200
Fax: 0121 254 7277
Web site: www.travelwm.co.uk
Acting Ch Exec/Ops Dir: Neil Barker
Fin Dir: Peter Coates **Eng Dir**: Jack Henry
Mktg & Dev Dir: Martin Hancock
Fleet: 1700 - 929 double-deck bus, 31 articulated bus, 689 single-deck bus, 51 minibus.
Chassis: 21 DAF. 434 Dennis. 150 MCW. 213 Mercedes. 100 Optare. 705 Volvo. 77 Scania.
Bodies: 529 Alexander. 150 MCW. 213 Mercedes. 121 Optare. 106 Plaxton. 504 Wright. 77 Scania.
Ops incl: local bus services, school contracts, private hire.
Livery: Red/White/Blue

MIDLAND METRO

METRO CENTRE, POTTERS LANE, WEDNESBURY WS10 0AR
Tel: 0121 502 2006
Fax: 0121 556 6299
Web site: www.centro.org.uk
Fleet: 16 articulated tramcars
General Manager: Fred Roberts
Chassis/Bodies: Ansaldo
Ops incl: tram service

Part of Travel West Midlands

W A SHEARINGS LTD

BAYTON ROAD, EXHALL CV7 9EJ.
Tel: 024 7664 4633.
Fax: 024 7636 0304.
Gen Man: Carol Carpenter.
See also W A Shearings Ltd, Greater Manchester.

WEST MIDLANDS SPECIAL NEEDS TRANSPORT

218-220 WINDSOR STREET, NECHELLS, BIRMINGHAM B7 4NE
Tel: 0121 333 3107
Fax: 0121 333 3345
E-mail: enquiries@wmsnt.org
Web site: www.wmsnt.org
Ch Exec: E B Connor **Ops Man**: D Rogers
Co Sec: J Frater
Fleet: 260 minibus.
Chassis: 260 Volkswagen.
Bodies: 260 Concept.
Ops incl: local bus services, school contracts.
Livery: Red/White/Blue Blue/Yellow
Ticket system: manual/receipts

*WHITTLE COACH & BUS LTD

See Worcestershire

WICKSONS TRAVEL

COPPICE ROAD, BROWNHILLS WS8 7DG
Tel: 01543 372247
Fax: 01543 374271
Web site: www.wicksons.co.uk
Fleet: 11 - 8 coach, 1 midibus, 2 midicoach
Chassis: 5 DAF. 1 MAN. 1 Mercedes. 4 Volvo
Bodies: 1 Autobus. 1 Noge. 9 Van Hool.
Ops incl: school contracts, excursions & tours, private hire, continental tours.
Livery: White/Blue/Orange

*WINDSOR-GRAY TRAVEL

186 GRIFFITHS DRIVE, WEDNESFIELD, WOLVERHAMPTON WV11 2JR
Tel: 01902 722392
Fax: 01902 722339
E-Mail: grahamwgt@hotmail.co.uk
Owner: Graham Williams
Fleet: 2 midicoach.
Chassis: 1 Bedford. 1 Dennis.
Bodies: 1 Duple. 1 Plaxton.
Ops incl: school contracts, private hire, excursions & tours.

A/c	Air conditioning	
	Vehicles suitable for disabled	
	Coach(es) with galley facilities	
wc	Coach(es) with toilet facilities	
	Seat belt-fitted vehicles	
R	Recovery service available (not 24 hr)	
R24	24hr recovery service	
	Replacement vehicle available	
T	Toilet-drop facilities available	
	Vintage vehicle(s) available	
	Open top vehicle(s)	

YARDLEY TRAVEL LTD

68 BERKELEY ROAD EAST, HAY MILLS, BIRMINGHAM B25 8MP
Tel: 0121 772 3700.
Fax: 0121 773 8649
Dirs: R A Meddings, R W Meddings, W J A Meddings
Fleet: 9 - 8 coach, 1 midicoach
Chassis: 1 Toyota. 8 Volvo.
Bodies: 2 Caetano. 7 Plaxton.
Ops incl: excursions & tours, private hire.
Livery: White/Yellow/Black.

*YOUNGS OF ROMSLEY

MALVERN VIEW, DAYHOUSE BANK, ROMSLEY, HALESOWEN B62 0EU
Tel/Fax: 01562 710717
Prop: R Young
Fleet: 3 - 1 coach, 2 minicoach
Chassis: 3 Mercedes.
Bodies: 3 Mercedes
Ops incl: excursions & tours, private hire, continental tours.
Livery: Bronze

WEST SUSSEX

ARUN COACHES/FAWLTY TOURS

1 NORFOLK TERRACE, HORSHAM RH12 1DA.
Tel: 01403 272999.
Fax: 01403 272777.
Prop/Ch Eng: H. Miller.
Fleet: 4 coach.
Chassis: 1 AEC. 1 Bristol. 2 Hestair/Duple.
Bodies: 2 Duple. 1 ECW. 1 Plaxton
Ops incl: private hire.
Livery: Red/Gold.

CHARIOTS OF CRAWLEY

12 FURNACE DRIVE, FURNACE GREEN, CRAWLEY RH10 6JA
Tel: 01293 513371
Prop: B D Cullip
Fleet: 1 midicoach.
Chassis: Iveco.
Ops incl: private hire.

C. L. COACHES

UNIT 13, CHARTWELL ROAD, LANCING BN15 8TU.
Tel: 01903 752555
Fax: 01903 752777
Man Dir: D Brown **Dir**: G Brown, D Brown
Man: H Ticehurst.
Fleet: 15 - 1 double-deck bus, 14 coach
Chassis: 15 Volvo
Bodies: 1 Alexander. 14 Plaxton.
Ops incl: private hire, school contracts.
Livery: Cream/Green/Grey

*COMPASS TRAVEL

FARADAY CLOSE, WORTHING BN13 3RB
Tel: 01903 690025
Fax: 01903 690015
E-mail: office@compass-travel.co.uk
Web site: www.compass-travel.co.uk
Man Dir: Chris Chatfield **Eng Dir**: Malcolm Gallichan **Co Sec**: Roger Cotterell
Fleet: 30 - 9 single-deck bus, 5 coach, 12 midibus, 2 midicoach, 2 minibus
Chassis: 3 DAF. 9 Dennis. 7 Mercedes. 9 Optare. 1 Scania. 1 Volvo.
Bodies: 1 Ikarus. 1 Jonckheere. 2 Mercedes. 12 Optare. 11 Plaxton. 3 Van Hool.

Ops incl: local bus services, school contracts, private hire.
Livery: White/Burgundy.
Ticket System: Wayfarer

CRAWLEY LUXURY

STEPHENSON WAY, THREE BRIDGES RH10 1TN.
Tel: 01293 521002
Fax: 01293 522450
E-mail: crawleylux@aol.com
Fleetname: Crawley Luxury Coaches.
Dirs: David Brown, Darren Brown, Gavin Brown **Ops Mans**: Stephen Burse, Howard Ticehurst
Fleet: 37 - 2 double-deck bus, 35 coach.
Chassis: 37 Volvo.
Bodies: 2 Alexander. 1 Duple. 1 Jonckheere. 33 Transbus.
Ops incl: private hire, school contracts.
Livery: Cream/Green/Grey.

*EXCEL PASSENGER LOGISTICS LTD

See Essex

*METROBUS LTD

WHEATSTONE CLOSE, CRAWLEY RH10 9UA
Tel: 01293 449192
Fax: 01293 404281
E-mail: info@metrobus.co.uk
Web site: www.metrobus.co.uk
Man Dir: Alan Eatwell **Dep Man Dir**: Kevin Lavender **Ops Dir**: Kevin Carey
Eng Dir: Dominic Moorhouse
Fleet: 365 - 145 double-deck bus, 150 single-deck bus, 69 midibus, 2 minibus.
Chassis: 1 AEC. 148 Dennis. 2 Optare. 189 Scania. 26 Volvo.
Bodies: 3 Alexander. 18 Caetano. 182 East Lancs. 11 Northern Counties. 4 Optare. 1 Park Royal. 99 Plaxton. 48 Scania.
Ops incl: local bus services
Livery: Red or Blue
Ticket system: Wayfarer

*PAVILION COACHES

See East Sussex

RICHARDSON TRAVEL LTD

RUSSELL HOUSE, BEPTON ROAD, MIDHURST GU29 9NB
Tel: 01730 813304
Fax: 01730 815985
E-mail: ast@richardson-travel.co.uk
Web site: www.richardson-travel.co.uk
Dirs: R W Richardson, C Richardson
Fleet: 14 - 7 double-deck bus. 7 single-deck coach.
Chassis: 14 Volvo
Bodies: 5 Alexander. 2 East Lancs. 7 Plaxton.
Ops incl: local bus services, school contracts, excursions & tours, private hire, continental tours.
Livery: Blue

*ROADMARK TRAVEL LTD

UNIT 1, WISTON BUSINESS PARK, LONDON ROAD, ASHINGTON, PULBOROUGH RH20 3DJ
Tel: 01903 893400
Fax: 01903 893700
E-mail: coaches@roadmarktravel.co.uk
Web site: www.roadmarktravel.co.uk
Dirs: Mark Anderson, David Coster
Co Sec: Les Anderson
Fleet: 3 - 2 coach, 1 open-top bus
Chassis/Bodies: 1 Leyland. 2 Neoplan
Ops incl: excursions & tours, private hire, continental tours.
Livery: White/Blue lettering

RUTHERFORDS INTERNATIONAL

BRAMFIELD HOUSE, CHURCH LANE, EASTERGATE, CHICHESTER PO20 3UZ
Tel: 01243 543673
Fax: 01403 782028
Owner: G R Bell
Fleet: coach
Chassis: Leyland. Neoplan. Scania.
Bodies: Irizar. Noge. Plaxton.
Ops incl: private hire, school contracts.
Livery: White

*SOUTHDOWN PSV LTD
SILVERWOOD, SNOW HILL, COPTHORNE RH10 3EN
Tel: 01342 715222
Fax: 01342 719617
E-mail: southdownpsv@btinternet.com
Web site: www.southdownpsv.co.uk
Man Dir: S J Swain **Eng Dir**: S Stanford
Fin Dir: P Larking **Ops Dir**: G Wood
Fleet: 17 - 5 double-deck bus, 12 single-deck bus.
Chassis: 5 DAF. 10 Dennis. 1 Volvo. 1 ADLEnviro300
Bodies: 2 Alexander. 2 East Lancs. 1 Optare. 11 Plaxton.
Ops incl: local bus services, school contracts
Livery: White/Blue/Green
Ticket System: Wayfarer TGX

*STAGECOACH (SOUTH) LTD
BUS STATION, SOUTHGATE, CHICHESTER PO19 8DG
Tel: 01243 536161
Fax: 01243 528743
E-mail: enquiries.south@stagecoachbus.com
Web site: www.stagecoachbus.com/south
Fleetname: Stagecoach
Man Dir: Andrew Dyer **Eng Dir**: Richard Alexander **Ops Dir**: Andrew Jarvis
Com Dir: Edward Hodgson
Fleet: 450 – 104 double-deck bus, 43 single-deck bus, 6 coach, 245 midibus, 52 minibus.
Chassis: 260 Dennis. 21 Leyland. 35 Mercedes. 17 Optare. 117 Volvo.
Bodies: 303 Alexander. 1 ECW. 6 Jonckheere. 2 Mercedes. 18 Northern Counties. 17 Optare. 64 Plaxton. 39 Transbus.
Ops incl: local bus services, school contracts, private hire, express.
Livery: Red/Blue/Orange/White
Ticket system: Wayfarer 3

*SUSSEX COUNTRY COACH HIRE
TERMINAL BUILDING, SHOREHAM AIRPORT BN43 5FF
Tel: 01273 465500
Fax: 01273 453040
E-mail: sxcountry@tiscali.co.uk
Web site: www.sussex-country.co.uk
Dirs: A Wright, Mrs M Keats
Fleet: 4 - 2 coach, 1 midicoach, 1 minibus
Chassis: 1 LDV. 1 Mercedes. 2 Volvo
Bodies: 1 Plaxton. 1 Van Hool. 1 other
Ops incl: private hire, school contracts, excursions & tours.
Livery: White

*W+H MOTORS
KELVIN WAY, CRAWLEY RH10 9SF
Tel: 01293 510220
Fax: 01293 513263
Recovery: 01293 548111
E-mail: coach@wandhgroup.co.uk
Web site: www.wandhgroup.co.uk
Man Dir: G M Heron **Co Sec**: Peter Phillips
Fleet: 16 - 10 coach, 2 double-deck coach, 4 midibus.
Chassis: 2 Ayats. 2 Iveco. 6 MAN. 6 Volvo.
Bodies: 3 Caetano. 2 Jonckheere. 1 Marshall/MCV. 3 Noge. 6 Sunsundegui. 1 Van Hool.
Ops incl: excursions and tours, private hire, school contracts, continental tours
Livery: White/Blue

*WESTRINGS COACHES LTD
3 CHURCH ROAD, EAST WITTERING, CHICHESTER PO20 8PS
Tel: 01243 672411
Fax: 01243 671366
E-mail: westringscoaches@btconnect.com
Web site: www.westringscoaches.co.uk
Dir: W J Buckland **Co Sec**: T S West
Fleet: 7 - 1 single-deck bus, 5 coach, 1 midicoach.

Chassis: 1 Dennis. 1 Scania. 1 Toyota, 3 Volvo.
Bodies: 1 Caetano. 1 East Lancs. 3 Jonckheere. 2 Plaxton.
Ops incl: school contracts, excursions & tours, private hire.

*WOODS TRAVEL LTD
PARK ROAD, BOGNOR REGIS PO21 5NF
Tel: 01243 871656
Fax: 01243 871669
Man Dir: R Elsmere **Dirs**: T Shaw-Morton, K Elsmere **Co Sec**: T Shaw-Morton **Traf Man**: G Hawkes **Tours man**: D Kirkby-Bott
Fleet: 16 - 15 coach, 1 midicoach.
Chassis: 15 DAF. 1 Mercedes.
Bodies: 15 Bova. 1 Mercedes
Ops incl: excursions & tours, private hire, continental tours, school contracts, private hire
Livery: Red/White/Blue.

WORTHING COACHES
117 GEORGE V AVENUE, WORTHING BN11 5SA.
Tel: 01903 505805
Prop: Lucketts of Fareham
Fleet: 7 coach.
Chassis: Volvo.
Bodies: incl: Irizar. Plaxton. Van Hool.
Ops incl: excursions & tours, private hire, continental tours.
Livery: Red/White/Yellow

YELLOWLINE TOURS LTD
34 TRULEIGH ROAD, UPPER BEEDING BN44 3JR.
Tel: 01903 813428.
Fax: 01243 829840.
Dir: Miss K. Fisher. **Co Sec**: G. Hanton.
Fleet: 1 coach.
Chassis: Leyland. **Body**: Plaxton.
Ops incl: excursions & tours, private hire.
Livery: Yellow/Black/White.

West Sussex / West Yorkshire

WEST YORKSHIRE, BRADFORD, CALDERDALE

ACRON TRAVEL
102 NEWLAITHES ROAD, HORSFORTH LS18 4SY
Tel: 0113 258 8923.
Fax: 0113 250 8204.
Fleetname: Travel Team.
Ptnrs: G. Navey, C. A. Goodmill
Fleet: 8 coach.
Chassis: 3 DAF. 1 MAN. 1 Neoplan. 2 Scania. 1 Volvo.
Bodies: 1 Berkhof. 1 Jonckheere. 2 LAG. 1 Neoplan. 3 Van Hool.
Ops incl: private hire, continental tours.
Livery: White with Blue splash.

*ANDERSON'S COACHES
HOLMFIELD HOUSE, STRANGLANDS LANE, FERRYBRIDGE WF11 8SD
Tel: 01977 552980
Fax: 01977 557823
E-mail: paulanthonyanderson@btinternet.com
Props: Paul Anderson, Gillian Anderson
Fleet: 2 coach
Chassis: 2 Setra.
Bodies: 2 Setra.
Ops incl: excursions & tours, private hire, continental tours

---

A/C	Air conditioning
	Vehicles suitable for disabled
	Coach(es) with galley facilities
WC	Coach(es) with toilet facilities
	Seat belt-fitted vehicles
R	Recovery service available (not 24 hr)
R24	24hr recovery service
	Replacement vehicle available
T	Toilet-drop facilities available
	Vintage vehicle(s) available
	Open top vehicle(s)

West Yorkshire

*ARRIVA YORKSHIRE LTD
24 BARNSLEY ROAD, WAKEFIELD WF1 5JX
Tel: 01924 231300
Fax: 01924 200106
Man Dir: Philip M Stone **Eng Dir:** Philip Cummins **Fin Dir:** David Cocker
Ops Dir: Paul Adcock
Fleet: 358 - 123 double-deck bus, 159 single-deck bus, 76 midibus.
Chassis: 149 DAF. 114 Dennis. 2 Leyland. 93 Volvo.
Bodies: 162 Alexander. 1 ECW. 35 East Lancs. 23 Ikarus. 14 Northern Counties. 42 Optare. 52 Plaxton. 2 Reeve Burgess. 1 UVG. 24 Wright.
Ops incl: local bus services.

B & H TOURS
52 WILSON AVENUE, MIRFIELD WF14 9AT.
Tel/Fax: 01924 497067.
Prop: Barbara Armitage.
Fleet: 1 coach. **Chassis/Body:** Bova.
Ops incl: excursions & tours, private hire, continental tours.
Livery: Cream/Brown.

B & J TRAVEL
3 SANDY LANE, MIDDLESTOWN, WAKEFIELD WF4 4PW.
Tel: 01924 263334.
Prop: J. S. Bendle.
Fleet: 2 coach.
Chassis: DAF. Volvo.
Bodies: Jonckheere. Plaxton.
Ops incl: school contracts, excursions & tours, private hire.
Livery: Red/White/Blue.

BRITANNIA TRAVEL
113 WESTON LANE, OTLEY LS21 2DX.
Tel/Fax: 01943 465591
Prop: A. Broome, Mrs S. Eastwood.
Fleet: 1 coach.
Chassis: Iveco. **Body:** Beulas.
Ops incl: excursions & tours, private hire, continental tours.
Livery: Silver/Red/Blue.

BROWNS COACHES (SK) LTD
WHITE APRON STREET, SOUTH KIRKBY WF9 3HQ
Tel: 01977 644777
Fax: 01977 643210
E-mail: browns.sk@speed-mail.co.uk
Web site: www.brownscoaches.com
Fleetname: Browns
Man Dir: Mrs J M Brown **Co Sec:** Miss M Brown **Gen Man:** A Griffith **Eng Dir:** D Brown **Ops Man:** S Covell
Fleet: 16 - 5 coach, 7 midicoach, 4 minibus.
Chassis: 2 Ford Transit. 3 Iveco. 8 Mercedes. 3 Scania.
Bodies: 2 Beulas. 1 Esker. 3 Irizar. 3 Plaxton. 7 other.
Ops incl: private hire, school contracts, continental tours.
Livery: Red/White/Blue

CLARKSONS HOLIDAYS
52 DONCASTER ROAD, SOUTH ELMSALL, PONTEFRACT WF9 2JN
Tel: 01977 642385
Fax: 01977 640158
E-mail: info@clarksonscoaches.co.uk
Web site: www.clarksoncoaches.co.uk
Chmn: Ken Clarkson **Dir/Co Sec:** JohnHancock **Dir:** Paul Clarkson
Fleet: 9 - 7 coach, 1 minicoach, 1 midicoach.
Chassis: 4 Mercedes. 5 Neoplan.
Bodies: 5 Mercedes. 4 Neoplan.
Ops incl: excursions & tours, continental tours.
Livery: Blue

DALESMAN
VICTORIA ROAD, GUISELEY LS20 8DG
Tel: 01943 870228
Fax: 01943 878227
E-mail: dalesman@lineone.net
Fleet: 14 - 8 coach, 3 midicoach, 3 minicoach.
Chassis: 8 DAF. 6 Mercedes.
Bodies: 3 Autobus. 3 Mercedes. 8 Van Hool.
Ops incl: school contracts, excursions & tours, private hire, continental tours.
Livery: White/Blue

*DEWHIRST COACHES LTD
THORNCLIFFE ROAD, BRADFORD BD8 7DD
Tel: 01274 481208
Fax: 01274 481208
E-mail: dewhirstcoaches@hotmail.co.uk
Dirs: S R Dewhirst
Fleet: 7 - 3 double-deck bus, 3 coach, 1 minibus.
Chassis: 2 DAF. 2 MAN. 1 Scania. 1 Toyota. 1 Volvo.
Bodies: 1 Alexander. 2 East Lancs. 3 Van Hool.
Ops incl: excursions & tours, private hire.
Livery: Blue/White

FIRST BRADFORD
BOWLING BACK LANE, BRADFORD BD4 8SP
Tel: 01274 734833
Fax: 01274 736768
E-mail: contact.us@firstgroup.com
Web site: www.firstgroup.com
Man Dir: Ian Davies
Fleet: includes double-deck bus, single-deck bus, minibus.
Chassis: Leyland. Leyland National. Optare. Volvo.
Bodies: Alexander. Leyland. Leyland National. Optare. Wright.
Ops incl: local bus services, school contracts.
Ticket System: Wayfarer

FIRST HALIFAX
SKIRCOAT ROAD, HALIFAX HX1 2RF.
Tel: 01422 305426
Fax: 01422 346323
Web site: www.firstcalderline.co.uk.
Man Dir: Mick Herdman **Ops Dir:** Graham Riley **Comm Dir:** Nigel Winter **Fin Dir:** Christine Haigh, **Eng Dir:** Mark Hargreaves, **Ops Man:** Adrian Arthur.
Fleet: 221 - 85 double-deck bus, 109 single-deck bus, 27 minibus.
Chassis: 2 Bluebird. 60 Dennis. 51 Leyland. 16 MCW. 27 Mercedes. 65 Volvo.
Bodies: Alexander. Bluebird. ECW. MCW. Optare. Plaxton. Roe. Wright.
Ops incl: local bus services, school contracts.
Livery: FirstGroup.
Ticket System: Wayfarer 3.

FIRST IN HUDDERSFIELD
OLD FIELDHOUSE LANE, HUDDERSFIELD HD2 1AG.
Tel: 01484 426313
Fax: 01484 431214
Web site: www.firsthuddersfield.co.uk.
Div Dir: Ian Davies **Man Dir:** Mark Herdman
Fleet: 160 - 48 double-deck bus. 103 single-deck bus. 9 minibus.
Chassis: 99 Dennis. 17 Leyland. 9 Mercedes. 31 MCW. 4 Scania.
Bodies: MCW. Northern Counties. Plaxton. Roe.
Ops incl: local bus services, school contacts.
Livery: White/Magenta/Blue
Ticket System: Wayfarer.

FIRST IN LEEDS
KIRKSTALL ROAD, LEEDS LS3 1LH.
Tel: 0113 245 1601
Fax: 0113 242 9721
Web site: www.firstgroup.com
www.firstleeds.co.uk
Fleetname: First in Leeds
Div Dir: Ian Davies
Fleet: 487 - 268 double-deck bus, 182 single-deck bus, 15 articulated bus, 22 minibus.
Chassis: 84 Dennis. Ford Transit. 33 MCW. 8 Mercedes. 14 Optare. 65Leyland. 150 Scania. 133 Volvo.
Bodies: Alexander. MCW. Optare. Plaxton. Roe. Wright.
Ops incl: local bus services, school contacts.
Livery: FirstGroup
Ticket System: Wayfarer 3.

*GAIN TRAVEL EXPERIENCE
6 FAIR ROAD, WIBSEY, BRADFORD BD6 1QN
Tel: 01274 603224
Fax: 01274 678274
E-mail: gail@gaintravel.co.uk
Web site: www.gaintravel.co.uk
Man Dir: Gail Bottomley
Dirs: Ian Bottomley, Darren Bottomley
Man: Beryl LeaRoyd
Fleet: 5 - 4 coach, 1 minibus.
Chassis: 3 DAF. 1 MAN.
Bodies: 4 Van Hool.
Ops incl: excursions & tours, private hire

*STANLEY GATH (COACHES) LTD
wc ❦ 🍴 A/c

LEES HALL ROAD, THORNHILL LEES, DEWSBURY WF12 9EQ
Tel: 01924 466766
Fax: 01924 458665
E-mail: info@stanleygath.co.uk
Web site: www.stanleygath.co.uk
Man Dir: A Gath-Bragg **Gen Man**: R Gara
Fleet: 13 - 11 coach, 1 midibus, 1minicoach.
Chassis: 1 DAF. 1 LDV. 11 Volvo.
Ops incl: excursions & tours, private hire, school contracts
Livery: Grey/Cream

GLENWAY COACHES (HALIFAX)
❦ wc A/c ✒

LEES HALL ROAD, THORNHILL LEES, DEWSBURY WF12 9EQ.
Tel: 01422 823244.
Fax: 01924 458665.
Dirs: J. R. Bragg, A. Gath-Bragg.
Gen Man: P. R. Emerton.
Fleet: 4 - 2 single-deck coach, 1 double-deck coach, 1 minicoach.
Chassis: 1 LDV. 1 Neoplan. 2 Volvo.
Ops incl: excursions & tours, private hire, school contracts, express, continental tours.
Livery: Grey/Cream

J D GODSON
3 SANDBED LANE, CROSSGATES LS15 8JH
Tel: 0113 264 6166.
Fax: 0113 390 9669.
E-mail: godsonscoaches@hotmail.com
Man Dir: David Godson
Fleet: 8
Chassis: 2 Bova. 3 DAF. 3 Volvo
Bodies: 2 Bova. 1 Caetano. 5 Plaxton.
Ops incl: school contracts, private hire.
Livery: Pink/White/Brown

G. W. GOULDING wc
64 THE RIDGEWAY, KNOTTINGLEY WF11 0JS.
Tel: 01977 672265, 672059.
Fax: 01977 670276.
Fleetname: B. Goulding.
Prop: G. W. Goulding.
Fleet: 5 - 3 coach, 1 midicoach, 1 minicoach.
Chassis: 1 Bristol. 1 Leyland. 1 Toyota. 2 Volvo.
Bodies: 1 Caetano. 4 Plaxton.
Ops incl: excursions & tours, private hire, continental tours.
Livery: White with Red/Yellow/Blue stripes.

GRA-CAR COACHES
THE GARAGE, FEATHERSTONE LANE, FEATHERSTONE WF7 6AN.
Tel: 01977 791950.
Fleet: 2 - 1 single-deck bus, 1 coach.

Chassis: DAF. Leyland.
Ops incl: local bus services, excursions & tours, private hire.

*GUEST AUTOMOTIVE LTD
❦

CENTRAL GARAGE, STANSFIELD ROAD, TODMORDEN OL14 5DL
Tel/Fax: 01706 813909
E-mail: tonygled@hotmail.co.uk
Man: A J Gledhill.
Fleet: 3 - 1 minibus, 1 minicoach.
Chassis/bodies: 3 Mercedes.
Ops incl: private hire, excursions & tours.

HOWIE'S OF ROBERTTOWN
♿ wc

194 ROBERTTOWN LANE, ROBERTTOWN, LIVERSEDGE WF15 7LF
Tel/Fax: 01924 400386.
Props: D. Howie, Susan Howie.
Fleet: 1 coach. **Chassis/Body**: Bova.
Ops incl: excursions & tours, private hire.
Livery: Cream/Purple/Gold.

ILLINGWORTH COACHES
wc 🍴 ❦ A/c ✒

UPPER WARRENGATE, WAKEFIELD WF1 4DT
Tel: 01924 373085
Fax: 01924 274110
Dirs: G Illingworth, P Illingworth
Fleet: 3 coach.
Chassis: 3 Scania.
Bodies: 3 Irizar
Ops incl: excursions & tours, private hire, continental tours.
Livery: White

*INDEPENDENT COACHWAYS LTD
❦ 🚌 wc 🚍 A/c ✒

LOW FOLD GARAGE, NEW ROAD SIDE, HORSFORTH LS18 4DR
Tel: 0113 258 6491
Fax: 0113 259 1125
E-mail: independentcoachways@yahoo.co.uk
Web site: www.independentcoachways.co.uk
Dirs: P & C Thornes **Gen Man**: Barry Rennison **Traf Man**: Peter Seaward
Fleet: 9 - 1 single-deck bus, 8 coach
Chassis: 1 Optare. 8 Volvo.
Bodies: 1 Optare. 7 Plaxton. 1 Van Hool.
Ops incl: private hire, school contracts.
Livery: Blue/Grey

KEIGHLEY & DISTRICT
CAVENDISH HOUSE, 91-93 CAVENDISH STREET, KEIGHLEY BD21 3DG
Tel: 01535 603284
Fax: 01535 610065
Web site: www.keighleyanddistrict.co.uk

Fleet name: The Zone
Chmn: G R Fearnley
Fleet: 103 - 40 double-deck bus, 63 single-deck bus.
Chassis: Dennis. Volvo.
Bodies: Alexander. Plaxton. Wright.
Ops incl: local bus services, school contracts
Livery: Blue/White, Blue/Red
Part of the Blazefield group which is owned by Transdev

*J J LONGSTAFF & SONS LTD
wc ❦ A/c

64 DAISY HILL, DEWSBURY WF13 1LH
Tel: 01924 463124
Fax: 01924 430345
Web site: www.longstaffofmirfield.com
Fleetname: Longstaff of Mirfield
Co Sec: S Kaye **Ops Man**: G Kaye
Fleet: 5 - 2 single-deck bus, 3 coach.
Chassis: 5 Volvo.
Bodies: 3 Van Hool. 2 Wright.
Ops incl: local bus services, school contracts, excursions & tours, private hire, continental tours.
Livery: Blue/Grey/White
Ticket system: Wayfarer

*A. LYLES & SON wc ❦ A/c
156 COMMONSIDE, BATLEY WF17 6LA
Tel: 01924 464771
Fax: 01924 469267
E-mail: alyles&son@aol.com
Senior Ptnr: Terence Lyles
Ptnr: Howard Lyles.
Fleet: 6 - 1 single-deck bus, 5 coach
Chassis: 2 DAF. 4 MAN.
Bodies: 1 Berkhof. 1 Duple. 1 Indcar. 1 Optare. 2 Van Hool.
Ops incl: local bus services, school contracts, excursions & tours, private hire, continental tours.
Livery: Beige/Brown/Red

DAVID PALMER COACHES LTD wc ❦ A/c ✒ T
THE TRAVEL OFFICE, WAKEFIELD ROAD, NORMANTON WF6 2BT
Tel: 01924 895849
Fax: 01924 897750
E-mail: info@davidpalmercoaches.co.uk
Web site: www.davidpalmercoaches.co.uk
Dirs: Andrew Palmer, Lisa Palmer, David Palmer, Margaret Palmer.
Fleet: 7 - 4 coach, 1 midicoach, 2 minibus.
Chassis: 2 DAF. 1 LDV. 2 MAN. 1 Mercedes. 1 Toyota.
Bodies: incl: 1 Mercedes. 4 Van Hool.
Ops incl: excursions & tours, private hire, continental tours.
Livery: Silver

A/c	Air conditioning	❦	Seat belt-fitted vehicles
♿	Vehicles suitable for disabled	R	Recovery service available (not 24 hr)
🍴	Coach(es) with galley facilities	R24	24hr recovery service
wc	Coach(es) with toilet facilities		
✒	Replacement vehicle available	T	Toilet-drop facilities available
🚍	Vintage vehicle(s) available	🚌	Open top vehicle(s)

West Yorkshire

West Yorkshire

PAUL'S TRAVEL
31 ST JOHN'S ROAD, HUDDERSFIELD HD1 5DX
Tel: 01484 454040.
Fax: 01484 300900.
Prop: P. Singh.
Fleet: 40 - 2 single-deck bus, 6 coach, 1 midibus, 1 midicoach, 30 minibus.
Chassis: 3 Bova, 2 DAF, 5 Ford Transit. 3 Iveco. 3 LDV. 2 Leyland. 15 Mercedes. 6 Optare. 1 Volvo.
Bodies: 3 Bova. 2 Leyland. 15 Mercedes. 6 Optare. 1 Plaxton.
Ops incl: local bus services, school contracts, excursions & tours, private hire, continental tours.

PULLMAN DINER
THE HAWTHORNES, GREAT NORTH ROAD, KNOTTINGLEY WF11 0BS
Tel: 07860 302018
Fax: 07860 677554
Web site: www.pullmandiner.co.uk
Prop: Michael Hartley
Fleet: 1 coach
Chassis: 1 MAN
Bodies: 1 Van Hool.
Ops incl: excursions & tours, private hire, continental tours

RED ARROW COACHES LTD
ASPLEY HOUSE, LINCOLN STREET, HUDDERSFIELD HD1 6RX.
Tel: 01484 420993.
Fax: 01484 540409.
E-mail: info@redarrowcoaches.co.uk
Web site: www.redarrowcoaches.co.uk
Dirs: Steven R. Moore, Suichwant Singh.
Fleet: 10 - 9 coach, 1 midicoach.
Chassis: 1 Ayats. 2 Bova. 2 DAF. 1 Dennis. 2 MAN. 2 Scania.
Bodies: 1 Ayats. 2 Bova. 1 Caetano. 2 Plaxton. 4 Van Hool.
Ops incl: excursions & tours, private hire, continental tours, school contracts.

JOHN RIGBY TRANSPORT & TRAVEL
SPRINGWELL MILLS, 231 BRADFORD ROAD, BATLEY WF17 6JL
Tel: 01924 485151
E-mail: rigbytransport@hotmail.co.uk
Web site: www.johnrigby.co.uk
Prop: John Rigby **Tran Man**: Steve Clayton
Fleet: 8 - 5 coach, 2 midicoach, 1 minicoach.
Chassis: 2 DAF. 1 Dennis. 2 MAN. 1 Mercedes. 2 Volvo.
Bodies: 3 Caetano. 1 Marcopolo. 1 Mercedes. 1 Plaxton. 2 Van Hool.
Ops incl: private hire, school contracts.
Livery: White

ROLLINSON SAFEWAY LTD
65 HALL LANE, LEEDS LS12 1PQ
Tel: 0113 231 1355
Fax: 0113 231 1344
Man Dir: Paul Rollinson. **Dir**: Peter Rollinson. **Contracts Man**: M. J. Joyce.
Fleet: 72 minibus.
Chassis: 1 Fiat. 3 Ford Transit. 3 Iveco. 20 Mercedes. 45 Renault.
Ops incl: private hire, school contracts.
Livery: Brown/Gold.

ROPERS COACHES
69 DUCKWORTH LANE, BRADFORD BD9 5EX
Tel: 01274 487973
Fax: 01274 543430
Dir: Vera Roper.
Fleet: 1 coach.
Chassis: 1 DAF
Body: 1 Bova.
Ops incl: excursions & tours, private hire, continental tours.
Livery: Blue/Silver.

*ROSS TRAVEL
THE GARAGE, ALLISON STREET, FEATHERSTONE WF7 6BB
Tel: 01977 791738
Fax: 01977 690109
E-mail: info@rosstravelgroup.co.uk
Web Site: www.rosstravelgroup.co.uk
Props: Peter Ross, Mary Ross.
Fleet: 17 - 10 single-deck bus, 5 coach, 1 midicoach, 1 minicoach.
Chassis: 1 DAF. 9 Mercedes. 3 Optare. 2 Scania. 2 Volvo
Bodies: 1 Alexander. 1 Bova. 1 Mercedes. 3 Optare. 6 Plaxton. 1 Setra. 3 Van Hool. 1 other.
Ops incl: local bus services, excursions & tours, private hire, school contracts, continental tours.
Livery: Red/White.
Ticket System: Almex A90

STEELS LUXURY COACHES
61 MAIN STREET, ADDINGHAM LS29 0PD
Tel: 01943 830206
Fax: 01943 831499
E-mail: info@steelscoaches.co.uk
Web site: www.steelscoaches.co.uk
Dir: Tim Steel **Co Sec**: Jane Steel
Fleet: 9 - 4 coach, 4 midicoach, 1 minicoach.
Chassis: 1 Dodge. 5 Mercedes. 3 Volvo.
Bodies: 1 Duple. 2 Jonckheere. 2 Optare. 2 Plaxton. 2 other.
Ops incl: excursions & tours, private hire, school contracts.
Livery: White/Red/Black

*E STOTT & SONS LTD
COLNE VALE GARAGE, SAVILE STREET, MILNSBRIDGE, HUDDERSFIELD HD3 4PG
Tel: 01484 460463
Fax: 01484 461634
E-mail: info@stottscoaches.co.uk
Web site: www.stottscoaches.co.uk
Dirs: Mark Stott, Carl Stott
Fleet: 25 - 4 single-deck bus, 11 coach, 10 minibus.
Chassis: 4 Leyland. 10 Mercedes. 11 Volvo.
Bodies: 4 Leyland. 7 Plaxton. 4 Sunsundegui.
Ops incl: local bus services, school contracts, private hire.
Livery: White/Red/Black/Silver
Ticket System: Wayfarer

STRINGERS PONTEFRACT MOTORWAYS
102 SOUTHGATE, PONTEFRACT WF8 1PN
Tel: 01977 600205
Fax: 01977 704178
E-mail: ms@stringerscoaches.fsnet.co.uk
Ptnrs: Sydney Stringer, Mark G Stringer
Tran Man: Mark S Stringer
Sec: Sonia Stringer **Ch Eng**: Chris Palmer
Fleet: 11 - 6 single-deck bus, 4 coach, 1 midicoach.
Chassis: 1 Mercedes. 6 Optare. 4 Volvo.
Bodies: 6 Optare. 1 Plaxton. 4 Van Hool.
Ops incl: local bus services, school contracts, excursions & tours, private hire.
Livery: Red/Black/White
Ticket system: Almex

T & S TRAVEL
INDUSTRIAL ESTATE, SOUTH KIRKBY, PONTEFRACT WF9 3NR.
Tel: 01977 644992.
Fax: 01977 608652.
Ptnrs: Mrs L. Stevenson, J. Tebbett.
Fleet: 9 - 4 midicoach, 5 minibus.
Chassis: 2 Ford Transit. 1 Freight Rover. 1 MCW. 3 Mercedes.
Ops incl: local bus services, excursions & tours.

*TETLEYS MOTOR SERVICES LTD
76 GOODMAN STREET, LEEDS LS10 1NY
Tel: 0113 276 2276
Fax: 0113 276 2277
E-mail: sales@tetleyscoaches.com
Web site: www.tetleyscoaches.com
Dir: Ian Tetley **Co Sec**: Joan Tetley
Ch Eng: David Leach **Ops Man**: Stephen Cunniff
Fleet: 16 - 13 coach. 1 midicoach. 2 minibus
Chassis: 1 Dennis. 1 Iveco. 1 Mercedes. 2 Renault. 11 Volvo.
Bodies: 11 Plaxton. 3 Van Hool. 2 other.
Ops incl: private hire, school contracts, express.
Livery: Blue lettering on White

TWIN VALLEY COACHES
INDUSTRIAL ROAD, SOWERBY BRIDGE HX6 2RA.
Tel/Fax: 01422 833358.
Dirs: D Pilling, E Pilling.
Fleet: 5 - 2 coach, 2 midicoach, 1 minicoach.
Chassis: 2 Dennis. 1 LDV. 1 MAN. 2 Mercedes.
Bodies: 1 Caetano. 2 Optare. 1 Plaxton.
Ops incl: private hire, school contracts.
Livery: Green/White.

W A SHEARINGS LTD
MILL LANE, NORMANTON WF6 1RF
Tel: 01977 603088
Fax: 01977 603114
Ops Man: Martin Guy
See also W A Shearings Ltd, Greater Manchester

WAKEFIELD TUTORIAL SCHOOL
COMMERICIAL STREET, MORLEY LS27 8HY
Tel: 0113 257 6165, 253 4033.
Fleetname: W. T. S. Travel.
Dirs: R. Favell (**Gen Man/Traf Man**), J. A. Crosby. **Sec**: S. Kelson.
Fleet: 1 minicoach.
Chassis: Freight Rover. **Body**: Concept.

Ops incl: excursions & tours, private hire.
Livery: White with Red/Green stripe.

*WELSH'S COACHES LTD
FIELD LANE, UPTON, PONTEFRACT WF9 1BH
Tel: 01977 643873
Fax: 01977 648143
E-mail: info@welshscoaches.com
Web site: www.welshscoaches.co.uk
Dir: John Welsh **Co Sec**: Judy Welsh
Fleet: 7 - 5 coach, 2 minicoach.
Chassis: 2 Mercedes. 5 Setra.
Bodies: 2 Mercedes. 5 Setra.
Ops incl: excursions & tours, private hire, continental tours.
Livery: White/Red/Green

*WTS MINICOACHES
49 PRIESTHORPE ROAD, FARSLEY, LEEDS LS28 5JR
Tel: 0113 257 6165
Fax: 0113 253 9581
Prop: Raymond Favell
Fleet: 1 minibus.
Chassis: 1 LDV
Bodies: 1 Onyx
Ops incl: school contracts, private hire, excursions & tours.
Livery: Green/White with Red/Yellow stripe

WILTSHIRE

ADRAINS OF BRINKWORTH
THE COACH YARD, THE COMMON, BRINKWORTH SN15 5DX
Tel: 01666 510874 5
Recovery: 07831 303295
Prop: Adrain Griffiths **Ops Man**: Colin Minchin
Fleet: 8 - 3 single-deck bus, 4 coach, 1 minibus.
Chassis: 1 LDV. 2 Leyland. 3 Mercedes. 2 Volvo.
Bodies: 7 Plaxton. 1 Reeve Burgess.
Ops incl: local bus services, school contracts, private hire.
Livery: White/Blue/Yellow
Ticket system: Wayfarer

*ANDREW JAMES QUALITY TRAVEL (ANDYBUS AND COACH LTD)
UNIT 6, WHITEWALLS, EASTON GREY, MALMESBURY SN16 0RD
Tel: 01666 825655
Fax: 01666 825651
Recovery: 07740 88710
E-mail: ajcoaches@andrew-james.co.uk
Web site: www.andrew-james.co.uk
Dir: Andrew James
Fleet: 16 - 3 coach, 6 single-deck bus, 6 midibus, 1 midicoach.
Chassis: 3 Bova. 2 DAF. 4 Dennis. 1 Leyland. 2 MAN. 1 Marshall. 5 Mercedes. 1 Optare. 1 Toyota.

Bodies: 3 Bova. 1 Caetano. 1 East Lancs. 1 Ikarus. 1 Marshall/MCV. 2 Optare. 8 Plaxton
Ops incl: local bus services, school contracts, private hire.
Livery: Bus - Cream/Orange, Coach - Yellow/Black
Ticket System: Wayfarer

APL TRAVEL
PEAR TREE COTTAGE, CRUDWELL SN16 9ES
Tel/Fax: 01666 577774
Prop: A.P. Legg

*BARNES COACHES
UNIT E, WOODSIDE ROAD, SOUTH MARSTON BUSINESS PARK, SWINDON SN3 4AQ
Tel: 01793 821303
Fax: 01793 828486
E-mail: travel@barnescoaches.co.uk
Web site: www.barnescoaches.co.uk
Dirs: Lionel Barnes, Terry Barnes, Luke Barnes, Matthew Barnes
Fleet: 29 - 26 coach, 2 minibus, 2 vintage
Chassis: 1 Bedford. 8 Bova. 2 Ford. 18 Volvo.
Bodies: 2 Berkhof. 8 Bova. 2 Jonckheere. 13 Van Hool
Ops incl: excursions & tours, school contracts, private hire, continental tours
Livery: Mint Green

BEELINE (R & R) COACHES LTD
BISHOPSTROW ROAD, WARMINSTER BA12 9HQ
Tel: 01985 213503
Fax: 01985 213922
Dirs: M N Hayball, A D Hayball
Gen Man: N Ennis
Fleet: 32 - 22 coach, 6 midicoach, 4 minibus.
Chassis: 4 LDV. 12 Mercedes. 16 Volvo.
Bodies: 2 Optare. 26 Plaxton. 4 other.
Ops incl: local bus services, school contracts, private hire
Livery: Beige/White
Ticket system: Setright

BELLS LUXURY COACHES
162 CASTLE STREET, SALISBURY SP1 3UA.
Tel: 01722 339422
Fax: 01722 412681
Man Dir: A Carter **Eng Dir**: G Parsons
Man: Chris Mills **Ops Dir**: A Wickham.
Fleet: 9 - 1 midicoach, 2 minicoach, 6 single-deck coach..
Chassis: 1 DAF. 1 Dennis. 2 Mercedes. 4 Volvo. 1 Toyota.
Bodies: 1 Caetano. 1 Jonckheere. 4 Plaxton. 1 Van Hool. 2 other.
Ops incl: excursions & tours, private hire, school contracts, continental tours.
Livery: Green/Cream
(Subsidiary of Wilts & Dorset)

A/c	Air conditioning	
	Vehicles suitable for disabled	
	Coach(es) with galley facilities	
wc	Coach(es) with toilet facilities	
	Seat belt-fitted vehicles	
R	Recovery service available (not 24 hr)	
R24	24hr recovery service	
	Replacement vehicle available	
T	Toilet-drop facilities available	
	Vintage vehicle(s) available	
	Open top vehicle(s)	

185

*BETTER MOTORING SERVICES

104A SWINDON ROAD, STRATTON-ST MARGARET SN3 4PT
Tel: 01793 823747
Fax: 01793 831898
Fleetname: BMS Coaches.
Prop: D G Miles **Fleet Eng**: M J Hopkins
Sec: Mrs M Mulhern
Fleet: 10 - 8 midicoach, 2 minicoach.
Chassis: 1 Ford. 9 Mercedes.
Bodies: 4 Autobus. 2 Mellor. 2 Optare. 2 other.
Ops incl: school contracts, excursions & tours, private hire, continental tours.
Livery: Coffee/Cream

C BODMAN & SONS

88 HIGH STREET, WORTON, DEVIZES SN10 5RU
Tel: 01380 722393
Fax: 01380 721969
Ptnrs: R J Bodman, D N Bodman, C J Bodman, K G Heath **Tran Man**: C J Bodman **Ops Man**: G Carter
Fleet: 41 - 21 single-deck bus, 19 coach, 1 minibus.
Chassis: 1 Bedford. 22 Dennis. 1 Iveco. 1 LDV. 3 Leyland. 2 Mercedes. 4 Optare. 6 Volvo.
Bodies: 3 Alexander. 3 Berkhof. 16 Carlyle. 2 Marshall. 1 Mellor. 4 Optare. 9 Plaxton. 2 UVG. 1 Wadham Stringer.
Ops incl: local bus services, school contracts, excursions & tours, private hire.

CHANDLERS COACH TRAVEL

158 CHEMICAL ROAD, WEST WILTS TRADING ESTATE, WESTBURY BA13 4JN
Tel: 01373 824500
Fax: 01373 824300
E-mail: info@chandlerscoach.co.uk
Web site: www.chandlerscoach.co.uk
Prop: Margaret l'Anson **Fleet Eng**: Christopher l'Anson
Fleet: 10 - 9 coach, 1 minibus.
Chassis: 1 Renault. 9 Volvo.
Bodies: 4 Plaxton. 1 Renault. 5 Van Hool.
Ops incl: school contracts, excursions & tours, private hire, continental tours.
Livery: White/Burgundy/Gold

COACHSTYLE LTD

HORSDOWN GARAGE, NETTLETON, CHIPPENHAM SN14 7LN
Tel/Fax: 01249 782224
Owners: Andrew Jones, Mrs A L Jones
Fleet: 15 - 2 single-deck bus, 13 coach.
Chassis: 4 DAF. 3 Leyland. 1 Scania. 6 Volvo.
Bodies: 3 Berkhof. 1 Caetano. 2 Duple. 3 Jonckheere. 2 Mercedes. 3 Van Hool.
Ops incl: local bus services, school contracts, excursions & tours, private hire, continental tours.

CROSS COUNTRY COACHES

BLACKFORD LANE, CASTLE EATON SN6 6LE
Tel: 01285 810000
Fax: 01285 810142
E-mail: sales@crosscountrycoaches.com
Dir: B. Telford.
Fleet: 12 - 5 double-deck bus, 5 coach, 1 double-deck coach, 1 vintage.
Chassis: 1 Bedford, 5 DAF. 5 Daimler. 1 Setra.
Ops incl: local bus services, excursions & tours, private hire, continental tours, school contracts.

*ELLISON'S COACHES

THE GARAGE, HIGH ROAD, ASHTON KEYNES, SWINDON SN6 6NX
Tel: 01285 861224
Fax: 01285 862115
E-mail: sales@ellisonscoaches.co.uk
Web site: www.ellisonscoaches.co.uk
Prop: Alan Ellison
Fleet: 18 coach - 2 single-deck bus, 16 coach
Chassis: 2 BMC. 16 Neoplan.
Ops incl: school contracts, private hire.

*FARESAVER BUSES

THE COACH YARD, VINCIENTS ROAD, BUMPERS FARM INDUSTRIAL ESTATE, CHIPPENHAM SN14 6AS
Tel: 01249 444444
Fax: 01249 448844
E-mail: sales@faresaver.co.uk
Web site: www.faresaver.co.uk
Prop: J V Pickford **Ops Man**: D J Pickford
Ops Man: D Beard **Ch Eng**: D Watts
Fleet: 60 - 30 midibus, 20 midicoach, 10 minicoach
Chassis: 60 Mercedes.
Bodies: 10 Alexander. 5 Carlyle. 5 Leicester. 40 Plaxton.
Ops incl: local bus services, school contracts, private hire.
Livery: White/Mauve.
Ticket System: Wayfarer 3

G-LINE MINICOACHES

15 BROAD TOWN ROAD, BROAD TOWN, SWINDON SN4 7RB.
Tel/Fax: 01793 814336.
E-mail: gline@btinternet.com
Chmn: P. McGarry. **Man Dir**: N. McGarry.
Service Dir: J. McGarry.
Tpt Man: N. McGarry.
Fleet: 30 - 4 minicoach, 26 midicoach
Chassis: 4 Ford Transit. 2 Iveco. 10 LDV. 5 Mercedes.
Ops incl: private hire, school contracts.

R. J. HARLEY

119 LONDON ROAD, MARLBOROUGH SN8 1LH.
Tel: 01672 52786.
Fleetname: Harley Travel.
Prop: R. J. Harley.
Gen Man/Traf Man: A. M. Harley.
Fleet: 2 minicoach. **Chassis**: 2 Ford Transit.
Ops incl: local bus services, school contracts, private hire.
Livery: Green/Red.
Ticket System: Setright

*HATTS COACHES

FOXHAM, CHIPPENHAM SN15 4NB
Tel: 01249 740444
Fax: 01249 740447
E-mail: info@hattstravel.co.uk
Web site: www.hattstravel.co.uk
Man Ptnr: Adrian Hillier **Ops Man**: Andy Bridgman **Traff Man**: Phil Turner **Wkshp Man**: M Henderson **Group Travel**: Marylin Nelson, Mark Fisher
Fleet: 48 - 6 single-deck bus, 24 coach, 11 midibus, 5 midicoach, 2 minicoach.
Chassis: 1 DAF. 1 Dennis. Iveco. 1 Leyland. 7 MAN. 14 Mercedes. 2 Optare. 3 Renault. 1 Toyota. 17 Volvo.
Bodies: 9 Autobus. 2 Ayats. 2 Berkhof. 1 Bova. 1 Caetano. 2 Marcopolo. 2 Mercedes. 1 Neoplan. 2 Noge. 4 Plaxton. 2 Reeve Burgess. 1 UVG. 14 Van Hool. 5 other.
Ops incl: local bus services, excursions & tours, private hire, continental tours, school contracts.

HI-DECK EUROCRUISERS

4 REEVES PLACE, WESTBURY BA13 4TH
Tel: 0800 328 2453
Web sitel: www.hideck.co.uk
Fleet: single-deck and double-deck coach
Chassis: incl: Neoplan
Ops incl: private hire, excursions.
Livery: Cream
Ticket system: Wayfarer

ANDREW JAMES QUALITY TRAVEL

FERRIS FARM, OLIVEMEAD LANE, DAUNTSEY SN15 4JF
Tel: 01666 505585
Fax: 01666 504647
E-mail: ajcoach@netcentral.co.uk
Web site: www.andrew-james.co.uk
Fleet: 18 - 12 single-deck bus, 4 coach, 1 midicoach, 1 minicoach.
Chassis: 2 Bova. 1 Dennis. 1 Dodge. 3 Iveco. 1 MAN. 6 Mercedes. 1 Neoplan. 1 Optare. 2 Renault.
Bodies: 2 Bova. 2 Duple. 1 ECW. 1 Neoplan. 3 Optare. 3 Plaxton. 1 Reeve Burgess. 1 Wadham Stringer.
Ops incl: local bus services, school contracts, private hire.
Livery: Yellow/Cream.
Ticket system: Wayfarer

KINGSTON COACHES

162 CASTLE STREET, SALISBURY SP1 3UA
Tel: 01722 337311
Fax: 01722 412681
Man: C Mills **Ops Man**: S Hursthouse
Fleet: 4 coach.
Chassis: 2 DAF. 1 Dennis. 1 Volvo.
Bodies: 3 Plaxton. 1 Van Hool.

Ops incl: private hire, continental tours, school contracts.
Livery: Red/Cream
(Subsidiary of Wilts & Dorset)

LEVER'S COACHES

162 CASTLE STREET, SALISBURY
SP1 3UA
Tel: 01722 417229
Fax: 01722 412681
Man: C Mills **Asst Man**: I Bassindale
Fleet: 6 - 5 coach, 1 midicoach.
Chassis: 3 DAF. 1 Dennis. 1 Mercedes. 1 Volvo.
Bodies: 1 Autobus. 1 Jonckheere. 1 Plaxton. 3 Van Hool.
Ops incl: local bus services, school contracts, private hire.
Livery: Cream/Blue.
Ticket system: Almex
(Subsidiary of Wilts & Dorset)

MANSFIELD'S COACHES

27 FINCHDALE, COVINGHAM, SWINDON SN3 5AL.
Tel/Fax: 01793 525375.
Prop: R. E. Mansfield. **Man**: A. Mansfield.
Tran Man: P. Mansfield.
Sec: Mrs M. S. Mansfield.
Fleet: 6.
Chassis: 3 MAN. 2 Mercedes. 1 Toyota.
Ops incl: excursions & tours, private hire, express, school contracts.
Livery: Yellow/Green/Red.
Ticket System: Setright.

PEWSEY VALE COACHES

HOLLYBUSH LANE, PEWSEY
SN9 5BB
Tel/Fax: 01672 562238
E-mail: pewseyvalecoaches@aol.com
Dirs: Andrew Thorne, Dawn Thorne, Anne Thorne
Fleet: coach, minicoach.
Chassis: Bova. Leyland. Mercedes. Volvo.
Bodies: Bova. Plaxton. Van Hool.
Ops incl: local bus services, school contracts, excursions & tours, continental tours
Livery: White/Blue/Red
Ticket system: Almex

ROBIN'S COACHES

TREDENA, FORD, CHIPPENHAM
SN14 8RR
Tel/Fax: 01249 782574
E-mail: info@robinscoaches.co.uk
Web site: robinscoaches.co.uk
Ptnrs: Robin Smith, D. P. Smith.
Fleet: 3 - 2 coach, 1 minibus.
Chassis: 2 Renault. 2 Volvo.
Bodies: 1 Berkhof. 1 Plaxton.
Ops incl: school contracts, excursions & tours, private hire, continental tours.
Livery: White/Blue/Pink

SEAGER'S COACHES LTD

AUDLEY ROAD, CHIPPENHAM
SN14 0EN.
Tel: 01249 654949
Fax: 01249 462006
E-mail: seagerscoaches@hotmail.com
Web site: www.seagers-coaches.co.uk
Dirs: Ms J Seager, T Woods, A Watts, Ms A Truscott
Fleet: 19 - 1 coach, 14 minibus, 2 midicoach
Chassis: 1 DAF. 9 Ford Transit. 4 Iveco. 3 LDV. 2 Mercedes.
Ops incl: private hire, school contracts.
Livery: White

*STAGECOACH WEST

See Gloucestershire

SWINDON VINTAGE OMNIBUS SOCIETY

10 FRASER CLOSE, NYTHE, SWINDON SN3 3RP
Tel: 01793 526001.
Chairm: M. Naughton. **Sec**: D. Nicol. **Treas**: D. Mundy.
Fleet: 1 double-deck bus.
Chassis: 1 Daimler.
Bodies: 1 Weymann.

*TEST VALLEY TRAVEL LTD

BANISTER BARN, NEWTON LANE, WHITEPARISH SP5 2QQ
Tel: 01794 884555
E-mail: testvalleytravel@btinternet.co.uk
Man Dir: J M Norman **Co Sec**: A N Norman
Fleet: 4 - 3 midicoach, 1 minibus.
Chassis/bodies: 1 Ford. 3 LDV.
Ops incl: private hire, school contracts.
Livery: White with Green/Gold relief.

*THAMESDOWN TRANSPORT

BARNFIELD ROAD, SWINDON
SN2 2DJ
Tel: 01793 428400
Fax: 01793 428405
Recovery: 01793 428432
Web site: www.thamesdown-transport.co.uk
Man Dir: Paul Jenkins **Eng Dir**: Nigel Mason **Fin Controller/Co Sec**: Cliff Connor
Ops Dir: David Burch
Fleet: 112 - 29 double-deck bus, 83 single-deck bus.
Chassis: 1 Daimler. 80 Dennis. 21 Leyland. 10 Scania.
Bodies: 17 Alexander. 4 ECW. 7 East Lancs. 1 Northern Counties. 73 Plaxton. 10 Wright.
Ops incl: local bus services, school contracts.
Livery: Blue/Green
Ticket System: Wayfarer TGX

TOURIST COACHES LTD

162 CASTLE STREET, SALISBURY
SP1 3UA
Tel: 01722 338359
Fax: 01722 412681
Man Dir: A Carter **Ops Dir**: A Wickham
Eng Dir: G Parsons **Man**: C Mills
Ops Man: S Hursthouse
Fleet: 32 - 21 coach, 4 midibus, 3 midicoach, 2 minicoach, 2 minibus
Chassis: 9 DAF. 5 Dennis. 2 LDV. 5 Mercedes. 3 Optare. 1 Toyota. 7 Volvo.
Bodies: 1 Autobus. 1 Caetano. 2 Ferqui. 1 Mercedes. 3 Optare. 11 Plaxton. 1 Reeve Burgess. 8 Van Hool. 5 other.
Ops incl: local bus services, school contracts, excursions & tours, private hire, continental tours
Livery: Orange/Cream.
Ticket System: Setright.
(Subsidiary of Wilts & Dorset)

A/c	Air conditioning		Seat belt-fitted vehicles
	Vehicles suitable for disabled	R	Recovery service available (not 24 hr)
	Coach(es) with galley facilities	R24	24hr recovery service
wc	Coach(es) with toilet facilities		

	Replacement vehicle available
T	Toilet-drop facilities available
	Vintage vehicle(s) available
	Open top vehicle(s)

WORCESTERSHIRE

*ASTONS COACHES

CLERKENLEAP, BROOMHALL, WORCESTER WR5 3HR
Tel: 01905 820201
Fax: 01905 829249
Recovery: 01905 820201
E-mail: info@astons-coaches.co.uk
Web site: www.astons-coaches.co.uk
Tran Man: Matthew Wells **Sales Man**: Anna Woodward **Man Dir**: T W Halford
Dir: Richard Conway
Fleet: 27 - 2 double-deck bus, 5 single-deck bus, 13 coach, 2 midicoach, 3 minibus, 2 midibus.
Chassis: 2 Dennis. 1 LDV. 1 MAN. 6 Mercedes. 1 Optare. 11 Scania. 5 Volvo.
Bodies: 3 Alexander. 1 Berkhof. 2 East Lancs. 3 Irizar. 1 Jonckheere. 6 Mercedes. 2 Optare. 1 Plaxton. 1 Reeve Burgess. 5 Van Hool. 1 Wright.
Ops incl: local bus services, school contracts, private hire, continental tours.
Ticket system: ERG

*N N CRESSWELL COACH HIRE

WORCESTER ROAD, EVESHAM WR11 4RA
Tel: 01386 48655
Fax: 01386 48656
Props: Mrs Mary Shephard, Mrs Sue Everatt **Ch Eng**: W G Fairbrother
Fleet: 20 - 16 coach, 3 minibus, 1 minicoach.
Chassis: 8 Bedford. 7 Dennis. 5 Mercedes.
Bodies: 20 Plaxton
Ops incl: local bus services, school contracts, private hire.
Livery: Wessex Bus/White
Ticket System: Setright.

DUDLEY'S COACHES

POPLAR GARAGE, ALCESTER ROAD, RADFORD, WORCESTER WR7 4LS
Tel: 01386 792206
E-mail: info@dudleys-coaches.co.uk
Web site: www.dudleys-coaches.co.uk
Dir: C Dudley
Fleet: 20 - 19 coach, 1 minibus.
Chassis: 3 Dennis. 1 Leyland. 1 VW. 15 Volvo.
Bodies: 1 Jonckheere. 13 Plaxton. 5 Van Hool. 1 other.
Ops incl: local bus services, school contracts, excursions & tours, private hire
Livery: Green/Cream.

FIRST WYVERN

HERON LODGE, LONDON ROAD, WORCESTER WR5 2EU.
Tel: 01905 359393.
Fax: 01905 351104.
Fleet: 240 - 119 single-deck bus, 7 coach, 114 minibus.
Chassis: Dennis. Leyland. Mercedes. Optare. Volvo.
Bodies: Alexander. Leyland. Marshall. Optare. Plaxton. Wright

Ops incl: local bus services, school contracts.
Livery: White/Magenta/Blue
Ticket System: Wayfarer

GOLD STAR TRAVEL

COOKSEY LODGE FARM, UPTON WARREN, BROMSGROVE B61 9HD
Tel/Fax: 01527 861685
Prop: Mrs Dorothy Homer.
Fleet: 1 single-deck bus
Chassis/Bodies: 1 Volvo/Van Hool.
Ops incl: private hire, excursions and tours
Livery: White/Gold

*HARDINGS INTERNATIONAL

OXLEASOW ROAD, REDDITCH B98 0RE
Tel: 01527 525200
Fax: 01527 523800
E-mail: john@hardingscoaches.com
Web site: www.hardingscoaches.co.uk
Man Dir: John Dyson
Co Sec: Malcolm Playford
Fleet Eng: Malcolm Chance
Fleet: 43 - 5 single-deck bus, 35 coach, 4 minibus.
Chassis: 3 DAF. 5 Leyland. 4 MAN. 9 Mercedes. 20 Scania. 3 Volvo.
Bodies: 2 Berkhof. 1 East Lancs. 1 Ikarus. 13 Irizar. 5 Leyland. 9 Mercedes. 13 Van Hool.
Ops incl: local bus services, school contracts, excursions & tours, private hire, continental tours
Livery: Silver/Red/Blue

HARRIS EXECUTIVE TRAVEL

58 MEADOW ROAD, CATSHILL, BROMSGROVE B61 0JL
Tel: 01527 872857
Fax: 01527 872708
E-mail: steve@harriscoaches.fsnet.co.uk
Dirs: J G Harris, S W Harris
Fleet: 7 - 6 coach, 1 mdnicoach.
Chassis: 7 Mercedes.
Bodies: 1 Caciamali. 6 Neoplan
Ops incl: excursions & tours, private hire, continental tours.
Livery: White/Red/Orange/yellow

J B C MALVERNIAN TOURS

NEWTOWN ROAD TRAVEL CENTRE, NEWTOWN ROAD, MALVERN WR14 1PJ.
Tel: 01684 575082.
Fax: 01684 568870.
Fleetname: Jones Bros Coaches
E-mail: info@malverncoaches.co.uk
Web site: www.malverncoaches.co.uk
Prop: M. A. Crump. **Gen Man**: Michael Yates. **Ch Eng**: A. Jackson.
Fleet: 11 - 10 coach, 1 midicoach.

Chassis: 2 Bova. 1 DAF. 2 Dennis. 2 Leyland. 1 MAN. 1 Toyota. 2 Volvo.
Bodies: 2 Bova. 3 Duple. 3 Plaxton. 1 Van Hool.
Ops incl: local bus services, school contracts, excursions & tours, private hire, continental tours.
Livery: Off-white/Orange.

KESTREL COACHES

UNITS 1&2, BARRACKS ROAD, SANDY LANE, STOURPORT-ON-SEVERN DY13 9QB
Tel/Fax: 01299 829689
Prop: M Wood.
Fleet: 10 - 4 coach, 3 midicoach, 3 minibus.
Chassis: 1 Bedford. 2 Bova. 1 DAF. 1 LDV. 2 Mercedes. 2 Toyota. 1 Citroën.
Bodies: 2 Bova. 3 Caetano. 1 Leyland. 2 Mercedes. 1 Van Hool. 1 Relay
Ops incl: local bus services, school contracts, private hire.
Livery: White
Ticket System: Almex

*THE TRANSPORT MUSEUM, WYTHALL

CHAPEL LANE, WYTHALL B47 6JX
Tel: 01564 826471
Trustees: David Taylor (**Chmn**), Paul Gray (**Fin**), Philip Ireland (**Museum Man**), Malcolm Keeley (**Collns Man**)
Fleet: 7 - 4 double-deck bus, 3 single-deck bus.
Chassis: 3 BMMO. 2 Bristol. 1 Daimler. 1 Guy.
Bodies: 3 BMMO. 2 ECW. 2 MCW.
Ops incl: local bus services, excursions & tours, private hire.
Livery: various
Ticket System: Setright

*WHITTLE COACH & BUS LTD

FOLEY BUSINESS PARK, STOURPORT ROAD, KIDDERMINSTER DY11 7QL
Tel: 01562 820002
Fax: 01562 820027
E-mail: webenquiries@whittlecoach.co.uk
Web site: www.whittlecoach.co.uk
Chmn: P J S Shipp **Man Dir**: D Shurden
Dir: P Harrison **Fl Eng**: T Jenkins
Co Sec: P A Leeman
Fleet: 53 - 8 single-deck bus, 31 coach, 12 midibus, 2 minicoach.
Chassis: 26 Dennis. 1 LDV. 8 Mercedes. 4 Optare. 14 Volvo.
Bodies: 3 Alexander. 4 Optare. 36 Plaxton. 6 UVG. 2 Wright. 2 other.
Ops incl: local bus services, school contracts, excursions & tours, private hire, continental tours.
Livery: White/Blue/Yellow.
Ticket system: Wayfarer III
(Subsidiary of East Yorkshire Motor Services)

*WOODSTONES COACHES LTD

ARTHUR DRIVE, HOO FARM INDUSTRIAL ESTATE, WORCESTER ROAD, KIDDERMINSTER DY11 7RA
Tel: 01562 823073
Man Dir: I Meredith **Dir**: R Meredith

Fleet: 6 coach
Chassis: 6 Volvo.
Bodies: 6 Plaxton.
Ops incl: local bus services, school contracts, excursions & tours, private hire
Livery: White/Orange/Yellow/Red

YARRANTON BROS LTD
[wc] [seat belt] [replacement]

EARDISTON GARAGE,
TENBURY WELLS WR15 8JL.
Tel: 01584 881229.

Dirs: A. L. Yarranton (**Gen Man**),
M. L. Yarranton, D. A. Yarranton.
Fleet: 12 - 10 coach, 1 minibus, 1 minicoach.
Chassis: 3 Bedford. 3 Dennis. 3 Mercedes. 2 Volvo. 1 Toyota.
Bodies: 2 Berkhof. 2 Caetano. 1 Jonckheere. 2 Mercedes. 4 Plaxton. 1 Duple.
Ops incl: local bus services, school contracts, excursions & tours, private hire, continental tours.
Livery: Green/White/Orange.

CHANNEL ISLANDS

ALDERNEY

RIDUNA BUSES
40C HIGH STREET, ALDERNEY GY9 3TG
Tel: 01481 823760
Fax: 01481 823030
Prop: A. J. Curtis.
Fleet: 5 - 2 single-deck bus, 2 coach, 1 minibus.
Chassis: 3 Bedford. 1 Freight Rover.
Bodies: 2 Duple. 1 Pennine. 1 Heaver.
Ops incl: local bus services, excursions & tours, private hire.
Livery: Cream/Maroon

GUERNSEY

ISLAND COACHWAYS LTD
[disabled] A/C

THE TRAMSHEDS, LES BANQUES, ST PETER PORT GY4 6SF
Tel: 01481 720210
Fax: 01481 710109
E-mail: sales@island-coachways.demon.co.uk
Web site: www.island-coachways.demon.co.uk
Man Dir: Mrs Hannah Beacom **Co Sec/Dir**:

George Boucher **Works Man/Dir**: Ben Boucher **Traf Man**: John Drillot **Off Man**: Mrs Jenny Down **Customer Care Man**: Mrs Ann Belben
Fleet: 56 - 38 single-deck bus, 14 coach, 1 midicoach, 3 minibus
Chassis: 1 Cannon. 33 Dennis. 4 Iveco. 9 Leyland. 4 Optare. 4 Renault. 1 Toyota.
Bodies: 1 Caetano. 4 Camo. 33 East Lancs. 3 Elme. 3 Iveco. 2 Leicester. 4 Optare. 6 Wadham Stringer.
Ops incl: local bus services, school contracts, excursions & tours, private hire
Livery: Bus: Green/Yellow Coach: Cream/Gold
Ticket System: Almex Smartfare.

JERSEY

CONNEX JERSEY
2 CALEDONIA PLACE, WEIGHBRIDGE, ST HELIER JE2 3NG
Tel: 01534 877772
Gen Man: Phillipe Juhles
Fleetname: Connex
Fleet: 46 single-deck buses
Chassis: 46 Dennis
Bodies: 46 Caetano

TANTIVY BLUE COACH TOURS [disabled] [vintage] A/C [R] [replacement]
70/72 LA COLOMBERIE, ST HELIER JE2 4QA
Tel: 01534 706706
Fax: 01534 706705
E-mail: info@jerseycoaches.com
Web site: www.jerseycoaches.com
Man Dir: Mike Cotilard **Ops Dir**: Paul Young
Fleet: 66 - 4 single-deck bus, 60 coach, 2 mdnicoach.
Chassis: 7 Bedford. 3 Cannon. 1 Iveco. 50 Leyland. 2 Optare.
Bodies: 2 Caetano. 6 Carlyle. 7 Duple. 3 Leicester. 2 Optare. 40 Wadham Stringer.
Ops incl: school contracts, excursions & tours, private hire.
Livery: Blue.

WAVERLEY COACHES LTD
UNIT 3, LA COLLETTE, ST HELIER JE2 3NX
Tel: 01534 758360
Fax: 01534 732627
Dir/Gen Man: S. E. Pedersen.
Ch Eng: Peter Evans.
Fleet: 18 - 12 coach, 2 midicoach, 4 minibus.
Chassis: 7 Bedford. 5 Leyland. 2 Mercedes. 1 Renault. 3 VW.
Bodies: 7 Duple. 5 Wadham Stringer. 4 other.
Ops incl: excursions & tours, private hire.
Livery: Yellow/White.

A/c	Air conditioning	[seat belt]	Seat belt-fitted vehicles	[replacement]	Replacement vehicle available
[disabled]	Vehicles suitable for disabled	[R]	Recovery service available (not 24 hr)	[T]	Toilet-drop facilities available
[galley]	Coach(es) with galley facilities			[vintage]	Vintage vehicle(s) available
[wc]	Coach(es) with toilet facilities	[R24]	24hr recovery service	[open top]	Open top vehicle(s)

Scottish Operators

ABERDEEN, CITY OF

*BLUEBIRD BUSES LTD

THE BUS STATION, GUILD STREET, ABERDEEN AB11 6GR
Tel: 01224 591381
Fax: 01224 584202
Recovery: 01224 591381
E-mail: eastscotland@stagecoachbus.com
Web site: www.stagecoachbus.com
Fleetname: Stagecoach Bluebird
Man Dir: Charlie Mullen **Ops Dir**: Robert Hall **Eng Dir**: John MacPherson **Ops Man**: George Devine **Depot Eng**: Iain Ferguson
Fleet: 369 - 65 double-deck bus, 141 single-deck bus, 17 coach, 61 midibus, 85 minibus.
Chassis: 42 Dennis. 52 Leyland. 38 MAN. 50 Mercedes. 25 Optare. 7 Scania. 155 Volvo.
Bodies: 268 Alexander. 5 Jonckheere. 11 Leyland. 10 Neoplan. 25 Optare. 43 Plaxton. 7 Wright.
Ops incl: local bus services, school contracts, excursions & tours, private hire, express.
Livery: Stagecoach/Megabus
Ticket System: Wayfarer TGX

FIRST

395 KING STREET, ABERDEEN AB24 5RP
Tel: 01224 650100
Web site: www.firstgroup.com
Man Dir: G Mair
Fleet: 185 - 34 double-deck bus, 107 single-deck bus, 12 coach, 20 articulated bus, 4 open top bus, 2 vintage, 6 minicoach.
Ops incl: local bus services, school contracts, excursions & tours, private hire, express, continental tours.
Livery: Coaches: Silver or White, Buses: Group Magenta Blue/Grey.

*FOUNTAIN EXECUTIVE

HILL OF GOVAL, DYCE, ABERDEEN AB21 7NX
Tel: 01224 729191
Fax: 01224 729898
E-mail: fountainexe@hotmail.com
Web site: www.fountainexecutive.co.uk
Prop: Michael Ewen
Fleet: 10 - 4 coach, 1 midicoach, 5 minicoach.
Chassis: 6 Mercedes. 4 Scania.
Bodies: incl 4 Jonckheere. Unvi
Ops incl: private hire, continental tours.
Livery: Gold

GRAMPIAN COACHES

FIRST ABERDEEN LTD, 395 KING STREET, ABERDEEN AB24 5RP
Tel: 01224 650151
Fax: 01224 650123
E-mail: tom.gordon@firstgroup.com
Web site: www.grampian-coaches.co.uk
Man Dir: George Mair **Sec**: Alan Paterson
Coaching Man: Tom Gordon
Fleet: 28 - 3 single-deck bus, 17 coach, 2 midicoach, 6 minibus.
Chassis: 1 Bluebird. 2 BMC. 1 Dennis. 6 Mercedes.1 Optare. 6 Scania. 11 Volvo.
Bodies: 6 Alexander. 2 BMC. 1 Duple. 6 Irizar. 5 Jonckheere. 1 Optare. 4 Plaxton. 2 Van Hool.
Ops incl: school contracts, excursions & tours, private hire, continental tours.
Livery: First ("Barbie")
Ticket System: Setright

MAIRS COACHES

395 KING STREET, ABERDEEN AB24 5RP.
Tel: 01224 650150.
Fax: 01224 650123.
Man Dir: G. Mair. **Eng Sup**: R. Elrick.
Comm Dir: J. Mackie
Fleet: 26 - 2 double-deck bus, 14 coach, 10 midicoach.
Chassis: 1 DAF. 1 Dennis. 3 Leyland. 8 Mercedes. 3 Renault. 1 Scania. 7 Volvo.
Bodies: 2 Alexander. 2 Duple. 8 Mercedes. 1 Irizar. 6 Plaxton. 2 Van Hool. 3 Dodge.
Ops incl: school contracts, excursions & tours, private hire, express, continental tours.
Livery: Silver/Grey or Maroon/Gold.
Ticket System: Wayfarer/Setright.
Part of FirstGroup.

*WHYTES COACH TOURS

SCOTSTOWN ROAD, NEWMACHAR, ABERDEEN AB21 7PP
Tel: 01651 862211
Fax: 01651 862918
Recovery: 01651 862724
E-mail: sales@whytescoachtours.co.uk
Web Site: www.whytescoachtours.co.uk
Ops incl: school contracts, excursions & tours, private hire, continental tours.
Livery: Two-tone Green

ABERDEENSHIRE

AMBER TRAVEL

CROSSFIELDS FARMHOUSE, TURRIFF AB53 7QY.
Tel: 01888 563474.
Fax: 01888 563474.
Props: D. Cheyne, S. Cheyne.
Fleet: 5 - 4 coach, 1 midibus.
Chassis: 1 Bedford. 1 Mercedes. 3 Volvo.
Ops incl: school contracts, private hire.
Livery: White/Red/Amber

CHEYNES COACHES

ALLANDALE, DAVIOT, INVERURIE AB51 0EJ
Tel: 01467 671400
Fax: 01467 671479
E-mail: lesley@cheynescoaches.co.uk
Web site: www.cheynescoaches.co.uk
Ptnrs: W A Cheyne, R Cheyne, L A Cheyne, M F Cheyne.
Fleet: 11 - 3 single-deck bus, 4 coach, 1 midibus, 1 minibus, 2 minicoach.
Chassis: 1 Ford Transit. 3 Leyland. 3 Mercedes. 4 Volvo.
Bodies:2 Optare. 1 Plaxton. 4 Van Hool.
Ops incl: school contracts, excursions & tours, private hire.
Livery: Silver/Pink/Purple

HAYS COACHES

HALLHILL, COBAIRDY, HUNTLY AB54 7YB
Tel: 01466 740283.
Fax: 01466 740283
Web site: www.hays.co.uk
Ptnr/Man: Stuart Hay
Fleet: 15 - 9 coach, 2 midicoach, 4 minibus.
Chassis: 1 Bedford. 1 Ford. 2 Ford Transit. 4 Iveco. 1 Leyland. 2 Mercedes. 3 Volvo.
Bodies: 4 Beulas. 1 Duple. 1 Marshall. 1 Mellor. 2 Mercedes. 3 Plaxton. 1 Van Hool. 2 Mazda.
Ops incl: local bus services, school contracts, excursions & tours, private hire, continental tours.
Livery: Grey/Blue/Red

J W COACHES LTD

DYKEHEAD GARAGE, BLACKHALL, BANCHORY AB31 6PS.
Tel/fax: 01330 823300.
Chmn/Man Dir: J. S. Westaby.
Dir: J. I. Westaby.
Ops Man: A. Anderson.
Fleet: 15 - 5 coach, 6 midibus, 1 midicoach, 3 minibus.
Chassis: 1 Bedford. 6 Freight Rover. 1 Iveco. 4 Leyland. 1 MAN. 2 Mercedes.
Bodies: 5 Carlyle. 3 Duple. 2 Plaxton. 2 Reeve Burgess. 1 Devon. 2 Dormobile.
Ops incl: local bus services, school contracts, excursions & tours, private hire.
Livery: Blue/Turquoise/White.
Ticket System: Setright.

KINEIL COACHES LTD

ANDERSON PLACE, WEST SHORE INDUSTRIAL ESTATE, FRASERBURGH AB43 9LG
Tel: 01346 510200
Fax: 01346 514774
Man Dir: Ian Neilson
Fleet: 24 - 2 single-deck bus, 14 coach, 1 midibus, 3 midicoach, 4 minicoach.
Chassis: 1 DAF. 2 Leyland. 13 Volvo.
Bodies: 2 Alexander. 1 Jonckheere. 3 Plaxton. 13 Van Hool. 5 other.
Ops incl: local bus services, school contracts, excursions & tours, private hire, continental tours.
Livery: Blue/White/Red
Ticket system: Wayfarer 2

*ALEX MILNE COACHES

THE GARAGE, 4 MAIN STREET, NEW BYTH AB53 5XD
Tel: 01888 544340
Tel: 01888 544154
Web site: www.alexmilnecoaches.co.uk
Ptnrs: Alex Milne, Brian Milne, Nettie Milne
Fleet: 13 - 2 coach, 1 midibus, 1 minicoach, 5 minibus, 4 minicoach.
Chassis: 5 Ford Transit. 6 Mercedes. 2 Volvo.
Bodies: 2 Esker. 5 Ford Transit. 4 Plaxton. 2 Van Hool.
Ops incl: local bus services, school contracts, private hire, excursions & tours
Livery: Blue/White
Ticket system: Wayfarer

M W NICOLL'S COACH HIRE

THE BUSINESS PARK, ABERDEEN ROAD, LAURENCEKIRK AB30 1EY
Tel: 01561 377262.
Fax: 01561 378822.
E-mail: malcolm.nicoll@lineone.net
Man Dir: M. W. Nicoll. **Dir**: I. J. Nicoll.
Service Man: A. Gordon.
Gen Man: H. Thomson.
Fleet: 24 - 2 single-deck bus, 6 coach, 3 midibus, 6 midicoach, 2 minibus, 5 minicoach.
Chassis: 1 Bova, 4 Ford Transit, 1 Leyland, 9 Mercedes, 1 Optare, Setra, 2 Toyota, 6 Volvo.
Bodies: 1 Bova, 2 Caetano, 1 Duple, 10 Mercedes, 1 Solo, 6 Van Hool, 4 others.
Ops incl: local bus services, private hire.
Livery: White.
Ticket System: Almex.

REIDS OF RHYNIE

22 MAIN STREET, RHYNIE, BY HUNTLY AB54 4HB
Tel/Fax: 01464 861212
Recovery: 07831 173681
Owner: Colin Reid.
Fleet: 14 - 4 coach, 2 midibus, 1 midicoach, 7 minibus.
Chassis: 4 Ford Transit. 4 LDV. 3 Mercedes. 4 Volvo.
Bodies: include: 3 Caetano. 2 Mercedes. 1 Van Hool.
Ops incl: local bus services, school contracts, private hire.
Livery: White/Blue/Water Green
Ticket system: Wayfarer 3

*SHEARER OF HUNTLY LTD

OLD TOLL ROAD, HUNTLY AB54 6JA.
Tel: 01466 792410
Fax: 01466 793926
Dlrs: James W Shearer, Irene E Shearer.
Fleet: 10 - 1 coach, 1 midicoach, 6 minibus, 2 mincoach
Chassis: 1 Dennis. 6 Ford Transit. 2 LDV. 1 Mercedes.

Bodies: incl: 1 UVG. 1 Wadham Stringer
Ops incl: school contracts, private hire.

SIMPSON'S COACHES

21 UNION STREET, ROSEHEARTY, FRASERBURGH AB43 7JQ
Tel: 01346 571610
Fax: 01346 571070
E-mail: info@simpsonscoaches.co.uk
Web site: www.simpsonscoaches.co.uk
Prop: Ron Simpson.
Fleet: 6 coach.
Chassis: 1 Iveco. 5 Volvo.
Bodies: 1 Beulas. 2 Berkhof. 3 Caetano.
Ops incl: excursions & tours, private hire, continental tours.
Livery: Silver/Blue.

ANGUS

*RIDDLER'S COACHES LIMITED

CAIRNIE LOAN, ARBROATH DD11 4DS
Tel: 01241 873464
Fax: 01241 873504
Dirs: C W Riddler, Mrs G M Riddler
Fleet: 6 coach.
Chassis: 6 Volvo.
Ops incl: excursions & tours, private hire

SIDLAW EXECUTIVE TRAVEL (SCOTLAND) LTD

LISHEEN, THE BRAE, AUCHTERHOUSE DD3 ORE
Tel: 01382 320280
Fax: 01382 320482
E-mail: travel@sidlaw.co.uk
Web site: www.sidlaw.co.uk
Dir: Bob Costello **Fleet Eng**: Jamie Costello
Fleet: 14 - 2 coach, 4 minicoach, 4 midicoach, 4 minicoach.
Chassis: 1 MAN. 13 Mercedes.
Ops incl: school contracts, excursions & tours, private hire.

ARGYLL & BUTE

BOWMAN'S COACHES (MULL) LTD

SCALLACASTLE, CRAIGNURE, ISLE OF MULL PA65 6BA.
Tel: 01680 812313.
Prop: A. Bowman, S. Bowman, I. Bowman, I. Bowman. **Gen Man**: A. Bowman.
Fleet: 12 coach.
Chassis: Bedford. Dennis. Ford. Leyland.
Bodies: Duple. Jonckheere. Plaxton.
Ops incl: local bus services, excursions & tours, private hire.
Livery: Cream/Red.
Ticket System: Setright, Almex.

CRAIG OF CAMPBELTOWN LTD

BENMHOR, CAMPBELTOWN PA28 6DN
Tel: 01586 552319.
Fax: 01586 552344
E-mail: d.halliday@westcoastmotors.co.uk
Web site: www.westcoastmotors.co.uk
Fleetname: West Coast Motors
Chmn/Man Dir: W G Craig **Dir**: C R Craig
Co Sec: J M Craig **Tran Man**: D M Halliday
Fleet Eng: D Martin
Fleet: 71 - 6 double-deck bus, 28 single-deck bus, 30 coach, 2 midibus, 3 midicoach, 1 minibus.
Chassis: 1 Bedford. 26 DAF. 17 Dennis. 1 Freight Rover. 5 Leyland. 1 MAN. 5 Mercedes. 5 Optare. 9 Volvo.
Bodies: 15 Alexander. 1 Ikarus. 1 Jonckheere. 1 Mellor. 1 Onyx. 5 Optare. 4 Park Royal. 13 Plaxton. 27 Van Hool. 2 Wright.
Ops incl: local bus services, school contracts, excursions & tours, private hire, express.
Livery: Multi-coloured
Ticket System: Wayfarer.

GARELOCHHEAD COACHES

WOODLEA GARAGE, MAIN ROAD, GARELOCHHEAD PA65 6BA
Tel: 01436 810200.
Fax: 01436 810050.
Prop: Stuart McQueen

HIGHLAND HERITAGE COACH TOURS

CENTRAL ADMINISTRATION OFFICE, DALMALLY PA33 1AY
Tel: 01838 200453
E-mail: info@highlandheritage.co.uk
Web site: www.highlandheritage.co.uk
Man Dir: Ian Cleaver
Fleet: 15 coach.
Chassis: 15 Volvo.
Bodies: 15 Van Hool.
Ops incl: excursions & tours
Livery: Gold

HIGHLAND ROVER COACHES

TAYNUILT PA35 1HT
Tel/Fax: 01866 822612
E-mail: angus.douglas@freeuk.com
Prop: Angus Douglas.
Fleet: 3 - 1 coach, 2 minibus.
Chassis: 1 Ford. 2 Mercedes.
Bodies: 2 Mercedes. 1 other
Ops incl: local bus services, school contracts, private hire
Ticket system: Setright.

Symbol	Meaning
A/c	Air conditioning
	Vehicles suitable for disabled
	Coach(es) with galley facilities
wc	Coach(es) with toilet facilities
	Seat belt-fitted vehicles
R	Recovery service available (not 24 hr)
R24	24hr recovery service
	Replacement vehicle available
T	Toilet-drop facilities available
	Vintage vehicle(s) available
	Open top vehicle(s)

Scottish Operators

McCOLLS OF ARGYLL LTD

MCCOLLS HOTEL, WEST BAY,
DUNOON PA23 7HN
Tel: 01369 702764
Fax: 01369 702764
Dir: David Wilkinson
Fleet: 8 coach
Chassis: 8 Iveco
Bodies: 8 Beulas
Ops incl: excursions & tours

OBAN & DISTRICT BUSES LTD

GLENGALLAN ROAD, OBAN
PA34 4HH
Tel: 01631 570500
Fax: 01631 570311
E-mail: enquiries@obanbuses.co.uk
Web site: www.obanbuses.co.uk
Fleetname: Oban & District.
Man Dir: Colin Craig **Dir**: W. G. Craig
Depot Controllers: David Hannah, Donnie McDougal **Workshop Supervisor**: Iain McDonald
Fleet: 23 - 16 single-deck bus, 2 coach, 2 midicoach, 2 minibus, 1 midibus.
Chassis: 4 DAF. 3 Dennis. 2 LDV. 10 Leyland. 2 Mercedes. 1 Optare. 1 Volvo.
Bodies: 10 Alexander. 1 Optare. 5 Plaxton. 4 Wright. 1 Onyx. 2 KL Conversion.
Ops incl: local bus services, school contracts, private hire, express.
Livery: Red/Blue/Honeysuckle
Ticket System: Wayfarer 3
Subsidiary of West Coast Motors

L. F STEWART & SON LTD

DALAYICH, BY TAYNUILT PA35 1HN.
Tel: 01866 833342.
Fax: 01866 833237.
Dirs: R. Maceachen, M. A. Stewart.
Fleet: 4 - 2 coach, 2 minibus.
Chassis: 2 Mercedes. 2 Volvo.
Bodies: 1 Plaxton. 2 Reeve Burgess. 1 Berkhof.
Ops incl: local bus services, school contracts, private hire.
Livery: Red/White/Yellow.

BORDERS

*AUSTIN TRAVEL

STATION ROAD, EARLSTON
TD4 6BZ
Tel: 01896 849360
Fax: 01896 849623
E-mail: austin@travel.gbtbroadband.co.uk
Web site: www.scotlnetours.co.uk
Ptnrs: Douglas Austin, Barry Austin.
Fleet: 7 - 4 coach, 2 midicoach, 1 minicoach.
Chassis: 2 Bova. 3 Mercedes. 2 Setra.
Bodies: 2 Bova. 2 Esker. 2 Setra. 1 other.
Ops incl: school contracts, excursions & tours, private hire, continental tours.
Livery: Pearlescent white

JAMES FRENCH & SON

THE GARAGE, COLDINGHAM, EYEMOUTH TD14 5NS.
Tel/Fax: 01890 771283.

Fleet: 12 coach.
Chassis: Volvo.
Bodies: Van Hool.
Ops incl: excursions & tours.

*MUNRO'S OF JEDBURGH LTD

OAKVALE GARAGE, BONGATE,
JEDBURGH TD8 6DU
Tel: 01835 862253
Fax: 01835 864297
E-mail: info@munrosofjedburgh.co.uk
Web site: www.munrosofjedburgh.co.uk
Co Sec: Ewan Farish **Ops Dir**: Donald Cameron **Eng Dir**: Bruce Campbell
Fleet: 43 - 15 double-deck bus, 7 coach, 18 midibus, 1 midicoach, 2 minicoach.
Chassis: 8 DAF. 9 Dennis. 2 Iveco. 7 MAN. 8 Mercedes. 7 Optare. 2 Plaxton Primo.
Bodies: 4 Alexander. 2 Crest. 1 Ikarus. 7 Marshall/MCV. 7 Optare. 10 Plaxton. 7 Van Hool. 5 other.
Ops incl: local bus services, school contracts, private hire.
Livery: White/Red stripe
Ticket System: Wayfarer 2

PERRYMAN BUSES

WOODBINE GARAGE, BURNMOUTH
TD14 5SL.
Tel: 01890 781533.
Fax: 01890 750481.
Web site: www.perrymansbuses.com
Man Dir: R. Perryman.
Fleet: 35 coach
Chassis: incl: 4 Volvo
Bodies: incl: 1 Wright
Ops incl: local bus services, private hire

*TELFORD'S COACHES LTD

I GEORGE STREET,
NEWCASTLETON TD9 0RA
Tel/Fax: 01387 375677
Recovery: 07711 280475
E-mail: info@telfordscoaches.com
Web site: www.telfordscoaches.com
Man Dir: Alistair S Telford **Ch Eng**: Rod Swan **Co Sec**: Shelagh Nixon
Fleet: 14 - 1 single-deck bus, 7 coach, 1 midibus, 5 minicoach.
Chassis: 1 Ford. 6 Mercedes. 1 Scania. 6 Volvo.
Bodies: 1 Jonckheere. 3 Mercedes-Benz. 9 Plaxton. 1 Van Hool.
Ops incl: local bus services, school contracts, excursions & tours, private hire, continental tours.
Livery: White with Blue vinyls
Ticket system: Almex

CLACKMANNANSHIRE

M. LINE INTERNATIONAL COACHES

THE COACH HOUSE, RIVERBANK,
ALLOA FK10 1NT.
Tel: 01259 212802.
Fax: 01259 213372.
E-mail: info@m-line.co.uk
Web Site: www.m-line.co.uk
Ops Man: T. Matchett.
Dir/Fleet Eng: C. W. Christie.

Fleet: 16 - 7 double-deck bus, 5 coach, 4 double-deck coach.
Chassis: 2 Bova. 2 Iveco. 4 Neoplan. 2 Volvo.
Bodies: 6 Alexander. 2 Bova. 4 Neoplan.
Ops incl: local bus services, school contracts, excursions & tours, private hire, continental tours.
Livery: Metallic Rainbow.
Ticket System: Almex.

MACKIE'S COACHES

32 GLASSHOUSE LOAN, ALLOA
FK10 1PE.
Tel: 01259 216180
Fax: 01259 217508
E-mail: enquiries@mackiescoaches.com
Web site: www.mackiescoaches.com
Fleet: 18 - single-deck bus, coach
Chassis: 3 Bova. 15 Volvo.
Bodies: 3 Bova. 2 Caetano. 1 Duple. 2 Jonckheere. 5 Van Hool. 5 Wright.
Ops incl: local bus services, school contracts, excursions & tours, private hire, continental tours.
Livery: White/Brown/Beige.
Ticket System: Wayfarer.

WOODS COACHES

2 GOLF VIEW, TILLICOULTRY
FK13 6DH
Tel: 01259 751753
Fax: 01259 751824
Fax: 07836 662919
E-mail: jwcoaches@btinternet.com
Web site: www.woodscoaches.net
Owner: James Woods
Ops Man: John Woods.
Fleet: 10 - coach, midicoach, minicoach
Chassis: 2 Bova, 8 Mercedes.
Bodies: 2 Bova. 2 Esker. 6 Mercedes.
Ops incl: school contracts, excursions & tours, private hire
Livery: Silver

DUMFRIES & GALLOWAY

ANDERSON'S COACHES

BLUE BELL HILL, SKIPPERS,
LANGHOLM DG13 0LH.
Tel: 01387 380553.
Fax: 01387 380553.
Ptnrs: I. R. Anderson, K. Irving.
Ch Eng: C. Anderson.
Fleet: 6 - 2 single-deck bus, 2 minibus, 2 minicoach.
Chassis: 1 AEC. 3 Ford Transit. 1 Freight Rover. 1 Leyland.
Bodies: 2 Plaxton. 1 Robin Hood. 1 PMT. 1 N/S Transit.
Ops incl: local bus services, school contracts, private hire.
Livery: Red/Orange/Yellow stripe.
Ticket System: Almex.

R. K. ARMSTRONG COACHES wc 🎟 A/c R24
THE PARK, BRIDGE-OF-DEE,
CASTLE DOUGLAS DG7 1TR.
Tel: 01556 503391
Fax: 01556 504656
Recovery: 01556 503391
E-mail: rkarmstrong8@aol.com
Web site: www.armstrongcoaches.com
Prop: R. K. Armstrong.
Fleet: 14 - 1 single-deck bus, 5 coach, 4 midibus, 2 midicoach, 1 minibus, 1 minicoach.
Chassis: 5 mercedes. 2 Optare. 1 Scania. 1 Toyota. 2 Volvo.
Bodies: 1 Jonckheere. 1 Leyland. 5 Mercedes. 2 Optare. 1 Plaxton. 2 Reeve Burgess. 1 Van Hool.
Ops incl: local bus services, school contracts, excursions and tours, private hire, continental tours.

WILLIAM BROWNRIGG 🎟
THE GARAGE, THORNHILL
DG3 5LZ.
Tel/Fax: 01848 330203
Fleet: 9 - 4 coach, 5 minibus
Chassis: Bova. Leyland. Mercedes. Scania. Volvo.
Bodies: Bova. Duple. Mercedes. Plaxton. Reeve Burgess.
Ops incl: local bus services, school contracts, excursions and tours, private hire
Livery: Orange/White

*JAMES GIBSON & SON
16 CHURCH STREET, MOFFAT
DG10 9HD
Tel: 01683 220200
Fax: 01683 221700
E-mail: enquiries@gibsonscoaches.co.uk
Web site: www.gibsonscoaches.co.uk
Fleet: 8 coach
Chassis: 5 Setra. 3 Volvo.
Bodies: 5 Setra. 3 Van Hool.
Ops incl: school contracts, excursions & tours, private hire, continental tours.
Livery: Red/Maroon/Orange

JAMES KING COACHES 🎟 wc
36 MAIN STREET, KIRKCOWAN,
NEWTON STEWART DG8 0HG
Tel: 01671 830284
Fax: 01671 830499
E-mail: enquiries@kingscoachhire.com
Fleet: 25 - 3 single-deck bus, 11 coach, 4 midibus, 7 midicoach.
Chassis: 9 Mercedes. 3 Optare. 13 Volvo.
Bodies: 2 East Lancs. 2 Jonckheere. 3 Optare. 6 Plaxton. 9 Van Hool. 3 other.
Ops incl: local bus services, school contracts, excursions & tours, private hire.

KIWI LUXURY TRAVEL wc 🎟 A/c
80 QUEEN STREET, NEWTON STEWART DG8 6JL
Tel: 01671 404294
Fax: 01671 403310
E-mail: kiwitravel@btconnect.com
Web site: www.kiwitravelltd.co.uk
Dirs: Ian Allison, Janet Allison
Fleet: 4 - 3 coach, 1 minicoach
Chassis: incl: 3 Volvo
Bodies: incl: 1 Caetano.
Ops incl: local bus services, school contracts, excursions & tours, private hire.

MacEWAN'S COACH SERVICES 🎟 wc A/c
JOHNFIELD, AMISFIELD, DUMFRIES DG1 3LS
Tel: 01387 256533
Fax: 01387 711123
Prop: John MacEwan
Ch Eng: Peter Maxwell
Fleet: 65 - 5 double-deck, 22 single-deck bus, 9 coach, 1 double-deck coach, 12 midibus, 4 midicoach, 12 minibus
Chassis: 1 AEC. 2 Bedford. 1 Bristol. 1 DAF. 3 Dennis. 3 Ford Transit. 1 Iveco. 4 LDV. 2 Leyland. 5 MAN. 5 MCW. 18 Mercedes. 3 Optare. 5 Scania. 2 Transbus. 9 Volvo.
Bodies: 10 Alexander. 2 Autobus. 2 Duple. 1 ECW. 1 East Lancs. 1 Irizar. 1 Jonckheere. 4 LDV. 4 Marshall/MCV. 5 MCW. 3 Optare. 17 Plaxton. 1 Crystal. 2 Drinkwater. 2 Transbus. 1 Van Hool. 3 Wright. 1 DAB. 2 Montano.
Ops incl: local bus services, school contracts
Livery: White/Red/Blue
Ticket system: ERG Transit 400

MCCULLOCH AND SON ♿ 🎟 wc A/c ✏
MAIN ROAD, STONEYKIRK, STRANRAER DG9 9DH.
Tel/Fax: 01776 830236.
E-mail: mcculloch.coaches@virgin.net
Fleetname: McCulloch Coaches
Ptnrs: D F McCulloch, E A McCulloch
Fleet: 8 - incl: 1 single-deck bus, 3 coach, 1 midibus, 1 midicoach, 1 minicoach.
Chassis: 1 Bedford. 4 Mercedes. 2 Optare. 3 Volvo.
Bodies: 1 Caetano. 1 Duple. 2 Optare. 4 Plaxton.
Ops incl: local bus services, excursions & tours, school contracts, private hire
Livery: White/Blue lettering
Ticket System: Ticket books

DUNDEE CITY

FISHERS TOURS wc 🎟 A/c ✏
MID CRAIGIE TRADING ESTATE, MID CRAIGIE ROAD, DUNDEE DD1 5EP
Tel/Fax: 01382 455177
E-Mail: fisherstours@btconnect.com
Web site: www.fisherstours.co.uk
Ptnrs: James Cosgrove, Catherine Cosgrove
Fleet: 16 - 3 single-deck bus (70seat), 11 coach, 1 midicoach, 1 midibus, 2 minibus.
Chassis: 3 Iveco. 7 Leyland. 4 Mercedes. 2 Volvo.
Bodies: 1 Beulas. 2 ECW. 1 Marshall. 3 Mercedes. 1 Optare. 6 Plaxton. 2 Van Hool.
Ops incl: school contracts, excursions & tours, private hire, continental tours.
Livery: White/Blue/Turquoise/Yellow.

SIDLAW EXECUTIVE TRAVEL (SCOTLAND) LTD ♿ 🎟 wc 🍽 A/c
LISHEEN, THE BRAE, AUCHTERHOUSE DD3 0RE
Tel: 01382 320280
Fax: 01382 320482
E-mail: travel@sidlaw.co.uk
Web site: www.sidlaw.co.uk
Dir: Bob Costello **Fleet Eng:** Jamie Costello
Fleet: 14 - 2 coach, 4 minicoach, 4 midicoach, 4 minicoach.
Chassis: 1 MAN. 13 Mercedes.
Ops incl: school contracts, excursions & tours, private hire.

*STRATHTAY SCOTTISH OMNIBUSES LTD ♿ wc 🎟 T
SEAGATE BUS STATION, DUNDEE DD1 2HR.
Tel: 01382 228345
Fax: 01382 202267
E-mail: eastscotland@stagecoachbus.com
Web site: www.stagecoachbus.com
Fleet Name: Stagecoach Strathtay
Man Dir: Doug Fleming **Ops Dir:** Steve Walker **Eng Dir:** Sandy Bryden
Assist Eng Dir: Tom Robertson **Ops Man:** Martin Hall **Depot Eng:** Alan Hughes
Fleet: 154 - 40 double-deck bus, 31 single-deck bus, 15 coach, 18 midibus, 50 minibus.
Chassis: 22 Dennis. 24 Leyland. 30 Mercedes. 17 Optare. 3 Renault. 58 Volvo.
Bodies: 58 Alexander. 33 East Lancs. 13 Northern Counties. 17 Optare. 18 Plaxton. 17 Wright. 3 Other.
Ops incl: local bus services, school contracts, excursions & tours, private hire, express.
Livery: Stagecoach.
Ticket System: Wayfarer 3

TRAVEL DUNDEE ♿ 🎟 wc T
44-48 EAST DOCK STREET, DUNDEE DD1 3JS
Tel: 01382 201121
Fax: 01382 201997
E-mail: mailbox@traveldundee.co.uk
Web site: www.traveldundee.co.uk
Man Dir: James Lee **Traff Man:** William Murphy **Ch Eng:** Frank Sheach
Business Man: Elsie Turbyne
Fleet: 127 - 18 double-deck, 88 single-deck, 19 coach, 2 double-deck coach
Chassis: 7 Dennis. 2 Leyland. 7 Mercedes. 12 Optare. 6 Scania. 93 Volvo.
Bodies: 3 East Lancs. 2 Leyland. 3 Mercedes. 12 Optare. 17 Plaxton. 90 Wright.
Ops incl: local bus services, school contracts, excursions & tours, private hire.
Livery: Travel Dundee/Travel Greyhound (Part of the National Express Group)

A/c	Air conditioning	
♿	Vehicles suitable for disabled	
🍽	Coach(es) with galley facilities	
wc	Coach(es) with toilet facilities	
🎟	Seat belt-fitted vehicles	
R	Recovery service available (not 24 hr)	
R24	24hr recovery service	
✏	Replacement vehicle available	
T	Toilet-drop facilities available	
	Vintage vehicle(s) available	
	Open top vehicle(s)	

Scottish Operators

EAST AYRSHIRE

LIDDELL'S COACHES
1 MAUCHLINE ROAD, AUCHINLECK KA18 2BJ.
Tel: 01290 424300/420717.
Fax: 01290 425637.
Prop: J. Liddell. **Ch Eng**: J. Quinn. **Co Sec**: Ms J. Samson. **Ops Man**: Ms M. Milroy.
Fleet: 24 - 8 double-deck bus, 10 coach, 4 midicoach, 2 minibus.
Chassis: 1 Bova. 3 DAF. 2 Dodge. 2 Freight Rover. 10 Leyland. 6 Volvo.
Bodies: 8 Alexander. 1 Bova. 1 Caetano. 3 Duple. 1 ECW. 1 East Lancs. 2 Jonckheere. 4 Plaxton. 2 Reeve Burgess. 1 Wright.
Ops incl: local bus services, school contracts, excursions & tours, private hire, express.
Livery: White with Brown/Orange/Lemon stripes.
Ticket System: Setright.

ROWE & TUDHOPE
WEST HILLHEAD, FARM ROAD, KILMARNOCK KA3 1PH
Tel: 01563 525631
Fax: 01563 571489
E-mail: geo.rowe@fsmail.net
Web site: www.roweandtudhope.com
Dir: George Rowe
Fleet: 22 - 1 double-deck bus, 3 single-deck bus, 12 coach, 2 midibus, 2 midicoach, 2 minicoach.
Chassis: 6 Dennis. 2 Ford Transit. 3 Leyland. 4 Mercedes. 2 Scania. 5 Volvo.
Bodies: 10 Alexander. 1 Irizar. 3 Jonckheere. 6 Plaxton. 2 other.
Ops incl: local bus services, school contracts, exursions & tours, private hire.
Livery: White/Blue flag
Ticket system: Wayfarer

EAST LOTHIAN

EVE CARS & COACHES
SPOTT ROAD, DUNBAR EH42 1RR.
Tel: 01368 865500.
Fax: 01368 865400.
Web site: www.eveinfo.co.uk
Ptnrs: Gary Scougall, Vona Scougall.

EAST RENFREWSHIRE

HENRY CRAWFORD COACHES LTD
SHILFORD MILL, NEILSTON, GLASGOW G78 3BA
Tel: 01505 850456
Fax: 01505 850479
E-mail: henrycrawford@talk21.com
Web site: www.henrycrawfordcoaches.co.uk
Ops Man: James Crawford(**Dir**)
Ch Eng: John Crawford(**Dir**)
Co Sec: Isobel Crawford(**Dir**)
Fleet: 26 - 21 coach, 5 minicoach.

Chassis: 1 Bova. 2 Leyland. 5 Mercedes. 18 Volvo.
Bodies: 1 Bova. 2 Duple. 1 Indcar. 1 Optare. 3 Plaxton. 16 Van Hool. 2 other.
Ops incl: private hire, school contracts.
Livery: White/Red

SOUTHERN COACHES (NM) LTD
LOCHLIBO ROAD, BARRHEAD G78 1LF.
Tel: 0141-881 1147.
Fax: 0141 881 1148.
E-mail: reservations@southern-coaches.co.uk.
Web site: southern-coaches.co.uk
Dirs: R. Wallace, D. Wallace, Mary Wallace.
Fleet: 19 - 17 coach, 2 minicoach.
Chassis: 2 DAF. 2 Toyota. 15 Volvo.
Bodies: 2 Caetano. 1 Jonckheere. 8 Plaxton. 8 Van Hool. 1 Ikarus.
Ops incl: school contracts, excursions & tours, private hire, express.
Livery: Cream/Blue/Orange.

EDINBURGH, CITY OF

AAA COACHES
UNIT 7, RAW CAMPS INDUSTRIAL ESTATE, KIRKNEWTON EH27 8DF
Tel: 01506 883000
Fax: 01506 884000
E-mail: aaacoaches@hotmail.com
Web site: www.aaacoaches.co.uk
Man Dir: Alan Sutherland
Fleet: 15 - 9 single-deck bus, 3 midibus, 3 minibus.
Chassis: 1 Dennis. 3 Ford. 2 Ford Transit. 1 LDV. 3 Mercedes. 2 Scania. 7 Volvo.
Bodies: 5 Jonckheere. 1 Leyland. 3 Mercedes. 2 Plaxton. 2 Sunsundegui. 2 Van Hool.
Ops incl: school contracts, excursions & tours, private hire
Livery: White with Highland scene.

*BROWNS OF EDINBURGH
DROVERS ROAD, EAST MAINS INDUSTRIAL ESTATE, BROXBURN EH52 5ND
Tel: 01506 857201
Fax: 01506 859096
E-mail: enquiries@brownscoaches.co.uk.
Web site: www.brownscoaches.co.uk.
Man Dir: Ronnie Brown
Fleet: 16 - 12 single-deck coach, 1 double-deck coach, 3 minicoach
Chassis: 3 Mercedes. 13 Volvo.
Bodies: 4 Berkhof. 9 Van Hool. 3 other.
Ops incl: excursions & tours, private hire, continental tours.
Livery: White/Blue

CITYCIRCLE UK LTD
BUTLERFIELD INDUSTRIAL ESTATE, BONNYRIGG EH19 3JQ
Tel: 01875 822862
Fax: 01875 822762
Web site: www.citycircleuk.com
Dir: Neil Pegg
Fleet: 5 coach.

Chassis/Bodies: 4 Setra. 1 Volvo.
Ops incl: private hire
(Subsidiary of City Circle, London)

*CITY SIGHTSEEING EDINBURGH LTD
ANNANDALE STREET, EDINBURGH EH7 4AZ
Tel: 0131 220 0770
E-mail: info@edinburghtour.com
Web site: www.edinburghtour.com
Fleet name: City Sightseeing
Ch Exec: Neil Renilson **Fin Dir**: Norman Strachan **Ops Dir**: William Campbell **Eng Dir**: William Devlin **Mktg Dir**: Iain Coupar
Fleet: 12 open-top bus
Chassis: 7 Dennis. 5 Leyland.
Bodies: 8 Alexander. 4 Plaxton.
Ops incl: excursions & tours
Livery: Red
Ticket system: Casio

*EDINBURGH BUS TOURS
ANNANDALE STREET, EDINBURGH EH7 4AZ
Tel: 0131 220 0770
E-mail: info@edinburghtour.com
Web site: www.edinburghtour.com
Ch Exec: Neil Renilson
Fin Dir: Norman Strachan **Ops Dir**: William Campbell **Eng Dir**: William Devlin
Mktg Dir: Iain Coupar
Fleet: 15 open-top bus
Chassis: 15 Leyland
Bodies: 12 Alexander. 3 Roe.
Livery: Cream/Green
Ticket system: Casio

FAIRWAY TRAVEL
6 BRIARBANK TERRACE, EDINBURGH EH11 1ST.
Tel: 0131 467 6717.
Fax: 0131 467 6717.
E-mail: davy@fairwaytravel.freeserve
Web site: www.fairwaytravel.co.uk
Prop: D. Innes.
Fleet: 4 - 1 coach, 2 midicoach, 1 minibus.
Chassis: 1 DAF. 1 Setra. 2 Toyota.
Bodies: 2 Caetano. 1 Leyland. 1 Setra.
Ops incl: school contracts, excursions & tours, private hire, continental tours.
Livery: Blue and Red on White.

FIRST IN EDINBURGH LTD
CARMUIRS HOUSE, 300 STIRLING ROAD, LARBERT FK5 3NJ
Tel: 01324 602200
Fax: 01324 611287
Web site: www.firstgroup.com
Man Dir: Brian Juffs **Ops Dir**: Juliette Turner
Eng Dir: Andrew Green **Fin Dir**: David Stewart
Fleet: 439 - 153 double-deck bus, 202 single-deck bus, 5 coach, 78 midibus, 1 minibus.
Chassis: 1 BMC. 78 Dennis. 21 Leyland. 2 MCW. 32 Mercedes. 188 Scania. 117 Volvo.
Bodies: 103 Alexander. 1 BMC. 24 East Lancs. 15 Northern Counties. 23 Optare. 80 Plaxton. 4 Transbus. 189 Wright.
Ops incl: local bus services
Livery: Pink/Purple/White

LIBERTON TRAVEL
🏷 wc 🍴 A/c

17-29 ENGINE ROAD, LOANHEAD
EH20 9RF
Tel: 0131 440 4400
Fax: 0131 448 0008
E-mail: sales@libertontravel.co.uk
Dirs: Iain Smith, Alan Boyd
Fleet: 10 - 7 coach, 2 minibus, 1 minicoach.
Chassis: 1 Dennis. 1 Ford Transit. 1 Freight Rover. 1 Mercedes. 6 Volvo.
Bodies: 1 Caetano. 1 Marcopolo. 4 Plaxton.
Ops incl: school contracts, excursions & tours, private hire.
Livery: White

*LOTHIAN BUSES PLC ♿
ANNANDALE STREET, EDINBURGH
EH7 4AZ
Tel: 0131 554 4494
Fax: 0131 554 3942
E-mail: mail@lothianbuses.co.uk
Web site: www.lothianbuses.co.uk
Ch Exec: Neil Renilson **Man Dir**: Ian Craig
Fin Dir: Norman Strachan **Ops Dir**: William Campbell **Eng Dir**: William Devlin **Mktg Dir**: Iain Coupar **Employee Dir**: Jim Dixon
Chmn: Pilmar Smith **Non Exec Dirs**: William Gallagher, Irene Kitson, A Ross, J Saren, A Guest, B Cox
Fleet: 680 - 545 double-deck bus, 135 single-deck bus.
Chassis: 280 Dennis. 96 Leyland. 5 Scania. 399 Volvo.
Bodies: 221 Alexander. 285 Plaxton. 169 Wright. 5 other.
Ops incl: local bus services.
Livery: Maroon/Red/White/Gold
Ticket system: Wayfarer 3

*MAC TOURS LTD 🚌 🚐
ANNANDALE STREET, EDINBURGH
EH7 4AZ
Tel: 0131 556 2244
E-mail: info@edinburghtour.com
Web site: www.edinburghtour.com
Ch Exec: Neil Renilson **Fin Dir**: Norman Strachan **Ops Dir**: William Campbell **Eng Dir**: William Devlin **Mktg Dir**: Iain Coupar
Fleet: 25 - 1 double-deck bus, 1 single-deck bus, 16 open-top bus, 6 midibus, 1 minibus.
Chassis: 14 AEC. 6 Dennis. 4 Leyland. 1 Mercedes.
Bodies: 8 Alexander. 14 Park Royal. 3 other.
Livery: Red/Cream
Ticket system: Wayfarer/Casio

*MAJESTIC TOURS EDINBURGH LTD 🚌
ANNANDALE STREET, EDINBURGH
EH7 4AZ
Tel: 0131 220 0770
E-mail: info@edinburghtour.com
Web site: www.edinburghtour.com
Ch Exec: Neil Renilson **Fin Dir**: Norman Strachan **Ops Dir**: William Campbell **Eng Dir**: William Devlin **Mktg Dir**: Iain Coupar
Fleet: 15 - 3 double-deck bus, 12 open-top bus.
Chassis: 6 AEC. 8 Leyland. 1 Volvo.
Bodies: 9 Alexander. 6 Park Royal.

Ops Incl: excursions & tours
Livery: Yellow/Blue
Ticket system: Casio

SCOTIA TRAVEL
🏷 wc 🍴 🔧 A/c T

ROSEBINE GARAGE, 29A MAIN STREET, COALTOWN,
GLENROTHES KY7 6HU
Tel: 0131 553 1455/01592 773900
Fax: 01592 775588
Recovery: 01592 773900
E-mail: enquiries@scotiatravel.co.uk
Web site: www.scotiatravel.co.uk
Prop: Alex Henderson
Fleet: 4 - 2 coach. 2 minicoach.
Chassis: 1 Bova. 1 DAF. 2 Mercedes.
Bodies: 1 Bova. 1 Reeve Burgess. 1 Van Hool.
Ops incl: private hire, excursions & tours, continental tours.
Livery: Blue/Gold/White.

EDINBURGH COACH LINES LTD
🏷 wc A/c R T

81 SALAMANDER STREET, LEITH, EDINBURGH EH6 7JZ
Tel: 0131 554 5413
Fax: 0131 553 3721
E-mail: enquiries@edinburghcoachlines.com.
Web site: www.edinburghcoachlines.com.
Dirs: Patric & Thomas Kavanagh **Gen Man**: Peter Fyvie **Traff Man**: John Blair
Bookings Cnsltnt: Jacquelie Bauld
Fleet: 25 - 20 coach, 4 midicoach, 1 minibus.
Chassis: 1 BMC. 1 MAN. 8 Mercedes. 14 Scania. 1 Volvo.
Bodies: 1 BMC. 1 Caetano. 1 Indcar. 8 Irizar. 4 Setra. 7 Van Hool.
Ops incl: excursions & tours, private hire, continental tours, school contracts.

FALKIRK

FIRST SCOTLAND EAST
♿ wc 🚌 🍴 🏷 R24 🔧 T

CARMUIRS HOUSE, 300 STIRLING ROAD, LARBERT FK1 5HP.
Tel: 01324 627175
Fax: 01324 611287.
Man Dir: B Juffs
Fleet: 481 - 176 double-deck bus, 247 single-deck bus, 22 coach, 36 midibus, 54 minibus.
Chassis: 91 Dennis. 91 Leyland. 12 Leyland-DAB. 37 MCW. 45 Mercedes. 23 Optare. 87 Scania. 95 Volvo.
Bodies: Alexander. East Lancs. MCW. Optare. Plaxton. Roe. Wright.
Ops incl: local bus services, school contracts, excursions & tours, private hire, express.
Livery: Cream/Blue or Cream/Green. New vehicles in First Group White/Blue/Magenta.
Ticket System: Wayfarer 3.

P. WOODS MINICOACHES
20 CALDER PLACE, HALLGLEN
FK1 2QQ.
Tel: 01324 613085.
Fax: 01324 717976.

FIFE

*FIFE SCOTTISH OMNIBUSES LTD
♿ 🚌 wc 🏷 T

GUTHRIE HOUSE, GLENFIELD INDUSTRIAL ESTATE, COWDENBEATH KY4 9HT
Tel: 01383 511911
Fax: 01383 516450
Recovery: 01383 511911
E-mail: eastscotland@stagecoachbus.com
Web site: www.stagecoachbus.com
Fleetname: Stagecoach in Fife
Man Dir: Doug Fleming **Ops Dir**: Steve Walker **Eng Dir**: Sandy Bryden
Assist Eng Dir: Tom Robertson
Fleet: 330 - 132 double-deck bus, 114 single-deck bus, 10 coach, 44 midibus, 34 minibus.
Chassis: 45 Dennis. 14 Leyland. 37 MAN. 19 Mercedes. 15 Optare. 10 Scania. 190 Volvo.
Bodies: 177 Alexander. 2 Jonckheere. 88 Northern Counties. 15 Optare. 48 Plaxton.
Ops incl: local bus services, school contracts, excursions & tours, private hire, express.
Livery: Stagecoach
Ticket System: ERG

KINGDOM COACHES
DEN WALK, METHIL KY8 3JH.
Tel: 01333 26109
Fleet: 3 coach.
Chassis: 2 DAF. 1 Ford.
Bodies: 2 Plaxton. 1 Van Hool.
Ops incl: private hire.
Livery: Yellow/White.

MOFFAT & WILLIAMSON LTD
♿ wc 🏷 🍴 A/c R 🔧

OLD RAILWAY YARD, ST FORT, NEWPORT-ON-TAY DD6 8RG
Tel: 01382 541159
Fax: 01382 541169
E-mail: enquiries@moffat-williamson.co.uk
Web site: www.moffat-williamson.co.uk
Gen Man: John Williamson **Ops Man**: Iain Williamson **Depot Man**: John Rodger
Fleet: 59 - 1 double-deck bus, 9 single-deck bus, 42 coach, 2 midibus, 3 midicoach, 2 minicoach.
Chassis: 1 DAF. 18 Dennis. 1 LDV. 1 Leyland. 4 MAN. 6 Mercedes. 5 Optare. 23 Volvo.

A/c	Air conditioning	🔧	Replacement vehicle available
♿	Vehicles suitable for disabled	T	Toilet-drop facilities available
🍴	Coach(es) with galley facilities	🚐	Vintage vehicle(s) available
wc	Coach(es) with toilet facilities	🚌	Open top vehicle(s)
🏷	Seat belt-fitted vehicles		
R	Recovery service available (not 24 hr)		
R24	24hr recovery service		

Scottish Operators

Ops incl: local bus services, school contracts, private hire, express.
Livery: Brown/Cream/Orange
Ticket System: Almex

RENNIES OF DUNFERMLINE LTD

WELLWOOD, DUNFERMLINE KY12 0PY
Tel: 01383 620600
Fax: 01383 620624
E-mail: gordon@rennies.co.uk
Web site: www.rennies.co.uk
Chmn: John Rennie **Gen Man**: Gordon Menzies **Tran Man**: Iain Robertson
Ch Eng: George Clark
Fleet: 52 - 20 double-deck bus, 25 coach, 3 midicoach, 4 minibus.
Chassis: 3 BMC. 10 Dennis. 1 Iveco. 1 LDV. 20 Leyland. 5 Mercedes. 12 Volvo.
Bodies: 1 Beulas. 3 BMC. 4 Caetano. 7 Jonckheere. 1 Mellor. 4 Mercedes. 4 Plaxton. 1 Sunsundegui. 4 Van Hool. 6 Wadham Stringer. 17 other.
Ops incl: local bus services, school contracts, excursions & tours, private hire, continental tours.
Livery: Blue/White.
Ticket system: Almex

*ST ANDREWS EXECUTIVE TRAVEL

UNIT 2, TOM STEWART LANE, ST ANDREWS KY16 8YB
Tel: 01334 470080
Fax: 01334 470081
E-mail: gordon@saxtravel.co.uk
Web Site: www.saxtravel.co.uk
Dir: Gordon Donaldson
Fleet: 8 - 2 coach, 6 midicoach.
Chassis/Bodies: 8 Mercedes
Ops incl: school contracts, excursions & tours, private hire.
Livery: Green/White

GLASGOW, CITY OF

*ALLANDER COACHES LTD

19 CLOBERFIELD INDUSTRIAL ESTATE, MILNGAVIE G62 7LN
Tel: 0141 956 5678
Fax: 0141 956 6669
E-mail: enquiries@allandertravel.co.uk
Web site: www.allandertravel.co.uk
Man Dir: J F Wilson **Dir**: E E Wilson
Ch Eng: G S Wilson **Co Sec**: M Brown
Ops Man: G F Wilson
Fleet: 26 - 3 double-deck bus, 3 single-deck bus, 18 coach, 2 midicoach.
Chassis: 16 Bova. 6 Dennis. 2 Mercedes. 2 Volvo.
Bodies: 16 Bova. 1 Esker. 2 Jonckheere. 2 Mercedes. 2 Wadham Stringer. 3 other.
Ops incl: excursions & tours, private hire, school contracts, continental tours.
Livery: Black/Gold/Orange.
Ticket system: Setright

*CITY SIGHTSEEING GLASGOW LTD

153 QUEEN STREET, GLASGOW G1 3BJ
Tel: 0141 204 0444
Fax: 0141 248 6582
Web site: www.scotguide.com
Dirs: A Pringle, Mrs C Pringle.
Fleet: 10 double-deck bus.
Chassis: 4 MCW. 6 Volvo.
Bodies: 6 Alexander. 4 East Lancs.
Ops incl: excursions & tours.
Livery: Red
Ticket system: Almex

DOIGS OF GLASGOW LTD

TRANSPORT HOUSE, SUMMER STREET, GLASGOW G40 3TB
Tel: 0141 554 5555
Fax: 0141 551 9000
E-mail: andy@doigs.com
Web site: www.doigs.com
Chmn/Man Dir: Andrew Forsyth
Co Sec: Iain Forsyth
Fleet: 15 - 1 double-deck bus, 1 single-deck bus, 1 articulated bus, 8 coach, 1 midicoach, 3 minicoach.
Chassis: incl: DAF. Dennis. LDV. Mercedes. Scania. 3 Volvo.
Bodies: 1 Caetano. 1 East Lancs. 7 Irizar. 1 Marcopolo. 2 Mercedes. 1 Optare. 3 Sunsundegui. 1 Wright.
Ops incl: school contracts, excursions & tours, private hire, continental tours.
Livery: Silver/Red lettering

FIRST GLASGOW

197 VICTORIA ROAD, GLASGOW G42 7AD.
Tel: 0141 423 6600
Fax: 0141 636 3228
Web Site: www.firstgroup.com.
Man Dir: Mark Savelli
Fleet: 953 - incl: double-deck bus, single-deck bus, minibus.
Chassis: 126 Dennis. 103 Leyland. 36 MCW. 85 Mercedes. 15 Optare. 130 Scania. 497 Volvo.
Bodies: Alexander. East Lancs. MCW. Optare. Plaxton. Wright.
Ops incl: local bus services.

NEIL MACKELLAIG

11 DUNSYRE PLACE, GLASGOW G23 5EB.
Tel: 0141 946 1895.
Prop: N. Mackellaig.
Fleet: 1 minicoach.
Chassis: Toyota. **Body**: Caetano.
Ops incl: school contracts, private hire.

*JOHN MORROW COACHES

18 ALBION INDUSTRIAL ESTATE, HALLEY STREET, YOKER, GLASGOW G13 4DJ
Tel: 0141 951 8888
Fax: 0141 952 6445
Prop: John Morrow.
Fleet: 15 - 1 single-deck bus, 2 coach, 11 midibus, 1 minicoach.
Bodies: 1 Caetano. 1 Leyland. 9 Mercedes. 2 Optare. 1 Plaxton. 1 Van Hool
Ops incl: local bus services, private hire,

school contracts, excursions & tours
Livery: Brown/Cream
Ticket system: Wayfarer 3

SCOTTISH CITYLINK COACHES LTD

BUCHANAN BUS STATION, KILLERMONT STREET, GLASGOW G2 3NP
Tel: 0141 352 4454
E-mail: info@citylink.co.uk
Web site: www.citylink.co.uk.
Ops incl: private hire, express.
Livery: Blue/yellow
Ticket system: Wayfarer

SELVEY'S COACHES

HILLCREST HOUSE, 33 HOWIESHILL ROAD, CAMBUSLANG G72 8PW.
Tel: 0141 641 1080.
Fax: 0141 641 2065.
Owner: A. G. Selvey.
Fleet: 8 - 5 coach, 2 midicoach, 1 minicoach.
Chassis: 3 Bedford. 2 Leyland. 1 Mercedes. 2 Volvo.
Bodies: 1 Duple. 1 Jonckheere. 1 Mercedes. 3 Plaxton.
Ops incl: excursions & tours, private hire, school contracts.
Livery: Maroon/Red/Yellow

HIGHLAND

BEAULY COACH HIRE

THE ROOKERY, WESTER BALBLAIR, BEAULY IV4 7BQ
Tel: 01463 782498
Fax: 01463 783298
E-mail: mhairicormack@aol.com
Prop: Gordon Cormack
Fleet: 4 - 2 midicoach, 2 minicoach
Chassis: Mercedes
Ops incl: school contracts, private hire

*BLUEBIRD BUSES LTD

6 BURNETT ROAD, LONGMAN INDUSTRIAL ESATE, INVERNESS IV1 1TF
Tel: 01463 239292
Fax: 01463 712338
Recovery: 01463 239292
E-mail: eastscotland@stagecoachbus.com
Web site: www.stagecoachbus.com
Fleetname: Stagecoach Inverness
Man Dir: Charlie Mullen **Ops Dir**: Robert Hall **Eng Dir**: John MacPherson
Ops Man: Scott Pearson **Depot Eng**: Callum MacGregor
Fleet: 63 - 7 double-deck bus, 12 single-deck bus, 9 coach, 27 midibus, 8 minibus.
Chassis: 27 Dennis. 1 Leyland. 3 MAN. 6 Mercedes. 2 Optare. 24 Volvo.
Bodies: 34 Alexander. 7 Jonckheere. 6 Northern Counties. 2 Optare. 14 Plaxton.
Ops incl: local bus services, school contracts, excursions & tours, private hire, express.
Livery: Stagecoach/Citylink/Megabus
Ticket System: Wayfarer TGX

*D&E COACHES LTD
♿ 🪑 wc 🍽 A/c R24 🔧 T
39 HENDERSON DRIVE,
INVERNESS IV1 1TR
Tel: 01463 222444
Fax: 01463 226700
Recovery: 07770 222612
E-mail: decoaches@aol.com
Web site: www.decoaches.co.uk
Dirs: Donald Mathieson,
Elizabeth Mathieson **Ops Man**: Willie Bell
Off Man: Gayle Pepples
Fleet: 19 - 2 single-deck bus, 6 coach,
3 midibus, 3 midicoach, 4 minibus,
1 minicoach.
Chassis: 2 Bova. 2 Dennis. 2 LDV.
7 Mercedes. 1 Toyota. 1 VW. 4 Volvo.
Bodies: 2 Alexander. 4 Berkhof. 2 Bova.
1 Caetano. 1 Esker. 1 Mercedes. 3 Plaxton.
2 Reeve Burgess. 2 Van Hool. 1 VW.
Ops incl: local bus services, school
contracts, private hire.
Livery: White on Black/Red
Ticket system: Thyron

DUNCAN MACLENNAN 🪑
HILL-SIDE, SHIELDAIG,
STRATHCARRON IV54 8XN
Tel/Fax: 01520 755239
Prop: Duncan MacLennan
Fleet: 2 - 1 midicoach, 1 minibus.
Chassis/bodies: 1 Ford. 1 Mercedes.
Ops incl: local bus services, school
contracts.

RAPSONS COACHES LTD
🍽 ♿ wc 🪑 🚌 A/c T
1 SEAFIELD ROAD, INVERNESS
IV1 1TN
Tel: 01463 710555
Fax: 01463 711488
E-mail: info@rapsons.co.uk
Web site: www.rapsons.co.uk
Chairman: Sandy Rapson **Man Dir**: John
Lornig **Ops Dir**: Neil MacDonald **Eng Dir**:
Russell Henderson **Comm Services Dir**:
Alistair Goodall.
Fleet: 250 - incl: 26 double-deck bus,
37 single-deck bus, 118 coach, 2 open-top
bus, 50 minibus.
Ops incl: local bus services, school
contracts, excursions & tours, private hire,
express.
Livery: Blue
Ticket System: Wayfarer 3

SHIEL BUSES 🪑 wc 🔧
BLAIN GARAGE, ACHARACLE
PH36 4JY.
Tel/Fax: 01967 431272.
E-mail: shiel.buses@virgin.net
Dir: Donnie MacGillivray.
Fleet: 10 - 4 single-deck coach, 6 midibus.
Chassis: 1 Ford Transit. 4 Mercedes.
4 Volvo.
Bodies: 2 Mercedes. 2 Plaxton. 2 Van Hool.
2 Onyx.
Ops incl: local bus services, school
contracts, private hire.
Livery: Red/White
Ticket system: Amex

SPA COACHES
wc 🪑 A/c R24 🔧 T
KINETTAS, STRATHPEFFER
IV14 9BH.
Tel: 01997 421311.
Fax: 01997 421983.
Web site: www.spacoaches.com
Prop: N. MacArthur.
Fleet: 28 - 6 double-deck bus, 13 coach,
5 midibus, 2 minibus.
Chassis: 1 DAF. 2 Ford Transit. 5 Mercedes.
14 Volvo.
Bodies: 1 Duple. 7 Alexander. 2 Caetano.
3 Jonckheere. 5 Plaxton. 6 Van Hool.
4 other.
Ops incl: local bus services, school
contracts, excursions & tours, private hire,
continental tours.
Livery: Orange/White.
Ticket System: Punch Tickets.

*GRAHAM URQUHART TRAVEL LTD
wc 🍽 🪑 A/c 🔧
28 MIDMILLS ROAD, INVERNESS
IV2 3NY
Tel: 01463 222292
Fax: 01463 238880
E-mail:
graham@urquharttravel.fsnet.co.uk
Web site:
www.grahamurquharttravel.co.uk
Dir: John G Urquhart **Sec**: John G Prant
Fleet: 8 - 4 coach, 2 midicoach, 2 minicoach
Chassis: 4 Mercedes. 4 Scania.
Bodies: 4 Irizar. 4 Esker.
Ops incl: excursions & tours, private hire.

*WHITE HEATHER TOURS
🪑
6 RIVERSIDE GROVE, LOCHY SIDE,
BANAVIE PH33 7RD
Tel/Fax: 01397 704704
E-mail:
enquiries@whitehertravel.co.uk
Web site:
www.whiteheathertravel.com
Prop: Adam A MacIntyre
Fleet: 5 midicoach.
Chassis/bodies: 2 Caetano. 3 Mercedes.
Ops incl: local bus service, school contracts,
excursions & tours, private hire.
Livery: Gold/Green/Red

INVERCLYDE

GILLEN'S COACHES LTD
UNIT 3, KINGSTON BUSINESS
PARK, PORT GLASGOW PA14 5DP
Tel/Fax: 01475 744618
Recovery: 07785 873299
Dir: Michael Gillen
Fleet: 14 - single-deck bus, midicoach,
minibus, minicoach
Ops incl: local bus services, excursions &
tours, private hire.
Livery: White
Ticket system: Wayfarer

GLEN COACHES LTD
wc 🍽 🪑 🔧 A/c
6 MACDOUGALL STREET,
GREENOCK PA15 2TG.
Tel: 01475 783399.
Fax: 01475 888446.
Owners: W. Wilson, Ms C. Wilson.
Fleet: 10 - 6 coach, 2 midibus, 1 midicoach,
1 minibus.
Chassis: 1 Iveco. 2 Mercedes. 6 Volvo.
Bodies: 1 Beulas. 1 Jonckheere. 2 Plaxton.
5 Van Hool.
Ops incl: local bus services, school
contracts, excursions & tours, private hire.
Livery: Blue/White.

MIDLOTHIAN

ALLAN'S GROUP
wc 🪑 A/c 🔧 T
NEWTONLOAN GARAGE,
GOREBRIDGE EH23 4LZ
Tel: 01875 820377.
Fax: 01875 822468
Recovery: 01875 820377
E-mail: allanscoaches@aol.co.uk
Web Site: www.allans-group.com
Dir: D W Allan **Ch Eng**: Neil Mitchell
Office Man: Mrs D Allan
Fleet: 14 - 9 single-deck bus, 5 midicoach.
Chassis: 5 Mercedes. 9 Scania.
Bodies: 5 Sitcar. 9 Van Hool.
Ops incl: school contracts, private hire.
Livery: Blue/Silver.

WILLIAM HUNTER
wc 🪑 A/c 🔧 T
OAKFIELD GARAGE, LOANHEAD
EH20 9AE
Tel: 0131 440 0704
Fax: 0131 448 2184
E-mail: sales@hunterscoaches.co.uk
Props: G I Hunter, W R Hunter.
Fleet: 14 - 12 coach, 2 minibus.
Chassis: 3 Toyota. 11 Volvo.
Bodies: 3 Caetano. 11 Van Hool.
Ops incl: school contracts, private hire.
Livery: Brown/Cream

FIRST SCOTLAND EAST
♿ wc 🚌 🍽 🪑 R 🔧 T
14-16 ESKBANK ROAD, DALKEITH
EH22 1HH.
Tel: 0131 663 1945.
Fax: 0131 660 3989.
Man Dir: Brian Juffs
Fleet: 481 - 176 double-deck bus,
247 single-deck bus, 22 coach, 36 minibus.
Chassis: 91 Dennis. 91 Leyland.12 Leyland-DAB. 37 MCW. 45 Mercedes. 23 Optare.
87 Scania. 95 Volvo.
Bodies: Alexander. East Lancs. MCW.
Optare. Plaxton. Roe. Wright.
Ops incl: local bus services, school
contracts, excursions & tours, private hire.
Livery: Cream/Yellow and Green, Light
Grey/Dark Blue and Magenta.
Ticket System: Wayfarer 3.
See also Edinburgh, Falkirk.

A/c	Air conditioning	🔧	Replacement vehicle available
♿	Vehicles suitable for disabled	T	Toilet-drop facilities available
🍽	Coach(es) with galley facilities	🚐	Vintage vehicle(s) available
wc	Coach(es) with toilet facilities	🚌	Open top vehicle(s)
🪑	Seat belt-fitted vehicles		
R	Recovery service available (not 24 hr)		
R24	24hr recovery service		

Scottish Operators

LIBERTON TRAVEL
See Edinburgh, City of

STANLEY MACKAY COACHES
See Edinburgh, City of

McKENDRY TRAVEL
RAMSAY COLLIERY, ENGINE ROAD, LOANHEAD EH20 9NP
Tel: 0131 440 1013
Fax: 0131 448 2160
E-mail: douglas.mckendry@virgin.net
Web site: www.mckendrycoaches.co.uk
Dir: Ann McKendry **Tran Man**: Stuart McCaw
Fleet: 15 - 1 double-deck bus, 12 coach, 2 minibus.
Chassis: 1 Dennis. 1 Ford Transit. 1 Freight Rover. 1 Leyland National. 4 Scania. 5 Volvo.
Bodies: 1 Caetano. 2 Jonckheere. 2 Plaxton. 5 Van Hool.
Ops incl: excursions & tours, private hire, school contracts.
Livery: White/Blue/Purple/Red vinyls

MORAY

*CENTRAL COACHES
CENTRAL GARAGE, CHURCH ROAD, KEITH AB55 5BR
Tel: 01542 882113
Fax: 01542 886945
E-mail: watson@centralcoaches.co.uk
Web site: www.centralcoaches.co.uk
Ptnrs: William Watson Smith, Veronica A Smith, William A Smith
Fleet: 8 - 6 coach, 2 minbus.
Chassis: 1 Bova. 2 DAF. 2 Mercedes. 3 Volvo.
Bodies: 1 Bova. 1 Caetano. 1 Jonckheere. 1 Leicester. 1 Mercedes. 2 Plaxton. 1 Van Hool.
Ops incl: local bus services, school contracts, private hire.
Livery: White/Red

MAYNES COACHES LTD   R24
4 MARCH ROAD WEST, BUCKIE AB56 4BU
Tel: 01542 831219
Fax: 01542 833572
E-mail: maynescoaches@talk21.com
Web site: www.maynes.co.uk
Man Dir: Gordon Mayne **Dirs**: Sandra Mayne, David Mayne (**Tran Man**), Kevin Mayne **Eng**: Mike Lapka
Co Sec: Jennifer Cowie
Fleet: 30 - 1 single-deck bus, 21 coach, 7 midicoach, 1 minicoach.
Chassis: 3 Bova. 1 Dennis. 1 Leyland. 3 MAN. 7 Mercedes. 13 Volvo.
Bodies: 4 Beluga. 2 Caetano. 3 Marcopolo. 1 Northern Counties. 4 Plaxton. 1 Reeve Burgess. 12 Van Hool.
Ops incl: local bus services, school contracts, excursions & tours, private hire, continental tours.
Livery: Blue/White/Gold

NORTH AYRSHIRE

CLYDE COAST COACHES LTD
55 MONTGOMERIE STREET, ARDROSSAN KA22 8HR
Tel: 01294 605454
Fax: 01294 605460
E-mail: enquiries@clydecoast.com
Web site: www.clydecoast.com
Dirs: Kenneth G McGregor, David H Frazer.
Fleet: 20 - 8 double-deck bus, 10 coach, 2 midibus.
Chassis: 1 Ford Transit. 8 Leyland. 1 VW. 10 Volvo.
Bodies: 3 Alexander. 5 ECW. 2 Sunsundegui. 8 Van Hool. 2 other.
Ops incl: excursions & tours, private hire, school contracts.
Livery: Silver Blue metallic

T & E DOCHERTY   R24   T
40 BANK STREET, IRVINE KA12 0LP
Tel/Recovery: 01294 278440
Fax: 01294 272510
E-mail: info@coach-hires.co.uk
Web Site: www.coach-hires.co.uk
Owner: Hugh Tait **Gen Man**: Tom Hamilton
Fleet: 31 - 2 double-deck bus, 6 single-deck bus, 11 coach, 4 minicoach, 8 minibus.
Chassis: 7 Bova. 1 Dodge. 2 LDV. 2 Leyland. 10 Mercedes. 2 Optare. 8 Volvo.
Bodies: 2 Alexander. 1 Autobus. 7 Bova. 1 Caetano. 1 East Lancs. 2 LDV. 2 Optare. 6 Plaxton. 1 Reeve Burgess. 2 Van Hool. 6 Wright. 1 Sitcar.
Ops incl: school contracts, excursions & tours, private hire, express, continental tours.
Livery: Buses: Blue/Cream. Coaches: Cream/Beige
Ticket System: Wayfarer 3.

MARBILL TRAVEL
HIGH MAINS GARAGE, MAINS ROAD, BEITH KA15 2AP
Tel: 01505 503367
Fax: 01505 504736
E-mail: marbill@btclick.com
Web site: www.marbillcoaches.com
Man Dir: Margaret Whiteman **Eng Dir**: David Barr **Ops Dir**: Connie Barr
Fleet: 66 - 26 double-deck bus, 20 single-deck bus, 18 coach, 2 minicoach.
Chassis: 2 Bova. 34 Leyland. 2 Mercedes. 28 Volvo
Bodies: 26 Alexander. 2 Bova. 25 Plaxton. 12 Van Hool. 1 Beluga.
Ops incl: school contracts, excursions & tours, private hire.

MILLPORT MOTORS LTD
16 BUTE TERRACE, MILLPORT KA28 0BA.
Tel: 01475 530555.
Fleet: 4 single-deck bus.
Chassis: 3 Leyland. 1 Volvo.
Ops incl: local bus services, private hire.
Livery: Blue/Cream.
Ticket System: Almex.

*SHUTTLE BUSES LTD
CALEDONIA HOUSE, LONGFORD AVENUE, KILWINNING KA13 6EX
Tel: 01294 550757
Fax: 01294 558822
E-mail: enquiries@shuttlebuses.co.uk
Web site: www.shuttlebuses.co.uk
Man Dir: David Granger
Fleet: 25 - 1 single-deck bus, 4 coach, 13 midibus, 3 midicoach, 2 minibus, 2 minicoach.
Chassis: 1 AEC. 5 Dennis. 3 Ford Transit. 2 Leyland. 6 Mercedes. 5 Optare. 1 Scania. 2 other.
Bodies: 3 Alexander. 1 Autobus. 1 Caetano. 2 Mercedes. 5 Optare. 3 Plaxton. 1 Reeve Burgess. 9 other.
Ops incl: local bus services, school contracts, private hire.
Livery: Yellow/White.
Ticket System: Wayfarer 3

NORTH LANARKSHIRE

A&C LUXURY COACHES
4 HILLHEAD AVENUE, MOTHERWELL ML1 4AQ
Tel: 01698 252652
Fax: 01698 259898
E-mail: enquiries@acluxurycoaches.co.uk
Web site: www.acluxurycoaches.co.uk
Prop: Alex Grenfell
Fleet: 6 - 3 coach, 2 midicoach, 1 minicoach.
Chassis: 3 Mercedes. 1 Neoplan. 2 Volvo.
Bodies: 1 Neoplan. 1 Plaxton. 1 Van Hool
Ops incl: school contracts, private hire, excursions & tours.

CANAVAN'S COACHES
CEDAR LODGE, COACH ROAD, KILSYTH G65 0DB.
Tel: 01236 822414.
Prop: M., G., H., & J. Canavan.
Ops incl: local bus services.

*DUNN'S COACHES
560 STIRLING ROAD, AIRDRIE ML6 7SS
Tel: 01236 722385
Fax: 01236 722385
E-mail: cdunn53@aol.com
Dirs: Fraser Dunn, Craig Dunn.
Fleet: 14 - double-deck bus, single-deck bus, coach, midibus.
Chassis: 3 Dennis. 1 Leyland. 1 Marshall. 2 Mercedes. 7 Volvo.
Bodies: 1 Marshall. 11 Plaxton. 1 Reeve Burgess.
Ops incl: local bus services, school contracts, private hire, express, continental tours.
Livery: White

ESSBEE COACHES (HIGHLANDS & ISLANDS)
7 HOLLANDHURST ROAD, GARTSHERRIE ML5 2EG

Tel: 01236 423621
Fax: 01236 433677
Man Dir: B. Smith. **Gen Man:** J. Kinnaird.
Ops Man: S. Stewart.
Fleet: 56 - 10 single-deck bus, 19 coach, 2 double-deck coach, 6 midicoach, 19 minibus.
Chassis: 2 DAF. 3 Ford Transit. 13 Leyland. 6 Leyland National. 21 Mercedes. 2 Neoplan. 10 Volvo.
Bodies: 7 Duple. 1 ECW. 1 Jonckheere. 6 Leyland National. 2 Neoplan. 15 Plaxton. 3 Autobus. 2 Crystals.
Ops incl: local bus services, school contracts, excursions & tours, private hire.
Livery: Red/Silver.
Ticket System: Wayfarer.

*GOLDEN EAGLE COACHES

MUIRHALL GARAGE, 197 MAIN STREET, SALSBURGH, BY SHOTTS ML7 4LS
Tel: 01698 870207
Fax: 01698 870217
E-mail: info@goldeneaglecoaches.com
Web site: www.goldeneaglecoaches.com
Dirs: Peter Irvine, Robert Irvine, Ishbel Irvine
Fleet: 17 - 4 single-deck bus, 13 coach.
Chassis: 1 Bova. 12 Volvo. 4 other.
Bodies: 1 Jonckheere. 4 MCW. 11 Van Hool. 1 other
Ops incl: private hire, excursions & tours, school contracts, .
Livery: White/Maroon/Gold

*HUTCHISON'S COACHES (OVERTOWN) LTD

5 CASTLEHILL ROAD, OVERTOWN, WISHAW ML2 0QS
Tel: 01698 372132
Fax: 01698 376933
E-mail: stewartanderson@hutchisoncoaches.co.uk
Web site: www.hutchisoncoaches.co.uk
Prop: Stewart Anderson
Fleet: 12 coach.
Chassis: 2 DAF. 4 Scania. 6 Volvo.
Bodies: 1 Berkhof. 4 Irizar. 7 Van Hool.
Ops incl: excursions & tours, private hire, continental tours
Livery: Silver/Blue/Red

IRVINE'S OF LAW

LAWMUIR ROAD, LAW ML8 5JB.
Tel: 01698 372452
Fax: 01698 376200
Prop: Peter Irvine **Man:** Gordon Graham
Ch Eng: Scott Fisher
Fleet: 40 - 14 double-deck bus, 13 coach, 13 midibus.
Chassis: DAF. Dennis. Optare. Scania. Volvo.
Bodies: Van Hool

Ops incl: local bus services, excursions & tours, school contracts, private hire, express, continental tours.
Livery: Red/Cream.
Ticket System: Wayfarer.

LONG'S COACHES LTD

157 MAIN STREET, SALSBURGH BY SHOTTS ML7 4LR.
Tel: 01698 870768.
Fax: 01698 870826.
E-mail: info@longscoaches.co.uk
Web site: www.longscoaches.co.uk
Dir: Peter I. Long **Co Sec:** Susan Long.
Fleet: 14 - 13 coach, 1 midicoach.
Chassis: 2 Bova. 12 Volvo.
Bodies: 2 Bova. 12 Van Hool.
Ops incl: excursions & tours, private hire, express, continental tours, school contracts.
Livery: Silver/Maroon.
Ticket System: Wayfarer.

MACPHAILS COACHES

409 HIGH STREET, NEWARTHILL, MOTHERWELL ML1 5SP
Tel: 01698 860249
Fax: 01698 861963
E-mail: macphailscoaches@hotmail.com
Web site: www.macphailscoaches.com
Dirs: Martin MacPhail, Henry MacPhail.
Fleet: 8 coach.
Chassis: 8 Volvo.
Bodies: 1 Plaxton. 7 Van Hool.
Ops incl: excursions & tours, private hire, continental tours.

MCKINDLESS EXPRESS

101 MAIN STREET, NEWMAINS, WISHAW ML2 9PP.
Tel: 01698 356990
Fax: 01698 356991
Web site: www.mckindlessgroup.co.uk
Prop: M. McKindless.
Ops Incl: local bus services, express, school contracts, private hire.
Chassis: includes King Long
Livery: Cream/Green
Ops incl: local bus sevices

*M.C.T. GROUP TRAVEL LTD

NETHAN STREET DEPOT, NETHAN STREET, MOTHERWELL ML1 3TF
Tel: 01698 253091
Fax: 01698 259208
Recovery: 01698 269301
E-mail: mctgrouptravel@hotmail.com
Web site: www.mctgrouptravel.com
Man Dir: Desmond Heenan **Dir:** Oswald Heenan **Fleet Eng:** Alan Bruce.
Fleet: 14 - 4 coach, 6 midicoach, 4 minicoach.
Chassis: 2 Mercedes. 8 Toyota. 4 Volvo.
Bodies: 6 Caetano. 1 Esker. 4 Jonckheere.

---

3 Mercedes.
Ops incl: excursions & tours, private hire, continental tours.
Livery: Turquoise/Silver

MILLER'S COACHES

22 WOODSIDE DRIVE, CALDERBANK, AIRDRIE ML6 9TN.
Tel: 01236 763671.
Owner: W. Miller. **Tran Man:** T. Miller.
Fleet: 12 - 8 coach, 4 minicoach.
Chassis: 8 Leyland. 4 Mercedes.
Bodies: 2 Alexander. 1 Mellor. 8 Plaxton. 1 Reeve Burgess.
Ops incl: local bus services, school contracts, private hire.
Livery: Black/White/Grey.

STEPEND COACHES

92 WADDELL AVENUE, GLENMAVIS, AIRDRIE ML6 0NZ.
Tel: 01236 760500.
Prop: S. Chapman.
Ops incl: local bus services.

*TRAMONTANA

CHAPELKNOWE ROAD, CARFIN, MOTHERWELL ML1 5LE
Tel: 01698 861790
Fax: 01698 860778
E-mail: wdt90@tiscali.co.uk
Prop: W D Telfer
Fleet: 6 coach
Chassis: 6 Volvo.
Bodies: 2 Caetano. 4 Plaxton.
Ops incl: private hire
Livery: White

ORKNEY

ORKNEY COACHES (FORMERLY PEACE'S COACHES)

SCOTTS ROAD, HATSTON INDUSTRIAL ESTATE, KIRKWALL KW15 1JY.
Tel: 01856 870555
Gen Man: Monty Smillie
Fleet: 42 - coach, midibus, midicoach, minibus.
Chassis: Bedford. Dennis. Ford. Mercedes. Optare. Toyota. Volvo.
Ops incl: local bus services, school contracts, excursions & tours, private hire. Subsidiary of Rapsons Coaches.

PERTH & KINROSS

*ABERFELDY MOTOR SERVICES

BURNSIDE GARAGE, ABERFELDY PH15 2DD
Tel: 01887 820433
Fax: 01887 829534

A/c	Air conditioning
	Vehicles suitable for disabled
	Coach(es) with galley facilities
wc	Coach(es) with toilet facilities
	Seat belt-fitted vehicles
R	Recovery service available (not 24 hr)
R24	24hr recovery service
	Replacement vehicle available
T	Toilet-drop facilities available
	Vintage vehicle(s) available
	Open top vehicle(s)

E-mail:
aberfeldymotors@btconnect.com
Web site:
www.aberfeldycoaches.co.uk
Prop: John Stewart **Co Sec**: Lynda Stewart
Ch Eng: David Matthew
Fleet: 9 - 7 coach, 1 midicoach, 1 minicoach.
Chassis: 2 Bova. 2 Mercedes. 5 Volvo.
Bodies: 2 Bova. 5 Van Hool. 2 other.
Ops incl: excursions & tours, private hire, continental tours, school contracts.
Livery: Blue

*CABER COACHES LTD

CHAPEL STREET GARAGE, ABERFELDY PH15 2AS
Tel: 01887 870090
Fax: 01887 829352
E-mail: cabercoaches@btinternet.com
Man Dir: Kenneth Carey **Sec**: Alexandre Carey
Fleet: 8 - 2 coach, 2 midicoach, 4 minibus.
Chassis: 2 Ford Transit. 2 LDV. 2 Mercedes.
Ops incl: local bus services, school contracts, private hire.
Livery: White
Ticket system: Almex

*DOCHERTY'S MIDLAND COACHES

PRIORY PARK, AUCHTERARDER PH3 1GB
Tel: 01764 662218
Fax: 01764 664228
E-mail: docherty.midland@virgin.net.
Web site:
www.dochertysmidlandcoaches.co.uk
Props: Jim & Edith Docherty **Ops**: Colin Docherty **Eng**: William Docherty
Fleet: 21 - 2 single-deck bus, 11 coach, 2 midibus, 4 midicoach, 1 minicoach, 1 vintage.
Chassis: 1 Leyland. 6 Mercedes. 1 Optare. 4 Scania. 9 Volvo.
Bodies: 2 Irizar. 1 Optare. 3 Plaxton. 1 UVG. 9 Van Hool. 2 Wright. 3 other.
Ops incl: local bus services, excursions & tours, school contracts, private hire
Livery: White/Black/Grey
Ticket System: Wayfarer

*EARNSIDE COACHES

GREENBANK ROAD, GLENFARG, PERTH PH2 9NW
Tel: 01577 830360
Fax: 01577 830599
E-mail: info@earnside.com.
Web site: www.earnside.com
Ptnrs: David Rutherford, Fiona Rutherford, Gary Rutherford, Elizabeth Rutherford
Fleet: 9 - 1 double-deck bus, 7 coach, 1 midibus.
Chassis: 1 DAF. 2 Leyland. 1 Renault. 1 Scania. 4 Volvo.
Bodies: 2 Berkhof. 1 Ikarus. 1 Irizar. 1 Leyland. 3 Plaxton. 1 other.
Ops incl: local bus services, school contracts, excursions & tours, private hire, continental tours.
Livery: Yellow/Maroon
Ticket system: Almex

*HIGHWAYMAN COACHES

STATION ROAD, ERROL PH2 7QB
Tel: 01821 642739
Fax: 01821 642683
E-mail: rng6@tesco.net.
Owner: Robin Gloag
Fleet: 12 - double-deck bus, coach, double-deck coach, midicoach, minicoach.
Chassis: 1 Bova. 2 Dennis. 3 Leyland. 1 Mercedes. 3 Neoplan. 1 Scania. 1 Toyota.
Bodies: 3 Alexander. 1 Bova. 1 Caetano. 1 Irizar. 1 Mercedes. 3 Neoplan. 1 Plaxton. 1 Van Hool.
Ops incl: school contracts, excursions & tours, private hire.
Livery: White/Blue lines

MEGABUS

10 DUNKELD ROAD, PERTH PH1 5TW
Tel: 01738 522456
Web site: www.megabus.com
Fleet: 60 - incl: 25 double-deck coach
Chassis: incl: 25 MAN
Bodies: incl: 25 MAN.
Ops incl: express.
Livery: Stagecoach (White/Blue/Orange/Red)/Megabus

PEGASUS TRAVEL LTD

28 INVERALMOND ROAD, PERTH PH1 3TW
Tel/Fax: 01738 444070
E-mail: enquiries@pegasus-travel.co.uk, info@pegasus-travel.co.uk
Web site: www.pegasus-travel.co.uk
Man Dir: Duncan Graham **Co Sec**: Mairi Graham **Ops Man**: Trevor White **Ch Eng**: Guy Batchelor
Fleet: 9 - 6 single-deck bus, 3 midicoach.
Chassis: 1 DAF. 1 Iveco. 3 Mercedes. 4 Volvo.
Bodies: 1 Autobus. 8 Plaxton.
Ops incl: local bus services, excursions & tours, private hire, school contracts
Livery: White

SMITH & SONS COACHES

THE COACH DEPOT, WOODSIDE, COUPAR ANGUS PH13 9LW
Tel: 01828 627310
Fax: 01828 628518
E-mail:
www.smithandsonscoaches.com
Prop: I. C. Smith. **Prop/Fleet Eng**: G. Smith.
Office Man: A. Osborne.
Prop/Traf Man: I. F. Smith.
Ops incl: local bus services, school contracts, excursions & tours, private hire, continental tours.
Livery: White/Orange.
Ticket System: Setright.

*STAGECOACH SCOTLAND LTD

RUTHENFIELD ROAD, INVERALMOND, PERTH PH1 3EE
Tel: 01738 629339
Fax: 01738 643264
Recovery: 01738 629339

E-mail:
eastscotland@stagecoachbus.com
Web site: www.stagecoachbus.com
Fleetname: Stagecoach Perth
Man Dir: Doug Fleming **Ops Dir**: Steve Walker **Eng Dir**: Sandy Bryden **Assist Eng Dir**: Tom Robertson **Ops Man**: Gus Beveridge **Depot Eng**: John Dick
Fleet: 77 - 16 double-deck bus, 25 single-deck bus, 6 coach, 10 midibus, 20 minibus.
Chassis: 10 Dennis. 16 Leyland. 16 MAN. 5 Mercedes. 15 Optare. 15 Volvo.
Bodies: 53 Alexander. 3 Jonckheere. 3 Neoplan. 15 Optare. 1 Plaxton. 2 Wright.
Ops incl: local bus services, school contracts, excursions & tours, private hire, express.
Livery: Stagecoach/Megabus
Ticket System: Wayfarer TGX

ELIZABETH YULE

STATION GARAGE, STATION ROAD, PITLOCHRY PH16 5AN
Tel: 01796 472290
Fax: 01796 474214
E-mail: info.elizabeth-yule@virgin.net
Web site:
www.perthshirecoaches.co.uk
Dirs: Elizabeth Yule, Alexandra M Bridges (Sandra)
Fleet: 9 - 5 coach, 3 midicoach, 1 minibus.
Chassis: 1 LDV. 3 Mercedes. 5 Volvo.
Ops incl: local bus services, school contracts, private hire.
Livery: White
Ticket System: Almex

RENFREWSHIRE

ALAN ARNOTT

16 TURNHILL CRESCENT, WEST FREELANDS, ERSKINE PA8 7AX
Fleetname: S & A Coaches, City Sprinter

ARRIVA SCOTLAND WEST

INCHINNAN, PAISLEY PA3
Web site: www.arrivabus.co.uk
Fleetnames: Arriva, SPT
Man Dir: Liz Esnouf
Ops Man: Murray Rogers
Fleet: 170 - incl double-deck bus, single-deck bus, midibus
Chassis: incl: Dennis, Leyland. Optare. Scania. Volvo.
Bodies: incl: Alexander, Northern Counties, Plaxton. Wright.
Ops incl: local bus services
Livery: Stone/Aquamarine

JAMES BURNS

24 GLENDOWER WAY, FOX BAR, PAISLEY PA2 0TH.
Fleetname: Green Line Coaches.

*CLASSIQUE SUN SALOON LUXURY COACHES

8 UNDERWOOD ROAD, PAISLEY PA3 1TD
Tel: 0141 889 4050
Fax: 0141 848 7616
Web site:

www.classiquecoaches.co.uk
Prop: David N Dean
Fleet: 9 coach.
Chassis: 1 AEC. 4 Leyland. 1 Setra. 3 Volvo.
Bodies: 1 Duple. 4 Plaxton. 2 Harrington. 1 Ramseier+Jenzer. 1 Setra.
Ops incl: excursions & tours, private hire, continental tours.
Livery: Various.

*MCGILLS BUS SERVICE LTD

99 EARNHILL ROAD, LARKFIELD INDUSTRIAL ESTATE PA16 0EQ
Tel: 01475 791720
Fax: 01475 711133
Ops incl: local bus services.
Livery: Blue/White

VIOLET GRAHAM COACHES

93 IVANHOE ROAD, FOX BAR, PAISLEY PA2 0LF.
Tel: 01505 349758.
Fax: 01505 349758.
Owner: V. Rosike.
Fleet: 2 midicoach.
Chassis: 1 Ford Transit. 1 Freight Rover.
Ops incl: school contracts, private hire.

SHETLAND

*R G JAMIESON & SON

MOARFIELD GARAGE, CULLIVOE, YELL ZE2 9DD
Tel: 01957 744214
Fax: 01957 744270
E-mail: rhjamieson@hotmail.com
Ptnr: Robert H Jamieson
Fleet: 5 - 1 single-deck bus, 2 coach, 2 minibus, 1 midicoach.
Chassis: 1 Dennis. 2 Ford Transit. 1 MAN. 2 Mercedes.
Bodies: incl: 1 Berkhof. 3 Plaxton
Ops incl: local bus services, school contracts, excursions & tours, private hire, continental tours.
Livery: White/Blue (three shades)

JOHN LEASK & SON

ESPLANADE, LERWICK ZE1 0LL
Tel: 01595 693162
Fax: 01595 693171
E-mail: info@leaskstravel.co.uk
Web site: www.leaskstravel.co.uk
Ptnrs: Peter R Leask, Andrew J N Leask
Fleet: 19 - 7 single-deck bus, 7 coach, 1 midibus, 1 midicoach, 2 minibus, 2 minicoach.
Chassis: 12 DAF. 2 Dennis. 1 LDV. 3 Mercedes. 1 Optare.
Bodies: 1 Alexander. 5 Ikarus. 1 Optare. 4 Plaxton. 2 Van Hool. 3 Wright. 3 other.
Ops incl: local bus services, school contracts, excursions & tours, private hire.
Livery: Ivory/Blue.
Ticket system: ERG

SOUTH AYRSHIRE

DODDS OF TROON LTD

4 EAST ROAD, AYR KA8 9BA
Tel: 01292 288100
Fax: 01292 287700
E-mail: info@doddsoftroon.com
Web site: www.doddsoftroon.com
Man Dir: James Dodds **Dirs**: Douglas Dodds, Norma Dodds
Fleet: 20 - 2 single-deck bus, 15 coach, 3 midicoach.
Chassis: 1 Dennis. 2 Leyland. 1 Scania. 3 Toyota. 13 Volvo.
Bodies: 2 Alexander. 3 Caetano. 1 Irizar. 6 Jonckheere. 3 Plaxton. 5 Van Hool.
Ops incl: school contracts, excursions & tours, private hire, express, continental tours.

IBT TRAVEL GROUP

CAIRN HOUSE, 15 SKYE ROAD, PRESTWICK KA9 2TA
Tel: 01292 477771
Fax: 01292 471770.
E-mail: briant@ibtravel.com
Partner: Ian Black
Fleet: 3 coaches
Chassis: Volvo
Bodies: Van Hool
Ops incl: continental tours, private hire
Livery: Blue/Gold flash

KEENAN OF AYR COACH TRAVEL

DARWIN GARAGE, COALHALL BY AYR KA6 6ND
Tel: 01292 591252
Fax: 01292 590980
Dirs: Tony Keenan, Jamie Keenan
Fleet: 20 - 2 double-deck bus, 6 single-deck bus, 10 coach, 1 midibus, 1 midicoach.
Chassis: incl: 8 Leyland. 8 Volvo.
Bodies: 8 Alexander. 4 Duple. 2 Plaxton. 6 Van Hool.
Ops incl: school contracts, excursions & tours, private hire.
Livery: Red/Yellow/Orange/White

*MILLIGANS COACH TRAVEL LTD

LOAN GARAGE, MAUCHLINE KA5 6AN
Tel: 01290 550365
Fax: 01290 553291
E-mail: milligans1@aol.com
Web Site: www.milliganscoachtravel.co.uk
Dir: William Milligan
Ops Man: Morag Milligan
Fleet: 20 coaches & midicoaches.
Chassis: 8 Bova. 8 Leyland. 4 Scania.
Bodies: 8 Bova. 3 Irizar. 9 Plaxton.
Ops incl: excursions & tours, private hire, school contracts, express.
Livery: Black/Red/Silver

*STAGECOACH WEST SCOTLAND

SANDGATE, AYR KA7 1DD
Tel: 01292 613700
Fax: 01292 613501
Web site: www.stagecoachbus.com
Man Dir: Sam Greer **Eng Dir**: Sam Greer
Ops Dir: Sarah Longair
Fleet: 449 - 2 open-top bus, 93 double-deck bus, 130 single-deck bus, 16 articulated bus, 54 coach, 92 midibus, 72 minibus.
Chassis: 3 AEC. 92 Dennis. 30 Leyland. 2 Leyland National. 44 MAN. 47 Mercedes. 25 Optare. 7 Scania. 209 Volvo.
Bodies: 276 Alexander. 1 Berkhof. 2 ECW. 11 East Lancs. 22 Jonckheere. 16 Leyland. 5 Neoplan. 2 Northern Counties. 25 Optare. 3 Park Royal. 91 Plaxton. 5 Wright.
Ops incl: local bus services, school contracts, private hire, express.
Livery: Stagecoach
Ticket System: Wayfarer

SOUTH LANARKSHIRE

ALFRA COACH HIRE

26 MACHAN ROAD, LARKHALL ML9 1HG.
Tel: 01698 887581.
Prop: F. Russell.
Fleet: 4 minibus.
Chassis: 2 Ford Transit. 1 Freight Rover. 1 Leyland.
Ops incl: private hire.
Livery: White.

R. & C. S. CRAIG

TOWNFOOT, ROBERTON, BY BIGGAR ML12 6RS.
Tel: 01899 850655.
Dirs: R. Craig, C. S. Craig.
Traf Man/Ch Eng: J. Harvie.
Gen Man: R. Craig.
Fleet: 3 - 2 minibus, 1 minicoach.
Chassis: Freight Rover.
Ops incl: school contracts, private hire.
Livery: White.

*MUIRS COACHES

1 POWELL STREET, DOUGLAS WATER ML11 9PP
Tel: 01555 880551
E-mail: coach@ruraldevtrust.co.uk
Web site: www.ruraldevtrust.co.uk
Man Dir: Gordon Muir.
Fleet: 8 - 2 single-deck bus, 1 midicoach, 5 minicoach.
Chassis: 1 LDV. 6 Mercedes. 1 Optare.
Ops incl: local bus services, school contracts, excursions & tours, private hire
Livery: Peacock Blue
Ticket system: TBC

A/C	Air conditioning	✔	Replacement vehicle available
♿	Vehicles suitable for disabled	T	Toilet-drop facilities available
🍽	Coach(es) with galley facilities	🚌	Vintage vehicle(s) available
WC	Coach(es) with toilet facilities		Open top vehicle(s)
🪑	Seat belt-fitted vehicles		
R	Recovery service available (not 24 hr)		
R24	24hr recovery service		

Scottish Operators

PARK'S OF HAMILTON LTD
wc ✂ A/c R24 ✎ T

14 BOTHWELL ROAD, HAMILTON
ML3 0AY
Tel: 01698 281222
Fax: 01698 303731
Chmn: Douglas Park **Ch Eng**:
Malcolm Fisher.
Co Sec/Dir: Gerry Donnachie. **Ops Man**:
Michael Andrews. **Dir**: Hugh McAteer.
Fleet: 100 - incl: coach, double-deck coach.
Chassis: incl: Neoplan. 30 Volvo. Iveco.
Bodies: incl: 30 Jonckheere.
Neoplan. Plaxton. Van Hool. Beulas.
Ops incl: local bus services, school
contracts, excursions & tours, private hire,
express, continental tours.
Livery: Black
Ticket System: Wayfarer

*SILVER CHOICE TRAVEL LTD
wc ✂ A/c ✎ T

1 MILTON ROAD, EAST KILBRIDE
G74 5BU
Tel: 01355 230403
Fax: 01355 249499
E-mail:
enquiries@silverchoicetravel.co.uk
Web site: www.silverchoicetravel.co.uk
Dirs: David W Gardiner **Ch Eng**: David Hunter
Fleet: 17 - 10 coach, 5 double-deck coach, 2 minicoach.
Chassis: 3 Bova. 1 Iveco. 2 Mercedes.
2 Neoplan. 3 Scania. 6 Volvo.
Ops incl: school contracts, excursions & tours, private hire, express, continental tours.
Livery: Silver

*WILLIAM STOKES & SONS LTD
wc A/c

22 CARSTAIRS ROAD, CARSTAIRS
ML11 8QD
Tel: 01555 870344
Fax: 01555 870601
E-mail: enquiries@stokescoaches.co.uk
Web site: www.stokescoaches.co.uk
Dirs: William Stokes, Alexander Stokes, John Stokes **Co Sec**: Walter Stokes,
Fleet: 21 - 8 single-deck bus, 7 coach, 3 midibus, 3 midicoach
Chassis: 3 DAF. 6 Dennis. 2 Leyland. 3 Mercedes. 7 Volvo.
Bodies: 2 Alexander. 3 Berkhof. 1 Caetano. 1 Carlyle. 1 Esker. 4 Ikarus. 1 Jonckheere. 6 Plaxton. 2 Van Hool.
Ops incl: local bus services, school contracts, excursions & tours, private hire.
Livery: Red/Cream
Ticket System: Almex A90

STONEHOUSE COACHES
48 NEW STREET, STONEHOUSE
ML9 3LT.
Tel: 01698 792145.
Prop: N. Collison.
Livery: White/Pink/Navy.

STUART'S OF CARLUKE
wc A/c

CASTLEHILL GARAGE, AIRDRIE
ROAD, CARLUKE ML8 4UF
Tel: 01555 773533
Fax: 01555 752220
Dir: Stuart Shevill **Ops**: John Hane
Fleet: 49 - 10 double-deck bus, 20 single-deck bus, 15 coach, 2 minibus, 2 minicoach

Chassis: 15 Dennis. 1 Ford Transit.
10 Leyland. 3 Mercedes. 1 Optare. 15 Volvo.
Bodies: Alexander. Caetano. ECW.
Jonckheere. Northern Counties. Optare.
Plaxton. Reeve Burgess. Van Hool.
Ops incl: local bus services, school
contracts, excursions and tours, private hire,
express, continental tours.
Livery: Silver/Blue
Ticket system: Wayfarer

WHITELAWS COACHES
wc ✂ A/c

LOCHPARK INDUSTRIAL ESTATE,
STONEHOUSE ML9 3LR
Tel: 01698 792800
Fax: 01698 793309
E-mail: enquiries@whitelaws.co.uk
Web site: www.whitelaws.co.uk
Fleet: 37 - 23 single-deck bus, 11 coach, 2 midicoach, 1 minibus.
Chassis: incl: 1 Iveco. 3 Mercedes.
Bodies: incl: 1 Marshall/MCV. 1 Plaxton.
3 Sunsundegui. 2 Van Hool. 1 Volvo.
Ops incl: local bus services, school
contracts, excursions & tours, private hire.
Livery: Silver with Red/White/Blue.
Ticket System: Wayfarer 3

STIRLING

*BILLY DAVIES EXECUTIVE COACHES
wc A/c R24

TRANSPORT HOUSE, PLEAN
INDUSTRIAL ESTATE, PLEAN,
STIRLING FK7 8BJ
Tel: 01786 816627
Fax: 01786 811433
Recovery: 01786 816627
Web site: www.daviescoaches.co.uk
E-mail: billy@daviescoaches.com
Prop: Billy Davies
Fleet: 10 - 4 double-deck bus, 3 coach, 2 midicoach, 1 minicoach.
Chassis: Ayats. MAN. Mercedes.
Bodies: Alexander. Ayats. Plaxton. Van Hool.
Ops incl: school contracts, private hire.
Livery: Red/Yellow
Ticket system: Wayfarer

FITZCHARLES COACHES LTD
wc ✂ A/c ✎ T

87 NEWHOUSE ROAD,
GRANGEMOUTH FK3 8NJ
Tel: 01324 482093
Fax: 01324 665411
E-mail: info@fitzcharles.co.uk
Web site: www.fitzcharles.co.uk
Man Dir: Ronnie Fitzcharles
Dir/Sec: Olive King **Ops**: David Fitzcharles
Fleet Eng: Stewart McArthur
Fleet: 16 - 15 coach, 1 midicoach.
Chassis: 3 DAF. 1 Mercedes. 12 Volvo.
Bodies: 2 Ayats. 4 Caetano. 8 Plaxton. 2 Sunsundegui.
Ops incl: excursions & tours, private hire, continental tours, school contracts, express.
Livery: Red/Cream.

WEST DUNBARTONSHIRE

D. P. BISHOP
14 LENNOX ROAD, MILTON,
DUMBARTON G82 2TL.
Fleetname: DB Travel.

LOCHS AND GLENS HOLIDAYS
SCHOOL ROAD, GARTOCHARN
G83 8RW
Tel: 01389 713 713
E-mail: enquiries@lochsandglens.com
Website: www.lochsandglens.com
Tran Man: Brian Nichols
Fleet: 15 coach
Chassis: 15 Volvo.
Bodies: 15 Jonckheere.
Ops incl: excursions & tours
Livery: White with blue letters

McCOLL'S COACHES LTD
wc ✂ A/c R ✎

BALLAGAN DEPOT, STIRLING
ROAD, BALLOCH G83 8LY
Tel: 01389 754321
Fax: 01389 755354
E-mail: mccolls@btconnect.com
Web site: www.mccolls.org.uk
Man: William McColl **Man Dirs**: Thomas McColl, Janet McColl **Co Sec**: Ann McKinlay
Ops Man: Liam McColl **Head mechanic**: Eddie McKinley
Fleet: double-deck bus, single-deck bus, coach, minibus.
Chassis: DAF. Dennis. Ford. Ford Transit. Leyland. leyland National. MCW. Mercedes. Volvo. other.
Bodies: Leyland National. MCW. Mercedes. other.
Ops incl: local bus services, school contracts, excursions & tours, private hire.

WEST LOTHIAN

LES BROWN TRAVEL
9 HARDHILL ROAD, BATHGATE
EH48 2BW
Tel: 01506 656129
Fax: 01506 656129
E-mail: les-brown@btconnect.com
Web Site: www.lesbrowntravel.com
Props: Les Brown, Colin Brown
Fleet: 8 - 2 midicoach, 6 minicoach.
Chassis: 5 Ford Transit. 3 Mercedes.
Ops incl: school contracts, excursions & tours, private hire.

BROWNINGS (WHITBURN) LTD
wc ✎

22 LONGRIDGE ROAD, WHITBURN
EH47 0DE
Tel: 01501 740234
Fax: 01501 741265
E-mail:
george@browningscoaches.fsnet.co.uk
Web site:
www.browningscoaches.co.uk
Man Dir: G D Browning

Co Sec: Mrs G Blyth
Fleet: 15 - 5 double-deck bus, 10 coach
Chassis: 5 Leyland. 10 Volvo.
Bodies: 2 Berkhof. 1 East Lancs. 1 Leyland. 2 Plaxton. 3 Roe. 6 Van Hool.
Ops incl: excursions & tours, private hire, school contracts.
Livery: Red/White/Blue.

*BULLDOG TRAVEL

UNIT 6, INCHCROSS, BATHGATE EH48 2HT
Tel: 01506 636366
Fax: 01506 657880
E-mail: autowater@btconnect.com
Props: G Torrance, K Nicoll
Fleet: 24 - 5 double-deck bus, 9 single-deck bus, 1 coach, 2 midibus, 1 minicoach, 6 minibus
Chassis: 7 Dennis. 2 Ford Transit. 2 Iveco. 1 LDV. 5 Mercedes. 1 Optare. 6 Volvo.
Bodies: 6 Leyland. 5 Mercedes. 1 Optare. 7 Plaxton. 5 other.
Ops incl: local bus services, private hire, school contracts.
Livery: Red/White/Blue
Ticket System: Wayfarer

E & M HORSBURGH

180 UPHALL STATION ROAD, PUMPHERSTON EH53 0PD
Tel: 01506 432251
Fax: 01506 438066
E-mail: horsburgh@btconnect.com
Web site: www.horsburghcoaches.com
Dirs: Eric Horsburgh, Mark Horsburgh
Fleet: 66 - 11 double-deck bus, 23 single-deck bus, 2 coach, 6 midibus, 4 minicoach, 22 minibus.
Chassis: 5 Dennis. 10 Ford Transit. 4 LDV. 14 Leyland. 18 Mercedes. 9 Optare.
Bodies: 4 LDV. 10 Ford. 14 Leyland. 8 Leyland National. 14 Mercedes. 9 Optare. 9 Plaxton.
Ops incl: local bus services, school contracts, private hire.
Livery: Golden Yellow/White
Ticket System: Almex

HOUSTOUN TRAVEL

110 PUMPHERSTON ROAD, UPHALL STATION, LIVINGSTON EH54 5PJ
Tel: 01506 437773.
Fax: 01506 437206.
Prop: Ian Horsburgh.
Fleet: 9 - 1 minibus, 8 minicoach.
Fleet: 1 DAF. 5 Ford Transit. 1 Freight Rover. 2 Mercedes.
Bodies: 1 Carlyle. 1 Leyland. 1 Mercedes. 1 Plaxton. 5 other.
Ops incl: local bus services, school contracts, private hire.

McKECHNIE OF BATHGATE LIMITED

2 EASTON ROAD, BATHGATE EH48 2QG
Tel: 01506 654337
Fax: 01506 654337
E-mail: pmkcoach@aol.com
Dir: Peter McKechnie **Co Sec**: Catherine McKechnie
Fleet: 8 - 4 coach, 2 midicoach, 2 minicoach
Chassis: 1 Leyland. 3 Volvo. 4 Mercedes
Ops incl: school contracts, private hire.

MARTIN'S COACH TRAVEL

1 SUMMERVILLE COURT, UPHALL STATION, LIVINGSTON EH54 5QG.
Tel: 01506 435968.
Fax: 01506 435968.
E-mail: martcoach@aol.com
Prop: Tony Martin
Fleet: 5 coach.
Chassis: 2 Bova. 1 MAN. 2 Volvo.
Bodies: 2 Bova. 3 Van Hool.
Ops incl: excursions & tours, private hire, school contracts.
Livery: White/Green/Orange/Blue

*PRENTICE WESTWOOD

WESTWOOD, WEST CALDER EH55 8PW
Tel: 01506 871231
Fax: 01506 871734
Recovery: 01506 871231
E-mail: sales@prenticewestwoodcoaches.co.uk
Web site: www.prenticewestwoodcoaches.co.uk
Dirs: Robbie Prentice, David Cowen **Ops Man**: Jock Johnston
Fleet: 49 - 8 double-deck bus, 32 coach, 5 double-deck coach, 2 midibus, 2 midicoach.
Chassis: 6 Bova. 1 DAF. 10 Leyland. 2 Mercedes. 3 Neoplan. 1 Optare. 1 Plaxton. 25 Volvo.
Bodies: 8 Alexander. 2 Berkhof. 6 Bova. 5 Caetano. 1 Ikarus. 5 Jonckheere. 3 Neoplan. 1 Optare. 8 Plaxton. 6 Van Hool. 2 Wadham Stringer. 2 other.
Ops incl: local bus services, school contracts, private hire, continental tours.
Livery: White/Blue/Red.
Ticket System: Wayfarer

WESTERN ISLES

GALSON-STORNOWAY MOTOR SERVICES LTD

1 LOWER BARVAS, ISLE OF LEWIS HS2 0QZ
Tel: 01851 840269.
Fax: 01851 840445.
E-mail: info@galsonmotorsltd.co.uk
Web site: www.galsonmotorsltd.co.uk
Dir: I. Morrison. **Ch Eng**: F. Smith.
Dir/Ops Man: I. Morrison.
Dir/Tran Man: C. Morrison.
Fleet: 17 - 1 double-deck, 12 coach, 1 midicoach, 3 minibus.
Chassis: 1 Autobus, 3 Ford Transit. 1 Leyland. 2 Mercedes. 11 Volvo.
Bodies: 1 Autobus. 3 Ford Transit. 2 Mercedes. 12 Plaxton. 2 others.
Ops incl: local bus services, school contracts, excursions & tours, private hire.
Livery: Yellow/Cream.
Ticket System: Wayfarer.

*HEBRIDEAN COACHES R24

HOWMORE, SOUTH UIST HS8 5SH
Tel: 01870 620345
Fax: 01870 620301
Recovery: 01870 620345
Props: D A MacDonald, S MacDonald
Fleet: 13 - coach, midibus, midicoach
Chassis: 2 Bedford. 4 Dennis. 2 Ford. 3 Leyland. 2 Mercedes.
Bodies: 4 Duple. 2 Mellor. 2 Plaxton.
Ops incl: local bus services, school contracts, private hire.
Livery: Cream/Green

LOCHS MOTOR TRANSPORT LTD

CAMERON TERRACE, LEURBOST, LOCHS, ISLE OF LEWIS HS2 9PE
Tel: 01851 860288.
Fax: 01851 705857.
Dirs: C. MacDonald, R. MacDonald, S. MacDonald, A. MacDonald.
Ch Eng: I. MacKinnon.
Fleet: 20 - 4 single-deck bus, 12 coach, 3 midibus, 1 midicoach.
Chassis: 12 Ford. 1 Freight Rover. 3 Leyland. 4 Mercedes.
Bodies: 5 Alexander. 1 Carlyle. 8 Duple. 2 Marshall. 2 M2M. 3 Plaxton.
Ops incl: local bus services, school contracts, private hire.
Livery: Blue/Cream.

Scottish Operators

A/c	Air conditioning	
	Vehicles suitable for disabled	
	Coach(es) with galley facilities	
wc	Coach(es) with toilet facilities	
	Seat belt-fitted vehicles	
R	Recovery service available (not 24 hr)	
R24	24hr recovery service	
	Replacement vehicle available	
T	Toilet-drop facilities available	
	Vintage vehicle(s) available	
	Open top vehicle(s)	

Isle of Man

*DOUGLAS CORPORATION TRAMWAY
STRATHALLAN CRESCENT, DOUGLAS IM2 4NR
Tel: 01624 696420
E-mail: pcannon@douglas.gov.im
Ops Supervisor: Peter Cannon
Fleet: 20 tramcars
Ops incl: tram services, private hire.

ISLE OF MAN TRANSPORT
TRANSPORT HEADQUARTERS, BANKS CIRCUS, DOUGLAS IM1 5PT
Tel: 01624 663366
Fax: 01624 663637
E-mail: info@busandrail.dtl.gov.im
Fleet: 109 - 75 double-deck bus, 10 single-deck bus, 24 tram.
Chassis: 33 DAF. 34 Dennis. 18 Leyland.
Bodies: 54 East Lancs. 8 Leyland. 10 Marshall. 10 Northern Counties. 3 Optare.
Ops incl: local bus/tram services, private hire
Livery: Red/Cream.
Ticket System: Wayfarer.

PROTOURS ISLE OF MAN LTD
SUMMERHILL, DOUGLAS IM2 4PF
Tel: 01624 674301
Fax: 01624 675656
Email: info@protours.co.im
Chmn & Man Dir: Roy Lightfoot
Dirs: D L Wilson, S F Cairns, F B Kinnear
Ops Man: Dave Bennett
Holiday Man: Colin Morgan
Ch Eng: Alan Lancaster
Fleet: 31 - 3 single-deck bus, 16 coach, 4 midicoach, 6 minibus, 2 minicoach.
Chassis: 8 Bedford. 1 Bova. 2 BMC. 6 DAF. 1 Ford Transit. 6 Iveco. 4 Leyland. 1 Scania. 1 Toyota. 2 LAG.
Bodies: 1 Berkhof. 1 Bova. 1 Caetano. 2 BMC. 1 Carlyle. 8 Duple. 5 Leicester. 7 Plaxton. 1 Reeve Burgess. 2 Van Hool. 1 Wadham Stringer. 1 other.
Ops incl: local bus services, excursions & tours, private hire, express, continental tours, school contracts.
Livery: White/Blue/Yellow

Isles of Scilly

HERITAGE TOURS
SANTAMANA, 9 RAMS VALLEY, ST MARY'S TR21 0JX
Tel: 01720 422387
Props: G. Twynham, Mrs P. Twynham.
Fleet: 1 single-deck bus (1948 vehicle).
Chassis: Austin K2. **Body**: Barnard.
Ops incl: excursions & tours, private hire.
Livery: Blue/Cream.

Do you want to keep your LITTLE RED BOOK up-to-date?
Buses magazine now carries updates every month.
See 248 page for Subscription details

Welsh Operators

ANGLESEY

CARREGLEFN COACHES
CARREGLEFN GARAGE, AMLWCH LL68 0PR
Tel: 01407 710139
Fax: 01407 710217
Prop: Alun Lewis
Fleet: 10 - 1 single-deck bus, 8 coach, 1 minicoach.
Chassis: 2 Bedford. 1 Toyota. 7 Volvo.
Bodies: 4 Caetano. 1 Duple. 5 Plaxton.
Ops incl: local bus services, school contracts, excursions & tours, private hire.
Livery: Blue/Cream

ELLIS COACHES
CHURCH STREET, LLANGEFNI LL77 7EB
Tel: 01248 750304
Prop: F. B. Ellis.
Fleet: 14 - 5 double-deck bus, 1 single-deck bus, 8 coach.
Chassis: Bedford. Bristol. Daimler. Ford. Leyland. Volvo.
Bodies: Duple. Plaxton.
Livery: D/D -Yellow/Mushroom/Red, S/D - White/Mauve/Red.

W C GOODSIR
30 TRENWFA ROAD, LANDS END, HOLYHEAD LL65 1LE
Tel: 01407 764340
Livery: White/Black/Yellow/Orange.

GWYNFOR COACHES
ANEYLFA, 1 GREENFIELD AVENUE, LLANGEFNI LL77 7NU
Tel: 01248 722694
Prop: H. Hughes.

*O R JONES & SONS
BUS & COACH DEPOT, LLANFAETHLU, HOLYHEAD LL65 4NW
Tel: 01407 730204
Fax: 01407 730083
Recovery: 01407 730759
Dir: J P Jones **Ops Man**: I O Jones
Tran Man: M O Jones
Fleet: 20 - 4 double-deck bus, 6 single-deck bus, 5 coach, 3 minibus, 1 minicoach, 1 vintage.
Chassis: 1 Bedford. 2 Bova. 4 Bristol. 3 DAF. 1 Dennis. 1 MAN. 3 Mercedes. 2 Optare. 3 Scania.
Bodies: 2 Bova. 1 Caetano. 1 Duple. 4 East Lancs. 1 Ikarus. 1 Irizar. 1 Jonckheere. 3 Mercedes. 2 Optare. 2 Plaxton. 2 Van Hool.
Ops incl: local bus services, school contracts, excursions & tours, private hire, express, continental tours.
Livery: Red/White/Green/Silver
Ticket system: Wayfarer

W E JONES & SON
THE GARAGE, LLANERCHYMEDD LL71 8EB
Tel: 01248 470228
Fax: 01248 852893
Prop: G E Jones
Fleet: 11 - 5 double-deck bus, 2 single-deck bus, 3 coach, 1 minibus.
Chassis: 1 Bedford. 1 Bristol. 1 DAF. 1 Daimler. 1 Dodge. 3 MCW. 1 Mercedes. 1 Volvo.
Bodies: 2 Alexander. 3 MCW. 1 Mercedes. 2 Northern Counties. 1 Plaxton.
Ops incl: school contracts, private hire.
Livery: Red/White

LEWIS-Y-LLAN
MADYN INDUSTRIAL ESTATE, AMLWCH LL68 9DL
Tel: 01407 832181
Fax: 01407 830112
Props: A. H. Lewis, R. M. Lewis.
Fleet: 10 - 2 double-deck bus, 4 coach, 4 midibus.
Chassis: 1 Bedford. 3 Leyland. 3 Mercedes. 2 Volvo. 1 Volkswagen.
Bodies: 1 Alexander. 1 East Lancs. 1 Jonckheere. 1 Leyland. 3 Optare. 3 Plaxton.
Livery: White/Blue.

BLAENAU GWENT

GARY'S COACHES OF TREDEGAR
42 COMMERCIAL STREET, TREDEGAR NP22 3DJ
Tel: 01495 726400
Fax: 01495 726500
Recovery: 01495 723264
E-mail: sales@garys-coaches.co.uk
Web site: www.garys-coaches.co.uk
Props: Mr & Mrs G A Lane **Ops Man**: D Williams **Ch Eng**: G Cresswell
Fleet: 14 - 12 coach, 1 midicoach, 1 midibus.
Chassis: 2 DAF. 1 Dennis. 1 Leyland. 2 Mercedes. 8 Volvo.
Bodies: 1 Bova. 4 Duple. 2 Mercedes. 5 Plaxton. 2 Van Hool.
Ops incl: excursions & tours, private hire, school contracts, continental tours.
Livery: White/Blue

HENLEYS BUS SERVICES LTD
HENLEYS COACH GARAGE, VICTOR ROAD, CWMTILLERY NP13 1HU
Tel: 01495 212288
Fax: 01495 320720
Dir: Martin Henley **Head Eng**: Michael Henley **Sec**: Daphne Henley
Fleet: 11 - 6 coach, 4 midibus, 1 minicoach.
Chassis: 4 Leyland. 4 Mercedes. 1 Setra. 2 Volvo.
Bodies: 1 Alexander. 1 Duple. 2 East Lancs. 1 Jonckheere. 1 Leicester. 5 Plaxton. 1 Setra.
Ops incl: local bus services, school contracts, excursions & tours, private hire.
Ticket system: Wayfarer

*STAGECOACH IN SOUTH WALES
See Torfaen

BRIDGEND

R & D BURROWS LTD
21 CEMETERY ROAD, OGMORE VALE CF32 7HR
Tel: 01656 840259
Fax: 01656 841866
E-mail: burrowscoaches@yahoo.co.uk
Web site: www.burrowscoaches.co.uk
Dirs: J G Jones, S A Jones, P J Jones
Fleet: 9 - 1 double-deck bus, 1 single-deck bus, 7 coach
Chassis: 1 DAF. 1 Ford. 3 Leyland. 1 Scania. 1 Setra. 2 Volvo.
Bodies: 1 Duple. 1 ECW. 3 Plaxton. 1 Setra. 2 Van Hool. 1 Wadham Stringer.
Ops incl: private hire, school contracts.

G M COACHES LTD
MOUNTAIN VIEW GARAGE, TY-FRY ROAD, CEFN CRIBWR CF32 0BB
Tel: 01656 740262
Fax: 01656 746040
E-mail: carl@gmcoaches.com
Web site: www.gmcoaches.com
Man Dir: Carl Hookings **Dirs**: Katherine Hookings, Andrea Lockwood **Man**: Idris Hall
Fleet: 32 - 10 double-deck bus, 14 coach, 2 double-deck coach, 1 open-top bus, 1 midicoach, 1 minicoach, 1 minibus.
Chassis: incl: 3 DAF. 1 Dennis. 2 MAN. 1 Mercedes. 2 Neoplan.
Bodies: 3 Alexander. 4 Berkhof. 2 ECW. 3 East Lancs. 1 Ikarus. 2 Jonckheere.

A/c	Air conditioning
♿	Vehicles suitable for disabled
🍽	Coach(es) with galley facilities
wc	Coach(es) with toilet facilities
♥	Seat belt-fitted vehicles
R	Recovery service available (not 24 hr)
R24	24hr recovery service
✦	Replacement vehicle available
T	Toilet-drop facilities available
🚌	Vintage vehicle(s) available
🚍	Open top vehicle(s)

1 Marshall/MCV. 1 Mercedes. 2 Neoplan. 1 Plaxton. 10 Van Hool.
Ops incl: local bus services, school contracts, excursions & tours, private hire, continental tours.
(Associated with EST Bus, Vale of Glamorgan)

GWYN JONES & SON LTD

WHITE CROFT GARAGE, BRYNCETHIN CF32 9YR
Tel: 01656 720300
Fax: 01656 725632
Recovery: 01656 720182
Chair: John Gwyn Jones
Dir: Miriam J. Jones
Fleet: coach.
Chassis: Leyland. Mercedes. Scania. Volvo.
Bodies: Berkhof. Jonckheere. Mercedes. Plaxton. Van Hool.
Ops incl: excursions & tours, private hire, continental tours, school contracts.
Livery: White/Gold/Maroon

*PENCOED TRAVEL LTD

18 CAER BERLLAN, PENCOED CF35 6RR
Tel: 01656 860200
Fax: 01656 864793
E-mail: info@pencoedtravel.co.uk
Web site: www.pencoedtravel.co.uk
Man Dir: Denise Cook **Ch Eng**: Neil Cook
Co Sec: Andrea Talbot **Ops**: David Morris
Fleet: 11 - 4 double-deck bus, 7 coach.
Chassis: 2 Bristol. 5 DAF. 1 Dennis. 3 Leyland.
Bodies: 1 Berkhof. 4 Leyland. 2 Plaxton. 4 Van Hool.
Ops incl: private hire, school contracts
Livery: White/Blue

*STAGECOACH IN SOUTH WALES
See Torfaen

CAERPHILLY

CASTELL COACHES LTD

UNITS 3 & 4 EUROPEAN TERMINAL BUILDING, PANTGLAS INDUSTRIAL ESTATE, BEDWAS CF83 8DR
Tel: 029 2086 1863.
Fax: 029 2086 1864
Recovery: 07967 636659
E-mail: sales@castellcoaches.co.uk
Web site: www.castellcoaches.co.uk
Co Sec: Mrs S Kerslake (**Tel**: 07801 515419)
Dir: C Kerslake. **Ops Man**: B Kerslake (**Tel**: 07801 515117)
Fleet: 21 - 5 double-deck bus, 12 coach, 3 midicoach, 1 minibus.
Chassis: 2 Bova. 4 DAF. 6 Leyland. 4 Mercedes. 7 Volvo.
Bodies: 2 Bova. 1 Duple. 2 Jonckheere. 4 Leyland. 4 Mercedes. 6 Plaxton. 2 Van Hool.
Ops incl: excursions & tours, private hire, continental tours, school contracts.
Livery: White with multicolour

GLYN WILLIAMS TRAVEL

PENNAR CROSSING, PONTLLANFRAITH NP12 2AW
Tel: 01495 229237
Fax: 01495 222880
Man Dir: G J Williams **Eng Dir**: T G Williams
Comm Man: I MacDonald
Fleet: 29 - 23 single-deck bus, 6 midibus.
Chassis: 23 Dennis. 6 BMC.
Bodies: 10 Caetano. 3 Marshall. 6 Plaxton. 4 UVG. 6 BMC.
Ops incl: local bus services.
Livery: Green/White.
Ticket System: Wayfarer TGX
Part of Stagecoach in Wales

HARRIS COACHES

BRYN GWYN STREET, FLEUR-DE-LIS NP2 1RZ
Tel: 01443 832290
Man Dir: John Harris
Fleetname: Shuttle
Ops incl: local bus services
Livery: Cream/Maroon/Red

*ISLWYN BOROUGH TRANSPORT LTD

PENMAEN ROAD DEPOT, PONTLLANFRAITH, BLACKWOOD NP12 2DY
Tel: 01495 235707
Fax: 01495 220871
E-mail: simsr@caerphilly.gov.uk
Web site: www.kingfishertravel.com
Chairmn: David Poole **Man Dir**: Roger Sims
Comm Dir: Paul Diapen **Traff Man**: Dow Jones
Fleet: 46 - 26 single-deck bus, 19 coach, 1 minibus.
Chassis: 3 Bova. 4 DAF. 2 Dennis. 1 Ford Transit. 2 Leyland. 17 MAN. 3 Mercedes. 14 Volvo.
Bodies: 1 Berkhof. 3 Bova. 2 Caetano. 6 East Lancs. 10 Jonckheere. 4 Marshall/MCV. 13 Optare. 3 Plaxton. 1 Setra. 1 Van Hool. 4 Transbus.
Ops incl: local bus services, school contracts, excursions & tours, private hire, continental tours.
Livery: Blue/White
Ticket System: Wayfarer

*STAGECOACH IN SOUTH WALES
See Torfaen

CARDIFF

*CARDIFF CITY TRANSPORT SERVICES LTD

SLOPER ROAD, LECKWITH, CARDIFF CF11 8TB
Tel: 029 2078 7710
Fax: 029 2078 7742
E-mail: headoffice@cardiffbus.com
Web site: www.cardiffbus.com
Chmn: Cllr Steve Pantak **Man Dir**: David Brown **Fin Dir/Co Sec**: Cynthia Ogbonna **Eng Dir**: Andrew Hoseason
Comm Man: Peter Heath

OpsMan: Gareth Mole
Fleet: 231 - 18 double-deck bus, 194 single-deck bus, 19 articulated bus
Chassis: 166 Dennis. 6 Leyland. 10 MCW. 19 Scania. 12 Transbus. 18 Volvo.
Bodies: 10 Alexander. 6 Leyland. 10 MCW. 15 Northern Counties. 138 Plaxton. 19 Scania. 12 Transbus.
Ops incl: local bus services
Livery: Burgess Blue/Cream
Ticket System: Wayfarer TGX

CROESO TOURS

13 WATERLOO ROAD, PENYLAN, CARDIFF CF23 5AD
Tel: 029 2047 2313
E-mail: jmforster13@hotmail.com
Owner: John M. Forster
Fleet: 3 - 1 midicoach, 1 minibus, 1 minicoach
Chassis: 1 Iveco. 1 LDV. 1 Renault
Ops incl: private hire, school contracts.

GREYHOUND COACHES CO

COACH DEPOT, STATION TERRACE, ELY BRIDGE, CARDIFF CF5 4AA
Tel: 029 2056 1467, 2055 2767
Ptnrs: T. James, Florence James.
Fleet: 14 - 13 coach, 1 minibus.
Chassis: 10 Bedford. 1 Ford Transit. 3 Volvo.
Ops incl: local bus services, excursions & tours, private hire.
Livery: White/Blue.

*STAGECOACH IN SOUTH WALES
See Torfaen

WALTONS COACHES

31 AVONDALE ROAD, GRANGETOWN CF1 7DT.
Tel: 029 2039 9511.
Dirs: B. J. Walton, Mrs S. F. Walton, R. J. Walton, D. McCarthy.
Fleet: 6 - 4 coach, 2 midicoach.
Chassis: Bedford. Ford. Mercedes.
Ops incl: private hire, school contracts.
Livery: Blue/White/Red.

WATTS COACHES

OLD POST GARAGE, BONVILSTON CF5 6TT.
Tel/Fax: 01446 781277.
Prop: C. P. Watts. **Tran Man**: J. B. Watts.
Fleet: 23 - 3 double-deck bus, 16 coach, 4 midicoach.
Chassis: 2 Bristol. 2 DAF. 5 Ford. 4 Leyland. 2 MAN. 4 Mercedes. 4 Volvo.
Bodies: 3 Alexander. 3 Caetano. 5 Duple. 1 Optare. 8 Plaxton. 1 Reeve Burgess. 1 Made-to-Measure. 1 Robin Hood.
Ops incl: school contracts, private hire.
Livery: Cream/Red/Gold.

*WHEADONS GROUP TRAVEL LTD

STATION TERRACE, ELY BRIDGE, CARDIFF CF5 4AA
Tel: 029 2057 5333
Fax: 029 2057 5384
E-mail: admin@wheadons-group.co.uk
Web site: www.wheadons-group.co.uk
Prop: Ernest Wheadon
Ch Eng: Steve Osling

Fleet: 34 - 20 coach, 10 midicoach, 4 midibus.
Chassis: Ford Transit. Scania. Toyota. Volvo.
Bodies: Autobus. Caetano. Mercedes. Plaxton. Van Hool.
Ops incl: private hire, school contracts, excursions & tours, continental tours.

CARMARTHENSHIRE

BYSIAU CWM TAF/ TAF VALLEY COACHES

PENRHEOL, WHITLAND SA34 0NH
Tel: 01994 240908
Fax: 01994 241264
Dirs: Clive Edwards, Heather Edwards
Fleet: 14 - 10 coach, 2 midibus, 1 midicoach, minicoach.
Chassis: Dennis. Iveco. LDV. Leyland. Mercedes. Optare. Volvo.
Bodies: Jonckheere. Mercedes. Optare. Plaxton. Reeve Burgess. Transbus. Van Hool
Ops incl: local bus services, excursions & tours, school contracts, private hire, continental tours.
Livery: White/Silver/Blue

CASTLE GARAGE LTD

BROAD STREET, LLANDOVERY
SA20 0AA
Tel: 01550 720335
Man Dir: Derek Jones
Fleet: 12 - 4 midibus, 4 midicoach, 4 minibus.
Chassis: 2 Ford Transit. 2 Freight Rover. 8 Mercedes.
Bodies: Mellor. Mercedes. Optare. Plaxton. Reeve Burgess. Wadham Stringer.
Ops incl: local bus services, school contracts, private hire.

GARETH EVANS COACHES

80 GLYN ROAD, BRYNAMMAN
SA18 1SS
Tel: 01269 823127
Fax: 01269 824533
Props: K. Davies, Mrs S. Davies.

GWYN WILLIAMS & SONS LTD

DERLWYN GARAGE, LOWER TUMBLE SA15 5YT
Fleet: 27 - 3 double-deck bus, 8 single-deck bus, 17 coach, 7 minibus
Livery: Two tone Blue/Red.

JONES INTERNATIONAL

STATION ROAD, LLANDEILO
SA19 6NG
Tel: 01558 822985
Fax: 01558 822984
Props: Meirion Jones, Myrddin Jones, Neil Jones **Office Man**: Carole Thompson
Ch Eng: Andrew Vale
Fleet: 7 - 2 single-deck bus, 5 coach.
Chassis: 3 DAF. 3 Leyland. 1 Volvo.
Bodies: 6 Van Hool. 1 Crossley.
Ops incl: excursions & tours, private hire, express, continental tours, school contracts.
Livery: Yellow/Blue

JONES MOTORS (LOGIN) LTD

LOGIN, WHITLAND SA34 0UX
Tel: 01437 563277
Fax: 01437 563393
E-mail: info@joneslogin.co.uk
Web Site: www.joneslogin.co.uk
Man Dirs: E A Jones, A T Jones, E H Jones
Fleet: 17 - 14 coach, 1 midicoach, 2 minibus.
Chassis: 8 Dennis. 2 LDV. 11 Mercedes. 1 Scania. 5 Volvo.
Bodies: 1 East Lancs. 1 Irizar. 2 Leyland. 1 Mercedes. 12 Plaxton.
Ops incl: local bus services, school contracts, excursions & tours, private hire, continental tours.

LEWIS COACHES WHITLAND

THE GARAGE, WHITLAND SA34 0AA
Tel: 01944 240274
Dirs: E Lewis
Fleet: 11 - 8 coach, 1 midibus, 2 minicoach.
Chassis: 1 Bedford. 3 Dennis. 2 LDV. 3 Leyland. 2 Volvo.
Bodies: 1 Berkhof. 1 Duple. 2 Leyland. 1 Optare. 6 Plaxton.
Livery: White with Green/Mink stripes.
Ops incl: local bus services, school contracts, private hire
Livery: White/Green with mink stripes
Ticket System: Wayfarer

*LEWIS-RHYDLEWIS

PENRHIW-PAL GARAGE, RHYDLEWIS, LLANDYSUL
SA44 5QG
Tel: 01239 851386
Fax: 01239 858899
E-mail: lewis_rhydlewis@hotmail.com
Ptnrs: Maldwyn Lewis, Meirion Lewis
Fleet: 20 - 16 coach, 1 midicoach, 3 minibus.
Chassis: 5 Bedford. 1 BMC. 1 Dennis. 2 Ford Transit. 1 Iveco. 5 Leyland. 1 Renault. 2 Setra. 2 Volvo.
Bodies: 1 BMC. 1 Duple. 13 Plaxton. 2 Setra. 3 other.
Ops incl: local bus services, school contracts, excursions & tours, private hire, continental tours.
Livery: Cream/Red/Orange/Maroon

MORRIS TRAVEL

ALLTYCNAP ROAD, JOHNSTOWN
SA31 3QY
Tel: 01267 235090.
Fax: 01267 238183.
E-mail: sales@morristravel.co.uk
Web site: www.morristravel.co.uk
Man Dir/Chmn: T J Freeman **Ops Dir**: C J Freeman. **Dir/Co Sec**: C M Freeman
Ch Eng: A Jones. **Traf Man**: V Shambrook
Traff Controller: P Davies.
Fleet: 29 - 1 single-deck bus, 19 coach, 1 midibus, 6 minibus, 1 minicoach, 1 midicoach.
Chassis: 4 Bedford. 3 DAF. 1 Ford. 1 Freight Rover 14 LDV. 2 Mercedes. 1 Optare. 4 Volvo.
Bodies: 1 Berkhof. 1 Duple. 14 Leyland. 1 Ford Transit. 2 Mercedes. 1 Optare. 9 Plaxton.
Ops incl: local bus services, school contracts, private hire.
Livery: Blue/Navy/White.
Ticket System: Wayfarer

THOMAS BROS

TOWY GARAGE, LLANGADOG
SA19 9LU.
Tel: 01550 777438
Fax: 01550 777807.
Prop: Gareth Thomas
Fleet: 19 - minibus, coach
Chassis/bodies: incl: 1 Mercedes/Optare Sorocco
Ops incl: local bus services, school contracts, excursions & tours, private hire.
Livery: Cream/Green.
Ticket System: Setright.

CEREDIGION

*BRODYR JAMES

GLANYRAFON, LLANGEITHO, TREGARON SY25 6TT
Tel: 01974 821255
Fax: 01974 251618
Dirs: T M G James, D E James
Fleet: 16 - 9 coach, 3 midibus, 2 midicoach, 2 minibus.
Chassis: 3 Dennis. 1 Ford Transit. 5 Mercedes. 1 Toyota. 6 Volvo.
Bodies: 2 Alexander. 2 Caetano. 1 Jonckheere. 1 Mellor. 1 Mercedes. 7 Plaxton. 2 Reeve Burgess.
Ops incl: local bus services, school contracts, private hire
Livery: White/Red/Gold
Ticket System: Almex

*LEWIS COACHES

BRYNEITHIN ROAD, LLANRHYSTUD
SY23 5DN
Tel/Fax: 01974 202495
Recovery: 01974 202495
E-mail: lewisllanrhystud@aol.com
Prop: Gwyn R Lewis
Fleet: 19 - 12 coach, 3 minibus, 4 minicoach.
Chassis: 1 Bedford. 2 DAF. 1 Dennis. 4 LDV. 3 Leyland. 2 Mercedes. 2 Toyota. 5 Volvo.
Bodies: 1 Berkhof. 2 Caetano. 1 Duple.

A/c	Air conditioning		Seat belt-fitted vehicles		Replacement vehicle available
	Vehicles suitable for disabled	R	Recovery service available (not 24 hr)	T	Toilet-drop facilities available
	Coach(es) with galley facilities				Vintage vehicle(s) available
wc	Coach(es) with toilet facilities	R24	24hr recovery service		Open top vehicle(s)

Welsh Operators

1 Jonckheere. 3 Marshall/MCV. 2 Plaxton. 4 Van Hool.
Ops incl: local bus services, school contracts, private hire, excursions & tours, continental tours.
Livery: White/Blue
Ticket System: Wayfarer

MID WALES TRAVEL

BRYNHYFRYD GARAGE, PENRHYNCOCH, ABERYSTWYTH SY23 3EH
Tel: 01970 828288
Fax: 01970 828940
Dir: J Melvyn Evans
Ops Man: Heddwyn Morgan
Fleet: coach, midibus, midicoach.
Chassis: 4 Dennis. 1 Leyland. 6 Mercedes. 6 Volvo
Bodies: 5 Alexander. 1 Autobus. 1 Jonckheere. 5 Plaxton. 4 UVG. 1 Wright.
Ops incl: local bus services, school contracts, private hire.
Livery: White/Blue

RED KITE COACHES

R24

UNIT 1, GLANDINAS, PENPARCIAU, ABERYSTWYTH SY23 1RR
Tel: 01970 627427
Fax: 01970 624412
E-mail: enquiries@redkitecoaches.co.uk
Web site: www.redkitecoaches.co.uk
Prop: P Bryan
Fleet: 4 - 2 single-deck bus, 1 double-deck coach, 1 midicoach.
Chassis: 1 DAF. 1 Leyland. 1 Scania. 1 Volvo.
Bodies: 2 Plaxton. 1 Wadham Stringer. 1 other
Ops incl: private hire, excursions & tours, express, continental tours.
Livery: White/Blue
Livery: Wayfarer

*RICHARDS BROS

MOYLGROVE GARAGE, PENTOOD INDUSTRIAL ESTATE, CARDIGAN SA43 3AG
Tel: 01239 613756
Fax: 01239 615193
E-mail: enquiries@richardsbros.co.uk
Web site: www.richardsbros.co.uk
Gen Man: W J M Richards **Ch Eng**: D N Richards **Traf Man**: R M Richards
Ops Man: S M Richards
Fleet: 67 - 23 single-deck bus, 22 coach, 4 midicoach, 4 minibus, 14 midibus.
Chassis: 8 Bedford. 23 DAF. 11 Dennis. 3 LDV. 1 MAN. 12 Mercedes. 2 Volvo.
Bodies: 5 Alexander. 1 Autobus. 1 Caetano. 3 Carlyle. 7 Duple. 2 Ikarus. 2 Marshall. 2 Northern Counties. 9 Optare. 15 Plaxton. 2 Reeve Burgess. 3 Transbus. 8 Van Hool. 3 Wright. 3 other.
Ops incl: local bus services, school contracts, excursions & tours, private hire, continental tours.
Livery: Blue/White/Maroon
Ticket System: Wayfarer

ROBERTS COACHES

UNIT 4, GLANYRAFON INDUSTRIAL ESTATE, ABERYSTWYTH SY23 3JQ
Tel: 01970 611085
Fax: 01970 626855
Prop: G Roberts
Fleet: 5 coach.
Chassis: 2 DAF. 3 Leyland.
Bodies: Plaxton. Duple.
Ops incl: school contracts, private hire, tours & excursions.
Livery: White or Blue

CONWY

ALPINE TRAVEL

CENTRAL COACH GARAGE, BUILDER STREET WEST, LLANDUDNO LL30 1HH
Tel: 01492 879133
Fax: 01492 876055
E-mail: chris@alpine-travel.co.uk
Web site: www.alpine-travel.co.uk
Dirs: Bryan Owens, Patricia Owens, Christopher Owens, Christopher Bryan Owens.
Fleet: 90 - double-deck bus, single-deck bus, coach, minibus.
Chassis: Bedford. Bova. Bristol. DAF. Dennis. Ford. Leyland. Leyland National. MAN. Mercedes. Volvo.
Bodies: Alexander. Bova. Duple. ECW. East Lancs. Leyland National. Marshall. Noge. Northern Counties. Plaxton. Sunsundegui. Wadham Stringer. Willowbrook. Robin Hood.
Ops incl: local bus services, school contracts, excursions & tours, private hire, continental tours.
Livery: Green/Cream or White
Ticket System: Setright

ARRIVA CYMRU LTD

IMPERIAL BUILDINGS, GLAN-Y-MOR ROAD, LLANDUDNO JUNCTION LL31 9RU
Tel: 01492 592111.
Fax: 01492 592968.
Man Dir: S. Green. **Eng Dir**: M. Evans.
Fin Dir: B. Pegg.
Fleet: 265 - 39 double-deck bus, 129 single-deck bus, 3 coach, 94 midibus.
Chassis: DAF. Dennis. Leyland. Mercedes. Scania. Volvo.
Bodies: Alexander. ECW. Northern Counties. Plaxton. Wright.
Ops incl: local bus services, school contracts, private hire, express.
Livery: Turquoise/Cotswold Stone
Ticket System: Wayfarer III.

GRWP ABERCONWY

MAESDU, LLANDUDNO LL30 1HF.
Tel: 01492 870870.
Fax: 01492 860821.
Fleetname: Great Orme Tours.
Dir: I. Trevette.
Tramway & Coach Man: Rosemary Sutton.
Fleet: 4 midicoach.
Chassis: 3 Bedford. 1 Guy.
Ops incl: local bus services, excursions & tours.
Livery: Blue/Cream.
Ticket System: Almex.

LLEW JONES INTERNATIONAL

STATION YARD, LLANRWST LL26 0EH
Tel: 01492 640320
Fax: 01492 642040
E-mail: info@llewjones.com
Web site: www.llewjones.com
ManDir: Stephen Jones
Ops Man: Kevin Williams **Fin Dir**: Eirlys Jones **Wkshp Man**: Erfyl Roberts
Fleet: 24 - 14 coach, 6 midibus, 4 midicoach.
Chassis: 6 DAF. 5 Dennis. 1 LDV. 1 MAN. 11 Mercedes. 1 Optare. 1 Setra. 1 Volvo.
Bodies: 3 Ayats. 1 Carlyle. 4 Duple. 1 Jonckheere. 2 Mercedes. 1 Noge. 1 Optare. 6 Plaxton. 1 Reeve Burgess. 2 UVG. 1 Van Hool. 2 Ovi.
Ops incl: local bus services, school contracts, excursions & tours, private hire, continental tours.
Livery: White/Silver/Magenta/Blue
Ticket system: Almex A90

ROBERTS MINI COACHES

RHANDIR GARAGE, RHANDIR LL22 8BW.
Tel: 01492 650449.
Prop: W. T. Roberts.

DENBIGHSHIRE

GHA COACHES

MILL GARAGE, BETWS GWERFIL GOCH, CORWEN LL21 9PU
Tel: 01978 753598
Fax: 01978 721441
E-mail: ghacoaches@aol.com
Web site: www.ghacoaches.co.uk
Man Dir: Gareth Davies
Fleet: incl 10 coaches
Chassis: includes 10 Volvo
Bodies: includes 10 Plaxton
Ops incl: school contracts, private hire
Livery: Grey/Red/Maroon.

M & H COACHES

8 TREWEN, DENBIGH LL16 3HF.
Tel: 01745 812057.
Prop: Mrs M. Owen.
Livery: Blue/White.

VOEL COACHES LTD

R

PENISA FILLING STATION, FFORD TALARGOCH, DYSERTH LL18 6BP
Tel: 01745 570309.
Fax: 01745 570307
Web site: www.voelcoaches.com
Man Dir: W M Kerfoot-Davies **Com Man**: Michelle Kerfoot Higginson.
Fleet: 25 - 7 double-deck bus, 4 single-deck bus, 12 coach, 1 minibus, 1 midicoach.
Chassis: Dennis. Mercedes. Scania. Volvo
Bodies: Berkhof. Van Hool.
Ops incl: local bus services, school contracts, excursions & tours, private hire, continental tours.
Livery: Orange

FLINTSHIRE

EAGLES AND CRAWFORD
wc

53 NEW STREET, MOLD CH7 1NY
Tel: 01352 700217/8
Fax: 01352 750211
E-mail: eaglesandcrawford@supanet.com
Ptnrs: J. F. J. K. & W. P. Eagles.
Fleet: 15 - 6 double-deck bus, 7 coach, 2 minibus.
Chassis: 6 Bristol. 2 Dennis. 1 Freight Rover. 4 Leyland. 1 Mercedes. 1 Toyota. 1 Van Hool.
Bodies: 1 Caetano. 1 Carlyle. 3 Duple. 6 ECW. 1 Mercedes. 1 Optare. 3 Plaxton. 1 Van Hool.
Ops incl: local bus services, excursions & tours, private hire, continental tours.
Livery: White/Blue/Orange.
Ticket System: Almex.

*FOUR GIRLS COACHES
wc

THE OLD POST OFFICE YARD, CORWEN ROAD, PONTYBODKIN, MOLD CH7 4TG
Tel: 01352 770438
Fax: 01352 770253
Ptnrs: Carolyn Thomas, Elaine Williams
Fleet: 9 - 7 coach, 1 minibus, 1 midicoach.
Chassis: 1 DAF. 1 LDV. 6 Volvo.
Bodies: incl: 1 Caetano
Ops incl: school contracts, private hire.
Livery: Turquoise/Red/Yellow

JONES MOTOR SERVICES
wc T

CHESTER ROAD, FLINT CH6 5DZ.
Tel: 01352 733292.
Fax: 01352 763353.
E-mail: tours@jonescoaches.co.uk
Ptnr: A. Jones.
Fleet: 10 - 9 coach, 1 midicoach.
Chassis: DAF, Iveco, Leyland.
Bodies: Caetano, Duple, Plaxton, Van Hool.
Ops incl: excursions & tours, private hire, express, continental tours, school contracts.
Livery: Blue.

OARE'S COACHES

TY DRAW. BRYNFORD, HOLYWELL CH8 8LP.
Tel: 01352 714868.
Fax: 01352 713339.
Prop: G. A. Oare.
Livery: White/Red/Silver.

P. & O. LLOYD
wc

RHYDWEN GARAGE, BAGILLT CH6 6JJ.
Tel: 01352 710682.
Man Dir: David Lloyd.
Fleet: 36 - 17 double-deck bus, 4 single-deck bus. 6 coach, 7 minibus.

Chassis: incl: Optare. Leyland. Volvo.
Bodies: incl: MCW. East Lancs. MCW. Optare. Plaxton. Van Hool.
Ops incl: local bus services, private hire, school contracts.
Livery: Cream/Red or Cream/Maroon/Gold.
Ticket System: Almex.

PIED BULL COACHES

53 WOODLANDS CLOSE, MOLD CH7 1UU.
Tel/Fax: 01352 754237.
Prop: R. Williams.
Livery: Blue/White.

TOWNLYNX

CAETIA LLWYD, NORTHOP ROAD, HOLYWELL CH8 8AE.
Tel: 01352 710489.
Prop: S. A. Lee.
Livery: White/Yellow/Blue.

GWYNEDD

ARVONIA COACHES
wc

THE SQUARE, LLANRUG LL55 4AA.
Tel: 01286 675175.
Fax: 01286 671126.
Prop: R. Morris.
Fleet: 9 - 6 coach, 2 midibus, 1 minibus.
Chassis: 1 Ford Transit. 1 MAN. 1 Mercedes. 1 Volvo. 3 EOS. 2 Van Hool.
Bodies: 2 Alexander. 1 Carlyle. 2 Van Hool. 3 EOS. 1 Noge.
Ops incl: local bus services, excursions & tours, private hire, continental tours.
Livery: White/Orange/Red.
Ticket System: Almex.

CAMBRIAN COAST COACH LINE

RIVERSIDE HOUSE, ABERGYNOLWYN LL36 9YR.
Tel/Fax: 01654 782235.
E-mail: ronbott@talyllyn.freeserve.co.uk.
Prop: Ronald C. Bott.
Fleet: 2 - 1 coach, 1 minicoach, plus 1 taxi.
Chassis: 1 Mercedes. 1 Toyota. 1 Seat.
Ops incl: excursions & tours, private hire.
Livery: Red/Blue.
Ticket System: Setright.

CERBYDAU BERWYN COACHES

BERWYN, TREFOR LL54 5LY
Tel: 01286 660315.
Fax: 01286 660110.
Prop: B. Japheth.
Livery: White/Yellow/Brown.

CAELLOI MOTORS (T. H. JONES & SON)
wc A/C T

UNIT 17, GLAN Y DON INDUSTRIAL ESTATE, PWLLHELI LL53 5YT
Tel: 01758 612719
Fax: 01758 612335
Fleet: 6 - 2 single-deck bus, 4 coach
Chassis: 1 DAF. 1 Marshall. 4 Volvo.
Bodies: 1 Berkhof. 1 Marshall. 3 Van Hool. 1 Wright.
Ops incl: local bus services, excursions & tours, private hire, continental tours
Livery: Multi
Ticket System: Almex

*CLYNNOG & TREFOR
wc A/C R24 T

TREFOR, CAERNARFON LL54 5HP
Tel: 01286 660208
Fax: 01286 660538
Dirs: D C Jones, E Griffiths
Fleet: 40 - 12 double-deck bus, 16 coach, 12 minibus.
Chassis: 3 Bristol. 9 Leyland. 12 Mercedes. 16 Volvo.
Bodies: 12 Alexander. 9 ECW. 3 Jonckheere. 3 Northern Counties. 13 Plaxton
Ops incl: local bus services, school contracts, private hire.
Livery: Red/Cream, White
Ticket system: Wayfarer TGX

EMMAS COACHES
wc A/C

BAKER STREET GARAGE, MARIAN ROAD, DOLGELLAU LL40 1EL
Tel: 01341 423934
Fax: 01341 423321
E-mail: info@emmascoaches.co.uk
Web site: www.emmascoaches.co.uk
Dir/Prop: Barry Thomas, **Sec**: Anita Thomas
Tran Man: Brett Thomas
Fleet: 11 - 1 single-deck bus, 5 coach, 1 double-deck coach, 1 midicoach, 2 minibus, 1 people carrier.
Chassis: 1 Bedford. 1 DAF. 1 Ford. 2 Leyland. 1 Leyland National. 2 Mercedes. 2 Scania. 1 Toyota.
Bodies: 1 Caetano. 2 Mercedes. 1 Optare. 23 Plaxton. 3 Van Hool. 1 other
Ops incl: local bus services, school contracts, excursions & tours, continental tours.
Livery: Green

EXPRESS MOTORS
wc A/C R24 T

THE GARAGE, LLYFNI ROAD, PENYGROES LL54 6ND
Tel: 01286 881108
Fax: 01286 882331
Web site: expressmotors.co.uk
Ptnrs: Eric Wyn Jones, Jean Ann Jones.
Managers: Ian Wyn Jones, Kevin Wyn Jones, Keith Jones.
Fleet: 36 - 2 double-deck bus, 8 single-deck bus, 8 coach, 2 double-deck coach, 1 open-

---

Welsh Operators

A/c	Air conditioning	✓	Replacement vehicle available
♿	Vehicles suitable for disabled	T	Toilet-drop facilities available
🍴	Coach(es) with galley facilities		Vintage vehicle(s) available
wc	Coach(es) with toilet facilities		Open top vehicle(s)
●	Seat belt-fitted vehicles		
R	Recovery service available (not 24 hr)		
R24	24hr recovery service		

top bus, 10 midibus, 2 midicoach, 2 minicoach, 1 vintage.
Chassis: 1 Bedford. 2 Bova. 2 Bristol. 4 DAF. 2 Dennis. 7 MAN. 10 Mercedes. 7 Optare.
Bodies: 3 Alexander. 2 Bova. 1 Duple. 2 ECW. 3 East Lancs. 1 Hispano. 1 Leyland. 3 Neoplan. 7 Optare. 3 Plaxton. 1 Transbus. 1 UVG. 3 Van Hool. 3 Wadham Stringer. 2 Wright.
Livery: buses - White/Yellw coaches - White

GRIFFITHS COACHES

3 ELIM COTTAGES, SILOH, PORTDINORWIC LL56 4JR
Tel: 01248 670530
Fax: 01248 671111
Prop: Hefin Griffiths
Fleet: 11 - 5 double-deck bus, 1 single-deck bus, 5 coach.
Chassis: 5 Bristol. 1 Leyland. 5 Volvo.
Bodies: 1 Berkhof. 5 ECW. 3 Jonckheere. 1 Plaxton. 1 Van Hool.
Ops incl: private hire, school contracts.
Livery: Red/Grey/White

JOHN'S COACHES

NORTH WESTERN ROAD, GLAN-Y-PWLL, BLAENEAU FFESTINIOG LL41 3NN
Tel: 01766 831781
Mobile: 0777 167735
Fax: 01766 831781
Prop: J R Edwards
Fleet: 6
Chassis: 1 Berkhof. 3 DAF. 2 Mercedes.
Bodies: Berkhof. Mercedes. Plaxton.
Ops incl: local bus service, school contracts, private hire.
Livery: White/Red
Ticket System: Wayfarer

KMP LLANBERIS LTD

Y ELYN INDUSTRIAL ESTATE, LLANBERIS LL55 4EL
Tel: 01286 870880
Fax: 01286 871191
E-mail: info@kmpbus.com
Web site: www.kmpbus.com
Man Dir: K A Williams **Co Sec**: E Williams
Eng Man: M A Williams **Ops Man**: D Hulme
Fleet: 28 - 4 double-deck bus, 15 single-deck bus, 4 coach, 1 open-top bus, 3 midibus.
Chassis: 9 Dennis. 1 Leyland. 4 MCW. 3 Mercedes. 1 Neoplan. 1 Optare. 9 Volvo.
Bodies: 3 Alexander. 1 Caetano. 2 East Lancs. 4 MCW. 3 Mellor. 1 Neoplan. 1 Optare. 5 Plaxton. 2 Reeve Burgess. 6 Wright.
Ops incl: local bus services, school contracts, private hire.
Livery: Blue/Black.
Ticket System: Wayfarer 3

NEFYN COACHES

WEST END GARAGE, ST DAVIDS ROAD, NEFYN LL53 6HE.
Tel: 01758 720904.
Fax: 01758 720331.
Props: B. G. Owen, M. A. Owen, A. G. Owen.
Fleet: 9 - 1 single-deck bus, 4 coach, 4 minicoach.
Chassis: 1 Freight Rover. 1 Leyland. 3 Mercedes. 3 Volvo. 1 Optare.
Bodies: Reeve Burgess, Plaxton.

Ops incl: local bus services, school contracts, excursions & tours, private hire.
Livery: Multi-colour.

SILVER STAR COACH HOLIDAYS LTD

13 CASTLE SQUARE, CAERNARFON LL55 2NF
Tel: 01286 672333
Fax: 01286 678118
Web site: www.silverstarholidays.com
Man Dir: Elfyn William Thomas **Co Sec**: Helen Jones **Ch Eng**: Barry Thomas
Ops Man: Eric Wyn Thomas
Fleet: 18 - 5 single-deck bus, 9 coach, 4 midibus. 1 vintage.
Chassis: 1 AEC. 1 Bedford, 3 Bristol. 3 Dennis. 1 Leyland. 8 Mercedes. 3 Neoplan. 1 Optare. 2 Setra. 2 Volvo.
Bodies: 1 Alexander. 3 ECW. 3 Neoplan. 1 Optare. 25 Plaxton. 2 Setra. 2 Van Hool. 1 Burlingham.
Ops incl: local bus services, school contracts, excursions & tours, private hire, continental tours.
Livery: Green coaches/Blue buses.
Ticket System: Wayfarer 3

MERTHYR TYDFIL

SIXTY SIXTY COACHES

THE COACH DEPOT, MERTHYR INDUSTRIAL PARK, PENTREBACH CF48 4DR
Tel: 01443 692060.
Fax: 01443 699061.
E-mail: enquiries@sixsixty.co.uk
Web site: www.sixtysixty.co.uk
Prop: G Handy, C T Handy.
Fleet: 18 - 3 single-deck bus, 9 coach, 2 double-deck coach, 3 midibus, 1 midicoach
Chassis: 6 DAF. 3 Dennis. 1 Leyland. 3 Mercedes. 2 Scania. 3 Volvo.
Bodies: 3 Alexander. 2 Caetano. 1 Duple. 3 Plaxton. 3 Reeve Burgess. 5 Van Hool. 1 LAG.
Ops incl: local bus services, school contracts, excursions & tours, private hire.
Livery: Silver
Ticket system: Wayfarer

*STAGECOACH IN SOUTH WALES
See Torfaen

MONMOUTHSHIRE

*REES COACH TRAVEL

WAUNLAPRA, LLANELLY HILL, ABERGAVENNY NP7 0PW
Tel: 01873 830210
Fax: 01873 832167
Snr Prtnr: Nigel A Rees
Ptnrs: Neville A Rees, Margo E Rees
Fleet: 10 coach.
Chassis: 1 Bedford. 1 Bova. 3 DAF. 2 Dennis. 1 LDV. 2 Neoplan
Bodies: 1 Bova. 3 Duple. 2 Jonckheere. 2 Neoplan. 2 Van Hool.

Ops incl: local bus services, school contracts, excursions & tours, private hire, continental tours.
Livery: Green/White

*STAGECOACH IN SOUTH WALES
See Torfaen

NEATH & PORT TALBOT

BLUEBIRD OF NEATH/ PONTARDAWE

9-10 LONDON ROAD, NEATH SA11 1HB.
Tel/Fax: 01639 643849.
Fleetname: Bluebird Coaches (Neath).
Prop: Ian S. Warren. **Ch Eng**: George Warren. **Sec**: Ms Melanie Evans.
Fleet: 21 - 2 double-deck bus, 18 coach, 1 midibus.
Chassis: 2 Bristol. 1 DAF. 1 Mercedes. 17 Volvo.
Bodies: 4 Jonckheere. 1 Mercedes. Leyland. 10 Plaxton. 6 Van Hool.
Ops incl: local bus services, excursions & tours, private hire, continental tours, school contracts.
Livery: White/Blue/Red.

NELSON & SON (GLYNNEATH) LTD

74A HIGH STREET, GLYNNEATH SA11 5AW.
Tel: 01639 722252.
Fax: 01639 720308.
Fleetname: Nelson's Coaches.
Man Dir: J. L. R. Nelson.
Dir/Co Sec: Mrs J. Nelson.
Fleet: 11 - 10 coach, 1 midicoach.
Chassis: 4 DAF. 1 Ford. 4 Leyland. 1 Mercedes. 1 Volvo.
Bodies: 1 Duple. 1 Jonckheere. 5 Plaxton. 3 Van Hool. 1 Other.
Ops incl: school contracts, excursions & tours, private hire, continental tours.
Livery: White/Red/Orange.

*D J THOMAS COACHES LTD

MILLAND ROAD INDUSTRIAL ESTATE, NEATH SA11 1NJ
Tel/Fax: 01639 635502
E-mail: mail@djthomascoaches.co.uk
Web site: www.djthomascoaches.co.uk
Man Dir/Co Sec: Mrs Andrea Gibson **Man Dir**: Richard Thomas **Ch Eng**: Lee Gibson
Fleet: 18 - 1 single-deck bus, 9 coach, 3 minicoach, 3 midicoach, 2 minibus.
Chassis: Ford. Ford Transit Tourneo. Mercedes. Renault. Volvo.
Bodies: Berkhof. Mercedes. Plaxton. Van Hool.
Ops incl: local bus services, excursions & tours, private hire, school contracts.
Ticket system: Wayfarer

Welsh Operators

TONNA LUXURY COACHES LTD

TENNIS VIEW GARAGE, HEOL-Y-GLO, TONNA SA11 3NJ
Tel: 01639 642727
Fax: 01639 646052
Dirs: K M Hopkins, A Hopkins
Fleet: 16 coach.
Chassis: 1 DAF. 1 Dennis. 3 Mercedes. 11 Volvo.
Bodies: incl 1 Alexander. Plaxton. Van Hool.
Ops incl: school contracts, private hire.
Livery: White/Blue

NEWPORT

*NEWPORT TRANSPORT LTD

160 CORPORATION ROAD, NEWPORT NP19 0WF
Tel: 01633 670563
Fax: 01633 242589
Web site: www.newporttransport.co.uk
E-mail: enquiries@newporttransport.co.uk
Fleetname: Newport Bus
Chmn: J G J Dally **Man Dir**: T G Roberts
Dir of Delivery: C D Blyth
Fin Dir: D Jenkins
Fleet: 76 - 6 double-deck bus, 51 single-deck bus, 7 coach, 1 open-top bus, 11 midibus.
Chassis: 17 Dennis. 59 Scania.
Bodies: 42 Alexander. 7 Irizar. 9 Wright. 18 Scania.
Ops incl: local bus services, school contracts, excursions & tours, private hire.
Livery: Green/Cream.
Ticket System: Wayfarer TGX150

*STAGECOACH IN SOUTH WALES
See Torfaen

WELSH DRAGON TRAVEL

21 BEAUFORT ROAD, NEWPORT NP19 7ND.
Tel: 01633 761397
E-mail: alan.smith5@ntworld.com
Prop: Alan Barrington Smith.
Fleet: 4 - 1 double-deck bus, 2 coach, 1 open-top bus.
Chassis: 1 Bedford. 1 Bristol. 2 Leyland.
Ops incl: local bus services, school contracts, private hire.
Livery: Red/Cream
Ticket System: Almex

PEMBROKESHIRE

W. H. COLLINS

CUFFERN GARAGE, ROCH, HAVERFORDWEST SA62 6HB.
Tel: 01437 710337.
Fleetname: Collins Coaches.
Prop: P. N. & M. Collins.
Fleet: 18 - 16 minibus, 2 minicoach.
Ops incl: school contracts, private hire.
Livery: Blue/Grey/White.

*EDWARDS BROS

THE GARAGE, BROAD HAVEN ROAD, TIERS CROSS, HAVERFORDWEST SA62 3BZ
Tel: 01437 890230
Fax: 01437 890337
Prop: Robert Edwards
Fleet: 18 - 8 coach, 3 midibus, 4 midicoach, 3 minibus.
Chassis: 1 Bova. 1 DAF. 1 Dennis. 2 LDV. 7 Mercedes. 6 Volvo.
Bodies: 1 Bova. 1 Marshall/MCV. 3 Mercedes. 7 Plaxton. 1 Reeve Burgess. 3 Van Hool. 2 other.
Ops incl: local bus services, school contracts, private hire.
Livery: Gold or White.
Ticket System: Wayfarer

*MIDWAY MOTORS

MIDWAY GARAGE, CRYMYCH SA41 3QU
Tel: 01239 831267
Fax: 01239 831279
E-mail: reesmidway@hotmail.com
Fleetname: W S Rees & Son
Props: Wyndham Rees, Elan Rees
Fleet: 15 - 3 single-deck bus, 5 coach, 4 midicoach, 2 minibus, 1 minicoach.
Chassis: 1 Bova. 1 DAF. 3 Dennis. 2 Ford. 1 Ford Transit. 1 Freight Rover. 1 Optare. 1 Toyota. 4 Volvo.
Bodies: incl: 1 Bova. 3 Caetano.
Ops incl: local bus services, school contracts, excursions & tours, continental tours.
Livery: Silver/Blue
Ticket system: Almex

SILCOX COACHES

WATERLOO GARAGE, PEMBROKE DOCK SA72 4RR.
Tel: 01646 683143.
Fax: 01646 621787.
Man Dir: K. W. Silcox
Fleet: 74 - 42 single-deck bus, 19 coach, 14 midibus, 1 midicoach.
Chassis: 25 Dennis. 38 Leyland. 1 MAN. 10 Mercedes. 1 Optare. 1 Volvo.
Bodies: 2 Berkhof. 7 Caetano. 5 Duple. 1 East Lancs. 3 Marco Polo. 4 Marshall. 2 Mellor. 1 Optare. 40 Plaxton. 2 UVG. 1 Van Hool. 6 Wadham Stringer. 2 Wright.

Ops incl: local bus services, school contracts, excursions & tours, private hire, continental tours.
Livery: Red/Cream/Blue.

SUMMERDALE COACHES

SUMMERDALE GARAGE, LETTERSTON SA62 5UB.
Tel: 01348 840270.
Props: D. G. Davies, B. J. L. Davies, G. R. Jones.
Livery: Yellow/Blue

POWYS

A. & E. HIRE

PENYBRYN, LLANGYNIEW, WELSHPOOL SY21 0JS
Tel: 01938 810518
Dir: Arwyn P Davies
Fleet: 5 minibus
Chassis/bodies: 4 Ford. 1 Freight Rover.
Ops incl: school contracts, private hire

ROY BROWNS COACHES

15 HIGH STREET, BUILTH WELLS LD2 3DN
Tel: 01982 552597
Tel: 01982 552286
E-mail: neil@rbci.fsnet.co.uk
Web site: www.roybrownscoaches.co.uk
Prop: N W Brown **Ops Man**: P H Davies
Fleet: 28 - 6 single-deck bus, 12 coach, 10 minibus.
Chassis: 4 Bedford. 5 DAF. 2 Dennis. 7 Leyland. 3 Optare. 1 Volvo
Bodies: 4 Caetano. 4 MCW. 10 Plaxton. 1 Wright. 1 other.
Ops incl: local bus services, school contracts, excursions & tours, private hire
Ticket System: Setright.

*CELTIC TRAVEL

NEW STREET, LLANIDLOES SY18 6EH
Tel/Fax: 01686 412231
E-mail: info@celtictravel.net
Web site: www.celtictravel.net
Props: W P L Davies, Mrs J Davies
Ops Man: P Davies
Fleet: 22 - 15 coach, 7 minibus.
Chassis: 2 Dennis. 7 Ford Transit. 3 Leyland. 10 Volvo
Bodies: 2 Duple. 1 Jonckheere. 7 Plaxton. 3 Van Hool. 2 Wadham Stringer.
Ops incl: school contracts, excursions & tours, private hire.
Livery: Grey with green/red lettering

CENTRAL TRAVEL

OLD BULK YARD, STATION YARD, NEWTOWN SY16 1BA
Tel: 07710 432832
Tel/Fax: 01686 610224
Props: Richard W Bowen

A/C	Air conditioning
	Vehicles suitable for disabled
	Coach(es) with galley facilities
WC	Coach(es) with toilet facilities
	Seat belt-fitted vehicles
R	Recovery service available (not 24 hr)
R24	24hr recovery service
	Replacement vehicle available
T	Toilet-drop facilities available
	Vintage vehicle(s) available
	Open top vehicle(s)

Welsh Operators

Fleet: 4 - 1 coach, 1 midicoach, 1 minicoach, 1 minibus.
Chassis: 1 Ford Transit. 1 Mercedes. 1 Scania. 1 Volvo
Bodies: 1 Mercedes. 1 Plaxton. 1 Van Hool.
Ops incl: school contracts, private hire.

COACHING CONNECTION
14 GREAT OAK STREET, LLANIDLOES SY18 6BN
Tel: 01686 413714
Fax: 01686 411065
Props: David Corfield, Miss Betty Tonks
Fleet: 1 coach
Chassis/Body: Setra
Ops incl: excursions & tours.
Livery: Cream with orange/brown flashes.

CROSS GATES COACHES
CROSS GATES, LLANDRINDOD WELLS LD1 6RE
Tel: 01597 852000
Fax: 01597 851748
E-mail: peter@llink.co.uk
Dir/ Ops Man: Peter Knill **Dir/Co Sec**: Reg Knill **Ch Eng**: Chris Prynne
Fleet: 15 - 4 single-deck bus, 10 coach, 1 midibus
Chassis: 2 DAF. 2 Dennis. 2 Mercedes. 4 Optare. 5 Scania.
Bodies: 1 Carlyle. 1 Duple. 1 Irizar. 4 Optare. 4 Plaxton. 4 Van Hool.
Ops incl: local bus services, school contracts, private hire.
Livery: Blue/Graphite
Ticket system: Wayfarer

D G DAVIES
AFON MARTEG GARAGE, PANT-Y-DWR LD6 5NA
Tel: 05978 8232
Prop: D G Davies
Fleet: 2
Chassis: Ford.
Bodies: Duple, Plaxton.
Ops incl: school contracts, private hire.
Livery: White with red/blue flashing

*R G GITTINS - COACHES
THE GARAGE, DOLANOG, WELSHPOOL SY21 0LQ
Tel/fax: 01938 810439
Prop: R G Gittins
Fleet: 3 - 1 coach, 1 midibus, 1 midicoach
Chassis: 1 Bova. 1 MAN. 1 Mercedes.
Ops incl: school contracts, excursions & tours, private hire.

GWYN JONES (MEIFORD)
THE GARAGE, MEIFOD SY22 6DB
Tel: 01938 500249
E-mail: gwynmeifod@talk21.com
Ptnrs: Gwyn Jones, Jean Jones, Martin Jones
Fleet: 3 - 2 single-deck bus, 1 midicoach
Chassis/Bodies: 1 DAF. 1 Caetano. 1 Mercedes.
Ops incl: school contracts, excursions & tours, private hire, continental tours.
Livery: Green/White

LAKELINE COACHES
EBRAN-DDU, FELINDRE, KNIGHTON LD7 1YN
Tel: 01547 7662
Dir: J E A Lakelin
Fleet: 4 - 3 coach, 1 minibus.
Chassis: 1 Bedford. 1 DAF. 1 Dennis. 1 Ford.
Bodies: 1 Duple. 1 LDV. 2 Plaxton.
Ops incl: school contracts, private hire
Livery: Pale Blue/Dark Blue

LLOYDS COACHES
R24
OLD CROSVILLE GARAGE, DOLL STREET, MACHYNLLETH SY20 8BH
Tel: 01654 702100
Fax: 01654 703900
Mobile: 07712 552953
E-mail: lloydscoaches@hotmail.com
Dirs: D W Lloyd
Fleet: 12 - 1 single-deck bus, 6 coach, 1 midicoach, 4 minibus
Chassis: 2 Leyland. 5 Mercedes. 5 Volvo.
Bodies: 3 Alexander. 1 Duple. 7 Plaxton. 1 other.
Ops incl: local bus services, school contracts, private hire.
Livery: Silver/Red/Yellow
Ticket system: Wayfarer

OWEN'S MOTORS LTD
TEMESIDE HOUSE, STATION ROAD, KNIGHTON LD7 1DT
Tel: 01547 528303
Fax: 01547 520512
Web site: www.owensmotors.co.uk
Ops Man: D. Owen. **Ch Eng**: T Owen.
Sec/Dir: J Owen
Fleet: 14 - 11 coach, 3 minibus.
Chassis: 3 Dennis. 1 Ford. 2 LDV. 7 Volvo.
Bodies: 2 Duple. 1 Ford Transit. 2 LDV. 8 Plaxton. 1 Van Hool.
Ops incl: local bus services, school contracts, excursions & tours, private hire, continental tours.
Livery: Blue/Grey

*STAGECOACH IN SOUTH WALES
See Torfaen

*STOCKHAMS COACH, MINIBUS & TAXIS
19 PLASDERWEN, LLANGATTOCK, CRICKHOWELL NP8 1HY
Tel: 01873 810559
Fax: 01873 810343
Dirs: Mrs Nancy Stockham, Melvyn Stockham, Derek Stockham
Fleet: 6 - 3 single-deck bus, 2 minibus, 1 minicoach.
Chassis: 2 Ford Transit. 1 Iveco. 1 Leyland. 2 Volvo
Ops incl: excursions & tours, private hire.
Livery: Green/Cream

STRATOS TRAVEL
2 SHORTBRIDGE STREET, NEWTOWN SY16 2LW
Tel: 01686 629021
Fax: 01686 626092
E-mail: info@stratostravel.co.uk
Web site: www.stratostravel.co.uk
Prop: M Owen
Fleet: 5 - 1 single-deck bus, 3 coach, 1 midicoach.
Chassis: 1 Ayats. 1 Bova. 1 Dennis. 1 Iveco.1 Toyota.
Bodies: 1 Ayats. 1 Beulas. 1 Bova. 1 Caetano. 1 Plaxton.
Ops incl: local bus services, excursions & tours, private hire, continental tours.
Livery: Silver/Blue

*TANAT VALLEY COACHES
THE GARAGE, LLANRHAEDR YM MOCHNANT, OSWESTRY SY10 0AD
Tel: 01691 780212
Fax: 01691 780634
E-mail: info@tanat.co.uk
Web site: www.tanat.co.uk
Dirs: Michael Morris, Sara Morris, Peter Morris, Nick Culliford
Fleet: 50 - 3 double-deck bus, 18 single-deck bus, 13 coach, 3 midibus, 1 midicoach, 12 minibus.
Chassis: 4 Dennis. 12 LDV. 13 Leyland. 3 Mercedes. 3 Optare. 1 Toyota. 9 Volvo.
Bodies: 3 Alexander. 1 Berkhof. 1 Caetano. 3 Carlyle. 2 Duple. 6 East Lancs. 3 Jonckheere. 6 Leyland. 2 Northern Counties. 3 Optare. 5 Plaxton. 2 UVG. 1 Van Hool. 12 other.
Ops incl: local bus services, school contracts, excursions & tours, private hire, express.
Livery: Maroon/Mustard
Ticket System: Almex A90

*WILLIAMS COACHES
R24 T
CAMBRIAN WAY, BRECON LD3 7BE
Tel: 01874 622223/611534
Fax: 01874 625218
E-mail: office@williams-coaches.co.uk
Web site: www.williams-coaches.co.uk
Dirs: J L Williams (Senr) (**Chmn**)
D M Williams (**Sec**), D G Williams,
J L Williams (Jnr), **Eng**: K Parry
Fleet: 40 - 20 coach, 6 midicoach, 14 minibus.
Chassis: 2 Bova. 2 DAF. 2 Dennis. 8 Ford Transit. 1 Fiat. 9 Ford transit.1 Irisbus. 3 LDV. 5 MAN. 14 Mercedes. 1 Scania. 6 Setra. 1 Volkswagen.
Bodies: 2 Bova. 1 Caetano. 1 Hispano. 1 Indcar. 1 Irizar. 1 Jonckheere. 5 Mercedes. 2 Plaxton. 2 Reeve Burgess. 6 Setra. 1 Van Hool.
Ops incl: school contracts, private hire, excursions & tours, continental tours.
Livery: Orange/Cream
Ticket System: Setright

RHONDDA, CYNON, TAFF

BEBB TRAVEL
♿ 💺 ♿wc A/c

THE COACH STATIOIN, LLANTWIT FARDRE CF38 2HB
Tel: 01443 215100
Fax: 01443 215134
E-mail: sales@bebbtravel.co.uk
Chmn: John O'Brien **Man Dir**: David Newman **Fleet Eng**: Dave Witte
Fleet: 44 - 26 single-deck bus, 18 coach.
Chassis: 26 Optare. 18 Volvo.
Bodies: 26 Optare. 18 Plaxton.
Ops incl: local bus services, school contracts, express
Livery: White/Blue/Red/Green
Ticket system: ERG
(Part of the Veolia Group)

EDWARDS COACHES
♿ wc 💺 🚌 A/c R 🔧 T

NEWTOWN INDUSTRIAL ESTATE, LLANTWIT FARDRE CF38 2EE
Tel: 01443 202048
Fax: 01443 217583
E-mail: admin@edwardscoaches.co.uk
Web site: www.edwardscoaches.co.uk
Owner: Mike Edwards **Dirs**: Shaun Edwards, Jason Edwards, Kelly Edwards, Jessica Edwards
Fleet: 84 - 28 double-deck bus, 47 coach, 5 midicoach, 4 minibus.
Chassis: 14 MCW. 14 Volkswagen.
Bodies: 13 Bova. 7 Irizar. 2 Jonckheere. 5 Marcopolo. 14 MCW. 1 Mellor. 5 Plaxton. 6 Setra.
Ops incl: school contracts, excursions & tours, private hire, continental tours.
Livery: White/Blue

GLOBE COACHES
wc A/c 💺 🍴 🔧

BROOKLANDS, FFORCHNEOL ROW, GODREAMAN, ABERDARE CF44 6HD.
Tel: 01685 873622.
Fax: 01685 876526
E-mail: wayne@globecoaches.entadsl.com
Web site: www.globecoaches.co.uk
Prop: Wayne Jarvis
Fleet: 18 - 16 coach, 2 midicoach.
Chassis: 2 DAF. 1 Leyland. 1 MAN. 2 Mercedes. 12 Volvo.
Bodies: 2 Berkhof. 2 Caetano. 2 Duple. 6 Jonckheere. 4 Plaxton.
Ops incl: excursions & tours, private hire, school contracts, continental tours.
Livery: White/Blue.

*MAISEY 💺
GELYNOG YARD, CASTELLAU ROAD, BEDDAU CF38 1ND
Tel/Fax: 01443 205462
E-mail: info@maiseybus.co.uk
Web site: www.maiseybus.co.uk
Ptnrs: Brian Evans, Graham Evans, Colin Evans.
Fleet: 10 minicoach.
Chassis: 2 Ford. 1 LDV. 7 Renault.
Bodies: 10 other
Ops incl: school contracts, private hire.
Livery: White/Red

*STAGECOACH IN SOUTH WALES
See Torfaen

THOMAS OF RHONDDA
♿ 💺 wc 🍴 A/c T

BUS DEPOT, PORTH CF39 0AG.
Tel: 01443 433714
Fleet: 56 - 20 double-deck bus, 6 single-deck bus, 22 coach, 3 double-deck coach, 3 midibus, 2 minibus.
Chassis: 7 Bova. 4 DAF. 4 Dennis. 26 Leyland. 3 MAN. 2 Scania. 10 Volvo.
Ops incl: local bus services, excursions & tours, school contracts, private hire, continental tours.
Livery: White
Ticket System: Almex

CITY & COUNTY OF SWANSEA

D'COACHES (DIAMOND HOLIDAYS)
wc A/c 💺 🔧

98/99 WOODFIELD STREET, MORRISTON SA6 8AS
Tel: 01792 795808
Fax: 01792 781173
E-mail: enquiry@diamondholidays.co.uk.
Web site: www.diamondholidays.co.uk.
Man Dir: Chris Roberts.
Ops Dir: Ryan Jones **Fin Dir**: David Rees
Fleet: 18 coach
Chassis: 18 DAF.
Bodies: 18 Bova.
Ops incl: excursions & tours, private hire, continental tours.
Livery: Cream/Gold/Green.

*FIRST CYMRU BUSES LIMITED ♿ 💺 wc
HEOL GWYROSYDD, PENLAN SA5 7BN
Tel: 01792 582233
Fax: 01792 561356
Web Site: www.firstgroup.com
Man Dir: J W Davies **Interim Ops Dir**: Mrs C Morgan **Fin Dir**: T McNiff
Ops Dir: P F Collier **Eng Dir**: P J Davies
Fleet: 360 - 3 double-deck bus, 25 single-deck bus, 45 coach, 270 midcoach, 17 minibus.
Chassis: 6 BMC. 296 Dennis. 3 Iveco. 3 Leyland. 14 Mercedes. 3 Optare. 4 Scania. 31 Volvo.
Bodies: 16 Alexander. 6 BMC. 4 Caetano. 1 Carlyle. 3 Ikarus. 42 Marshall/MCV. 1 Northern Counties. 3 Optare. 279 Plaxton. 4 Reeve Burgess. 1 Willowbrook.
Ops incl: local bus services, school contracts, excursions & tours, private hire, express.
Livery: FirstGroup.
Ticket System: Wayfarer III

HAWKES COACHES LTD
💺 wc A/c

BRIDGE ROAD, WAUNARLWYDD, SWANSEA SA5 4SP
Tel: 01792 873336
Fax: 01792 875172
E-mail: hawkescoaches@btconnect.com
Fleet: 22 - 2 single-deck bus, 19 coach, 1 midibus.
Chassis: 1 DAF. 3 Dennis. 1 Optare. 17 Volvo.
Bodies: 2 Alexander. 4 Duple. 4 Jonckheere. 12 Plaxton.
Ops incl: local bus services, private hire, school contracts.
Ticket System: Wayfarer
(part of the Veolia Group)

BRIAN ISAAC COACHES LTD 💺 wc 🍴 A/c 🔧
COACH HOLIDAY CENTRE, 99 WOODFIELD STREET, MORRISTON, SWANSEA SA6 8AS
Tel: 01792 701644
Fax: 01792 310233
E-mail: enquiries@brianisaac.co.uk
Web Site: www.brianisaac.co.uk
Man Dir: Brian H Isaac **Fin Dir**: David Rees
Ops Dir: Ryan Jones
Fleet: 10 coach
Chassis: 10 DAF.
Bodies: 10 Bova.
Ops incl: excursions & tours, private hire, continental tours.
Livery: Blue/Magenta/White

PULLMAN COACHES LTD
UNIT 41, PENCLAWDD INDUSTRIAL ESTATE, CROFTY SA4 3RT.
Tel: 01792 851430
E-mail: pullmancoaches@aol.com
Web site: www.pullmancoaches.co.uk
Dirs: C. W. Lewis, H. S. Rees.
Fleet: 34 - 8 single-deck bus, 25 coach, 1 minicoach.
Livery: Cream/White/Red/Fawn
(Part of Veolia Transport)

*STAGECOACH IN SOUTH WALES
See Torfaen

A/c	Air conditioning	💺 Seat belt-fitted vehicles	🔧 Replacement vehicle available
♿	Vehicles suitable for disabled	R Recovery service available (not 24 hr)	T Toilet-drop facilities available
🍴	Coach(es) with galley facilities	R24 24hr recovery service	🚌 Vintage vehicle(s) available
wc	Coach(es) with toilet facilities		Open top vehicle(s)

Welsh Operators

TORFAEN

B'S TRAVEL
13 EAST VIEW, GRIFFITHSTOWN NP4 5DW.
Tel/Fax: 01495 756889.
E-mail: kay@bstravel.fsnet.co.uk
Ptnrs: James Benning, Kay Benning.
Fleet: 4 - 1 coach, 1 midicoach, 1 minibus, 1 minicoach.
Chassis: 1 LDV. 1 MAN. 2 Mercedes.
Bodies: 1 Autobus. 1 Jonckheere. 1 Gem. 1 LDV.
Ops incl: private hire, school contracts.
Livery: White

*JENSON TRAVEL
UNIT 10, PONTNEWYNDD INDUSTRIAL ESTATE, PONTNEWYNDD, PONTYPOOL NP4 6YW
Tel/Fax: 01495 760539
E-mail: jenson01@btconnect.com
Tran Man: Nicola Jenkins **Props:** Gwyn & Nicola Jenkins **Ch Eng:** Peter Ryan
Fleet: 19
Chassis: 6 Dennis. 3 LDV. 1 MAN. 5 Mercedes. 1 Peugeot. 3 Volvo.
Bodies: 2 Jonckheere. 1 EOS. 3 LDV. 1 Optare. 1 Plaxton. 1 Renault. 4 Reeve Burgess. 1 Wadham Stringer.
Ops incl: school contracts, excursions & tours, private hire.
Livery: White with Blue logo

*STAGECOACH IN SOUTH WALES
1 ST DAVID'S ROAD, CWMBRAN NP44 1PD
Tel: 01633 838856
Fax: 01633 865299
Web site: www.stagecoachbus.com
Man Dir: John Gould **Comm Dir:** Richard Davies **Eng Dir:** David Howe
Fleet: 347 - 4 double-deck bus, 56 single-deck bus, 34 coach, 8 double-deck coach, 148 midibus, 97 minibus.
Chassis: 134 Dennis. 52 Mercedes. 6 Neoplan. 50 Optare. 14 Transbus. 91 Volvo.
Bodies: 159 Alexander. 6 Caetano. 9 Marshall/MCV. 6 Neoplan. 19 Northern Counties. 52 Optare. 74 Plaxton. 14 Transbus. 5 UVG. 3 Wright.
Ops incl: local bus services, school contracts, express.
Livery: Stagecoach
Ticket System: ERG, Wayfarer III

VALE OF GLAMORGAN

EST BUS LTD
UNIT 26, TUMULUS WAY, LLANDOW TRADING ESTATE, LLANDOW CF71 7PB
Tel: 01446 793100
Dir: C Hookings
Ops incl: local bus services, school contracts
Livery: Maroon/Cream

HAYWARD TRAVEL (CARDIFF)
2 MURCH CRESCENT, DINAS POWYS CF64 4RF
Tel: 029 2051 5551
Fax: 029 2051 5113
E-mail: info@haywardtravel.co.uk
Web site: www.haywardtravel.co.uk
Ops incl: private hire

THOMAS OF BARRY
12 PARK CRESCENT, BARRY CF62 6HD
Tel/Recovery: 01446 722800
Fax: 01446 722766
E-mail: thomasofbarry@hotmail.com
Web site: www.thomasofbarry.com
Ops Man: K Jones
Fleet: 71 - 5 double-deck bus, 15 single-deck bus, 30 coach, 2 double-deck coach, 4 open-top bus, 5 midibus, 3 midicoach, 2 minibus, 5 minicoach.
Chassis: 20 Dennis. 2 Irisbus. 2 MAN. 20 Mercedes. 5 Optare. 20 Scania. 2 Volvo.
Bodies: 4 Beulas. 3 Caetano. 5 Duple. 12 Irizar. 6 Leyland. 5 MCW. 9 Mercedes. 15 Plaxton. 2 Sunsundegui. 3 UVG. 6 Van Hool.
Ops incl: local bus services, school contracts, excursions & tours, private hire, express, continental tours.
Livery: White/Maroon.
Ticket System: Wayfarer 3 (part of the Veolia Group)

WREXHAM

ACTON COACHES
109 HERBERT JENNING AVENUE, ACTON PARK LL12 7YA
Tel/Fax: 01978 352470
Prop: D B Evans.
Fleet: 4 - 3 coach, 1 midibus
Chassis: 1 DAF. 2 Volvo. 1 Mercedes.
Bodies: 1 Plaxton. 1 Caetano. 1 Van Hool. 1 Optare.
Livery: Blue/White
Ops incl: school contracts, private hire

GEORGE EDWARDS & SON
BERWYN, BWLCHYWYN LL11 5UE.
Tel/Fax: 01978 757281
Props: G F & G Edwards.
Fleet: 7 - includes single-deck bus, coach
Chassis: 1 Bedford. 6 DAF
Bodies: 2 Duple. 1 Optare. 4 Van Hool
Ops incl: local bus services, school contracts, private hire.
Livery: Red/Ivory/Maroon

HAYDN'S TOURS & TRAVEL
BEVERLEY, FIELD HEAD, CHIRK LL14 5PU.
Tel/Fax: 01691 773267
E-mail: christopherwilliams@virgin.net
Ptnrs: M Williams, Chris Williams.
Fleet: 2 coach
Chassis: 1 DAF. 1 Volvo.
Bodies: 1 Duple. 1 Plaxton.
Ops incl: excursions & tours, private hire, school contracts.
Livery: Red/White/Yellow/Orange

JOHN'S TRAVEL WREXHAM
1 BRYN MAELOR, SOUTHSEA LL11 6RD.
Tel: 01978 753364
Prop: John F H Ithell
Fleet: 4 - 2 midibus, 2 minibus
Chassis: 4 Mercedes
Bodies: 1 Carlyle. 2 Plaxton. 1 Reeve Burgess.
Ops incl: local bus services, private hire
Livery: White with red lettering
Ticket system: Wayfarer

D. JONES & SON
CLYDFAN, HALL STREET, RHOSLLANERCRUGOG LL14 2LG.
Tel: 01978 842540
Mobile: 07739 206623
Props: D. & G. Jones.
Fleet: 7 - 1 coach, 6 single-deck bus
Chassis: 1 DAF. 4 Dennis. 2 Mercedes.
Bodies: 3 Caetano. 1 Mercedes. 3 Plaxton.
Ops incl: local bus services, school contracts, private hire.
Ops incl: local bus services, private hire
Livery: Blue/Cream.
Ticket system: Wayfarer

E JONES & SONS
MOUNTAIN VIEW, BANK STREET, PONCIAU LL14 1EN.
Tel: 01978 841613.
Props: J B & G Jones.
Fleet: 7
Livery: Blue/White/Orange.

PAT'S COACHES LTD
GATEWEN ROAD, NEW BROUGHTON LL11 6YA
Tel: 01978 720171
Fax: 01978 758459
E-mail: enquiries@patscoaches.co.uk.fsnet.co.uk
Web site: www.patscoaches.co.uk
Ptnr: P C Davies, J M Davies, D K Davies
Chassis: 1 DAF. 1 LDV. 2 Mercedes. 2 Neoplan. 2 Scania. 8 Volvo.
Bodies: 1 Autobus. 4 Berkhof. 1 Jonckheere. 1 Marcopolo. 1 Marshall/MCV. 2 Mercedes. 2 Neoplan. 2 Plaxton. 1 Van Hool. 1 Wright. 1 other.
Livery: White/Red/Yellow

PRICES COACHES
THE HAVEN, BERSHAM ROAD, SOUTHSEA LL11 6TF
Tel/Fax: 01978 756834
Prop: Tecwyn Price
Fleet: 7 - 2 double-deck bus, 4 coach, 1 midibus
Chassis: 2 Leyland. 1 Mercedes. 1 Setra. 3 Volvo.
Bodies: 2 Leyland. 1 Kassbohrer. 1 Mercedes. 2 Plaxton. 1 Van Hool.
Ops incl: school contracts, private hire
Livery: Primrose/Green/Orange

*STRAFFORDS COACHES

UNITS 7/8, FIVE CROSSES INDUSTRIAL ESTATE, MINERA LL11 3RD.
Tel: 01978 756106
Fax: 01978 722705
Fleet: 12 - 8 coach, 2 midicoach, 2 minicoach.
Chassis: DAF. MAN. Mercedes. Scania.
Ops incl: school contracts, private hire, excursions & tours, continental tours. .
Livery: White, with stars

T WILLIAMS & SONS

CLARKE STREET BUS GARAGE, PONCIAU LL14 1RT
Tel: 01978 840062.
Prop: J S Williams.
Fleet: 4 coach.
Chassis: 2 Bedford, 1 DAF, 1 Volvo.
Bodies: Duple, Plaxton, Jonckheere.
Ops incl: private hire, school contracts, excursions & tours.
Livery: Blue/Cream.
Ticket System: Setright.

Do you want to keep your LITTLE RED BOOK up-to-date?
Buses magazine now carries updates every month.
See 248 page for Subscription details

A/c	Air conditioning		Seat belt-fitted vehicles
	Vehicles suitable for disabled	R	Recovery service available (not 24 hr)
	Coach(es) with galley facilities	R24	24hr recovery service
WC	Coach(es) with toilet facilities		
	Replacement vehicle available		
T	Toilet-drop facilities available		
	Vintage vehicle(s) available		
	Open top vehicle(s)		

Interested in Transport subjects?

Like a good read?
FREE?
send for our illustrated catalogue

Call 01455 254 470 or write to:

**Midland Counties Publications
4 Watling Drive, Hinckley,
Leicestershire LE10 3EY**

E-mail midlandbooks@compuserve.com
www.midlandcountiessuperstore.com

NORTHERN IRELAND

A1 COACH TRAVEL
35 NORBURGH PARK, FOYLE SPRINGS, DERRY/LONDONDERRY BT48 0RG
Tel/Fax: 028 7130 9323
Prop: J. Bradshaw
Fleet: 2 midicoach
Chassis: 1 Mercedes. 1 Renault.
Ops incl: private hire, continental tours, school contracts.

CHAMBERS COACH HIRE LTD
11 CIRCULAR ROAD, MONEYMORE BT45 7PY
Tel: 028 8674 8152
Fax: 028 8674 8152
Web site: www.coachireland.com
Non-Exec Chmn: Ted Hesketh **Dirs:** Des Chambers, Mary Chambers, Paul Chambers, Philip Harkness **Ops Man:** Mary McIver
Fleet: 48 - 16 coach, 2 double-deck coach, 4 midibus, 8 midicoach, 6 minicoach, 12 minibus.
Chassis: 2 Ford Transit. 1 Mercedes. 16 Scania.
Bodies: 2 Berkhof. 15 Irizar. 18 Mercedes. 12 Plaxton.
Ops incl: school contracts, excursions & tours, private hire

*CROSS COUNTRY COACHES LTD
63 BALLYLINTAGH ROAD, COLERAINE BT51 3SP
Tel: 028 7086 8989
Fax: 028 7086 9191
E-mail: sales@crosscountrycoaches.com
Dirs: J R Telford, B Telford
Fleet: 6 - 5 coach, 1 midicoach.
Chassis: 1 Bedford. 1 DAF. 1 MAN. 1 Volvo.
Bodies: 1 Duple. 5 Van Hool.
Ops incl: excursions & tours, private hire, continental tours.
Livery: White

DARRAGHS COACHES
22 LISHEEGHAN ROAD, BALLYMONEY BT53 7JY
Tel: 028 2954 0684
Fax: 028 2954 0785
E-mail: kdarragh@aol.com
Man: Robert Darragh

GILES TOURS
63 ABBEYDALE AVENUE, NEWTOWNARDS BT23 8RT
Tel/Fax: 028 9181 1099
E-mail: enquiries@gilestours.co.uk
Web site: www.gilestours.co.uk
Dirs: Neil Giles, Patricia Giles
Fleet: 4 - 3 coach, 1 midicoach.
Chassis: 1 Mercedes. 3 Van Hool.
Ops incl: excursions & tours, private hire, continental tours.

LAKELAND TOURS
47 MAIN STREET, TEMPO BT94 3LU
Tel: 028 8954 1646
Fax: 028 8954 1424
Recovery: 07779 026597
E-mail: lakelandtours@btconnect.com
Web site: www.lakelandtours.co.uk
Prop: Ian McCutcheon
Fleet: 5 - 3 coach, 1 midicoach, 1 minicoach.
Chassis: 1 DAF. 1 Leyland. 2 MAN. 1 Mercedes.
Bodies: 1 Mercedes. 1 Noge. 1 Plaxton. 1 Setra. 1 Van Hool.
Ops incl: excursions & tours, private hire, school contracts.

LOGANS EXECUTIVE TRAVEL
58 GALDANAGH ROAD, DUNLOY, BALLYMENA BT44 9DB
Tel: 028 2765 7203
Fax: 028 2765 7559
E-mail: coaches@loganstravel.com
Web site: www.loganstravel.com
Prop: Sean Logan
Fleet: 49 - coach, midicoach, minicoach, minibus.
Chassis: 6 Iveco. 5 LDV. 1 MAN. 12 Mercedes. 25 Volvo.
Ops incl: local bus services, school contracts, private hire, continental tours.

LONDONDERRY & LOUGH SWILLY BUS COMPANY LTD
STRAND ROAD, DERRY/LONDONDERRY BT48 7PY
Tel: 00 353 74 22863
Fleet: 88 - single-deck bus, coach.
Ops incl: local bus services.

POOTS COACH HIRE LTD
118A PORTADOWN ROAD, TANDRAGEE BT62 2JX
Tel: 028 3884 1504
Fax: 028 3884 1724
Dirs: Jim T Poots, Samuel Poots
Fleet: 6 - 3 coach, 3 midicoach.
Chassis: 1 DAF. 3 Mercedes. 2 Leyland.
Bodies: 3 Plaxton. 3 Reeve Burgess
Ops incl: excursions & tours, private hire, express, school contracts.
Livery: White
Ticket system: Wayfarer

O. ROONEY COACH HIRE LTD
4 DANA PLACE, HILLTOWN, NEWRY BT34 5UE
Tel: 028 4063 0825
Fax: 028 4063 8028
Recovery: 077721 510955
E-mail: oliver@orcoachireland.com
Web site: www.orcoachireland.com
Man Dir: Oliver Rooney
Ops Man: Aaron Rooney
Fleet: 12 - 2 single-deck bus, 3 coach, 2 midibus, 5 minibus.
Chassis: 2 Dennis. 1 Leyland. 6 Mercedes. 1 Renault. 2 Volvo.
Bodies: 3 Alexander. 3 Plaxton. 6 Reeve Burgess.
Ops incl: local bus services, excursions & tours, school contracts, private hire.
Livery: White/Yellow

SLOAN TRAVEL
51 KILLOWEN OLD ROAD, ROSTREVOR, NEWRY BT34 3AE.
Tel: 028 4173 8459
Fax: 028 4173 9459
Dir/Ch Eng: B. M. Sloan. **Sec:** Ms M. Sloan.
Fleet: 7 - 6 coach, 1 minibus.
Chassis: 4 Bedford. 3 Ford.
Bodies: 2 Duple. 4 Plaxton.
Ops incl: local bus services, school contracts, excursions & tours, private hire, express, continental tours.
Livery: Mixed.

TRANSLINK
CENTRAL STATION, EAST BRIDGE STREET, BELFAST BT1 3PB
Tel: 028 9089 9400
E-mail: feedback@translink.co.uk
Web site: www.translink.co.uk
Fleetnames: Ulsterbus, Citybus
Chmn: Dr Joan Smyth **Dir of HR:** Alan Mercer **Dir of Ops:** Philip O'Neil **Fin Dir:** Stephen Armstrong **Mktg Exec:** Ciaran Rogan **Head of Projects:** David Laird **Infrastructure Exec:** Clive Bradberry
Fleet: 1,469 – 20 double-deck bus, 1,274 single-deck bus, 40 coach, 2 double-deck coach, 8 articulated bus, 4 open-top bus, 98 minibus, 23 minicoach.
Chassis: 1 Ayats. 84 Bristol. 10 DAF. 43 Dennis. 819 Leyland. 97 Mercedes. 23 Optare. 5 Renault. 43 Scania. 346 Volvo.
Bodies: 1,023 Alexander. 1 Ayats. 7 Caetano. 4 Duple. 3 ECW. 4 Irizar. 10 Mercedes. 23 Optare. 135 Plaxton. 2 Reeve Burgess. 6 Van Hool. 247 Wright. 6 Other makes.

A/c	Air conditioning		Replacement vehicle available
	Vehicles suitable for disabled	T	Toilet-drop facilities available
	Coach(es) with galley facilities	R	Recovery service available (not 24 hr)
WC	Coach(es) with toilet facilities		Vintage vehicle(s) available
		R24	24hr recovery service
			Open top vehicle(s)

Northern Ireland

REPUBLIC OF IRELAND

AIRCOACH
DUBLIN
Web site: www.aircoach.ie
Chassis: incl Setra
Ops incl: express
Livery: Blue

ALLIED COACHES
113 GRANGE WAY, BALDOYLE INDUSTRIAL ESTATE, BALDOYLE, DUBLIN D13
Tel: 00 353 1 832 8300
Fax: 00 353 1 832 8299
E-mail: info@alliedcoaches.ie
Web site: www.alliedcoaches.ie
Man Dir: Jim Nolan **Man**: Seamus Nolan
Fleet: 7 - 3 coach, 2 minicoach, 2 minibus.
Chassis: incl: 1 DAF. 2 Mercedes.
Bodies: incl: 1 BMC. 2 Marcopolo
Ops incl: excursions & tours, private hire
Livery: Silver

ARAN TOURS LTD
14 LOWER ALBERT ROAD, SANDYCOVE, Co DUBLIN
Tel: 00 353 1 280 1899
Fax: 00 353 1 280 1799

BARRY'S COACHES LTD
THE GLEN, MAYFIELD, CORK CITY
Tel: 00 353 21 450 5390, 450 1669 (emergencies only)
Fax: 00 353 21 450 9628
Fleet: 15 - 12 coach, 2 minibus, 1 minicoach.
Chassis: 1 AEC. 3 Bedford. 6 Leyland. 2 Mercedes. 2 Volvo.
Bodies: 7 Duple. 1 Jonckheere. 2 Mercedes. 3 Plaxton. 2 Van Hool.
Livery: Blue/White

*BARTON TRANSPORT
STRAFFAN ROAD, MAYNOOTH, CO KILDARE.
Tel: 00 353 1 628 6026
Fax: 00 353 1 628 6026
E-mail: info@barton-transport.ie
Web site: www.bartons-transport.ie
Man Dir: Patrick Barton **Man**: Fergal Barton
Fleet: 35 - 1 double-deck bus, 10 single-deck bus, 20 coach, 4 minicoach.
Chassis: 2 BMC. 26 DAF. 3 Irisbus. 3 MAN. 1 Mercedes.
Bodies: 2 Beulas. 13 Berkhof. 2 BMC. 5 Ikarus. 2 Marcopolo. 2 Optare. 5 Plaxton. 4 Temsa.
Ops incl: local bus services, private hire, excursions & tours, school contracts.

RONNIE BRUEN T/A BLUEBIRD COACHES
72 KILBARRON DRIVE, COOLOCK, DUBLIN 5.
Tel/Fax: 00 353 1 847 7896.
Dirs: Ronnie Bruen, Keith Bruen.
Fleet: 7 - 3 coach, 2 midicoach, 2 minibus.
Chassis: Ford Transit. Leyland. Mercedes. Volvo.
Bodies: Mercedes. Duple.

Ops incl: private hire, express, school contracts.
Livery: Cream/Red.

BUCKLEY'S TOURS
KILLARNEY, Co KERRY
Tel: 00 353 64 31945
E-mail: buckleys@iol.ie

BURKE BROS (COACHES) LTD
CLARETUAM, TUAM, Co GALWAY
Tel: 00 353 93 55416
Fax: 00 353 93 55356
Dirs: P. Burke, Ms M. Burke.
Ops Man: P. Steede.
Fleet: 12 - 10 coach, 2 midicoach.
Chassis: Mercedes-Benz, Toyota, Volvo.
Bodies: Caetano, Jonckheere, Plaxton.
Ops incl: local bus services, private hire, continental tours.
Livery: White with Blue/Orange stripes.

BUS EIREANN/IRISH BUS
BROADSTONE, PHIBSBOROUGH, DUBLIN 7
Tel: 00 353 1 830 2222
Fax: 00 353 1 830 9377
E-mail: info@buseireann.ie
Web site: www.buseireann.ie
Chmn: Dr John Lynch **Ch Exec**: Tim Hayes
Co Sec: Martin Nolan **Ch Mech Eng**: Joe Neiland **Man HR**: Des Tallon
Man Sales&Mktg: Barry Doyle
Fleet: 1,396 - 23 double-deck bus, 567 single-deck bus, 640 coach, 2 open-top bus, 87 midibus, 27 minibus.
Chassis: 201 DAF. 43 Dennis. 2 Ford. 155 GAC. 278 Leyland. 76 Mercedes. 20 Optare. 156 Scania. 415 Volvo.
Bodies: 86 Alexander. 176 Caetano. 24 East Lancs. 31 Hispano. 156 Irizar. 184 Leyland. 20 Mercedes. 1 Northern Counties. 20 Optare. 322 Plaxton. 20 Sunsundegui. 18 Van Hool. 106 Wright. 182 other.
Ops incl: local bus services, school contracts, excursions & tours, private hire, express.
Livery: White/Red.
Ticket System: Wayfarer.

BUTLERS BUSES
17 BROOKVALE, COBH, Co CORK
Tel/Fax: 00 353 21 811660
E-mail: butlersb@gofree.indigo.ie
Prop: Ian Butler

CAHALANE COACHES
UNIT 6, KILBARRY ENTERPRISE CENTRE, DUBLIN HILL, CORK
Tel: 00 353 21 430 4606
Fax: 00 353 21 430 1200
Fleet: includes 14, 24, 29 and 35-seat coaches

CALLINAN COACHES LTD
KINISKA, GLAREGALWAY, Co GALWAY

Tel: 00 353 91 798324
Fax: 00 353 91 798962
Recovery: 00 353 8724 13691
E-mail: info@callinancoaches.ie
Web site: www.callinancoaches.ie
Fleet: 22 single-deck bus
Chassis: 22 Volvo.
Ops incl: excursions & tours, continental tours, private hire

*GERRY CARROLL COACH HIRE
BALLYMAKENNY ROAD, DROGHEDA, CO LOUTH
Tel: 00 353 41 98 36074
Prop: Gerry Carroll **Dir**: Patrick Caroll
Sec: Betty Carroll
Fleet: 3 coach.
Chassis: Bedford.
Bodies: Plaxton
Ops incl: local bus services, excursions & tours, private hire.
Livery: White/Blue

*CIRCLE LINE BUS CO LTD
STRAFFAN ROAD, MAYNOOTH, CO KILDARE
Tel: 00 353 1 628 6250
E-mail: info@circlelinebus.ie
Web site: www.circlelinebus.ie
Dirs: Paul Morton, Patrick Barton
Man: Nigel O'Connor
Fleet: 23 - 16 double-deck bus, 7 single-deck bus
Chassis: 6 MAN. 17 Volvo.
Bodies: 14 East Lancs. 3 Ikarus. 4 Marcopolo.
Ops incl: local bus services

COLLIN'S COACHES
CARRICKAMOSS, Co MONAGHAN
Tel: 00 353 42 9661 631
Fax: 00 353 42 9663 462
E-mail: colcoach@iol.ie

CONWAY COACH AND CHAUFFEUR DRIVE
WILLOW GROVE, REDGATE, LIMERICK
Tel: 00 353 61 53366
Prop: R. Conway (Gen Man), Val Conway.
Prop/Ch Eng: Patrick Conway. **Prop/Sec**: Audrey Hurley. **Traf Man**: R. Hurley.
Fleet: 11 midicoach.
Livery: White/Red.

CORCORANS EXECUTIVE TOURS
10 COLLEGE STREET, KILLARNEY, CO KERRY
Tel: 00 353 64 36666
Fax: 00 353 64 35666
Fleet: coach, midicoach
Chassis: incl: Mercedes
Ops incl: private hire

COYLES COACHES
GWEEDORE, Co DONEGAL
Tel: 00 353 75 31208.
E-mail: coylescoaches@eircom.net

CREMIN COACHES
BANTRY, Co CORK
Tel/Fax: 00 353 2 766 906
E-mail: info@cremincoaches.com
Web site: www.cremincoaches.com
Fleet: incl: minicoach
Chassis: incl: Mercedes
Livery: White
Ops incl: private hire

CRONIN'S COACHES LTD [wc] A/c
SHANNON BUILDINGS, MALLOW ROAD, CORK
Tel: 00 353 21 430 9090
Fax: 00 353 21 430 5508
Email: cork@croninscoaches.com.
Web Site: www.croninscoaches.com.
Dirs: D. & Joan Cronin. **Ch Eng:** Niall Cronin. **Gen Man:** Nora Cronin.
Fleet: 50 - 47 coach, 3 midicoach.
Chassis: DAF. Leyland. Volvo.
Bodies: Van Hool
Ops incl: private hire
Livery: White with red flash.

CROSSON MOTOR GROUP
UNIT 10/12 NEWTOWN INDUSTRIAL ESTATE, COOLOCK, DUBLIN 17
Tel: 00 353 1 848 5811
Fax: 00 353 1 848 5721
Fleetname: Crosson Coaches.
Chmn: S. Crosson. **Man Dir:** A. Kennedy.
Dirs: J. O'Reilly, B. Cullen, S. Crosson.
Fleet: 1 midicoach.
Chassis: Mercedes. **Body:** Euro Coach.
Ops incl: private hire, continental tours.
Livery: White

MARTIN CROWLEY
CLANCOOL BEG, BANDON, Co CORK
Tel/Fax: 00 353 23 42150
Fleet: incl: minicoach, midicoach
Ops incl: private hire

DERO'S COACH TOURS
[R24]
22 MAIN STREET, KILLARNEY, Co KERRY
Tel: 00 353 64 31251
Fax: 00 353 64 34077
Email: deroscoachtours@eircom.net.
Web site: www.derostours.com
Prop: Ms E. O'Sullivan Quille. **Sales Dir:** Ms C. O'Sullivan, D O'Sullivan.
Fleet: 18 - 12 coach, 4 midicoach, 2 minicoach.
Chassis: 10 DAF. 6 Mercedes. 2 Volvo.
Livery: White with multi red/Silver/Red/Orange.
Relief drivers and guiding agency also.

JIMMY DONNELLY & SON
46 IRISH STREET, ENNISCORTHY, Co WEXFORD.
Tel: 00 353 54 33956
Fleet: 7 - 5 coach, 2 minibus

DONOVAN'S COACH HIRE
HEADFORD, KILLARNEY, Co KERRY
Tel: 00 353 64 54041.
Fax: 00 353 64 54041
Props: Joe & Maureen Donovan.
Fleet: 8 - 5 coach, 2 midicoach, 1 minibus.
Chassis: 1 Ford Transit. 3 LDV. 2 Mercedes. 2 Volvo.
Bodies: 2 Jonckheere. 1 Duple. 2 Mercedes. 1 Plaxton.
Ops incl: school contracts, excursions & tours, private hire.

P. DOYLE LTD
ROUNDWOOD, Co WICKLOW
Tel: 00 353 1 281 8119
Fleetname: St Kevins Bus Service.
Prop/Traf Man: P. Doyle.
Gen Man/Ch Eng: J. Doyle.
Sec: John Doyle.
Fleet: 5 single-deck bus.
Chassis: 5 Leyland.
Bodies: 1 Plaxton. 4 others.
Livery: Blue/Cream.
Ticket System: Setright.

*TONY DOYLE COACHES LTD
[wc] A/c
BALLYORNEY, ENNISKERRY, Co WICKLOW
Tel: 00 353 1 286 7427
Fax: 00 353 1 286 7427
Email: info@tonydoyle.com
Web site: www.tonydoyle.com
Fleet: 14 - 8 coach, 2 midicoach, 3 minicoach.
Chassis: 1 Irisbus. 2 Iveco. 3 MAN. 2 Mercedes. 3 Scania. 1 Volvo.
Bodies: 5 Beulas. 1 Esker. 2 Indcar. 3 Irizar. 1 Noge. 1 Sunsundegui.
Ops incl: excursions & tours, school contracts, private hire.

THE DUALWAY GROUP
A/c
KEATINGS PARK, RATHCOOLE, Co DUBLIN
Tel: 00 353 1 458 0054
Fax: 00 353 1 458 0808
E-mail: info@dualwaycoaches.com
Web site: www.dualwaycoaches.com
Fleetnames: Dualway, City Sightseeing, Grayline
Man Dir: Anthony McConn **Gen Man:** David McConn **Fin Controller:** Trish McConn
Admin Man: Dawn Nolan
Fleet: 35 - 23 double-deck bus, 6 coach, 20 open-top bus, 6 midicoach
Chassis: 8 AEC. 1 Daimler. 14 Leyland. 7 Mercedes. 4 Volvo.
Bodies: 14 Alexander. 3 East Lancs. 1 Esker. 1 Jonckheere. 10 Leyland. 2 Marcopolo. 1 Northern Counties. 1 Optare. 2 Park Royal.
Ops incl: local bus services, excursions & tours, school contracts, private hire.

DUBLIN BUS (BUS ATHA CLIATH)
59 UPPER O'CONNELL STREET, DUBLIN 1.
Tel: 00 353 1 872 0000
Fax: 00 353 1 873 1195
Email: info@dublinbus.ie
Web site: www.dublinbus.ie
Chmn: John Lynch **Ch Exec:** Joe Meagher
Dirs: David Egan, Arnold O'Byrne, Tom Coffey, Peter Webster **Head of Finance:** Paul O'Neill **Ch Eng:** Shane Doyle
Business Dev Man: Paddy Doherty
Human Resources Man: Gerry Maguire
Ops Man: Mick Matthews
Fleet: 1,076 - 966 double-deck bus, 39 single-deck bus, 51 midibus, 20 articulated bus
Chassis: includes DAF. Dennis. Leyland. Volvo.
Bodies: includes: Alexander. ECW. Wright.
Ops incl: local bus services.
Livery: Blue/Yellow with Dublin Blue/White/Darker Blue swoosh

*DUBLIN MINI COACHES & CHAUFEUR HIRE
A/c
THE TRAVEL BANK LTD, WASDALE HOUSE, 14 CAMAC PARK, OLD NAAS ROAD, DUBLIN 12
Tel: 00 353 861 780049
Fax: 00 353 1 6961001
Email: info.dmc@o2.ie
Web site: www.dublinminicoaches.com
Man Dir: Stephen Millar
Fleet: 12 - 8 midicoach, 4 minicoach.
Chassis/Bodies: 12 Mercedes.
Ops incl: excursions & tours, private hire.

EIREBUS LTD
CORDUFF ROAD, BLANCHARDSTOWN, DUBLIN 15
Tel: 00 353 1 824 2626
Fax: 00 353 1 824 2627
E-mail: eirebus@iol.ie
Web site: www.eirebus.ie
Man Dir: Patrick Kavanagh **Dir:** Thomas Kavanagh **Tran Man:** Derek Graham
Gen Man: Paul Curtis
Fleet: 37 - 29 coach, 2 midicoach, 2 minicoach, 4 minibus.
Chassis: 2 MAN. 6 Mercedes. 24 Scania. 2 Toyota. 3 Volvo.
Bodies: 2 Indcar. 14 Irizar. 2 Jonckheere. 4 Plaxton. 11 Van Hool. 4 other.

ENFIELD COACHES LTD
RATHCORE, ENFIELD, Co MEATH
Tel: 00 353 1 824 2626
Fleet: 3 - 1 coach, 3 minibus

A/c Air conditioning	Seat belt-fitted vehicles	Replacement vehicle available
Vehicles suitable for disabled	R Recovery service available (not 24 hr)	T Toilet-drop facilities available
Coach(es) with galley facilities		Vintage vehicle(s) available
[wc] Coach(es) with toilet facilities	R24 24hr recovery service	Open top vehicle(s)

Republic of Ireland

FAHERTY'S COACH HIRE
DRUMONEY, MOYCULLEN,
Co GALWAY
Tel: 00 353 91 85228
Fleet: 5 - 4 coach, 1 minicoach

FINEGAN COACH HIRE
29 MAIN STREET,
CARRICKMACROSS,
Co MONAGHAN
Tel: 00 353 42 61313
Fleet: 7 - 5 coach, 1 minicoach, 1 minibus

FINNEGAN - BRAY
OLD COURT INDUSTRIAL ESTATE,
BOGHALL ROAD, BRAY, Co
WICKLOW
Tel: 00 353 1 286 0061
Fax: 00 353 1 286 8121
E-mail: finnegan-bray@oceanfree.net
Dir: Eugene Finnegan
Fleet: 15 - 2 double-deck bus, 3 single-deck bus, 3 coach, 2 midicoach, 4 midibus, 1 minibus.
Chassis: 4 DAF. 1 Dennis. 6 Mercedes. 1 Optare. 3 Volvo.
Bodies: 1 Alexander. 2 Ikarus. 1 Leyland. 6 Mercedes. 1 Northern Counties. 1 Optare. 2 Plaxton. 1Van Hool.
Ops incl: local bus services, excursions & tours, school contracts, private hire.
Livery: Red

DECLAN FINNEGAN
THE COACH & CAB CAFE, 10 MAIN STREET, KENMARE, CO KERRY
Tel: 00 353 64 41491
Fax: 00 353 64 42636
Fleet: coach, minicoach
Ops incl: private hire.

TOM FOX
MONAGHAN ROAD, ROCKCORRY,
Co MONAGHAN
Tel: 00 353 42 42284
Fleet: 2 coach

MARTIN FUREY COACHES LTD
MILLTOWN, DRUMCLIFFE, Co SLIGO
Tel: 00 353 71 63092
Fleet: 5 - 3 coach, 2 minibus

GALVINS COACHES
MAIN STREET, DUNMANWAY,
Co CORK
Tel: 00 353 23 45125
Fax: 00 353 23 45407
Dir: R. E. Galvin
Chassis: Ford. Ford Transit. Leyland National. Scania. Volvo.
Bodies: Leyland National. Mercedes. Plaxton. Van Hool. Willowbrook. Duple.
Fleet: single-deck bus, coach, double-deck coach, midibus, midicoach.

GLYNNS COACH HIRE (ENNIS) LTD
KNOCKADERRY, TULLA ROAD,
ENNIS, Co CLARE
Tel: 00 353 65 682 8234
Fax: 00 353 65 684 0678
Recovery: 00 353 8625 97037
Email: info@glynnscoaches.com
Web site: www.glynnscoaches.com
Fleetname: Glynns of Ennis
Chmn: Jackie Cronin. **Sec:** Niamh Cronin.
Fleet: 14 - 5 coach, 4 midicoach, 2 minibus, 3 minicoach. 2 Irisbus.
Chassis: 2 Beulas. 1 DAF. 1 Iveco. 3 MAN. 5 Mercedes. 1 Setra. 3 Volvo.
Bodies: 1 Ikarus. 3 Indcar. 5 Mercedes. 1 Noge. 2 Plaxton. 1 Setra. 1 Euro.

JAMES GLYNN
GRAIGUE NA SPIDOGUE (POST GRAIGUECULLEN), NURNEY
Tel: 00 353 503 46616
Prop/Gen Man/Traf Man: J. Glynn
Prop/Ch Eng: A. Glynn **Prop/Sec:** Mrs J. Glynn.
Fleet: 4 - 3 single-deck bus, 1 coach.
Livery: Cream/Blue.

HALPENNY TRANSPORT
ASHVILLE, THE SQUARE,
BLACKROCK, DUNDALK
Tel: 00 353 42 21608
Fleetname: Halpenny Transport
Man Dir: John Halpenny
Fleet: 14 - includes 2 double-deck bus, 2 single-deck bus, 8 coach
Chassis: mainly Volvo.
Bodies: include 1 Sunsundegui
Ops incl: local bus services, private hire, continental tours
Livery: White with Red/Blue/Green, Blue/Cream

HEALY COACHES
CASTLEGAR, GALWAY
Tel: 00 353 91 770066
Fax: 00 353 91 753335
Web site: www.healybus.com
Email: healybus@iol.ie
Prop: Michael Healy
Fleet: 13 - 2 single-deck bus, 8 coach, 1 open-top bus, 2 midicoach
Chassis: 6 Leyland. 1 MAN. 1 Mercedes. 4 Volvo.
Bodies: 2 Alexander. 1 Duple. 1 ECW. 2 Ikarus. 2 Leyland. 1 Mellor. 1 Noge. 2 Plaxton.

M. HOGAN
LIBERTY STREET, THURLES,
Co TIPPERARY
Tel: 00 353 50 421622
Fleetname: Shamrock Bus Service.
Prop/Gen Man: M. Hogan.
Ch Eng: T. Maher. **Sec:** J. Maher.
Fleet: 2 coach.
Livery: Cream/Orange.
Ticket System: Setright.

IRELAND COACHES
COOLQUAY, THE WARD, Co DUBLIN
Tel: 00 353 1 835 2714
Fax: 00 353 1 835 2715
E-mail: irelandcoaches@eircom.net
Fleet: 30 coaches, midicoaches, minicoaches

IRISH COACHES
R24
ULSTER BANK CHAMBERS,
2-4 LOWER O'CONNELL STREET,
DUBLIN
Tel: 00 353 1 878 8894/8898
Fax: 00 353 1 878 8916
E-mail: dch@irishcoaches.ie
Web site: www.irishcoaches.ie
Chmn: Patric Barton **Dir:** Dermot Cronin
Man Dir: D C Hughes
Fleet: 4 - 3 coach, 1 midicoach
Chassis: 4 DAF
Bodies: 1 Ayats. 1 Berkhof. 2 Marcopolo.
Livery: yellow

DONAL JOYCE MINIBUS HIRE
GENTIAN HILL HOUSE,
KNOCKNACARRA, Co GALWAY
Tel: 00 353 91 521427
Fax: 00 353 91 52 4284
Fleet: 8 - 2 minicoaches,8 midibus
Ops incl: excursions & tours, private hire

BERNARD KAVANAGH & SONS LTD
BRIDGE GARAGE, URLINGFORD,
Co KILKENNY
Tel: 00 353 56 31189
Fax: 00 353 56 31314
Email: info@bkavcoaches.com.
Web Site: www.bkavcoaches.com.
Fleet: 54 - 50 coach, 4 midicoach.
Chassis: incl 3 Bova. 7 MAN. 2 Setra. 4 Volvo.
Bodies: 5 Beulas. 2 Indcar. 10 Irizar. 2 Jonckheere. 3 Plaxton. 2 Setra. 30 Van Hool.
Ops incl: excursions & tours, private hire, express, continental tours.
Livery: White/Multi

J J KAVANAGH & SONS
MAIN STREET, URLINGFORD,
Co KILKENNY
Tel: 00 353 56 31106
Fax: 00 353 56 31116
E-mail: info@jjkavanagh.ie
Web site: www.jjkavanagh.ie
Joint Man Dir/Fin Cont: J. J. Kavanagh
Joint Man Dir/Ops Man: Paul Kavanagh
Maintenance Man: Edward Scully
Fleet: 38 - 1 double-deck bus, 36 coach, 1 open-top bus
Chassis: 6 MAN. 25 Setra. 45 Volvo.
Bodies: 15 Caetano. 2 Leyland. 4 Mercedes. 2 Northern Counties. 20 Plaxton. 25 Setra. 7 Van Hool. 1 Wright.
Ops incl: local bus services

M. KAVANAGH
LIMERICK ROAD, TIPPERARY
Tel: 00 353 62 51563
Fax: 00 353 62 51593
E-mail: mattkavanagh3@aol.net
Fleet: 19 - 12 coaches, 5 single-deck bus, 2 minibus

PIERCE KAVANAGH COACHES

CHURCH VIEW, URLINGFORD, COKILKENNY
Tel: 00 353 56 31213
Fax: 00 353 56 31599
E-mail: info@kavanaghscoaches.com
Web site: www.kavanaghscoaches.com
Dirs: Pierce Kavanagh, John Kavanagh **Ch Eng**: John Kenny
Co Sec: Jim Bannon
Fleet: 20 - 1 single-deck bus, 18 coach, 1 midicoach.
Chassis: 1 Bova. 1 DAF. 2 Ford. 5 Ford Transit. 4 Leyland. 5 MAN. 1 Mercedes. 3 Scania. 2 Volvo

KEENAN COMMERCIALS LTD

BELLURGAN, DUNDALK, Co LOUTH
Tel: 00 353 42 937 1405
Fax: 00 353 42 937 1893
Fleetname: Anchor Coaches
Man Dir: Seamus Keenan
Fleet: 17 - 8 single-deck bus, 7 coach, 2 minibus.

KENNEALLY'S BUS SERVICE LTD

BLENHEIM, WATERFORD
Tel: 00 353 51 872777
Fax: 00 353 51 872770
Joint Man Dirs: J J Kavanagh, Paul Kavanagh **Tran Man**: Tony Crean
Ops Man: Michael Ryan
Fleet: 27 - 6 double-deck bus, 3 single-deck bus, 18 coach
Chassis: 1 AEC. 2 Leyland. 5 MAN. 15 Setra. 30 Volvo.
Bodies: 4 Alexander. 5 Caetano. 4 Northern Counties. 15 Setra. 10 Van Hool. 1 Wright.
Ops incl: local bus services, excursions & tours, private hire, express, continental tours.
Livery: Green/Blue/Red on White
Subsidiary of J J Kavanagh, Urlingford

KENNEDY COACHES

ANNASCAUL, TRALEE, Co KERRY
Tel: 00 353 66 91 57106
Fax: 00 353 66 91 57427
Fleet: 5 - 3 double-deck bus, 3 minibus

K. M. KEOGH

39A WEXFORD ROAD, ARKLOW
Tel: 00 353 40 22560
Fleet: 4 coach

KERRY COACHES LTD

INISFALLEN, 15 MAIN STREET, KILLARNEY, Co KERRY
Tel: 00 353 64 31945
Fax: 00 353 64 31903
Email: buckleys@iol.ie
Web site: www.kerrycoaches.com

Ops Man: Alan O'Connor
Fleetnames: Buckley Tours, Kerry Tours
Man Dir: M Buckley
Fleet: 19 - 14 coach, 2 midicoach, 3 minibus.
Chassis: incl: 2 Setra

DAVE LONG COACH TRAVEL

CURRAGH, SKIBBEREEN
Tel: 00 353 28 21138
Fleet: 1 coach

LESCLACHA LTD

28 AVONDALE, NEWMARKET-ON-FERGUS
Tel: 00 353 61 71233
Fleetname: Lovetts Coaches
Fleet: 9 - 1 single-deck bus, 6 coach, 1 midibus, 1 minibus.
Chassis: Leyland.

LUAS

LUAS DEPOT, RED COW ROUNDABOUT, CLONDALKIN, DUBLIN 22
Tel: 00 353 1 461 4910
Web site: www.luas.ie
Man Dir: Richard Dujardin
Gen Man: Brian Brennan
Fleet: 40 tram
Chassis/bodies: Alstom Citadis
Ops: tram service

P. J. McCONNON

GREENLEE, CLONES ROAD, MONAGHAN
Tel: 00 353 47 82020
Fleet: 4 coaches
Chassis: Volvo
Bodies: Plaxton

JAMES McGEE (BUSES)

BALLINA MAIN ROAD, FALCARRAGH, LETTERKENNY
Tel: 00 353 74 35174
Fleet: 8 minibus
Chassis: 1 Ford. 3 Toyota.
Ops incl: private hire.
Livery: White

JOHN McGINLEY COACH TRAVEL

MAGHEERCARTY, GORTAHEEK, Co DONEGAL
Tel: 00 353 7491 35201
Fax: 00 353 7491 35960
E-mail: info@jchhmcginley.com
Web site: www.jchhmcginley.com
Prop: James McGinley
Fleet: 16 - 8 coach, 8 minibus.
Chassis: Ford Transit. Mercedes. Volvo.
Bodies: Plaxton. Van Hool.
Ops incl: local bus services, excursions & tours, continental tours, school contracts, private hire, express, continental tours.

GERALD MANNING

CASTLE ROAD, CROOM, LIMERICK
Tel: 00 353 61 88311
E-mail: gmanning@indigo.ie
Fleet: 13 - 10 coach, 2 minibus, 1 midibus.

ALAN MARTIN COACHES

R24

1 KIRKFIELD COTTAGE, CLONSILLA, DUBLIN 15
Tel: 00 353 1 835 1560
Fax: 00 353 1 835 1816
Dirs: A. Martin, B. C. Martin.
Ch Eng: M. Reilly. **Traf Man**: M. Clarke.
Fleet: 8 - 6 single-deck bus, 1 double-deck bus, 1 minibus.
Chassis: 6 Ford. 2 Leyland. 4 MAN. 2 Mercedes. 3 Scania. 2 Toyota. 5 Volvo.
Ops incl: local bus services, school contracts, excursions & tours, private hire, express.
Livery: White with two Blue stripes.

MARTIN'S COACHES (CAVAN) LTD

CORRATILLION, CORLOUGH, BELTURBET, Co CAVAN
Tel: 00 353 49 26222
Fax: 00 353 49 23116
E-mail: jimmartin@eircom.net
Dir: James G Martin
Fleet: 16 - 5 coach, 4 midicoach, 7 minibus.
Chassis: 5 DAF. 7 Ford Transit. 3 Mercedes. 1 Toyota.
Bodies: 4 Bova. 2 Caetano. 3 Mercedes.

MD COACH HIRE

25 TARA LAWN, THE DONAHIES, RAHENY, DUBLIN 13
Tel/Fax: 00 353 1 847 9591
Prop: Michael Dunne.

MICHAEL MEERE COACH HIRE

33 CHURCH DRIVE, CLARECASTLE, ENNIS, Co CLARE
Tel: 00 353 65 682 4833
Fax: 00 353 65 684 4544
E-mail: michaelmeere@clarelive.com

MIDLAND BUS CO LTD

LOUGHNASKIN, ATHLONE
Tel: 00 353 90 22427
Dir/Gen Man: N. Henry
Fleet: 14 coach
Chassis: Leyland, Volvo, Mercedes.
Ops incl: local bus services, excursions & tours.

JOE MORONEY

HERMITAGE, ENNIS, Co CLARE.
Tel: 00 353 66 824146
Fax: 00 353 65 686 9480
E-mail: mcoachesennis@eire.com
Fleet: 7 - 1 double-deck coach, 1 coach

A/c	Air conditioning	♥ Seat belt-fitted vehicles	✓ Replacement vehicle available
	Vehicles suitable for disabled	R Recovery service available (not 24 hr)	T Toilet-drop facilities available
	Coach(es) with galley facilities		Vintage vehicle(s) available
WC	Coach(es) with toilet facilities	R24 24hr recovery service	Open top vehicle(s)

Republic of Ireland

MORTON'S COACHES DUBLIN
TAYLORS LANE, BALLYBODEN, DUBLIN 16
Tel: 00 353 1 494 4927
E-mail: mortonscoaches@clubi.ie, info@circlelinebus.com
Fleet: Circle Line Bus Co
Prop: Paul Morton
Fleet: 13 - 1 double-deck bus, 3 single-deck bus, 6 coach, 3 double-deck coach
Chassis: Ayats. DAF. MAN. Mercedes. Volvo.
Bodies: Ayats. East Lancs. Marcopolo. Wright.
Ops incl: local bus services, school contracts, excursions & tours, private hire, continental tours.
Livery: White

THOMAS MURPHY & SONS
KILBRIDE HOUSE, KILBRIDE LANE, BRAY, Co WICKLOW
Tel: 00 353 1 286 2471
Fleet: 11 - 8 coach, 1 minibus, 2 minicoach.
Chassis: Volvo, Mercedes, Scania.

NAUGHTON COACH TOURS
SHANAGURRANE, SPIDDAL, Co GALWAY
Tel: 00 353 91 553188
Fax: 00 353 91 553302
E-mail: naugtour@iol.ie
Web site: www.wombat.ie/pages/oneachtain-tours
Dir: Steve Naughton **Dir/Sec:** Maureen Naughton
Fleet: 8 - 5 coach, 1 double-deck bus, 2 midicoach.
Chassis: 1 Daimler. 1 MAN. 3 Mercedes. 1 Toyota. 2 Volvo
Bodies: 1 Caetano. 1 Jonckheere. 1 Leyland. 2 Plaxton.
Ops incl: excursions & tours, private hire

NESTORBUS LTD, GALWAY & DUBLIN
TURLOUGHMORE, ATHENRY, Co GALWAY
Tel: 00 353 91 797144, 00 353 1 832 0094
Fax: 00 353 91 797244
E-mail: busnestor@eircom.net
Web Site: www.busnestor.galway.net
Prop: P. Nestor
Fleet: 9 - 8 coach, 1 double-deck coach.
Chassis: 8 Mercedes. 1 Setra.
Ops incl: excursions & tours, private hire, express, continental tours.
Livery: Red/Cream

NOLAN COACHES
19 CLONSHAUGH LAWN, COOLOCK, DUBLIN 17
Tel: 00 353 1 847 3487
Mobile: 0862 592000
Prop: David Nolan
Fleet: 1 coach
Ops incl: school contracts, private hire.

O'CONNELL COACHES
PORTUMNA ROAD, BALLINASLOE
Tel: 00 353 905 43339
Prop: J. O'Connell
Fleet: 5 coach
Chassis: Ford. **Bodies:** Plaxton
Ops incl: private hire.

O'CONNOR AUTOTOURS LTD
ROSS ROAD, KILLARNEY
Tel: 00 353 64 31052
Fax: 00 353 64 31703
Dir/Gen Man: B. O'Connor.
Ch Eng: R. Downing. **Sec:** C. Enright.
Traf Man: D. Fenton
Fleet: 5 - 1 midibus, 4 minicoach.
Chassis: Leyland. Mercedes. Volvo.
Bodies: Reeve Burgess. Van Hool. Euro.
Ops incl: excursions & tours, private hire.
Livery: Maroon/Yellow.

TOM O'CONNOR
CLOGHANE, TRALEE, Co KERRY
Tel: 00 353 66 713 8140

FEDA O'DONNELL COACHES
RANAFAST, Co DONEGAL
Tel/Fax: 00 353 75 48114
Prop: Pat O'Flaherty.
Fleet: 13 - 9 coach, 2 minibus, 2 minicoach.
Ops incl: express

O'FLAHERTY TRANSPORT LTD
LISDOONVARNA, Co CLARE
Tel/Fax: 00 353 65 74117.
Fleet: 1 midicoach.
Prop: Pat O'Flaherty

LARRY O'HARA
13 SKIBBEREEN LAWN, WATERFORD CITY
Tel: 00 353 51 372232
Fax: 00 353 51 357566
E-mail: larryohara@eircom.net
Fleetname: O'Hara Autotours
Props: Larry O'Hara, Helen O'Hara
Fleet: 6 - 2 midicoach, 2 minibus, 2 minicoach.
Chassis/Bodies: 1 Ford Transit. Mercedes.

O'MALLEY COACHES
FOILDARRIG, NEWPORT, Co TIPPERARY
Tel: 00 353 61 378119
Fax: 00 353 61 378002
Owner: E. O'Malley
Fleet: 16 - 2 single-deck bus, 9 coach, 2 midibus, 2 midicoach, 1 minibus.
Ops incl: local bus services, school contracts, excursions & tours, private hire, express.
Livery: Blue/White.

O'S COACHES
HOSPITAL, Co LIMERICK
Tel: 00 353 61 383 222
Fax: 00 353 61 383 222
E-mail: oscoaches@eircom.net
Prop: Sean F. O'Sullivan
Ch Eng: Patrick Leahy.
Fleet: double-deck bus

Chassis: Leyland, Leyland National, Mercedes
Bodies: Leyland, Leyland National, Mercedes
Ops incl: school contracts
Livery: Blue/Cream

O'SULLIVANS COACHES
FARRAHY ROAD, KILDORRERY, MALLOW, Co CORK
Tel: 00 353 22 25185
Fax: 00 353 22 25731
Prop: C O'Sullivan
Fleet: 12 - 9 coach, 3 midicoach.
Chassis: 2 Bedford. 1 Ford Transit. 1 Leyland. 2 Mercedes. 4 Volvo.
Bodies: 1 Duple. 3 Plaxton. 3 Van Hool. 3 Van Conversions.

GEORGE PLANT
ARDNAGEEHA, BANTRY, Co CORK
Tel/Fax: 00 353 27 5064
Fleet: incl: minicoach, minibus
Ops incl: private hire, excursions & tours

JACKY POWER TOURS
2 LOWER ROCK STREET, TRALEE, Co KERRY
Tel: 00 353 66 713 6300
Fax: 00 353 66 712 9444
Fleet: 7 - 5 midicoach, 2 midibus.

JOHN ROSS
97 SLIAGH BREAGH, PEPPERSTOWN, ARDEE, Co LOUTH
Tel: 00 353 41 53158
Fleet: 8 - 3 coach, 2 midicoach, 2 minibus, 1 midibus

*O'BRIEN COACHES LTD T/A ROVER COACHES
LYNN ROAD, MULLINGAR, Co WESTMEATH
Tel: 00 353 44 934 4429
Fax: 00 353 44 938 5020
Recovery: 086 2571 645
E-mail: info@rovercoaches.ie
Fleet Name: Rover
Dirs: Patrick O'Brien, John Farrell
Fleet: 16 - 9 coach, 4 midibus, 2 midicoach, 1 minibus.
Chassis: 1 DAF. 2 Ford Transit. 1 Iveco. MAN. 3 Mercedes. 2 Renault. 1 Toyota. 8 Volvo.
Bodies: 3 Caetano. 1 Esker. 2 Jonckheere. 4 Plaxton. 1 Setra. 3 other.
Ops incl: excursions & tours, school contracts, private hire, express, continental tours.

SEALANDAIR COACHING (IRELAND) LTD/PAB TOURS
51 MIDDLE ABBEY STREET, DUBLIN 1
Tel: 00 353 1 873 3411
Fax: 00 353 1 873 2639
E-mail: info@pabtours.com
Web site: www.pabtours.com
Fleetname: PAB Tours
Man Dir: Anthony Kelly
Fleet: 5 coach

Chassis: Leyland
Bodies: Duple

MATT SHANAHAN COACHES
ST MARTINS, LACKEN ROAD, KILBARRY, WATERFORD
Tel: 00 353 51 74192
Fleet: 2 - single-deck bus

ST KEVINS BUS SERVICE
See P Doyle, above

*SUIRWAY BUS & COACH SERVICES LTD
PASSAGE EAST, Co WATERFORD
Tel: 00 353 51 382209
Fax: 00 353 51 382676
E-mail: suirway@eircom.net
Web site: www.suirway.com
Fleetname: Suirway
Dir: Brian Lynch

Fleet: 10 - 6 coach, 2 single-deck bus, 2 midicoach.
Chassis: 2 Mercedes. 8 Volvo.
Bodies: 2 Esker. 2 Jonckheere. 4 Van Hool. 2 Wright.
Ops incl: local bus services, excursions & tours, private hire.
Livery: White

SWILLY BUS SERVICE
LETTERKENNY, Co DONEGAL
Tel: 00 353 74 22863
Ops incl: local bus service

TREACY COACHES
ERRIGAL, KILLALA ROAD, BALLINA, Co MAYO
Tel: 00 353 96 22563
Fax: 00 353 96 70968
E-mail: treacycoaches@eipcom.net
Dirs: A. Treacy (**Gen Man**). Sec: M. Treacy.
Fleet: 8 - 1 minibus, 7 coach.
Ops incl: excursions & tours, private hire, express.
Livery: White/Blue

Do you want to keep your LITTLE RED BOOK up-to-date?
Buses magazine now carries updates every month.
See 248 page for Subscription details

A/c	Air conditioning		Seat belt-fitted vehicles		Replacement vehicle available
	Vehicles suitable for disabled	R	Recovery service available	T	Toilet-drop facilities available
	Coach(es) with galley facilities		(not 24 hr)		Vintage vehicle(s) available
wc	Coach(es) with toilet facilities	R24	24hr recovery service		Open top vehicle(s)

Revised / Additional / Late Entries

Do you want to keep your
LITTLE RED BOOK
up-to-date?
Buses magazine now carries
updates every month.
See 248 page for Subscription details

section 5
Indices

TRADE INDEX

Several of the traders listed in this index will have more than one entry; only the first is shown here in each case.

A

ABACUS TUBULAR PRODUCTS LTD	34
ABBOT BROWN & SONS LTD	19
AC IS	49
ACT	43
ACTIA UK Ltd	27
AD COACH SALES	12
ADGROUP	48
ADG TRANSPORT CONSULTANCY	48
ADVANCED VEHICLE BUILDERS	11
AFTERMARKET COACH SUPPLIES	18
AIRCONCO	18
AIR DOOR SERVICES	24
AJP COMMERCIALS	12
AKM TECHSERVICES	51
ALBATROSS TRAVEL GROUP	57
ALBION AUTOMOTIVE LTD	25
ALCOA	47
ALEXANDER DENNIS LTD	8
ALLEN & DOUGLAS CORPORATE CLOTHING LTD	46
ALLIED VEHICLES	12
ALLISON TRANSMISSION	33
ALMEX INFORMATION SYSTEMS	43
ALSTOM TRANSPORT	9
ALTRO	32
AMA LTD	18
ANTAL INTERNATIONAL NETWORK	51
AP BORG & BECK / AP LOCKHEED — see Automotive Products	
ARDEE COACH TRIM LTD	40
ARRIVA BUS AND COACH	12
ARVIN MERITOR	20
ASHLEY BANKS LTD	22
ASHTREE GLASS LTD	36
ATLANTIS INTERNATIONAL	47
ATLAS LIGHTING COMPONENTS	35
ATOS ORIGIN	43
AUSTIN ANALYTICS	48
AUTOGLASS	47
AUTOLIFT LTD	35
AUTOMATE WHEEL COVERS	32
AUTOMOTIVE PRODUCTS GROUP LTD	20
AUTOMOTIVE TEXTILE INDUSTRIES LTD	32
AUTOPRO SOFTWARE UK	49
AUTOSAN	8
AUTOSOUND LTD	18
AVENTA	49
AVONDALE INTERNATIONAL LTD	12
AVS STEPS	19
AVT SYSTEMS	18
AYATS (GB) LTD	8

B

BALFOUR BEATTY RAIL PLANT LTD	38
BARNWELL SERVICES	37
BARRONS CHARTERED ACCOUNTANTS	48
B A S E	12
BBA FRICTION LTD	20
BELMONT INTERNATIONAL LTD	53
BELVOIR CASTLE	58
BEMROSEBOOTH LTD	43
BERNSTEIN ENGINEERING LTD	40
BESTCHART LTD	51
BEST IMPRESSIONS	49
BETA RESEARCH (ZEBRA)	19
M. BISSELL DISPLAY	31
BLACKPOOL COACH SERVICES	19
BLACKPOOL TRIM SHOPS LTD	46
BLUEBIRD VEHICLES LTD	11
BLYTHSWOOD MOTORS LTD	13
BMC UK	8
BOB VALE COACH SALES	13
BOMBARDIER TRANSPORTATION	9
BORLAND, WINDER-DIXON LLP	51
BOTEL LTD	57
BRADTECH LTD	25
BRECKNELL WILLIS	38
BRIAN NOONE	13
BRIDGE OF WEIR LEATHER CO LTD	46
BRIGADE ELECTRONICS	39
BRIGHT-TECH DEVELOPMENTS	24
BRISTOL BUS & COACH SALES	13
BRISTOL ELECTRIC RAILBUS	38
BRITAX PMG LTD	26
BRITISH BUS PUBLISHING	56
BRITISH BUS SALES	13
BRITTANY FERRIES	53
BROADWATER MOULDINGS LTD	44
DAVID BROWN VEHICLE TRANSMISSIONS LTD	33
BRT BEARINGS LTD	37
COLIN BUCHANAN & PARTNERS	48
BULWARK BUS & COACH ENGINEERING LTD	19
BURNT TREE VEHICLE SOLUTIONS	11
BUS & COACH BUYER	56
BUS AND COACH PROFESSIONAL	56
BUSES	56
BUS USER	56
BUS SHELTERS LTD	41
BUSS BIZZ	22
BUTTS OF BAWTRY	33
BUZZLINES LTD	49

C

SALVADOR CAETANO (UK) LTD	9

CALEDONIAN MACBRAYNE LTD	53
CALOTELS HOTELS	53
CAMIRA	40
CANN PRINT	43
CAPOCO DESIGN	48
CAREYBROOK LTD	48
CARLYLE BUS & COACH LTD	19
CARMANAH TECHNOLOGIES	41
CARRIER SUTRAK	18
CASH PROCESSING SOLUTIONS LTD	22
CHAPMAN DRIVERS SEATING	40
CHASSIS DEVELOPMENTS	11
CI COACHLINES	57
CIE TOURS	53
CLAN TOOLS & PLANT LTD	39
CLAYTON HEATERS LTD	18
COACH-AID	22
COACH & BUS	52
COACH & BUS WEEK	56
COACH CARPETS	32
COACH DISPLAYS LTD	52
COACH DIRECT	48
COACHFINDER LIMITED	49
COBUS UK	19
COGENT PASSENGER SEATING LTD	40
COLIN BUCHANAN & PARTNERS	48
COMPAK RAMPS	35
CONCEPT COACHCRAFT	11
CONDOR FERRIES	53
CONSERVE UK LTD	18
COURTSIDE CONVERSIONS	11
CRAIG TILSLEY & SON LTD	28
CREATIVE MANAGEMENT DEVELOPMENT	55
CRESCENT FACILITIES LTD	25
CREST COACH CONVERSIONS	19
CREWE ENGINES	28
CRONER CCH GROUP LTD	51
CROWN COACHBUILDERS LTD	11
CRYSTALKLEEN LTD	47
CSM LIGHTING	36
CUBIC TRANSPORTATION SYSTEMS LTD	31
CUMMINS UK	19
CUMMINS-ALLISON LTD	22
CVI	11
CYBERLYNE COMMUNICATIONS LTD	42

D

DAF COMPONENTS LTD	28
DATS (DAVE'S ACCIDENT & TRAINING SERVICES)	52
DAVID BROWN VEHICLE TRANSMISSIONS LTD	33
DAVID FISHWICK	13
R. L. DAVISON & CO LTD	53
DAWSONRENTALS	13
DAYCO — TRANSPORT & TRADE DISTRIBUTION LTD	28
DCA DESIGN INTERNATIONAL	51
DE LA RUE	43
DEANS SYSTEMS (UK) LTD	24
DECKER MEDIA LTD	55

DFDS SEAWAYS	53
DIESEL POWER ENGINEERING	28
DINEX EXHAUSTS LTD	27
DIRECT PARTS LTD	18
DISTINCTIVE SYSTEMS LTD	49
T & E DOCHERTY	49
DRINKMASTER LTD	25
DRIVER HIRE	49
DRURY & DRURY	19
DUNLOP TYRES	44
DUOFLEX LTD	34

E

EAST LANCASHIRE COACHBUILDERS LTD	9
EASTGATE COACH TRIMMERS	20
EATON LTD	23
EBERSPACHER (UK) LTD	18
KEITH EDMONSON	43
ELECTRONIC TICKET MACHINE SOFTWARE SERVICES (UK)	22
ELITE SERVICES LTD	39
ELLIS TRANSPORT SERVICES	51
ELSAN LTD	25
EMINOX LTD	30
ENECO	19
ENSIGN BUS COMPANY LTD	13
ERENTEK	22
ERF MEADWAY	42
ERRINGTONS OF EVINGTON LTD	13
ESKER BUS & COACH SALES, IRELAND	10
ESKER BUS & COACH, UK	11
E T M SOFTWARE SERVICES	22
EURO COACH BUILDERS LTD	11
EUROTUNNEL	53
EVOBUS (UK) LTD	13
EXCEL CONVERSIONS	11
EXPO MANAGEMENT LTD	52
EXPRESS COACH REPAIRS LTD	18

F

R. W. FAULKS FCIT	51
FCAV & CO	18
FIGUREHEAD DATA SYSTEMS	49
FINANCIAL INSPECTION SERVICES LTD	51
FIREMASTER EXTINGUISHER LTD	31
FIRTH FURNISHINGS LTD	32
FIRST CHOICE NAMEPLATES	35
DAVID FISHWICK COACH SALES	13
FJORD LINE	57
FLEET AUCTION GROUP	13
FLEETMASTER BUS & COACH LTD	13
FLIGHTS COACH TRAVEL LTD	37
FORD	10
FRASER EAGLE MANAGEMENT SERVICES	49
FTA VEHICLE INSPECTION SERVICE	28
FUMOTO ENGINEERING OF EUROPE LTD	30
FURROWS COMMERCIAL VEHICLES	13
FWT	49

G

GABRIEL & COMPANY LTD	34
GARDNER PARTS	33
GEMCO	33
GHE	20
GLIDE RITE	41
GM COACHWORK	12
IAN GORDON COMMERCIALS	13
GOSKILLS	49
GRAMPIAN SOFTWARE	51
GRASSHOPPER INN	53
GREATDAYS TRAVEL GROUP, MANCHESTER	57
GREATDAYS TRAVEL GROUP, LONDON	58
TONY GREAVES GRAPHICS	49
LEONARD GREEN ASSOCIATES	51
JOHN GROVES TICKET SYSTEMS	22

H

HANDLEY COACH UNIFORMS	46
HANOVER DISPLAYS LTD	24
HANSAR FINANCE LTD	53
HANTS & DORSET TRIM LTD	20
HAPPICH V&I COMPONENTS LTD	31
THOMAS HARDIE - WIGAN	19
HART BROTHERS	22
HATCHER COMPONENTS LTD	47
HATTS COACHWORKS	20
P J HAYMAN	53
HAYWARD TRAVEL (CARDIFF)	49
HENRY BOOTH GROUP *(see BEMROSE BOOTH)*	
B HEPWORTH & CO	47
HILTECH DEVELOPMENTS LTD	28
J. HIPWELL & SON	47
HISPACOLD	18
HL SMITH TRANSMISSIONS	25
JOHN HOLDSWORTH & CO LTD	47
HOLLOWAY COMMERCIALS	13
B D HOLT	13
HWP (H W PICKRELL)	14

I

IAN ALLAN PRINTING LTD	56
IAN GORDON	13
IBPTS	43
IMAGE & PRINT GROUP	46
IMAGE FIRST CORPORATE CLOTHING LTD	46
IMEXPART LTD	22
IMPERIAL ENGINEERING	22
INDEPENDENT COACH TRAVEL	58
INDCAR	12
INDICATORS INTERNATIONAL LTD	24
INDUSTRIAL & COMMERCIAL WINDOW CO LTD	47
INIT	43
INOVAS LTD	18
INTELLITEC	26
INTERLUBE SYSTEMS LTD	33
INVERTEC	20
IRISBUS (UK) LTD	8
IRISH COMMERCIALS	13
IRISH FERRIES	53
IRIZAR	10
ISLE OF MAN STEAM PACKET COMPANY	53
IVECO	29
ANDY IZATT	48

J

J W GLASS LTD	48
JACOBS BABTIE GROUP LTD	51
THE JANE AUSTEN CENTRE	58
JANES URBAN TRANSPORT SYSTEMS	56
JAYCAS	18
JBF SERVICES LTD	28
JDC	12
JES BUSCYCLE	20
JMW	33
JOHN GROVES TICKET SYSTEMS	22
JOHN BRADSHAW	10
JOHN HOLDSWORTH & CO LTD	47
JONCKHEERE	10
JOURNEYPLAN	38
JUBILEE AUTOMOTIVE GROUP	12

K

KAB SEATING LTD	40
KARIVE LTD	24
KEITH EDMONDSON	43
KELLETT (UK) LTD	22
KERNOW ASSOCIATES	48
KING LONG	8
KNORR-BREMSE SYSTEMS	22
THOMAS KNOWLES - TRANSPORT CONSULTANT	51
KVC	10

L

LANCES MOBILE PAINTING	36
LANTERN RECOVERY SPECIALISTS	49
THE LAWTON MOTOR BODY BUILDING CO LTD	18
LDV PLC	11
LEICESTER CARRIAGE BUILDERS	10
LEINSTER VEHICLE DISTRIBUTORS/LVD	13
LEISUREWEAR DIRECT	46
LEONARD GREEN ASSOCIATES	51
LEXCEL POWER SYSTEMS PLC	19
LEYLAND PRODUCT DEVELOPMENTS	28
LH GROUP SERVICES LTD	25
LHE FINANCE LTD	53
LONDON BUS EXPORT	13
LOOK CCTV	42
LOUGHSHORE AUTOS LTD	13
LRTA PUBLICATIONS see *TRAMWAYS & URBAN TRANSIT*	
LUNAR SEATING LTD	40

M

M A C LTD	18
MACEMAIN + AMSTAD	41
MAJORLIFT HYDRAULIC EQUIPMENT LTD	33

MAJORLINE ENGINEERING LTD	13
MAN TRUCK & BUS UK LTD (MENTOR)	8
MARK TERRILL PSV BADGES	19
MARK TERRILL TICKET MACHINERY	22
MARKET ENGINEERING	58
MARTYN INDUSTRIALS LTD	20
MASS SPECIAL ENGINEERING LTD	13
MAUN INTERNATIONAL	52
MARSHALLS COMMERCIAL ENGINEERING LTD	28
MCI EXHIBITIONS LTD	52
MCV BUS & COACH LTD	10
McKENNA BROTHERS LTD	24
MELLOR COACHCRAFT	12
MENTOR COACH & BUS LTD	13
MERCEDES-BENZ	8
METRONET REW LTD	40
MID WEST BUS & COACH SALES LTD	14
MIDLAND COUNTIES PUBLICATIONS	56
MINIBUS OPTIONS LTD	12
MINIMISE YOUR RISK	49
MINITRAM SYSTEMS LTD	9
MIRROR IMAGE MODELS	36
MISTRAL GROUP (UK) PLC	14
MOCAP LIMITED	37
MONOWASH (BRUSH REPLACEMENT SERVICE)	47
STEPHEN C MORRIS	49
MOSELEY DISTRIBUTORS	10
MOSELEY (PCV) LTD	20
MOSELEY IN THE SOUTH LTD	14
MOTIONAL MEDIA LTD	38
MOTT MACDONALD	52
MTB EQUIPMENT LTD	39
MULTIPART PSV	19
MVA	49

N

NATIONWIDE CLEANING & SUPPORT	47
NEALINE WINDSCREEN WIPER PRODUCTS	18
NEERMAN & PARTNERS	49
NEOPLAN (MENTOR)	8
NEXT BUS LTD	14
NOGE (MENTOR)	10
NORBURY BLINDS	24
NORFOLKLINE	53
W. NORTHS (PV) LTD	14
NORTON FOLGATE	53
NU-TRACK	11

O

OLYMPUS COACHCRAFT LTD	12
OMNI WHITTINGTON	53
OMNIBUS	51
OMNIBUS TRAINING LTD	52
OPTARE COACH SALES	14
OPTARE GROUP	8
ORVEC INTERNATIONAL	34
OWENS OF OSWESTRY BMC	14

P

P&O FERRIES	53
PACEL ELECTRONICS	27
PACET MANUFACTURING	23
PARTLINE LTD	22
PARRY PEOPLE MOVERS	9
PASSENGER LIFT SERVICES LTD	35
PAYPOINT	43
PERCY LANE PRODUCTS LTD	24
PENINSULA GROUP	49
PERKINS GROUP LTD	29
PETERS DOOR SYSTEMS LTD	25
PHOENIX SEATING	40
H W PICKRELL	14
PINDAR	55
PIONEER WESTON	31
PLAXTON LTD	8
PLAXTON COACH SALES CENTRE	14
PLUM PUBLISHING	53
PNEUMAX LTD	25
POLYBUSH	41
POWER BATTERIES (GB) LTD	19
POWERTRAIN PRODUCTS LTD	19
PRE METRO OPERATIONS	39
PRESTOLITE	27
PROFESSIONAL TRANSPORT SERVICES	49
PSS - STEERING & HYDRAULICS DIVISION	42
PSV GLASS	48
PSV PRODUCTS	19
PVS MANUFACTURING LTD	12

Q

Q'STRAINT	40
QUEENSBRIDGE (PSV) LTD	28
QUEENSBURY SHELTERS	41

R

RAINBOW CORPORATEWEAR	46
RATCLIFF TAIL LIFTS LTD	35
RED FUNNEL	53
RENAULT UK LTD	11
RESCROFT LTD	40
RH BODYWORKS	20
RICON UK LTD	35
RIGTON INSURANCE SERVICES	54
ROADLEASE	53
ROADLINK INTERNATIONAL LTD	22
ROBERTSON TRANSPORT CONSULTING	52
ROEVILLE COMPUTER SYSTEMS	51
ROUTE ONE	56

S

SAFEGUARD	32
SAFETEX LTD	40
SALTIRE COMMUNICATIONS	49
SALVADOR CAETANO (UK) LTD	9
SAMMYS GARAGE	49
SC COACHBUILDERS	9

SCAN COIN	22
SCANDUS UK	40
SCANIA (GB) LTD	8
SCHADES LTD	43
SEAFRANCE	53
SECURON (AMERSHAM) LTD	40
SERGEANT (B&A) LTD	22
SETRA	8
SHADES-TECHNICS	25
SHAWSON SUPPLY LTD	23
SIEMENS TRAFFIC CONTROLS	39
SIEMENS VDO	43
SILFLEX LTD	24
SKILLPLACE TRAINING	52
SMART CENTRAL COACH	47
SMITH BROS & WEBB	47
H L SMITH	25
SNOWCHAINS EUROPRODUCTS	46
SOMERS TOTALKARE	37
SOMERBUS	14
SOUTHDOWN PSV	14
SOUTHERN VECTIS PLC	57
SPECIALIST TRAINING & CONSULTANCY SERVICES	52
SSL	38
STAFFORD BUS CENTRE	14
STAGE HOTEL — LEICESTER	54
STANFORD COACHWORKS	12
STENA LINE	53
STERTIL UK	33
STEPHEN C MORRIS	49
STEPHENSONS OF ESSEX	14
JOHN STEWART & CO	12
PHIL STOCKFORD GARAGE EQUIPMENT	33
STOKE TRUCK & BUS CENTRE	14
STUART MANUFACTURING CO LTD	43
SUPERFAST FERRIES	39
SUSTRACO	39
SUTRAK: See CARRIER SUTRAK	
T	
TAGTRONICS LTD	51
TALISMAN	46
TARA SUPPORT SERVICES	49
TAS PARTNERSHIP	52
TAWE COACHBUILDERS	12
TAYLORS COACH SALES	14
TELMA RETARDER LTD	39
TERENCE BARKER TANKS	33
MARK TERRILL PSV BADGES	19
MARK TERRILL TICKET MACHINERY	22
THOMAS AUTOMATICS CO LTD	22
THOMAS HARDIE - WIGAN	19
THOMAS KNOWLES	51
TIFLEX LTD	32
TIME TRAVEL (UK)	49
TITAN BUS UK LTD	49
TONY GREAVES GRAPHICS	49
TOP GEARS DESTINATIONS	24

TOP LINE TRAVEL OF YORK LTD	49
TOWERGATE CHAPMAN STEVENS	54
TOYOTA	11
TRAMONTANA COACH DISTRIBUTORS	14
TRAM POWER LTD	9
TRAMWAYS & URBAN TRANSIT	57
TRANMAN SOLUTIONS	58
TRANSIT MAGAZINE	57
TRANSMANCHE FERRIES	53
TRANSPORT DESIGN INTERNATIONAL	28
TRANSPORT STATIONERY SERVICES	56
TRANSPORT TICKET SERVICES	22
TRANSPORT & TRAINING SERVICES LTD	58
TRANSPORTATION MANAGEMENT SOLUTIONS	19
TRAVEL INFORMATION SYSTEMS	51
TRAVELGREEN	50
TRAVELPATH 3000	54
TREVOR WIGLEY & SON BUS LTD	15
TRIMPLEX SAFETY TREAD LTD	32
TRUCK ALIGN CO LTD	20
TRUEFORM ENGINEERING LTD	41
TUBE PRODUCTS LTD	40
TVAC	12
U	
UK COACH & BUS	14
UNITEC PARTS & SERVICE LTD	19
UNITEC	18
UNITEC LONDON	18
UNITEC ROTHERHAM	18
UNITEC SCOTLAND	18
UNWIN SAFETY SYSTEMS	34
USED COACH SALES	14
UVMODULAR	12
V	
BOB VALE COACH SALES	12
VAN HOOL	8
VAPOR STONE	25
VARLEY & GULLIVER LTD	33
VARTA AUTOMOTIVE BATTERIES LTD	19
VAUXHALL	11
VBI TRISCAN	33
VCA	52
VDL BOVA	9
VDL BUS INTERNATIONAL	9
VDO KIENZLE UK LTD	27
VENTURA	14
VETRO DESIGN	49
VICTORIA COACH STATION	50
VISECT LTD (TACH:TRAK)	43
V L TEST SYSTEMS LTD	33
VOITH TURBO LTD	33
VOLKSWAGEN COMMERCIAL VEHICLES	11
VOLVO BUS LTD	9
VOLVO BUS & COACH CENTRE	14
VOLVO FINANCIAL SERVICES	53
VOLVO INSURANCE SERVICES	54
VOR TRANSMISSIONS LTD	44

VOSA	52
VULTRON INTERNATIONAL LTD	38

W

W. NORTHS (PV) LTD	14
WABCO AUTOMOTIVE UK LTD	22
WACTON COACH SALES & SERVICES	14
WALLMINSTER LTD	30
WALSH'S ENGINEERING	29
WARD INTERNATIONAL CONSULTING LTD	52
WAYFARER TRANSIT SYSTEMS	44
WEALDEN PSV LTD	15
WEALDSTONE ENGINEERING	30
WEBASTO PRODUCT LTD	18
WEBB'S	52
WEDLAKE SAINT	54
WIDNEY UK LTD	39
ALAN WHITE COACH SALES	15
WHITELEY ELECTRONICS	41
WIGHTLINK ISLE OF WIGHT FERRIES	53
WIGLEY TREVOR	15
WILKER	12
WILLIS LTD	54
WILSURE INSURANCE BROKERS	54
WINDOW CLEAN SERVICES	40
WOODBRIDGE FOAM UK LTD	40
WRIGHT GROUP	9
WRIGHTSURE INSURANCE SERVICES	54
WS ATKINS *see* ATKINS	

Y

YORKSHIRE BUS & COACH SALES	15

Z

ZF POWERTRAIN	26

Do you want to keep your
LITTLE RED BOOK
up-to-date?
Buses **magazine is now carrying updates**
every month.
See opposite title page or page 248
for Subscription details

OPERATOR INDEX

1ST CHOICE SCORPIO TRAVEL, SLOUGH	82

A

AAA COACHES, KIRKNEWTON	194
A1 COACH TRAVEL, LONDONDERRY	217
A1 TRAVEL, YEOVIL	169
A1A LTD, BIRKENHEAD	143
A.2.B TRAVEL UK LTD, PRENTON	143
AtoB TRAVEL LTD, LUTON	81
A & C LUXURY COACHES, MOTHERWELL	198
A & E HIRE, WELSHPOOL	211
A & J COACHES OF WASHINGTON CO LTD, WASHINGTON, TYNE & WEAR	174
AA, KNIGHTS OF THE ROAD, GREATER LONDON	137
A B COACHES LTD, TOTNES	99
A M K, LIPHOOK	125
A R TRAVEL, HEMEL HEMPSTEAD	123
ABBEY COACHWAYS LTD, CARLTON, Nr GOOLE	149
ABBEY TRAVEL LTD, HITCHIN	123
G. ABBOTT & SONS, LEEMING	149
ABERFELDY MOTOR SERVICES,	199
ABUS, BRISTOL	84
ACE TRAVEL, BURNTWOOD	167
ACKLAMS COACHES, BEVERLEY	109
ACRON TRAVEL, HORSFORTH	181
ACTON COACHES, WREXHAM	214
ADAMS TOURS, BLOXWICH	176
ADAMSON'S COACHES, CRAMLINGTON	154
ADBEY TRAVEL, LEICESTER	133
ADLINGTON TAXIS AND MINICOACHES, HORWICH	116
ADRAINS OF BRINKWORTH	185
AINTREE COACHLINE, BOOTLE	143
AIRCOACH, DUBLIN	218
AIRLINKS — THE AIRPORT COACH CO LTD, WEST DRAYTON	137
AIRLYNX LTD, SOUTHAMPTON	118
ALAN ARNOTT, ERSKINE	200
ALANSWAY COACHES, NEWTON ABBOTT	99
ALDERMASTON COACHES, ALDERMASTON	82
ALEC HEAD, LUTTON, PETERBOROUGH	153
ALEX MILNE, NEW BYTH BY TURRIFF	191
ALEXCARS LTD, CIRENCESTER	114
ALFA COACHES LTD, STOCKTON-ON-TEES	105
ALFA TRAVEL, CHORLEY	130
ALFRA COACH HIRE, LARKHALL	201
A LINE COACHES, GATESHEAD	174
ALLAN'S GROUP, GOREBRIDGE	197
ALLANDER COACHES LTD, MILNGAVIE	196
ALLIED COACHES, BALDOYLE, DUBLIN	218
ALLIED COACHLINES LTD, HAYES	144
ALMAR TRAVEL, CHESTER-le-STREET	105
ALPHA COACH CO, HULL	109
ALPHA PERSONALISED TRAVEL LTD, WATFORD	123
ALPINE TRAVEL, LLANDUDNO	208

ALTONA COACH SERVICES & TRAVEL CONSULTANT, GATESHEAD	174
ALTONIAN COACHES, ALTON	118
AMBASSADOR TRAVEL (ANGLIA) LTD, GREAT YARMOUTH	146
AMBER TRAVEL, TURRIFF	190
AMK CHAUFFEUR DRIVEN, LIPHOOK	119
GEOFF AMOS COACHES, DAVENTRY	153
AMPORT & DISTRICT COACHES LTD, ANDOVER	119
ANDERSON COACHES LTD, SHEFFIELD	164
ANDERSON TRAVEL LTD, LONDON SE1	137
ANDERSON'S COACHES, FERRYBRIDGE	181
ANDERSON'S COACHES, LANGHOLM	192
ANDREW JAMES QUALITY TRAVEL, MALMESBURY	186
ANDREW'S OF TIDESWELL LTD	96
ANDREWS COACHES, FOXTON, CAMBRIDGE	87
ANDYBUS AND COACH LTD, MALMESBURY	193
ANGEL MOTORS (EDMONTON) LTD, TOTTENHAM	137
ANGEL TRAVEL, WARRINGTON	89
ANGELA COACHES LTD, BURSLEDON	119
ANGLIAN COACHES LTD, BECCLES	169
ANITAS BRITISH & CONTINENTAL TOURS LTD, STANSTED AIRPORT	109
ANTHONYS TRAVEL, RUNCORN	89
APL TRAVEL, CRUDWELL	185
APPLEBYS COACHES, LOUTH	148
APT COACHES LTD, RAYLEIGH	109
ARAN TOURS, SANDYCOVE, Co DUBLIN	218
ARLEEN COACH HIRE & SERVICES LTD, PEASEDOWN ST JOHN	161
R. K. ARMSTRONG COACHES, CASTLE DOUGLAS	193
ARNOLD LIDDELL COACHES, BRISTOL	85
ARON COACHLINES LTD, HAYES	144
ARRIVA CYMRU LTD, LLANDUDNO JUNCTION	208
ARRIVA DERBY LTD	96
ARRIVA LONDON	137
ARRIVA MIDLANDS, LEICESTER	133
ARRIVA MIDLANDS, CANNOCK	167
ARRIVA NORTH EAST LTD, SUNDERLAND	174
ARRIVA NORTH WEST & WALES, AINTREE	143
ARRIVA PLC	80
ARRIVA SCOTLAND WEST, PAISLEY	200
ARRIVA SOUTHERN COUNTIES, MAIDSTONE	126
ARRIVA SURREY & WEST SUSSEX, GUILDFORD	171
ARRIVA THE SHIRES & ESSEX, LUTON	8
ARRIVA YORKSHIRE, WAKEFIELD	182
ARROWEBROOK COACHES, CHESTER	89
ARUN COACHES/FAWLTY TOURS, HORSHAM	180
ARVONIA COACHES, CAERNARFON	209
ASHALL'S COACHES, MANCHESTER	116
ASHFORD LUXURY COACHES, FELTHAM	144
ASHLEY TRAVEL LTD t/a GRANT & McALLIN, SHEFFIELD	164

Operator Index

232

Operator	Page
G. ASHTON COACHES, *ST HELENS*	143
ASM COACHES, *WHITSTABLE*	126
ASMAL COACHES, *LEICESTER*	133
J. & F. ASPDEN (BLACKBURN) LTD	130
ASTONS COACHES, *WORCESTER*	188
ASTONS OF NEWPORT, *SHROPSHIRE*	159
H. ATKINSON & SONS (INGLEBY), *NORTHALLERTON*	149
AUSDEN CLARK LTD, *LEICESTER*	133
AUSTIN TRAVEL, *EARLSTON*	192
AUTOCAR BUS & COACH, *TONBRIDGE*	126
AUTODOUBLE LTD, *MILTON KEYNES*	85
AVENSIS COACH TRAVEL, *ROMSEY*	119
AVON COACH & BUS COMPANY, *BIRKENHEAD*	143
AWAY DAYS, *SHANKLIN*	125
AWAYDAYS LTD T/A GEMINI TRAVEL, *IPSWICH*	178
AXE VALE COACHES, *AXBRIDGE*	161
AXE VALLEY MINI TRAVEL, *SEATON*	99
AYREVILLE COACHES, *PLYMOUTH*	99
AZTEC COACH TRAVEL, *BRISTOL*	84

B

Operator	Page
B & H TOURS, *MIRFIELD*	182
B & J TRAVEL, *MIDDLESTOWN*	182
B B COACHES LTD, *HALESOWEN*	176
B'S TRAVEL, *PONTYPOOL*	214
BACK ROADS TOURING CO LTD, *LONDON W5*	137
BAGNALLS COACHES, *SWADLINCOTE*	96
BAILEY'S COACHES LTD, *WATNALL*	155
BAILISS TOURS, *BARTON-IN-THE-BEANS*	133
BAKERS COACHES, *BIDDULPH*	167
BAKERS COACHES, *MORETON-IN-MARSH*	114
BAKERS COACHES, *YEOVIL*	169
BAKERS COMMERCIAL SERVICES, *ENSTONE*	158
BAKERS DOLPHIN COACH TRAVEL, *WESTON-SUPER-MARE*	161
BAKEWELL COACHES, *BAKEWELL*	96
IAN BALDRY, *FELIXSTOWE*	169
BALDRY'S COACHES, *YORK*	149
BANBURYSHIRE ETA LTD, *BANBURY*	158
BANSTEAD COACHES LTD, *BANSTEAD*	171
BARCROFT TOURS & EVENTS, *HASTINGS*	107
BARFORDIAN COACHES LTD, *BEDFORD*	81
BARNES COACHES LTD, *SWINDON*	185
BARNSLEY & DISTRICT TRACTION CO	164
BARRATT'S COACHES, *SANDBACH*	89
BARRY'S COACHES LTD, *CORK*	218
BARRY'S COACHES LTD, *WEYMOUTH*	103
BARTON TRANSPORT, *MAYNOOTH*	218
BASFORDS COACHES LTD, *TOWCESTER*	153
BATH BUS COMPANY	161
BATTERSBY SILVER GREY, *MORECAMBE*	130
BATTERSBY'S COACHES, *WALKDEN*	116
BEACON COACHES, *CHELMSLEY WOOD*	176
K. W. BEARD LTD, *CINDERFORD*	114
BEAULY COACH HIRE, *WESTER BALBLAIR, BY BEAULY*	196
BEAVIS HOLIDAYS, *BUSSAGE*	114
BEBB TRAVEL, *LLANTWIT FARDRE*	213
BEECHES TRAVEL, *TWICKENHAM*	144
BEECROFT COACHES, *FEWSTON, NR HARROGATE*	150
BEELINE (R&R) COACHES LTD, *WARMINSTER*	185
BEESTONS COACHES LTD, *HADLEIGH*	169
BELLS LUXURY COACHES, *SALISBURY*	185
BEN GEORGE TRAVEL, *BROUGHTON*	148
BEN JOHNSON COACHES, *BRANDESBURTON*	109
BENNETT'S COACHES, *GLOUCESTER*	114
BENNETT'S TRAVEL, *WARRINGTON*	89
BENNETTS TRAVEL (CRANBERRY) LTD, *GATES HEATH*	167
BERKELEY COACH AND TRAVEL LTD, *PAULTON, BRISTOL*	84
BERRY'S COACHES (TAUNTON) LTD	162
BESSWAY TRAVEL, *WEST HARROW*	144
BEST WAY TRAVEL, *SALTBURN*	105
BETTER MOTORING SERVICES, *STRATTON-ST MARGARET*	186
JAMES BEVAN LTD, *LYDNEY*	114
BIBBY'S OF INGLETON	150
BIG BUS COMPANY, *LONDON SW1W*	137
BILLIES COACHES LTD, *ROTHERHAM*	164
BIRMINGHAM COACH COMPANY LTD, THE, *WARLEY*	176
BIRMINGHAM INTERNATIONAL COACHES LTD, *TILE CROSS*	176
D. P. BISHOP, *DUMBARTON*	202
B J S TRAVEL, *GREAT WAKERING*	109
BLACKBURN BOROUGH TRANSPORT LTD	130
BLACKPOOL TRANSPORT LTD	130
BLAGDON LIONESS COACHES LTD, *BRISTOL*	162
BLAZEFIELD HOLDINGS	80
BLUE DIAMOND COACHES, *HARLOW*	109
BLUE IRIS COACHES, *NAILSEA*	84
BLUEBIRD BUS & COACH, *MIDDLETON*	116
BLUEBIRD BUSES, *ABERDEEN*	190
BLUEBIRD BUSES, *INVERNESS*	196
BLUEBIRD COACHES (WEYMOUTH) LTD	103
BLUEBIRD COACHES, *COOLOCK, DUBLIN*	218
BLUEBIRD OF NEATH/PONTARDAWE	210
BLUELINE COACHES, *MAGHULL*	143
BLUE TRIANGLE BUSES, *RAINHAM*	109
BLUEWAYS GUIDELINE COACHES LTD, *LONDON*	137
BLUNSDON'S COACH TRAVEL, *BLADON*	158
C. BODMAN & SONS, *DEVIZES*	186
A. S. BONE & SONS, *HOOK*	119
A & H BOOTH LTD, *HYDE*	116
BORDACOACH, *RAYLEIGH*	109
BOSTOCK'S COACHES LTD, *CONGLETON*	89
BOTTERILLS, *THORNTON DALE*	150
BOULTONS OF SHROPSHIRE, *CHURCH STRETTON*	159
BOURNEMOUTH TRANSPORT LTD	103
L F BOWEN LTD, *TAMWORTH*	153
BOWERS COACHES LTD, *CHAPEL-EN-LE-FRITH*	96
D K & N BOWMAN, *WREAY, CARLISLE*	93
BOWMAN'S COACHES (MULL) LTD, *CRAIGNURE*	191
BOWYER'S COACHES, *HEREFORD*	122
BRADSHAWS TRAVEL, *KNOTT END ON SEA*	130

Operator	Page
BRAZIERS MINI COACHES, *BUCKINGHAM*	85
BRENTONS OF BLACKHEATH, *LONDON SE3*	138
BRENTWOOD COACHES	109
BRIAN ISAAC COACHES LTD, *SWANSEA*	213
BRIGHTON & HOVE BUS & COACH CO LTD	107
BRIGHTONIAN COACHES, *BRIGHTON*	107
BRIJAN TOURS, *CULDRIDGE*	119
BRISTOL ELECTRIC RAILBUS	84
BRITANNIA COACHES, *DOVER*	127
BRITANNIA TRAVEL, *OTLEY*	182
BRITTAINS COACHES LTD, *NORTHAMPTON*	153
BRODYR JAMES, *TREGARON*	207
BROMYARD OMNIBUS COMPANY, *BROMYARD*	122
A T BROWN, *TELFORD*	159
EDDIE BROWN TOURS LTD, *YORK*	150
H E BROWN, *CONGLETON*	89
LES BROWN TRAVEL, *BATHGATE*	202
BROWNINGS (WHITBURN) LTD	202
S H BROWNRIGG LTD, *EGREMONT*	93
WILLIAM BROWNRIGG, *THORNHILL*	193
BROWNS COACHES LTD, *PONTEFRACT*	182
BROWNS COACHES, *ASHFORD*	127
BROWNS OF DURHAM, *DURHAM*	105
BROWNS OF EDINBURGH, *BROXBURN*	194
ROY BROWNS COACHES, *BUILTH WELLS*	211
RONNIE BRUEN, *COOLOCK, DUBLIN*	218
BRYANS OF ENFIELD	138
BRYLAINE TRAVEL, *BOSTON*	135
BUCKBY'S COACHES, *ROTHWELL*	153
BUCKLEYS, *DONCASTER*	164
BUCKLEY'S TOURS, *KILLARNEY*	218
BUDDENS COACHES LTD, See AVENSIS	
BUGLERS COACHES LTD, *BRISTOL*	84
R. BULLOCK & CO (TRANSPORT) LTD, *CHEADLE HULME*	116
BULLDOG TRAVEL, *BATHGATE*	116, 203
BURDETTS COACHES LTD, *MOSBOROUGH*	164
BURGHFIELD MINI COACHES LTD, *READING*	82
BURKE BROS (COACHES) LTD, *TUAM, Co GALWAY*	218
BURNHAM PARK COACHES, *PLYMOUTH*	99
BURNLEY & PENDLE	130
JAMES BURNS, *PAISLEY*	200
BURRELLS (BARNARD CASTLE COACHES), *RICHMOND*	150
R & D BURROWS LTD, *OGMORE VALE, BRIDGEND*	205
BURTONS COACHES LTD, *HAVERHILL*	170
BURTONS COLCHESTER, *COLCHESTER*	109
BUS EIREANN/IRISH BUS, *DUBLIN*	218
TERRY BUSHELL TRAVEL, *BURTON-ON-TRENT*	167
BUSES4U, *TANDRIDGE*	171
BUTLER BROTHERS, *KIRKBY IN ASHFIELD*	155
BUTLERS BUSES, *COBH, Co CORK*	218
BUTTERS COACHES, *MARKET DRAYTON*	159
BU-VAL, *LITTLEBOROUGH*	116
BUZZLINES, *HYTHE*	127
BYNGS INTERNATIONAL COACHES, *PORTSMOUTH*	119
BYRAN COACHES LTD, *SHEFFIELD*	164
BYSIAU CWM TAF/TAF VALLEY COACHES, *WHITLAND*	207
LES BYWATER & SONS LTD, *ROCHDALE*	116

C

Operator	Page
C & G COACH SERVICES, *CHATTERIS*	87
C & S COACHES, *HEATHFIELD*	107
C I COACHLINES, *CHELMSFORD*	109
C. L. COACHES, *LANCING*	180
C N ENTERPRISES, *ROMFORD*	109
CABER COACHES, *ABERFELDY*	208
CABIN COACHES, *HAYES*	145
CAELLOI MOTORS, *PWLLHELI*	209
CAHALANE COACHES, *CORK*	218
CALDEW COACHES, *CARLISLE*	93
CALL-A-COACH, *WALTON-ON-THAMES*	171
CALLINAN COACHES, *GLAREGALWAY*	218
CAMBRIAN COAST COACH LINE, *ABERGYNOLWYN*	209
CAMPBELL'S COACHES, *SOUTH SHIELDS*	174
CANAVAN'S COACHES, *KILSYTH*	198
DEN CANEY COACHES LTD, *BIRMINGHAM*	177
CANTABRICA COACHES, *WATFORD*	123
CARADOC COACHES, *CHURCH STRETTON*	159
CARADON RIVIERA TOURS, *LISKEARD*	91
CARAVELLE COACHES, *EDGWARE*	145
CARDIFF BUS, *CARDIFF*	206
CARMEL COACHES, *OKEHAMPTON*	99
J. W. CARNELL LTD, *SUTTON BRIDGE*	135
PETER CAROL PRESTIGE COACHING, *WHITCHURCH, BRISTOL*	84
CARR'S COACHES, *SILLOTH*	94
CARREGLEFN COACHES, *AMLWCH*	205
CAROUSEL BUSES, *HIGH WYCOMBE*	85
GERRY CARROLL COACH HIRE, *DROGHEDA*	218
CARS INTERNATIONAL A. C. T., *ASH*	171
CARSVILLE COACHES, *URMSTON*	116
CASTELL COACHES LTD, *BEDWAS*	206
CASTLE GARAGE LTD, *LLANDOVERY*	207
CASTLEWAYS LTD, *WINCHCOMBE*	114
CATTERALLS OF SOUTHAM, *SOUTHAM*	175
CAVALIER TRAVEL, *LONG SUTTON*	135
CAVALIER TRAVEL SERVICES, *BRENTFORD*	138
CEDAR COACHES, *BEDFORD*	81
CEDRIC COACHES, *WIVENHOE*	109
CELTIC TRAVEL, *LLANIDLOES*	211
CENTAUR TRAVEL MINICOACHES, *SIDCUP*	138
CENTRAL COACHES, *KEITH*	198
CENTRAL MINI COACHES, *DOVER*	127
CENTRAL TRAVEL, *NEWTOWN*	211
CENTREBUS, *LUTON*	81
CENTURION TRAVEL, *MIDSOMER NORTON*	162
CERBYDAU BERWYN COACHES, *TREFOR, PWLLHELI*	209
CHADWELL HEATH COACHES, *ROMFORD*	109
CHALFONT COACHES OF HARROW LTD, *SOUTHALL*	145
CHALFONT LINE LTD, *WEST DRAYTON*	145

CHALKWELL COACH HIRE & TOURS, SITTINGBOURNE	127
CHAMBERS COACH HIRE LTD, MONEYMORE	217
CHAMBERS COACHES (STEVENAGE) LTD	123
H. C. CHAMBERS & SON LTD, BURES	170
CHANDLERS COACH TRAVEL, WESTBURY	186
CHAPEL END COACHES, NUNEATON	175
CHARIOTS OF CRAWLEY	180
CHARIOTS OF ESSEX LTD, STANFORD-LE-HOPE	109
CHARLTON-ON-OTMOOR SERVICES, OXFORD	158
CHARTER COACH LTD, YORK	150
CHAUFFEURS OF BIRMINGHAM, EDGBASTON	177
CHEAM COACHES, CHEAM, SUTTON	171
CHENERY, DISS	146
CHENEY COACHES LTD, BANBURY	158
CHERRYBRIAR, LONDON E3	138
CHESTERBUS, CHESTER	89
CHEYNE'S COACHES, INVERURIE	190
CHILTERN TRAVEL, HENLOW	81
CHIVERS COACHES LTD, WALLINGTON	172
CIRCLE LINE, MAYNOOTH, IRELAND	218
CITYCIRCLE UK, BONNYRIGG	194
CITY SIGHTSEEING EDINBURGH LTD, EDINBURGH	196
CITY SIGHTSEEING GLASGOW LTD, GLASGOW	204
CLAPTON COACHES LTD, RADSTOCK	162
CLARIBEL COACHES, TILE CROSS	177
CLARKES OF LONDON, LONDON SE26	138
CLARKSON COACHWAYS, BARROW IN FURNESS	94
CLARKSONS HOLIDAYS, SOUTH ELMSALL	182
CLASSIC COACHES LTD, ANNFIELD PLAIN	105
CLASSIC COACHES, LUTON	81
CLASSIC GOLD COACHES, SOUTH CLEVEDON	84
CLASSIQUE SUN SALOON LUXURY COACHES, PAISLEY	200
CLEGG & BROOKING COACHES, STOCKBRIDGE	119
CLH TRAVEL, PAIGNTON	99
CLINTONA MINICOACHES, BRENTWOOD	111
CLOWES COACHES, LONGNOR	96
CLYDE COAST COACHES LTD, ARDROSSAN	198
CLYNNOG & TREFOR MOTORS, CAERNARFON	209
COACH COMPANIONS LTD, LEOMINSTER	122
COACH HOUSE TRAVEL, DORCHESTER	108
COACHLINERS, SOUTH SHIELDS	103
COACH OPTIONS, ROCHDALE	116
COACH SERVICES LTD, THETFORD	146
COACHING CONNECTION, LLANIDLOES	212
COACHSTYLE LTD, CHIPPENHAM	186
COAST TO COAST PACKHORSE, KIRKBY STEPHEN	94
COASTAL & COUNTRY COACHES LTD, WHITBY	150
COASTAL COACHES, NEWICK, LEWES	105
COCHRANE'S, PETERLEE	119
COLISEUM COACHES LTD, WEST END, SOUTHAMPTON	125
COLLIN PHILLIPSON, GOOLE	109, 166
COLLIN'S COACHES, CARRICKAMOSS, Co MONAGHAN	218
COLLINS COACHES LTD, LONDON W7	138
COLLINS COACHES, CAMBRIDGE	87
COLLINS COACHES, SELBY	150
W. H. COLLINS, ROCH	211
COLRAY COACH HIRE, BLACKPOOL	130
COMPASS ROYSTON COACHES, DURHAM	105
COMPASS TRAVEL, WORTHING	180
CONFIDENCE BUS/COACH HIRE, LEICESTER	133
CONISTON COACHES LTD, BROMLEY	138
CONNEX BUS UK LTD, St HELIER, JERSEY	189
CONWAY COACH AND CHAUFFEUR DRIVE, LIMERICK	218
COOKS COACHES, WELLINGTON, SOMERSET	162
COOKS COACHES, WESTCLIFF-ON-SEA	111
COOMBS TRAVEL, WESTON-SUPER-MARE	162
HENRY COOPER, ANNITSFORD	174
COOPERS COACHES, WOOLSTON	119
COOPERS TOURS LTD, KILLAMARSH	164
COPELAND TOURS (STOKE-ON-TRENT) LTD, MEIR	167
DAVID CORBEL OF LONDON LTD, EDGWARE	138
CORCORANS EXECUTIVE TOURS, KILLARNEY, Co KERRY	218
CORPORATE COACHING, LUTON	81
COSY COACHES, KILLAMARSH	164
COTTRELL'S COACHES, MITCHELDEAN	114
COUNTRY HOPPER, IBSTOCK	134
COUNTRYBUS, ADDLESTONE	172
COUNTRY LION (NORTHAMPTON) LTD	153
COUNTRYLINER COACH HIRE LTD, GUILDFORD	172
COUNTRYSIDE BUS SERVICES, SCARBOROUGH	150
COUNTY COACHES, BRENTWOOD	111
COUNTY MINI COACHES, LEICESTER	134
L. S. COURT LTD, FILLONGLEY	176
COURTESY TRAVEL, SHREWSBURY	159
COURTNEY COACHES, BERKSHIRE	82
COX'S OF BELPER	96
COYLES COACHES, GWEEDORE, Co DONEGAL	219
R. & C. S. CRAIG, ROBERTON	201
CRAIG OF CAMPBELTOWN, CAMPBELTOWN	191
CRAIGGS TRAVEL EUROPEAN, AMBLE	154
HENRY CRAWFORD COACHES LTD, NEILSTON	202
CRAWLEY LUXURY, THREE BRIDGES	180
CREMIN COACHES, BANTRY, WEST CORK	219
CRESSWELLS COACHES (GRESLEY) LTD, SWADLINCOTE	96
N N CRESSWELL, EVESHAM	188
CRISTAL HIRE COACHES OF SWANWICK	96
CROESO TOURS, PENYLAN	206
CRONIN'S COACHES LTD, CORK	219
CROPLEY, FOSDYKE	135
CROPPER COACHES, TOTTINGTON	116
CROSS COUNTRY COACHES, COLERAINE	217
CROSS COUNTRY COACHES, SWINDON	186
CROSS COUNTRY HIRE, POOLE	103
CROSS GATES COACHES, LLANDRINDOD WELLS	212
CROSSKEYS COACHES, FOLKESTONE	127

CROSSON MOTOR GROUP, *COOLOCK, DUBLIN*	219
MARTIN CROWLEY, *BANDON Co CORK*	219
CROWN COACHES, *BICKLEY*	138
CROWN COACHES, *LEIGH-ON-SEA*	111
CROYDON TRAMLINK	138
CRUISERS LTD, *REDHILL*	172
CRUSADE TRAVEL, *PENKRIDGE*	167
CRUSADER HOLIDAYS, *CLACTON-ON-SEA*	111
CRYSTALS COACHES LTD, *LONDON SW10*	138
CUCKMERE COMMUNITY BUS, *POLEGATE*	107
CUMBRIA COACHES, *CARLISLE*	94
CUMFI-LUX COACHES, *HILLINGDON*	145
CUMFY COACHES, *SOUTHPORT*	143
CUNNINGHAM CARRIAGE CO, *CORRINGHAM*	111

D

Operator	Page
D & E COACHES, *INVERNESS*	197
D & G COACH & BUS LTD, *STOKE ON TRENT*	167
D & H TRAVEL, *KENDAL*	94
D A C COACHES, *GUNNISLAKE*	91
D H CARS OF DENSTONE LTD, *UTTOXETER*	168
D R M BUS & CONTRACT SERVICES, *BROMYARD*	122
D.R.M. MINIBUS & COACH TRAVEL, *CHASE TERRACE*	176
D. R. P. MINIBUS TRAVEL, *NEWPORT PAGNELL*	91
D-WAY TRAVEL, *BUNGAY*	170
DAGLISH COACHES, *FRIZINGTON*	94
DAIMLER, *BIRMINGHAM*	177
DAISHS TRAVEL, *TORQUAY*	105
DALESMAN, *GUISELEY*	182
DAM EXPRESS, *ARDWICK GREEN*	116
DAMORY COACHES, *BLANDFORD FORUM*	103
DANS MINI-BUSES, *LONDON E18*	138
DARLEY FORD TRAVEL, *LISKEARD*	92
DARRAGHS COACHES, *BALLYMONEY*	217
DARTLINE COACHES, *EXETER*	99
DAVIAN COACHES, *LONDON*	139
DAVID PALMER COACHES LTD, *NORMANTON*	183
BILLY DAVIES EXECUTIVE COACHES, *STIRLING*	202
D G DAVIES, *RHAYADER*	212
DAWLISH COACHES LTD	100
ALAN DAWNEY COACH HIRE, *SHEPPEY*	127
DAWSON'S MINICOACHES, *ALFRETON*	97
MIKE DE COURCEY TRAVEL LTD, *COVENTRY*	177
DELAINE BUSES LTD, *BOURNE*	135
DEN CANEY COACHES LTD, *BIRMINGHAM*	177
DERBY COMMUNITY TRANSPORT	97
DEREK HIRCOCKS COACHES, *UPWELL, Nr WISBECH*	87
DEROS COACH TOURS, *KILLARNEY*	219
DERWENT COACHES LTD, *STANLEY, CO DURHAM*	174
DEWHIRST COACHES, *BRADFORD*	182
DEWS COACHES, *SOMERSHAM*	87
D'COACHES (DIAMOND HOLIDAYS), *MORRISTON*	213
DIRECT COACH TOURS, *BIRMINGHAM*	177
DOBSON'S BUSES LTD, *NORTHWICH*	90

Operator	Page
T. & E. DOCHERTY, *IRVINE*	198
DOCHERTY'S MIDLAND COACHES, *AUCHTERARDER*	208
DOCKLANDS MINIBUSES, *SILVERTOWN E16*	139
DODDS OF TROON LTD, *AYR*	201
J. DODSWORTH (COACHES) LTD, *BOROUGHBRIDGE*	150
DOIGS OF GLASGOW LTD	196
JIMMY DONNELLY & SON, *ENNISCORTHY, Co WEXFORD*	219
DONOVAN'S COACH HIRE, *KILLARNEY*	219
DONS COACHES DUNMOW LTD, *GREAT DUNMOW*	111
DORSET COUNTY COUNCIL, PASSENGER TRANSPORT SECTION	104
DOUGLAS CORPORATION TRAMWAY	204
P. DOYLE LTD, *ROUNDWOOD, Co WICKLOW*	219
TONY DOYLE COACHES, *ENNISKERRY, Co WICKLOW*	219
K&H DOYLE, *RIPLEY*	97
TIM DRAPER HOLIDAYS, *ALFRETON*	97
DRP TRAVEL, *MILTON KEYNES*	86
DRURY COACHES, *GOOLE*	109
DUALWAY COACHES, *RATHCOOLE, Co DUBLIN*	219
DUBLIN BUS	219
DUBLIN MINI COACHES, *DUBLIN*	219
DUDLEY'S COACHES LTD, *WORCESTER*	188
DUNCAN MACLENNAN, *STRATH-CARRON*	197
DUNN'S COACHES, *AIRDRIE*	198
DUNN-LINE, *NOTTINGHAM*	155
DURHAM CITY COACHES LTD	105
DURHAM TRAVEL, *SEAHAM*	105

E

Operator	Page
'E' COACHES OF ALFRETON	97
EAGLE COACHES, *BRISTOL*	84
EAGLE LINE TRAVEL, *CHELTENHAM*	115
EAGLE TRAVEL, *STAFFORD*	168
EAGLES & CRAWFORD, *MOLD*	209
EAGRE, *MORTON*	135
EALING COMMUNITY TRANSPORT, *LONDON W3*	139
EARNSIDE COACHES, *GLENFARG*	208
EASSONS COACHES LTD, *ITCHEN*	119
EAST LONDON BUS GROUP, *ILFORD*	*139*
EAST TEIGNBRIDGE COMMUNITY TRANSPORT *DAWLISH*	100
EAST YORKSHIRE MOTOR SERVICES LTD, *HULL*	109
EASTBOURNE BUSES LTD	107
A. W. EASTON'S COACHES LTD, *STRATTON STRAWLESS, NORWICH*	146
EASTONWAYS LTD, *RAMSGATE*	127
EASTVILLE COACHES LTD, *BRISTOL*	84
EASTWARD COACHES, *IVYBRIDGE*	100
EAVESWAY TRAVEL LTD, *ASHTON-IN-MAKERFIELD*	130
EBLEY COACH SERVICES, *NAILSWORTH*	115
EDS MINIBUS & COACH HIRE, *EAST TILBURY*	111
EDINBURGH BUS TOURS, *EDINBURGH*	194
EDINBURGH COACH LINES, *EDINBURGH*	195

EDWARDS BROS, *TIERS CROSS*	211
EDWARDS COACHES, *LLANTWIT FARDRE*	213
GEORGE EDWARDS & SON, *BWLCHYWYN*	223
L J EDWARDS COACH HIRE, *HAILSHAM*	108
EIREBUS LTD, *DUBLIN*	219
ELCOCK REISEN LTD, *MADELEY*	160
ELITE SERVICES LTD, *STOCKPORT*	116
ELIZABETH YULE, *PITLOCHRY*	200
ELLEN SMITH (TOURS) LTD, *ROCHDALE*	116
ELLENDERS COACHES, *SHEFFIELD*	164
ELLIS COACHES, *LLANGEFNI*	205
P & J ELLIS LTD, *LONDON NW10*	139
ELLISON'S COACHES, *ASHTON KEYNES*	186
ELTHAM EXECUTIVE CHARTER, *LONDON SE9*	139
EMBLINGS COACHES, *GUYHIRN*	87
EMMERSON COACHES, *IMMINGHAM*	148
EMMAS COACHES, *DOLGELLAU*	209
EMPRESS COACHES LTD, *ST LEONARDS-ON-SEA*	108
EMPRESS MOTORS LTD, *LONDON E2*	108, 139
EMSWORTH & DISTRICT, *SOUTHBOURNE*	120
ENDEAVOUR COACHES, *BIRMINGHAM*	177
ENFIELD COACHES, *ENFIELD, Co MEATH*	219
ENNIS COACHES, *MATLOCK*	97
ENSIGNBUS COMPANY, *PURFLEET*	111
ENTERPRISE TRAVEL, *DARLINGTON*	105
EPSOM COACHES GROUP, *EPSOM*	172
ERB SERVICES, *BYKER*	174
ESSBEE COACHES, *COATBRIDGE*	198
E.S.T. BUS LTD, *LLANDOW*	214
EUROLINK FOLKESTONE	127
EUROSUN COACHES, *CROMER*	147
EUROTAXIS, *BRISTOL*	84
EUROLINERS, *REDNAL, BIRMINGHAM*	127
GARETH EVANS COACHES, *BRYNAMMAN*	207
EVE CARS & COACHES, *DUNBAR*	194
EXCALIBUR COACHES, *LONDON SE15*	111
EXCALIBUR COACH TRAVEL, *SOUTHMINSTER*	139
EXCEL PASSENGER LOGISTICS LTD, *STANSTED AIRPORT*	111
EXCELSIOR COACHES LTD, *BOURNEMOUTH*	104
EXPERT COACH SERVICES LTD, *GRIMSBY*	148
EXPRESS MOTORS, *PENYGROES CAERNARFON*	209
EXPRESSLINES LTD, *BEDFORD*	81
EXPRESSWAY COACHES, *ROTHERHAM*	164
F	
FAHERTY'S COACH HIRE, *MOYCULLEN, Co GALWAY*	220
FAIRWAY TRAVEL, *EDINBURGH*	193
FALCON TRAVEL, *SHEPPERTON*	145
FARELINE BUS & COACH SERVICES, *EYE*	170
FARESAVER BUSES, *CHIPPENHAM*	186
FARGO COACHLINES, *BRAINTREE*	111
FARLEIGH COACHES, *ROCHESTER*	127
FARNHAM COACHES, *FARNHAM*	172
FELIX BUS SERVICES LTD, *STANLEY, DERBYS*	97
FENN HOLIDAYS LTD, *MARCH*	87
FERRERS COACHES LTD, *SOUTH WOODHAM FERRERS*	112
FERRYMAN TRAVEL, *LEYBOURNE*	127
DAVID FIELD, *NEWENT*	115
FIFE SCOTTISH OMNIBUSES LTD, *COWDENBEATH*	195
FILERS TRAVEL, *ILFRACOMBE*	100
FINEGAN COACH HIRE, *CARRICKMACROSS, Co MONAGHAN*	220
FINGLANDS COACHWAYS, *RUSHOLME*	117
DECLAN FINNEGAN, *KENMARE, Co KERRY*	220
EUGENE FINNEGAN (TRANSPORT), *BRAY, Co WICKLOW*	220
FIRST IN ABERDEEN	190
FIRST BERKSHIRE, *BRACKNELL*	82
FIRST BRADFORD	182
FIRST CHOICE TRAVEL, *PETERBOROUGH*	87
FIRST BRISTOL, *WESTON-SUPER-MARE*	84
FIRST CYMRU, *SWANSEA*	213
FIRST IN CHESTER & THE WIRRAL	90, 143
FIRST DEVON & CORNWALL	100
FIRST EASTERN COUNTIES, *NORWICH*	147
FIRST EDINBURGH	193
FIRST ESSEX BUSES, *CHELMSFORD*	112
FIRST GLASGOW	196
FIRST HALIFAX, *HALIFAX*	182
FIRST HAMPSHIRE & DORSET LTD, *SOUTHAMPTON*	120
FIRST IN HUDDERSFIELD	182
FIRST IN LEEDS	182
FIRST LEICESTER	134
FIRST LONDON	139
FIRST IN MANCHESTER, *OLDHAM*	117
FIRST NORTHAMPTON	153
FIRST POTTERIES (NORTH STAFFS)	168
FIRST SCOTLAND EAST	197
FIRST SOMERSET & AVON, *WESTON-SUPER-MARE*	162
FIRST SOUTH YORKS, *ROTHERHAM*	164
FIRST IN WYVERN, *WORCESTER*	188
FIRST YORK	150
FIRSTGROUP PLC	80
FISHERS TOURS, *DUNDEE*	193
JOHN FISHWICK & SONS, *LEYLAND*	130
FITZCHARLES COACHES LTD, *GRANGEMOUTH*	202
FIVE STAR GROUP TRAVEL, *PRESCOTT*	143
JOHN FLANAGAN COACH TRAVEL, *GRAPPENHALL, WARRINGTON*	90
FLIGHTS HALLMARK LTD, *BIRMINGHAM*	177
FLYGHT TRAVEL, *COSHAM*	120
FOCUS COACHES, *PRESTON*	130
FORDS COACHES, *ALTHORNE*	112
FOREST COACHES, *LONDON E6*	139
FORESTDALE COACHES LTD, *CROYDON*	139
FORGET-ME-NOT (TRAVEL) LTD, *IPSWICH*	170
FORMBY COACHWAYS LTD, *FORMBY*	143
FOUNTAIN EXECUTIVE, *ABERDEEN*	190
FOUR GIRLS COACHES, *PONTYBODKIN*	209
FOWLERS TRAVEL, *HOLBEACH DROVE*	135

TOM FOX, *ROCKCORRY, Co MONAGHAN*	220
FRASER EAGLE LTD, *PADIHAM*	130
FREEBIRD, *BURY*	117
FREEBIRD, *TOTTINGTON*	138
FREESTONES COACHES, *BEETLEY, DEREHAM*	147
JAMES FRENCH & SON, *EYEMOUTH*	192
FRODINGHAM COACHES, *DRIFFIELD*	109
MARTIN FUREY COACHES LTD, *DRUMCLIFFE, Co SLIGO*	220
L. FURNESS & SONS, *HIGH GREEN*	164

G

G & S TRAVEL, *RAMSGATE*	127
G. J. TRAVEL LTD, *CHERTSEY*	172
G. M. COACHES, *CEFN CRIBWR*	205
G. P. D. TRAVEL, *HEYWOOD*	131
GAIN TRAVEL EXPERIENCE LTD, *BRADFORD*	182
GALES COACHES LTD, *HASLEMERE*	172
GALLEON TRAVEL LTD, *HERTFORD*	123
GALLOWAY EUROPEAN, *MENDLESHAM*	170
GALSON-STORNOWAY, *ISLE OF LEWIS*	203
GALVINS COACHES, *DUNMANWAY, Co CORK*	220
GANGE'S COACHES, *COWES*	125
GARDINERS TRAVEL, *SPENNYMOOR*	105
GARELOCHEAD COACHES	191
GARETH EVANS COACHES, *BRYNAMMAN*	215
GARNETT'S COACHES, *BISHOP AUCKLAND*	106
GARRETT COACHES LTD, *NEWTON ABBOT*	100
GARY'S COACHES OF TREDEGAR	205
STANLEY GATH (COACHES) LTD, *DEWSBURY*	183
GATWICK FLYER, *ROMFORD*	112
GEE-VEE TRAVEL, *BARNSLEY*	164
GEMINI TRAVEL, *IPSWICH*	170
GEMINI TRAVEL, *MARCHWOOD*	120
GENIAL TRAVEL, *STANWAY*	112
BEN GEORGE TRAVEL, *BRIGG*	148
GHA COACHES, *CORWEN*	208
JAMES GIBSON & SON, *MOFFAT*	193
GILES TOURS, *NEWTOWNARDS*	217
GILLEN COACHES, *PORT GLASGOW*	197
R G GITTINS, *WELSHPOOL*	212
G-LINE, *St ANNES*	131
G-LINE MINICOACHES, *SWINDON*	186
GLEN COACHES LTD, *GREENOCK*	197
GLENVIC OF BRISTOL LTD	84
GLENWAY COACHES, *DEWSBURY*	183
GLIDER TRAVEL, *BROWNHILLS*	177
G-LINE MINICOACHES, *SWINDON*	194
GLOBE COACHES, *ABERDARE*	213
GLOVERS COACHES LTD, *ASHBOURNE*	97
JAMES GLYNN, *NURNEY*	220
GLYNNS COACH HIRE (ENNIS) LTD	220
GO NORTH EAST, *GATESHEAD*	175
GO-AHEAD GROUP	80
J D GODSON, *CROSSGATES*	183
PETER GODWARD COACHES, *SOUTH WOODHAM FERRERS*	112
GOLD STANDARD, THE, *GREENFORD*	140, 145
GOLD STAR COACHES, *TORQUAY*	100
GOLD STAR TRAVEL, *BROMSGROVE*	188
GOLDEN BOY COACHES LTD, *HODDESDON*	123
GOLDEN EAGLE COACHES, *SALSBURGH*	199
GOLDEN GREEN LUXURY TOURS, LONGNOR *BUXTON*	97
GOLDEN PIONEER TRAVEL, *HEREFORD*	122
GOLDENSTAND SOUTHERN LTD, *LONDON, NW10*	139
GOODE COACHES, *NORTHAMPTON*	153
GOODE'S COACHWAYS, *WEDNESBURY*	177
W. C. GOODSIR, *HOLYHEAD*	205
GOODWIN'S COACHES, *BRAINTREE*	112
W. GORDON & SONS, *ROTHERHAM*	155
GOSPEL'S COACHES, *HUCKNALL*	164
G. W. GOULDING, *KNOTTINGLEY*	191
GRA-CAR COACHES, *FEATHERSTONE*	183
GRAHAM URQUHART TRAVEL, *INVERNESS*	197
VIOLET GRAHAM COACHES, *PAISLEY*	201
GRAHAM'S COACHES, *BRISTOL*	85
GRAHAM'S, *KELVEDON*	125
GRAND HOTEL TOURS, *SANDOWN*	132
GRAMPIAN COACHES, *ABERDEEN*	190
GRAND PRIX COACHES, *BROUGH*	94
GRANGEWOOD TRAVEL, *POTTER HEIGHAM*	147
GRANT PALMER PASSENGER SERVICES, *DUNSTABLE*	81
GRAVES COACHES, *BROXBOURNE*	123
GRAY'S TRAVEL OF COVENTRY	177
GRAYLINE COACHES, *BICESTER*	158
GRAYS LUXURY TRAVEL, *HOYLAND COMMON*	165
GRAYSCROFT BUS SERVICES LTD, *MABLETHORPE*	136
A. GREEN COACHES LTD, *WALTHAMSTOW*	140
GREEN BUS SERVICE (WARSTONE MOTORS), *GREAT WYRLEY*	177
GRETTON'S COACHES, *PETERBOROUGH*	87
GREYHOUND COACHES CO, *CARDIFF*	206
GREYS OF ELY	87
GRIERSONS COACHES, *STOCKTON-ON-TEES*	106
GRIFFIN BUS, *SEVENOAKS*	128
GRIFFITHS COACHES, *PORTDINORWIC*	210
JEFF GRIFFITHS COACHES, *ST ANNES*	131
GRIMSHAW COACHES, *BURNLEY*	138
GRINDLES COACHES LTD, *CINDERFORD*	121
GROUP TRAVEL, *BODMIN*	92
GROVE COACHES, *HERTFORD*	123
GRWP ABERCONWY, *LLANDUDNO*	208
GUEST AUTOMOTIVE, *TODMORDEN*	183
GUSCOTT'S COACHES LTD, *BEAWORTHY*	100
GWYN JONES (MEIFORD), *MYFORD*	212
GWYN WILLIAMS & SONS LTD, *LOWER TUMBLE*	207
GWYNFOR COACHES, *LLANGEFNI*	213

H

HAGUES COACHES, *ROTHERHAM*	165
HAILSTONE TRAVEL, *LITTLE BURSTEAD*	112
PHIL HAINES COACHES, *BOSTON*	136
MIKE HALFORD, *BRIDPORT*	104
A. HALPENNY, BLACKROCK, *DUNDALK*	220

HALTON BOROUGH TRANSPORT LTD, *WIDNES*	90
HAMILTON OF UXBRIDGE	145
R. HANDLEY & SONS LTD, *MIDDLEHAM*	150
HAPPY AL'S COACHES, *BIRKENHEAD*	143
HAPPY DAYS COACHES, *WHITCHURCH*	168
HAPPY DAYS COACHES, *STAFFORD*	168
HARDINGS COACHES, *BETCHWORTH*	172
HARDINGS INTERNATIONAL, *REDDITCH*	188
HARDINGS TOURS LTD, *HUYTON*	144
HARDYS, *ILFRACOMBE*	100
HARGREAVES COACHES, *HEBDEN, Nr SKIPTON*	150
HARLEQUIN TRAVEL, *IPSWICH*	170
R. J. HARLEY, *MARLBOROUGH*	186
HARPUR'S COACHES, *DERBY*	97
HARRIS COACHES, *BLACKWOOD*	206
HARRIS EXECUTIVE TRAVEL, *BROMSGROVE*	188
HARRISON'S TRAVEL, *ALFRETON*	97
D & H HARROD (COACHES) LTD, *KING'S LYNN*	147
HARROGATE & DISTRICT TRAVEL LTD	150
HARWOOD COACHES, *WEYBRIDGE*	172
HATTS COACHES, *CHIPPENHAM*	186
HAWKES COACHES LTD, *SWANSEA*	213
HAYS COACHES, *HUNTLY*	190
HAYDN'S TOURS & TRAVEL, *CHIRK*	214
HAYTON'S COACHES, *BURNAGE*	117
HAYWARD TRAVEL (CARDIFF)	214
HAYWARDS COACHES, *NEWBURY*	82
HEALINGS INTERNATIONAL COACHES, *OLDHAM*	117
HEALY COACHES, *GALWAY*	220
HEARD'S COACHES, *BIDEFORD*	100
HEARNS COACHES, *HARROW WEALD*	140
HEATON'S OF SHEFFIELD	165
HEBRIDEAN COACHES, *HOWMORE, SOUTH UIST*	203
HEDINGHAM & DISTRICT OMNIBUSES LTD, *SIBLE HEDINGHAM*	112
HEMMINGS COACHES, *HOLSWORTHY*	100
HENLEYS BUS SERVICES, *ABERTILLERY*	205
HENRY CRAWFORD COACHES LTD, *NEILSTON*	194
HENSHAWS COACHES, *JACKSDALE*	155
HERBERTS TRAVEL, *SHEFFORD*	81
HERITAGE TOURS, *ST MARY'S, ISLES OF SCILLY*	204
HERRINGTON COACHES LTD, *FORDINGBRIDGE*	120
HEYFORDIAN TRAVEL LTD, *BICESTER*	158
HI-DECK EUROCRUISERS, *WESTBURY*	186
HIGHLAND HERITAGE, *DALLMALLY*	191
HIGHLAND ROVER COACHES, *TAYNUILT*	191
HIGHWAYMAN COACHES, *PERTH*	208
HILLS OF HERSHAM, *HERSHAM*	172
HILLS SERVICES, *TORRINGTON*	100
HILLARYS COACHES, *PRUDHOE*	154
DEREK HIRCOCKS COACHES, *UPWELL, Nr WISBECH*	87
JOHN HOBAN TRAVEL LTD, *WORKINGTON*	94
HODDER MOTOR SERVICES LTD, *CLITHEROE*	131
HODGE'S COACHES (SANDHURST) LTD, *SANDHURST*	82
HODGSONS COACHES, *BARNARD CASTLE*	106
HODSON COACHES LTD, *NAVENBY*	136
M. HOGAN, *THURLES, Co TIPPERARY*	220
HOGG EUROPEAN COACHES, *SHEFFIELD*	165
HOLLINSHEAD COACHES LTD, *BIDDULPH*	168
HOLLOWAY COACHES LTD, *SCUNTHORPE*	148
J. R. HOLLYHEAD INTERNATIONAL, *WILLENHALL*	178
G & J HOLMES, *CLAY CROSS*	97
HOLMES GROUP TRAVEL, *NEWPORT*	160
HOLMESWOOD COACHES LTD, *ORMSKIRK*	131
HOMEWARD BOUND TRAVEL, *WIMBORNE*	104
HOOKWAYS CLASSIC TOURS, *PAIGNTON*	100
HOOKWAYS GREENSLADES, *EXETER*	101
HOOKWAYS JENNINGS, *BUDE*	92
HOOKWAYS PLEASUREWAYS, *OKEHAMPTON*	101
HOPLEYS BUS & COACH, *TRURO*	92
HOPWOOD COACHES, *ASKHAM BRYAN, YORK*	151
HORNSBY TRAVEL, *SCUNTHORPE*	137
HORROCKS, *LYDBURY NORTH*	160
E & M HORSBURGH, *PUMPHERSTON*	203
HORSEMAN COACHES LTD, *READING*	82
JOHN HOUGHTON, *LONDON W5*	140
HOUNSLOW COMMUNITY TRANSPORT	153
HOUNSLOW MINI COACHES, *FELTHAM*	145
HOUSTON'S OF LONDON, *LONDON N15*	140
HOUSTOUN TRAVEL, *LIVINGSTON*	203
HOWIE'S OF ROBERTTOWN, *LIVERSEDGE*	183
HOWLETTS COACHES, *WINSLOW*	86
JIM HUGHES COACHES, *SUNDERLAND*	175
VIC HUGHES & SON LTD, *FELTHAM*	145
HULLEYS OF BASLOW, *BAKEWELL*	97
HULME HALL COACHES LTD, *CHEADLE HULME*	90
HUMBLES COACHES, *SHILDON*	106
HUNTS TRAVEL, *ALFORD*	136
WILLIAM HUNTER, *LOANHEAD*	197
HUNTINGDON & DISTRICT	87
HUTCHISON'S COACHES (OVERTOWN) LTD, *WISHAW*	199
HUTTON COACH HIRE, *WESTON-SUPER-MARE*	162
J. F. HUXLEY, *MALPAS*	90
HYLTON & DAWSON, *GLENFIELD*	134
HYTHE & WATERSIDE COACHES, *HYTHE*	120

I

Operator	Page
IAN BALDRY, *FELIXSTOWE*	169
IBT TRAVEL GROUP, *PRESTWICK*	201
ILLINGWORTH COACHES, *WAKEFIELD*	183
IMPACT OF LONDON, *GREENFORD*	140
IMPERIAL BUS CO LTD, *RAINHAM*	112
INDEPENDENT COACHWAYS LTD, *HORSFORTH*	183
INGLEBY'S LUXURY COACHES LTD, *YORK*	151
INTERNATIONAL COACH LINES LTD, *THORNTON HEATH*	140
IPSWICH BUSES LTD	170
IRELAND COACHES, *Co DUBLIN*	220
IRISH COACHES, *DUBLIN*	220
IRVINE'S OF LAW, *LAW*	199
IRVINGS COACH HIRE LTD, *CARLISLE*	94
BRIAN ISAAC COACHES LTD, *SWANSEA*	213
ISLAND COACH SERVICES, *LAKE, IoW*	126
ISLAND COACHWAYS, *ST PETER PORT*	189

Operator Index

Operator	Page
ISLE COACHES, *OWSTON FERRY*	165
ISLE OF MAN TRANSPORT, *DOUGLAS*	204
ISLE OF WIGHT COUNCIL, *NEWPORT*	126
ISLWYN BOROUGH TRANSPORT LTD, *BLACKWOOD*	206
IVYBRIDGE & DISTRICT, *IVYBRIDGE*	100

J

Operator	Page
J & C COACHES, *NEWTON AYCLIFFE*	106
J & D EURO TRAVEL, *HARROW*	145
J & Y COACHES, *CLITHEROE*	131
J B C MALVERNIAN TOURS, *MALVERN*	188
J C S COACHES, *CORBY*	153
J R J COACHES, *CORBY*	154
J R TRAVEL, *YORK*	151
J W COACHES LTD, *BANCHORY*	190
JACKSON'S COACHES, *BLACKPOOL*	131
ANDREW JAMES QUALITY TRAVEL, *CHIPPENHAM*	186
BRODYR JAMES, *TREGARON*	216
JAMES KING COACHES, *NEWTON STEWART*	193
PAUL JAMES COACHES, *COALVILLE*	134
R. G. JAMIESON & SON, *YELL*	201
JANS COACHES, SOHAM, *ELY*	87
JAYLINE BAND SERVICES, *HORDEN,*	106
JEFFS COACHES LTD, *HELMDON*	151
JEMS TRAVEL, *STANNINGTON*	165
JENSON TRAVEL, *PONTYPOOL*	214
JOHN MORROW COACHES, *GLASGOW*	196
JOHN'S COACHES, *BLAENAU-FFESTINIOG*	210
JOHN'S TRAVEL, *WREXHAM*	214
BEN JOHNSON, *BRANDESBURTON*	109
JOHNSON'S TOURS, *HODTHORPE*	156
JOHNSONS COACH & BUS TRAVEL, *HENLEY-IN-ARDEN*	178
D JONES & SON, *RHOSLLANERCRUGOG*	214
E JONES & SONS, *PONCIAU*	214
JONES EXECUTIVE COACHES LTD, *WALKDEN*	117
JONES INTERNATIONAL, *LLANDEILO*	207
JONES MOTOR SERVICES, *FLINT*	209
JONES MOTORS (LOGIN) LTD, *WHITLAND*	207
O R JONES & SONS LTD, *LLANFAETHLU*	205
P W JONES COACHES, *HEREFORD*	122
W E JONES & SON, *LLANERCHYMEDD*	205
JOSEPHS MINI COACHES, *NEWCASTLE-UNDER-LYME*	168
DONAL JOYCE MINIBUS HIRE, *GALWAY*	220
JUMBO MINI COACHES, *NOTTINGHAM*	156

K

Operator	Page
K & B TRAVEL, *CLIBURN*	94
K & S COACHES, *MANSFIELD*	156
K. M. MOTORS LTD, *BARNSLEY*	165
KARDAN TRAVEL, *COWES, IoW*	126
BERNARD KAVANAGH & SONS LTD, *URLINGFORD*	220
J. J. KAVANAGH & SONS, *URLINGFORD*	220
M. KAVANAGH, *TIPPERARY*	220
PIERCE KAVANAGH COACHES, *URLINGFORD*	221
KEENAN OF AYR COACH TRAVEL, *COALHALL*	201
KEENAN COMMERCIALS, *DUNDALK, CO LOUTH*	220
KEIGHLEY & DISTRICT TRAVEL	183
KENNEALLY'S BUS SERVICE LTD, *WATERFORD*	220
KENNEDY COACHES, *TRALEE*	220
KENT COACH TOURS LTD, *ASHFORD*	128
KENT COUNTY COUNCIL, *AYLESFORD*	128
KENZIES COACHES LTD, *ROYSTON*	123
K. M. KEOGH, *ARKLOW*	220
KERRY COACHES, *KILLARNEY, Co KERRY*	220
KESTREL COACHES, *STOURPORT ON SEVERN*	188
KETTLEWELL (RETFORD) LTD	156
R. KIME & CO LTD, *FOLKINGHAM*	136
KINCH BUS LTD, *HEANOR*	98
KINEIL COACHES, *FRASERBURGH*	190
JAMES KING COACHES, *NEWTON STEWART*	201
KINGDOM COACHES, *LEVEN*	195
KINGDOM'S TOURS LTD, *TIVERTON*	100
KINGFISHER MINICOACHES, *READING*	83
KINGS COACHES, *STANWAY*	112
THE KINGS FERRY, *GILLINGHAM*	128
KINGS LUXURY COACHES, *MIDDLESBROUGH*	151
KINGSNORTON COACHES, *BIRMINGHAM*	177
KINGSLEY COACHES, *BIRTLEY*	175
KINGSMAN INTERNATIONAL TRAVEL, *FAVERSHAM*	128
KINGSTON COACHES, *SALISBURY*	186
KINGSWINFORD COACHWAYS, *BRIERLY HILL*	177
KIRBYS COACHES, *RAYLEIGH*	112
KIRKBY LONSDALE COACH HIRE, *CARNFORTH*	131
KIWI LUXURY TRAVEL, *NEWTON STEWART*	193
KMP LLANBERIS LTD	210
KONECTBUS, *DEREHAM*	147
K-VALLEY MINI-COACHES, *WOKING*	172

L

Operator	Page
LADYBIRD TRAVEL, *WORKINGTON*	94
LADYLINE, *RAWMARSH*	165
LAKELAND TOURS, *TEMPO, Co FERMANAGH*	217
LAKELINE COACHES, *KNIGHTON*	212
LAKES SUPERTOURS, *WINDERMERE*	94
LAKESIDE COACHES, *ELLESMERE (SHROPSHIRE)*	160
LAMBS COACHES, *STOCKPORT*	117
LAMBERT'S COACHES (BECCLES) LTD	170
LANCASHIRE UNITED, *BLACKBURN*	132
LANGSTON & TASKER, *BUCKINGHAM*	86
LEANDER COACH TRAVEL, *SWADLINCOTE*	97
JOHN LEASK & SON, *LERWICK*	201
LEE'S COACHES, *LANGLEY MOOR*	106
LENDOR, *MOSSLEY*	117
LEOLINE TRAVEL, *HAMPTON*	145
LEON MOTOR SERVICES LTD, *FINNINGLEY*	165
LEONS COACH TRAVEL, *STAFFORD*	168
LE-RAD COACHES & LIMOUSINES *WOODLEY Nr STOCKPORT*	90
LESCLACHA LTD, *NEWMARKET-ON-FERGUS*	220
LEVERS COACHES LTD, *SALISBURY*	187
LEWIS-RHYDLEWIS, *RHYDLEWIS*	207
LEWIS COACHES, *LLANDRHYSTUD*	207

LEWIS TRAVEL UK, *LONDON SE1*	140
LEWIS'S COACHES, *WHITLAND*	207
LEWIS-Y-LLAN, *AMLWCH*	205
LIBERTON TRAVEL, *EDINBURGH*	195
ARNOLD LIDDELL COACHES, *BRISTOL*	85
LIDDELL'S COACHES, *AUCHINLECK*	193
LINK LINE COACHES LTD, *LONDON*	140
LINKFAST LTD T/A S&M COACHES, *BENFLEET*	112
LISKEARD & DISTRICT OMNIBUS CO LTD *LAUNCESTON*	92
LITTLE BUS COMPANY, THE, *ELSTREE*	140
LITTLE JIM'S BUSES, *BERKHAMSTED*	123
LITTLE TRANSPORT LTD, *ILKESTON*	98
LIVERPOOL CITY COACHES	144
LLEW JONES INTERNATIONAL, *LLANWRST*	208
P&O LLOYD, *BAGILLT*	209
LLOYDS COACHES, *MACHYNLLETH*	212
LOCHS MOTOR TRANSPORT LTD, *LEWIS*	203
LOCHS & GLENS HOLIDAYS, *GARTOCHAN*	202
LODGE COACHES, *HIGH EASTER*	112
LOGANS EXECUTIVE TRAVEL, *DUNLOY*	217
LOGANS TOURS, *NORTHFLEET GREEN*	128
LONDON BUSES, *LONDON E8*	140
LONDON CENTRAL, *MITCHAM*	140
LONDON GENERAL, *MITCHAM*	141
LONDONDERRY & LOUGH SWILLY, *LONDONDERRY*	217
LONDON SOVEREIGN, *TWICKENHAM*	145
LONDON UNITED BUS CO, *TWICKENHAM*	145
DAVE LONG COACH TRAVEL, *SKIBBEREEN*	221
LONG'S COACHES LTD, *SALSBURGH*	199
LONGMYND TRAVEL, *SHREWSBURY*	160
J. J. LONGSTAFF & SONS LTD, *DEWSBURY*	183
LONGSTAFF'S COACHES, *MORPETH*	162
LOTHIAN BUSES, *EDINBURGH*	195
LOVERINGS COACHES (see TAW & TORRIDGE)	107
LUAS, *DUBLIN*	221
LUCKETTS TRAVEL, *FAREHAM*	120
LUDLOWS OF HALESOWEN	178
LUGG VALLEY PRIMROSE TRAVEL, *LEOMINSTER*	122
LUXURY MINI COACH, GREENFORD	141, 146
A. LYLES & SON, *BATLEY*	183

M

Operator	Page
M. LINE INTERNATIONAL COACHES, *ALLOA*	192
M & B COACHES & MINIBUSES, *TELFORD*	160
M & E COACHES, *HERSHAM*	172
M & H COACHES, *DENBIGH*	208
M & J TRAVEL, *CRAVEN ARMS*	160
M & M COACH LINES, *HARROW WEALD*	146
M & S COACHES, *LEOMINSTER*	122
M.C.T. GROUP TRAVEL LTD, *MOTHERWELL*	199
M D COACH HIRE, *DUBLIN*	221
M P MINICOACHES, *TELFORD*	160
M T P CHARTER COACHES, *LONDON E11*	141
MAC TOURS LTD, *EDINBURGH*	195
MacEWAN'S COACH SERVICES, *AMISFIELD*	193
NEIL MacKELLAIG, *GLASGOW*	196
MACKIE'S COACHES OF ALLOA, *ALLOA*	192
DUNCAN MacLENAN, *STRATH-CARRON*	197
MacPHAILS COACHES, *MOTHERWELL*	199
MacPHERSON COACHES LTD, *SWADLINCOTE*	103
MAGPIE TRAVEL, HIGH *WYCOMBE*	86
MAIRS COACHES, *ABERDEEN*	190
MAISEY, *PONTYPRIDD*	213
MAJESTIC TOURS EDINBURGH LTD	195
MALCYS, *SHEFFIELD*	165
GERALD MANNING, CROOM, *LIMERICK*	221
MANOR TRAVEL, *BEEFORD*	109
MANSFIELD'S COACHES, *SWINDON*	187
MARBILL COACH SERVICES LTD, *BEITH*	198
MARCHANTS COACHES LTD, *CHELTENHAM*	115
MARCHWOOD MOTORWAYS LTD, *TOTTON*	120
MARPLE MINI COACHES	90, 117
MARSHALLS COACHES, *LEIGHTON BUZZARD*	81, 124
MARSHALLS OF SUTTON-ON-TRENT, *NEWARK*	156
ALAN MARTIN COACHES, *DUBLIN*	221
WALTER MARTIN COACHES, *SHEFFIELD*	165
MARTIN'S OF TYSOE	176
MARTIN'S COACH TRAVEL, *LIVINGSTON*	203
MARTINS COACHES, *LONDON*	141
MARTINS COACHES, *CHAPELTOWN*	165
MARTINS COACHES, *KETTERING*	154
MARTINS SELF DRIVE, *REDFIELD*	85
MARTIN'S COACHES, *CAVAN*	221
MASS TRANSIT, *ANSTON*	165
MASTER TRAVEL, *WELWYN GARDEN CITY*	124
MATTHEWS COACHES, *KINGS LYNN*	147
MAUDES COACHES, *BARNARD CASTLE*	106
MAUN CRUSADER TOURS, *SUTTON-IN-ASHFIELD*	156
MAYDAY TRAVEL, *CROYDON*	172
MAYFIELD COACHES	165
MAYNE COACHES LTD, *WARRINGTON*	90
MAYNE OF MANCHESTER, *MANCHESTER*	117
MAYNES COACHES, *BUCKIE*	198
MAYPOLE COACHES, *MELLING*	144
ROY McCARTHY COACHES, *MACCLESFIELD*	90
McCOLLS OF ARGYLL, *DUNOON*	192
McCOLLS COACHES, *ALEXANDRIA*	202
P. J. McCONNON, *MONAGHAN*	221
McCULLOCH AND SON, *STRANRAER*	193
JAMES McGEE (BUSES), *LETTERKENNY*	221
JOHN McGINLEY COACHES, *LETTERKENNY, Co DONEGAL*	221
McGILLS BUS SERVICE LTD, *GREENOCK*	201
McKECHNIE OF BATHGATE LTD	203
McKENDRY TRAVEL, *LOANHEAD*	198
McKINDLESS EXPRESS, *WISHAW*	199
McLAUGHLIN'S TOURS, *PENWORTHAM*	132
McLEANS COACHES, *WITNEY*	158
MEADWAY PRIVATE HIRE, *BIRMINGHAM*	177
MICHAEL MEERE COACH HIRE, *ENNIS*	221
MEGABUS, *PERTH*	208
MEMORY LANE COACHES, *OLD BOLINGBROKE*	136
MEMORY LANE VINTAGE OMNIBUS SERVICES, *MAIDENHEAD*	83

Operator Index

MEREDITHS COACHES, *MALPAS*	90
MERTON COMMUNITY TRANSPORT, *MITCHAM*	172
MERVYN'S COACHES, *MICHELDEVER*	120
MESSENGER COACHES, *WIGTON*	94
METRO COACHES, *STOCKTON-ON-TEES*	151
METROBUS LTD, *CRAWLEY*	180
METROLINE TRAVEL LTD, *HARROW*	146
METROLINK, *MANCHESTER*	117
MID DEVON COACHES, *CREDITON*	101
MIDLAND BUS CO LTD, *ATHLONE*	221
MIDLAND METRO, *WEDNESBURY*	187
MID WALES TRAVEL, *PENRHYNCOCH*	208
MIDWAY MOTORS, *CRYMYCH*	211
MIKES COACHES, *BASILDON*	113
MIL-KEN TRAVEL LTD, *LITTLEPORT*	88
MIL-KEN TRAVEL LTD, *NEWMARKET*	170
KEN MILLER TRAVEL, *SHENSTONE*	177
MILLER'S COACHES, *AIRDRIE*	199
MILLIGANS COACH TRAVEL, *MAUCHLINE*	201
MILLMAN COACHES, *GRIMSBY*	149
MILLMAN'S OF *WARRINGTON*	90
MILLPORT MOTORS LTD	198
ALEX MILNE, *NEW BYTH*	191
MINIBUS & COACH HIRE, *EARL STONHAM*	170
MINIBUS SERVICES, *WATFORD*	124
MINSTERLEY MOTORS, *SHREWSBURY*	160
MK METRO LTD, *MILTON KEYNES*	86
MOFFAT & WILLIAMSON LTD, *GAULDRY*	195
MOOR TO SEA, *NEWTON ABBOT*	101
MOORE'S COACHES LTD, *HOLMES CHAPEL*	90
MOORLAND BUSES, *WESTON COYNEY*	168
JOE MORONEY, *ENNIS*	221
MORRIS TRAVEL, *CARMARTHEN*	207
JOHN MORROW COACHES, *GLASGOW*	196
MORTON'S COACH, *MAYNOOTH, IRELAND*	222
MOSLEYS TOURS, *DEWSBURY*	165
MOTTS COACHES (AYLESBURY) LTD, *AYLESBURY*	86
MOUNTAIN GOAT LTD, *WINDERMERE*	95
MOUNTS BAY COACHES, *PENZANCE*	92
C. W. MOXON LTD, *OLDCOTES*	156
MUIRS COACHES, *DOUGLAS WATER*	201
MULLEYS MOTORWAYS LTD, *IXWORTH*	171
MUNRO'S OF JEDBURGH	192
THOMAS MURPHY & SONS, *BRAY, Co WICKLOW*	222
GAVIN MURRAY & ELLISONS COACHES, *ST HELENS*	144
MYKANN COACH HIRE, *SWADLINCOTE*	98
MYTTON TRAVEL, *MINSTERLEY*	160

N

NASHS COACHES LTD, *SMETHWICK*	178
NATIONAL EXPRESS GROUP PLC	80
NATIONAL EXPRESS LTD, *EDGBASTON*	178
NATIONAL HOLIDAYS, *HULL*	109
NAUGHTON COACH TOURS, *SPIDDAL*	222
NBM HIRE LTS, *PENRITH*	95
N.C.B. MOTORS LTD, *WEM*	160
NCP CHALLENGER, *TWICKENHAM*	146

NEAL'S TRAVEL LTD, *ISLEHAM, ELY*	88
NEFYN COACHES, *NEFYN, PWLLHELI*	210
NEIL MACKELLAIG, *GLASGOW*	204
NELSON & SON (GLYNNEATH) LTD, *NEATH*	210
W. H. NELSON (COACHES) LTD, *WICKFORD*	113
NESBIT BROS LTD, *MELTON MOWBRAY*	134
NESTORBUS LTD, *GALWAY & DUBLIN*	222
NEW BHARAT COACHES LTD, *SOUTHALL*	141
NEW ENTERPRISE COACHES, *TONBRIDGE*	128
NEWBOURNE COACHES, *LEIGHTON BUZZARD*	141
NEWBURY COACHES, *LEDBURY*	122
NEWBURY & DISTRICT, *NEWBURY*	83
NEWBURY TRAVEL, *OLDBURY*	178
NEWPORT TRANSPORT LTD	211
M. W. NICOLL'S COACH HIRE, *LAUREiNCEKIRK*	191
NIDDRIE COACHES, *MIDDLEWICH*	91
NIELSEN TRAVEL SERVICES, *SHEFFIELD*	166
NIGEL JACKSON TRAVEL, *QUENIBOROUGH*	134
NITEFLITE BUS LEASING, *CLEVEDON*	162
NOLAN COACHES, *COOLOCK, DUBLIN*	222
NORFOLK GREEN, *KINGS LYNN*	147
NORTH BIRMINGHAM BUSWAYS LTD, *ERDINGTON*	178
NORTH SOMERSET COACHES, *NAILSEA*	85
NORTHERN BLUE, *BURNLEY*	132
NORTH WEST COACHES & LIMOS *THORNTON CLEVELEYS*	132
NORTON MINI TRAVEL, *STOCKTON-ON-TEES*	106
NOTTINGHAM CITY TRANSPORT LTD	156
NOTTINGHAM EXPRESS TRANSIT	156
NOTTS & DERBY TRACTION CO LTD, *HEANOR*	98
NU-VENTURE COACHES LTD, *AYLESFORD*	128

O

OTS MINIBUS & COACH HIRE, *CONSTANTINE*	92
O'CONNELL COACHES, *BALLINASLOE*	222
O'CONNOR AUTOTOURS LTD, *KILLARNEY*	222
TOM O'CONNOR, *TRALEE*	222
FEDA O'DONNELL, *DONEGAL*	222
O'FLAHERTY TRANSPORT, *LISDOONVARNA*	222
LARRRY O'HARA, *WATERFORD*	222
O'MALLEY COACHES, *NEWPORT, Co TIPPERARY*	222
O'S COACHES, *HOSPITAL, Co LIMERICK*	222
O'SULLIVANS COACHES, *MALLOW, Co CORK*	222
OARE'S COACHES, *HOLYWELL*	209
OBAN & DISTRICT BUSES LTD	192
OCEAN COACHES, *PORTSLADE*	108
DAVID OGDEN COACHES, *ST HELENS*	144
OLYMPIA TRAVEL, *HINDLEY*	132
OLYMPIAN COACHES LTD, *HARLOW*	113
THE ORIGINAL LONDON TOUR, *WANDSWORTH*	141
ORKNEY COACHES, *KIRKWALL*	199
OTTER COACHES, *OTTERY ST MARY*	101
OWEN'S MOTORS LTD, *KNIGHTON*	212
OWENS COACHES, *OSWESTRY*	160
OXFORD BUS COMPANY	158
OXFORD INTERNATIONAL, *BASINGSTOKE*	158

P

P&M COACHES, *WICKFORD*	113
DAVID PALMER COACHES LTD, *NORMANTON*	183
PARAGON TRAVEL, *UTTOXETER*	168
PARAMOUNT MINI-COACHES, *PLYMOUTH*	101
PARK TOURS AND TRAVEL (MOUNTAIN GOAT), *WINDERMERE*	100
PARK'S OF HAMILTON	202
PARKERS COACHES, *SWADLINCOTE*	98
PARKSIDE TRAVEL, *BROXBOURNE*	124
PARRYS INTERNATIONAL TOURS LTD, *CHESLYN HAY*	168
PAT'S COACHES, *NEW BROUGHTON*	214
PATRON TRAVEL, *FLINTHAM*	156
PAUL'S TRAVEL, *HUDDERSFIELD*	183
PAVILION COACHES, *HOVE*	108
D. A. PAYNE COACH HIRE, *ST NEOTS*	88
PAYNES COACHES & CAR HIRE LTD, *BUCKINGHAM*	86
PC COACHES OF LINCOLN	136
PEARCES PRIVATE HIRE, *WALLINGFORD*	158
PEARSON COACHES, *HULL*	109
PEELINGS COACHES, *KING'S LYNN*	147
PEGASUS COACHWAYS LTD, *RETFORD*	165
PEGASUS TRAVEL, *PERTH*	156
PENCOED TRAVEL LTD, *BRIDGEND*	206
PENMERE MINIBUS SERVICES, *FALMOUTH*	92
PERRY'S COACHES, *MALTON*	151
PERRYMAN BUSES, *BURNMOUTH*	192
PETER CAROL PRESTIGE COACHING, *WHITCHURCH, BRISTOL*	84
PETERBOROUGH TRAVEL CONSULTANTS, *PETERBOROUGH*	88
PETE'S TRAVEL - see PEOPLES EXPRESS	
PEWSEY VALE COACHES, *PEWSEY*	187
PHILLIPS COACHES, *SOUTH WOODHAM FERRERS*	113
COLLIN PHILLIPSON MINICOACHES, *OUSEFLEET*	109, 166
PICKERING COACHES, *SOUTH GODSTONE*	172
PIED BULL COACHES, *MOLD*	209
JOHN PIKE COACHES, *ANDOVER*	120
PLANET TRAVEL, *EARITH*	88
GEORGE PLANT, *BANTRY, Co CORK*	222
PLANTS LUXURY TRAVEL, *CHEADLE, STAFFS*	168
PLASTOWS COACHES, *WHEATLEY*	158
DAVID PLATT COACHES & MINITRAVEL OF LEES, *OLDHAM*	117
PLYMOUTH CITYBUS LTD	101
POOTS COACH HIRE, *TANDRAGEE*	217
JOHN POWELL TRAVEL, *HELLABY*	166
POWELLS COACHES, *CREDITON*	101
POWELLS COACHES, *SHERBORNE*	104
JACKY POWER TOURS, *TRALEE*	222
POYNTERS COACHES, *ASHFORD, KENT*	128
PRE METRO, *KINGS NORTON*	178
PREMIER TRAVEL, *BRISTOL*	85
PRENTICE WESTWOOD, *WEST CALDER*	203
PRESTON BUS LTD	132
PRICES COACHES, *SOUTHSEA, WALES*	214
PRIMROSE COACHES OF CORNWALL, *HAYLE*	92
PRINCESS COACHES, *WEST END, SOUTHAMPTON*	120
PRIORY MOTOR COACH CO LTD, *NORTH SHIELDS*	175
F PROCTER & SON LTD, *FENTON*	168
PROCTERS COACHES (NORTH YORKSHIRE), *LEEMING BAR*	151
PROSPECT COACHES (WEST) LTD, *STOURBRIDGE*	179
PROTOURS (ISLE OF MAN), *DOUGLAS*	204
PROVENCE PRIVATE HIRE, *ST ALBANS*	124
PULFREYS COACHES, *GRANTHAM*	136
PULLMAN COACHES LTD, *SWANSEA*	213
PULLMAN DINER , *KNOTTINGLEY*	183

Q

QUANTOCK MOTOR SERVICES, *TAUNTON*	162

R

R & B COACHES, *LUDLOW*	160
R. & R. COACHES LTD (BEELINE), *WARMINSTER*	185
R. K. F. TRAVEL, *STROOD*	128
RADLEY COACH TRAVEL, *BRIGG*	149
RADMORES COACHES, *PLYMPTON*	101
RAINHAM COACH CO, THE, *GILLINGHAM*	128
RAMBLER COACHES, *HASTINGS*	108
RAMON TRAVEL, *BOSCOMBE*	104
RAPSONS GROUP, *INVERNESS*	197
RAYS COACHES, *PLYMOUTH*	102
RB TRAVEL, *PYTCHLEY*	154
READING & WOKINGHAM COACHES, *WOKINGHAM*	83
READING HERITAGE TRAVEL, *READING*	83
READING TRANSPORT LTD	83
REAYS COACHES LTD, *WIGTON*	95
RED ARROW COACHES LTD, *HUDDERSFIELD*	183
RED KITE COMMERCIAL SERVICES, *LEIGHTON BUZZARD*	82
RED ROSE TRAVEL LTD, *AYLESBURY*	86
REDROUTE BUSES, *NORTHFLEET*	128
REDBY BUS & COACH, *SUNDERLAND*	175
REDFERN COACHES (MANSFIELD) LTD	156
RED KITE COACHES, *ABERYSTWYTH*	208
REDLINE COACHES, *LEYLAND*	132
REDWING COACHES, *LONDON SE24*	141
REDWOODS TRAVEL, *CULLOMPTON*	102
REES MOTOR (TRAVEL), *LLANELLY HILL, ABERGAVENNY*	210
REEVES COACH HOLIDAYS, *CHORLEY*	132
REG'S COACHES LTD, *HERTFORD*	124
REGAL BUSWAYS, *CHELMSFORD*	113
REGENT COACHES, *WHITSTABLE*	128
REIDS OF RHYNIE, *RHYNIE, BY HUNTLY*	191
RELIANCE, *BENFLEET*,	113
RELIANCE MOTOR SERVICES, *SUTTON-ON-FOREST*	151
RENNIES OF DUNFERMLINE LTD	196
RENOWN COACHES, *BEXHILL*	108

Operator	Page
REYNOLDS COACHES OF CAISTER, GREAT YARMOUTH	147
REYNOLDS DIPLOMAT COACHES, WATFORD	124
RICHARDS BROS, CARDIGAN	208
RICHARDSON COACHES, HARTLEPOOL	106
RICHARDSON TRAVEL LTD, MIDHURST	180
RICHMOND'S COACHES, BARLEY	124
RIDDLER'S COACHES, ARBROATH	191
RIDLERS, DULVERTON	162
RIDUNA BUSES, ALDERNEY	189
JOHN RIGBY TRANSPORT & TRAVEL, BATLEY	183
RIGBY'S EXECUTIVE COACHES, ALTHAM	131
RINGWOOD COACHES, STAVELEY	98
RIVERSIDE COACHES, TELFORD	161
ROADLINER PASSENGER TRANSPORT, POOLE	104
ROADMARK TRAVEL LTD, ASHINGTON	180
ROBERTS COACHES, ABERYSTWYTH	216
ROBERTS COACHES, HUGGLESCOTE	134
ROBERTS TOURS, WINGATE	106
ROBIN HOOD TRAVEL LTD, LEEK	176
ROBIN'S COACHES, CHIPPENHAM	187
ROBINSON KIMBOLTON, KIMBOLTON	88
ROBINSONS HOLIDAYS, GREAT HARWOOD	132
ROBINSONS COACHES, APPLEBY	95
RODGER'S COACHES, CORBY	154
ROEVILLE TOURS LTD, ADWICK-LE-STREET	166
ROWLANDS GILL TAXIS & COACHES, ROWLANDS GILL	175
ROLLINSON SAFEWAY LTD, LEEDS	183
RONDO TRAVEL, HARROGATE	151
O. ROONEY, HILLTOWN	217
ROPERS COACHES, BRADFORD	183
ROSELYN COACHES, PAR	92
JOHN ROSS, ARDEE, Co LOUTH	222
ROSS TRAVEL, FEATHERSTONE	183
ROSSENDALE TRANSPORT LTD, RAWTENSTALL	132
ROUNDABOUT BUSES, BEXLEYHEATH	141
ROVER COACHES, MULLINGAR, IRELAND	222
ROVER EUROPEAN TRAVEL, HORSLEY, STROUD	115
ROWE & TUDHOPE, KILMARNOCK	193
ROWELL COACHES, LOW PRUDHOE	154
ROY BROWNS COACHES, BUILTH WELLS	211
ROYLES TRAVEL, SHEFFIELD	166
ROY PHILLIPS, SLEAFORD	136
RUTHERFORDS TRAVEL, EASTERGATE	180

S

Operator	Page
SAFEGUARD COACHES, GUILDFORD	172
SAFFORDS COACHES LTD, SANDY	88
SANDERS COACHES, HOLT	148
SANDGROUNDER, SOUTHPORT	132
SARGANTS BROS LTD, KINGTON	122
SCARBOROUGH & DISTRICT	151
SCARLET BAND, WEST CORNFORTH	106
SCHOFIELD TRAVEL LTD, LOUGHBOROUGH	134
SCOTIA TRAVEL, GLENROTHES	195
SCOTLAND & BATES, APPLEDORE	129
SCOTTISH CITYLINK COACHES LTD, GLASGOW	196
SEAVIEW SERVICES, SANDOWN	126

Operator	Page
SEA VIEW COACHES (POOLE) LTD	104
SEAGER'S COACHES LTD, CHIPPENHAM	187
SEALANDAIR COACHING (IRELAND), DUBLIN	222
SEARLE'S AUTO SERVICES, THORNHAUGH, Nr PETERBOROUGH	88
SEATH COACHES, EAST STUDDAL, Nr DOVER	129
SELVEY'S COACHES, CAMBUSLANG	196
SELWYNS TRAVEL, MANCHESTER AIRPORT	91, 118
H. SEMMENCE & CO LTD, WYMONDHAM	148
SERENE TRAVEL, BEDLINGTON	154
SEWARDS COACHES, AXMINSTER	102
SHAFTESBURY & DISTRICT MOTOR SERVICES	104
MATT SHANAHAN COACHES, WATERFORD	223
SHARPE & SONS (NOTTINGHAM), NOTTINGHAM	157
HARRY SHAW, COVENTRY	179
SHAWS OF MAXEY, PETERBOROUGH	88
SHEARER OF HUNTLY LTD, HUNTLEY	191
SHEARINGS see W.A. SHEARINGS	
SHEN CARE VOLUNTARY TRANSPORT, SELLY OAK	179
SHERBURN VILLAGE COACHES	112
SHERWOOD TRAVEL, IMMINGHAM	157
SHIEL BUSES, ACHARACLE	197
SHIRE COACHES, ST ALBANS	124
SHIRE TRAVEL INTERNATIONAL, HEDNESFORD	169
SHOREY'S TRAVEL & TRANSPORT, MAULDEN	82
B. R. SHREEVE & SONS LTD, LOWESTOFT	171
SHROPSHIRE COUNTY COUNCIL, SHREWSBURY	161
SHUTTLE BUSES LTD, KILWINNING	198
SIDLAW EXECUTIVE TRAVEL, AUCHTERHOUSE	193
SIESTA INTERNATIONAL, MIDDLESBROUGH	151
SILCOX COACHES, PEMBROKE DOCK	211
SILVER CHOICE TRAVEL LTD, EAST KILBRIDE	202
SILVER STAR COACH HOLIDAYS LTD, CAERNARFON	210
SILVERDALE LONDON LTD, LONDON NW10	142
SILVERDALE TOURS (NOTTINGHAM) LTD, NOTTINGHAM	157
SILVERLINE LANDFLIGHT, SOLIHULL	179
SIMS TRAVEL, BOOT	95
SIMONDS COACH & TRAVEL, DISS	148
SIMPSON'S COACHES, ROSEHEARTY	191
SIXTY SIXTY COACHES, PENTREBACH	210
D. W. SKELTON, BRIDGWATER	163
SKILLS MOTOR COACHES, BULWELL	157
SKINNERS OF OXTED	172
SKYLINERS LTD, NUNEATON	184
SLACKS TRAVEL, MATLOCK	98
SLEAFORDIAN COACHES. SLEAFORD	136
H. & A. SLEEP, BERE ALSTON	102
SLEIGHTS COACHES, SWINTON	166
SLOAN TRAVEL, ROSTREVOR	217
SMITH & SONS COACHES, COUPAR ANGUS	200
JOHN SMITH & SONS, THIRSK	152
SMITH'S COACHES (BE & GW SMITH), SHEPTON MALLET	163
SMITH BUNTINGFORD	124

Operator	Page
SMITHS COACHES (MARPLE) LTD	91, 118
SMITHS COACHES, *CORBY GLEN, Nr GRANTHAM*	136
G. A. SMITHS COACHES LTD, *TRING*	124
SMITHS MOTORS (LEDBURY) LTD	122
SNOWDON COACHES, *EASINGTON*	107
SOLENT BLUE LINE, *SOUTHAMPTON*	121
SOLENT COACHES, *RINGWOOD*	121
SOLID ENTERTAINMENTS, *GRIMSBY*	149
SOMERBUS, *BRISTOL*	163
SOULS COACHES LTD, *OLNEY*	86
SOUTH COAST MOTOR SERVICES, *CROYDON*	172
SOUTH GLOUCESTERSHIRE BUS & COACH COMPANY, *PATCHWAY, BRISTOL*	85
SOUTH LANCS TRAVEL, *ATHERTON*	118
SOUTH MIMMS TRAVEL LTD	124
SOUTH WEST COACHES LTD, *WINCANTON*	163
SOUTHDOWN PSV, *COPTHORNE*	181
SOUTHERN COACHES (NM) LTD, *BARRHEAD*	194
SOUTHERN VECTIS, *NEWPORT, IoW*	126
SOUTHGATE & FINCHLEY COACHES LTD, *LONDON N11*	142
SOVEREIGN COACHES, *LYME REGIS*	104
SPA COACHES, *STRATHPEFFER*	197
SPENCERS COACHES, *NEWARK*	157
SPOT HIRE TRAVEL, *BEARSTED*	129
SPRATTS COACHES LTD, *WRENINGHAM*	148
SQUIRRELL'S COACHES, *HITCHAM*	171
ST ANDREWS EXECUTIVE TRAVEL	196
ST KEVINS BUS SERVICE (P. DOYLE), *ROUNDWOOD, Co WICKLOW*	227
STAGECOACH CAMBRIDGESHIRE, *CAMBRIDGE*	88
STAGECOACH EAST, *NORTHAMPTON*	154
STAGECOACH IN EAST KENT & HASTINGS	129
STAGECOACH IN HASTINGS, *ST LEONARDS ON SEA*	108
STAGECOACH EAST MIDLANDS, *CHESTERFIELD*	98
STAGECOACH GROUP	80
STAGECOACH IN HAMPSHIRE, *BASINGSTOKE*	121
STAGECOACH HANTS & SURREY, *ALDERSHOT*	121
STAGECOACH IN HULL	109
STAGECOACH LINCOLNSHIRE,	136
STAGECOACH MANCHESTER, *ARDWICK*	118
STAGECOACH MERSEYSIDE, *LIVERPOOL*	144
STAGECOACH NORTH EAST, *SUNDERLAND*	175
STAGECOACH NORTH WEST, *CARLISLE*	95
STAGECOACH IN OXFORDSHIRE	159
STAGECOACH SCOTLAND, *PERTH*	200
STAGECOACH (SOUTH), *CHICHESTER*	181
STAGECOACH IN SOUTH WALES, *CWMBRAN*	214
STAGECOACH SOUTH WEST, *EXETER*	102
STAGECOACH YORKSHIRE, *BARNSLEY*	166
STAGECOACH SUPERTRAM, *SHEFFIELD*	166
STAGECOACH TRANSIT, *STOCKTON*	112
STAGECOACH IN WARWICKSHIRE, *RUGBY*	176
STAGECOACH WEST SCOTLAND, *AYR*	201
F. W. STAINTON & SON LTD, *KENDAL*	95
STALLION COACHES, *CHELMSFORD*	113
STAN'S COACHES, *MALDON*	113
STANLEY MACKAY COACHES OF EDINBURGH, *BONNYRIGG*	203
STANLEY TAXIS & MINICOACHES	107
STANSTED TRANSIT, *STANSTED*	113
STANWAYS COACHES, *KIDSGROVE*	169
STEELS LUXURY COACHES, *ADDINGHAM*	183
STEPEND COACHES, *GLENMAVIS*	199
STEPHENSONS OF *EASINGWOLD*	152
STEPHENSONS OF ESSEX LTD, *ROCHFORD*	113
STEVE'S OF AMBLESIDE LTD	95
L. F. STEWART & SON LTD, *DALAYICH, BY TAYNUILT*	192
STEVE STOCKDALE COACHES, *SELBY*	152
STODDARDS LTD, *CHEADLE, STAFFS*	169
STOCKHAMS COACHES, *CRICKHOWELL*	212
WILLIAM STOKES & SONS LTD, *CARSTAIRS*	202
STONEHOUSE COACHES	202
JIM STONES COACHES	91
STONES COACHES OF BATH	163
E STOTT & SONS, *MILNSBRIDGE*	183
STOTT'S TOURS (OLDHAM) LTD	118
STRAFFORD'S COACHES, *MINERA*	215
STRATHTAY SCOTLAND OMNIBUSES LTD, *DUNDEE*	193
STRATOS TRAVEL LTD, *NEWTOWN, POWYS*	212
STREAMLINE, *MAIDSTONE*	129
STREETS COACHWAYS LTD, *BARNSTAPLE*	102
STRINGERS PONTEFRACT MOTORWAYS	183
STUARTS OF CARLUKE	202
SUIRWAY BUS & COACH SERVICES LTD, *PASSAGE EAST, Co WATERFORD, IRELAND*	223
SULLIVAN BUSES, *POTTERS BAR*	125
SUMMERCOURT TRAVEL, *SUMMERCOURT*	92
SUMMERDALE COACHES, *LETTERSTON*	211
SUMMERFIELD COACHES LTD, *SOUTHAMPTON*	121
SUNBEAM COACHES LTD, *NORWICH*	148
SUNBURY COACHES, *SHEPPERTON*	146
SUNRAY TRAVEL, *EPSOM*	172
SUNSET COACHES, *PENZANCE*	92
SUPERTRAVEL MINICOACHES, *SPEKE*	144
SURELINE, *PORTLAND*	104
SURELINE COACHES, *WOKING*	173
SUSSEX COUNTRY COACH HIRE, *SHOREHAM*	181
SUSSEX PIONEER COACHES, *BRIGHTON*	108
SUTTON COMMUNITY TRANSPORT	173
SWALLOW COACH CO LTD, *RAINHAM, ESSEX*	113
SWANBROOK TRANSPORT LTD, *CHELTENHAM*	121
SWEYNE COACHES, *GOOLE*	109
SWIFTS HAPPY DAYS TRAVEL, *DONCASTER*	166
SWIFTSURE TRAVEL (BURTON UPON TRENT) LTD	169
SWILLY BUS, *LETTERKENNY, Co DONEGAL*	223
SWINDON VINTAGE OMNIBUS, *SWINDON*	187

T

Operator	Page
T & S TRAVEL, *PONTEFRACT*	183
TF MINI COACHES, *BARKING*	113
T M TRAVEL, *STAVELEY*	98
T N C COACHES, *CASTLE BROMWICH*	179

F. T. TAGG COACHES, *SUTTON-IN-ASHFIELD*	157
TALLY HO! COACHES, *KINGSBRIDGE*	102
TANAT VALLEY COACHES, *LLANRHAEDR YM, OSWESTRY*	212
TANTIVY BLUE COACH TOURS, *ST HELIER, JERSEY*	189
TAPPINS COACHES, *DIDCOT*	159
TATES COACHES, *MARKYATE*	125
TAVISTOCK COMMUNITY TRANSPORT, *GREENLANDS*	93
TAW & TORRIDGE COACHES LTD, *OKEHAMPTON*	102
TAYLORS COACH TRAVEL, *YEOVIL*	163
TELFORD'S COACHES, *NEWCASTLETON*	192
TELLINGS GOLDEN MILLER COACHES LTD, *HEATHROW AIRPORT*	142
TERRYS COACH HIRE, *COVENTRY*	179
TERRY'S COACHES, *HEMEL HEMPSTEAD*	125
TEST VALLEY TRAVEL, *WHITEPARISH*	187
TETLEYS MOTOR SERVICES, *LEEDS*	183
THAMESDOWN TRANSPORT LTD, *SWINDON*	187
ARTHUR THOMAS COACHES, *GORSEINON*	222
THOMAS BROS, *LLANGADOG*	207
D J THOMAS COACHES OF NEATH	210
EDWARD THOMAS & SON, *WEST EWELL*	173
THOMAS OF BARRY	214
THOMAS OF RHONDDA, *PORTH*	213
THOMAS PATERSON & BROWN LTD, *KILBIRNIE*	206
THOMPSON'S, *FRAMLINGHAM*	171
THOMSETT'S COACHES, *DEAL*	129
THORNES INDEPENDENT LTD, *HEMINGBROUGH*	152
THREE STAR COACH HIRE	82
TILLEY'S COACHES, *BUDE*	93
TIMEBUS TRAVEL, *ST ALBANS*	142
TITTERINGTON COACHES LTD, *BLENCOW*	95
TOMORROWS TRANSPORT, *ENFIELD*	142
TONNA LUXURY COACHES LTD, *NEATH*	211
TOP LINE TRAVEL, *YORK*	152
TOP TRAVEL, *READING*	121
TOTNES & DARTMOUTH RING & RIDE, *TOTNES*	102
TOURIST COACHES LTD, *SALISBURY*	187
TOWER COACHES, *WIGTON*	95
TOWLERS COACHES, *WISBECH*	88
TOWN & COUNTRY COACHES, *NEWTON ABBOT*	102
TOWN & COUNTRY MOTOR SERVICES LTD, *HURWORTH MOOR, Nr DARLINGTON*	107
TOWNLYNX, *HOLYWELL*	209
TRACKS VEHICLE SERVICES, *ROMNEY MARSH*	129
TRAMONTANA, *MOTHERWELL*	199
TRANSDEV	80
TRANSIT EXPRESS TRAVEL, *LENTON*	157
TRANSLINC LTD, *LINCOLN*	136
TRANSLINK, *BELFAST*	217
THE TRANSPORT MUSEUM, *WYTHALL*	188
TRATHENS TRAVEL SERVICES, *PLYMOUTH*	102
TRAVEL DUNDEE	193
TRAVEL LONDON, *LONDON SE5*	142
TRAVELMASTERS, *SHEERNESS*	129
TRAVELPATH 3000, *GRANTHAM*	136
TRAVEL WEST MIDLANDS, *BIRMINGHAM*	179
TRAVEL WRIGHT, *NEWARK-ON-TRENT*	157
TRAVELGREEN COACHES, *DONCASTER*	166
TRAVELINE, *MINEHEAD*	163
TRAVELLERS CHOICE, THE, *CARNFORTH*	133
TRAVELSPEED - see NORTHERN BLUE	
TRAVELSURE, *SEAHOUSES*	155
TRAVEL-WRIGHT, *MOUNTSORREL*	134
TREACY COACHES, *BALLINA, Co MAYO*	223
TRELEY MOTORS, *PENZANCE*	93
TRENT BARTON, *HEANOR*	98
TRINGWOOD TRAVEL, *WALTON ON THAMES*	173
TRURONIAN LTD, *TRURO*	93
TRUSTLINE SERVICES LTD, *HERTFORD*	125
TUERS MOTORS LTD, *PENRITH*	96
TURNERS TOURS, *CHULMLEIGH*	102
TURNERS COACHWAYS (BRISTOL) LTD, *BRISTOL*	85
T W COACHES LTD, *SOUTH MOLTON*	102
TWIN VALLEY COACHES, *SOWERBY BRIDGE*	183
TYNE VALLEY COACHES LTD, *HEXHAM*	155
TYNEDALE GROUP TRAVEL, *HALTWISTLE*	155
TYRERS OF ADLINGTON, *CHORLEY*	133
TYRER TOURS LTD, *PADIHAM*	133

U

Operator	Page
UNICORN COACHES LTD, *HATFIELD*	125
UNI-LINK,	121
UNITY COACHES, *RETFORD*	157
UNO LTD, *HATFIELD*	125
GRAHAM URQUHART TRAVEL, *INVERNESS*	197

V

Operator	Page
VALES COACHES (MANCHESTER) LTD	118
VENTURE TRANSPORT (HENDON) (1965) LTD, *HARROW*	146
VEOLIA TRANSPORT,	80
VICEROY OF ESSEX LTD, *SAFFRON WALDEN*	114
VIKING MINICOACHES, *BROADSTAIRS*	129
VIKING TOURS & TRAVEL, *SWADLINCOTE*	98
VILLAGER MINIBUS, *SHARNBROOK*	82
VINCE COACHES, *BURGHCLERE, Nr NEWBURY*	83
VISCOUNT CENTRAL COACHES, *BURNLEY*	133
VISION TRAVEL INTERNATIONAL LTD, *WATERLOOVILLE*	121
VISTA COACHWAYS, *CLEEVE*	163
VOEL COACHES LTD, *DYSERTH*	208

W

Operator	Page
W+H MOTORS, *CRAWLEY*	181
W M TRAVEL, *WISBECH*	89
W T S MINICOACHES, *FARSLEY*	185
WA SHEARINGS LTD, *EXHALL*	179
WA SHEARINGS LTD, *NORMANTON*	185
WA SHEARINGS LTD, *TORQUAY*	103
WA SHEARINGS LTD, *WARRINGTON*	91
WA SHEARINGS LTD, *WIGAN*	118
WAKEFIELD TUTORIAL SCHOOL, *MORLEY*	185

WALDEN TRAVEL LTD, *SAFFRON WALDEN*	114	T. WILLIAMS & SONS, *PONCIAU*	223
WALLIS COACHWAYS, *BILSTHORPE, Nr NEWARK*	157	WILLIAMSONS OF *ROTHERHAM*	166
WALTONS COACHES, *GRANGETOWN, CARDIFF*	206	WILLS MINI COACHES, *KINGSBRIDGE*	103
WARRINGTON BOROUGH TRANSPORT LTD	91	WILSON'S COACHES, *ROSSINGTON*	167
WARRINGTON COACHES, *ILAM*	98	WILTAX BUSES LTD, *ADDLESTONE*	173
WARSTONE MOTORS LTD, *GREAT WYRLEY*	169	WILTS & DORSET BUS COMPANY LTD, *POOLE*	104
WATERSIDE TOURS - see HYTHE & WATERSIDE		WINDSOR-GRAY TRAVEL, *WOLVERHAMPTON*	179
PAUL WATSON TRAVEL, *DARLINGTON*	107	WINDSORIAN COACHES LTD, *WINDSOR*	83
WATTS COACHES, *BONVILSTON, Nr CARDIFF*	206	WINGS LUXURY TRAVEL LTD, *HAYES*	142
WAVERLEY COACHES LTD, *ST HELIER, JERSEY*	189	WINN BROS, *NORTHALLERTON*	152
WEARDALE MOTOR SERVICES LTD, *STANHOPE*	107	PAUL S. WINSON COACHES LTD, *LOUGHBOROUGH*	134
WEAVAWAY TRAVEL, *NEWBURY*	83	WINTS COACHES, *BUTTERTON, Nr LEEK*	169
WEBB'S *PETERBOROUGH*	88	WISE COACHES LTD, *HAILSHAM*	108
WEBBER BUS, *BRIDGWATER*	163	WISTONIAN COACHES, *SELBY*	152
WELLGLADE LTD	80	MAL WITTS EXECUTIVE TRAVEL, *GLOUCESTER*	115
WELSH DRAGON TRAVEL *NEWPORT, MONMOUTHSHIRE*	211	WOOD BROTHERS TRAVEL LTD, *BUCKFASTLEIGH*	103
WELSH'S COACHES, *PONTEFRACT*	185	JOHN WOODHAMS VINTAGE TOURS, *RYDE IoW*	126
WEST END/RUTLAND TRAVEL, *MELTON MOWBRAY*	134	WOODS COACHES LTD, *LEICESTER*	135
WEST MIDLANDS SPECIAL NEEDS TRANSPORT, *BIRMINGHAM*	179	WOODS COACHES, *TILLICOULTRY*	192
		P. WOODS MINICOACHES, *HALLGLEN*	195
WESTBUS COACH SERVICES LTD, *HOUNSLOW*	142	WOODS TRAVEL LTD, *BOGNOR REGIS*	181
WESTERHAM COACHES, *OXTED*	173	WOODSTONES COACHES LTD, *KIDDERMINSTER*	188
WESTERN GREYHOUND, *NEWQUAY*	93	WOODWARD'S COACHES LTD, *GLOSSOP*	99
WESTRINGS COACHES, *EAST WITTERING*	181	WOOTTENS, *CHESHAM*	86
WEST'S COACHES LTD, *WOODFORD GREEN*	142	J.P.A. WORTH, *BUXTON*	169
WESTWAY COACH SERVICES, *LONDON SW20*	142	WORTHEN TRAVEL, *LITTLE MINSTERLEY*	161
WHEADONS GROUP TRAVEL, *CARDIFF*	206	WORTHING COACHES	181
WHEELERS TRAVEL, *SOUTHAMPTON*	121	WORTHS MOTOR SERVICES LTD, *ENSTONE*	159
WHEAL BRITON COACHES, *TRURO*	93	WRIGHT BROS (COACHES) LTD, *NENTHEAD*	96
WHIPPET COACHES LTD, *FENSTANTON*	89	LEN WRIGHT BAND SERVICES LTD, *WATFORD*	125
WHITE BUS SERVICES, *WINDSOR*	83	WRIGLEY'S COACHES, *IRLAM*	118
WHITE HEATHER TOURS, *FORT WILLIAM*	197		
WHITEGATE TRAVEL, *NORTHWICH*	91	**Y**	
WHITELAWS COACHES, *STONEHOUSE*	202	YARDLEY TRAVEL LTD, *BIRMINGHAM*	180
WHITTLE COACH & BUS, *KIDDERMINSTER*	188	YARRANTON BROS LTD, *TENBURY WELLS*	189
WHYTES COACH TOURS, *NEWMACHAR*	190	YELLOW ROSE COACHES, *CARNFORTH*	133
WICKSONS TRAVEL, *BROWNHILLS*	179	YELLOWLINE TOURS LTD, *UPPER BEEDING*	181
WIDE HORIZON LUXURY TRAVEL, *HINCKLEY*	134	YEOMANS CANYON TRAVEL LTD, *HEREFORD*	122
WIGHTROLLERS, *SANDOWN, ISLE OF WIGHT*	126	YESTERYEAR MOTOR SERVICES, *DISEWORTH, DERBY*	99
ALBERT WILDE COACHES, *HEAGE*	99	YORKS COACHES, *COGENHOE*	153
WILFREDA BEEHIVE, *ADWICK-LE-STREET*	166	YORKSHIRE COASTLINER LTD, *MALTON*	160
WILKINSONS TRAVEL, *ROTHERHAM*	166	YOUNGS OF ROMSLEY, *HALESOWEN*	180
F R WILLETTS & CO, *PILLOWELL, Nr LYDNEY*	121	YULE, *PITLOCHRY*	200
T WILLIAMS & SONS, *WREXHAM*	215		
WILLIAMS COACHES, *BRECON*	212	**Z**	
F. T. WILLIAMS TRAVEL, *CAMBORNE*	93	ZAK'S BUS & COACH SERVICES, *GREAT BARR* see Central Connect	
GLYN WILLIAMS TRAVEL, *BLACKWOOD*	206		
GWYN WILLIAMS & SONS LTD, *LOWER TUMBLE*	207		

The UK's biggest selling PSV magazine

Subscribe today and SAVE 10% on the normal price

Delivering prompt and informed coverage every month, **BUSES** magazine has provided an essential overview of the UK's PSV industry for over fifty-five years.

Supported by quality editorial features and the latest news, **BUSES** magazine is essential reading for decision-makers within the bus industry.

The magazine is notable for its most unique feature, 'Fleet News', now an 18-page section detailing the latest additions to and departures from major and less major bus and coach fleets in the UK and Ireland.

Every month BUSES editorial features cover key areas of interest, including vehicle operation, technical developments, ticketing and publicity.

Subscribe today to receive **BUSES** on your desk every month, and keep abreast of the latest news and developments in the bus industry.

12 ISSUES	NORMAL RATE	DISCOUNT RATE	YOU SAVE
UK	£44.40	£39.96	£4.44
EUROPE	£53.20	£47.88	£5.32
ROW	£58.20	£52.38	£5.82

Great subscriber benefits!

A subscription to BUSES comes with FREE MEMBERSHIP to the **Ian Allan Publishing Subs Club.**

As a member of the **Ian Allan Publishing Subs Club**, you will receive a personalised Subscription Loyalty Card, plus a quarterly newsletter with great subscriber benefits, discounts, offers and competitions!

Offer valid until 30/09/08

BUSES PRIORITY SUBSCRIPTION FORM

LRB08

I would like to subscribe to *BUSES*, starting with the.................................... issue

- 12 issues UK　　DISCOUNT RATE　£39.96
- 12 issues Europe　DISCOUNT RATE　£47.88
- 12 issues ROW　　DISCOUNT RATE　£52.38

Mr/Mrs/Miss/Ms: .... Forename: ....
Surname: ....
Address: ....
....
....
Post Code: ....
Tel No: ....
Email: ....

1. Debit / Credit Card

Please debit my card for the amount £..........................

☐ Mastercard　　☐ Visa　　☐ Switch / Maestro Card

Exp date: .... Start date:................... Issue No: ....
Cardholders signature: .... Date: ....

2. Cheque

I enclose a cheque to the value of ....
(Please make cheque payable to Ian Allan Publishing Ltd. Eurocheques are not accepted.)

3. Invoice

☐ Please invoice me

Please complete and send to: Buses Subscriptions Department, Ian Allan Publishing Ltd, Riverdene Business Park, Molesey Road, Hersham, Surrey, KT12 4RG
Tel: +44 (0)1932 266622　Fax: +44 (0)1932 266633　Email: subs@ianallanpublishing.co.uk